HERITAGE OF WESTERN CIVILIZATION

VOLUME II

EDITED AND WITH INTRODUCTIONS BY

JOHN LOUIS BEATTY *University of California, Riverside*
OLIVER A. JOHNSON *University of California, Riverside*

PRENTICE-HALL, INC., ENGLEWOOD CLIFFS, NEW JERSEY

HERITAGE OF WESTERN CIVILIZATION

Select Readings

SECOND EDITION

[redacted]

HERITAGE OF WESTERN CIVILIZATION
Select Readings
SECOND EDITION

VOLUME II

edited by
JOHN LOUIS BEATTY
OLIVER A. JOHNSON

Current printing (last digit):
10 9 8 7 6 5 4 3

PRENTICE-HALL INTERNATIONAL, INC., *London*
PRENTICE-HALL OF AUSTRALIA, PTY. LTD., *Sydney*
PRENTICE-HALL OF CANADA, LTD., *Toronto*
PRENTICE-HALL OF INDIA (PRIVATE) LTD., *New Delhi*
PRENTICE-HALL OF JAPAN, INC., *Tokyo*

Library of Congress Catalog Card No.: 66–14746

Printed in the United States of America C-38701

[redacted]

PREFACE TO THE SECOND EDITION

Books, generally, are the result of their author's reaction to a specific situation or problem. Either he feels some discontent with the level of knowledge about a subject or he has a special message to convey or a new story to relate; or else his experience indicates a present inadequacy that he believes his volume will remedy. The original reason for the preparation of this book was the last. The inadequacy we felt arose from the difficulties encountered in attempting to teach beginning college students something of their own heritage by using the available collections of readings drawn from the history of Western civilization.

The fault in most of these collections stems either from the lack of a clearly defined editorial rationale or from a rationale that has been too narrowly defined. In addition, most of them suffer from a serious pedagogical flaw—the almost inescapable urge on the part of the editors to be as broadly inclusive as possible, to include parts of the work of as many people of major importance (as well as many of minor importance) as can be jammed between the covers of a book. It is hoped by this means to introduce the student to virtually all the names he should be expected to remember as he pursues his course of study.

This seems to be a laudable educational aim, but it tends to fall between two stools. On the one hand, such a book provides many names and little by which to remember those names. On the other hand, it forces the editors to use such short selections that the quality of the work of the author and the intent of his writing tend to be lost, again leaving the student with little or nothing.

We have sought to avoid these pitfalls by permitting normal course structure to determine the general outlines of our book. Believing that the most a student could be expected to assimilate with understanding each week would be about two selections, especially if these were of sufficient length really to acquaint him with the personality, the mind, and the work of the author, and assuming the normal academic year to be about thirty weeks long, we arrived at the approximate total number of selections to include, hoping always that the result would be pedagogically sound and intellectually rewarding. To suggest, however, that we have reduced the entire heritage of the West to a set of about sixty readings would be flagrant arrogance on our part. And certainly the decisions concerning inclusion or exclusion have been in many cases painful. Why Polybius and not Livy? Why Luther and not Loyola? Why *Unam Sanctam* without *De Rerum Novarum*? These questions (and many others) can be answered only on the level of thoughtful, careful, and painful editorial fiat. In any event, we are convinced that the materials included here will provide the beginning student with a significant introduction to and sampling of his civilization's past. If these two goals are met, this book will have served him well.

The plan of the work is relatively simple. We have arrayed the readings in rough chronological sequence, but have altered that order in a few cases where it did not seem most fitting. Thus, Cellini precedes Erasmus, and Bertrand Russell follows Franklin Roosevelt. The sixty or so readings have been divided into eight sections—the Ancient Near East, Greece, Rome, the Middle Ages, Renaissance and Reformation, Early Modern Europe, the Nineteenth Century, and the Contemporary World. Each section begins with a general introduction to the period that aims at providing a broad framework into which the selections may be fitted. Each of these selections is introduced individually as well.

There is no single theme or central thread running through the book, such as the growth of freedom, the evolution of democracy, or the relationship of man to God. As a matter of fact, we have deliberately avoided organizing the book around a central theme. This decision arose out of the conviction that such an organization would inevitably result in a distorted picture of the past. Instead, we have presented selections that we believe throw light on *many* of the major issues and attitudes of Western civilization. Our hope is that the student himself will detect the relevance of a variety of themes to his own experience.

Our obligations to those who assisted us in this work are real, many, and varied. It is impossible to single out particular persons for special citation. Our colleagues at the University of California, Riverside, other colleagues at various colleges and universities throughout the country, and the librarians of at least eight libraries have all been most generous of their time and effort. We are particularly indebted, in this, the second edition, to those teachers throughout the country who have taken the time to question our choices and who have made meaningful suggestions for additions and amendments. Naturally, not all their advice and counsel has been accepted, but even a rejected criticism forces re-examination and further thought, and so is helpful. Our greatest debt, of course, is that owed the authors of the works here included and the translators of those works. Without them there would be no book of readings.

J. L. B.
O. A. J.

TABLE OF CONTENTS

The Contemporary World

HERITAGE OF WESTERN CIVILIZATION

RENAISSANCE AND REFORMATION

THE RENAISSANCE was a cultural and intellectual revival that had its beginnings in the city-states of northern Italy during the fourteenth and fifteenth centuries. The gradual change from the medieval outlook was probably caused by several factors—the great economic prosperity of these city-states, their contacts through trade with other cultures, the reduction of the papacy to the role of an Italian principality, and the Church's loss of emotional prestige. These elements combined to produce the highly secular outlook that is the essence of the Renaissance.

This secular outlook is commonly referred to as "humanism," a term that may be defined in two ways. According to the narrower definition, humanism was a rebirth, or renaissance, of interest in classical antiquity. Men turned to a re-reading of the great (and not so great) works of Greek and Roman literature, a re-examination and preservation of classical architecture and sculpture, and a re-study of the classical languages themselves. This very interest in the glories of Greece and Rome, however, exacted its price, for Renaissance literature and some of its art tended to be imitative, to rely too heavily on the models of a by-gone day. The conviction that it was impossible to surpass or even to equal the achievements of the ancients tended to inhibit the mind and imagination of the men of the Renaissance.

The broader definition of humanism states the typically Renaissance notion that man and his activities are the most important and interesting elements of the universe. Thus, man himself, rather than God, is the proper subject of contemplation and examination. This secular, humanistic outlook posed many interesting problems. If man and his life on this earth are the most important concern of man, how may the "good" man or the "good" life be determined? Castiglione, in his manual on conduct, *The Book of the Courtier,* claimed that virtue is its own reward, that one does not do good or bad out of hope for reward or fear of punishment in an afterlife, but only because it is good to be good. Some of the same secular ethic is implied in the political theories of Machiavelli, whose ideal prince was not concerned with or troubled by an angry or beneficent God but only with the problems of acquiring and maintaining power to ensure a stable political order in which the citizenry could live in peace and plenty.

During the fifteenth and sixteenth centuries the Renaissance spread from Italy to France, England, Spain, the Lowlands, and throughout Germany and Poland. Italian manners and customs were widely adopted and it became fashionable to build "in the Italian fashion" and to dress "in the Italian mode." More important, however, than the adoption of these cultural superficialities was the ready acceptance by scholars in northern Europe of the critical methods developed by Pico, Valla, and others, of reading and analyzing documents, literature, and writings of all kinds. Moreover, the scientific attitude and the widespread curiosity about the physical world led many Europeans to inquire, to study, to dissect, to experiment, and to seek a fuller understanding of the nature of the universe and man's place in it.

Among the leaders of the New Learning in the North was Sir Thomas

More of England, who looked closely at his society and found it mean and corrupt. This conclusion he elaborated in his brilliant and immensely popular satire, *Utopia,* which was published in 1516 in Latin and subsequently translated into English, French, Spanish, German, and Italian. More's close friend, Erasmus of Rotterdam, was also deeply influenced by the skeptical, critical thought of the Renaissance. Erasmus translated the New Testament from Greek into Latin, wrote various *Colloquies* containing observations and commentaries on the contemporary world, and, more lasting perhaps, published his penetrating analysis of people and affairs under the title *The Praise of Folly.*

Not everyone, however, received the New Learning with the same enthusiasm. A German monk, Martin Luther, though he accepted the typically humanistic ideas regarding the critical examination of texts, could not accept the Renaissance notion that this world and its affairs were of primary importance. For he was unwilling to divorce himself from the crucial problem of the salvation of man's soul. Most of the men of the Renaissance simply shelved the problem of salvation—for them, life was for the living, to be enjoyed and possibly to be remembered without remorse or regret. Benvenuto Cellini, an Italian goldsmith, was a perfect example of this attitude. But for Luther (a contemporary of Cellini) life on this earth was but a transient aspect of the eternal life of the soul. In this one sense, Luther represented a reversion to the medieval outlook. But at the same time he shared in the new intellectual movements, being convinced that everyone was competent to read and understand the holy writings and to find his own salvation through faith.

Justification by faith lay at the heart of the Lutheran break with the Catholic Church. Originally, Luther sought only the reform of church practice, not doctrine. But the indifference of the church leaders, together with what seemed to him an almost institutionalized acceptance of abuses, made Luther's outcries go unheard. The Church finally became seriously enough concerned over Luther's protests to excommunicate him, thereby laying the ground for the Protestant movement. Launched by Luther, Protestantism quickly gained adherents in many parts of Europe. The most influential of these was a Frenchman transplanted to Geneva, John Calvin, who supplied the movement with a theology. Anything but an innovator, Calvin returned to the writings of St. Paul and St. Augustine and the doctrine of original sin, which he reiterated with a rare combination of legalistic precision and evangelical fervor.

For centuries, the Catholic Church had been flexible enough in its thinking and its practices to adjust to reform movements from within—for example, the Cluniac movement of the eleventh century, the Cistercian of the twelfth, and the Franciscan of the thirteenth. But by the end of the fifteenth century the Church was no longer able to provide the spiritual comfort required to sustain a great number of loyal and devoted followers. During the fifteenth century a group of mystics, who dedicated their lives to poverty and the education of the young, had appeared in Germany —the Brotherhood of the Common Life. This relatively obscure group felt that the conventional Catholic Church was somehow failing in its purposes, and sought to restore a measure of fervor to the traditional faith. Even Erasmus was concerned about the abuses in church practice and the indifference of church leadership to the needs of the people. He presented his solutions to these problems in what he called "the philosophy of Christ."

One of the outcomes of the conflict between the Protestant movement and the Catholic Church was a revitalization of the Catholic faith. Led mostly by the militant order of the Society of Jesus, founded in 1540 by Saint Ignatius of Loyola, the Catholics re-converted Poland, Bohemia, and large areas of France and Germany. Of course, this revitalization was not accomplished without bitterness, heroism, and conflict from both Protestant and Catholic. The Peasants Revolt in Germany in the early sixteenth century, the religious wars in France in the late sixteenth century, and the Thirty Years' War in the early seventeenth century were only outstanding examples of the hatred, fear, and bloodshed provoked by conflicting religious opinions.

During the Renaissance, then, Europe was expanding intellectually and culturally through scientific investigation and literary and artistic innovation, and was attempting to find some solution to religious controversy. Europe was expanding geographically as well. For the time of the Renaissance and Reformation was also the age of exploration and commercial revolution. To the west new continents were discovered, new colonies were planted, and new empires were created. The discovery of a sea route around Africa immensely stimulated traffic between western Europe and the Orient, leading finally to a relative decline in the economic status of the great Italian cities and the emergence of Portugal, Spain, the Dutch Republic, and finally France and England as world powers with great fleets and vast overseas holdings. The influx of wealth (both in goods and precious metals) from East and West created severe economic dislocations and upheavals in Europe, thus adding another source of strife and discontent to a culture already troubled by the ferment of Renaissance skepticism and Reformation religious enthusiasm. It was from this matrix that the modern world emerged; many of the problems posed then remain today.

PICO DELLA MIRANDOLA

Giovanni Pico, the Count of Mirandola (1463–1494), epitomized both in his life and in his writings the Renaissance ideal of manhood. Wealthy, nobly born, handsome, and brilliant, he was well embarked on a distinguished intellectual career which would certainly have made him the undisputed leader of the humanistic movement when he fell victim to fever at the age of thirty. Unwilling to limit himself, as many other humanists did, to translating and imitating the literature of classical Greece and Rome, he undertook the task of assimilating all the great writings of the past, searching out the elements of truth contained in each of them, and assembling these truths into a new philosophical synthesis of his own.

The Oration on the Dignity of Man *is a part of this ambitious project. After seven years of study in various European universities, Pico arrived in Rome at the age of twenty-three and announced that he was prepared to defend in public debate against anyone in Europe a list of nine hundred theses representing the conclusions that he had derived from his studies. (He even offered to pay the travel expenses of scholars coming long distances.) The debate, scheduled for January, 1487, never took place. Pope Innocent VIII, suspicious that Pico was straying from orthodoxy, appointed a commission to examine the list of theses. When the commission confirmed the pope's suspicions by labeling a number of them heretical, Innocent forced the debate to be canceled.*

The nature of the Oration, *which Pico had intended as an introductory address for the debate, is evident from its title. Apart from the intrinsic interest of the discussion itself, including the many references which Pico makes to the most diverse literary sources, the significance of the* Oration *lies in its eloquent summation of the Renaissance interest in man and the belief in the dignity of human life. The selection that follows includes the first seven sections of the* Oration.

On the Dignity of Man

Most reverend fathers: I have read in the writings of the Arabs that Azdallah the Saracen, when asked what thing on this worldly stage appeared most marvelous to him, replied that he perceived nothing more wonderful than Man. This opinion is concurred in by that famous statement of Hermes Trismegistus:

Man, Asclepius, is a great miracle.

As I pondered the sense of these sayings, I became dissatisfied with those arguments which are brought forth in profusion by many people to establish the excellence

Giovanni Pico Della Mirandola, DE HOMINIS DIGNITATE, *trans. Douglass S. Parker of the University of California, Riverside.*

of Humanity: namely, that Man is the intermediary of all created things, slave to those above him, king to those below; that Man is the interpreter of nature, by virtue of the sharpness of his senses, the searching of his reason, and the light of his understanding; that Man is the interval between time and eternity, the copula of the universe (as the Persians say), or even its wedding, a little lower, on David's authority, than the angels. These are great things, certainly, but not of prime importance; not so great that they lay just claim to the highest admiration. For, under these conditions, why should we not give even greater admiration to the angels themselves, and to the blessed choir of Heaven?

At length, I felt that I had come to understand both why Man is the most fortunate of creatures, and thus worthy of all admiration, and what, finally, this situation is which he has received in the scheme of the universe—a position to be envied, not only by the beasts, but by the stars, by the spirits beyond the world. The answer is marvelous and incredible. How could it be otherwise? For it is on this account that Man is rightly said and believed to be a great miracle, truly a being to be admired.

Hear now, Fathers, what this solution is, and, in your courtesy, grant my discourse a friendly audience.

The Supreme Father, God the Creator, had already fashioned this worldly residence which we see about us, the majestic temple of His Godhood, after the laws of His secret wisdom. He had adorned the zone beyond the heavens with intellects; He had quickened the ethereal spheres into life with eternal souls; He had filled the foul and filthy regions of the lower world with a multitude of animals of every sort. But, His work completed, the Demiurge desired that there be someone to contemplate the reason of such a great work, to love its beauty, to wonder at its vastness. Thus, when everything had been finished (as Moses and Timaeus bear witness), He turned His thoughts last of all to bringing forth Man. But there remained no archetype on which to pattern the new creature, no treasure to bestow on the new son as an inheritance, no place in all the world where that contemplator of the universe might sit. By this time, all things were full; all things had been distributed in the highest, middle, and lowest orders. But it was not the nature of the Father's power to fail, as though exhausted, in the last act of creation; nor of His wisdom, to waver in a necessary deed through lack of a plan; nor of His beneficent love, to compel the very being who was to praise the divine generosity in other things to impugn that generosity in himself. At length the Greatest Craftsman decided that this being, to whom He could give nothing of its own, should share in everything which he had assigned to each of the other beings. Thus he received Man as a work of undefined pattern, and, placing him in the center of the world, addressed him as follows:

I have given you, O Adam, neither a fixed location, nor an especial appearance, nor any gift peculiarly your own; therefore, you may attain and possess, as you wish and as you will, whatever location, whatever appearance, whatever gifts you yourself desire. The nature of all other things is limited and confined within laws which I have laid down. You, confined by no limits, will determine your nature for yourself by your judgment, into whose power I have consigned you. I have placed you in the middle of the world, whence you may survey the more conveniently everything which is in the world. I have made you neither heavenly nor earthly, neither mortal nor immortal; thus, as a free and sovereign craftsman, you may mold yourself whatever form you choose. You will be able to degenerate into those lower creatures, which are brutes; you will be able, by the determination of your mind, to be reborn into those higher creatures, which are divine.

How great is the generosity of God the Father! How great and admirable is the happiness of Man, whose gift it is to have that which he wishes! Upon their birth, beasts bring with them from their mother's bag (as Lucilius says) all that they will ever possess. From the beginning of time, or soon after, the supreme spirits have been that which they will be throughout all eternity. But as Man is born, the Father has planted in him seeds of every sort, shoots of every life; those which each man cultivates will grow, and bear their fruits in him. If these are vegetable, he will become a plant; if sensual, a brute; if rational, a heavenly being; if intellectual, an angel and son of God. But if Man, not contented with any creature's lot, betakes himself into the center of his oneness, then, made one with God, in the solitary darkness of the Father he who was created above all things will excell all things.

Who would not admire this chameleon of ours? Or, rather, who would admire anything else more greatly? Asclepius of Athens does no wrong when he says of man that, in accordance with his changing aspect and his self-transforming nature, he was symbolized in the mysteries by Proteus. Hence those metamorphoses celebrated among the Hebrews and the Pythagoreans: indeed, the most secret Hebrew theology makes transformations, now of holy Enoch into an angel of the divinity, now of other men into other divine spirits; the Pythagoreans transform evildoers into beasts, and even (if we may believe Empedocles) into plants. Imitating this, Mohammed would often say, "He who departs from the divine law becomes a beast," and rightly so. For not the bark, but the dull and insensible nature makes the plants; not the hide, but the brutish and sensual soul the beast; not the circular body, but correct reason the heavens; not separation from the body, but spiritual intelligence the angel. For should you see a man given up to his belly and creeping on the ground, you see a plant, not a man; should you see someone blinded by the empty illusions of an apparition like Calypso, enticed by titillating allurements, a slave to his senses, you see a beast, not a man; should you see a philosopher perceiving all by his correct reasoning, you would revere him—he is a being of heaven, not of earth; should you see a pure contemplator, unconscious of his body, completely withdrawn into the sanctuary of his mind, this is no earthly, no celestial being:—this is a most majestic spirit dressed in human flesh.

Is there anyone, then, who would not admire man? Not wrongly, in both the Mosaic and the Christian scriptures, is he called now by the name of "all flesh," now by the name of "every creature," since he molds, fashions, and transforms himself after the appearance of all flesh and after the nature of every creature. Therefore Evanthes the Persian, in his account of the Chaldean theology, writes that Man possesses no innate form of his own, but many extraneous and foreign ones, whence that saying of the Chaldeans that man is an animal of varied and manifold and unstable nature.

But to what end do I record this? So that, after we have been born in this condition—that of being what we wish—we shall understand that we must take especial care that it not be said against us, that we were in honor and knew it not, and became as brutes and foolish beasts. Rather, may the words of the prophet Asaph apply —"Ye are gods, and all of you are children of the most High,"—lest we, abusing the Father's most indulgent generosity, render that unfettered choice which He gave us harmful rather than beneficial. May some holy aspiration enter our hearts, so that we are not content with middling things, but pant for the highest and strain to achieve them, since we can if we will.

Let us scorn the earthly, despise the

heavenly, and thus, disdaining everything which is of the world, fly to that assembly beyond the world which is nearest God, who towers over all. There, as the holy mysteries tell, Seraphim, Cherubim, and Thrones occupy the first place; let us strive to equal their dignity and glory. And, if we wish it, we shall be in no wise lower than they.

NICCOLÒ MACHIAVELLI

A reading of The Prince *by Machiavelli (1469–1527) makes it easy to understand the evil connotations that have come to surround the term "Machiavellian." Written as a handbook for political leaders,* The Prince *is most famous as the source of the doctrine that, in politics, the end always justifies the means. With Machiavelli, this doctrine was no theoretical assumption; it was a conclusion derived from acute observation and analysis of the political practices of the day. As a diplomat in the service of his native city of Florence, Machiavelli was able to observe the tactics of the men who were struggling for control of the Italian peninsula in the early sixteenth century. The most colorful of these power-hungry men was the notorious Caesar Borgia, son of Pope Alexander VI, whom Machiavelli met on numerous occasions during his diplomatic career. For Borgia, power clearly was an end in itself.*

Although, in The Prince, *Machiavelli praises Borgia and advocates the pursuit of power without regard to the methods employed, to be fair we must realize that Machiavelli himself was not an unqualified Machiavellian. In the final chapter of* The Prince, *he urges Lorenzo de' Medici to exert his princely power to unify Italy and drive out foreign oppressors, an end that Machiavelli valued more highly than the mere pursuit of power for its own sake. And in his* Discourses *he concludes that the best-governed state is a state ruled, not by a Machiavillian prince, but by the people themselves. In spite of these qualifications, however, Machiavelli is commonly regarded as the champion of power politics and of the doctrine that the end justifies the means.*

To capture something of the flavor and diversity of the Italian Renaissance, we have only to realize that Machiavelli and Pico della Mirandola were contemporaries living in the city of Florence. Yet while Pico was writing on the dignity of man, Machiavelli was observing, "For it may be truly affirmed of mankind in general, that they are ungrateful, fickle, timid, dissembling, and self-interested. . . ."

The Prince

NICCOLÒ MACHIAVELLI, CITIZEN AND SECRETARY OF FLORENCE, TO THE MOST MAGNIFICENT LORENZO DE MEDICI:

Those who court the favour of princes generally present them with whatever they possess that is most rare, curious, or valuable; as horses, armour, embroidered cloths, precious stones, &c., according to the dignity of the personage they seek to propitiate. For my part, my anxiety to present myself to the notice of your highness, with the best proof of my devotion, has not enabled me to discover, amongst all I possess, anything that I esteem more, or account so valuable, as a knowledge of the actions of celebrated men; a knowledge acquired by a long experience of modern times, and a diligent perusal of the ancients. The observations which I have made with all the accuracy, reflection, and care of which I am capable, are contained in the small volume now addressed to you. And although I have not the vanity to deem it worthy of your acceptance, yet I am persuaded that your goodness will not refuse the offering, since it is impossible to present you with anything more valuable than a work which will place before you, in a small compass, all the experience I have acquired during many years of continual meditation and suffering in the school of adversity.

You will find in this fragment neither a glowing and lofty style, nor any of those meretricious ornaments with which authors seek to embellish their works. Its interest must depend upon the importance of the subject, the solidity of the reflections, and the truth of the facts recorded.

It will, perhaps, appear presumptuous in me, a man of humble birth, to propose rules of conduct to those who govern; but as the painter when about to sketch a mountainous country places himself in the plain, and in order to draw the scenery of a vale, ascends an eminence, even so, I conceive, that a person must be a prince to discover the nature and character of a people, and one of the people to judge properly of a prince.

I am therefore bold enough to hope that you will accept this feeble tribute in reference to the intention with which it is offered; and if you condescend to read it with attention, you will have evidence of my ardent desire to see you fill with glory those high destinies, to which fortune and your splendid talents have called you.

If from your elevated position you should condescend to look down on a person in my lowly station, you will see how long and how unworthily I have been persecuted by the extreme and unrelenting malevolence of fortune.

Niccolò Machiavelli

. . .

Chapter XIV

OF THE DUTIES OF A PRINCE RELATIVE TO HIS MILITARY FORCE

Princes ought . . . to make the art of war their sole study and occupation, for it is peculiarly the science of those who govern. War, and the several sorts of discipline and institutions relative to it, should be his only study, the only pro-

Niccolò Machiavelli, "The Prince," from THE HISTORY OF FLORENCE AND THE AFFAIRS OF ITALY *(London, 1854).*

fession he should follow, and the object he ought always to have in view. By this means princes can maintain possession of their dominions; and private individuals are sometimes raised thereby to supreme authority; whilst, on the other hand, we frequently see princes shamefully reduced to nothing, by suffering themselves to be enfeebled by slothful inactivity. I repeat, therefore, that by a neglect of this art it is that states are lost, and by cultivating it they are acquired.

Francis Sforza, from a private station, attained the rank of duke of Milan, by having an army always at his disposal; and by a deviation from this rule his children, who succeeded to the dukedom, were reduced to the station of private individuals. And this is not surprising: for, in the first place, nothing is so likely to impair our esteem for the character of a prince as to see him destitute of a military force; and, as I shall endeavour to prove hereafter, that a prince should most particularly beware of falling into general contempt.

We cannot establish a comparison between men who are armed, and those who are not so; and it would be equally absurd to suppose that the disarmed should command, and the others obey. A prince who is ignorant of the art of war can never enjoy repose or safety amongst armed subjects; he will always be to them an object of contempt, as they to him will justly be subjects of suspicion; how is it possible then that they should act in concert? In short, a prince who does not understand the art of war can never be esteemed by his troops, nor can he ever confide in them.

It is necessary therefore that princes should pay their whole attention to the art of war, which includes mental labour and study as well as the military exercise. To begin with the latter, the prince should take the utmost care that his troops be well disciplined and regularly exercised. The chase is well adapted to inure the body to fatigue, and to all the intemperances of weather. This exercise will also teach him to observe the sources and situations, as well as the nature of rivers and marshes; to measure the extent of plains, and the declivity of mountains. By these means he will acquire a knowledge of the topography of a country which he has to defend, and will easily habituate himself to select the places where war may be best carried on. For the plain and valleys of Tuscany resemble more or less those of other countries; so that a perfect knowledge of one will enable them to form a tolerably accurate judgment of the other.

This study is particularly useful to commanders. A general who neglects it will never know where to look for an enemy, nor how to conduct his troops, nor to encamp, nor the proper time to attack. The Greek and Roman historians deservedly praised Philopomenes, prince of Achaia, for his application to the study of war in time of peace. He was accustomed in his travels to stop and ask his friends, which of two armies would have the advantage, if one posted on such or such a hill, and the other in such a particular place? In what manner this, if commanded by himself, should join and give battle to the other? What steps he ought to take in order to secure a retreat, or pursue the enemy, in case he should retire? He thus proposed to them in every case which might happen in war, listened attentively to their opinion, and then gave his own, together with the reasons on which it was founded. By these means he was always prepared to meet unforeseen events.

As to that part of military science which is learned in the closet, a prince ought to read history, and to pay particular attention to the achievements of great generals, and the cause of their victories and defeats; but above all he should follow the example of those great men who, when they select a model, resolve to follow in his steps. It was thus that Alexander the Great immortalized himself by following the example of Achilles, Caesar by imitating Alexander, and Scipio by copying Cyrus. If we take the trouble to compare the life of the latter Roman with that of Cyrus, we shall see how nearly Scipio copied the modesty, affability, humanity, liberality, and the other virtues with which Xenophon adorns his hero.

It is thus a wise prince should conduct himself, and so employ his time during peace, that if fortune should change, he may be prepared equally for her frowns or her favours.

Chapter XV

WHAT DESERVES PRAISE OR BLAME IN MEN, AND ABOVE ALL IN PRINCES

It now remains to show in what manner a prince should behave to his subjects and friends. This matter having been already discussed by others, it may seem arrogant in me to pursue it farther, especially if I should differ in opinion from them; but as I write only for those who possess sound judgment, I thought it better to treat this subject as it really is, in fact, than to amuse the imagination with visionary models of republics and governments which have never existed. For the manner in which men now live is so different from the manner in which they ought to live, that he who deviates from the common course of practice, and endeavours to act as duty dictates, necessarily ensures his own destruction. Thus, a good man, and one who wishes to prove himself so in all respects, must be undone in a contest with so many who are evilly disposed. A prince who wishes to maintain his power ought therefore to learn that he should not be always good, and must use that knowledge as circumstances and the exigencies of his own affairs may seem to require.

Laying aside, then, the false ideas which have been formed as to princes, and adhering only to those which are true, I say, that all men, and especially princes, are marked and distinguished by some quality or other which entails either reputation or dishonour. For instance, men are liberal or parsimonious, honourable or dishonourable, effeminate or pusillanimous, courageous or enterprising, humane or cruel, affable or haughty, wise or debauched, honest or dishonest, good tempered or surly, sedate or inconsiderate, religious or impious, and so forth.

It would, doubtless, be happy for a prince to unite in himself every species of good quality; but as our nature does not allow so great a perfection, a prince should have prudence enough to avoid those defects and vices which may occasion his ruin; and as to those which can only compromise his safety and the possession of his dominions, he ought, if possible, to guard against them; but if he cannot succeed in this, he need not embarrass himself in escaping the scandal of those vices, but should devote his whole energies to avoid those which may cause his ruin. He should not shrink from encountering some blame on account of vices which are important to the support of his states; for everything well considered, there are some things having the appearance of virtues, which would prove the ruin of a prince, should he put them in practice, and others, upon which, though seemingly bad and vicious, his actual welfare and security entirely depend.

Chapter XVI

OF LIBERALITY AND ECONOMY

To begin with the first qualities of the above-mentioned, I must observe that it is for the interest of a prince to be accounted liberal, but dangerous so to exercise his liberality, that he is thereby neither feared nor respected. I will explain myself. If a prince be only liberal, as far as it suits his purposes, that is to say, within certain bounds, he will please but few, and will be called selfish. A prince who wishes to gain the reputation of being liberal, should be regardless of expense; but then to support this reputation, he will often be reduced to the necessity of levying taxes on his subjects, and adopting every species of fiscal resource which cannot fail to make him odious. Besides exhausting the public treasure by his prodigality, his credit will be destroyed, and he will run the risk of losing his dominions on the first reverse of fortune, his liberality, as it always happens, having ensured him more enemies than friends. And which is worse, he cannot retrace his steps and replenish his finances, without being charged with avarice.

A prince, therefore, who cannot be liberal without prejudicing his state, should not trouble himself much about the imputation of being covetous; for he will be esteemed liberal in time, when people see that by parsimony he has improved his revenue, become able to defend his dominions, and even to undertake useful enterprises without the aid of new taxes; then the many from whom he takes nothing will deem him sufficiently liberal, and the few only, whose expectations he has failed to realize, will accuse him of avarice. In our own times we have seen no great exploits performed, except by those who have been accounted avaricious; all the others have failed. Julius II attained the pontifical chair by means of his bounty; but he judged rightly in supposing, that in order to enable him to prosecute the war against France, it would do him injury to preserve his reputation for liberality. By his parsimony he was able to support the expense of all his wars without the imposition of new taxes. The present king of Spain could never have accomplished all his great enterprises, if he had felt any ambition to be thought liberal.

A prince, then, who would avoid poverty, and always be in a condition to defend his dominions without imposing new taxes on his subjects, should care little for being charged with avarice, since the imputed vice may be the very means of incuring the prosperity and stability of his government.

It may however be alleged that Caesar would never have attained the empire but by his liberality, and that many others have arrived at the highest honours by the same means. I answer, you are either in possession of dominion already, or you are not. In the first place, liberality would be prejudicial; in the second, the reputation of it is serviceable and necessary. Ceasar endeavoured to appear liberal whilst he aspired to the empire of Rome. But if he had lived longer, he would have lost that reputation for liberality which had paved him the way to empire, or he would have lost himself in the attempt to preserve it.

There have been, however, some princes who have performed splendid actions, and who have distinguished themselves by their liberality; but then their prodigality did not come from the public purse. Such were Cyrus, Alexander, and Caesar. A prince ought to be very sparing of his own and his subjects' property; but he should be equally lavish of that which he takes from the enemy, if he desires to be popular with his troops; for that will not diminish his reputation, but rather add to it. He who is too liberal cannot long continue so; he will become poor and contemptible unless he grinds his subjects with new taxes—which cannot fail to render him odious to them. Now there is nothing a prince ought to dread so much as his subjects' hatred; unless, indeed, it be their contempt. And both these evils may be occasioned by over liberality. If he must choose between extremes, it is better to submit to the imputation of parsimony than to make a show of liberality; since the first, though it may not be productive of honour, never gives birth to hatred and contempt.

Chapter XVII

ON CRUELTY AND CLEMENCY, AND WHETHER IT IS BETTER TO BE LOVED THAN FEARED

To proceed to other qualities which are requisite in those who govern. A prince ought unquestionably to be merciful, but should take care how he executes his clemency. Caesar Borgia was accounted cruel; but it was to that cruelty that he was indebted for the advantage of uniting Romagna to his other dominions, and of establishing in that province peace and tranquillity, of which it had been so long deprived. And, every thing well considered, it must be allowed that this prince showed greater clemency than the people of Florence, who, to avoid the reproach of cruelty, suffered Pistoia to be destroyed. When it is necessary for a prince to restrain his subjects within the bounds of duty, he should not regard the imputation of cruelty, because by making a few examples, he will find that he really showed more humanity in the end, than he, who by too great indulgence, suffers disorders to arise, which commonly terminate in rapine and murder. For such disorders disturb a whole community, whilst punishments inflicted by the prince affect only a few individuals.

This is particularly true with respect to a new prince, who can scarcely avoid the reproach of cruelty, every new government being replete with dangers. Thus Virgil makes Dido excuse her severity, by the necessity to which she was reduced of maintaining the interests of a throne which she did not inherit from her ancestors:—

Res dura et regni novitas me talia cogunt
Moliri, et late fines custode tueri.

A prince, however, should not be afraid of phantoms of his own raising; neither should he lend too ready an ear to terrifying tales which may be told him, but should temper his mercy with prudence, in such a manner, that too much confidence may not put him off his guard, nor causeless jealousies make him insupportable. There is a medium between a foolish security and an unreasonable distrust.

It has been sometimes asked, whether it is better to be loved than feared; to which I answer, that one should wish to be both. But as that is a hard matter to accomplish, I think, if it is necessary to make a selection, that it is safer to be feared than be loved. For it may be truly affirmed of mankind in general, that they are ungrateful, fickle, timid, dissembling, and self-interested; so long as you can serve them, they are entirely devoted to you; their wealth, their blood, their lives, and even their offspring are at your disposal, when you have no occasion for them; but in the day of need, they turn their back upon you. The prince who relies on professions, courts his own destruction, because the friends whom he acquires by means of money alone, and whose attachment does not spring from a regard for personal merit, are seldom proof against reverse of fortune, but abandon their benefactor when he most requires their services. Men are generally more inclined to submit to him who makes himself dreaded, than to one who merely strives to be beloved; and the reason is obvious, for friendship of this kind, being a mere moral tie, a species of duty resulting from a benefit, cannot endure against the calculations of interest: whereas fear carries with it the dread of punishment, which never loses its influence. A prince, however, ought to make himself feared, in such a manner, that if he cannot gain the love, he may at least avoid the hatred, of his subjects; and he may attain this object by respecting his subjects' property and the honour of their wives. If he finds it absolutely necessary to inflict the punishment of death, he should avow the reason for it, and above all things, he should abstain from touching the property of the condemned party. For certain it is that men sooner forget the death of their relations than the loss of their patrimony. Besides, when he once begins to live by means of rapine, many occasions offer for seizing the wealth of his subjects; but there will be little or no necessity for shedding blood.

But when a prince is at the head of his army, and has under his command a multitude of soldiers, he should make little account of being esteemed cruel; such a character will be useful to him, by keeping his troops in obedience, and preventing every species of faction.

Hannibal, among many other admirable talents, possessed in a high degree that of making himself feared by his troops; insomuch, that having led a very large army, composed of all kinds of people, into a foreign country, he never had occasion, either in prosperity or adversity, to punish the least disorder or the slightest want of discipline: and this can only be attributed to his extreme severity, and such other qualities as caused him to be feared and respected by his soldiers, and without which his extraordinary talents and courage would have been unavailing.

There have been writers notwithstanding, but, in my opinion, very injudicious ones who, whilst they render every degree of justice to his talents and his splendid achievements, still condemn the principle on which he acted. But nothing can in this respect more fully justify him than the example of Scipio, one of the greatest generals mentioned in history. His extreme indulgence towards the troops he commanded in Spain occasioned disorders, and at length a revolt, which drew on him from Fabius Maximus, in full senate, the reproach of having destroyed the Roman soldiery. This general having suffered the barbarous conduct of one of his lieutenants toward the Locrians to go unpunished, a senator, in his justification, observed that there were some men who knew better how to avoid doing ill themselves than to punish it in others. This excess of indulgence would in time have tarnished the glory and reputation of Scipio, if he had been a prince; but as he lived under a republican government, it was not only connived at, but redounded to his glory.

I conclude, then, with regard to the question, whether it is better to be loved than feared,—that it depends on the inclinations of the subjects themselves, whether they will love their prince or not; but the prince has it in his own power to make them fear him, and if he is wise, he will rather rely on his own resources than on the caprice of others, remembering that he should at the same time so conduct himself as to avoid being hated.

Chapter XVIII

WHETHER PRINCES OUGHT TO BE FAITHFUL TO THEIR ENGAGEMENTS

It is unquestionably very praiseworthy in princes to be faithful to their engagements; but among those of the present day, who have been distinguished for great exploits, few indeed have been remarkable for this virtue, or have scrupled to deceive others who may have relied on their good faith.

It should therefore be known, that there are two ways of deciding any contest: the one by laws, the other by force. The first is peculiar to men, the second to beasts; but when laws are not sufficiently powerful, it is necessary to recur to force: a prince ought therefore to understand how to use both these descriptions of arms. This doctrine is admirably illustrated to us by the ancient poets in the allegorical history of the education of Achilles, and many other princes of antiquity, by the centaur Chiron, who, under the double form of man and beast, taught those who were destined to govern, that it was their duty to use by turns the arms adapted to both these natures, seeing that one without the other cannot be of any durable advantage. Now, as a prince must learn how to act the part of a beast sometimes, he should make the fox and the lion his patterns. The first can but feebly defend himself against the wolf, and the latter readily falls into such snares as are laid for him. From the fox, therefore, a prince will learn dexterity in avoiding snares; and from the lion, how to employ his strength to keep the wolves in awe. But they who entirely rely upon the lion's strength, will not always meet with success: in other words, a prudent prince cannot and ought not to keep his word, except when he can do it without injury to himself, or when the circumstances under which he contracted the engagement still exist.

I should be cautious in inculcating such a precept if all men were good; but as the generality of mankind are wicked, and ever ready to break their words, a prince should not pique himself in keeping his more scrupulously, especially as it is always easy to justify a breach of faith on his part. I could give numerous proofs of this, and show numberless engagements and treaties which have been violated by the treachery of princes, and that those who enacted the part of the fox, have always succeeded best in their affairs. It is necessary, however, to disguise the appearance of craft, and thoroughly to understand the art of feigning and dissembling; for men are generally so simple and so weak, that he who wishes to deceive easily finds dupes.

One example, taken from the history of our own times, will be sufficient. Pope Alexander VI played during his whole life a game of deception; and notwithstanding his faithless conduct was extremely well known, his artifices always proved successful. Oaths and protestations cost him nothing; never did a prince so often break his word or pay less regard to his engagements. This was because he so well understood this chapter in the art of government.

It is not necessary, however, for a prince to possess all the good qualities I have enumerated, but it is indispensable that he should appear to have them. I will even venture to affirm, that it is sometimes dangerous to use, though it is always useful to seem to possess them. A prince should earnestly endeavour to gain the reputation of kindness, clemency, piety, justice, and fidelity to his engagements. He ought to possess all these good qualities, but still retain such power over himself as to display their opposites whenever it may be expedient. I maintain, that a prince, and especially a new prince, cannot with impunity exercise all the virtues, because his own self-preservation will often compel him to violate the laws of charity, religion, and humanity. He should habituate himself to bend easily to the various circumstances which may from time to time surround him. In a word, it will be as useful to him to persevere in the path of rectitude, while he feels no inconvenience in doing so, as to know how to deviate from it when circumstances dictate such a course. He should make it a rule above all things, never to utter anything which does not breathe of kindness, justice, good faith, and piety: this last quality it is most important for him to appear to possess, as men in general judge more from appearances than from reality. All men have eyes, but few have the gift of penetration. Every one sees your exterior, but few can discern what you have in your heart; and those few dare not oppose the voice of the multitude, who have the majesty of their prince on their side. Now, in forming a judgment of the minds of men, and more especially of princes, as we cannot recur to any tribunal, we must attend only to results. Let it then be the prince's chief care to maintain his authority; the means he employs, be what they may, will, for this purpose, always appear honourable and meet applause; for the vulgar are ever caught by appearances, and judge only by the event. And as the world is chiefly composed of such as are called the vulgar, the voice of the few is seldom or never heard or regarded.

There is a prince now alive (whose name it may not be proper to mention) who ever preaches the doctrines of peace and good faith; but if he had observed either the one or the other, he would long ago have lost both his reputation and dominions [*Ferdinand of Spain*].

. . .

Chapter XXV

HOW FAR FORTUNE INFLUENCES THE THINGS OF THIS WORLD, AND HOW FAR SHE MAY BE RESISTED

I know that several have thought, and many still are of opinion, that all sublunary events are governed either by Divine Providence or by chance, in such a manner that human wisdom has no share in their direction; and hence they infer that man should abstain from interfering with their course, and leave everything to its natural tendency.

The revolutions which in our times are of such frequent recurrence, seem to support this doctrine, and I own, that I, myself, am almost inclined to favour such opinions, particularly when I consider how far those events surpass all human conjecture; yet, as we confessedly possess a free will, it must, I think, be allowed, that chance does not so far govern the world as to leave no province for the exercise of human prudence.

For my own part, I cannot help comparing the blind power of chance to a rapid river, which, having overflowed its banks, inundates the plain, uproots trees, carries away houses and lands, and sweeps all before it in its destructive progress; everybody flies possessing neither resolution nor power to oppose its fury. But this should not discourage us, when the river has returned within its natural limits, from constructing dykes and banks to prevent a recurrence of similar disasters. It is the same with fortune; she exercises her power when we oppose no barrier to her progress.

If we cast our eyes on Italy, which has been the theatre of these revolutions, and consider the causes by which they have been provoked, we shall find it to be a defenceless country. If she had been properly fortified like Germany, Spain, or France, such inundations of foreigners would never have happened, or at least their irruptions would have been attended with less devastation.

Let this suffice in general concerning the necessity of opposing fortune. But to descend to particulars. It is no uncommon thing to see a prince fall from prosperity to adversity, without our being able to attribute his fate to any change in conduct or character; for, as I have already shown at large, he who relies solely on fortune must be ruined inevitably whenever she abandons him.

Those princes who adapt their conduct to circumstances are rarely unfortunate. Fortune is only changeable to those who cannot conform themselves to the varying exigencies of the times; for we see different men take different courses to obtain the end they have in view; for instance, in pursuit of riches or glory, one prosecutes his object at random, the other with caution and prudence: one employs art, the other force; one is impetuosity itself, the other all patience; means by which each may severally succeed. It also happens that of two who follow the same route, one may arrive at his destination, and the other fail; and that if two other persons, whose dispositions are diametrically opposite, pursue the same object by wholly different means, yet both shall equally prosper; which is entirely owing to the temper of the times, which always prove favourable or adverse, according as men conform to them.

Circumstances also frequently decide whether a prince conducts himself well or ill on any particular occasion. There are times when an extraordinary degree of prudence is necessary; there are others when the prince should know how to trust some things to chance; but there is nothing more difficult than suddenly to change his conduct and character; sometimes from inability to resist his old habits and inclinations, at others, from want of resolution to quit a course in which he had always been successful.

Julius II, who was of a fiery and violent disposition, succeeded in all his enterprises; doubtless, because a prince of such a character was best adapted to the circumstances under which the church was then governed by this pontiff. Witness his first invasion of the territory of Bologna, in the life of John Bentivoglio, which gave great umbrage to the Venetians and the kings of France and Spain, but none of them dared to interfere. The first, because they did not feel themselves strong enough to cope with a pontiff of his character; Spain, because she was engaged in the conquest of Naples; and France, besides having an interest in keeping fair with Julius, wished still to humble the Venetians; so that she, without hesitation, granted the pope all the assistance he required.

Julius II, therefore, by a precipitate mode of proceeding, succeeded in an enterprise which could not have been accomplished by cool and deliberate measures. He would unquestionably have failed had he given Spain and the Venetians time to reflect on his designs, and if he had allowed France the opportunity of amusing him by excuses and delays.

Julius II displayed in all his enterprises the same character of violence; and his successes have in that respect fully justified him; but he did not perhaps live long enough to experience the inconstancy of fortune; for had an occasion unexpectedly occurred in which it would have been necessary to act with prudence and circumspection, he would infallibly have been ruined, in consequence of that impetuosity and inflexibility of character which wholly governed him.

From all these circumstances we may conclude, that those who cannot change their system when occasion requires it, will no doubt continue prosperous as long as they glide with the stream of fortune; but when that turns against them, they are ruined, from not being able to follow that blind goddess through all her variations.

Besides, I think that it is better to be bold than too circumspect; because fortune is of a sex that likes not a tardy wooer, and repulses all who are not ardent; she declares also, more frequently, in favour of those who are young, because they are bold and enterprising.

Chapter XXVI

EXHORTATION TO DELIVER ITALY FROM FOREIGN POWERS

When I take a review of the subject matter treated of in this book, and examine whether the circumstances in which we are now placed would be favourable to the estabishment of a new government, honourable alike to its founder and advantageous to Italy, it appears to me that there never was, nor ever will be, a period more appropriate for the execution of so glorious an undertaking.

If it was necessary that the people of Israel should be slaves to Egypt, in order to elicit the rare talents of Moses; that the Persians should groan under the oppression of the Medes, in order to prove the courage and magnanimity of Cyrus; and that the Athenians should be scattered and dispersed, in order to make manifest the rare virtues of Theseus, it will be likewise necessary, for the glory of some Italian hero, that his country should be reduced to its present miserable condition, that they should be greater slaves than the Israelites, more oppressed than the Persians, and still more dispersed than the Athenians; in a word, that they should be without laws and without chiefs, pillaged, torn to pieces, and enslaved by foreign powers.

And though it has sometimes unquestionably happened that men have risen, who appeared to be sent by Heaven to achieve our deliverance; yet jealous fortune has ever abandoned them in the midst of their career; so that our unfortunate country still groans and pines away in the expectation of a deliverer, who may put an end to the devastations in Lombardy, Tuscany, and the kingdom of Naples. She supplicates Heaven to raise up a prince who may free her from the odious and humiliating yoke of foreigners, who may close the numberless wounds with which she has been so long afflicted, and under whose standard she may march against her cruel oppressors.

But on whom can Italy cast her eyes except upon your illustrious house, which, visibly favoured by Heaven and the church, the government of which is confided to its care, possesses also the wisdom and the power necessary to undertake so glorious an enterprise? and I cannot think that the execution of this project will seem difficult if you reflect on the actions and conduct of the heroes whose examples I have above adduced. Though their exploits were indeed wonderful, they were still but men; and although their merit raised them above others, yet none of them certainly were placed in a situation so favourable as that in which you now stand. You have justice on your side; their cause was not more lawful than yours, and the blessing of God will attend you no less than them. Every war that is necessary is just; and it is humanity to take up arms for the defence of a people to whom no other resource is left.

All circumstances concur to facilitate the execution of so noble a project, for the accomplishment of which it will only be necessary to tread in the steps of those great men whom I have had an opportunity of mentioning in the course of this work. For though some of them, it is true, were conducted by the hand of God in a wonderful manner, though the sea divided to let them pass, a cloud directed their course, a rock streamed with water to assuage their thirst, the manna fell from heaven to appease their hunger, yet there is no occasion for such miracles at present, as you possess in yourself sufficient power to execute a plan you ought by no means to neglect. God will not do everything for us; much is left to ourselves, and the free exercise of our will, that so our own actions may not be wholly destitute of merit.

If none of our princes have hitherto been able to effect what is now expected from your illustrious house, and if Italy has continually been unfortunate in her wars, the evil has arisen from the defects in military discipline, which no person has possessed the ability to reform.

Nothing reflects so much honour on a new prince as the new laws and institutions established under his direction, especially when they are good, and bear the character of grandeur. Now it must be acknowledged that Italy soon accommodates herself to new forms. Her inhabitants are by no means deficient in courage, but they are destitute of proper chiefs; the proof of this is in the duels and other individual combats in which the Italians have always evinced consummate ability, whilst their valour in battles has appeared well-nigh extinguished. This can only be attributed to the weakness of the officers, who are unable to ensure obedience from those who know, or think they know, the art of war. Thus we have seen the greatest generals of the present day, whose orders were never executed with exactness and celerity. These are the reasons why, in the wars in which we have been for the last twenty years engaged, the armies raised in Italy have been almost always beaten. Witness Tarus, Alexandria, Capua, Genoa, Vaila, Bologna, and Mestri.

If therefore your illustrious house is willing to regulate its conduct by the example of our ancestors, who have delivered their country from the rule of foreigners, it is necessary, above all things, as the only true foundation of every enterprise, to set on foot a national army; you cannot have better or more faithful soldiers, and though every one of them may be a good man, yet they will become still better when they are all united, and see themselves honoured, caressed, and rewarded by a prince of their own.

It is therefore absolutely necessary to have troops raised in our own country, if we wish to protect it from the invasion of foreign powers. The Swiss as well as the Spanish infantry are highly esteemed, but both have defects which may be avoided in the formation of our troops, which would render them superior to both of those powers. The Spaniards cannot support the shock of cavalry, and the Swiss cannot maintain their ground against infantry that is equally resolute with themselves.

Experience has fully shown that the Spanish battalions cannot resist the French cavalry, and that the Swiss have been beaten by the infantry of Spain. And though there has not been any thorough trial with regard to the Swiss on this point, yet there was a sort of specimen at the battle of Ravenna, where the Spanish infantry came in contact with the German troops, who fought in the same order as the Swiss. Upon that occasion, the Spaniards, having with their accustomed vivacity, and under the protection of their bucklers, thrown themselves across the pikes of the Germans, the latter were obliged to give way, and would have been entirely defeated, if their cavalry had not come to their relief.

It is necessary therefore to institute a military force possessing neither the defects of the Swiss or the Spanish infantry, and that may be able to maintain its ground against the French cavalry, and this is to be effected, not by changing their arms, but by altering their discipline. Nothing is more likely to make a new prince esteemed, and to render his reign illustrious.

Such an opportunity ought eagerly to be embraced, that Italy, after her long sufferings, may at last behold her deliverer appear. With what demonstrations of joy and gratitude, with what affection, with what impatience for revenge, would he not be received by those unfortunate provinces, who have so long groaned under such odious oppression. What city would shut her gates against him, and what people would be so blind as to refuse him obedience? What rivals would he have to dread? Is there one Italian who would not hasten to pay him homage? All are weary of the tyranny of these barbarians. May your illustrious house, strong in all the hopes which justice gives our cause, deign to undertake this noble enterprise, that so, under your banners, our nation may resume its ancient splendour, and, under your auspices, behold the prophecy of Petrarch at last fulfilled.

When virtue takes the field,
Short will the conflict be,
Barbarian rage shall yield
The palm to Italy:
For patriot blood still warms Italian veins,
Though low the fire, a spark at least remains.

BENVENUTO CELLINI

The term "Renaissance man" has come to suggest one who has an almost universal genius, an ability to do all things well. It also implies a confidence in the human potential, a conviction that a man with reason and taste can do anything if he merely applies his human resources to the task at hand. Leonardo da Vinci once wrote a letter to Lodovico Sforza, who afterward became the Duke of Milan, applying for a job. In cataloguing his abilities, Leonardo exudes self-confidence. He claims that he can ". . . construct very light bridges, easy to transport from one place to another . . . [in case of siege] remove the water from the ditches, and make an infinite variety of scaling-ladders . . . [make] a kind of cannon that is easy and convenient to carry, and that will throw out inflammable matters, causing great affright and damage to the enemy . . . make cannon, mortars, and field pieces of beautiful and useful shape, and different from those in common use . . . equal all others in architecture, in designing both public and private edifices, and in conducting water from one place to another . . . undertake in sculpture works in marble, bronze, or terra-cotta; likewise in painting can do what can be done equal to any other, whoever he may be. . . ." The letter closes with this assurance: "And if any of the abovementioned things seem to any impossible and impracticable, I offer to make trial of them in your park, or in any other place that may please your Excellency, to whom I commend myself with all possible humility." And the remarkable thing is that Leonardo could actually do what he said he could.

Another Renaissance figure with the same kind of brash assurance was Benvenuto Cellini (1500–1571), who, though a lesser artist than Leonardo, was his equal in confidence and probably his superior in the ability to live life to its fullest. Actually, Cellini was a semi-frustrated sculptor who is best known for his work as a goldsmith. Although little of his work has survived, Cellini's great masterpiece, the gold salt-cellar made for Francis I of France, is preserved at the Kunsthistorisches Museum in Vienna.

Cellini's Autobiography, *from which the following selections are taken, was written between 1558 and 1562, but was not published until the early eighteenth century. It enjoyed enormous popularity as a highly revealing personal document and as an intimate portrait of the sixteenth century—nor has it lost its fascination for modern readers.*

The Life of Benvenuto Cellini

BOOK FIRST

I

All men of whatsoever quality they be, who have done anything of excellence, or which may properly resemble excellence, ought, if they are persons of truth and honesty, to describe their life with their own hand; but they ought not to attempt so fine an enterprise till they have passed the age of forty. This duty occurs to my own mind, now that I am travelling beyond the term of fifty-eight years, and am in Florence, the city of my birth. Many untoward things can I remember, such as happen to all who live upon our earth; and from those adversities I am now more free than at any previous period of my career—nay, it seems to me that I enjoy greater content of soul and health of body than ever I did in bygone years. I can also bring to mind some pleasant goods and some inestimable evils, which, when I turn my thoughts backward, strike terror in me, and astonishment that I should have reached this age of fifty-eight, wherein, thanks be to God, I am still travelling prosperously forward.

II

It is true that men who have laboured with some show of excellence, have already given knowledge of themselves to the world; and this alone ought to suffice them; I mean the fact that they have proved their manhood and achieved renown. Yet one must needs live like others; and so in a work like this there will always be found occasion for natural bragging, which is of divers kinds, and the first is that a man should let others know he draws his lineage from persons of worth and most ancient origin.

I am called Benvenuto Cellini, son of Maestro Giovanni, son of Andrea, son of Cristofano Cellini; my mother was Madonna Elisabetta, daughter to Stefano Granacci; both parents citizens of Florence. It is found written in chronicles made by our ancestors of Florence, men of old time and of credibility, even as Giovanni Villani writes, that the city of Florence was evidently built in imitation of the fair city of Rome; and certain remnants of the Colosseum and the Baths can yet be traced. These things are near Santa Croce. The capitol was where is now the Old Market. The Rotonda is entire, which was made for the temple of Mars, and is now dedicated to our Saint John. That thus it was, can very well be seen, and cannot be denied; but the said buildings are much smaller than those of Rome. He who caused them to be built, they say, was Julius Caesar, in concert with some noble Romans, who, when Fiesole had been stormed and taken, raised a city in this place, and each of them took in hand to erect one of these notable edifices.

. . .

Thus then we find; and thus we believe that we are descended from a man of worth. Furthermore, we find that there are Cellinis of our stock in Ravenna, that most ancient town of Italy, where too are plenty of gentle folk. In Pisa also there are some, and I have discovered them in many parts of Christendom; and in this state also the breed exists, men devoted to the profession of arms; for not many years ago a young man, called Luca Cellini, a beardless

THE LIFE OF BENVENUTO CELLINI, *4th ed. [autobiography], trans. J. A. Symonds (New York, 1896).*

youth, fought with a soldier of experience and a most valorous man, named Francesco da Vicorati, who had frequently fought before in single combat. This Luca, by his own valour, with sword in hand, overcame and slew him, with such bravery and stoutness that he moved the folk to wonder, who were expecting quite the contrary issue; so that I glory in tracing my descent from men of valour.

As for the trifling honours which I have gained for my house, under the well-known conditions of our present ways of living, and by means of my art, albeit the same are matters of no great moment, I will relate these in their proper time and place, taking much more pride in having been born humble and having laid some honourable foundation for my family, than if I had been born of great lineage and had stained or overclouded that by my base qualities. So then I will make a beginning by saying how it pleased God I should be born.

. . .

When I reached the age of fifteen, I put myself, against my father's will, to the goldsmith's trade with a man called Antonio, son of Sandro, known commonly as Marcone the goldsmith. He was a most excellent craftsman and a very good fellow to boot, high-spirited and frank in all his ways. My father would not let him give me wages like the other apprentices; for having taken up the study of this art to please myself, he wished me to indulge my whim for drawing to the full. I did so willingly enough; and that honest master of mine took marvellous delight in my performances. He had an only son, a bastard, to whom he often gave his orders, in order to spare me. My liking for the art was so great, or, I may truly say, my natural bias, both one and the other, that in a few months I caught up the good, nay, the best young craftsmen in our business, and began to reap the fruits of my labours. I did not, however, neglect to gratify my good father from time to time by playing on the flute or cornet. Each time he heard me, I used to make his tears fall accompanied with deep-drawn sighs of satisfaction. My filial piety often made me give him that contentment, and induced me to pretend that I enjoyed the music too.

. . .

XII

When I had recovered my health, I returned to my old friend Marcone, the worthy goldsmith, who put me in the way of earning money, with which I helped my father and our household. About that time there came to Florence a sculptor named Piero Torrigiani; he arrived from England, where he had resided many years; and being intimate with my master, he daily visited his house; and when he saw my drawings and the things which I was making, he said: "I have come to Florence to enlist as many young men as I can; for I have undertaken to execute a great work for my king, and want some of my own Florentines to help me. Now your method of working and your designs are worthy rather of a sculptor than a goldsmith; and since I have to turn out a great piece of bronze, I will at the same time turn you into a rich and able artist." This man had a splendid person and a most arrogant spirit, with the air of a great soldier more than of a sculptor, especially in regard to his vehement gestures and his resonant voice, together with a habit he had of knitting his brows, enough to frighten any man of courage. He kept talking every day about his gallant feats among those beasts of Englishmen.

In course of conversation he happened to mention Michel Agnolo Buonarroti, led thereto by a drawing I had made from a cartoon of that divinest painter. This cartoon was the first masterpiece which Michel Agnolo exhibited, in proof of his stupendous talents. He produced it in competition with another painter, Lionardo da Vinci, who also made a cartoon; and both were intended for the council-hall in the palace of the Signory. They represented the taking of Pisa by the Florentines; and our admirable Lionardo had chosen to depict a battle of horses, with the capture of some standards, in as divine a style as could possibly be imagined. Michel Agnolo in his cartoon portrayed a number of foot-soldiers, who, the season being summer, had gone to bathe in Arno. He drew them at the very moment the alarm is sounded, and the men all naked run to arms; so splendid in their action that nothing survives of ancient or of modern art which touches the same lofty point of excellence; and as I have already said, the design of the great Lionardo was itself most admirably beautiful. These two cartoons stood, one in the palace of the Medici, the other in the hall of the Pope. So long as they remained intact, they were the school of the world. Though the divine Michel Agnolo in later life finished that great chapel of Pope Julius, he never rose halfway to the same pitch of power; his genius never afterwards attained to the force of those first studies.

XIII

Now let us return to Piero Torrigiani, who, with my drawing in his hand, spoke as follows: "This Buonarroti and I used, when we were boys, to go into the Church of the Carmine, to learn drawing from the chapel of Masaccio. It was Buonarroti's habit to banter all who were drawing there; and one day, among others, when he was annoying me, I got more angry than usual, and clenching my fist, gave him such a blow on the nose, that I felt bone and cartilage go down like biscuit beneath my knuckles; and this mark of mine he will carry with him to the grave." These words begat in me such hatred of the man, since I was always gazing at the masterpieces of the divine Michel Agnolo, that although I felt a wish to go with him to England, I now could never bear the sight of him.

All the while I was at Florence, I studied the noble manner of Michel Agnolo, and from this I have never deviated. About that time I contracted a close and familiar friendship with an amiable lad of my own age, who was also in the goldsmith's trade. He was called Francesco, son of Filippo, and grandson of Fra Lippo Lippi, that most excellent painter. Through intercourse together, such love grew up between us that, day or night, we never stayed apart. The house where he lived was still full of the fine studies which his father had made, bound up in several books of drawings by his hand, and taken from the best antiquities of Rome. The sight of these things filled me with passionate enthusiasm; and for two years or thereabouts we lived in intimacy. At that time I fashioned a silver bas-relief of the size of a little child's hand. It was intended for the clasp to a man's belt; for they were then worn as large as that. I carved on it a knot of leaves in the antique style, with figures of children and other masks of great beauty. This piece I made in the workshop of one Francesco Salimbene; and on its being exhibited to the trade, the goldsmiths praised me as the best young craftsman of their art.

There was one Giovan Battista, surnamed Il Tasso, a woodcarver, precisely of my own age, who one day said to me that if I was willing to go to Rome, he should be glad to join me. Now we had this conversation together immediately after dinner; and I being angry with my father for the same old reason of the music, said to Tasso: "You are a fellow of words, not deeds." He answered: "I too have come to anger with my mother; and if I had cash enough to take me to Rome, I would not turn back to lock the door of that wretched little workshop I call mine." To these words I replied that if that was all that kept him in Florence I had money enough in my pockets to bring us both to Rome. Talking thus and walking onwards, we found ourselves at the gate San Piero Gattolini without noticing that we had got there; whereupon I said: "Friend Tasso, this is God's doing that we have reached this gate without either you or me noticing that we were there; and now that I am here, it seems to me that I have finished half the journey." And so, being of one accord, we pursued our way together, saying, "Oh, what will our old folks say this evening?" We then made an agreement not to think more about them till we reached Rome. So we tied our aprons behind our backs, and trudged almost in silence to Siena. When we arrived at Siena, Tasso said (for he had hurt his feet) that he would not go farther, and asked me to lend him money to get back. I made answer: "I should not have enough left to go forward; you ought indeed to have thought of this on leaving Florence; and if it is because of your feet that you shirk the journey, we will find a return horse for Rome, which will deprive you of the excuse." Accordingly I hired a horse; and seeing that he did not answer, I took my way toward the gate of Rome. When he knew that I was firmly resolved to go, muttering between his teeth, and limping as well as he could, he came on behind me very slowly and at a great distance. On reaching the gate, I felt pity for my comrade, and waited for him, and took him on the crupper, saying: "What would our friends speak of us to-morrow, if, having left for Rome, we had not pluck to get beyond Siena?" Then the good Tasso said I spoke the truth; and as he was a pleasant fellow, he began to laugh and sing; and in this way, always singing and laughing, we travelled the whole way to Rome. I had just nineteen years then, and so had the century.

When we reached Rome, I put myself under a master who was known as Il Firenzuola. His name was Giovanni, and he came from Firenzuola in Lombardy, a most able craftsman in large vases and big plate of that kind. I showed him part of the model for the clasp which I had made in Florence at Salimbene's. It pleased him exceedingly; and turning to one of his journeymen, a Florentine called Giannotto Giannotti, who had been several years with him, he spoke as follows: "This fellow is one of the Florentines who know something, and you are one of those who know nothing." Then I recognised the man, and turned to speak with him; for before he went to Rome, we often went to draw together, and had been very intimate comrades. He was so put out by the words his master flung at him, that he said he did not recognise me or know who I was; whereupon I got angry, and cried out: "O Giannotto, you who were once my friend—for have we not been together in such and such places, and drawn, and ate, and drunk, and slept in company at your house in the country? I don't want you to bear witness on my behalf to this worthy man, your master, because I hope my hands are such that without aid from you they will declare what sort of a fellow I am."

XIV

When I had thus spoken, Firenzuola, who was a man of hot spirit and brave, turned to Giannotto, and said to him: "You vile rascal, aren't you ashamed to treat a man who has been so intimate a comrade with you in this way?" And with the same movement of quick feeling, he faced round and said to me: "Welcome to my workshop; and do as you have promised; let your hands declare what man you are."

He gave me a very fine piece of silver plate to work on for a cardinal. It was a little oblong box, copied from the porphyry sarcophagus before the door of the Rotonda. Beside what I copied, I enriched it with so many elegant masks of my invention, that my master went about showing it through the art, and boasting that so good a piece of work had been turned out from his shop. It was about half a cubit in size, and was so constructed as to serve for a salt-cellar at table. This was the first earning that I touched at Rome, and part of it I sent to assist my good father; the rest I kept for my own use, living upon it while I went about studying the antiquities of Rome, until my money failed, and I had to return to the shop for work. Battista del Tasso, my comrade, did not stay long in Rome, but went back to Florence.

After undertaking some new commissions, I took it into my head, as soon as I had finished them, to change my master; I had indeed been worried into doing so by a certain Milanese, called Pagolo Arsago. My first master, Firenzuola, had a great quarrel about this with Arsago, and abused him in my presence; whereupon I took up speech in defence of my new master. I said that I was born free, and free I meant to live, and that there was no reason to complain of him, far less of me, since some few crowns of wages were still due to me; also that I chose to go, like a free journeyman, where it pleased me, knowing I did wrong to no man. My new master then put in with his excuses, saying that he had not asked me to come, and that I should gratify him by returning with Firenzuola. To this I replied that I was not aware of wronging the latter in any way, and as I had completed his commissions, I chose to be my own master and not the man of others, and that he who wanted me must beg me of myself. Firenzuola cried: "I don't intend to beg you of yourself; I have done with you; don't show yourself again upon my premises." I reminded him of the money he owed me. He laughed me in the face; on which I said that if I knew how to use my tools in handicraft as well as he had seen, I could be quite as clever with my sword in claiming the just payment of my labour. While we were exchanging these words, an old man happened to come up, called Maestro Antonio, of San Marino. He was the chief among the Roman goldsmiths, and had been Firenzuola's master. Hearing what I had to say, which I took good care that he should understand, he immediately espoused my cause, and bade Firenzuola pay me. The dispute waxed warm, because Firenzuola was an admirable swordsman, far better than he was a goldsmith. Yet reason made itself heard; and I backed my cause with the same spirit, till I got myself paid. In course of time Firenzuola and I became friends, and at his request I stood godfather to one of his children.

XV

I went on working with Pagolo Arsago, and earned a good deal of money, the greater part of which I always sent to my good father. At the end of two years, upon my father's entreaty, I returned to Florence, and put myself once more under Francesco Salimbene, with whom I earned a great deal, and took continual pains to improve in my art. I renewed my intimacy with Francesco di Filippo; and though I was too much given to pleasure, owing to that accursed music, I never neglected to devote some hours of the day or night to study. At that time I fashioned a silver heart's-key (*chiavaquore*), as it was then called. This was a girdle three inches broad, which used to be made for brides and was executed in half relief with some small figures in the round. It was a commission from a man called Raffaello Lapaccini. I was very badly paid; but the honour which it brought me was worth far more than the gain I might have justly made by it. Having at this time worked with many different persons in Florence, I had come to know some worthy men among the goldsmiths, as, for instance, Marcone, my first master; but I also met with others reputed honest, who did all they could to ruin me, and robbed me grossly. When I perceived this, I left their company, and held them for thieves and blackguards. One of the goldsmiths, called Giovanbattista Sogliani, kindly accommodated me with part of his shop, which stood at the side of the New Market near the Landi's bank. There I finished several pretty pieces, and made good gains, and was able to give my family much help. This roused the jealousy of the bad men among my former masters, who were called Salvadore and Michele Guasconti. In the guild of the goldsmiths they had three big shops, and drove a thriving trade. On becoming aware of their evil will against me, I complained to certain worthy fellows, and remarked that they ought to have been satisfied with the thieveries they practised on me under the cloak of hypocritical kindness. This coming to their ears, they threatened to make me sorely repent of such words; but I, who knew not what the colour of fear was, paid them little or no heed.

. . .

XIX

At Siena I waited for the mail to Rome, which I afterwards joined; and when we passed the Paglia, we met a courier carrying news of the new Pope Clement VII. Upon my arrival in Rome, I went to work in the shop of the master-goldsmith Santi. He was dead; but a son of his carried on the business. He did not work himself, but entrusted all his commissions to a young man named Lucagnolo from Iesi, a country fellow, who while yet a child had come into Santi's service. This man was short but well proportioned, and was a more skilful craftsman than any one whom I had met with up to that time; remarkable for facility and excellent in design. He executed large plate only; that is to say, vases of the utmost beauty, basons, and such pieces. Having put myself to work there, I began to make some candelabra for the Bishop of Salamanca, a Spaniard. They were richly chased, so far as that sort of work admits. A pupil of Raffaello da Urbino called Gian Francesco, and commonly known as Il Fattore, was a painter of great ability; and being on terms of friendship with the Bishop, he introduced me to his favour, so that I obtained many commissions from that prelate, and earned considerable sums of money.

During that time I went to draw sometimes in Michel Agnolo's chapel, and sometimes in the house of Agostino Chigi of Siena, which contained many incomparable paintings by the hand of that great master Raffaello. This I did on feast-days, because the house was then inhabited by Messer Gismondo, Agostino's brother. They plumed themselves exceedingly when they saw young men of my sort coming to study in their palaces. Gismondo's wife, noticing my frequent presence in that house—she was a lady as courteous as could be, and of surpassing beauty—came up to me one day, looked at my drawings, and asked me if I was a sculptor or a painter; to whom I said I was a goldsmith. She remarked that I drew too well for a goldsmith; and having made one of her waiting-maids bring a lily of the finest diamonds set in gold, she showed it to me, and bade me value it. I valued it at 800 crowns. Then she said that I had very nearly hit the mark, and asked me whether I felt capable of setting the stones really well. I said that I should much like to do so, and began before her eyes to make a little sketch for it, working all the better because of the pleasure I took in conversing with so lovely and agreeable a gentlewoman. When the sketch was finished, another Roman lady of great beauty joined us; she had been above, and now descending to the ground-floor, asked Madonna Porzia what she was doing there. She answered with a smile: "I am amusing myself by watching this worthy young man at his drawing; he is as good as he is handsome." I had by this time acquired a trifle of assurance, mixed, however, with some honest bashfulness; so I blushed and said: "Such as I am, lady, I shall ever be most ready to serve you." The gentlewoman, also slightly blushing, said: "You know well that I want you to serve me;" and reaching me the lily, told me to take it away; and gave me besides twenty golden crowns which she had in her bag, and added: "Set me the jewel after the fashion you have sketched, and keep for me the old gold in which it is now set." On this the Roman lady observed: "If I were in that young man's body, I should go off without asking leave." Madonna Porzia replied that virtues rarely are at home with vices, and that if I did such a thing, I should strongly belie my good looks of an honest man. Then turning round, she took the Roman lady's hand, and with a pleasant smile said: "Farewell, Benvenuto." I stayed on a short while at the drawing I was making, which was a copy of a Jove by Raffaello. When I had finished it and left the house, I set myself to making a little model of wax, in order to show how the jewel would look when it was completed. This I took to Madonna Porzia, whom I found with the same Roman lady. Both of them were highly satisfied with my work, and treated me so kindly that, being somewhat emboldened, I promised the jewel should be twice as good as the model. Accordingly I set hand to it, and in twelve days I finished it in the form of a fleur-de-lys, as I have said above, ornamenting it with little masks, children, and animals, exquisitely enamelled, whereby the diamonds which formed the lily were more than doubled in effect.

XX

While I was working at this piece, Lucagnolo, of whose ability I have before spoken, showed considerable discontent, telling me over and over again that I might acquire far more profit and honour by helping him to execute large plate, as I had done at first. I made him answer that, whenever I chose, I should always be capable of working at great silver pieces; but that things like that on which I was now engaged were not commissioned every day; and beside their bringing no less honour than large silver plate, there was also more profit to be made by them. He laughed me in the face, and said: "Wait and see Benvenuto; for by the time that you have finished that work of yours, I will make haste to have finished this vase, which I took in hand when you did the jewel; and then experience shall teach you what profit I shall get from my vase, and what you will get from your ornament." I answered that I was very glad indeed to enter into such a competition with so good a craftsman as he was, because the end would show which of us was mistaken. Accordingly both the one and the other of us, with a scornful smile upon our lips, bent our heads in grim earnest to the work, which both were now desirous of accomplishing; so that after about ten days, each had finished his undertaking with great delicacy and artistic skill.

Lucagnolo's was a huge silver piece, used at the table of Pope Clement, into which he flung away bits of bone and the rind of divers fruits, while eating; an object of ostentation rather than necessity. The vase was adorned with two fine handles, together with many masks, both small and great, and masses of lovely foliage, in as exquisite a style of elegance as could be imagined; and seeing which I said it was the most beautiful vase that ever I set eyes on. Thinking he had convinced me, Lucagnolo replied: "Your work seems to me no less beautiful, but we shall soon perceive the difference between the two." So he took his vase and carried it to the Pope, who was very well pleased with it, and ordered at once that he should be paid at the ordinary rate of such large plate. Meanwhile I carried mine to Madonna Porzia, who looked at it with astonishment, and told me I had far surpassed my promise. Then she bade me ask for my reward whatever I liked; for it seemed to her my desert was so great that if I craved a castle she could hardly recompense me; but since that was not in her hands to bestow, she added laughing that I must beg what lay within her power. I answered that the greatest reward I could desire for my labour was to have satisfied her ladyship. Then, smiling in my turn, and bowing to her, I took my leave, saying I wanted no reward but that. She turned to the Roman lady and said: "You see that the qualities we discerned in him are companied by virtues, and not vices." They both expressed their admiration, and then Madonna Porzia continued: "Friend Benvenuto, have you never heard it said that when the poor give to the rich, the devil laughs?" I replied: "Quite true! and yet, in the midst of all his troubles, I should like this time to see him laugh"; and as I took my leave, she said that this time she had no will to bestow on him that favour.

When I came back to the shop, Lucagnolo had the money for his vase in a paper packet; and on my arrival he cried out: "Come and compare the price of your jewel with the price of my plate." I said that he must leave things as they were till the next day, because I hoped that even as my work in its kind was not less excellent than his, so I should be able to show him quite an equal price for it.

XXI

On the day following, Madonna Porzia sent a major-domo of hers to my shop, who called me out, and putting into my hands a paper packet full of money from his lady, told me that she did not choose the devil should have his whole laugh out: by which she hinted that the money sent me was not the entire payment merited by my industry, and other messages were added worthy of so courteous a lady. Lucagnolo, who was burning to compare his packet with mine, burst into the shop; then in the presence of twelve journeymen and some neighbours, eager to behold the result of this competition, he seized his packet, scornfully exclaiming "Ou! ou!" three or four times, while he poured his money on the counter with a great noise. They were twenty-five crowns in giulios; and he fancied that mine would be four or five crowns *di moneta.* I for my part, stunned and stifled by his cries, and by the looks and smiles of the bystanders, first peeped into my packet; then, after seeing that it contained nothing but gold, I retired to one end of the counter, and, keeping my eyes lowered and making no noise at all, I lifted it with both hands suddenly above my head, and emptied it like a mill hopper. My coin was twice as much as his; which caused the onlookers, who had fixed their eyes on me with some derision, to turn round suddenly to him and say: "Lucagnolo, Benvenuto's pieces, being all of gold and twice as many as yours, make a far finer effect." I thought for certain that, what with jealousy and what with shame, Lucagnolo would have fallen dead upon the spot; and though he took the third part of my gain, since I was a journeyman (for such is the custom of the trade, two-thirds fall to the workman and one-third to the masters of the shop), yet inconsiderate envy had more power in him than avarice: it ought indeed to have worked quite the other way, he being a peasant's son from Iesi. He cursed his art and those who taught it him, vowing that thenceforth he would never work at large plate, but give his whole attention to those whoreson gewgaws, since they were so well paid. Equally enraged on my side, I answered that every bird sang its own note; that he talked after the fashion of the hovels he came from; but that I dared swear that I should succeed with ease in making his lubberly lumber, while he would never be successful in my whoreson gewgaws. Thus I flung off in a passion, telling him that I would soon show him that I spoke truth. The bystanders openly declared against him, holding him for a lout, as indeed he was, and me for a man, as I had proved myself.

XXII

Next day, I went to thank Madonna Porzia, and told her that her ladyship had done the opposite of what she said she would; for that while I wanted to make the devil laugh, she had made him once more deny God. We both laughed pleasantly at this, and she gave me other commissions for fine and substantial work.

Meanwhile, I contrived, by means of a pupil of Raffaello da Urbino, to get an order from the Bishop of Salamanca for one of those great water-vessels called *acquereccia,* which are used for ornaments to place on sideboards. He wanted a pair made of equal size; and one of them he intrusted to Lucagnolo, the other to me. Giovan Francesco, the painter I have mentioned, gave us the design. Accordingly I set hand with marvellous good-will to this piece of plate, and was accommodated with a part of his workshop by a Milanese named Maestro Giovan Piero della Tacca. Having made my preparations, I calculated how much money I should need for certain affairs of my own, and sent all the rest to assist my poor father.

It so happened that just when this was being paid to him in Florence, he stumbled upon one of those Radicals who were in the Eight at the time when I got into that little trouble there. It was the very man who had abused him so rudely, and who swore that I should certainly be sent into the country with the lances. Now this fellow had some sons of very bad morals and repute; wherefore my father said to him: "Misfortunes can happen to anybody, especially to men of choleric humour when they are in the right, even as it happened to my son; but let the rest of his life bear witness how virtuously I have brought him up. Would God, for your wellbeing, that your sons may act neither worse nor better towards you than mine do to me. God rendered me able to bring them up as I have done; and where my own power could not reach, 'twas He who rescued them, against your expectation, out of your violent hands." On leaving the man, he wrote me all this story, begging me for God's sake to practise music at times, in order that I might not lose the fine accomplishment which he had taught me with such trouble. The letter so overflowed with expressions of the tenderest fatherly affection, that I was moved to tears of filial piety, resolving, before he died, to gratify him amply with regard to music. Thus God grants us those lawful blessings which we ask in prayer, nothing doubting.

XXIII

While I was pushing forward Salamanca's vase, I had only one little boy as help, whom I had taken at the entreaty of friends, and half against my own will, to be my workman. He was about fourteen years of age, bore the name of Paulino, and was son to a Roman burgess, who lived upon the income of his property. Paulino was the best-mannered, the most honest, and the most beautiful boy I ever saw in my whole life. His modest ways and actions, together with his superlative beauty and his devotion to myself, bred in me as great an affection for him as a man's breast can hold. This passionate love led me oftentimes to delight the lad with music; for I observed that his marvellous features, which by complexion wore a tone of modest melancholy, brightened up, and when I took my cornet, broke into a smile so lovely and so sweet, that I do not marvel at the silly stories which the Greeks have written about the deities of heaven. Indeed, if my boy had lived in those times, he would probably have turned their heads still more. He had a sister, named Faustina, more beautiful, I verily believe, than that Faustina about whom the old books gossip so. Sometimes he took me to their vineyard, and, so far as I could judge, it struck me that Paulino's good father would have welcomed me as a son-in-law. This affair led me to play more than I was used to do.

It happened at that time that one Giangiacomo of Cesena, a musician in the Pope's band, and a very excellent performer, sent word through Lorenzo, the trumpeter of Lucca, who is now in our Duke's service, to inquire whether I was inclined to help them at the Pope's Ferragosto, playing soprano with my cornet in some motets of great beauty selected by them for that occasion. Although I had the greatest desire to finish the vase I had begun, yet, since music has a wondrous charm of its own, and also because I wished to please my old father, I consented to join them. During eight days before the festival we practised two hours a day together; then on the first of August we went to the Belvedere, and while Pope Clement was at table, we played those carefully studied motets so well that his Holiness protested he had never heard music more sweetly executed or with better harmony of parts. He sent for Giangiacomo, and asked him where and how he had procured so excellent a cornet for soprano, and inquired particularly who I was. Giangiacomo told him my name in full. Whereupon the Pope said: "So, then, he is the son of Maestro Giovanni?" On being assured I was, the Pope expressed his wish to have me in his service with the other bandsmen. Giangiacomo replied: "Most blessed Father, I cannot pretend for certain that you will get him, for his profession, to which he devotes himself assiduously, is that of a goldsmith, and he works in it miraculously well, and earns by it far more than he could do by playing." To this the Pope added: "I am the better inclined to him now that I find him possessor of a talent more than I expected. See that he obtains the same salary as the rest of you; and tell him from me to join my service, and that I will find work enough by the day for him to do at his other trade." Then stretching out his hand, he gave him a hundred golden crowns of the Camera in a handkerchief, and said: "Divide these so that he may take his share."

When Giangiacomo left the Pope, he came to us, and related in detail all that the Pope had said; and after dividing the money between the eight of us, and giving me my share, he said to me: "Now I am going to have you inscribed among our company." I replied: "Let the day pass; to-morrow I will give my answer." When I left them, I went meditating whether I ought to accept the invitation, inasmuch as I could not but suffer if I abandoned the noble studies of my art. The following night my father appeared to me in dream, and begged me with tears of tenderest affection, for God's love and his, to enter upon this engagement. Methought I answered that nothing would induce me to do so. In an instant he assumed so horrible an aspect as to frighten me out of my wits, and cried: "If you do not, you will have a father's curse; but if you do, may you be ever blessed by me!" When I woke, I ran, for very fright, to have myself inscribed. Then I wrote to my old father, telling him the news, which so affected him with extreme joy that a sudden fit of illness took him, and well-nigh brought him to death's door. In his answer to my letter, he told me that he too had dreamed nearly the same as I had.

XXIV

Knowing now that I had gratified my father's honest wish, I began to think that everything would prosper with me to a glorious and honourable end. Accordingly, I set myself with indefatigable industry to the completion of the vase I had begun for Salamanca. That prelate was a very extraordinary man, extremely rich, but difficult to please. He sent daily to learn what I was doing; and when his messenger did not find me at home, he broke into fury, saying that he would take the work out of my hands and give it to others to finish. This came of my slavery to that accursed music. Still I laboured diligently night and day, until, when I had brought my work to a point when it could be exhibited, I submitted it to the inspection of the Bishop. This so increased his desire to see it finished, that I was sorry I had shown it. At the end of three months I had it ready, with little animals and foliage and masks, as beautiful as one could hope to see. No sooner was it done than I sent it by the hand of my workman, Paulino, to show that able artist Lucagnolo, of whom I have spoken above. Paulino, with the grace and beauty which belonged to him, spoke as follows: "Messer Lucagnolo, Benvenuto bids me say that he has sent to show you his promises and your lumber, expecting in return to see from you his gewgaws." This message given, Lucagnolo took up the vase, and carefully examined it; then he said to Paulino: "Fair boy, tell your master that he is a great and able artist, and that I beg him to be willing to have me for a friend, and not to engage in aught else." The mission of that virtuous and marvellous lad caused me the greatest joy; and then the vase was carried to Salamanca, who ordered it to be valued. Lucagnolo took part in the valuation, estimating and praising it far above my own opinion. Salamanca, lifting up the vase, cried like a true Spaniard: "I swear by God that I will take as long in paying him as he has lagged in making it." When I heard this, I was exceedingly put out, and fell to cursing all Spain and every one who wished well to it.

Amongst other beautiful ornaments, this vase had a handle, made all of one piece, with most delicate mechanism, which, when a spring was touched, stood upright above the mouth of it. While the prelate was one day ostentatiously exhibiting my vase to certain Spanish gentlemen of his suite, it chanced that one of them, upon Monsignor's quitting the room, began roughly to work the handle, and as the gentle spring which moved it could not bear his loutish violence, it broke in his hand. Aware what mischief he had done, he begged the butler who had charge of the Bishop's plate to take it to the master who had made it, for him to mend, and promised to pay what price he asked, provided it was set to rights at once. So the vase came once more into my hands, and I promised to put it forthwith in order, which indeed I did. It was brought to me before dinner; and at twenty-two o'clock the man who brought it returned, all in a sweat, for he had run the whole way, Monsignor having again asked for it to show to certain other gentlemen. The butler, then, without giving me time to utter a word, cried: "Quick, quick, bring the vase." I, who wanted to act at leisure and not to give it up to him, said that I did not mean to be so quick. The serving-man got into such a rage that he made as though he would put one hand to his sword, while with the other he threatened to break the shop open. To this I put a stop at once with my own weapon, using therewith spirited language, and saying: "I am not going to give it to you! Go and tell Monsignor, your master, that I want the money for my work before I let it leave this shop." When the fellow saw he could not obtain it by swaggering, he fell to praying me, as one prays to the Cross, declaring that if I would only give it up, he would take care I should be paid. These words did not make me swerve from my purpose; but I kept on saying the same thing. At last, despairing of success, he swore to come with Spaniards enough to cut me in pieces. Then he took to his heels; while I, who inclined to believe partly in their murderous attack, resolved that I would defend myself with courage. So I got an admirable little gun ready, which I used for shooting game, and muttered to myself: "He who robs me of my property and labour may take my life too, and welcome." While I was carrying on this debate in my own mind, a crowd of Spaniards arrived, led by their major-domo, who, with the headstrong rashness of his race, bade them go in and take the vase and give me a good beating. Hearing these words, I showed them the muzzle of my gun, and prepared to fire, and cried in a loud voice: "Renegade Jews, traitors, is it thus that one breaks into houses and shops in our city of Rome? Come as many of you thieves as like, an inch nearer to this wicket, and I'll blow all their brains out with my gun." Then I turned the muzzle toward their major-domo, and making as though I would discharge it, called out: "And you big thief, who are egging them on, I mean to kill you first." He clapped spurs to the jennet he was riding, and took flight headlong. The commotion we were making stirred up all the neighbours, who came crowding round, together with some Roman gentlemen who chanced to pass and cried: "Do but kill the renegades, and we will stand by you." These words had the effect of frightening the Spaniards in good earnest. They withdrew, and were compelled by the circumstances to relate the whole affair to Monsignor. Being a man of inordinate haughtiness, he rated the members of his household, both because they had engaged in such an act of violence, and also because, having begun, they had not gone through with it. At this juncture the painter, who had been concerned in the whole matter, came in, and the Bishop bade him go and tell me that if I did not bring the vase at once, he would make mincemeat of me; but if I brought it, he would pay its price down. These threats were so far from terrifying me, that I sent him word I was going immediately to lay my case before the Pope.

In the meantime, his anger and my fear subsided; whereupon, being guaranteed by some Roman noblemen of high degree that the prelate would not harm me, and having assurance that I should be paid, I armed myself with a large poniard and my good coat of mail, and betook myself to his palace, where he had drawn up all his household. I entered, and Paulino followed with the silver vase. It was just like passing through the Zodiac, neither more nor less; for one of them had the face of the lion, another of the scorpion, a third of the crab. However, we passed onward to the presence of the rascally priest, who spouted out a torrent of such language as only priests and Spaniards have at their command. In return I never raised my eyes to look at him, nor answered word for word. That seemed to augment the fury of his anger; and causing paper to be put before me, he commanded me to write an acknowledgment to the effect that I had been amply satisfied and paid in full. Then I raised my head and said I should be very glad to do so when I had received the money. The Bishop's rage continued to rise; threats and recriminations were flung about; but at last the money was paid, and I wrote the receipt. Then I departed, glad at heart and in high spirits.

DESIDERIUS ERASMUS

In contrast to the Italian Renaissance, which became quite secular and pagan in temper, the Renaissance in northern Europe retained more of the medieval Christian outlook. The combination of Renaissance humanism with Christianity, characteristic of the northern Renaissance, is exemplified most clearly in the writings of Erasmus of Rotterdam (1466–1536). Intensely aware of the shortcomings of the Catholic Church of his day, Erasmus was nevertheless convinced that the elimination of these evils lay not in a rejection of Christianity but rather in a return to it. Believing that the Church had departed from the true teachings of its founder, he urged a reform of religious beliefs and practices based on a return to the gospel of the New Testament or, as he called it, the "philosophy of Christ." Erasmus felt that such a reform should be inaugurated and carried forward by the Church itself through a program of widespread education. He broke off a long-standing friendship with Martin Luther because he was unwilling to go along with Luther's insistence that, since gradual reform from within based on an appeal to reason was futile, the only solution lay in violent revolt against the Church. Although Erasmus refused to join the Protestant movement, he contributed significantly to the Reformation by appealing for a return to the original teachings of Christ and by directing pointed satires against abuses within the Church.

The following selection is from the most famous work of Erasmus, The Praise of Folly *(1509). In it are most of the major Erasmian theses, in language that reveals the literary genius of its author.*

The Praise of Folly

However mortal folk may commonly speak of me (for I am not ignorant how ill the name of Folly sounds, even to the greatest fools), I am she—the only she, I may say—whose divine influence makes gods and men rejoice. One great and sufficient proof of this is that the instant I stepped up to speak to this crowded assembly, all faces at once brightened with

Desiderius Erasmus, THE PRAISE OF FOLLY, *trans. H. H. Hudson (Princeton: Princeton University Press, 1941), pp. 7, 15–19, 22–25, 67–70, 76–79, 85–88, 93–100, 125. Used by permission of Princeton University Press.*

a fresh and unwonted cheerfulness, all of you suddenly unbent your brows, and with frolic and affectionate smiles you applauded; so that as I look upon all present about me, you seem flushed with nectar, like gods in Homer, not without some nepenthe, also; whereas a moment ago you were sitting moody and depressed, as if you had come out of the cave of Trophonius. Just as it commonly happens, when the sun first shows his splendid golden face to the earth or when, after a bitter winter, young spring breathes mild west winds, that a new face comes over everything, new color and a sort of youthfulness appear; so at the mere sight of me, you straightway take on another aspect. And thus what great orators elsewhere can hardly bring about in a long, carefully planned speech, I have done in a moment, with nothing but my looks. . . .

Can life be called life at all if you take away pleasure? . . . You applaud! I knew that none of you is so wise—or rather so foolish—no, I prefer to say so wise—as to err on that point. Even the famous Stoics do not really scorn pleasure, but they studiously dissemble and attack it in public with a thousand reproaches, only to the end that, with other people scared off, they may enjoy it more liberally. But let them tell me, by Jove, what part of life is not sad, unpleasant, graceless, flat, and burdensome, unless you have pleasure added to it, that is, a seasoning of folly? As proof of this, there is extant that lovely tribute to me by Sophocles, who can never be sufficiently praised, "To know nothing affords the happiest life"; and he would be authority enough but come, I will open the whole matter, step by step.

First of all, who does not know that the earliest period of a man's life is by far the happiest for him and by far the most pleasant for all about him? What is it in children, that we should kiss them the way we do, and cuddle them, and fondle them —so that even an enemy would give aid to one of that age—except this enchantment of folly, which prudent nature carefully bestows on the newly born; so that by this pleasure, as a sort of prepayment, they win the favor of their nurses and parents and make these forget the pains of bringing them up. After this comes adolescence. How welcome it is in every home! How well everyone wishes it! How studiously does everyone promote it, how officiously they lend it the helping hand! But, I ask, whence comes this grace of youth? Whence but from me, by whose favor the young know so little—and how lightly worn is that little! And presently when lads grown larger begin, through experience and discipline, to have some smack of manhood, I am a liar if by the same token the brightness of their beauty does not fade, their quickness diminish, their wit lose its edge, their vigor slacken. The farther one gets from me, then, the less and less he lives, until *molesta senectus* (that is, irksome old age) arrives, hateful to others, to be sure, but also and more so to itself.

Old age would not be tolerable to any mortal at all, were it not that I, out of pity for its troubles, stand once more at its right hand; and just as the gods of the poets customarily save, by some metamorphosis or other, those who are dying, in like manner I bring those who have one foot in the grave back to their infancy again, for as long as possible; so that the folk are not far off in speaking of them as "in their second childhood." If anyone would like to know the method of bringing about this alteration, I shall not conceal it. I lead them to my spring of Lethe —for that stream rises in the Fortunate Isles, and only a little rivulet of it flows in the underworld—so that then and there they may drink draughts of forgetfulness. With their cares of mind purged away, by gentle stages they become young again. But now, you say, they merely dote, and play the fool. Yes, quite so. But precisely this it is to renew one's infancy. Is to be childish anything other than to dote and play the fool? As if in that age the greatest joy were not this, that one knows nothing! For who does not dread and shun as a prodigy the boy who has a man's wisdom? As the proverb current among the folk has it, "I hate a boy of premature wisdom." Who could bear to converse or transact business with an old man who should join to his long experience of things, an equal vigor of mind and sharpness of judgment? Hence it is that an old man dotes, thanks to me.

Yet this dotard of mind, meanwhile, is exempt from those carking cares by which your wise man is distracted. My dotard, too, is still an acceptable pot-companion. He does not feel life's tedium, which a younger constitution can scarce abide. Occasionally, like the old gentleman in Plautus, he goes back to conning those three letters, *a, m, o*—the unhappiest man in the world if he had his wits about him; but meanwhile happy, through my grace, a source of pleasure to his friends, a hail-fellow-well-met. Thus it is that, in Homer, speech sweeter than honey flows from the lips of Nestor, while that of Achilles is bitter; and in the same author the old men sitting on the wall utter gracious and elegant discourse. On this one score, indeed, the old even have an advantage over real childhood, which is sweet but tongue-tied, and lacks the chief solace of life, uninhibited garrulousness. Add to this that the old take great pleasure in children, and children in turn are delighted with the old. "God ever brings like to like." For wherein do they differ, except that age is more wrinkled and has counted more birthdays? Otherwise, their whitish hair, mouth without teeth, shortened body, appetite for milk, babbling, chatter, toying, shortness of memory, heedlessness, and all their other traits, agree exactly. And the farther the old proceed in age, the nearer they come back to the semblance of childhood; until like children indeed, having no weariness of life or sense of death, they take leave of the world.

Now let anyone that will compare this boon of mine with the metamorphoses produced by other gods. Those which they worked when angry it is not well to mention; but take the stories of people toward whom they were especially friendly. They would transform somebody into a tree, or a bird, or a cicada, or even into a snake; as if this were not to perish indeed—to be made into something else! But I restore the very same man to the best and happiest part of his life. And if mortals would abstain utterly from any contact with wisdom, and live out their span continuously in my company, there would not be any such thing as old age, but in happiness they would enjoy perpetual youth. . . .

But now the time has come when, following the pattern of Homer, we should turn our backs on the heavens and travel down again to earth, where likewise we shall perceive nothing joyous or fortunate except by my favor. First of all, you see with what foresight nature, the source and artificer of the human race, has made provision that this race shall never lack its seasoning of folly. For since, by the Stoic definitions, wisdom is no other than to be governed by reason, while folly is to be moved at the whim of the passions, Jupiter, to the end, obviously, that the life of mankind should not be sad and harsh, put in—how much more of passions than of reason? Well, the proportions run about one pound to half an ounce. Besides, he imprisoned reason in a cramped corner of the head, and turned over all the rest of the body to the emotions. After that he instated two most violent tyrants, as it were, in opposition to reason: anger, which holds the citadel of the breast, and consequently the very spring of life, the heart; and lust, which rules a broad empire lower down, even to the privy parts. How much reason is good for, against these twin forces, the ordinary life of men sufficiently reveals when reason—and it is all she can do—shouts out her prohibitions until she is hoarse and dictates formulas of virtue. But the passions simply bid their so-called king go hang himself, and more brazenly roar down the opposition, until the man, tired out as well, willingly yields and knuckles under.

But a tiny bit more than a grain of reason is vouchsafed to the male, born as he is for handling affairs; and in order that he might give and take counsel in manly fashion, he brought me into the council chamber, as everywhere else. Right off I gave him advice worthy of myself: namely, that he should form an alliance with woman—a stupid animal, God wot, and a giddy one, yet funny and sweet—so that in domestic familiarity her folly might leaven the lumpishness of the male temperament. When Plato shows himself in doubt whether to place woman in the class of rational creatures or in that of brutes, he only wishes to point out how flagrant is the folly of the sex. For if by chance some woman wishes to be thought of as wise, she does nothing but show herself twice a fool. It is as if one took a bull to the masseuse, a thing quite "against the grain," as the phrase is. It is doubly a fault, you know, when against nature one assumes the color of a virtue, warping one's character in a direction not its own. Just as, according to the proverb of the Greeks, "an ape is always an ape, though dressed in scarlet," so a woman is always a woman —that is, a fool—whatever part she may have chosen to play.

And yet I do not suppose the female sex is so foolish as to become incensed at me for this, that I, a woman and Folly as well, attribute folly to women. For if they rightly consider the matter, they are bound to score up a credit to Folly for this, that in many respects they are better off than men. For one thing, they have the gift of beauty, which with good reason they prefer above all things else. Assisted by it, they wield a tyranny over tyrants themselves. Whence but from the malady of prudence comes that horrendous visage, rough as to skin, with an undergrowth of beard and a suggestion of senility, in men? Whereas the cheeks of women are always bare and smooth, their voice gentle, their skin soft, as if presenting a picture of perpetual youth. Furthermore, what else do they want in life but to be as attractive as possible to men? Do not all their trimmings and cosmetics have this end in view, and all their baths, fittings, creams, scents, as well—and all those arts of making up, painting, and fashioning the face, eyes, and skin? Just so. And by what other sponsor are they better recommended to men than by folly? What is there that men will not permit to women? But for what consideration, except pleasure? And women please by no other thing than their folly. The truth of this no one will deny who has considered what nonsense a man talks with a woman, and what quaint tricks he plays, as often as he has a mind to enjoy the delights of feminine society. . . .

And if I should seem at this point to be speaking more rashly than truly, I suggest that for a time we shall look into the lives of men, and it will be apparent how much they owe to me and how many, the greatest along with the humble, follow me. We shall not run over the lives of everybody, for that would take too long, but only the most notable; from which it will be easy to form an opinion about the others. For why should I spend time on the common and baser sort, who are wholly mine beyond controversy? They everywhere teem with so many forms of folly and daily devise so many new ones that a thousand Democrituses would not suffice for laughing at them—and there would be work, then, for one more Democritus to laugh at the laughers.

You would never believe what sport and entertainment your mortal manikins provide daily for the gods. These gods, you know, set aside their sober forenoon hours for composing quarrels and giving ear to prayers. But after that, when they are well moistened with nectar and have no desire for the transaction of business, they seek out some promontory of heaven and, sitting there with faces bent downward, they watch what mortal men are adoing. There is no show like it. Good God, what a theater! How various the action of fools! (I may say that now and then I take a seat alongside the gods of the poets.) Here is a fellow dying for love of a sweet young thing, and the less he is loved in return, the more helplessly he is in love. This one marries a dowry, not a wife. This one prostitutes his own wife. The jealousy of another keeps watch like Argus. Here is a man in mourning, but mercy me, what fool things he says and does! Hiring mourners as if they were actors, to play a comedy of grief! Another man squeezes out a tear at the tomb of his mother-in-law. This one spends on his belly whatever he can scrape together by hook or crook, but presently he will be just as hungry again. Another finds nothing better than sleep and idleness. There are those who get themselves into a stew working at what is other people's business, while they neglect their own. There is also the broker, who accounts himself rich on other people's money, but is on the way to bankruptcy. Another thinks that the happy life consists in living like a pauper in order that his heir may be wealthy. Another, for the sake of a small and uncertain profit, sails the seven seas, exposing his life, which no money could pay for, to the hazard of waves and winds. This one prefers seeking riches in war to passing a safe and quiet life at home. Some decide that they can most conveniently attain to wealth by courting and fawning upon childless old men. There are even those who prefer to do the same to rich old women. Both kinds furnish rare sport to the gods who are spectators, because they are usually cheated by the parties they set out to catch.

But the most foolish and sordid of all are your merchants, in that they carry on the most sordid business of all and this by the most sordid methods; for on occasion they lie, they perjure themselves, they steal, they cheat, they impose on the public. Yet they make themselves men of importance—because they have gold rings on their fingers. Nor do they lack for flattering friars who admire them and call them Right Honorable in public, with the purpose, surely, that some little driblet from the ill-gotten gains may flow to themselves. Elsewhere you will see certain Pythagoreans, in whose eyes all things are common—to such a degree, in fact, that whatever they light upon that is lying around loose they carry off with a tranquil spirit, as if it passed to them by inheritance. There are others who are rich only in wishes; they build beautiful air-castles and conceive that doing so is enough for happiness. Some delight in passing for wealthy men away from home, though they starve meanly enough in their own houses. One man hastens to put into circulation what money he has; his neighbor hoards his up through thick and thin. This one pushes forward as a candidate for public honors; that one finds his pleasure by his fireside. A good many people bring suits which are destined never to end; once and again they eagerly strive to outdo each other—in enriching the judge who sets the postponements and the advocate who colludes with him. One burns with zeal for revolutions; another is toiling upon his Grand Scheme. This man leaves wife and children at home and sets out on a pilgrimage to Jerusalem, Rome, or the shrine of St. James, where he has no particular business. In sum, if you might look down from the moon, as Menippus did of old, upon the numberless agitations among mortal men, you would think you were seeing a swarm of flies or gnats, quarreling among themselves, waging wars, setting snares for each other, robbing, sporting, wantoning, being born, growing old, and dying. And one can scarce believe what commotions and what tragedies this animalcule, little as he is and so soon to perish, sets agoing. For sometimes a trivial war or a spell of the plague will sweep off and utterly wipe out thousands of them at once.

But I should be most foolish myself and worthy of the manifold laughter of Democritus, if I should go on counting forms of folly and madness among the folk. Let me turn to those who maintain among mortals an appearance of wisdom and, as the saying is, seek for the golden bough. . . .

Among men of learned professions, the lawyers may claim first place for themselves, nor is there any other class quite so self-satisfied; for while they industriously roll up the stone of Sisyphus by dint of weaving together six hundred laws in the same breath, no matter how little to the purpose, and by dint of piling glosses upon glosses and opinions upon opinions, they contrive to make their profession seem the most difficult of all. What is really tedious commends itself to them as brilliant. Let us put in with them the logicians and sophists, a breed of men more loquacious than the famed brass kettles at Dodona; any one of them can out-chat twenty picked women. They would be happier, however, if they were merely talkative, and not quarrelsome as well, to such a degree that they will stubbornly cut and thrust over a lock of goat's wool, quite losing track of the truth in question while they go on disputing. Their self-love makes them happy, and equipped with three syllogisms they will unhesitatingly dare to join battle upon any subject with any man. Mere frowardness brings them back unbeaten, though you match Stentor against them.

Near these march the scientists, reverenced for their beards and the fur on their gowns, who teach that they alone are wise while the rest of mortal men flit about as shadows. How pleasantly they dote, indeed, while they construct their numberless worlds, and measure the sun, moon, stars, and spheres as with thumb and line. They assign causes for lightning, winds, eclipses, and other inexplicable things, never hesitating a whit, as if they were privy to the secrets of nature, artificer of things, or as if they visited us fresh from the council of the gods. Yet all the while nature is laughing grandly at them and their conjectures. For to prove that they have good intelligence of nothing, this is a sufficient argument: they can never explain why they disagree with each other on every subject. Thus knowing nothing in general, they profess to know all things in particular; though they are ignorant even of themselves, and on occasion do not see the ditch or the stone lying across their path, because many of them are blear-eyed or absent-minded; yet they proclaim that they perceive ideas, universals, forms without matter, primary substances, quiddities, and ecceities—things so tenuous, I fear, that Lynceus himself could not see them. When they especially disdain the vulgar crowd is when they bring out their triangles, quadrangles, circles, and mathematical pictures of the sort, lay one upon the other, intertwine them into a maze, then deploy some letters as if in line of battle, and presently do it over in reverse order—and all to involve the uninitiated in darkness. Their fraternity does not lack those who predict future events by consulting the stars, and promise wonders even more magical; and these lucky scientists find people to believe them.

Perhaps it were better to pass over the theologians in silence, and not to move such a Lake Camarina, or to handle such an herb *Anagyris foetida,* as that marvellously supercilious and irascible race. For they may attack me with six hundred arguments, in squadrons, and drive me to make a recantation; which if I refuse, they will straightway proclaim me an heretic. By this thunderbolt they are wont to terrify any toward whom they are ill-disposed. No other people are so loth to acknowledge my favors to them; yet the divines are bound to me by no ordinary obligations. They are happy in their self-love, and as if they already inhabited the third heaven they look down from a height on all other mortal men as on creatures that crawl on the ground, and they come near to pitying them. They are protected by a wall of scholastic definitions, arguments, corollaries, implicit and explicit propositions; they have so many hideaways that they could not be caught even by the net of Vulcan; for they slip out on their distinctions, by which also they cut through all knots as easily as with a double-bitted axe from Tenedos; and they abound with newly-invented terms and prodigious vocables. Furthermore, they explain as pleases them the most arcane matters, such as by what method the world was founded and set in order, through what conduits original sin has been passed down along the generations, by what means, in what measure, and how long the perfect Christ was in the Virgin's womb, and how accidents subsist in the Eucharist without their subject.

But those are hackneyed. Here are questions worthy of the great and (as some call them) illuminated theologians, questions to make them prick up their ears—if ever they chance upon them. Whether divine generation took place at a particular time? Whether there are several sonships in Christ? Whether this is a possible proposition: God the Father hates the Son? Whether God could have taken upon Himself the likeness of a woman? Or of a devil? Of an ass? Of a gourd? Of a piece of flint? Then how would that gourd have preached, performed miracles, or been crucified? Also, what would Peter have consecrated if he had administered the sacrament while Christ's body hung upon the Cross? Also whether at that moment Christ could be said to be a man? And whether after the resurrection it will be forbidden to eat and drink? (Now, while there is time, they are providing against hunger and thirst!) . . .

Coming nearest to these in felicity are the men who generally call themselves "the religious" and "monks"—utterly false names both, since most of them keep as far away as they can from religion and no people are more in evidence in every sort of place. But I do not see how anything could be more dismal than these monks if I did not succor them in many ways. For though people as a whole so detest this race of men that meeting one by accident is supposed to be bad luck, yet they flatter themselves to the queen's taste. For one thing, they reckon it the highest degree of piety to have no contact with literature, and hence they see to it that they do not know how to read. For another, when with asinine voices they bray out in church those psalms they have learned, by rote rather than by heart, they are convinced that they are anointing God's ears with the blandest of oil. Some of them make a good profit from their dirtiness and mendicancy, collecting their food from door to door with importunate bellowing; nay, there is not an inn, public conveyance, or ship where they do not intrude, to the great disadvantage of the other common beggars. Yet according to their account, by their very dirtiness, ignorance, want of manners, and insolence, these delightful fellows are representing to us the lives of the apostles.

What is funnier than to find that they do everything by rule, employing, as it were, the methods of mathematics; and to slip up is a great crime. There must be just so many knots for each shoe and the shoe-string must be of a certain color; the habit must be decked with just so much trimming; the girdle must be of a certain material and the width of so many straws; the cowl of a certain shape and a certain number of bushels in capacity; the hair so many fingers long; and one must sleep just so many hours. Who does not see that all this equality is really very unequal, in view of the great diversity of bodies and temperaments? Yet on the basis of such details they hold other people as mere nutshells. What is more, the members of one order, amid all their professions of apostolic charity, will turn and condemn the members of some other, making an admirable hubbub over the way their habit is belted or the slightly darker color of it. Among the monks you will see some so rigorously pious that they will wear no outer garment unless it be of Cilician goat's hair, while their inner garment is of Milesian wool; some others, on the contrary, are linen on the outside, but still wool underneath. Members of certain orders start back from the mere touch of a piece of money as if it were aconite. They do not, however, withdraw from the touch of a glass of wine, or of a woman. In short, all orders take remarkable care that nothing in their way of life shall be consistent; nor is it so much their concern to be like Christ as to be unlike each other. Thus a great part of their felicity derives from their various names. Those of one order delight to call themselves Cordeliers, but among them some are Coletes, some Minors, some Minims, some Crutched. Again, there are the Benedictines and the Bernardines; the Bridgetines and the Augustinians; the Williamists and the Jacobines; as if it were not enough to be called Christians.

The greater number of them work so hard at their ceremonies and at maintaining the minutiae of tradition that they deem one heaven hardly a suitable reward for their labors; never recalling that the time will come when, with all these things held of no account, Christ will demand a reckoning of that which He has prescribed, namely, charity. One friar will then show a paunch which has been padded out with every kind of fish; another will spill out a hundred bushels of hymns. Another will count off so many myriads of fasts, and will lay the blame for his almost bursting belly upon his having always broken his fasts by a single dinner. Another will point to a pile of ceremonies so big that seven ships could scarcely carry it. Another will boast that for sixty years he never touched money, except when his fingers were protected by two pairs of gloves. Another will wear a cowl so dirty and greasy that no sailor would deign to put it on. Another will celebrate the fact that for more than fifty-five years he lived the life of a sponge, always fastened to one spot. Another will show a voice grown hoarse with assiduous chanting; another, a lethargy contracted by living alone; another, a tongue grown dumb under his vow of silence. But Christ, interrupting their boasts, which otherwise would go on endlessly, will say: "Whence comes this new race of Jews? I recognize one commandment which is truly mine, and of that I hear nothing. Of old in the sight of all men and using no device of parable I promised the inheritance of my Father, not to cowls, orisons, or fasts, but to works of charity. Nor do I acknowledge those who acknowledge too well their own good works; let those that wish to seem holier than myself dwell, if they like, in those six hundred heavens of Basilides, or let them command a new heaven to be built for themselves by the very ones whose petty traditions they have preferred above my commandments." When they shall hear these words and shall see common sailors and teamsters preferred above them, with what faces, think you, will they look wistfully on each other! Yet meanwhile, with some assistance from me, they are happy in their good hope. . . .

In truth I am glad to get away from these actors and dissemblers, who are as grateful for my benefits as they are false in their pretensions to piety. And at this point it pleases me to touch upon kings and nobles of the court, by whom I am worshipped sincerely and, as becomes gentlemen, frankly. And indeed, if they had so much as half an ounce of sound wisdom, what life were more dismal than theirs or more to be avoided? For let a person weigh in his mind how heavy a burden rests on the shoulders of anyone wishing to act the true prince, and he will not conclude that sovereignty is a thing worth using perjury and parricide to gain. He will consider that one who grasps the helm of great affairs must further the public, not his private, interest and give his mind to nothing except as it concerns the general good; he must not deviate a finger's breadth from the laws of which he is author and executor; he must himself be warrant for the integrity of all officials and magistrates; he is one person who is exposed to all eyes, and like a favorable star he has power, by the good influence of his conduct, to bring salvation in human affairs; or like a fatal comet he may bring destruction in his train. The vices of other men are not so deeply felt or so widely communicated. A prince is in such a position that if he lapses ever so slightly from honesty, straightway a dangerous and vital infection spreads to many people. Then the lot of princes brings with it a host of things which tend to lead them from righteousness, such as pleasure, liberty, adulation, and excess; so that he must endeavour more earnestly and watch more vigilantly lest, beguiled by these, he fail of his duty. Finally, to say nothing of treasons, hatreds, and other perils or dreads, there stands above his own crown that true King who will call him to account for even the least of his trespasses; and the accounting will be the more severe as the empire he ruled was the more mighty. I say that if the prince weighed these things, and many more like them, within himself—and he would do so, were he wise—I am afraid he could neither sleep nor eat in any joy.

But as it is, with my assistance, kings leave all these concerns to the gods, take care of themselves nicely, and grant no hearing to anyone unless he knows how to speak pleasant things, because solicitude must not get a foothold in their minds. They believe they have played the part of a sovereign to the hilt if they diligently go hunting, feed some fine horses, sell dignities and offices at a profit to themselves, and daily devise new measures by which to drain away the wealth of citizens and sweep it into their own exchequer. All this, of course, is done in due form, under new-found names, so that even when most unjust it shall carry some appearance of equity; and they take care to add a little sweetening so that in any event they may secure for themselves the hearts of the people. Fashion me now a man such as princes commonly are, a man ignorant of the laws, almost an enemy of the public welfare, intent upon private gain, addicted to pleasure, a hater of learning, a hater, too, of liberty and truth, thinking about anything except the safety of the state, and measuring all things by his own desire and profit. Then put on him a golden chain, symbolizing the union of all virtues linked together; set on him a crown adorned with gems, which is to remind him that he ought to surpass others in every heroic quality. In addition, give him a scepter, emblem of justice and of a heart in no way corrupted, and finally a scarlet robe, badge of a certain eminent love for the realm. If a prince really laid his own life alongside these symbols, I believe he would have the grace to be ashamed of his finery. He would be afraid some nosy satirist might turn the whole spectacle, suited as it is for high tragedy, into laughter and derision.

Now what shall I say about the noble courtiers? Though nothing is more venal, more servile, more witless, or more contemptible than most of them, yet they desire to seem the foremost of created things. Here is one point, however, in which they are as modest as one could wish: they are satisfied to carry about on their bodies gold, gems, scarlet, and the other insignia of wisdom and the virtues, but the reality of these they leave for the use of others. They find themselves abundantly happy in being allowed to speak of the king as "our master," in having learned how to turn a compliment in three words, and in knowing how to repeat on occasion those courteous titles of Your Grace, Your Lordship, and Your Majesty; in having cast off shame beyond other men, and in flattering handsomely. For these are the arts which truly become the nobleman and courtier. For the rest, if you look more closely at their whole way of life, you are sure to find them "mere Phaeacians, suitors of Penelope, and"—you know the rest of the verse, which Echo can give you better than I. They sleep until noon, when a hired chaplain comes to their bedside and swiftly runs through matins before they are half up. Then to breakfast, which is barely got through when dinner-time comes along. After dinner come dice, checkers, cards, jesters, fools, whores, dalliance, and horse-play. Meanwhile there must be a round or two of drinks. Then back to supper, with toasts after it—not just a toast, by Jove! And in this fashion do their hours, days, months, years, and lives glide away with no boredom. For myself it is as good as a hearty meal to watch these high-flyers, observing how every one of the ladies will think herself nearer to gods the longer train she trails; while one of the noblemen will shove past another by using his elbow, in order that he may seem to stand a little closer to Jove; and each is the more pleased with himself the heavier chain he can carry about on his neck, as if he were showing off his strength rather than his wealth.

Our popes, cardinals, and bishops for some time now have earnestly copied the state and practice of princes, and come near to beating them at their own game. Let a bishop but consider what his alb, the white emblem of sincerity, should teach him, namely, a life in every way blameless; and what is signified on his part by the two-horned miter, the two peaks bound by the same knot—I suppose it is a perfect knowledge of the Old and New Testaments; what is meant by covering his hands with gloves, a clean administration of the sacrament and one unsullied by any taint of human concerns; what the crozier symbolizes, most watchful care of the flock put under his charge; what is indicated by the cross that is carried before him, to wit, a victory over all carnal affections. If he would contemplate these and other lessons of the sort, I say, would he not lead a sad and troubled life? But as it is, they do well enough by way of feeding themselves; as for the other, the care of the sheep, they delegate that to Christ himself, or else refer it to their suffragans, as they call them, or other deputies. Nor do they keep in mind the name they bear, or what the word "bishop" means—labor, vigilance, solicitude. Yet in raking in moneys they truly play the bishop, overseeing everything—and overlooking nothing.

In a similar way the cardinals, if they considered the fact that they have succeeded to the places of the apostles, would see that the same works are required of them as were performed by their predecessors; that they are not lords, but stewards, of spiritual things, and that shortly they are to render an exact account of what they hold in trust. Yes, let them too philosophize a bit concerning their vestments, and question themselves in this fashion: "What does the whiteness of this upper garment mean? Is it not a notable and singular purity of heart? What the crimson lower garment? Is it not a burning love of God? What, again, that outer robe flowing down in broad folds and spreading over the mule of his Exalted Reverence, though it would suffice to cover a camel? Is it not charity ample enough to embrace all men in its helpfulness, by way of teaching, exhorting, chastising, admonishing, ending wars, resisting wicked princes, and freely spending blood—not money alone—for the flock of Christ? And wherefore all this money, anyway, for those who hold the places of the needy apostles?" If they would weigh these things, I repeat, they would not be so ambitious for the post, and would willingly give it up, or at least they would lead a toilsome and watchful life of the sort lived by those ancient apostles.

As to these Supreme Pontiffs who take the place of Christ, if they tried to emulate His life, I mean His poverty, labors, teaching, cross, and contempt for safety, if even they thought upon the title of Pope—that is, Father—or the addition "Most Holy," who on earth would be more afflicted? Who would purchase that seat at the price of every resource and effort? Or who defend it, when purchased, by the sword, by poison, or by anything else? Were wisdom to descend upon them, how it would inconvenience them! Wisdom, did I say? Nay, even a grain of salt would do it—a grain of that salt which is spoken of by Christ. It would lose them all that wealth and honor, all those possessions, triumphal progresses, offices, dispensations, tributes, and indulgences; it would lose them so many horses, mules, and retainers; so many pleasures. (See how I have comprehended in a few words many marketsful, a great harvest, a wide ocean, of goods!) In place of these it would bring vigils, fasts, tears, prayers, sermons, studies, sighs, and a thousand troublesome tasks of the sort. Nor should we pass over the circumstance that all those copyists and notaries would be in want, as would all those advocates, promoters, secretaries, muleteers, grooms, bankers, and pimps—I was about to add something more tender, though rougher, I am afraid, on the ears. In short, that great host of men which burdens—I beg your pardon, I mean adorns—the Roman See would beg for their bread. This would be inhuman and downright abominable, and, what is more accursed, those very princes of the church and true lights of the world would themselves be reduced to a staff and a wallet.

As it is now, what labor turns up to be done they hand over to Peter and Paul, who have leisure for it. But the splendor and the pleasure they take care of personally. And so it comes about—by my doing, remember—that scarcely any kind of men live more softly or less oppressed with care; believing that they are amply acceptable to Christ if with a mystical and almost theatrical finery, with ceremonies, and with those titles of Beatitude and Reverence and Holiness, along with blessing and cursing, they perform the office of bishops. To work miracles is primitive and old-fashioned, hardly suited to our times; to instruct the people is irksome; to interpret the Holy Scriptures is pedantry; to pray is otiose; to shed tears is distressing and womanish; to live in poverty is sordid; to be beaten in war is dishonorable and less than worthy of one who will hardly admit kings, however great, to kiss his sacred foot; and finally, to die is unpleasant, to die on the cross a disgrace.

There remain only those weapons and sweet benedictions of which Paul speaks, and the popes are generous enough with these: interdictions, excommunications, re-excommunications, anathematizations, pictured damnations, and the terrific lightning-bolt of the bull, which by its mere flicker sinks the souls of men below the floor of hell. And these most holy fathers in Christ, and vicars of Christ, launch it against no one with more spirit than against those who, at the instigation of the devil, try to impair or to subtract from the patrimony of Peter. Although this saying of Peter's stands in the Gospel, "We have left all and followed Thee," yet they give the name of his patrimony to lands, towns, tribute, imposts, and moneys. On behalf of these things, inflamed by zeal for Christ, they fight with fire and sword, not without shedding of Christian blood; and then they believe they have defended the bride of Christ in apostolic fashion, having scattered what they are pleased to designate as "her enemies." As if the church had any enemies more pestilential than impious pontiffs who by their silence allow Christ to be forgotten, who enchain Him by mercenary rules, adulterate His teaching by forced interpretations, and crucify Him afresh by their scandalous life! . . .

But indeed I have long since forgotten myself and run out of bounds. If anything I have said shall seem too saucy or too glib, stop and think: 'tis Folly, and a woman, that has spoken. But of course you will also remember that Greek proverb, "Even a foolish man will often speak a word in season," unless, perhaps, you assume that this does not extend to women. I see that you are expecting a peroration, but you are just too foolish if you suppose that after I have poured out a hodgepodge of words like this I can recall anything that I have said. There is an old saying, "I hate a pot-companion with a memory." Here is a new one: "I hate a hearer that remembers anything."

And so farewell. . . . Applaud . . . live . . . drink . . . O most distinguished initiates of Folly!

MARTIN LUTHER

The theory that all events are interrelated receives dramatic confirmation in the relationship between the Renaissance and the Reformation. In order to raise money to build St. Peter's Cathedral in Rome, the greatest monument of Renaissance art, Pope Leo X authorized the granting of papal indulgences in return for suitable donations to the Church. In 1517, one of the papal agents, a Dominican friar named John Tetzel, appeared in Central

Germany, to grant these indulgences. Martin Luther (1483–1546), a professor at the University of Wittenberg, responded by posting a list of Ninety-Five Theses, in which he attacked the entire theory and practice of indulgences, on the door of the Castle Church. Luther's act, in turn, set in motion a series of events that resulted finally in the Protestant Reformation.

Although it was Tetzel's activities that set him off, Luther based his opposition to the Church on grounds far deeper than the problem of indulgences. Basically, the question centered on the salvation of man's soul. From his studies of St. Paul and St. Augustine, Luther became convinced that, since all men are utterly condemned and lost as a result of original sin, it is impossible for them to achieve salvation by any works of their own. Rather, salvation is the free gift of God's grace through faith. This doctrine of justification by faith rather than works undercut the position of the Catholic Church, which maintained that, since the works necessary to salvation (e.g., the sacraments) could be performed only with the aid of the priesthood, the Church provided the only means to salvation. In place of the priestly hierarchy, Luther substituted the notion of "the priesthood of all believers."

An Open Letter to the Christian Nobility of the German Nation Concerning the Reform of the Christian Estate, 1520

TO HIS MOST ILLUSTRIOUS AND MIGHTY IMPERIAL MAJESTY, AND TO THE CHRISTIAN NOBILITY OF THE GERMAN NATION,

DOCTOR MARTIN LUTHER

Grace and power from God, Most illustrious Majesty, and most gracious and dear Lords.

It is not out of sheer forwardness or rashness that I, a single, poor man, have undertaken to address your worships. The distress and oppression which weigh down all the Estates of Christendom, especially of Germany, and which move not me alone, but everyone to cry out time and again, and to pray for help, have forced me even now to cry aloud that God may inspire some one with His Spirit to lend this suffering nation a helping hand. Ofttimes the councils have made some pretence at reformation, but their attempts have been cleverly hindered by the guile of certain men and things have gone from bad to worse. I now intend, by the help of God, to throw some light upon the wiles and wickedness of these men, to the end that when they are known, they may not henceforth be so hurtful and so great a hindrance. God has given us a noble youth to be our head and thereby has awakened great hopes of good in many hearts; wherefore it is meet that we should do our part and profitably use this time of grace.

In this whole matter the first and most important thing is that we take earnest heed not to enter on it trusting in great might or in human reason, even though all power in the world were ours; for God

"An Open letter to the Christian Nobility of the German Nation Concerning the Reform of the Christian Estate," trans. C. M. Jacobs, in WORKS OF MARTIN LUTHER *(Philadelphia: Muhlenberg Press, 1915), II, 63–84. Courtesy of the Fortress Press.*

cannot and will not suffer a good work to be begun with trust in our own power or reason. Such works He crushes ruthlessly to earth, as it is written in the xxxiii Psalm, "There is no king saved by the multitude of an host: a mighty man is not delivered by much strength." On this account, I fear, it came to pass of old that the good Emperors Frederick I and II, and many other German emperors were shamefully oppressed and trodden under foot by the popes, although all the world feared them. It may be that they relied on their own might more than on God, and therefore they had to fall. In our own times, too, what was it that raised the bloodthirsty Julius II to such heights? Nothing else, I fear, except that France, the Germans, and Venice relied upon themselves. The children of Benjamin slew forty-two thousand Israelites because the latter relied on their own strength.

That it may not so fare with us and our noble young Emperor Charles, we must be sure that in this matter we are dealing not with men, but with the princes of hell, who can fill the world with war and bloodshed, but whom war and bloodshed do not overcome. We must go at this work despairing of physical force and humbly trusting God; we must seek God's help with earnest prayer, and fix our minds on nothing else than the misery and distress of suffering Christendom, without regard to the deserts of evil men. Otherwise we may start the game with great prospect of success, but when we get well into it the evil spirits will stir up such confusion that the whole world will swim in blood, and yet nothing will come of it. Let us act wisely, therefore, and in the fear of God. The more force we use, the greater our disaster if we do not act humbly and in God's fear. The popes and the Romans have hitherto been able, by the devil's help, to set kings at odds with one another, and they may well be able to do it again, if we proceed by our own might and cunning, without God's help.

I. THE THREE WALLS OF THE ROMANISTS

The Romanists, with great adroitness, have built three walls about them, behind which they have hitherto defended themselves in such wise that no one has been able to reform them; and this has been the cause of terrible corruption throughout all Christendom.

First, when pressed by the temporal power, they have made decrees and said that the temporal power has no jurisdiction over them, but, on the other hand, that the spiritual is above the temporal power. Second, when the attempt is made to reprove them out of the Scriptures, they raise the objection that the interpretation of the Scriptures belongs to no one except the pope. Third, if threatened with a council, they answer with the fable that no one can call a council but the pope.

In this wise they have slyly stolen from us our three rods, that they may go unpunished, and have ensconced themselves within the safe stronghold of these three walls, that they may practise all the knavery and wickedness which we now see. Even when they have been compelled to hold a council they have weakened its power in advance by previously binding the princes with an oath to let them remain as they are. Moreover, they have given the pope full authority over all the decisions of the council, so that it is all one whether there are many councils or no councils,—except that they deceive us with puppet-shows and sham-battles. So terribly do they fear for their skin in a really free council! And they have intimidated kings and princes by making them believe it would be an offence against God not to obey them in all these knavish, crafty deceptions.

Now God help us, and give us one of the trumpets with which the walls of Jericho were overthrown, that we may blow down these walls of straw and paper, and may set free the Christian rods for the punishment of sin, bringing to light the craft and deceit of the devil, to the end that through punishment we may reform ourselves, and once more attain God's favor.

Against the first wall we will direct our first attack.

It is pure invention that pope, bishops, priests and monks are to be called the "spiritual estate"; princes, lords, artisans, and farmers the "temporal estate." That is indeed a fine bit of lying and hypocrisy. Yet no one should be frightened by it; and for this reason—*viz.,* that all Christians are truly of the "spiritual estate," and there is among them no difference at all but that of office, as Paul says in I Corinthians xii, We are all one body, yet every member has its own work, whereby it serves every other, all because we have one baptism, one Gospel, one faith, and are all alike Christians; for baptism, Gospel and faith alone make us "spiritual" and a Christian people.

But that a pope or a bishop anoints, confers tonsures, ordains, consecrates, or prescribes dress unlike that of the laity, —this may make hypocrites and graven images, but it never makes a Christian or "spiritual" man. Through baptism all of us are consecrated to the priesthood, as St. Peter says in I Peter ii, "Ye are a royal priesthood, a priestly kingdom," and the book of Revelation says, "Thou hast made us by Thy blood to be priests and kings." For if we had no higher consecration than pope or bishop gives, the consecration by pope or bishop would never make a priest, nor might anyone either say mass or preach a sermon or give absolution. Therefore when the bishop consecrates it is the same thing as if he, in the place and stead of the whole congregation, all of whom have like power, were to take one out of their number and charge him to use this power for the others; just as though ten brothers, all king's sons and equal heirs, were to choose one of themselves to rule the inheritance for them all,—they would all be kings and equal in power, though one of them would be charged with the duty of ruling.

To make it still clearer. If a little group of pious Christian laymen were taken captive and set down in a wilderness, and had among them no priest consecrated by a bishop, and if there in the wilderness they were to agree in choosing one of themselves, married or unmarried, and were to charge him with the office of baptising, saying mass, absolving and preaching, such a man would be as truly a priest as though all bishops and popes had consecrated him. That is why in cases of necessity any one can baptise and give absolution, which would be impossible unless we were all priests. This great grace and power of baptism and of the Christian Estate they have well-nigh destroyed and caused us to forget through the canon law. It was in the manner aforesaid that Christians in olden days chose from their number bishops and priests, who were afterwards confirmed by other bishops, without all the show which now obtains. It was thus that Sts. Augustine, Ambrose, and Cyprian became bishops.

Since, then, the temporal authorities are baptised with the same baptism and have the same faith and Gospel as we, we must grant that they are priests and bishops, and count their office one which has a proper and a useful place in the Christian community. For whoever comes out of the water of baptism can boast that he is already consecrated priest, bishop, and pope, though it is not seemly that every one should exercise the office. Nay, just because we are all in like manner priests, no one must put himself forward and undertake, without our consent and election, to do what is in the power of all of us. For what is common to all, no one dare take upon himself without the will and the command of the community; and should it happen that one chosen for such an office were deposed for malfeasance, he would then be just what he was before he held office. Therefore a priest in Christendom is nothing else than an office-holder. While he is in office, he has precedence; when deposed, he is a peasant or a townsman like the rest. Beyond all doubt, then, a priest is no longer a priest when he is deposed. But now they have invented *characteres indelebiles,* and prate that a deposed priest is nevertheless something different from a mere layman. They even dream that a priest can never become a layman, or be anything else than a priest. All this is mere talk and man-made law.

From all this it follows that there is really no difference between laymen and priests, princes and bishops, "spirituals" and "temporals," as they call them, except that of office and work, but not of "estate"; for they are all of the same estate,—true priests, bishops, and popes,—though they are not all engaged in the same work, just as all priests and monks have not the same work. This is the teaching of St. Paul in Romans xii and I Corinthians xii, and of St. Peter in I Peter ii, as I have said above, *viz.*, that we are all one body of Christ, the Head, all members one of another. Christ has not two different bodies, one "temporal," the other "spiritual." He is one Head, and He has one body.

Therefore, just as those who are now called "spiritual"—priests, bishops or popes —are neither different from other Christians nor superior to them, except that they are charged with the administration of the Word of God and the sacraments, which is their work and office, so it is with the temporal authorities,—they bear sword and rod with which to punish the evil and to protect the good. A cobbler, a smith, a farmer, each has the work and office of his trade, and yet they are all alike consecrated priests and bishops, and every one by means of his own work or office must benefit and serve every other, that in this way many kinds of work may be done for the bodily and spiritual welfare of the community, even as all the members of the body serve one another.

See, now, how Christian is the decree which says that the temporal power is not above the "spiritual estate" and may not punish it. That is as much as to say that the hand shall lend no aid when the eye is suffering. Is it not unnatural, not to say unchristian, that one member should not help another and prevent its destruction? Verily, the more honorable the member, the more should the others help. I say then, since the temporal power is ordained of God to punish evil-doers and to protect them that do well, it should therefore be left free to perform its office without hindrance through the whole body of Christendom without respect of persons, whether it affect pope, bishops, priests, monks, nuns or anybody else. For if the mere fact that the temporal power has a smaller place among the Christian offices than has the office of preachers or confessors, or of the clergy, then the tailors, cobblers, masons, carpenters, pot-boys, tapsters, farmers, and all the secular tradesmen, should also be prevented from providing pope, bishops, priests and monks with shoes, clothing, houses, meat and drink, and from paying them tribute. But if these laymen are allowed to do their work unhindered, what do the Roman scribes mean by their laws, with which they withdraw themselves from the jurisdiction of the temporal Christian power, only so that they may be free to do evil and to fulfil what St. Peter has said:

"There shall be false teachers among you, and through covetousness shall they with feigned words make merchandise of you."

On this account the Christian temporal power should exercise its office without let or hindrance, regardless whether it be pope, bishop, or priest whom it affects; whoever is guilty, let him suffer. All that the canon law has said to the contrary is sheer invention of Roman presumption. For thus saith St. Paul to all Christians: "Let every soul (I take that to mean the pope's soul also) be subject unto the higher powers; for they bear not the sword in vain, but are the ministers of God for the punishment of evil-doers, and for the praise of them that do well." St. Peter also says: "Submit yourselves unto every ordinance of man for the Lord's sake, for so is the will of God." He has also prophesied that such men shall come as will despise the temporal authorities, and this has come to pass through the canon law.

So then, I think this first paper-wall is overthrown, since the temporal power has become a member of the body of Christendom, and is of the "spiritual estate," though its work is of a temporal nature. Therefore its work should extend freely and without hindrance to all the members of the whole body; it should punish and use force whenever guilt deserves or necessity demands, without regard to pope, bishops, and priests, —let them hurl threats and bans as much as they will.

This is why guilty priests, if they are surrendered to the temporal law, are first deprived of their priestly dignities, which would not be right unless the temporal sword had previously had authority over them by divine right.

Again, it is intolerable that in the canon law so much importance is attached to the freedom, life and property of the clergy, as though the laity were not also as spiritual and as good Christians as they, or did not belong to the Church. Why are your life and limb, your property and honor so free, and mine not? We are all alike Christians, and have baptism, faith, Spirit, and all things alike. If a priest is killed, the land is laid under interdict,—why not when a peasant is killed? Whence comes this great distinction between those who are equally Christians? Only from human laws and inventions!

Moreover, it can be no good spirit who has invented such exceptions and granted to sin such license and impunity. For if we are bound to strive against the works and words of the evil spirit, and to drive him out in whatever way we can, as Christ commands and His Apostles, ought we, then, to suffer it in silence when the pope or his satellites are bent on devilish words and works? Ought we for the sake of men to allow the suppression of divine commandments and truths which we have sworn in baptism to support with life and limb? Of a truth we should then have to answer for all the souls that would thereby be abandoned and led astray.

It must therefore have been the very prince of devils who said what is written in the canon law: "If the pope were so scandalously bad as to lead souls in crowds to the devil, yet he could not be deposed." On this accursed and devilish foundation they build at Rome, and think that we should let all the world go to the devil, rather than resist their knavery. If the fact that one man is set over others were sufficient reason why he should escape punishment, then no Christian could punish another, since Christ commands that every man shall esteem himself the lowliest and the least.

Where sin is, there is no escape from punishment; as St. Gregory also writes that we are indeed all equal, but guilt puts us in subjection one to another. Now we see how they whom God and the Apostles have made subject to the temporal sword deal with Christendom, depriving it of its liberty by their own wickedness, without warrant of Scripture. It is to be feared that this is a game of Antichrist or a sign that he is close at hand.

The second wall is still more flimsy and worthless. They wish to be the only Masters of the Holy Scriptures, even though in all their lives they learn nothing from them. They assume for themselves sole authority, and with insolent juggling of words they would persuade us that the pope, whether he be a bad man or a good man, cannot err in matters of faith; and yet they cannot prove a single letter of it. Hence it comes that so many heretical and unchristian, nay, even unnatural ordinances have a place in the canon law, of which, however, there is no present need to speak. For since they think that the Holy Spirit never leaves them, be they never so unlearned and wicked, they make bold to decree whatever they will. And if it were true, where would be the need or use of the Holy Scriptures? Let us burn them, and be satisfied with the unlearned lords at Rome, who are possessed of the Holy Spirit,—although He can possess only pious hearts! Unless I had read it myself, I could not have believed that the devil would make such clumsy pretensions at Rome, and find a following.

But not to fight them with mere words, we will quote the Scriptures. St. Paul says in I Corinthians xiv: "If to anyone something better is revealed, though he be sitting and listening to another in God's Word, then the first, who is speaking, shall hold his peace and give place." What would be the use of this commandment, if we were only to believe him who does the talking or who has the highest seat? Christ also says in John vi, that all Christians shall be taught of God. Thus it may well happen that the pope and his followers are wicked men, and no true Christians, not taught of God, not having true understanding. On the other hand, an ordinary man may have true understanding; why then should we not follow him? Has not the pope erred many times? Who would help Christendom when the pope errs, if we were not to believe another, who had the Scriptures on his side, more than the pope?

Therefore it is a wickedly invented fable, and they cannot produce a letter in defence of it, that the interpretation of Scripture or the confirmation of its interpretation belongs to the pope alone. They have themselves usurped this power; and although they allege that this power was given to Peter when the keys were given to him, it is plain enough that the keys were not given to Peter alone, but to the whole community. Moreover, the keys were not ordained for doctrine or government, but only for the binding and loosing of sin, and whatever further power of the keys they arrogate to themselves is mere invention. But Christ's word to Peter, "I have prayed for thee that thy faith fail not," cannot be applied to the pope, since the majority of the popes have been without faith, as they must themselves confess. Besides, it is not only for Peter that Christ prayed, but also for all Apostles and Christians, as he says in John xvii: "Father, I pray for those whom Thou hast given Me, and not for these only, but for all who believe on Me through their word." Is not this clear enough?

Only think of it yourself! They must confess that there are pious Christians among us, who have the true faith, Spirit, understanding, word and mind of Christ. Why, then, should we reject their word and understanding and follow the pope, who has neither faith nor Spirit? That would be to deny the whole faith and the Christian Church. Moreover, it is not the pope alone who is always in the right, if the article of the Creed is correct: "I believe in one holy Christian Church"; otherwise the prayer must run: "I believe in the pope at Rome," and so reduce the Christian Church to one man,—which would be nothing else than a devilish and hellish error.

Besides, if we are all priests, as was said above, and all have one faith, one Gospel, one sacrament, why should we not also have the power to test and judge what is correct or incorrect in matters of faith? What becomes of the words of Paul in I Corinthians ii: "He that is spiritual judgeth all things, yet he himself is judged of no man," and II Corinthians iv: "We have all the same Spirit of faith"? Why, then, should not we perceive what squares with faith and what does not, as well as does an unbelieving pope?

All these and many other texts should make us bold and free, and we should not allow the Spirit of liberty, as Paul calls Him, to be frightened off by the fabrications of the popes, but we ought to go boldly forward to test all that they do or leave undone, according to our interpretation of the Scriptures, which rests on faith, and compel them to follow not their own interpretation, but the one that is better. In the olden days Abraham had to listen to his Sarah, although she was in more complete subjection to him than we are to anyone on earth. Balaam's ass, also, was wiser than the prophet himself. If God then spoke by an ass against a prophet, why should He not be able even now to speak by a righteous man against the pope? In like manner St. Paul rebukes St. Peter as a man in error. Therefore it behooves every Christian to espouse the cause of the faith, to understand and defend it, and to rebuke all errors.

The third wall falls of itself when the first two are down. For when the pope acts contrary to the Scriptures, it is our duty to stand by the Scriptures, to reprove him, and to constrain him, according to the Lord of Christ in Matthew xviii: "If thy brother sin against thee, go and tell it him between thee and him alone; if he hear thee not, then take with thee one or two more; if he hear them not, tell it to the Church; if he hear not the Church, consider him a heathen." Here every member is commanded to care for every other. How much rather should we do this when the member that does evil is a ruling member, and by his evil-doing is the cause of much harm and offence to the rest! But if I am to accuse him before the Church, I must bring the Church together.

They have no basis in Scripture for their contention that it belongs to the pope alone to call a council or confirm its actions; for this is based merely upon their own laws, which are valid only in so far as they are not injurious to Christendom or contrary to the laws of God. When the Pope deserves punishment, such laws go out of force, since it is injurious to Christendom not to punish him by means of a council.

Thus we read in Acts xv that it was not St. Peter who called the Apostolic Council, but the Apostles and elders. If, then, that right had belonged to St. Peter alone, the council would not have been a Christian council, but an heretical *conciliabulum*. Even the Council of Nicaea—the most famous of all—was neither called nor confirmed by the Bishop of Rome, but by the Emperor Constantine, and many other emperors after him did the like, yet these councils were the most Christian of all. But if the pope alone had the right to call councils, then all these councils must have been heretical. Moreover, if I consider the councils which the pope has created, I find that they have done nothing of special importance.

Therefore, when necessity demands, and the pope is an offence to Christendom, the first man who is able should, as a faithful member of the whole body, do what he can to bring about a truly free council. No one can do this so well as the temporal authorities, especially since now they also are fellow-Christians, fellow-priests, "fellow-spirituals," fellow-lords over all things, and whenever it is needful or profitable, they should give free course to the office and work in which God has put them above every man. Would it not be an unnatural thing, if a fire broke out in a city, and every body were to stand by and let it burn on and on and consume everything that could burn, for the sole reason that nobody had the authority of the burgomaster, or because, perhaps, the fire broke out in the burgomaster's house? In such case is it not the duty of every citizen to arouse and call the rest? How much more should this be done in the spiritual city of Christ, if a fire of offence breaks out, whether in the papal government, or anywhere else? In the same way, if the enemy attacks a city, he who first rouses the others deserves honour and thanks; why then should he not deserve honour who makes known the presence of the enemy from hell, and awakens the Christians, and calls them together?

But all their boasts of an authority which dare not be opposed amount to nothing after all. No one in Christendom has authority to do injury, or to forbid the resisting of injury. There is no authority in the Church save for edification. Therefore, if the pope were to use his authority to prevent the calling of a free council, and thus became a hindrance to the edification of the Church, we should have regard neither for him nor for his authority; and if he were to hurl his bans and thunderbolts, we should despise his conduct as that of a madman, and relying on God, hurl back the ban on him, and coerce him as best we could. For this presumptuous authority of his is nothing; he has no such authority, and he is quickly overthrown by a text of Scripture; for Paul says to the Corinthians, "God has given us authority not for the destruction, but for the edification of Christendom." Who is ready to overleap this text? It is only the power of the devil and of Antichrist which resists the things that serve for the edification of Christendom; it is, therefore, in no wise to be obeyed, but is to be opposed with life and goods and all our strength.

Even though a miracle were to be done in the pope's behalf against the temporal powers, or though someone were to be stricken with a plague—which they boast has sometimes happened—it should be considered only the work of the devil, because of the weakness of our faith in God. Christ Himself prophesied in Matthew xxiv: "There shall come in My Name false Christs and false prophets, and do signs and wonders, so as to deceive even the elect," and Paul says in II Thessalonians ii, that Antichrist shall, through the power of Satan, be mighty in lying wonders.

Let us, therefore, hold fast to this: No Christian authority can do anything against Christ; as St. Paul says, "We can do nothing against Christ, but for Christ." Whatever does aught against Christ is the power of Antichrist and of the devil, even though it were to rain and hail wonders and plagues. Wonders and plagues prove nothing, especially in these last evil times, for which all the Scriptures prophesy false wonders. Therefore we must cling with firm faith to the words of God, and then the devil will cease from wonders.

Thus I hope that the false, lying terror with which the Romans have this long time made our conscience timid and stupid, has been allayed. They, like all of us, are subject to the temporal sword; they have no power to interpret the Scriptures by mere authority, without learning; they have no authority to prevent a council or, in sheer wantonness, to pledge it, bind it, or take away its liberty; but if they do this, they are in truth in the communion of Antichrist and of the devil, and have nothing at all of Christ except the name.

II. ABUSES TO BE DISCUSSED IN COUNCILS

We shall now look at the matters which should be discussed in the councils, and with which popes, cardinals, bishops, and all the scholars ought properly to be occupied day and night if they love Christ and His Church. But if they neglect this duty, then let the laity and the temporal authorities see to it, regardless of bans and thunders; for an unjust ban is better than ten just releases, and an unjust release worse than ten just bans. Let us, therefore, awake, dear Germans, and fear God rather than men, that we may not share the fate of all the poor souls who are so lamentably lost through the shameful and devilish rule of the Romans, in which the devil daily takes a larger and larger place,—if indeed, it were possible that such a hellish rule could grow worse, a thing I can neither conceive nor believe.

1. It is a horrible and frightful thing that the ruler of Christendom, who boasts himself vicar of Christ and successor of St. Peter, lives in such worldly splendor that in this regard no king nor emperor can equal or approach him, and that he who claims the title of "most holy" and "most spiritual" is more worldly than the world itself. He wears a triple crown, when the greatest kings wear but a single crown; if that is like the poverty of Christ and of St. Peter, then it is a new kind of likeness. When a word is said against it, they cry out "Heresy!" but that is because they do not wish to hear how unchristian and ungodly such a practice is. I think, however, that if the pope were with tears to pray to God he would have to lay aside these crowns, for our God can suffer no pride; and his office is nothing else than this,—daily to weep and pray for Christendom, and to set an example of all humility.

However that may be, this splendour of his is an offence, and the pope is bound on his soul's salvation to lay it aside, because St. Paul says, "Abstain from all outward shows, which give offence," and in Rom. xii, "We should provide good, not only in the sight of God, but also in the sight of all men." An ordinary bishop's crown would be enough for the pope; he should be greater than others in wisdom and holiness, and leave the crown of pride to Antichrist, as did his predecessors several centuries ago. They say he is a lord of the world; that is a lie; for Christ, Whose vicar and officer he boasts himself to be, said before Pilate, "My kingdom is not of this world," and no vicar's rule can go beyond his lord's. Moreover he is not the vicar of the glorified, but of the crucified Christ, as Paul says, "I was willing to know nothing among you save Christ, and Him only as the Crucified"; and in Philippians ii, "So think of yourselves as ye see in Christ, Who emptied Himself and took upon Him the appearance of a servant"; and again in I Corinthians i, "We preach Christ, the Crucified." Now they make the pope a vicar of the glorified Christ in heaven, and some of them have allowed the devil to rule them so completely that they have maintained that the pope is above the angels in heaven and has authority over them. These are indeed the very works of the very Antichrist.

2. What is the use in Christendom of those people who are called the cardinals? I shall tell you. Italy and Germany have many rich monasteries, foundations, benefices, and livings. No better way has been discovered to bring all these to Rome than by creating cardinals and giving them the bishoprics, monasteries, and prelacies, and so overthrowing the worship of God. For this reason we now see Italy a very wilder-

ness—monasteries in ruins, bishoprics devoured, the prelacies and the revenues of all the churches drawn to Rome, cities decayed, land and people laid waste, because there is no more worship or preaching. Why? The cardinals must have the income. No Turk could have so devastated Italy and suppressed the worship of God.

Now that Italy is sucked dry, they come into Germany, and begin oh so gently. But let us beware, or Germany will soon become like Italy. Already we have some cardinals; what the Romans seek by that the "drunken Germans" are not to understand until we have not a bishopric, a monastery, a living, a benefice, a *heller* or a *pfennig* left. Antichrist must take the treasures of the earth, as it was prophesied. So it goes on. They skim the cream off the bishoprics, monasteries, and benefices, and because they do not yet venture to turn them all to shameful use, as they have done in Italy, they only practise for the present the sacred trickery of coupling together ten or twenty prelacies and taking a yearly portion from each of them, so as to make a tidy sum after all. The priory of Würzburg yields a thousand *gulden;* that of Bamberg, something; Mainz, Trier and the others, something more; and so from one to ten thousand *gulden* might be got together, in order that a cardinal might live at Rome like a rich king.

"After they are used to this, we will create thirty or forty cardinals in a day, and give to one Mount St. Michael at Bamberg and the bishopric of Würzburg to boot, hang on to these a few rich livings, until churches and cities are waste, and after that we will say, 'We are Christ's vicars and shepherds of Christ's sheep; the mad, drunken Germans must put up with it.' "

I advise, however, that the number of the cardinals be reduced, or that the pope be made to keep them at his own expense. Twelve of them would be more than enough, and each of them might have an income of a thousand *gulden* a year. How comes it that we Germans must put up with such robbery and such extortion of our property, at the hands of the pope? If the Kingdom of France has prevented it, why do we Germans let them make such fools and apes of us? It would all be more bearable if in this way they only stole our property; but they lay waste the churches and rob Christ's sheep of their pious shepherds, and destroy the worship and the Word of God. Even if there were not a single cardinal, the Church would not go under. As it is they do nothing for the good of Christendom; they only wrangle about the incomes of bishoprics and prelacies, and that any robber could do.

3. If ninety-nine parts of the papal court were done away and only the hundredth part allowed to remain, it would still be large enough to give decisions in matters of faith. Now, however, there is such a swarm of vermin yonder in Rome, all boasting that they are "papal," that there was nothing like it in Babylon. There are more than three thousand papal secretaries alone; who will count the other offices, when they are so many that they scarcely can be counted? And they all lie in wait for the prebends and benefices of Germany as wolves lie in wait for the sheep. I believe that Germany now gives much more to the pope at Rome than it gave in former times to the emperors. Indeed, some estimate that every year more than three hundred thousand *gulden* find their way from Germany to Rome, quite uselessly and fruitlessly; we get nothing for it but scorn and contempt. And yet we wonder that princes, nobles, cities, endowments, land, and people are impoverished! We should rather wonder that we still have anything to eat!

JOHN CALVIN

The success of Protestantism as an international reform movement was due largely to the work of a younger contemporary of Luther, the Frenchman John Calvin. Born Jean Cauvin in Picardy in 1509, Calvin went to Paris in 1523 to study first for a clerical and later for a legal career. During his student days he became acquainted with the writings of Luther, which were beginning to circulate through France at the time. His growing sympathy for the German "heresies" brought him to the attention of the authorities and he was forced to flee from the country. After some wandering he finally established himself permanently in the small city of Geneva, Switzerland. Thus began one of the most remarkable social and political experiments of modern times. Under Calvin's leadership Geneva was organized as a theocratic state. The clergy assumed control not only of the political affairs of the city but of the moral life of its citizens. In his attempt to realize a society of saints, Calvin systematically set about to banish gaiety, frivolity, and sin from the city. Although he was unusually successful, and Geneva became a city of piety and sobriety, Calvin was never fully satisfied. Sin, he discovered, could not be eradicated completely but would periodically rear its ugly head in the midst of his saintly society.

From Geneva, which came to be known as the Protestant Rome, Calvinism spread throughout most of Europe, into Germany, Poland, Bohemia, Hungary, and the Low Countries. The French Huguenots were Calvinists as were the Scottish Presbyterians and the English Puritans, who brought both the religious doctrines and the theocratic social organization of Calvin across the Atlantic to the colony of Massachusetts.

Calvin was not only a religious and social reformer but also one of the greatest of all Christian theologians. In his Institutes of the Christian Religion, *which he first published at the age of twenty-seven, he reiterated and defended the Augustinian doctrine of original sin, with its implied notions of election, faith, and grace. On the subject of predestination, about which most theologians had spoken in muted tones, Calvin was particularly vehement. God in his omnipotence has decreed from all eternity the ultimate destiny of every individual soul. We, guilty sinners, can do nothing to alter this divine decree; all that rests with us is to praise God's infinite grace if he has elected us for salvation or to accept his just condemnation if he has damned us to hell.*

The selection from the Institutes *that follows outlines the main features of Calvin's theology.*

Institutes of the Christian Religion

DISCUSSION OF HUMAN NATURE AS CREATED, OF THE FACULTIES OF THE SOUL, OF THE IMAGE OF GOD, OF FREE WILL, AND OF THE ORIGINAL INTEGRITY OF MAN'S NATURE

We must now speak of the creation of man: not only because among all God's works here is the noblest and most remarkable example of his justice, wisdom, and goodness; but because, as we said at the beginning, we cannot have a clear and complete knowledge of God unless it is accompanied by a corresponding knowledge of ourselves. This knowledge of ourselves is twofold: namely, to know what we were like when we were first created and what our condition became after the fall of Adam. While it would be of little benefit to understand our creation unless we recognized in this sad ruin what our nature in its corruption and deformity is like, we shall nevertheless be content for the moment with the description of our originally upright nature. And to be sure, before we come to the miserable condition of man to which he is now subjected, it is worth-while to know what he was like when first created. Now we must guard against singling out only those natural evils of man, lest we seem to attribute them to the Author of nature. For in this excuse, impiety thinks it has sufficient defense, if it is able to claim that whatever defects it possesses have in some way proceeded from God. It does not hesitate, if it is reproved, to contend with God himself, and to impute to him the fault of which it is deservedly accused. And those who wish to seem to speak more reverently of the Godhead still willingly blame their depravity on nature, not realizing that they also, although more obscurely, insult God. For if any defect were proved to inhere in nature, this would bring reproach upon him.

Since, then, we see the flesh panting for every subterfuge by which it thinks that the blame for its own evils may in any way be diverted from itself to another, we must diligently oppose this evil intent. Therefore we must so deal with the calamity of mankind that we may cut off every shift, and may vindicate God's justice from every accusation. Afterward, in the proper place, we shall see how far away men are from the purity that was bestowed upon Adam. . . .

In this integrity man by free will had the power, if he so willed, to attain eternal life. Here it would be out of place to raise the question of God's secret predestination because our present subject is not what can happen or not, but what man's nature was like. Therefore Adam could have stood if he wished, seeing that he fell solely by his own will. But it was because his will was capable of being bent to one side or the other, and was not given the constancy to persevere, that he fell so easily. Yet his choice of good and evil was free, and not that alone, but the highest rectitude was in his mind and will, and all the organic parts were rightly composed to obedience, until in destroying himself he corrupted his own blessings.

Hence the great obscurity faced by the

philosophers, for they were seeking in a ruin for a building, and in scattered fragments for a well-knit structure. They held this principle, that man would not be a rational animal unless he possessed free choice of good and evil; also it entered their minds that the distinction between virtues and vices would be obliterated if man did not order his life by his own planning. Well reasoned so far—if there had been no change in man. But since this was hidden from them, it is no wonder they mix up heaven and earth! They, as professed disciples of Christ, are obviously playing the fool when, by compromising between the opinions of the philosophers and heavenly doctrine, so that these touch neither heaven nor earth, in man—who is lost and sunk down into spiritual destruction—they still seek after free choice. But these matters will be better dealt with in their proper place. Now we need bear only this in mind: man was far different at the first creation from his whole posterity, who, deriving their origin from him in his corrupted state, have contracted from him a hereditary taint. For, the individual parts of his soul were formed to uprightness, the soundness of his mind stood firm, and his will was free to choose the good. If anyone objects that his will was placed in an insecure position because its power was weak, his status should have availed to remove any excuse; nor was it reasonable for God to be constrained by the necessity of making a man who either could not or would not sin at all. Such a nature would, indeed, have been more excellent. But to quarrel with God on this precise point, as if he ought to have conferred this upon man, is more than iniquitous, inasmuch as it was in his own choice to give whatever he pleased. But the reason he did not sustain man by the virtue of perseverance lies hidden in his plan; sobriety is for us the part of wisdom. Man, indeed, received the ability provided he exercised the will; but he did not have the will to use his ability, for this exercising of the will would have been followed by perseverance. Yet he is not excusable, for he received so much that he voluntarily brought about his own destruction; indeed, no necessity was imposed upon God of giving man other than a mediocre and even transitory will, that from man's Fall he might gather occasion for his own glory.

GOD BY HIS POWER NOURISHES AND MAINTAINS THE WORLD CREATED BY HIM, AND RULES ITS SEVERAL PARTS BY HIS PROVIDENCE

Moreover, to make God a momentary Creator, who once for all finished his work, would be cold and barren, and we must differ from profane men especially in that we see the presence of divine power shining as much in the continuing state of the universe as in its inception. For even though the minds of the impious too are compelled by merely looking upon earth and heaven to rise up to the Creator, yet faith has its own peculiar way of assigning the whole credit for Creation to God. To this pertains that saying of the apostle's to which we have referred before, that only "by faith we understand that the universe was created by the word of God." For unless we pass on to his providence —however we may seem both to comprehend with the mind and to confess with the tongue—we do not yet properly grasp what it means to say: "God is Creator." Carnal sense, once confronted with the power of God in the very Creation, stops there, and at most weighs and contemplates only the wisdom, power, and goodness of the author in accomplishing such handiwork. (These matters are self-evident, and even force themselves upon the unwilling.) It contemplates, moreover, some general preserving and governing activity, from which the force of motion derives. In short, carnal sense thinks there is an energy divinely bestowed from the beginning, sufficient to sustain all things.

But faith ought to penetrate more deeply, namely, having found him Creator of all, forthwith to conclude he is also everlasting Governor and Preserver—not only in that he drives the celestial frame as well as its several parts by a universal motion, but also in that he sustains, nourishes, and cares for everything he has made, even to the least sparrow. Thus David, having briefly stated that the universe was created by God, immediately descends to the uninterrupted course of His providence, "By the word of Jehovah the heavens were made, and all their host by the breath of his mouth." Soon thereafter he adds, "Jehovah has looked down upon the sons of men," and what follows is in the same vein. For although all men do not reason so clearly, yet, because it would not be believable that human affairs are cared for by God unless he were the Maker of the universe, and nobody seriously believes the universe was made by God without being persuaded that he takes care of his works, David not inappropriately leads us in the best order from the one to the other. In general, philosophers teach and human minds conceive that all parts of the universe are quickened by God's secret inspiration. . . .

But because we know that the universe was established especially for the sake of mankind, we ought to look for this purpose in his governance also. The prophet Jeremiah exclaims, "I know, O Lord, that the way of man is not his own, nor is it given to man to direct his own steps." Moreover, Solomon says, "Man's steps are from the Lord and how may man dispose his way?" Let them now say that man is moved by God according to the inclination of his nature, but that he himself turns that motion whither he pleases. Nay, if that were truly said, the free choice of his ways would be in man's control. Perhaps they will deny this because he can do nothing without God's power. Yet they cannot really get by with that, since it is clear that the prophet and Solomon ascribe to God not only might but also choice and determination. Elsewhere Solomon elegantly rebukes this rashness of men, who set up for themselves a goal without regard to God, as if they were not led by his hand. "The disposition of the heart is man's, but the preparation of the tongue is the Lord's." It is an absurd folly that miserable men take it upon themselves to act without God, when they cannot even speak except as he wills!

Indeed, Scripture, to express more plainly that nothing at all in the world is undertaken without his determination, shows that things seemingly most fortuitous are subject to him. For what can you attribute more to chance than when a branch breaking off from a tree kills a passing traveler? But the Lord speaks far differently, acknowledging that he has delivered him to the hand of the slayer. Likewise, who does not attribute lots to the blindness of fortune? But the Lord does not allow this, claiming for himself the determining of them. He teaches that it is not by their own power that pebbles are cast into the lap and drawn out, but the one thing that could have been attributed to chance he testifies to come from himself. In the same vein is that saying of Solomon, "The poor man and the usurer meet together; God illumines the eyes of both." He points out that, even though the rich are mingled with the poor in the world, while to each his condition is divinely assigned, God, who lights all men, is not at all blind. And so he urges the poor to patience; because those who are not content with their own lot try to shake off the burden laid upon them by God. Thus, also, another prophet rebukes the impious who ascribe to men's toil, or to fortune, the fact that some lie in squalor and others rise up to honors. "For not from the east, nor from the west, nor from the wilderness comes lifting up; because God is judge, he humbles one and lifts up another." Because God cannot put off the office of judge, hence he reasons that it is by His secret plan that some distinguish themselves, while others remain contemptible. . . .

HOW WE MAY APPLY THIS DOCTRINE TO OUR GREATEST BENEFIT

. . . All who will compose themselves to this moderation will not murmur against God on account of their adversities in time past, nor lay the blame for their own wickedness upon him as did the Homeric Agamemnon, saying: "I am not the cause, but Zeus and fate." And they will not, as if carried off by the fates, out of desperation cast themselves to destruction like that youth of Plautus: "Unstable is the lot of things, the fates drive men according to their own pleasure. I will betake myself to the precipice, that there I may lose my goods with my life." And they will not follow the example of another, and cover up their own evil deeds with the name "God." For thus Lyconides says in another comedy: "God was the instigator; I believe the gods willed it. For I know if they had not so willed, it would not have happened." But rather let them inquire and learn from Scripture what is pleasing to God so that they may strive toward this under the Spirit's guidance. At the same time, being ready to follow God wherever he calls, they will show in very truth that nothing is more profitable than the knowledge of this doctrine.

Profane men with their absurdities foolishly raise an uproar, so that they almost, as the saying is, mingle heaven and earth. If the Lord has indicated the point of our death, they say, we cannot escape it. Therefore it is vain for anyone to busy himself in taking precautions. One man does not dare take a road that he hears is dangerous, lest he be murdered by thieves; another summons physicians, and wears himself out with medicines to keep himself alive; another is afraid of living in tumble-down houses. In short, all devise ways and forge them with great purpose of mind, to attain what they desire. Now either all these remedies which attempt to correct God's will are vain; or else there is no fixed decree of God that determines life and death, health and disease, peace and war, and other things that men, as they desire or hate them, so earnestly try by their own toil either to obtain or to avoid. Also they conclude that believers' prayers, by which the Lord is asked to provide for things that he has already decreed from eternity, are perverse, not to say superfluous. To sum up, they cancel all those plans which have to do with the future, as militating against God's providence, which, without their being consulted, has decreed what he would have happen. Then whatever does happen now, they so impute to God's providence that they close their eyes to the man who clearly has done it. Does an assassin murder an upright citizen? He has carried out, they say, God's plan. Has someone stolen, or committed adultery? Because he has done what was foreseen and ordained by the Lord, he is the minister of God's providence. Has a son, neglecting remedies, with never a care awaited the death of a parent? He could not resist God, who had so appointed from eternity. Thus all crimes, because subject to God's ordinance, they call virtues. . . .

The same men wrongly and rashly lay the happenings of past time to the naked providence of God. For since on it depends everything that happens, therefore, say they, neither thefts, nor adulteries, nor murders take place without God's will intervening. Why therefore, they ask, should a thief be punished, who has plundered someone whom the Lord would punish with poverty? Why shall a murderer be punished, who has killed one whose life the Lord had ended? If all such men are serving God's will, why shall they be punished? On the contrary, I deny that they are serving God's will. For we shall not say that one who is motivated by an evil inclination, by only obeying his own wicked desire, renders service to God at His bidding. A man, having learned of His will, obeys God in striving toward the goal to which he is called by that same will. From what source do we learn but from his Word? In such fashion we must in our deeds search out God's will which he declares through his Word. God requires of us only what he commands. If we contrive anything against his commandment, it is not obedience but obstinacy and transgression. Yet, unless he willed it, we would not do it. I agree. But do we do evil things to the end that we may serve him? Yet he by no means commands us to do them; rather we rush headlong, without thinking what he requires, but so raging in our unbridled lust that we deliberately strive against him. And in this way we serve his just ordinance by doing evil, for so great and boundless is his wisdom that he knows right well how to use evil instruments to do good. And see how absurd their argument is: they would have transgressors go unpunished, on the ground that their misdeeds are committed solely by God's dispensation.

I grant more: thieves and murderers and other evildoers are the instruments of divine providence, and the Lord himself uses these to carry out the judgments that he has determined with himself. Yet I deny that they can derive from this any excuse for their evil deeds. Why? Will they either involve God in the same iniquity with themselves, or will they cloak their own depravity with his justice? They can do neither.

. . .

BY THE FALL AND REVOLT OF ADAM THE WHOLE HUMAN RACE WAS DELIVERED TO THE CURSE, AND DEGENERATED FROM ITS ORIGINAL CONDITION; THE DOCTRINE OF ORIGINAL SIN

With good reason the ancient proverb strongly recommended knowledge of self to man. For if it is considered disgraceful for us not to know all that pertains to the business of human life, even more detestable is our ignorance of ourselves, by which, when making decisions in necessary matters, we miserably deceive and even blind ourselves!

But since this precept is so valuable, we ought more diligently to avoid applying it perversely. This, we observe, has happened to certain philosophers, who, while urging man to know himself, propose the goal of recognizing his own worth and excellence. And they would have him contemplate in himself nothing but what swells him with empty assurance and puffs him up with pride.

But knowledge of ourselves lies first in considering what we were given at creation and how generously God continues his favour toward us, in order to know how great our natural excellence would be if only it had remained unblemished; yet at the same time to bear in mind that there is in us nothing of our own, but that we hold on sufferance whatever God has bestowed upon us. Hence we are ever dependent on him. Secondly, to call to mind our miserable condition after Adam's fall; the awareness of which, when all our boasting and self-assurance are laid low, should truly humble us and overwhelm us with shame. In the beginning God fashioned us after his image that he might arouse our minds both to zeal for virtue and to meditation upon eternal life. Thus, in order that the great nobility of our race (which distinguishes us from brute beasts) may not be buried beneath our own dullness of wit, it behooves us to recognize that we have been endowed with reason and understanding so that, by leading a holy and upright life, we may press on to the appointed goal of blessed immortality.

But that primal worthiness cannot come to mind without the sorry spectacle of our foulness and dishonour presenting itself by way of contrast, since in the person of the first man we have fallen from our original condition. From this source arise abhorrence and displeasure with ourselves, as well as true humility; and thence is kindled a new zeal to seek God, in whom each of us may recover those good things which we have utterly and completely lost. . . .

Because what God so severely punished must have been no light sin but a detestable crime, we must consider what kind of sin there was in Adam's desertion that enkindled God's fearful vengeance against the whole of mankind. To regard Adam's sin as gluttonous intemperance (a common notion) is childish. As if the sum and head of all virtues lay in abstaining solely from one fruit, when all sorts of desirable delights abounded everywhere; and not only abundance but also magnificent variety was at hand in that blessed fruitfulness of earth!

We ought therefore to look more deeply. Adam was denied the tree of the knowledge of good and evil to test his obedience and prove that he was willingly under God's command. The very name of the tree shows the sole purpose of the precept was to keep him content with his lot and to prevent him from becoming puffed up with wicked lust. But the promise by which he was bidden to hope for eternal life so long as he ate from the tree of life, and conversely, the terrible threat of death once he tasted of the tree of knowledge of good and evil, served to prove and exercise his faith. Hence it is not hard to deduce by what means Adam provoked God's wrath upon himself. Indeed, Augustine speaks rightly when he declares that pride was the beginning of all evils. For if ambition had not raised man higher than was meet and right, he could have remained in his original state.

But we must take a fuller definition from the nature of the temptation which Moses describes. Since the woman through unfaithfulness was led away from God's Word by the serpent's deceit, it is already clear that disobedience was the beginning of the Fall. This Paul also confirms, teaching that all were lost through the disobedience of one man. Yet it is at the same time to be noted that the first man revolted from God's authority, not only because he was seized by Satan's blandishments, but also because, contemptuous of truth, he turned aside to falsehood. And surely, once we hold God's Word in contempt, we shake off all reverence for him. For, unless we listen attentively to him, his majesty will not dwell among us, nor his worship remain perfect. Unfaithfulness, then, was the root of the Fall. But thereafter ambition and pride, together with ungratefulness, arose, because Adam by seeking more than was granted him shamefully spurned God's great bounty, which had been lavished upon him. To have been made in the likeness of God seemed a small matter to a son of earth unless he also attained equality with God—a monstrous wickedness! If apostasy, by which man withdraws from the authority of his Maker—indeed insolently shakes off his yoke—is a foul and detestable offense, it is vain to extenuate Adam's sin. Yet it was not simple apostasy, but was joined with vile reproaches against God. These assented to Satan's slanders, which accused God of falsehood and envy and ill will. Lastly, faithlessness opened the door to ambition, and ambition was indeed the mother of obstinate disobedience; as a result, men, having cast off the fear of God, threw themselves wherever lust carried them. Hence Bernard rightly teaches that the door of salvation is opened to us when we receive the gospel today with our ears, even as death was then admitted by those same windows when they were opened to Satan. For Adam would never have dared oppose God's authority unless he had disbelieved in God's Word. Here, indeed, was the best bridle to control all passions: the thought that nothing is better than to practice righteousness by obeying God's commandments; then, that the ultimate goal of the happy life is to be loved by him. Therefore Adam, carried away by the devil's blasphemies, as far as he was able extinguished the whole glory of God.

As it was the spiritual life of Adam to remain united and bound to his Maker, so estrangement from him was the death of his soul. Nor is it any wonder that he consigned his race to ruin by his rebellion when he perverted the whole order of nature in heaven and on earth. "All creatures," says Paul, "are groaning," "subject to corruption, not of their own will." If the cause is sought, there is no doubt that they are bearing part of the punishment deserved by man, for whose use they were created. Since, therefore, the curse, which goes about through all the regions of the world, flowed hither and yon from Adam's guilt, it is not unreasonable if it is spread to all his offspring. Therefore, after the heavenly image was obliterated in him, he was not the only one to suffer this punishment—that, in place of wisdom, virtue, holiness, truth, and justice, with which adornments he had been clad, there came forth the most filthy plagues, blindness, impotence, impurity, vanity, and injustice—but he also entangled and immersed his offspring in the same miseries.

This is the inherited corruption, which the church fathers termed "original sin," meaning by the word "sin" the depravation of a nature previously good and pure. There was much contention over this matter, inasmuch as nothing is farther from the usual view than for all to be made guilty by the guilt of one, and thus for sin to be made common. This seems to be the reason why the most ancient doctors of the church touched upon this subject so obscurely. At least they explained it less clearly than was fitting. Yet this timidity could not prevent Pelagius from rising up with the profane fiction that Adam sinned only to his own loss without harming his posterity. Through this subtlety Satan attempted to cover up the disease and thus to render it incurable. But when it was shown by the clear testimony of Scripture that sin was transmitted from the first man to all his posterity, Pelagius quibbled that it was transmitted through imitation, not propagation. Therefore, good men (and Augustine above the rest) labored to show us that we are corrupted not by derived wickedness, but that we bear inborn defect from our mother's womb. . . .

So that these remarks may not be made concerning an uncertain and unknown matter, let us define original sin. It is not my intention to investigate the several definitions proposed by various writers, but simply to bring forward the one that appears to me most in accordance with truth. Original sin, therefore, seems to be a hereditary depravity and corruption of our nature, diffused into all parts of the soul, which first makes us liable to God's wrath, then also brings forth in us those works which Scripture calls "works of the flesh." And that is properly what Paul often calls sin. The works that come forth from it—such as adulteries, fornications, thefts, hatreds, murders, carousings—he accordingly calls "fruits of sin," although they are also commonly called "sins" in Scripture, and even by Paul himself.

We must, therefore, distinctly note these two things. First, we are so vitiated and perverted in every part of our nature that by this great corruption we stand justly condemned and convicted before God, to whom nothing is acceptable but righteousness, innocence, and purity. And this is not liability for another's transgression. For, since it is said that we became subject to God's judgment through Adam's sin, we are to understand it not as if we, guiltless and undeserving, bore the guilt of his offense but in the sense that, since we through his transgression have become entangled in the curse, he is said to have made us guilty. Yet not only has punishment fallen upon us from Adam, but a contagion imparted by him resides in us, which justly deserves punishment. For this reason, Augustine, though he often calls sin "another's" to show more clearly that it is distributed among us through propagation, nevertheless declares at the same time that it is peculiar to each. And the apostle himself most eloquently testifies that "death has spread to all because all have sinned." That is, they have been enveloped in original sin and defiled by its stains. For that reason, even infants themselves, while they carry their condemnation along with them from the mother's womb, are guilty not of another's fault but of their own. For, even though the fruits of their iniquity have not yet come forth, they have the seed enclosed within them. Indeed, their whole nature is a seed of sin; hence it can be only hateful and abhorrent to God. From this it follows that it is rightly considered sin in God's sight, for without guilt there would be no accusation.

Then comes the second consideration: that this perversity never ceases in us, but continually bears new fruits—the works of the flesh that we have already described—just as a burning furnace gives forth flame and sparks, or water ceaselessly bubbles up from a spring. Thus those who have defined original sin as "the lack of the original righteousness, which ought to reside in us," although they comprehend in this definition the whole meaning of the term, have still not expressed effectively enough its power and energy. For our nature is not only destitute and empty of good, but so fertile and fruitful of every evil that it cannot be idle. . . .

MAN HAS NOW BEEN DEPRIVED OF FREEDOM OF CHOICE AND BOUND OVER TO MISERABLE SERVITUDE

We have now seen that the domination of sin, from the time it held the first man bound to itself, not only ranges among all mankind, but also completely occupies individual souls. It remains for us to investigate more closely whether we have been deprived of all freedom since we have been reduced to this servitude; and, if any particle of it still survives, how far its power extends. But in order that the truth of this question may be more readily apparent to us, I shall presently set a goal to which the whole argument should be directed. The best way to avoid error will be to consider the perils that threaten man on both sides. (1) When man is denied all uprightness, he immediately takes occasion for complacency from that fact; and, because he is said to have no ability to pursue righteousness on his own, he holds all such pursuit to be of no consequence, as if it did not pertain to him at all. (2) Nothing, however slight, can be credited to man without depriving God of his honour, and without man himself falling into ruin through brazen confidence. Augustine points out both these precipices.

Here, then, is the course that we must

follow if we are to avoid crashing upon these rocks: when man has been taught that no good thing remains in his power, and that he is hedged about on all sides by most miserable necessity, in spite of this he should nevertheless be instructed to aspire to a good of which he is empty, to a freedom of which he has been deprived. In fact, he may thus be more sharply aroused from inactivity than if it were supposed that he was endowed with the highest virtues. Everyone sees how necessary this second point is. I observe that too many persons have doubts about the first point. For since this is an undoubted fact, that nothing of his own ought to be taken away from man, it ought to be clearly evident how important it is for him to be barred from false boasting. At the time when man was distinguished with the noblest marks of honor through God's beneficence, not even then was he permitted to boast about himself. How much more ought he now to humble himself, cast down as he has been—due to his own ungratefulness—from the loftiest glory into extreme disgrace! At that time, I say, when he had been advanced to the highest degree of honor, Scripture attributed nothing else to him than that he had been created in the image of God, thus suggesting that man was blessed, not because of his own good actions, but by participation in God. What, therefore, now remains for man, bare and destitute of all glory, but to recognize God for whose beneficence he could not be grateful when he abounded with the riches of his grace; and at least, by confessing his own poverty, to glorify him in whom he did not previously glory in recognition of his own blessings?

Also, it is no less to our advantage than pertinent to God's glory that we be deprived of all credit for our wisdom and virtue. Thus those who bestow upon us anything beyond the truth add sacrilege to our ruin. When we are taught to wage our own war, we are but borne aloft on a reed stick, only to fall as soon as it breaks! Yet we flatter our strength unduly when we compare it even to a reed stick! For whatever vain men devise and babble concerning these matters is but smoke. . . .

If this be admitted, it will be indisputable that free will is not sufficient to enable man to do good works, unless he be helped by grace, indeed by special grace, which only the elect receive through regeneration. For I do not tarry over those fanatics who babble that grace is equally and indiscriminately distributed. But it has not yet been demonstrated whether man has been wholly deprived of all power to do good, or still has some power, though meager and weak; a power, indeed, that can do nothing of itself, but with the help of grace also does its part. The Master of the Sentences meant to settle this point when he taught: "We need two kinds of grace to render us capable of good works." He calls the first kind "operating," which ensures that we effectively will to do good. The second he calls "co-operating," which follows the good will as a help. The thing that displeases me about this division is that, while he attributes the effective desire for good to the grace of God, yet he hints that man by his very own nature somehow seeks after the good—though ineffectively. Thus Bernard declares the good will is God's work, yet concedes to man that of his own impulse he seeks this sort of good will. But this is far from Augustine's thought, from whom Peter Lombard pretended to have taken this distinction. The ambiguity in the second part offends me, for it has given rise to a perverted interpretation. They thought we co-operate with the assisting grace of God, because it is our right either to render it ineffectual by spurning the first grace, or to confirm it by obediently following it. This the author of the work *The Calling of the Gen-*

tiles expresses as follows: "Those who employ the judgment of reason are free to forsake grace, so that not to have forsaken it is a meritorious act; and what could not be done without the co-operation of the Spirit is counted meritorious for those whose own will could not have accomplished it." I chose to note these two points in passing that you, my reader, may see how far I disagree with the sounder Schoolmen. I differ with the more recent Sophists to an even greater extent, as they are farther removed from antiquity. However, we at least understand from this division in what way they grant free will to man. For Lombard finally declares that we have free will, not in that we are equally capable of doing or thinking good and evil, but merely that we are freed from compulsion. According to Lombard, this freedom is not hindered, even if we be wicked and slaves of sin, and can do nothing but sin.

Man will then be spoken of as having this sort of free decision, not because he has free choice equally of good and evil, but because he acts wickedly by will, not by compulsion. Well put, indeed, but what purpose is served by labeling with a proud name such a slight thing? A noble freedom, indeed—for man not to be forced to serve sin, yet to be such a willing slave that his will is bound by the fetters of sin!

. . .

ETERNAL ELECTION, BY WHICH GOD HAS PREDESTINED SOME TO SALVATION, OTHERS TO DESTRUCTION

In actual fact, the covenant of life is not preached equally among all men, and among those to whom it is preached, it does not gain the same acceptance either constantly or in equal degree. In this diversity the wonderful depth of God's judgment is made known. For there is no doubt that this variety also serves the decision of God's eternal election. If it is plain that it comes to pass by God's bidding that salvation is freely offered to some while others are barred from access to it, at once great and difficult questions spring up, explicable only when reverent minds regard as settled what they may suitably hold concerning election and predestination. A baffling question this seems to many. For they think nothing more inconsistent than that out of the common multitude of men some should be predestined to salvation, others to destruction. But how mistakenly they entangle themselves will become clear in the following discussion. Besides, in the very darkness that frightens them not only is the usefulness of this doctrine made known but also its very sweet fruit. We shall never be clearly persuaded, as we ought to be, that our salvation flows from the wellspring of God's free mercy until we come to know his eternal election, which illumines God's grace by this contrast: that he does not indiscriminately adopt all into the hope of salvation but gives to some what he denies to others.

How much the ignorance of this principle detracts from God's glory, how much it takes away from true humility, is well known. Yet Paul denies that this which needs so much to be known can be known unless God, utterly disregarding works, chooses those whom he has decreed within himself. "At the present time," he says, "a remnant has been saved according to the election of grace. But if it is by grace, it is no more of works; otherwise grace would no more be grace. But if it is of works, it is no more of grace; otherwise work would not be work." If—to make it clear that our salvation comes about solely from God's mere generosity—we must be called back to the course of election, those who wish to get rid of all this are obscuring as maliciously as they can what ought to have been gloriously and vociferously proclaimed, and they tear humility up by the very roots. Paul clearly testifies that, when the salvation of a remnant of the people is ascribed to the election of grace, then only is it acknowledged that God of his mere good pleasure preserves whom he will, and moreover that he pays no reward, since he can owe none.

They who shut the gates that no one may dare seek a taste of this doctrine wrong men no less than God. For neither will anything else suffice to make us humble as we ought to be nor shall we otherwise sincerely feel how much we are obliged to God. And as Christ teaches, here is our only ground for firmness and confidence: in order to free us of all fear and render us victorious amid so many dangers, snares, and mortal struggles, he promises that whatever the Father has entrusted into his keeping will be safe. From this we infer that all those who do not know that they are God's own will be miserable through constant fear. Hence, those who by being blind to the three benefits we have noted would wish the foundation of our salvation to be removed from our midst, very badly serve the interests of themselves and of all other believers. How is it that the church becomes manifest to us from this, when, as Bernard rightly teaches, "it could not otherwise be found or recognized among creatures, since it lies marvelously hidden . . . both within the bosom of a blessed predestination and within the mass of a miserable condemnation?"

But before I enter into the matter itself, I need to mention by way of preface two kinds of men.

Human curiosity renders the discussion of predestination, already somewhat difficult of itself, very confusing and even dangerous. No restraints can hold it back from wandering in forbidden bypaths and thrusting upward to the heights. If allowed, it will leave no secret to God that it will not search out and unravel. Since we see so many on all sides rushing into this audacity and impudence, among them certain men not otherwise bad, they should in due season be reminded of the measure of their duty in this regard.

First, then, let them remember that when they inquire into predestination they are penetrating the sacred precincts of divine wisdom. If anyone with carefree assurance breaks into this place, he will not succeed in satisfying his curiosity and he will enter a labyrinth from which he can find no exit. For it is not right for man unrestrainedly to search out things that the Lord has willed to be hid in himself, and to unfold from eternity itself the sublimest wisdom, which he would have us revere but not understand that through this also he should fill us with wonder. He has set forth by his Word the secrets of his will that he has decided to reveal to us. These he decided to reveal in so far as he foresaw that they would concern us and benefit us. . . .

Profane men, I admit, in the matter of predestination abruptly seize upon something to carp, rail, bark, or scoff at. But if their shamelessness deters us, we shall have to keep secret the chief doctrines of the faith, almost none of which they or their like leave untouched by blasphemy. An obstinate person would be no less insolently puffed up on hearing that within the essence of God there are three Persons than if he were told that God foresaw what would happen to man when he created him. And they will not refrain from guffaws when they are informed that but little more than five thousand years have passed since the creation of the universe, for they ask why God's power was idle and asleep for so long. Nothing, in short, can be brought forth that they do not assail with their mockery. Should we, to silence these blasphemies, forbear to speak of the deity of Son and Spirit? Must we pass over in silence the creation of the universe? No! God's truth is so powerful, both in this respect and in every other, that it has nothing to fear from the evil-speaking of wicked men.

So Augustine stoutly maintains in his little treatise *The Gift of Perseverance*. For we see that the false apostles could not make Paul ashamed by defaming and accusing his true doctrine. They say that this whole discussion is dangerous for godly minds—because it hinders exhortations, because it shakes faith, because it disturbs and terrifies the heart itself—but this is nonsense! Augustine admits that for these reasons he was frequently charged with preaching predestination too freely, but, as it was easy for him, he overwhelmingly refuted the charge. We, moreover, because many and various absurdities are obtruded at this point, have preferred to dispose of each in its own place. I desire only to have them generally admit that we should not investigate what the Lord has left hidden in secret, that we should not neglect what he has brought into the open, so that we may not be convicted of excessive curiosity on the one hand, or of excessive ingratitude on the other. For Augustine also skillfully expressed this idea: we can safely follow Scripture, which proceeds at the pace of a mother stooping to her child, so to speak, so as not to leave us behind in our weakness. But for those who are so cautious or fearful that they desire to bury predestination in order not to disturb weak souls—with what color will they cloak their arrogance when they accuse God indirectly of stupid thoughtlessness, as if he had not foreseen the peril that they feel they have wisely met? Whoever, then, heaps odium upon the doctrine of predestination openly reproaches God, as if he had unadvisedly let slip something hurtful to the church.

No one who wishes to be thought religious dares simply deny predestination, by which God adopts some to hope of life, and sentences others to eternal death. But our opponents, especially those who make foreknowledge its cause, envelop it in numerous petty objections. We, indeed, place both doctrines in God, but we say that subjecting one to the other is absurd.

When we attribute foreknowledge to God, we mean that all things always were, and perpetually remain, under his eyes, so that to his knowledge there is nothing future or past, but all things are present. And they are present in such a way that he not only conceives them through ideas, as we have before us those things which our minds remember, but he truly looks upon them and discerns them as things placed before him. And this foreknowledge is extended throughout the universe to every creature. We call predestination God's eternal decree, by which he determined with himself what he willed to become of each man. For all are not created in equal condition; rather, eternal life is foreordained for some, eternal damnation for others. Therefore, as any man has been created to one or the other of these ends, we speak of him as predestined to life or to death. . . .

As Scripture, then, clearly shows, we say that God once established by his eternal and unchangeable plan those whom he long before determined once for all to receive into salvation, and those whom, on the other hand, he would devote to destruction. We assert that, with respect to the elect, this plan was founded upon his freely given mercy, without regard to human worth; but by his just and irreprehensible but incomprehensible judgment he has barred the door of life to those whom he has given over to damnation. Now among the elect we regard the call as a testimony of election. Then we hold justification another sign of its manifestation, until they come into the glory in which the fulfillment of that election lies. But as the Lord seals his elect by call and justification, so, by shutting off the reprobate from knowledge of his name or from the sanctification of his Spirit, he, as it were, reveals by these marks what sort of judgment awaits them. Here I shall pass over many fictions that stupid men have invented to overthrow predestination. They need no refutation, for as soon as they are brought forth they abundantly prove their own falsity.

THE COUNTER REFORMATION

The Counter Reformation of the Catholic Church expressed itself in three major institutions: the Society of Jesus (usually called the Jesuits), the Inquisition (or Holy Office), and the Council of Trent. The Company or Society of Jesus was founded by St. Ignatius of Loyola (1491–1556), an unlettered Spanish soldier who, as the result of a religious experience he underwent after being wounded in battle, resolved to become a "soldier of Christ." Once he had recovered, he set about educating himself, starting with elementary school and continuing through the University of Paris, where he began organizing the Jesuit order. Loyola's new Society was established along military lines; and iron discipline demanded that each member show complete obedience to his immediate superiors and ultimately to his supreme commander, the pope. During the religious conflicts of the sixteenth and seventeenth centuries, the Jesuits were always to be found on the side of the papal forces, in opposition primarily to the Protestants but to Catholic liberals as well.

The Inquisition was an old organization, which had been developed by the Dominican order in the thirteenth century primarily to combat the Albigensian heresy in southern France. It gained its greatest strength, however, in Spain, where it was used as the prime agent of persecution against the Moors and Jews, particularly under the leadership of the notorious Torquemada. After the Reformation the Inquisition joined forces with the Jesuits to combat the "Protestant heresy."

The Council of Trent, called originally by Pope Paul III in 1545, met at irregular intervals over a period of nearly twenty years under three different popes in the capital of the Italian Tyrol. The Council responded to the Protestant movement by reaffirming the basic doctrines of the Catholic Church while at the same time calling for a reform of abuses within the Church. The selection that follows includes some of the more important decrees, concerning both doctrine and practice, adopted by the Council.

The Canons and Decrees of the Council of Trent

DECREE TOUCHING THE OPENING OF THE COUNCIL

Doth it please you,—unto the praise and glory of the holy and undivided Trinity, Father, and Son, and Holy Ghost; for the increase and exaltation of the Christian faith and religion; for the extirpation of heresies; for the peace and union of the Church; for the reformation of the Clergy and Christian people; for the depression and extinction of the enemies of the Christian name,—to decree and declare that the sacred and general council of Trent do begin, and hath begun?

They answered: It pleaseth us.

DECREE CONCERNING THE CANONICAL SCRIPTURES

The sacred and holy, oecumenical, and general Synod of Trent,—lawfully assembled in the Holy Ghost, the same three legates of the Apostolic See presiding therein,—keeping this always in view, that, errors being removed, the purity itself of the Gospel be preserved in the Church; which (Gospel), before promised through the prophets in the holy Scriptures, our Lord Jesus Christ, the Son of God, first promulgated with His own mouth, and then commanded to be preached by His Apostles to every creature, as the fountain of all, both saving truth, and moral discipline; and seeing clearly that this truth and books, and the unwritten traditions which, received by the Apostles from the mouth of Christ himself, or from the Apostles themselves, the Holy Ghost dictating, have come down even unto us, transmitted as it were from hand to hand; (the Synod) following the examples of the orthodox Fathers, receives and venerates with an equal affection of piety, and reverence, all the books both of the Old and of the New Testament—seeing that one God is the author of both—as also the said traditions, as well those appertaining to faith as to morals, as having been dictated, either by Christ's own word of mouth, or by the Holy Ghost, and preserved in the Catholic Church by a continuous succession.

. . .

DECREE CONCERNING THE EDITION, AND THE USE, OF THE SACRED BOOKS

Moreover, the same sacred and holy Synod,—considering that no small utility may accrue to the Church of God, if it be made known which out of all the Latin editions, now in circulation, of the sacred books, is to be held as authentic,—ordains and declares, that the said old and vulgate edition, which, by the lengthened usage of so many ages, has been approved of in the Church, be, in public lectures, disputations, sermons and expositions, held as authentic; and that no one is to dare, or presume to reject it under any pretext whatever.

Furthermore, in order to restrain petulant spirits, It decrees, that no one, relying on his own skill, shall,—in matters of faith, and of morals pertaining to the edification of Christian doctrine,—wresting the sacred Scripture to his own senses, presume to interpret the said sacred Scripture contrary to that sense which holy mother Church, —whose it is to judge of the true sense and interpretation of the holy Scriptures,—

THE CANONS AND DECREES OF THE SACRED AND OECUMENICAL COUNCIL OF TRENT, *trans.* J. *Waterworth (London, 1848).*

hath held and doth hold; or even contrary to the unanimous consent of the Fathers; even though such interpretations were never (intended) to be at any time published. . . .

DECREE CONCERNING ORIGINAL SIN

That our Catholic *faith, without which it is impossible to please God,* may, errors being purged away, continue in its own perfect and spotless integrity, and that the Christian people may not *be carried about with every wind of doctrine;* whereas that old serpent, the perpetual enemy of mankind, amongst the very many evils with which the Church of God is in these our times troubled, has also stirred up not only new, but even old, dissensions touching original sin, and the remedy thereof; the sacred and holy, oecumenical and general Synod of Trent,—lawfully assembled in the Holy See presiding therein,—wishing now to come to the reclaiming of the erring, and the confirming of the wavering—following the testimonies of the sacred Scriptures, of the holy Fathers, of the most approved councils, and the judgment and consent of the Church itself, ordains, confesses, and declares these things touching the said original sin:

1. If any one does not confess that the first man, Adam, when he had transgressed the commandment of God in Paradise, immediately lost the holiness and justice wherein he had been constituted; and that he incurred, through the offence of that prevarication, the wrath and indignation of God, and consequently death, with which God had previously threatened him, and, together with death, captivity under his power who thenceforth *had the empire of death, that is to say, the devil,* and that the entire Adam, through that offence of prevarication, was changed, in body and soul, for the worse; let him be anathema.

2. If any one asserts, that the prevarication of Adam injured himself alone, and not his posterity; and that the holiness and justice, received of God, which he lost, he lost for himself alone, and not for us also; or that he, being defiled by the sin of disobedience, has only transfused death, and pains of the body, into the whole human race, but not sin also, which is the death of the soul; let him be anathema:—whereas he contradicts the apostle who says; *By one man sin entered into the world, and by sin death, and so death passed upon all men, in whom all have sinned.*

3. If any one asserts, that this sin of Adam,—which in its origin is one, and being transfused into all by propagation, not by imitation, is in each one as his own,—is taken away either by the powers of human nature, or by any other remedy than the merit of the *one mediator, our Lord Jesus Christ, who hath reconciled us to God in his own blood, made unto us justice, sanctification, and redemption;* or if he denies that the said merit of Jesus Christ is applied, both to adults and to infants, by the sacrament of baptism rightly administered in the form of the Church; let him be anathema: *For there is no other name under heaven given to men, whereby we must be saved.* Whence that voice; *Behold the lamb of God, behold him who taketh away the sins of the world;* and that other; *As many as have been baptized, have put on Christ.*

. . .

THAT A RASH PRESUMPTUOUSNESS IN THE MATTER OF PREDESTINATION IS TO BE AVOIDED

No one, moreover, so long as he is in this mortal life, ought so far to presume as regards the secret mystery of divine predestination, as to determine for certain that he is assuredly in the number of the predestinate; as if it were true, that he that is justified, either cannot sin any more, or, if he do sin, that he ought to promise himself an assured repentance; for except by special revelation, it cannot be known whom God hath chosen unto Himself.

. . .

ON THE SACRAMENTS IN GENERAL

Canon I. If any one saith, that the sacraments of the New Law were not all instituted by Jesus Christ, our Lord; or, that they are more, or less, than seven, to wit, Baptism, Confirmation, the Eucharist, Penance, Extreme Unction, Order, and Matrimony; or even that any one of these seven is not truly and properly a sacrament; let him be anathema.

Canon II. If any one saith, that these said sacraments of the New Law do not differ from the sacraments of the Old Law, save that the ceremonies are different, and different the outward rites; let him be anathema.

Canon III. If any one saith, that these seven sacraments are in such wise equal to each other, as that one is not in any way more worthy than another; let him be anathema.

Canon IV. If any one saith, that the sacraments of the New Law are not necessary unto salvation, but superfluous; and that, without them, or without the desire thereof, men obtain of God, through faith alone, the grace of justification;—though all (the sacraments) are not indeed necessary for every individual; let him be anathema.

Canon V. If any one saith, that these sacraments were instituted for the sake of nourishing faith alone; let him be anathema.

Canon VI. If any one saith, that the sacraments of the New Law do not contain the grace which they signify; or, that they do not confer that grace on those who do not place an obstacle thereunto; as though they were merely outward signs of grace or justice received through faith, and certain marks of the Christian profession, whereby believers are distinguished amongst men from unbelievers; let him be anathema.

Canon VII. If any one saith, that grace, as far as God's part is concerned, is not given through the said sacraments, always, and to all men, even though they receive them rightly, but (only) sometimes, and to some persons; let him be anathema.

Canon VIII. If any one saith, that by the said sacraments of the New Law grace is not conferred through the act performed, but that faith alone in the divine promise suffices for the obtaining of grace; let him be anathema.

Canon IX. If any one saith, that, in the three sacraments, Baptism, to wit, Confirmation, and Order, there is not imprinted in the soul a character, that is, a certain spiritual and indelible sign, on account of which they cannot be repeated; let him be anathema.

Canon X. If any one saith, that all Christians have power to administer the word, and all the sacraments; let him be anathema.

Canon XI. If any one saith, that, in ministers, when they effect, and confer the sacraments, there is not required the intention at least of doing what the Church does; let him be anathema.

Canon XII. If any one saith, that a minister, being in mortal sin,—if so be that he observe all the essentials which belong to the effecting, or conferring of, the sacrament,—neither effects, nor confers the sacrament; let him be anathema.

Canon XIII. If any one saith, that the received and approved rites of the Catholic Church, wont to be used in the solemn administration of the sacraments, may be condemned, or without sin be omitted at pleasure by the ministers, or be changed, by every pastor of the churches, into other new ones; let him be anathema.

. . .

ON THE REAL PRESENCE OF OUR LORD JESUS CHRIST IN THE MOST HOLY SACRAMENT OF THE EUCHARIST

Lord's Supper

In the first place, the holy Synod teaches, and openly and simply professes, that, in the august sacrament of the holy Eucharist, after the consecration of the bread and wine, our Lord Jesus Christ, true God and man, is truly, really, and substantially contained under the species of those sensible things. For neither are these things mutually repugnant,—that our Saviour Himself always sitteth at the right hand of the Father in heaven, according to the natural mode of existing, and that, nevertheless, He be, in many other places, sacramentally present to us in his own substance, by a manner of existing, which, though we can scarcely express it in words, yet can we, by the understanding illuminated by faith, conceive, and we ought most firmly to believe, to be possible unto God: for thus all our forefathers, as many as were in the true Church of Christ, who have treated of this most holy Sacrament have most openly professed, that our Redeemer instituted this so admirable a sacrament at the last supper, when, after the blessing of the bread and wine, He testified, in express and clear words, that He gave them His own very Body, and His own Blood; words which,—recorded by the holy Evangelists, and afterwards repeated by Saint Paul, whereas they carry with them that proper and most manifest meaning in which they were understood by the Fathers,—it is indeed a crime the most unworthy that they should be wrested, by certain contentious and wicked men, to fictitious and imaginary tropes, whereby the verity of the flesh and blood of Christ is denied, contrary to the universal sense of the Church, which, as *the pillar and ground of truth,* has detested, as satanical, these inventions devised by impious men; she recognising, with a mind ever grateful and unforgetting, this most excellent benefit of Christ.

. . .

ON THE MOST HOLY SACRAMENT OF THE EUCHARIST

Canon I. If any one denieth, that, in the sacrament of the most holy Eucharist, are contained truly, really, and substantially, the body and blood together with the soul and divinity of our Lord Jesus Christ, and consequently the whole Christ; but saith that He is only therein as in a sign, or in figure, or virtue; let him be anathema.

Canon II. If any one saith, that, in the sacred and holy sacrament of the Eucharist, the substance of the bread and wine remains conjointly with the body and blood of our Lord Jesus Christ, and denieth that wonderful and singular conversion of the whole substance of the bread into the Body, and of the whole substance of the wine into the Blood—the species only of the bread and wine remaining—which conversion indeed the Catholic Church most aptly calls Transubstantiation; let him be anathema.

. . .

Canon IX. If any one denieth, that all and each of Christ's faithful of both sexes are bound, when they have attained to years of discretion, to communicate every year, at least at Easter, in accordance with the precept of the holy Mother Church; let him be anathema.

. . .

Canon XI. If any one saith, that faith alone is a sufficient preparation for receiving the sacrament of the most holy Eucharist; let him be anathema. And for fear lest so great a sacrament may be received unworthily, and so unto death and condemnation, this holy Synod ordains and declares, that sacramental confession, when a confessor may be had, is of necessity to be made beforehand, by those whose conscience is burthened with mortal sin, how contrite even soever they may think themselves. But if any one shall presume to teach, preach, or obstinately to assert, or even in public disputation to defend the contrary, he shall be thereupon excommunicated.

. . .

ON THE ECCLESIASTICAL HIERARCHY, AND ON ORDINATION

But, forasmuch as in the sacrament of Order, as also in Baptism and Confirmation, a character is imprinted, which can neither be effaced nor taken away; the holy Synod with reason condemns the opinion of those, who assert that the priests of the New Testament have only a temporary power; and that those who have once been rightly ordained, can again become laymen, if they do not exercise the ministry of the word of God. And if any one affirm, that all Christians indiscriminately are priests of the New Testament, or that they are all mutually endowed with an equal spiritual power, he clearly does nothing but confound the ecclesiastical hierarchy, which is *as an army set in array;* as if, contrary to the doctrine of blessed Paul, *all* were *apostles, all prophets, all evangelists, all pastors, all doctors.* Wherefore, the holy Synod declares that, besides the other ecclesiastical degrees, bishops, who have succeeded to the place of the apostles, principally belong to this hierarchical order; that they are *placed,* as the same apostle says, *by the Holy Ghost, to rule the Church of God;* that they are superior to priests; administer the sacrament of Confirmation; ordain the ministers of the Church; and that they can perform very many other things; over which functions others of an inferior order have no power. Furthermore, the sacred and holy Synod teaches, that, in the ordination of bishops, priests, and of the other orders, neither the consent, nor vocation, nor authority, whether of the people, or of any civil power or magistrate whatsoever, is required in such wise as that, without this, the ordination is invalid: yea rather doth It decree, that all those who, being only called and instituted by the people, or by the civil power and magistrate, ascend to the exercise of these ministrations, and those who of their own rashness assume them to themselves, are not ministers of the Church, but are to be looked upon as *thieves and robbers, who have not entered by the door.* These are the things which it hath seemed good to the sacred Synod to teach the faithful of Christ, in general terms, touching the sacrament of Order.

. . .

ON THE SACRAMENT OF MATRIMONY

. . .

Canon IX. If any one saith, that clerics constituted in sacred orders or Regulars, who have solemnly professed chastity, are able to contract marriage, and that being contracted it is valid, notwithstanding the ecclesiastical law, or vow; and that the contrary is nothing else than to condemn marriage; and, that all who do not feel that they have the gift of chastity, even though they have made a vow thereof, may contract marriage; let him be anathema: seeing that God refuses not that gift to those who ask for it rightly, neither does *He suffer us to be tempted above that which we are able.*

Canon X. If any one saith, that the marriage state is to be placed above the state of virginity, or of celibacy, and that it is not better and more blessed to remain in virginity, or in celibacy, than to be united in matrimony; let him be anathema.

. . .

ON THE INVOCATION, VENERATION, AND RELICS, OF SAINTS, AND ON SACRED IMAGES

The holy Synod enjoins on all bishops, and others who sustain the office and charge of teaching, that, agreeably to the usage of the Catholic and Apostolic Church, received from the primitive times of the Christian religion, and agreeably to the consent of the holy Fathers, and to the decrees of sacred Councils, they especially instruct the faithful diligently concerning the intercession and invocation of saints; the honour (paid) to relics; and the legitimate use of images: teaching them, that the saints, who reign together with Christ, offer up their own prayers to God for men; that it is good and useful suppliantly to invoke them, and to have recourse to their prayers, aid, (and) help for obtaining benefits from God, through His Son, Jesus Christ our Lord, who is our alone Redeemer and Saviour; but that they think impiously, who deny that the saints, who enjoy eternal happiness in heaven, are to be invocated; or who assert either that they do not pray for men; or, that the invocation of them to pray for each of us even in particular, is idolatry; or, that it is repugnant to the word of God; and is opposed to the honour of the *one mediator of God and men, Christ Jesus;* or, that it is foolish to supplicate, vocally, or mentally, those who reign in heaven. Also, that the holy bodies of holy martyrs, and of others now living with Christ,—which bodies were the living members of Christ, and *the temple of the Holy Ghost,* and which are by Him to be raised unto eternal life, and to be glorified,—are to be venerated by the faithful; through which (bodies) many benefits are bestowed by God on men; so that they who affirm that veneration and honour are not due to the relics of saints; or, that these, and other sacred monuments, are uselessly honoured by the faithful; and that the places dedicated to the memories of the saints are in vain visited with the view of obtaining their aid; are wholly to be condemned, as the Church has already long since condemned, and now also condemns them.

Moreover, that the images of Christ, of the Virgin Mother of God, and of the other saints, are to be had and retained particularly in temples, and that due honour and veneration are to be given them; not that any divinity, or virtue, is believed to be in them, on account of which they are to be worshipped; or that anything is to be asked of them; or, that trust is to be reposed in images, as was of old done by the Gentiles who placed their hope in idols; but because the honour which is shown them is referred to the prototypes which those images represent; in such wise that by the images which we kiss, and before which we uncover the head, and prostrate ourselves, we adore Christ; and we venerate the saints, whose similitude they bear: as by the decrees of Councils, and especially of the second Synod of Nicaea, has been defined against the opponents of images.

. . .

CARDINALS AND ALL PRELATES OF THE CHURCHES SHALL BE CONTENT WITH MODEST FURNITURE AND A FRUGAL TABLE: THEY SHALL NOT ENRICH THEIR RELATIVES OR DOMESTICS OUT OF THE PROPERTY OF THE CHURCH

It is to be wished, that those who undertake the office of a bishop should understand what their portion is; and comprehend that they are called, not to their own convenience, not to riches or luxury, but to labours and cares for the glory of God. For it is not to be doubted, that the rest of the faithful also will be more easily excited to religion and innocence, if they shall see those who are set over them, not fixing their thoughts on the things of this world, but on the salvation of souls, and on their heavenly country. Wherefore the holy Synod, being minded that these things are of the greatest importance toward restoring ecclesiastical discipline, admonishes all bishops, that, often meditating thereon, they show themselves conformable to their office, by their actual deeds, and the actions of their lives; which is a kind of perpetual sermon; but above all that they so order their whole conversation, as that others may thence be able to derive examples of frugality, modesty, continency, and of that holy humility which so much recommends us to God.

Wherefore, after the example of our fathers in the Council of Carthage, It not only orders that bishops be content with modest furniture, and a frugal table and diet, but that they also give heed that in the rest of their manner of living, and in their whole house, there be nothing seen that is alien from this holy institution, and which does not manifest simplicity, zeal toward God, and a contempt of vanities. Also, it wholly forbids them to strive to enrich their own kindred or domestics out of the revenues of the Church: seeing that even the canons of the Apostles forbid them to give to their kindred the property of the church, which belongs to God; but if their kindred be poor, let them distribute to them thereof as poor, but not misapply, or waste, it for their sakes: yea, the holy Synod with the utmost earnestness, admonishes them completely to lay aside all this human and carnal affection toward brothers, nephews and kindred, which is the seed-plot of many evils in the Church. And what has been said of bishops, the same is not only to be observed by all who hold ecclesiastical benefices, whether Secular or Regular, each according to the nature of his rank, but the Synod decrees that it also regards the cardinals of the holy Roman Church; for whereas, upon their advice to the most holy Roman Pontiff, the administration of the universal Church depends, it would seem to be a shame, if they did not at the same time shine so pre-eminent in virtue and in the discipline of their lives, as deservedly to draw upon themselves the eyes of all men.

. . .

DECREE CONCERNING INDULGENCES

Whereas the power of conferring Indulgences was granted by Christ to the Church; and she has, even in the most ancient times, used the said power, delivered unto her of God; the sacred holy Synod teaches, and enjoins, that the use of Indulgences, for the Christian people most salutary, and approved of by the authority of sacred Councils, is to be retained in the Church; and It condemns with anathema those who either assert, that they are useless; or who deny that there is in the

Church the power of granting them. In granting them, however, It desires that, in accordance with the ancient and approved custom in the Church, moderation be observed; lest, by excessive facility, ecclesiastical discipline be enervated. And being desirous that the abuses which have crept therein, and by occasion of which this honourable name of Indulgences is blasphemed by heretics, be amended and corrected, It ordains generally by this decree, that all evil gains for the obtaining thereof, —whence a most prolific cause of abuses amongst the Christian people has been derived,—be wholly abolished. But as regards the other abuses which have proceeded from superstition, ignorance, irreverance, or from whatsoever other source, since, by reason of the manifold corruptions in the places and provinces where the said abuses are committed, they cannot conveniently be specially prohibited; It commands all bishops, diligently to collect, each in his own church, all abuses of this nature, and to report them in the first provincial Synod; that, after having been reviewed by the opinions of the other bishops also, they may forthwith be referred to the Sovereign Roman Pontiff, by whose authority and prudence that which may be expedient for the universal Church will be ordained; that thus the gift of holy Indulgences may be dispensed to all the faithful, piously, holily, and incorruptly.

EARLY MODERN EUROPE

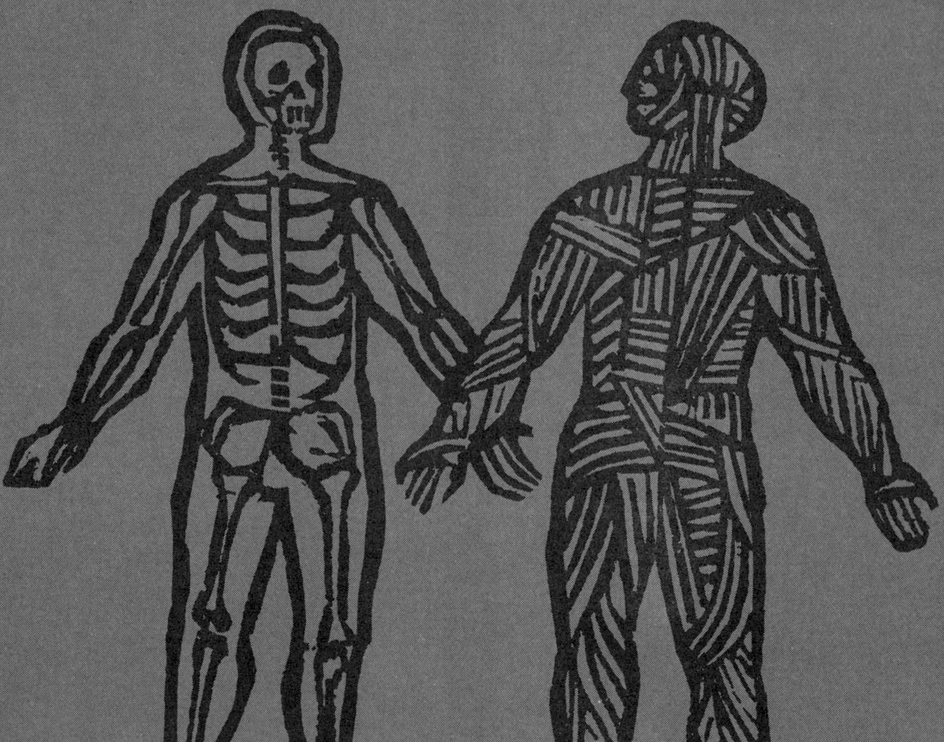

THE PEACE OF WESTPHALIA (1648) ended the Thirty Years' War and marked the beginning of a new era in the history of Europe. In addition to territorial changes, the treaty incorporated two major principles that were to influence events for many years to come.

First, the Peace fairly definitely ended the wars over religion and effectively ended the notion of Protestant versus Catholic. The idea that religious beliefs were matters for the individual's own conscience to settle had grown up slowly during the hundred years before 1648, and with the Peace of Westphalia religious liberty became rather well established. The treaty left it to each prince to determine the religion of his subjects; if a subject felt that he could not accept his prince's religion, he could move to another country where a more acceptable faith was practiced.

Second, the Thirty Years' War and its conclusion clearly answered the question of whether or not Europe would have a universal monarchy, such as the Holy Roman Empire. Henceforth, there was to be a system of independent sovereign powers balancing one another in the contest for power. The political, economic, and diplomatic history of Europe from the Peace of Westphalia to the fall of Napoleon was dominated by the rivalries of dynastic families, each seeking to expand its holdings at the expense of the others.

To implement this rivalry—some prefer to describe the situation as anarchy, but that depends on how you look at it—the entire machinery of international politics was either created or refined. Diplomatic services were called into being and sanctioned, international law was developed to regulate affairs between states, the law of war was formulated (a curious contradiction in itself), elaborate alliance systems were negotiated, and numerous wars were fought. There were even visionary projects for seventeenth- and eighteenth-century versions of a United Nations organization.

All these developments provide us with clues to an understanding of early modern European history, for they reflect a self-conscious attempt to regularize and limit the effects of competition among states. Thus, even the wars were fought for very limited objectives, such as the conquest of a particular bit of land. The idea of limited warfare with limited objectives differs radically from the twentieth-century notion of unlimited, total war fought to destroy an entire people or a government or a philosophy. In the seventeenth and eighteenth centuries, war tended to be an honorable game between princes who could accept defeat gracefully, knowing their thrones were secure even if a war were lost.

Another reason for limiting warfare was to protect the domestic scene from serious disruption. Whenever possible, the general population was not disturbed or its daily routines changed. The armies themselves were recruited from among those who were least essential to the functioning of the economy—the beggar, the ne'er-do-well, and the unskilled worker constituted the raw material that was molded into highly trained, severely disciplined armies by a corps of officers drawn mostly from the hereditary nobility. Thus, there was a deliberate attempt to isolate and confine both warfare and the military organizations that carried it on.

The purpose of even limited war, of course, was to increase the power and territory of the prince. But war was not the sole means of accomplishing these ends. Since agriculture, industry, and commerce could also contribute to the strength of the ruler, these activities were carefully fostered and protected from the effects of war. Stimulation and protection, however, meant control and regulation. In industry, for example, the quality of manufactures was maintained at a high level, costs were kept low, and the most advantageous commodities were produced. This system of regulation, called *mercantilism,* was adopted in one form or another in all the countries of Western Europe.

The mercantilists started from two basic principles: One, that the wealth of a state was determined by the quantity of gold and silver it possessed; two, that the total amount of trade in the world was fixed. It was from these two assumptions that most of the mercantilist practices were deduced. Wealth—that is, bullion—was necessary to support the prince in his wars and other activities; and if his country lacked adequate gold and silver mines, the only way it could obtain this wealth was to export more goods than it imported. Furthermore, since wealth was power, it followed that the power of one's rivals could be reduced by cutting down their supplies of gold and silver—that is, by selling them goods and by taking gold and silver in payment. Also, since the mercantilists thought that the total amount of trade was fixed, if one country could increase its share, the shares of all the others would be smaller and, consequently, they would be less able to accumulate wealth.

This same logic operated in the creation and administration of overseas empires. Colonies were intended to produce raw materials that could be shipped to the mother country for fabrication and then exported, either back to the colonies or, better, to the political and economic rivals of the mother country. The colonies were prohibited from trading with any state other than the parent.

By the end of the eighteenth century, however, mercantilism was falling under heavy criticism. The most telling attack on the system was published in 1776 by Adam Smith, who argued that the wealth of nations lay not so much in bullion as in productive capacity.

Smith's work was an expression of the major intellectual movement of the eighteenth century, which is often called the Age of Reason or the Enlightenment. The writers and thinkers of this century were convinced that the universe was regulated by natural laws, and that these laws could be discovered through the use of man's power to think and reason. This conviction was bolstered by the discoveries of Sir Isaac Newton, who in the late seventeenth century had worked out the laws of the physical universe by means of experimentation, observation, and deduction. The task the men of the Enlightenment set for themselves was to find the equivalent laws that governed human relationships, politics, and economics. Their search for the natural laws of society led them to examine and to criticize existing ideas and institutions. The theory of divine-right monarchy, for example, presented by Bishop Bossuet the century before, was held up to ridicule by both John Locke and Jean Jacques Rousseau; mercantilism was attacked as an interference with the natural laws of supply and demand; the Catholic Church was severely criticized (particularly by Voltaire) on the grounds that it rested on superstition rather than on reason, and that it undertook to censor and condemn books and articles.

We find one insistent emphasis throughout the Age of Reason. The mind must be free to inquire, to learn, and to communicate. Any social institution or tradition that interfered with this freedom had to be either recast according to the dictates of reason or else discarded. Remnants from the past that were no longer useful or that had survived only because of tradition were to be abolished. Dramatic evidence of this insistence appears in the lists of grievances (*Cahiers de Doléances*) that were drawn up in France on the eve of the French Revolution.

If the desire for liberty was strong in the eighteenth century, so too was the desire for equality. In a sense, the idea of social and political equality stemmed from the idea of liberty, for, if a man was free to do and think as he pleased, he should be judged on the basis of his thoughts and actions, rather than on the basis of hereditary rights, ranks, and privileges. Nor should his freedom be limited by arbitrary prohibitions on what he could or could not do. It was felt, for example, that a man should be able to rise to the highest ranks in the army if he had the necessary talent and ability, and that to require noble birth for high rank was unreasonable and senseless. "Equality of opportunity" and "the career open to talent" were later pointed to by Napoleon as the very essence of the French Revolution.

The eighteenth century ended in violence, revolution, terror, and tumult. Western civilization had come to the end of one era and the beginning of another. The gracious aristocrat was rapidly becoming an anachronism, and his political and economic power was being taken over by a middle class whose position rested on commercial and industrial wealth, not on patents of rank and the titles of ennobled ancestors. This new middle class found the doctrines of the Enlightenment acceptable also—liberty and equality were very appealing to men who chose to rely on themselves for prestige and social status. But they faced one major problem: If these high ideals were accepted, how could they be practiced? It is around attempts to answer this question that much of the history of the next century centers.

FRANCIS BACON

Francis Bacon (1561–1626) was a prophet of the scientific revolution of the seventeenth century—a revolution that transformed the foundations of European thought and ushered in the new Age of Science. To accomplish such an intellectual revolution, Bacon believed that men must turn their backs on medieval scholastic philosophy and develop a new science based on a true knowledge, derived from careful and continued observation, of the workings of nature. This observational method, which Bacon called induction, is explained and illustrated in his major work, The Great Instauration, *which, in his opinion, represented a "total reconstruction of the sciences, arts, and all human knowledge."*

Although he was a prophet of the new science, Bacon himself did not fully grasp the nature of the method that men like Galileo and Newton were to employ in their work. His concept of induction, or the careful examination of particular occurrences in nature, fails to take adequate account of two other elements that are basic to modern scientific method: the formulation of hypotheses, and the deduction and verification of the consequences of these.

Living at the height of the English Renaissance (which followed a hundred years behind that of Italy), Bacon exemplifies many of the attitudes found in previous Renaissance writers—the rejection of the medieval world-view as pernicious error, the somewhat naive optimism about his ability to take the whole of human knowledge as his sphere of activity, and the faith that he stood on the threshold of a new intellectual era. Finally, in his assertion that "knowledge is power" Bacon repeated a central concept of Machiavelli. But with a significant difference. For, although both men were interested in power, Machiavelli was concerned with the power that a prince could wield over his subjects, while Bacon was concerned with the power, derived from scientific understanding, that all men could wield over nature.

The selection that follows is Bacon's plan for his Great Instauration.

The Great Instauration

THE PLAN OF THE WORK

The work is in six Parts:—

1. *The Divisions of the Sciences.*
2. *The New Organon; or Directions concerning the Interpretation of Nature.*
3. *The Phenomena of the Universe; or a Natural and Experimental History for the foundation of Philosophy.*
4. *The Ladder of the Intellect.*
5. *The Forerunners; or Anticipations of the New Philosophy.*
6. *The New Philosophy; or Active Science.*

THE PHILOSOPHICAL WORKS OF FRANCIS BACON *(London, 1905).*

The Arguments of the Several Parts

It being part of my design to set everything forth, as far as may be, plainly and perspicuously (for nakedness of the mind is still, as nakedness of the body once was, the companion of innocence and simplicity), let me first explain the order and plan of the work. I distribute it into six parts.

The first part exhibits a summary or general description of the knowledge which the human race at present possesses. For I thought it good to make some pause upon that which is received; that thereby the old may be more easily made perfect and the new more easily approached. And I hold the improvement of that which we have to be as much an object as the acquisition of more. Besides which it will make me the better listened to; for "He that is ignorant (says the proverb) receives not the words of knowledge, unless thou first tell him that which is in his own heart." We will therefore make a coasting voyage along the shores of the arts and sciences received; not without importing into them some useful things by the way.

In laying out the division of the sciences, however, I take into account not only things already invented and known, but likewise things omitted which ought to be there. For there are found in the intellectual as in the terrestial globe waste regions as well as cultivated ones. It is no wonder therefore if I am sometimes obliged to depart from the ordinary divisions. For in adding to the total you necessarily alter the parts and sections; and the received divisions of the sciences are fitted only to the received sum of them as it stands now.

With regard to those things which I shall mark as omitted, I intend not merely to set down a simple title or a concise argument of that which is wanted. For as often as I have occasion to report anything as deficient, the nature of which is at all obscure, so that men may not perhaps easily understand what I mean or what the work is which I have in my head, I shall always (provided it be a matter of any worth) take care to subjoin either directions for the execution of such work, or else a portion of the work itself executed by myself as a sample of the whole; thus giving assistance in every case either by work or by counsel. For if it were for the sake of my own reputation only and other men's interests were not concerned in it, I would not have any man think that in such cases merely some light and vague notion has crossed my mind, and that the things which I desire and offer at are no better than wishes; when they are in fact things which men may certainly command if they will, and of which I have formed in my own mind a clear and detailed conception. For I do not propose merely to survey these regions in my mind, like an augur taking auspices, but to enter them like a general who means to take possession.—So much for the first part of the work.

Having thus coasted past the ancient arts, the next point is to equip the intellect for passing beyond. To the second part therefore belongs the doctrine concerning the better and more perfect use of human reason in the inquisition of things, and the true helps of the understanding: that thereby (as far as the condition of mortality and humanity allows) the intellect may be raised and exalted, and made capable of overcoming the difficulties and obscurities of nature. The art which I introduce with this view (which I call *Interpretation of Nature*) is a kind of logic; though the difference between it and the ordinary logic is great; indeed immense. For the ordinary logic professes to contrive and prepare helps and guards for the understanding, as mine does; and in this one point they agree. But mine differs from it in three points especially; viz., in the end aimed at; in the order of demonstration; and in the starting point of the inquiry.

For the end which this science of mine proposes is the invention not of arguments but of arts; not of things in accordance with principles, but of principles themselves; not of probable reasons, but of designations and directions for works. And as the intention is different, so accordingly is the effect; the effect of the one being to overcome an opponent in argument, of the other to command nature in action.

In accordance with this end is also the nature and order of the demonstrations. For in the ordinary logic almost all the work is spent about the syllogism. Of induction the logicians seem hardly to have taken any serious thought, but they pass it by with a slight notice, and hasten on to the formulæ of disputation. I on the contrary reject demonstration by syllogism, as acting too confusedly, and letting nature slip out of its hands. For although no one can doubt that things which agree in a middle term agree with one another (which is a proposition of mathematical certainty), yet it leaves an opening for deception; which is this. The syllogism consists of propositions; propositions of words; and words are the tokens and signs of notions. Now if the very notions of the mind (which are as the soul of words and the basis of the whole structure) be improperly and over-hastily abstracted from facts, vague, not sufficiently definite, faulty in short in many ways, the whole edifice tumbles. I therefore reject the syllogism; and that not only as regards principles (for to principles the logicians themselves do not apply it) but also as regards middle propositions; which, though obtainable no doubt by the syllogism, are, when so obtained, barren of works, remote from practice, and altogether unavailable for the active department of the sciences. Although therefore I leave to the syllogism and these famous and boasted modes of demonstration their jurisdiction over popular arts and such as are matter of opinion (in which department I leave all as it is), yet in dealing with the nature of things I use induction throughout, and that in the minor propositions as well as the major. For I consider induction to be that form of demonstration which upholds the sense and closes with nature, and comes to the very brink of operation, if it does not actually deal with it.

Hence it follows that the order of demonstration is likewise inverted. For hitherto the proceeding has been to fly at once from the sense and particulars up to the most general propositions, as certain fixed poles for the argument to turn upon, and from these to derive the rest by middle terms: a short way, no doubt, but precipitate; and one which will never lead to nature, though it offers an easy and ready way to disputation. Now my plan is to proceed regularly and gradually from one axiom to another, so that the most general are not reached till the last; but then when you do come to them you find them to be not empty notions but well defined, and such as nature would really recognize as her first principles, and such as lie at the heart and marrow of things.

But the greatest change I introduce is in the form itself of induction and the judgment made thereby. For the induction of which the logicians speak, which proceeds by simple enumeration, is a puerile thing; concludes at hazard; is always liable to be upset by a contradictory instance; takes into account only what is known and ordinary; and leads to no result.

Now what the sciences stand in need of is a form of induction which shall analyse experience and take it to pieces, and by a due process of exclusion and rejection lead to an inevitable conclusion. And if that ordinary mode of judgment practised by the logicians was so laborious, and found exercise for such great wits, how much more labour must we be prepared to bestow upon this other, which is extracted not merely out of the depths of the mind, but out of the very bowels of nature.

Nor is this all. For I also sink the foundations of the sciences deeper and firmer; and I begin the inquiry nearer the source than men have done heretofore; submitting to examination those things which the common logic takes on trust. For, first, the logicians borrow the principles of each science from the science itself; secondly, they hold in reverence the first notions of the mind; and lastly, they receive as conclusive the immediate informations of the sense, when well disposed. Now upon the first point, I hold that true logic ought to enter the several provinces of science armed with a higher authority than belongs to the principles of those sciences themselves, and ought to call those putative principles to account until they are fully established. Then with regard to the first notions of the intellect; there is not one of the impressions taken by the intellect when left to go its own way, but I hold it for suspected, and no way established, until it has submitted to a new trial and a fresh judgment has been thereupon pronounced. And lastly, the information of the sense itself I sift and examine in many ways. For certain it is that the senses deceive; but then at the same time they supply the means of discovering their own errors; only the errors are here, the means of discovery are to seek.

The sense fails in two ways. Sometimes it gives no information, sometimes it gives false information. For first, there are very many things which escape the sense, even when best disposed and no way obstructed; by reason either of the subtlety of the whole body, or the minuteness of the parts, or distance of place; or slowness or else swiftness of motion, or familiarity of object, or other causes. And again when the sense does apprehend a thing its apprehension is not much to be relied upon. For the testimony and information of the sense has reference always to man, not to the universe; and it is a great error to assert that the sense is the measure of things.

To meet these difficulties, I have sought on all sides diligently and faithfully to provide helps for the sense—substitutes to supply its failures, rectifications to correct its errors; and this I endeavour to accomplish not so much by instruments as by experiments. For the subtlety of experiments is far greater than that of the sense itself, even when assisted by exquisite instruments; such experiments, I mean, as are skilfully and artificially devised for the express purpose of determining the point in question. To the immediate and proper perception of the sense therefore I do not give much weight; but I contrive that the office of the sense shall be only to judge of the experiment, and that the experiment itself shall judge of the thing. And thus I conceive that I perform the office of a true priest of the sense (from which all knowledge in nature must be sought, unless men mean to go mad) and a not unskilful interpreter of its oracles; and that while others only profess to uphold and cultivate the sense, I do so in fact. Such then are the provisions I make for finding the genuine light of nature and kindling and bringing it to bear. And they would be sufficient of themselves, if the human intellect were even, and like a fair sheet of paper with no writing upon it. But since the minds of men are strangely possessed and beset, so that there is no true and even surface left to reflect the genuine rays of things, it is necessary to seek a remedy for this also.

Now the idols, or phantoms, by which the mind is occupied are either adventitious or innate. The adventitious come into the mind from without; namely, either from the doctrines and sects of philosophers, or from perverse rules of demonstration. But the innate are inherent in the very nature of the intellect, which is far more prone to error than the sense is. For let men please themselves as they will in admiring and almost adoring the human mind, this is certain: that as an uneven mirror distorts the rays of objects according to its own figure and section, so the mind, when it receives impressions of objects through the sense, cannot be trusted to report them truly, but in forming its notions mixes up its own nature with the nature of things.

And as the first two kinds of idols are hard to eradicate, so idols of this last kind cannot be eradicated at all. All that can be done is to point them out so that this insidious action of the mind may be marked and reproved (else as fast as old errors are destroyed new ones will spring up out of the ill complexion of the mind itself, and so we shall have but a change of errors, and not a clearance); and to lay it down once for all as a fixed and established maxim, that the intellect is not qualified to judge except by means of induction, and induction in its legitimate form. This doctrine then of the expurgation of the intellect to qualify it for dealing with truth, is comprised in three refutations: the refutation of the Philosophies; the refutation of the Demonstrations; and the refutation of the Natural Human Reason. The explanation of which things, and of the true relation between the nature of things and the nature of the mind, is as the strewing and decoration of the bridal chamber of the Mind and the Universe, the Divine Goodness assisting; out of which marriage let us hope (and be this the prayer of the bridal song) there may spring helps to man, and a line and race of inventions that may in some degree subdue and overcome the necessities and miseries of humanity. This is the second part of the work.

But I design not only to indicate and mark out the ways, but also to enter them. And therefore the third part of the work embraces the Phenomena of the universe; that is to say, experience of every kind, and such a natural history as may serve for a foundation to build philosophy upon. For a good method of demonstration or form of interpreting nature may keep the mind from going astray or stumbling, but it is not any excellence of method that can supply it with the material of knowledge. Those however who aspire not to guess and divine but to discover and know; who propose not to devise mimic and fabulous worlds of their own, but to examine and dissect the nature of this very world itself; must go to facts themselves for everything. Nor can the place of this labour and search and worldwide perambulation be supplied by any genius or meditation or argumentation; no, not if all men's wits could meet in one. This therefore we must have, or the business must be for ever abandoned. But up to this day such has been the condition of men in this matter, that it is no wonder if nature will not give herself into their hands.

For first, the information of the sense itself, sometimes failing, sometimes false; observation, careless, irregular, and led by chance; tradition, vain and fed on humour; practise, slavishly bent upon its work; experiment, blind, stupid, vague, and prematurely broken off; lastly, natural history trivial and poor;—all these have contributed to supply the understanding with very bad materials for philosophy and the sciences.

Then an attempt is made to mend the matter by a preposterous subtlety and winnowing of argument. But this comes too late, the case being already past remedy; and is far from setting the business right or sifting away the errors. The only hope therefore of any greater increase or progress lies in a reconstruction of the sciences.

Of this reconstruction the foundation must be laid in natural history, and that of a new kind and gathered on a new principle. For it is in vain that you polish the mirror if there are no images to be reflected; and it is as necessary that the intellect should be supplied with fit matter to work upon, as with safeguards to guide its working. But my history differs from that in use (as my logic does) in many things,—in end and office, in mass and composition, in subtlety, in selection also and setting forth, with a view to the operations which are to follow.

For first, the object of the natural history which I propose is not so much to delight with variety of matter or to help with present use of experiments, as to give light to the discovery of causes and supply a suckling philosophy with its first food. For though it be true that I am principally in pursuit of works and the active department of the sciences, yet I wait for harvest-time, and do not attempt to mow the moss or to reap the green corn. For I well know that axioms once rightly discovered will carry whole troops of works along with them, and produce them, not here and there one, but in clusters. And that unseasonable and puerile hurry to snatch by way of earnest at the first works which come within reach, I utterly condemn and reject, as an Atlanta's apple that hinders the race. Such then is the office of this natural history of mine.

Next, with regard to the mass and composition of it: I mean it to be a history not only of nature free and at large (when she is left to her own course and does her work her own way),—such as that of the heavenly bodies, meteors, earth and sea, minerals, plants, animals,—but much more of nature under constraint and vexed; that is to say, when by art and the hand of man she is forced out of her natural state, and squeezed and moulded. Therefore I set down at length all experiments of the mechanical arts, of the operative part of the liberal arts, of the many crafts which have not yet grown into arts properly so called, so far as I have been able to examine them and as they conduce to the end in view. Nay (to say the plain truth) I do in fact (low and vulgar as men may think it) count more upon this part both for helps and safeguards than upon the other; seeing that the nature of things betrays itself more readily under the vexations of art than in its natural freedom.

Nor do I confine the history to Bodies; but I have thought it my duty besides to make a separate history of such Virtues as may be considered cardinal in nature. I mean those original passions or desires of matter which constitute the primary elements of nature; such as Dense and Rare, Hot and Cold, Solid and Fluid, Heavy and Light, and several others.

Then again, to speak of subtlety: I seek out and get together a kind of experiments much subtler and simpler than those which occur accidentally. For I drag into light many things which no one who was not proceeding by a regular and certain way to the discovery of causes would have thought of inquiring after; being indeed in themselves of no great use; which shows that they were not sought for on their own account; but having just the same relation to things and works which the letters of the alphabet have to speech and words—which, though in themselves useless, are the elements of which all discourse is made up.

Further, in the selection of the relations and experiments I conceive I have been a more cautious purveyor than those who have hitherto dealt with natural history. For I admit nothing but on the faith of eyes, or at least of careful and severe examination; so that nothing is exaggerated for wonder's sake, but what I state is sound and without mixture of fables or vanity. All received or current falsehoods also (which by strange negligence have been allowed for many ages to prevail and become established) I proscribe and brand by name; that the sciences may be no more troubled with them. For it has been well observed that the fables and superstitions and follies which nurses instil into children do serious injury to their minds; and the same consideration makes me anxious, having the management of the childhood as it were of philosophy in its course of natural history, not to let it accustom itself in the beginning to any vanity. Moreover, whenever I come to a new experiment of any subtlety (though it be in my own opinion certain and approved), I nevertheless subjoin a clear account of the manner in which I made it; that men knowing exactly how each point was made out, may see whether there be any error connected with it, and may arouse themselves to devise proofs more trustworthy and exquisite, if such can be found; and finally, I interpose everywhere admonitions and scruples, and cautions, with a religious care to eject, repress, and as it were exorcise every kind of phantasm.

Lastly, knowing how much the sight of man's mind is distracted by experience and history, and how hard it is at the first (especially for minds either tender or preoccupied) to become familiar with nature, I not unfrequently subjoin observations of my own, being as the first offers, inclinations, and as it were glances of history towards philosophy; both by way of an assurance to men that they will not be kept for ever tossing on the waves of experience, and also that when the time comes for the intellect to begin its work, it may find everything the more ready. By such a natural history then as I have described, I conceive that a safe and convenient approach may be made to nature, and matter supplied of good quality and well prepared for the understanding to work upon.

And now that we have surrounded the intellect with faithful helps and guards, and got together with most careful selection a regular army of divine works, it may seem that we have no more to do but to proceed to philosophy itself. And yet in a matter so difficult and doubtful there are still some things which it seems necessary to premise, partly for convenience of explanation, partly for present use.

Of these the first is to set forth examples of inquiry and invention according to my method, exhibited by anticipation in some particular subjects; choosing such subjects as are at once the most noble in themselves among those under inquiry, and most different one from another; that there may be an example in every kind. I do not speak of those examples which are joined to the several precepts and rules by way of illustration (for of these I have given plenty in the second part of the work); but I mean actual types and models, by which the entire process of the mind and the whole fabric and order of invention from the beginning to the end, in certain subjects, and those various and remarkable, should be set as it were before the eyes. For I remember that in the mathematics it is easy to follow the demonstration when you have a machine besides you; whereas without that help all appears involved and more subtle than it really is. To examples of this kind,—being in fact nothing more than an application of the second part in detail and at large,—the fourth part of the work is devoted.

The fifth part is for temporary use only, pending the completion of the rest; like interest payable from time to time until the principle be forthcoming. For I do not make so blindly for the end of my journey, as to neglect anything useful that may turn up by the way. And therefore I include in this fifth part such things as I have myself discovered, proved, or added,—not however according to the true rules and methods of interpretation, but by the ordinary use of the understanding in inquiring and discovering. For besides that I hope my speculations may in virtue of my continual conversancy with nature have a value beyond the pretensions of my wit, they will serve in the meantime for wayside inns, in which the mind may rest and refresh itself on its journey to more certain conclusions. Nevertheless I wish it to be understood in the meantime that they are conclusions by which (as not being discovered and proved by the true form of interpretation) I do not at all mean to bind myself. Nor need any one be alarmed at such suspension of judgment, in one who maintains not simply that nothing can be known, but only that nothing can be known except in a certain course and way; and yet establishes provisionally certain degrees of assurance, for use and relief until the mind shall arrive at a knowledge of causes in which it can rest. For even those schools of philosophy which held the absolute impossibility of knowing anything were not inferior to those which took upon them to pronounce. But then they did not provide helps for the sense and understanding, as I have done, but simply took away all their authority: which is quite a different thing —almost the reverse.

The sixth part of my work (to which the rest is subservient and ministrant) discloses and sets forth that philosophy which by the legitimate, chaste, and severe course of inquiry which I have explained and provided is at length developed and established. The completion however of this last part is a thing both above my strength and beyond my hopes. I have made a beginning of the work—a beginning, as I hope, not unimportant:—the fortune of the human race will give the issue;—such an issue, it may be, as in the present condition of things and mens' minds cannot easily be conceived or imagined. For the matter in hand is no mere felicity of speculation, but the real business and fortunes of the human race, and all power of operation. For man is but the servant and interpreter of nature: what he does and what he knows is only what he has observed of nature's order in fact or in thought; beyond this he knows nothing and can do nothing. For the chain of causes cannot by any force be loosed or broken, nor can nature be commanded except by being obeyed. And so those twin objects, human Knowledge and human Power, do really meet in one; and it is from ignorance of causes that operation fails.

And all depends on keeping the eye steadily fixed upon the facts of nature and so receiving their images simply as they are. For God forbid that we should give out a dream of our own imagination for a pattern of the world; rather may he graciously grant to us to write an apocalypse or true vision of the footsteps of the Creator imprinted on his creatures.

Therefore do thou, O Father, who gavest the visible light as the first fruits of creation, and didst breathe into the face of man the intellectual light as the crown and consummation thereof, guard and protect this work, which coming from thy goodness returneth to thy glory. Thou when thou turnedst to look upon the works which thy hands had made, sawest that all was very good, and didst rest from thy labours. But man, when he turned to look upon the work which his hands had made, saw that all was vanity and vexation of spirit, and could find no rest therein. Wherefore if we labour in thy works with the sweat of our brows thou wilt make us partakers of thy vision and thy sabbath. Humbly we pray that this mind may be steadfast in us, and that through these our hands, and the hands of others to whom thou shalt give the same spirit, thou wilt vouchsafe to endow the human family with new mercies.

RENÉ DESCARTES

Unlike his contemporary, Francis Bacon, who tried to break completely with the medieval scholastic intellectual tradition, René Descartes (1596–1650) thought it possible to find a basis for traditional beliefs by using the methods of scientific inquiry. His attempt to combine the old with the new is clearly shown in the selection that follows. In it, after severely criticizing his own scholastic education, he gives a list of rules for the discovery of scientific truth. Through the application of these rules he is then able, by means of deductive reasoning, to prove the existence of God. Descartes was, thus, a transitional figure, living partly in the old intellectual world of the scholastics and partly in the new world of the seventeenth-century scientists.

Despite his unwillingness to break completely with the past, Descartes was one of the most important of early modern scientists. In mathematics he was the founder of analytic geometry. And in physics he developed an explanation of the universe which for a century rivaled Newton's theory of universal gravitation. Although Descartes engaged in experimentation, he did not, like Bacon, believe that induction was the most fruitful scientific method. Instead, he was an advocate of the deductive method, his preference being undoubtedly a result of his successful use of deduction in mathematics.

Discourse on Method

Part One

Good Sense is, of all things among men, the most equally distributed; for every one thinks himself so abundantly provided with it, that those even who are the most difficult to satisfy in everything else, do not usually desire a larger measure of this quality than they already possess. And in this it is not likely that all are mistaken: the conviction is rather to be held as testifying that the power of judging aright and of distinguishing Truth from Error, which is properly what is called Good Sense or Reason, is by nature equal in all men; and that the diversity of our opinions, consequently, does not arise from some being endowed with a larger share of Reason than others, but solely from this, that we conduct our thoughts along different ways, and

René Descartes, DISCOURSE ON METHOD OF RIGHTLY CONDUCTING THE REASON AND SEEKING TRUTH IN THE SCIENCES, *4th ed., trans. J. Veitch (Edinburgh, 1870).*

do not fix our attention on the same objects. For to be possessed of a vigorous mind is not enough; the prime requisite is rightly to apply it. The greatest minds, as they are capable of the highest excellencies, are open likewise to the greatest aberrations: and those who travel very slowly may yet make far greater progress, provided they keep always to the straight road, than those who, while they run, forsake it.

For myself, I have never fancied my mind to be in any respect more perfect than those of the generality; on the contrary, I have often wished that I were equal to some others in promptitude of thought, or in clearness and distinctness of imagination, or in fulness and readiness of memory. And besides these, I know of no other qualities that contribute to the perfection of the mind; for as to the Reason or Sense, inasmuch as it is that alone which constitutes us men, and distinguishes us from the brutes, I am disposed to believe that it is to be found complete in each individual; and on this point to adopt the common opinion of philosophers, who say that the difference of greater and less holds only among the *accidents,* and not among the *forms* or *natures of individuals* of the same *species.*

I will not hesitate, however, to avow my belief that it has been my singular good fortune to have very early in life fallen in with certain tracks which have conducted me to considerations and maxims, of which I have formed a Method that gives me the means, as I think, of gradually augmenting my knowledge, and of raising it by little and little to the highest point which the mediocrity of my talents and the brief duration of my life will permit me to reach. For I have already reaped from it such fruits that, although I have been accustomed to think lowly enough of myself, and although when I look with the eye of a philosopher at the varied courses and pursuits of mankind at large, I find scarcely one which does not appear vain and useless, I nevertheless derive the highest satisfaction from the progress I conceived myself to have already made in the search after truth, and cannot help entertaining such expectations of the future as to believe that if, among the occupations of men as men, there is any one really excellent and important, it is that which I have chosen.

After all, it is possible I may be mistaken; and it is but a little copper and glass, perhaps, that I take for gold and diamonds. I know how very liable we are to delusion in what relates to ourselves, and also how much the judgments of our friends are to be suspected when given in our favour. But I shall endeavour in this Discourse to describe the paths I have followed, and to delineate my life as in a picture, in order that each one may be able to judge of them for himself, and that in the general opinion entertained of them, as gathered from current report, I myself may have a new help towards instruction to be added to those I have been in the habit of employing.

My present design, then, is not to teach the Method which each ought to follow for the right conduct of his Reason, but solely to describe the way in which I have endeavoured to conduct my own. They who set themselves to give precepts must of course regard themselves as possessed of greater skill than those to whom they prescribe; and if they err in the slightest particular, they subject themselves to censure. But as this Tract is put forth merely as a history, or, if you will, as a tale, in which, amid some examples worthy of imitation, there will be found, perhaps, as many more which it were advisable not to follow, I hope it will prove useful to some without being hurtful to any, and that my openness will find some favour with all.

From my childhood, I have been familiar with letters; and as I was given to believe that by their help a clear and certain knowledge of all that is useful in life might be acquired, I was ardently desirous of instruction. But as soon as I had finished the entire course of study, at the close of which it is customary to be admitted into the order of the learned, I completely changed my opinion. For I found myself involved in so many doubts and errors, that I was convinced that I had advanced no farther in all my attempts at learning, than the discovery at every turn of my own ignorance. And yet I was studying at one of the most celebrated Schools in Europe, in which I thought there must be learned men, if such were anywhere to be found. I had been taught all that others learned there; and not contented with the sciences actually taught us, I had, in addition, read all the books that had fallen into my hands, treating of such branches as are esteemed the most curious and rare. I knew the judgment which others had formed of me; and I did not find that I was considered inferior to my fellows, although there were among them some who were already marked out to fill the places of our instructors. And, in fine, our age appeared to me as flourishing, and as fertile in powerful minds as any preceding one. I was thus led to take the liberty of judging of all other men by myself, and of concluding that there was no science in existence that was of such a nature as I had previously been given to believe.

I still continued, however, to hold in esteem the studies of the Schools. I was aware that the Languages taught in them are necessary to the understanding of the writings of the ancients; that the grace of Fable stirs the mind; that the memorable deeds of History elevate it; and, if read with discretion, aid in forming the judgment; that the perusal of all excellent books is, as it were, to interview with the noblest men of past ages, who have written them, and even a studied interview, in which are discovered to us only their choicest thoughts; that Eloquence has incomparable force and beauty; that Poesy has its ravishing graces and delights; that in the Mathematics there are many refined discoveries eminently suited to gratify the inquisitive, as well as further all the arts and lessen the labour of man; that numerous highly useful precepts and exhortations to virtue are contained in treatises on Morals; that Theology points out the path to heaven; that Philosophy affords the means of discoursing with an appearance of truth on all matters, and commands the admiration of the more simple; that Jurisprudence, Medicine, and the other Sciences, secure for their cultivators honours and riches; and, in fine, that it is useful to bestow some attention upon all, even upon those abounding the most in superstition and error, that we may be in a position to determine their real value, and guard against being deceived.

But I believed that I had already given sufficient time to Languages, and likewise to the reading of the writings of the ancients, to their Histories and Fables. For to hold converse with those of other ages and to travel, are almost the same thing. It is useful to know something of the manners of different nations, that we may be enabled to form a more correct judgment regarding our own, and be prevented from thinking that everything contrary to our customs is ridiculous and irrational,—a conclusion usually come to by those whose experience has been limited to their own country. On the other hand, when too much time is occupied in travelling, we become strangers to our native country; and the over curious in the customs of the past are generally ignorant of those of the present. Besides, fictitious narratives lead us to imagine the possibility of many events that are impossible; and even the most faithful histories, if they do not wholly misrepresent matters, or exaggerate their importance to render the account of them more worthy of perusal, omit, at least, almost always the meanest and least striking of the attendant circumstances; hence it happens that the remainder does not represent the truth, and that such as regulate their conduct by examples drawn from this source, are apt to fall into the extravagances of the knight-errants of Romance, and to entertain projects that exceed their powers.

I esteemed Eloquence highly, and was in raptures with Poesy; but I thought that both were gifts of nature rather than fruits of study. Those in whom the faculty of Reason is predominant, and who most skillfully dispose their thoughts with a view to render them clear and intelligible, are always the best able to persuade others of the truth of what they lay down, though they should speak only in the language of Lower Brittany, and be wholly ignorant of the rules of Rhetoric; and those whose minds are stored with the most agreeable fancies, and who can give expression to them with the greatest embellishment and harmony, are still the best poets, though unacquainted with the Art of Poetry.

I was especially delighted with the Mathematics, on account of the certitude and evidence of their reasonings: but I had not as yet a precise knowledge of their true use; and thinking that they but contributed to the advancement of the mechanical arts, I was astonished that foundations, so strong and solid, should have had no loftier superstructure reared on them. On the other hand, I compared the disquisitions of the ancient Moralists to very towering and magnificent palaces with no better foundation than sand and mud: they laud the virtues very highly, and exhibit them as estimable far above anything on earth; but they give us no adequate criterion of virtue, and frequently that which they designate with so fine a name is but apathy, or pride, or despair, or parricide.

I revered our Theology, and aspired as much as any one to reach heaven: but being given assuredly to understand that the way is not less open to the most ignorant than to the most learned, and that the revealed truths which lead to heaven are above our comprehension, I did not presume to subject them to the impotency of my Reason; and I thought that in order competently to undertake their examination, there was need of some special help from heaven, and of being more than man.

Of Philosophy I will say nothing, except that when I saw that it had been cultivated for many ages by the most distinguished men, and that yet there is not a single matter within its sphere which is not still in dispute, and nothing, therefore, which is above doubt, I did not presume to anticipate that my success would be greater in it than that of others; and further, when I considered the number of conflicting opinions touching a single matter that may be upheld by learned men, while there can be but one true, I reckoned as well-nigh false all that was only probable.

As to the other Sciences, inasmuch as these borrow their principles from Philosophy, I judged that no solid superstructures could be reared on foundations so infirm; and neither the honour nor the gain held out by them was sufficient to determine me to their cultivation: for I was not, thank heaven, in a condition which compelled me to make merchandise of Science for the bettering of my fortune; and though I might not profess to scorn glory as a Cynic, I yet made very slight account of that honour which I hoped to acquire only through fictitious titles. And, in fine, of false Sciences I thought I knew the worth sufficiently to escape being deceived by the professions of an alchemist, the predictions of an astrologer, the impostures of a magician, or by the artifices and boasting of any of those who profess to know things of which they are ignorant.

For these reasons, as soon as my age permitted me to pass from under the control of my instructors, I entirely abandoned the study of letters, and resolved no longer to seek any other science than the knowledge of myself, or of the great book of the world. I spent the remainder of my youth in travelling, in visiting courts and armies, in holding intercourse with men of different dispositions and ranks, in collecting varied experience, in proving myself in the different situations into which fortune threw me, and, above all, in making such reflection on the matter of my experience as to secure my improvement. For it occurred to me that I should find much more truth in the reasonings of each individual with reference to the affairs in which he is personally interested, and the issue of which must presently punish him if he has judged amiss, than in those conducted by a man of letters in his study, regarding speculative matters that are of no practical moment, and followed by no consequences to himself, farther, perhaps, than that they foster his vanity the better the more remote they are from common sense; requiring, as they must in this case, the exercise of greater ingenuity and art to render them probable. In addition, I had always a most earnest desire to know how to distinguish the true from the false, in order that I might be able clearly to discriminate the right path in life, and proceed in it with confidence.

It is true that, while busied only in considering the manners of other men, I found here, too, scarce any ground for settled conviction, and remarked hardly less contradiction among them than in the opinions of the philosophers. So that the greatest advantage I derived from the study consisted in this, that, observing many things which, however extravagant and ridiculous to our apprehension, are yet by common consent received and approved by other great nations, I learned to entertain too decided a belief in regard to nothing of the truth of which I had been persuaded merely by example and custom: and thus I gradually extricated myself from many errors powerful enough to darken our Natural Intelligence, and incapacitate us to great measure from listening to Reason. But after I had been occupied several years in thus studying the book of the world, and in essaying to gather some experience, I at length resolved to make myself an object of study, and to employ all the powers of my mind in choosing the paths I ought to follow; an undertaking which was accompanied with greater success than it would have been had I never quitted my country or my books.

Part Two

I was then in Germany, attracted thither by the wars in that country, which have not yet been brought to a termination; and as I was returning to the army from the coronation of the Emperor, the setting in of winter arrested me in a locality where, as I found no society to interest me, and was besides fortunately undisturbed by any cares or passions, I remained the whole day in seclusion, with full opportunity to occupy my attention with my own thoughts. Of these one of the very first that occurred to me was, that there is seldom so much perfection in works composed of many separate parts, upon which different hands have been employed, as in those completed by a single master. Thus it is observable that the buildings which a single architect has planned and executed, are generally more elegant and commodious than those which several have attempted to improve, by making old walls serve for purposes for which they were not originally built. Thus also, those ancient cities which, from being at first only villages, have become, in course of time, large towns, are usually but ill laid out compared with the regularly constructed towns which a professional architect has freely planned on an open plain; so that although the several buildings of the former may often equal or surpass in beauty those of the latter, yet when one observes their indiscriminate juxtaposition, there a large one and here a small, and the consequent crookedness and irregularity of the streets, one is disposed to allege that chance rather than any human will guided by reason, must have led to such an arrangement. And if we consider that nevertheless there have been at all times certain officers whose duty it was to see that private buildings contributed to public ornament, the difficulty of reaching high perfection with but the materials of others to operate on, will be readily acknowledged. In the same way I fancied that those nations which, starting from a semi-barbarous state and advancing to civilization by slow degrees, have had their laws successively determined, and, as it were, forced upon them simply by experience of the hurtfulness of particular crimes and disputes, would by this process come to be possessed of less perfect constitutions than those which, from the commencement of their association as communities, have followed the appointments of some wise legislator. It is thus quite certain that the constitution of the true religion, the ordinances of which are derived from God, must be incomparably superior to that of every other. And, to speak of human affairs, I believe that the past pre-eminence of Sparta was due not to the goodness of each of its laws in particular, for many of these were very strange, and even opposed to good morals, but to the circumstance that, originated by a single individual, they all tended to a single end. In the same way I thought that the sciences contained in books, (such of them at least as are made up of probable reasonings, without demonstrations), composed as they are of the opinions of many different individuals massed together, are farther removed from truth than the simple inferences which a man of good sense using his natural and unprejudiced judgment draws respecting the matters of his experience. And because we have all to pass through a state of infancy to manhood, and have been of necessity, for a length of time, governed by our desires and preceptors, (whose dictates were frequently conflicting, while neither perhaps always counselled us for the best), I farther concluded that it is almost impossible that our judgments can be so correct or solid as they would have been, had our Reason been mature from the moment of our birth, and had we always been guided by it alone.

It is true, however, that it is not customary to pull down all the houses of a town with the single design of rebuilding them differently, and thereby rendering the streets more handsome; but it often happens that a private individual takes down his own with the view of erecting it anew, and that people are even sometimes constrained to this when their houses are in danger of falling from age, or when the foundations are insecure. With this before me by way of example, I was persuaded that it would indeed be preposterous for a private individual to think of reforming a state by fundamentally changing it throughout, and overturning it in order to set it up amended; and the same I thought was true of any similar project for reforming the body of the Sciences, or the order of teaching them established in the Schools: but as for the opinions which up to that time I had embraced, I thought that I could not do better than resolve at once to sweep them wholly away, that I might afterwards be in a position to admit either others more correct, or even perhaps the same when they had undergone the scrutiny of Reason. I firmly believed that in this way I should much better succeed in the conduct of my life, than if I built only upon old foundations, and leant upon principles which, in my youth, I had taken upon trust. For although I recognised various difficulties in this undertaking, these were not, however, without remedy, nor once to be compared with such as attend the slightest reformation in public affairs. Large bodies, if once overthrown, are with great difficulty set up again, or even kept erect when once seriously shaken, and the fall of such is always disastrous. Then if there are any imperfections in the constitutions of states, (and that many such exist the diversity of constitutions is alone sufficient to assure us), custom has without doubt materially smoothed their inconveniencies, and has even managed to steer altogether clear of, or insensibly corrected a number which sagacity could not have provided against with equal effect; and, in fine, the defects are almost always more tolerable than the change necessary for their removal; in the same manner that highways which wind among mountains, by being much frequented, become gradually so smooth and commodious, that it is much better to follow them than to seek a straighter path by climbing over the tops of rocks and descending to the bottoms of precipices.

Hence it is that I cannot in any degree approve of those restless and busy meddlers who, called neither by birth nor fortune to take part in the management of public affairs, are yet always projecting reforms; and if I thought that this Tract contained aught which might justify the suspicion that I was a victim of such folly, I would by no means permit its publication. I have never contemplated anything higher than the reformation of my own opinions, and basing them on a foundation wholly my own. And although my own satisfaction with my work has led me to present here a draft of it, I do not by any means therefore recommend to every one else to make a similar attempt. Those whom God has endowed with a larger measure of genius will entertain, perhaps, designs still more exalted; but for the many I am much afraid lest even the present undertaking be more than they can safely venture to imitate. The single design to strip one's self of all past beliefs is one that ought not to be taken by every one. The majority of men is composed of two classes, for neither of which would this be at all a befitting resolution: in the *first* place, of those who with more than a due confidence in their own powers, are precipitate in their judgments and want the patience requisite for orderly and circumspect thinking; whence it happens, that if men of this class once take the liberty to doubt of their accustomed opinions, and quit the beaten highway, they will never be able to thread the byeway that would lead them by a shorter course, and will lose themselves and continue to wander for life; in the *second* place, of those who, possessed of sufficient sense or modesty to determine that there are others who excel them in the power of discriminating between truth and error, and by whom they may be instructed, ought rather to content themselves with the opinions of such than trust for more correct to their own Reason.

For my own part, I should doubtless have belonged to the latter class, had I received instruction from but one master, or had I never known the diversities of opinion that from time immemorial have prevailed among men of the greatest learning. But I had become aware, even so early as during my college life, that no opinion, however absurd and incredible, can be imagined, which has not been maintained by some one of the philosophers; and afterwards in the course of my travels I remarked that all those whose opinions are decidedly repugnant to ours are not on that account barbarians and savages, but on the contrary that many of these nations make an equally good, if not a better, use of their Reason than we do. I took into account also the very different character which a person brought up from infancy in France or Germany exhibits, from that which, with the same mind originally, this individual would have possessed had he lived always among the Chinese or with savages, and the circumstance that in dress itself the fashion which had pleased us ten years ago, and which may again, perhaps, be received into favour before ten years have gone, appears to us at this moment extravagant and ridiculous. I was thus led to infer that the ground of our opinions is far more custom and example than any certain knowledge. And, finally, although such be the ground of our opinions, I remarked that a plurality of suffrages is no guarantee of truth where it is at all of difficult discovery, as in such cases it is much more likely that it will be found by one than by many. I could, however, select from the crowd no one whose opinions seemed worthy of preference, and thus I found myself constrained, as it were, to use my own Reason in the conduct of my life.

But like one walking alone and in the dark, I resolved to proceed so slowly and with such circumspection, that if I did not advance far, I would at least guard against falling. I did not even choose to dismiss summarily any of the opinions that had crept into my belief without having been introduced by Reason, but first of all took sufficient time carefully to satisfy myself of the general nature of the task I was setting myself, and ascertain the true Method by which to arrive at the knowledge of whatever lay within the compass of my powers.

Among the branches of Philosophy, I had, at an earlier period, given some attention to Logic, and among those of the Mathematics to Geometrical Analysis and Algebra,—three Arts or Sciences which ought, as I conceived, to contribute something to my design. But, on examination, I found that, as for Logic, its syllogisms and the majority of its other precepts are of avail rather in the communication of what we already know, or even as the Art of Lully, in speaking without judgment of things of which we are ignorant, than in the investigation of the unknown; and although this Science contains indeed a number of correct and very excellent precepts, there are, nevertheless, so many others, and these either injurious or superfluous, mingled with the former, that it is almost quite as difficult to effect a severance of the true from the false as it is to extract a Diana or a Minerva from a rough block of marble. Then as to the Analysis of the ancients and the Algebra of the moderns, besides that they embrace only matters highly abstract, and, to appearance, of no use, the former is so exclusively restricted to the consideration of figures, that it can exercise the Understanding only on condition of greatly fatiguing the Imagination; and, in the latter, there is so complete a subjection to certain rules and formulas, that there results an art full of confusion and obscurity calculated to embarrass, instead of a science fitted to cultivate the mind. By these considerations I was induced to seek some other Method which would comprise the advantages of the three and be exempt from their defects. And as a multitude of laws often only hampers justice, so that a state is best governed when, with few laws, these are rigidly administered; in like manner, instead of the great number of precepts of which Logic is composed, I believed that the four following would prove perfectly sufficient for me, provided I took the firm and unwavering resolution never in a single instance to fail in observing them.

The *first* was never to accept anything for true which I did not clearly know to be such; that is to say, carefully to avoid precipitancy and prejudice, and to comprise nothing more in my judgment than what was presented to my mind so clearly and distinctly as to exclude all ground of doubt.

The *second,* to divide each of the difficulties under examination into as many parts as possible, and as might be necessary for its adequate solution.

The *third,* to conduct my thoughts in such order that, by commencing with objects the simplest and easiest to know, I might ascend by little and little, and, as it were, step by step, to the knowledge of the more complex; assigning in thought a certain order even to those objects which in their own nature do not stand in a relation of antecedence and sequence.

And the *last,* in every case to make enumerations so complete, and reviews so general, that I might be assured that nothing was omitted.

The long chains of simple and easy reasonings by means of which geometers are accustomed to reach the conclusions of their most difficult demonstrations, had led me to imagine that all things, to the knowledge of which man is competent, are mutually connected in the same way, and that there is nothing so far removed from us as to be beyond our reach, or so hidden that we cannot discover it, provided only we abstain from accepting the false for the true, and always preserve in our thoughts the order necessary for the deduction of one truth from another. And I had little difficulty in determining the objects with which it was necessary to commence, for I was already persuaded that it must be with the simplest and easiest to know, and, considering that of all those who have hitherto sought truth in the Sciences, the mathematicians alone have been able to find any demonstrations, that is, any certain and evident reasons, I did not doubt but that such must have been the rule of their investigations. I resolved to commence, therefore, with the examination of the simplest objects, not anticipating, however, from this any other advantage than that to be found in accustoming my mind to the love and nourishment of truth, and to a distaste for all such reasonings as were unsound. But I had no intention on that account of attempting to master all the particular Sciences commonly denominated Mathematics: but observing that, however different their objects, they all agree in considering only the various relations or proportions subsisting among those objects, I thought it best for my purpose to consider these proportions in the most general form possible, without referring them to any objects in particular, except such as would most facilitate the knowledge of them, and without by any means restricting them to these, that afterwards I might thus be the better able to apply them to every other class of objects to which they are legitimately applicable. Perceiving further, that in order to understand these relations I should sometimes have to consider them one by one, and sometimes only to bear them in mind, or embrace them in the aggregate, I thought that, in order the better to consider them individually I should view them as subsisting between straight lines, than which I could find no objects more simple, or capable of being more distinctly represented to my imagination and senses; and on the other hand, that in order to retain them in the memory, or embrace an aggregate of many, I should express them by certain characters the briefest possible. In this way I believed that I could borrow all that was best both in Geometrical Analysis and in Algebra, and correct all the defects of the one by help of the other.

And, in point of fact, the accurate observance of these few precepts gave me, I take the liberty of saying, such ease in unravelling all the questions embraced in these two sciences, that in the two or three months I devoted to their examination, not only did I reach solutions of questions I had formerly deemed exceedingly difficult, but even as regards questions of the solution of which I continued ignorant, I was enabled, as it appeared to me, to determine the means whereby, and the extent to which, a solution was possible; results attributable to the circumstance that I commenced with the simplest and most general truths, and that thus each truth discovered was a rule available in the discovery of subsequent ones. Nor in this perhaps shall I appear too vain, if it be considered that, as the truth on any particular point is one, whoever apprehends the truth, knows all that on that point can be known. The child, for example, who has been instructed in the elements of Arithmetic, and has made a particular addition, according to rule, may be assured that he has found, with respect to the sum of the numbers before him, all that in this instance is within the reach of human genius. Now, in conclusion, the Method which teaches adherence to the true order, and an exact enumeration of all the conditions of the thing sought includes all that gives certitude to the rules of Arithmetic.

But the chief ground of my satisfaction with this Method, was the assurance I had of thereby exercising my reason in all matters, if not with absolute perfection, at least with the greatest attainable by me: besides, I was conscious that by its use my mind was becoming gradually habituated to clearer and more distinct conceptions of its objects; and I hoped also, from not having restricted this Method to any particular matter, to apply it to the difficulties of the other Sciences, with not less success than to those of Algebra. I should not, however, on this account have ventured at once on the examination of all the difficulties of the Sciences which presented themselves to me, for this would have been contrary to the order prescribed in the Method, but observing that the knowledge of such is dependent on principles borrowed from Philosophy, in which I found nothing certain, I thought it necessary first of all to endeavour to establish its principles. And because I observed, besides, that an inquiry of this kind was of all others of the greatest moment, and one in which precipitancy and anticipation in judgment were most to be dreaded, I thought that I ought not to approach it till I had reached a more mature age (being at that time but twenty-three), and had first of all employed much of my time in preparation for the work, as well by eradicating from my mind all the erroneous opinions I had up to that moment accepted, as by amassing variety of experience to afford materials for my reasonings, and by continually exercising myself in my chosen Method with a view to increased skill in its application.

. . .

Part Four

I am in doubt as to the propriety of making my first meditations in the place above mentioned matter of discourse; for these are so metaphysical, and so uncommon, as not, perhaps, to be acceptable to every one. And yet, that it may be determined whether the foundations that I have laid are sufficiently secure, I find myself in a measure constrained to advert to them. I had long before remarked that, in relation to practice, it is sometimes necessary to adopt, as if above doubt, opinions which we discern to be highly uncertain, as has been already said; but as I then desired to give my attention solely to the search after truth, I thought that a procedure exactly the opposite was called for, and that I ought to reject as absolutely false all opinions in regard to which I could suppose the least ground for doubt, in order to ascertain whether after that there remained aught in my belief that was wholly indubitable. Accordingly, seeing that our senses sometimes deceive us, I was willing to suppose that there existed nothing really such as they presented to us; and because some men err in reasoning, and fall into paralogisms, even on the simplest matters of Geometry, I, convinced that I was as open to error as any other, rejected as false all the reasonings I had hitherto taken for demonstrations; and finally, when I considered that the very same thoughts (presentations) which we experience when awake may also be experienced when we are asleep, while there is at that time not one of them true, I supposed that all the objects (presentations) that had ever entered into my mind when awake, had in them no more truth than the illusions of my dreams. But immediately upon this I observed that, whilst I thus wished to think that all was false, it was absolutely necessary that I, who thus thought, should be somewhat; and as I observed that this truth, *I think, therefore I am,* was so certain and of such evidence, that no ground of doubt, however extravagant, could be alleged by the Sceptics capable of shaking it, I concluded that I might, without scruple, accept it as the first principle of the Philosophy of which I was in search.

In the next place, I attentively examined what I was, and as I observed that I could suppose that I had no body, and that there was no world nor any place in which I might be; but that I could not therefore suppose that I was not; and that, on the contrary, from the very circumstance that I thought to doubt of the truth of other things, it most clearly and certainly followed that I was; while, on the other hand, if I had only ceased to think, although all the other objects which I had ever imagined had been in reality existent, I would have had no reason to believe that I existed; I thence concluded that I was a substance whose whole essence or nature consists only in thinking, and which, that it may exist, has need of no place, nor is dependent on any material thing; so that "I," that is to say, the mind by which I am what I am, is wholly distinct from the body, and is even more easily known than the latter, and is such, that although the latter were not, it would still continue to be all that it is.

After this I inquired in general into what is essential to the truth and certainty of a proposition; for since I had discovered one which I knew to be true, I thought that I must likewise be able to discover the ground of this certitude. And as I observed that in the words *I think, therefore I am,* there is nothing at all which gives me assurance of their truth beyond this, that I see very clearly that in order to think it is necessary to exist, I concluded that I might take, as a general rule, the principle, that all the things which we very clearly and distinctly conceive are true, only observing, however, that there is some difficulty in rightly determining the objects which we distinctly conceive.

In the next place, from reflecting on the circumstance that I doubted, and that consequently my being was not wholly perfect, (for I clearly saw that it was a greater perfection to know than to doubt), I was led to inquire whence I had learned to think of something more perfect than myself; and I clearly recognised that I must hold this notion from some Nature which in reality was more perfect. As for the thoughts of many other objects external to me, as of the sky, the earth, light, heat, and a thousand more, I was less at a loss to know whence these came; for since I remarked in them nothing which seemed to render them superior to myself, I could believe that, if these were true, they were dependencies on my own nature, in so far as it possessed a certain perfection, and, if they were false, that I held them from nothing, that is to say, that they were in me because of a certain imperfection of my nature. But this could not be the case with the idea of a Nature more perfect than myself; for to receive it from nothing was a thing manifestly impossible; and, because it is not less repugnant that the more perfect should be an effect of, and dependent on the less perfect, than that something should proceed from nothing, it was equally impossible that I could hold it from myself: accordingly, it but remained that it had been placed in me by a Nature which was in reality more perfect than mine, and which even possessed within itself all the perfections of which I could form any idea; that is to say, in a single word, which was God. And to this I added that, since I knew some perfections which I did not possess, I was not the only being in existence, (I will here, with your permission, freely use the terms of the Schools); but, on the contrary, that there was of necessity some other more perfect Being upon whom I was dependent, and from whom I had received all that I possessed; for if I had existed alone, and independently of every other being, so as to have had from myself all the perfection, however little, which I actually possessed, I should have been able, for the same reason, to have had from myself the whole remainder of perfection, of the want of which I was conscious, and thus could of myself have become infinite, eternal, immutable, omniscient, all-powerful, and, in fine, have possessed all the perfections which I could recognise in God. For in order to know the nature of God, (whose existence has been established by the preceding reasonings), as far as my own nature permitted, I had only to consider in reference to all the properties of which I found in my mind some idea, whether their possession was a mark of perfection; and I was assured that no one which indicated any imperfection was in him, and that none of the rest was awanting. Thus I perceived that doubt, inconstancy, sadness, and such like, could not be found in God, since I myself would have been happy to be free from them. Besides, I had ideas of many sensible and corporeal things; for although I might suppose that I was dreaming, and that all which I saw or imagined was false, I could not, nevertheless, deny that the ideas were in reality in my thoughts. But, because I had already very clearly recognised in myself that the intelligent nature is distinct from the corporeal, and as I observed that all composition is an evidence of dependency, and that a state of dependency is manifestly a state of imperfection, I therefore determined that it could not be a perfection in God to be compounded of these two natures, and that consequently he was not so compounded; but that if there were any bodies in the world, or even any intelligences, or other natures that were not wholly perfect, their existence depended on his power in such a way that they could not subsist without him for a single moment.

I was disposed straightway to search for other truths; and when I had represented to myself the object of the geometers, which I conceived to be a continuous body, or a space indefinitely extended in length, breadth, and height or depth, divisible into divers parts which admit of different figures and sizes, and of being moved or transposed in all manner of ways, (for all this the geometers suppose to be in the object they contemplate), I went over some of their simplest demonstrations. And, in the first place, I observed, that the great certitude which by common consent is accorded to these demonstrations, is founded solely upon this, that they are clearly conceived in accordance with the rules I have already laid down. In the next place, I perceived that there was nothing at all in these demonstrations which could assure me of the existence of their object: thus, for example, supposing a triangle to be given, I distinctly perceived that its three angles were necessarily equal to two right angles, but I did not on that account perceive anything which could assure me that any triangle existed: while, on the contrary, recurring to the examination of the idea of a Perfect Being, I found that the existence of the Being was comprised in the idea in the same way that the equality of its three angles to two right angles is comprised in the idea of a triangle, or as in the idea of a sphere, the equidistance of all points on its surface from the centre, or even still more clearly; and that consequently it is at least as certain that God, who is this Perfect Being, is, or exists, as any demonstration of Geometry can be.

But the reason which leads many to persuade themselves that there is a difficulty in knowing this truth, and even also in knowing what their mind really is, is that they never raise their thoughts above sensible objects, and are so accustomed to consider nothing except by way of imagination, which is a mode of thinking limited to material objects, that all that is not imaginable seems to them not intelligible. The truth of this is sufficiently manifest from the single circumstance, that the philosophers of the Schools accept as a maxim that there is nothing in the Understanding which was not previously in the Senses, in which however it is certain that the ideas of God and of the soul have never been; and it appears to me that they who make use of their imagination to comprehend these ideas do exactly the same thing as if, in order to hear sounds or smell odours, they strove to avail themselves of their eyes; unless indeed that there is this difference, that the sense of sight does not afford us an inferior assurance to those of smell or hearing; in place of which, neither our imagination nor our senses can give the assurance of anything unless our Understanding intervene.

Finally, if there be still persons who are not sufficiently persuaded of the existence of God and of the soul, by the reasons I have adduced, I am desirous that they should know that all the other propositions, of the truth of which they deem themselves perhaps more assured, as that we have a body, and that there exist stars and an earth, and such like, are less certain; for, although we have a moral assurance of these things, which is so strong that there is an appearance of extravagance in doubting of their existence, yet at the same time no one, unless his intellect is impaired, can deny, when the question relates to a metaphysical certitude, that there is sufficient reason to exclude entire assurance, in the observation that when asleep we can in the same way imagine ourselves possessed of another body and that we see other stars and another earth, when there is nothing of the kind. For how do we know that the thoughts which occur in dreaming are false rather than those other which we experience when awake, since the former are often not less vivid and distinct than the latter? And though men of the highest genius study this question as long as they please, I do not believe that they will be able to give any reason which can be sufficient to remove this doubt, unless they presuppose the existence of God.

THOMAS HOBBES

The great revolutions in seventeenth-century England produced two major political philosophers, Thomas Hobbes (1588–1679) and John Locke (1632–1704). Their writings, which coincided respectively with the Puritan Revolution and the Glorious Revolution, reflect the ways in which these political upheavals compared with one another.

Hobbes's Leviathan, *published in 1651, is filled with overtones of the insecurity, fear, and violence of the civil war just finished. Hobbes himself, because of his associations with the English aristocracy, had been forced to flee during the revolution to France, where he tutored the future King Charles II, also a refugee, in mathematics. The* Leviathan, *beyond mirroring its own troubled times, is a carefully argued defense of the theory of political absolutism. Hobbes found a philosophical justification for absolutism in the ancient theory of materialism, which had been revived during the seventeenth century in the scientific writings of men like Galileo and Descartes. Applying the assumptions of these scientists to human nature, Hobbes then deduced his absolutistic position in politics from them.*

Hobbes's theory of absolutism is sometimes confused with the theory of the divine right of kings, as elaborated, for example, by his contemporary, Bishop Bossuet. Although both theories provide defenses of political absolutism, the defenses given are very different. While Bossuet's is based on an interpretation of Christianity, Hobbes's rests on philosophical materialism, which logically cannot admit the existence of God. Also, for Bossuet the sovereign is justified in his rule by reason of his hereditary right of succession to the throne, but for Hobbes the "right" to rule reduces simply to the sovereign's ability to maintain himself in power.

In his emphasis on power, Hobbes picks up a theme from Machiavelli, but he transforms it into one element in a complete philosophy of society and government—something that the Florentine, for all his insight into practical politics, had not succeeded in doing.

Leviathan

THE INTRODUCTION

Nature, the art whereby God hath made and governs the world, is by the *art* of man, as in many other things, so in this also imitated, that it can make an artificial animal. For seeing life is but a motion of limbs, the beginning whereof is in some principal part within; why may we not say, that all *automata* (engines that move themselves by springs and wheels as doth a watch) have an artificial life? For what is the *heart,* but a *spring;* and the *nerves,* but so many *strings;* and the *joints,* but

THE ENGLISH WORKS OF THOMAS HOBBES, *Vol. III, ed. W. Molesworth (London, 1839).*

so many *wheels*, giving motion to the whole body, such as was intended by the artificer? *Art* goes yet further, imitating that rational and most excellent work of nature, *man*. For by art is created that great LEVIATHAN called a COMMONWEALTH, or STATE, in Latin CIVITAS, which is but an artificial man; though of greater stature and strength than the natural, for whose protection and defence it was intended; and in which the *sovereignty* is an artificial *soul*, as giving life and motion to the whole body; the *magistrates*, and other *officers* of judicature and execution, artificial *joints; reward* and *punishment*, by which fastened to the seat of the sovereignty every joint and member is moved to perform his duty, are the *nerves*, that do the same in the body natural; the *wealth* and *riches* of all the particular members, are the *strength; salus populi*, the *people's safety*, its *business; counsellors*, by whom all things needful for it to know are suggested unto it, are the *memory; equity*, and *laws*, an artificial *reason* and *will; concord, health; sedition, sickness;* and *civil war, death*. Lastly, the *pacts* and *covenants*, by which the parts of this body politic were at first made, set together, and united, resemble that *fiat*, or the *let us make man*, pronounced by God in the creation.

. . .

Chapter XIII

OF THE NATURAL CONDITION OF MANKIND AS CONCERNING THEIR FELICITY, AND MISERY

Nature hath made men so equal, in the faculties of the body, and mind; as that though there be found one man sometimes manifestly stronger in body, or of quicker mind than another; yet when all is reckoned together, the difference between man, and man, is not so considerable, as that one man can thereupon claim to himself any benefit, to which another may not pretend, as well as he. For as to the strength of body, the weakest has strength enough to kill the strongest, either by secret machination, or by confederacy with others, that are in the same danger with himself.

And as to the faculties of the mind, setting aside the arts grounded upon words, and especially that skill of proceeding upon general, and infallible rules, called science; which very few have, and but in few things; as being not a native faculty, born with us; nor attained, as prudence, while we look after somewhat else, I find yet a greater equality amongst men, than that of strength. For prudence, is but experience; which equal time, equally bestows on all men, in those things they equally apply themselves unto. That which may perhaps make such equality incredible, is but a vain conceit of one's own wisdom, which almost all men think they have in a greater degree, than the vulgar; that is, than all men but themselves, and a few others, whom by fame, or for concurring with themselves, they approve. For such is the nature of men, that howsoever they may acknowledge many others to be more witty, or more eloquent, or more learned; yet they will hardly believe there be many so wise as themselves; for they see their own wit at hand, and other men's at a distance. But this proveth rather that men are in that point equal, than unequal. For there is not ordinarily a greater sign of the equal distribution of any thing, than that every man is contented with his share.

From this equality of ability, ariseth equality of hope in the attaining of our ends. And therefore if any two men desire the same thing, which nevertheless they cannot both enjoy, they become enemies; and in the way to their end, which is principally their own conservation, and sometimes their delectation only, endeavour to destroy, or subdue one another. And from hence it comes to pass, that where an invader hath no more to fear, than another man's single power; if one plant, sow, build, and possess a convenient seat, others may probably be expected to come prepared with forces united, to dispossess, and deprive him, not only of the fruit of his labour, but also of his life, or liberty. And the invader again is in the like danger of another.

And from this diffidence of one another, there is no way for any man to secure himself, so reasonable, as anticipation; that is, by force, or wiles, to master the persons of all men he can, so long, till he see no other power great enough to endanger him: and this is no more than his own conservation requireth, and is generally allowed. Also because there be some, that taking pleasure in contemplating their own power in the acts of conquest, which they pursue farther than their security requires; if others, that otherwise would be glad to be at ease within modest bounds, should not by invasion increase their power, they would not be able, long time, by standing only on their defence, to subsist. And by consequence, such augmentation of dominion over men being necessary to a man's conservation, it ought to be allowed him.

Again, men have no pleasure, but on the contrary a great deal of grief, in keeping company, where there is no power able to over-awe them all. For every man looketh that his companion should value him, at the same rate he sets upon himself: and upon all signs of contempt, or undervaluing, naturally endeavours, as far as he dares, (which amongst them that have no common power to keep them in quiet, is far enough to make them destroy each other), to extort a greater value from his contemners, by damage; and from others, by the example.

So that in the nature of man, we find three principal causes of quarrel. First, competition; secondly, diffidence; thirdly, glory.

The first, maketh men invade for gain; the second, for safety; and the third, for reputation. The first use violence, to make themselves masters of other men's persons, wives, children, and cattle; the second, to defend them; the third, for trifles, as a word, a smile, a different opinion, and any other sign of undervalue, either direct in their persons, or by reflection in their kindred, their friends, their nation, their profession, or their name.

Hereby it is manifest, that during the time men live without a common power to keep them all in awe, they are in that condition which is called war; and such a war, as is of every man, against every man. For WAR, consisteth not in battle only, or the act of fighting; but in a tract of time, wherein the will to contend by battle is sufficiently known: and therefore the notion of *time,* is to be considered in the nature of war; as it is in the nature of weather. For as the nature of foul weather, lieth not in a shower or two of rain; but in an inclination thereto of many days together: so the nature of war, consisteth not in actual fighting; but in the known disposition thereto, during all the time there is no assurance to the contrary. All other time is PEACE.

Whatsoever therefore is consequent to a time of war, where every man is enemy to every man; the same is consequent to the time, wherein men live without other security, than what their own strength, and their own invention shall furnish them withal. In such condition, there is no place for industry; because the fruit thereof is uncertain: and consequently no culture of the earth; no navigation, nor use of the commodities that may be imported by sea; no commodious building; no instruments of moving, and removing, such things as require much force; no knowledge of the face of the earth; no account of time; no arts; no letters; no society; and which is worst of all, continual fear, and danger of violent death; and the life of man, solitary, poor, nasty, brutish, and short.

It may seem strange to some man, that has not well weighed these things; that nature should thus dissociate, and render men apt to invade, and destroy one another: and he may therefore, not trusting to this inference, made from the passions, desire perhaps to have the same confirmed by experience. Let him therefore consider with himself, when taking a journey, he arms himself, and seeks to go well accompanied; when going to sleep, he locks his doors; when even in his house he locks his chests; and this when he knows there be laws, and public officers, armed, to revenge all injuries shall be done him; what opinion he has of his fellow-subjects, when he rides armed; of his fellow citizens, when he locks his doors; and of his children, and servants, when he locks his chests. Does he not there as much accuse mankind by his actions, as I do by my words? But neither of us accuse man's nature in it. The desires, and other passions of man, are in themselves no sin. No more are the actions, that proceed from those passions, till they know a law that forbids them: which till laws be made they cannot know: nor can any law be made, till they have agreed upon the person that shall make it.

It may peradventure be thought, there was never such a time, nor condition of war as this; and I believe it was never generally so, over all the world: but there are many places, where they live so now. For the savage people in many places of America, except the government of small families, the concord whereof dependeth on natural lust, have no government at all; and live at this day in that brutish manner, as I said before. Howsoever, it may be perceived what manner of life there would be, where there were no common power to fear, by the manner of life, which men that have formerly lived under a peaceful government, use to degenerate into, in a civil war.

But though there had never been any time, wherein particular men were in a condition of war one against another; yet in all times, kings, and persons of sovereign authority, because of their independency, are in continual jealousies, and in the state and posture of gladiators; having their weapons pointing, and their eyes fixed on one another; that is, their forts, garrisons, and guns upon the frontiers of their kingdoms; and continual spies upon their neighbours; which is a posture of war. But because they uphold thereby, the industry of their subjects; there does not follow from it, that misery, which accompanies the liberty of particular men.

To this war of every man, against every man, this also is consequent; that nothing can be unjust. The notions of right and wrong, justice and injustice have there no place. Where there is no common power, there is no law: where no law, no injustice. Force, and fraud, are in war the two cardinal virtues. Justice, and injustice are none of the faculties neither of the body, or mind. If they were, they might be in a man that were alone in the world, as well as his senses, and passions. They are qualities, that relate to men in society, not in solitude. It is consequent also to the same condition, that there be no propriety, no dominion, no *mine* and *thine* distinct; but only that to be every man's, that he can get; and for so long, as he can keep it. And thus much for the ill condition, which man by mere nature is actually placed in; though with a possibility to come out of it, consisting partly in the passions, partly in his reason.

The passions that incline men to peace, are fear of death; desire of such things as are necessary to commodious living; and a hope by their industry to obtain them. And reason suggesteth convenient articles of peace, upon which men may be drawn to agreement. These articles, are they, which otherwise are called the Laws of Nature, whereof I shall speak more particularly, in the two following chapters.

Chapter XIV

OF THE FIRST AND SECOND NATURAL LAWS, AND OF CONTRACTS

The RIGHT OF NATURE, which writers commonly call *jus naturale,* is the liberty each man hath, to use his own power, as he will himself, for the preservation of his own nature; that is to say, of his own life; and consequently, of doing any thing, which in his own judgment, and reason, he shall conceive to be the aptest means thereunto.

By LIBERTY, is understood, according to the proper signification of the word, the absence of external impediments: which impediments, may oft take away part of a man's power to do what he would; but cannot hinder him from using the power left him, according as his judgment, and reason shall dictate to him.

A LAW OF NATURE, *lex naturalis,* is a precept or general rule, found out by reason, by which a man is forbidden to do that, which is destructive of his life, or taketh away the means of preserving the same; and to omit that, by which he thinketh it may be best preserved. For though they that speak of this subject, use to confound *jus,* and *lex, right* and *law:* yet they ought to be distinguished; because RIGHT, consisteth in liberty to do, or to forbear; whereas LAW, determineth, and bindeth to one of them: so that law, and right, differ as much, as obligation, and liberty; which in one and the same matter are inconsistent.

And because the condition of man, as hath been declared in the precedent chapter, is a condition of war of every one against every one: in which case every one is governed by his own reason; and there is nothing he can make use of, that may not be a help unto him, in preserving his life against his enemies; it followeth, that in such a condition, every man has a right to every thing; even to one another's body. And therefore, as long as this natural right of every man to every thing endureth, there can be no security to any man, how strong or wise soever he be, of living out the time, which nature ordinarily alloweth men to live. And consequently it is a precept, or general rule of reason, *that every man, ought to endeavour peace, as far as he has hope of obtaining it; and when he cannot obtain it, that he may seek, and use, all helps, and advantages of war.* The first branch of which rule, containeth the first, and fundamental law of nature; which is, *to seek peace, and follow it.* The second, the sum of the right of nature; which is, *by all means we can, to defend ourselves.*

From this fundamental law of nature, by which men are commanded to endeavour peace, is derived this second law; *that a man be willing, when others are so too, as far-forth, as for peace, and defence of himself he shall think it necessary, to lay down this right to all things; and be contented with so much liberty against other men, as he would allow other men against himself.* For as long as every man holdeth this right, of doing any thing he liketh; so long are all men in the condition of war. But if other men will not lay down their right, as well as he; then there is no reason for any one, to divest himself of his: for that were to expose himself to prey, which no man is bound to, rather than to dispose himself to peace. This is that law of the Gospel; *whatsoever you require that others should do to you, that do ye to them.* And that law of all men, *quod tibi fieri non vis, alteri ne feceris.*

To *lay down* a man's *right* to any thing, is to *divest* himself of the *liberty,* of hindering another of the benefit of his own right to the same. For he that renounceth, or passeth away his right, giveth not to any other man a right which he had not before; because there is nothing to which every man had not right by nature: but only standeth out of his way, that he may enjoy his own original right, without hindrance from him; not without hindrance from another. So that the effect which redoundeth to one man, by another man's defect of right, is but so much diminution of impediments to the use of his own right original.

Right is laid aside, either by simply renouncing it; or by transferring it to another. By *simply* RENOUNCING; when he cares not to whom the benefit thereof redoundeth. By TRANSFERRING; when he intendeth the benefit thereof to some certain person, or persons. And when a man hath in either manner abandoned, or granted away his right, then is he said to be OBLIGED, or BOUND, not to hinder those, to whom such right is granted, or abandoned, from the benefit of it: and that he *ought,* and it is his DUTY, not to make void that voluntary act of his own: and that such hindrance is INJUSTICE, and INJURY, as being *sine jure;* the right being before renounced, or transferred. So that *injury,* or *injustice,* in the controversies of the world, is somewhat like to that, which in the disputations of scholars is called *absurdity.* For as it is there called an absurdity, to contradict what one maintained in the beginning: so in the world, it is called injustice, and injury, voluntarily to undo that, which from the beginning he had voluntarily done. The way by which a man either simply renounceth, or transferreth his right, is a declaration, or signification, by some voluntary and sufficient sign, or signs, that he doth so renounce, or transfer; or hath so renounced, or transferred the same, to him that accepteth it. And these signs are either words only, or actions only; or, as it happeneth most often, both words, and actions. And the same are the BONDS, by which men are bound, and obliged: bonds, that have their strength, not from their own nature, for nothing is more easily broken than a man's word, but from fear of some evil consequence upon the rupture.

Whensoever a man transferreth his right, or renounceth it; it is either in consideration of some right reciprocally transferred to himself; or for some other good he hopeth for thereby. For it is a voluntary act: and of the voluntary acts of every man the object is some *good to himself.* And therefore there be some rights, which no man can be understood by any words, or other signs, to have abandoned, or transferred. As first a man cannot lay down the right of resisting them, that assault him by force, to take away his life; because he cannot be understood to aim thereby, at any good to himself. The same may be said of wounds, and chains, and imprisonment; both because there is no benefit consequent to such patience; as there is to the patience of suffering another to be wounded, or imprisoned: as also because a man cannot tell, when he seeth men proceed against him by violence, whether they intend his death or not. And lastly the motive, and end for which this renouncing, and transferring of right is introduced, is nothing else but the security of a man's person, in his life, and in the means of so preserving life, as not to be weary of it. And therefore if a man by words, or other signs, seem to despoil himself of the end, for which those signs were intended; he is not to be understood as if he meant it, or that it was his will; but that he was ignorant of how such words and actions were to be interpreted.

The mutual transferring of right, is that which men call CONTRACT.

. . .

If a covenant be made, wherein neither of the parties perform presently, but trust one another; in the condition of mere nature, which is a condition of war of every man against every man, upon any reasonable suspicion, it is void: but if there be a common power set over them both, with right and force sufficient to compel performance, it is not void. For he that performeth first, has no assurance the other will perform after; because the bonds of words are too weak to bridle men's ambition, avarice, anger, and other passions, without the fear of some coercive power; which in the condition of mere nature, where all men are equal, and judges of the justness of their own fears, cannot possibly be supposed. And therefore he which performeth first, does but betray himself to his enemy; contrary to the right, he can never abandon, of defending his life, and means of living.

But in a civil estate, where there is a power set up to constrain those that would otherwise violate their faith, that fear is no more reasonable; and for that cause, he which by the covenant is to perform first, is obliged so to do.

. . .

The force of words, being, as I have formerly noted, too weak to hold men to the performance of their covenants; there are in man's nature, but two imaginable helps to strengthen it. And those are either a fear of the consequence of breaking their word; or a glory, or pride in appearing not to need to break it. This latter is a generosity too rarely found to be presumed on, especially in the pursuers of wealth, command, or sensual pleasure; which are the greatest part of mankind. The passion to be reckoned upon, is fear.

. . .

Chapter XV

OF OTHER LAWS OF NATURE

From that law of nature, by which we are obliged to transfer to another, such rights, as being retained, hinder the peace of mankind, there followeth a third; which is this, *that men perform their covenants made:* without which, covenants are in vain, and but empty words; and the right of all men to all things remaining, we are still in the condition of war.

And in this law of nature, consisteth the fountain and original of JUSTICE. For where no covenant hath preceded, there hath no right been transferred, and every man has right to every thing; and consequently, no action can be unjust. But when a covenant is made, then to break it is *unjust:* and the definition of INJUSTICE, is no other than *the not performance of covenant.* And whosoever is not unjust, is *just.*

But because covenants of mutual trust, where there is a fear of not performance on either part, as hath been said in the former chapter, are invalid; though the original of justice be the making of covenants; yet injustice actually there can be none, till the cause of such fear be taken away; which while men are in the natural condition of war, cannot be done. Therefore before the names of just, and unjust can have place, there must be some coercive power, to compel men equally to the performance of their covenants, by the terror of some punishment, greater than the benefit they expect by the breach of their covenant; and to make good that propriety, which by mutual contract men acquire, in recompense of the universal right they abandon: and such power there is none before the erection of a commonwealth. And this is also to be gathered out of the ordinary definition of justice in the Schools: for they say, that *justice is the constant will of giving to every man his own.* And therefore where there is no *own,* that is no propriety, there is no injustice; and where there is no coercive power erected, that is, where there is no commonwealth, there is no propriety; all men having right to all things:

therefore where there is no commonwealth, there nothing is unjust. So that the nature of justice, consisteth in keeping of valid covenants: but the validity of covenants begins not but with the constitution of a civil power, sufficient to compel men to keep them: and then it is also that propriety begins.

. . .

Chapter XVII

OF THE CAUSES, GENERATION, AND DEFINITION OF A COMMONWEALTH

The final cause, end, or design of men, who naturally love liberty, and dominion over others, in the introduction of that restraint upon themselves, in which we see them live in commonwealths, is the foresight of their own preservation, and of a more contented life thereby; that is to say, of getting themselves out from that miserable condition of war, which is necessarily consequent, as hath been shown in Chapter XIII, to the natural passions of men, when there is no visible power to keep them in awe, and tie them by fear of punishment to the performance of their covenants, and observation of those laws of nature set down in the fourteenth and fifteenth chapters.

For the laws of nature, as *justice, equity, modesty, mercy,* and, in sum, *doing to others, as we would be done to,* of themselves, without the terror of some power, to cause them to be observed, are contrary to our natural passions, that carry us to partiality, pride, revenge, and the like. And covenants, without the sword, are but words, and of no strength to secure a man at all. Therefore notwithstanding the laws of nature, which every one hath then kept, when he has the will to keep them, when he can do it safely, if there be no power erected, or not great enough for our security; every man will, and may lawfully rely on his own strength and art, for caution against all other men. And in all places, where men have lived by small families, to rob and spoil one another, has been a trade, and so far from being reputed against the law of nature, that the greater spoils they gained, the greater was their honour; and men observed no other laws therein, but the laws of honour; that is, to abstain from cruelty, leaving to men their lives, and instruments of husbandry. And as small families did then; so now do cities and kingdoms which are but greater families, for their own security, enlarge their dominions, upon all pretences of danger, and fear of invasion, or assistance that may be given to invaders, and endeavour as much as they can, to subdue, or weaken their neighbours, by open force, and secret arts, for want of other caution, justly; and are remembered for it in after ages with honour.

Nor is it the joining together of a small number of men, that gives them this security; because in small numbers, small actions on the one side or the other, make the advantage of strength so great, as is sufficient to carry the victory; and therefore gives encouragement to an invasion. The multitude sufficient to confide in for our security, is not determined by any certain number, but by comparison with the enemy we fear; and is then sufficient, when the odds of the enemy is not of so visible and conspicuous moment, to determine the event of war, as to move him to attempt.

And be there never so great a multitude; yet if their actions be directed according to their particular judgments, and particular appetites, they can expect thereby no defence, nor protection, neither against a common enemy, nor against the injuries of one another. For being distracted in opinions concerning the best use and application of their strength, they do not help but hinder one another; and reduce their strength by mutual opposition to nothing: whereby they are easily, not only subdued by a very few that agree together; but also when there is no common enemy, they make war upon each other, for their particular interests. For if we could suppose a great multitude of men to consent in the observation of justice, and other laws of nature, without a common power to keep them all in awe; we might as well suppose all mankind to do the same; and then there neither would be, nor need to be any civil government, or commonwealth at all; because there would be peace without subjection.

Nor is it enough for the security, which men desire should last all the time of their life, that they be governed, and directed by one judgment, for a limited time; as in one battle, or one war. For though they obtain a victory by their unanimous endeavour against a foreign enemy; yet afterwards, when either they have no common enemy, or he that by one part is held for an enemy, is by another part held for a friend, they must needs by the difference of their interest dissolve, and fall again into a war amongst themselves.

It is true, that certain living creatures, as bees, and ants, live sociably one with another, which are therefore by Aristotle numbered amongst political creatures; and yet have no other direction, than their particular judgments and appetites; nor speech, whereby one of them can signify to another, what he thinks expedient for the common benefit: and therefore some man may perhaps desire to know, why mankind cannot do the same. To which I answer,

First, that men are continually in competition for honour and dignity, which these creatures are not; and consequently amongst men there ariseth on that ground, envy and hatred, and finally war; but amongst these not so.

Secondly, that amongst these creatures, the common good differeth not from the private; and being by nature inclined to their private, they procure thereby the common benefit. But man, whose joy consisteth in comparing himself with other men, can relish nothing but what is eminent.

Thirdly, that these creatures, having not, as man, the use of reason, do not see, nor think they see any fault, in the administration of their common business; whereas amongst men, there are very many, that think themselves wiser, and abler to govern the public, better than the rest; and these strive to reform and innovate, one this way, another that way; and thereby bring it into distraction and civil war.

Fourthly, that these creatures, though they have some use of voice, in making known to one another their desires, and other affections; yet they want that art of words, by which some men can represent to others, that which is good, in the likeness or evil; and evil, in the likeness of good; and augment, or diminish the apparent greatness of good and evil; discontenting men, and troubling their peace at their pleasure.

Fifthly, irrational creatures cannot distinguish between *injury,* and *damage;* and therefore as long as they be at ease, they are not offended with their fellows: whereas man is then most troublesome, when he is most at ease: for then it is that he loves to shew his wisdom, and control the actions of them that govern the commonwealth.

Lastly, the agreement of these creatures is natural; that of men, is by covenant only, which is artificial: and therefore it is no wonder if there be somewhat else required, besides covenant, to make their agreement constant and lasting; which is a common power, to keep them in awe, and to direct their actions to the common benefit.

The only way to erect such a common power, as may be able to defend them from the invasion of foreigners, and the injuries of one another, and thereby to secure them in such sort, as that by their own industry, and by the fruits of the earth, they may nourish themselves and live contentedly; is, to confer all their power and strength upon one man, or upon one assembly of men, that may reduce all their wills, by plurality of voices, unto one will: which is as much as to say, to appoint one man, or assembly of men, to bear their person; and every one to own, and acknowledge himself to be author of whatsoever he that so beareth their person, shall act, or cause to be acted, in those things which concern the common peace and safety; and therein to submit their wills, every one to his will, and their judgments, to his judgment. This is more than consent, or concord; it is a real unity of them all, in one and the same person, made by covenant of every man with every man, in such manner, as if every man should say to every man, *I authorise and give up my right of governing myself, to this man, or to this assembly of men, on this condition, that thou give up thy right to him, and authorise all his actions in like manner*. This done, the multitude so united in one person, is called a COMMONWEALTH, in Latin CIVITAS. This is the generation of that great LEVIATHAN, or rather, to speak more reverently, of that *mortal god,* to which we owe under the *immortal God,* our peace and defence. For by this authority, given him by every particular man in the commonwealth, he hath the use of so much power and strength conferred on him, that by terror thereof, he is enabled to perform the wills of them all, to peace at home, and mutual aid against their enemies abroad. And in him consisteth the essence of the commonwealth; which, to define it, is *one person, of whose acts a great multitude, by mutual covenants one with another, have made themselves every one the author, to the end he may use the strength and means of them all, as he shall think expedient, for their peace and common defence.*

And he that carrieth this person, is called SOVEREIGN, and said to have *sovereign power;* and every one besides, his SUBJECT.

BISHOP BOSSUET

Bishop Bossuet's Politics Drawn from the Very Words of Holy Scripture *presents a doctrine that was popular in the royal courts of Europe during the seventeenth century—the doctrine of the divine right of kings. Written for the instruction of the Dauphin (the heir to the throne of Louis XIV), over whose education Bossuet had charge, the text amply justifies its title; for every conclusion which the author reaches is reinforced with copious references from scripture.*

To Bossuet (1627–1704), living amidst the splendor of the court of Louis XIV, the theory of divine right undoubtedly provided a seemingly rational justification of the social order. Other political theorists of the time, however, were beginning to view the situation in another light. Among these was the Englishman John Locke. In his First Treatise of Civil Government, *written within a few years of Bossuet's* Politics, *Locke turned to the scriptures to find arguments with which to refute the divine-right theory defended by Bishop Bossuet.*

Politics Drawn from the Very Words of Holy Scripture

Third Book

IN WHICH WE BEGIN TO EXPLAIN THE NATURE AND PROPERTIES OF ROYAL AUTHORITY

Article I. Essential characteristics are noted.

SINGLE PROPOSITION: *There are four characteristics or qualities essential to royal authority:* Firstly, royal authority is sacred; Secondly, it is paternal; Thirdly, it is absolute; Fourthly, it is subject to reason. This is what must be established systematically in the following articles.

Article II. Royal authority is sacred.

FIRST PROPOSITION: *God establishes kings as his ministers and reigns through them over the peoples of the world.*—We have already seen that all power comes from God.

"The ruler," adds St. Paul, "is God's minister for good. But if you do evil, be afraid, for he does not wield the sword in vain. He is a minister of God, an avenger of evil deeds."

Rulers thus act as God's ministers and as His lieutenants on earth. It is through them that He exercises his dominion. "Do you believe yourselves capable of resisting the kingdom of the Lord, that He possesses through the children of David?"

It is for this reason that we have seen that the royal throne is not the throne of a man, but the throne of God himself. "God has chosen my son Solomon in order to place him on the throne where the Lord reigns over Israel." And furthermore: "Solomon sits on the throne of the Lord."

And in order that we should not believe that to have kings established by God is characteristic only of the Israelites, here is what Ecclesiastes says: "God gives to each people their governor; and Israel is manifestly reserved for Himself."

He thus governs all peoples, and gives to all of them their kings. However He governs Israel in a more particular and more direct fashion.

SECOND PROPOSITION: *The person of the king is sacred.*—It follows from the above that the person of the king is sacred, and any attempt upon the lives of kings is a sacrilege.

God has had them anointed by His prophets with a sacred ointment, as He has had His pontiffs and His altars anointed.

But even without the application of this ointment to their bodies, they are sacred by virtue of their charge, as the representatives of the divine majesty, delegated by His providence to the execution of His designs. It is thus that God, Himself, calls Cyrus His anointed. "Here is what the Lord said to Cyrus, my anointed, whom I have taken by the hand to subject all peoples to him."

The title of christ is given to kings, and everywhere they are seen to be called christs, or the anointed of the Lord.

Under this venerable name, even the prophets revere them, and regard them as associated with the sovereign power of God, whose authority they exercise over the people. "Speak of me boldly before the Lord, and before His christ. Speak out if I have taken someone's bull or someone's ass, if I have taken bribes from someone, if I have oppressed someone. And they replied: Never. And Samuel said: the Lord and

Jacques Bénigne Bossuet, POLITIQUE TIRÉE DE L'ECRITURE SAINTE, *trans. Owen Ulph of Reed College.*

His christ are thus witnesses that you have no complaint against me."

It is thus that Samuel, after having judged the people for God with absolute power for twenty-one years, gives an account of his conduct before God and before Saul, to whom he appeals as witnesses to the testimony establishing his innocence.

Kings must be protected as sacred objects; and whoever neglects to protect them is worthy of death. "Long live the Lord," said David to Saul's captains, "all of you who do not safeguard your master, the anointed of the Lord, are the children of death."

. . .

THIRD PROPOSITION: *The ruler must be obeyed out of the principle of religion and conscience.*—St. Paul, after having stated that the ruler is the minister of God, concluded as follows: "It is thus necessary that you subject yourself to him not only through fear of his wrath, but through the obligation of your conscience."

This is why "it is necessary to serve him not merely in a way to meet the eye as if to please men, but with pure intent, with fear, with respect, and with a heart as sincere as that of Jesus Christ."

And furthermore: "Servants, obey your temporal masters in all things, never serving only in a way to meet the eye as if to please men, but in simplicity of heart and in the fear of God. Do all that you do with a good heart as though serving God and not men, assured of receiving from God Himself the reward for your services. Look upon Jesus Christ as your master."

If the apostle speaks thus of servitude, a state contrary to nature, what ought we to think of legitimate subjection to rulers and magistrates, protectors of public liberty!

That is why St. Peter said: "For the love of God, be thus subjected to the order which is established among men. Be subjected to the king as to God, possessor of the supreme power. Be subjected to those to whom He gives His authority and who are sent by Him to praise good deeds and punish evil ones."

Even though they may not acquit themselves of this duty, their charge and their ministry must be respected. "Obey your masters, not only those who are good and moderate, but even those who are vexatious and unjust."

There is thus something religious in the respect one renders to the ruler. Service to God and respect for kings are one, and St. Peter links these two duties together: "Fear God, honor the king."

Thus has God put into rulers something divine. "I have said: You are gods, and you are all children of the Almighty." It is God Himself whom David causes to speak thus.

From this it ensues that the servants of God swear by the safety and life of the king, as by a divine and sacred thing. Uriah speaking to David: "By your safety and by the conservation of your life, I will never do that thing."

Even though the king should prove unfaithful, according to the view we must hold of the order of God: "By the safety of Pharoah, I will not let you leave here."

It is necessary to listen to the first Christians, and to Tertullian who speaks for all of them as follows: "We swear not by the ghosts of the Caesars; but by their life and safety, which is more august than all their ghosts. Don't you know that spirits are demons? But we, who see in the emperors the choice and judgment of God who has given them command over all peoples, respect in them what God has placed there and we hold these things at great oath."

He adds: "What more shall I say for our religion and our piety towards the emperor than that we should respect the one whom our God has chosen. In a manner I can say that Caesar is more ours than yours because it is our God who has established him."

It is therefore the spirit of Christianity to

cause kings to be respected religiously. So much so that the same Tertullian appropriately calls our faith, "the religion of the second majesty."

The second majesty is but a derivative of the first, that is to say, of the divine being, Who, for the good of human things, has wished to cause some portion of His splendor to shine forth upon kings.

FOURTH PROPOSITION: *King's must respect their own power and use it only for the public good.*—Since their power, as it has thus been said, comes from on high, they must not believe that they are the masters to use it as they please. They must use it with fear and moderation as a thing which comes to them from God, and for which God will demand an accounting. "Listen, O kings, and understand! Learn, judges of the earth! Lend an ear, O you who hold the peoples under your power, and be pleased to see the multitudes that surround you. It is God who has given you power. Your strength comes from the Almighty who will examine your work and sound the depths of your thoughts. Because, being ministers of His kingdom, you have not judged well and you have not proceeded according to His will, He will soon appear to you in a terrible manner. Because to those who command is reserved the most harsh punishment, the small and the weak will be pitied but the powerful will be severely tormented. God fears the power of no one, because He has made both the great and the small and He is equally concerned for one and the other. And the strongest will be tormented most strongly. I speak unto you, O kings! so that you may be wise, and so that you fall not from grace."

Kings must, therefore, tremble as they use the power that God gives them, and reflect how horrible is the sacrilege of using a power that comes from God for evil.

We have seen the kings seated on the throne of the Lord, holding the sword that He has placed in their hands. How profane and audacious are those unjust kings who sit on the throne of God and use the sword, which He puts into their hands, to commit violent deeds, and to cut the throats of His children!

Thus they respect their power because it is not their power, but the power of God which it is necessary to employ in a holy and religious manner. St. Gregory of Nazianzus speaks thus to the emperors: "Respect your purple. Recognize within your persons the mystery of God. He governs celestial things alone, He shares those of the earth with you. Be thus gods to your subjects." That is to say, govern them as God governs, in a noble, impartial, beneficial, and, in a word, in a manner divine.

Article III. Royal authority is paternal, and its fundamental quality is benevolence. After what has been said, this truth needs no further proofs.

We have seen that kings hold rank from God, who is the true father of the human race. We have also seen that the first concept of power that existed among men is that of paternal power and that kings have been molded in the image of fathers. Also, everyone is in agreement that the obedience which is due to public power is found in the *Decalogue* only in the precept that obliges us to honor our fathers. From all this it seems that the appellation *king* is synonymous with the appellation *father*, and that benevolence is the most natural characteristic of kings.

. . .

Fourth Book

CONTINUATION OF THE CHARACTERISTICS OF ROYALTY

Article I. Royal authority is absolute.

In order to render this term odious and insufferable, many persons attempt to confuse absolute government with arbitrary government. But there are no terms more distinguished by their difference as we shall see when we speak of justice.

FIRST PROPOSITION: *The prince need render account to no one for what he orders.*—"Observe the commandments that come from the mouth of the king, and keep the oath that you have made to him. Do not seek to escape his view, and do not indulge in evil undertakings, because he will do what he wishes. The word of the king is powerful. And no one can say to him: Why do you act thus? He who obeys will come to no harm."

Without this absolute authority he can neither do good nor suppress evil. His power must be such that no one may hope to escape from it. And finally, the only defense of individuals against public power must be their innocence.

This doctrine conforms to the words of St. Paul: "If you do not want to fear power, do good."

SECOND PROPOSITION: *Once the prince has judged there is no other judgment.*—Sovereign judgments are attributed to God Himself. When Joseph established the judges to judge the people, he said: "It is not in the name of men that you judge, but in the name of God."

That is what causes Ecclesiastes to say: "Do not judge against the judge." This is even more important when the sovereign judge is the king. And the reason that supports this, "is that he is judging according to justice." It is not that he is always so judging, but that he is assumed to be so judging and no one has the right to judge or to review after him.

It is thus necessary to obey rulers as though they were identical with justice, without which there is neither order nor justice in affairs.

They are gods, and in a manner they share divine independence. "I have said: You are gods and you are all children of the Almighty."

Only God is able to judge their judgments and their persons. "God has taken His seat in the assembly of the gods and, seated in the center, He judges the gods."

It is for that reason that St. Gregory, bishop of Tours, said to King Chilperic in a council: "We speak to you, but you listen to us only if you want to. If you don't want to, who will condemn you other than He who has said that He was justice itself?"

It follows that he who does not want to obey the ruler is not referred to another tribunal, but is condemned irremissably to death as an enemy of the public peace and of human society. "Whoever will be proud and will not obey the command of the pontiff and the ordinance of the judge will die and you will thus eradicate the evil from among you." And furthermore: "Whoever shall refuse to obey all your orders, may he die." It is the people who speak thus to Joshua.

The ruler can correct himself when he knows that he has done badly, but against his authority there can be no remedy except his authority.

That is why he must certainly be careful what he orders. "Be careful of what you order. All that you judge will fall back upon you. Fear God. Do everything with great care."

It is thus that Joseph instructed the judges to whom he was entrusting his authority. How much of this he recollected when he himself had to judge.

THIRD PROPOSITION: *There is no co-active force against the ruler.*—A co-active force is a power to constrain and to execute what is legitimately ordained. Legitimate power belongs to the ruler alone. To him alone belongs the co-active force.

It is for that reason also that St. Paul gives the sword to him alone. "If you do not do well, be afraid, because it is not in vain that he wields the sword."

In the state only the ruler should be

armed, otherwise everything is in confusion and the state falls back into anarchy.

He who creates a sovereign ruler puts everything together into his hands, all the sovereign authority to judge and all the forces of the state. "Our king will judge and he will march before us and he will conduct our wars." This is what the Jewish people said when they asked for a king. Samuel declares to them upon this basis that the power of their ruler will be absolute, incapable of being restrained by any other power. Here is the right of the king who will reign over you, sayeth the Lord: "He will take your children and place them into his service. He will seize some of your lands and the best of that which you have in order to give it to his servants," and so forth.

Will they have the right to do all that legally? God forbid! Because God does not grant such powers. But they will have the right to do it with impunity and without regard for human justice. That is why David said: "I have sinned against you alone. O Lord, have pity on me!" Commenting on this passage, St. Jerome said: "Because he was king, he had only God to fear."

. . .

To the ruler alone belongs the general care of the people. That is the first article and the foundation of all others. To him the public works; to him the squares and arms; to him the decrees and ordinances; to him the marks of distinction; no power but that which is dependent on his; no assembly except by his authority.

It is thus that for the good of a state all the power is united in one. To put the power somewhere else is to divide the state. It is to destroy the public peace. It is to create two masters against which the oracle of the Scriptures states: "No man can serve two masters."

The ruler is by his charge the father of the people. He is by his grandeur above petty interests. Even more, all his grandeur and all his natural interest is that the people be conserved, since lacking the people he is no longer ruler. There is nothing better than to leave all the power of the state to the one who has the greatest interest in the conservation and the glory of the state itself.

. . .

SIXTH PROPOSITION: *The people must fear the ruler; but the ruler must only fear doing evil.*—"Whoever will be proud and will not obey the commandment of the pontiff and the ordinance of the judge will die and you shall remove the evil from within Israel. And all who shall hear his torment will be afraid so that no one shall allow himself to succumb to pride."

Fear is a restraint necessary to men because of their pride and their natural indocility.

The people must thus fear the ruler, but if the ruler fears the people all is lost. The weakness of Aaron, to whom Moses had left the command while he was on the mountain, was the cause of the adoration of the golden calf. "What have these people done to you?" Moses said to him, "And why have you led them to so great an evil." He blames the crime of the people on Aaron who had not repressed it even though it was within his power to do so.

Note closely the following terms: "What have these people done to you for you to lead them to so great an evil?" One is the enemy of the people by not resisting them on such occasions.

Aaron answered him: "May my Lord not be angry with me. You know that these people are inclined toward evil. They came to tell me: Create gods to lead us because we do not know what has happened to Moses who has rescued us from Egypt."

What an excuse for a sovereign magistrate to fear angering the people. God does not receive it, "and irritated to the last degree against Aaron, He wanted to crush him, but Moses prayed for him."

Saul attempts to place the blame on the people for not having executed the orders of God. It is a vain excuse that God rejects for he was established on the throne to resist the people whenever they drifted into evil. Samuel said to him: "Listen to what the Lord has pronounced against you. You have rejected His word. Also He has rejected you and you shall not be king." Saul replied to Samuel, "By fearing the people and ceding to their harangues, I have sinned in having disobeyed the Lord and you."

The ruler must firmly repulse importunate persons who ask him for unjust things.

The fear of angering, pushed too far, degenerates into a criminal weakness. "There are people who lose their souls through misguided humility. The impudent one that they dare not refuse causes them to perish."

Fifth Book

FOURTH AND FINAL CHARACTERISTIC OF ROYAL AUTHORITY

Article I. Royal authority is subject to reason.

FIRST PROPOSITION: *Government is a work of reason and intelligence.*—"Now, listen, O kings, and be instructed, judges of the earth."

All men are created capable of understanding. But principally you upon whom reposes an entire nation, you who should be the soul and intelligence of a State, in whom must be found the first reason for all its movements, the less it is necessary for you to justify yourself to others, the more you must have justification and intelligence within yourself.

The contrary of acting out of reason is to act out of passion or anger. To act out of anger as Saul acted against David, driven by his jealousy or possessed by his black melancholy, entails all kinds of irregularities, inconsistencies, inequalities, anomalies, injustices, and confusion in one's conduct.

Though one has only a horse to lead and a flock to guide, one cannot do it without reason. How much more is needed for the leadership of men and a rational flock!

"The Lord took David from the care of his sheep to have him conduct Jacob, his servant, and Israel, his inheritance. And he led them in the innocence of his heart with an able and intelligent hand."

Everything among men is accomplished through intelligence and through counsel. "Houses are built out of wisdom and become solid through prudence. Ability fills the granaries and amasses riches. The wise man is courageous. The able man is robust and strong because war is waged by strategy and by industry, and salvation is found where there is much counsel."

Wisdom herself says: "It is through me that kings rule and through me legislators prescribe what is just."

She is so born to command that she gives the empire even to those born in servitude. "The wise servant will command the children of the house who lack wisdom, and he will apportion their lots." And furthermore: "Free people will subject themselves to a judicious servant."

God, upon installing Joshua, orders him to study the law of Moses which was the law of the kingdom, "in order," He says, "that you should understand all that you do." And furthermore: "And then you will carry out your designs and you will understand what you do."

David said as much to Solomon in the last instructions he gave to him upon dying. "Take care to observe the laws of God so that you may understand all that you do and to which side you are to turn.

"So that you may not be turned, turn

yourself knowingly. Let reason direct all your movements. Know what you do and why you are doing it."

. . .

Article IV. Consequences of the Preceding Doctrine of Majesty and its Attendant Features.

FIRST PROPOSITION: *What majesty is.*— I do not call majesty that pomp which surrounds kings, or that external brilliance which dazzles the vulgar. That is the reflection of majesty and not majesty itself.

Majesty is the image of the grandeur of God in the ruler.

God is infinite. God is all. The ruler in his capacity as ruler is not looked upon as a private individual. He is a public figure. The entire state is in him. The will of all the people is contained in his. As all perfection and all virtue is united in God, thus all the power of individuals is reunited in the person of the ruler. What grandeur that a single man should contain so much of it!

The power of God makes itself felt in an instant from one end of the world to the other. Royal power acts simultaneously throughout the entire kingdom. It holds the whole kingdom in a state of polity as God holds the whole world.

Should God withdraw His hand, the world will fall back into nothingness. Should authority cease in the kingdom, all will be in confusion.

Consider the ruler in his cabinet. From there all orders emanate which make the magistrates and the captains, the citizens and the soldiers, the provinces and the armies on land and sea, act in concert. It is the image of God who seated on His throne in the highest part of the heavens directs all of nature.

"What movement is caused," said St. Augustine, "simply by the command of the emperor! He only moves his lips—there is no slighter movement—and the whole empire moves. It is the image of God who does all by His word. He has spoken and things have been done. He has commanded and they have been created."

We admire His works. Nature is a matter to expound upon for the curious. "God gives them the world to meditate upon, but they will never discover the secret of His work from the beginning to the end." We see some portion of it, but the depth is impenetrable. Thus is the secret of the ruler.

The designs of the ruler are only known through their execution. Thus are the counsels of God likewise manifested, and no one shares them save those whom God admits.

If the power of God extends everywhere, magnificence accompanies it. There is no corner of the universe where shining examples of His goodness do not appear. Behold the order, behold the justice, behold the tranquility in all the kingdom! It is the natural effect of the authority of the ruler.

There is nothing more majestic than kindness widely displayed, and there is no greater vilification of majesty than the misery of the people caused by the ruler.

The evil hide in vain. God's light follows them everywhere. His arm reaches them from the highest heavens to the depths of the abyss. "Where shall I go before your spirit and where shall I flee before your face? If I climb to heaven you are there. If I throw myself into the depths of hell, I find you there. If I rise in the morning and retreat to the most distant seas it is your hand that leads me there and your right hand holds me there. And I have said that perhaps the shadows will cover me, but night has been as day around me. Before you, darkness is not dark. The night is lighted as the day. Darkness and light are one and the same." The evil find God everywhere, high and low, night and day. Whatever morning they get up, He warns them. However far they should travel, His hand is on them.

Thus God gives the ruler the power of discovering the most secret conspiracies. He has eyes and hands everywhere. We have seen that the birds of the sky report to him what is going on. He has even received from God through practiced experience a certain insight which makes one suspect him of powers of divination. Once he has penetrated intrigue, his long arms reach out to seize his enemies from the extremities of the world. He ferrets them out from the depths of the abyss. There is no asylum secure against such power.

Finally, let yourself gather before your eyes those things so great and so august that we have said concerning royal authority. Behold an immense people united in a single person. Behold the sacred power, paternal and absolute. Behold the secret reason which governs the entire body of the state enclosed in a single head. See the image of God in the king and you have the concept of royal majesty.

God is holiness itself, goodness itself, power itself, reason itself. In these things resides the majesty of God. In the image of these things is the majesty of the ruler.

This majesty is so great that it cannot be the same in the ruler as it is in the source. It is borrowed from God who gives it to him for the good of the people for whom it is good to be constrained by a superior force.

I do not know what divine attribute attaches itself to the ruler and inspires fear in the people. May the king not forget himself for that reason. "I have said that it is God who speaks. I have said: You are gods and you are all children of the Almighty but you will die like men and you will fall like the great." I have said, you are gods. That is to say, you have authority in you. You carry on your forehead a divine character. You are the children of the Almighty. It is He who has established your power for the welfare of mankind. But, O gods of flesh and blood, O gods of mud and dust, you will die like men, you will fall like the great. Greatness separates men for a time. A common fall at the end makes them all equal.

O kings, exercise your power thus boldly because it is divine and beneficial to mankind! But exercise it with humility. It is applied to you from without. In the end it leaves you feeble, it leaves you mortal, it leaves you sinners and makes you all the more responsible before God.

JEAN BAPTISTE COLBERT

The leading minister of France during many of the years of Louis XIV's reign was Jean-Baptiste Colbert. Born in 1619 into a thoroughly middle-class family, Colbert did not rise to power particularly rapidly, nor did his early career show signs of great distinction. He first attracted the attention of Le Tellier, the Secretary of State for War, by his devotion to duty, his tirelessness, and his administrative talents. In 1647, Colbert was elevated to the post of personal secretary to the Minister, Le Tellier. Two years later (after a financially judicious marriage), he left Le Tellier's service and entered the household of Cardinal Mazarin, who was in effect the ruler of France.

Again Colbert's talents and perseverance brought him advancement. When Mazarin died in 1661 and Louis XIV took over control of the government, Colbert moved easily into the top rank of ministers and advisers to the king. In 1665 he was made Comptroller-General, and later he became Secretary of State for Naval Affairs as well as Superintendent of Buildings—a highly significant post, for he was responsible for all government construction, including the great palace of Versailles.

One of the results of this first minister's tireless industry was that he stamped his name upon that brand of state activity which attempts to regulate everything for the sake of the political power and prestige of the country and its monarch. In fact, the term "Colbertism" came to stand for state interest and activity in all sorts of enterprises—encouraging new commerce and industry, fostering agriculture, establishing price and wage levels, fixing standards of quality for goods, forbidding certain imports and exports, supporting the arts and crafts, developing a large, well-trained army and navy, simplifying the legal system and procedures for tax assessment and collection, and abolishing accretions of custom and practice that infringed on the power of the state.

The three selections that follow give a good picture of the busy Frenchman's activities. In the first he tells of some of the measures taken by the king to stimulate commerce and industry; in the second—this was ostensibly a letter from Louis XIV, but it was actually written by Colbert—he exhorts the commercial class to ever greater effort; and in the third, he reveals the lengths to which he is willing to go in order to acquire a greater share of the world's wealth. The translation has been left awkward, involved, and rough, because that was Colbert's own style.

Memoirs on the Financial Affairs of France to Serve as a History, 1663

. . . Not being content to seek means of obtaining relief for his people, the King again wanted to act with the same application to procure some benefits for them; and, thinking that the means of reestablishing abundance and wealth among his subjects could not help but follow the restoration of manufacturing within the Kingdom and of domestic and foreign commerce, after being carefully informed on all details, he found:

The internal commerce, which consists of nothing but the communication of one city with the others and the easy transportation of merchandise, entirely ruined. . . .

The transportation of merchandise almost ruined by the number of tolls which have been established upon many pretexts.

All manufacturing, which was once so great within the Kingdom, entirely gone, the Dutch and the English having taken nearly all by various evil means outside their State, except the lone manufacture of silk which still exists at Lyons and Tours, although muchly diminished.

As for external commerce, it is not known, so to speak, in the kingdom except by the Dutch who come to take all the excess merchandise in our ports, and who

Jean-Baptiste Colbert, LETTRES, INSTRUCTIONS ET MÉMOIRES, *trans. by the editor, John Louis Beatty.*

bring us all those of which we could have need; in short that he does not find, according to the research that His Majesty has made, that on the three hundred leagues of coastline on the Ocean sea and on the more than one hundred leagues on the Mediterranean sea, there were two hundred vessels of all burden belonging to his subjects, and he finds more than six thousand sailors who serve the foreigners. This deplorable state of commerce which no other prince before this one thought of recognizing, being clearly known everywhere else, His Majesty, well realizing that, not having ships in his realm, which was the only way to attract wealth, resolved to give that all his protection and made it a customary affair of his councils.

To begin, he named some councillors to his councils; and by some decrees which he gave them, he ordered the masters of requests in the provinces to work at the verification of all the debts of the towns, of all the tolls and of all the titles by which these were established. . . .

He willed that all the records on the liquidation (of the debts) be reported before him, in order that he himself with the advice of his council might rule on the validity or invalidity of these debts.

He determined to observe the same thing in regard to the tolls established on the rivers; and after a report long and boring to all others, he suppressed by means of decrees issued over a period of five or six months, all the tolls on the rivers of Garonne, Dordogne, Charente, Loire, Seine, Somme, Marne, Oise, Saône and Rhone, for the titles were vicious, in such a way he made the great rivers navigable and by these means settled the transportation of merchandise within the kingdom. . . .

With regard to manufacturing, since it is a difficult matter and one which takes much time to resolve, His Majesty gives all the necessary care to raise the spirits of his people and to give them the means (of improving manufacturing).

As to foreign trade, having recognized that, his power at sea being entirely withered away, he must of necessity begin by re-establishing his maritime forces, in order to give courage to his peoples and to the principal merchants of his kingdom to buy and have built some vessels and to give themselves up in earnest to the sea service.

To this end His Majesty, having had the condition of his ships and galleys inspected, found that for ten years one could see no more than two or three French warships at sea, that the shipyards were denuded entirely of all stores, that the number of vessels was reduced to twenty or twenty-two, many of which in an unfit condition to serve having almost been destroyed in port without serving for lack of repairs; that the captains were inexperienced because of the long cessation of activity; that the better sailors and an infinity of others had passed into the service of foreigners because they could find no employment in France.

In regard to the galleys: all the rowers reduced to eight or nine hundred galley slaves, most of them sick and enfeebled by the misery they have suffered in the years past; six miserable hulls of galleys, all the others sunk in the port of Toulon; finally, this state of affairs, on which rests the larger part of the glory of the prince and the respect and veneration of his name in foreign countries, reduced to the most pitiable condition one can imagine.

This, having been clearly recognized by the King, he gave both his orders and the necessary funds for the re-establishment of both of these two powers. To achieve this, he ordered a general refitting of all his vessels. He got from Holland and sent to Sweden in order to buy not only all the needed supplies to refit and build ships, but also two hundred thousands of copper for the casting of large cannon and set about madly to put a powerful force to sea.

At the same time he cut timber in the forests of Bourgogne and Brittany and began to have some vessels built at Toulon and Brest.

In regard to the galleys he gave orders to buy all the slaves to be found at Malta and wrote vigorously to the grand master of that religion there (*i.e.*, the Grand Master of the Order of St. John of Malta). He gave orders to his procurers-general in the sovereign companies that they take the opportunity to sentence to the galleys guilty persons who could be executed. . . .

For the liberal arts His Majesty has established, formed and given the necessary funds for the Academy of Painting and Sculpture, in which all the young people are taught by the most excellent masters of these two arts. And not only has he given salaries for this purpose to the directors and teachers, but also he has given divers prizes now and then to stimulate the young people, and every year he has taken one or two of the best prepared in each art to send to Rome, where he gives them a pension on which to live for two or three years until their art is perfected, and then to return to France and be employed in the buildings of the royal house.

He has established the royal manufacture of tapestry at the house of Gobelins, and he put people to work at the designs by Monsieur Le Brun, his premier painter, who is certainly recognized as the first painter in Europe. At the same time he put people to work at an infinity of new kinds of goldsmithing, embroidery and all sorts of furniture, having already furnished two of his country houses more superbly than the Louvre had ever been furnished.

Louis XIV to the Municipal Magistrates and Inhabitants of Marseilles

August 26, 1664

Very dear and well-loved, having considered that it would be useful to this kingdom to re-establish the commerce inside and outside of this place . . . we have resolved to hold, for this purpose, every fifteenth day in our presence, a special Council of commerce, in which all the interests of merchants and the means of achieving this re-establishment will be examined and resolved, as also all that which relates to manufacturing. We say to you also that we assign, in the expenses of our State, one million livres each year for the rehabilitation of manufacturing and the improvement of navigation, exclusive of the other larger amounts which we have caused to be raised to supply the companies of the East and West Indies;

That we also work constantly to abolish all the tolls which are asked on the navigable rivers;

That already more than one million livres have been spent on the restoration of the public roads, a project at which we will also work without ceasing;

That we will with the funds of our royal treasury assist all those who want to undertake the restoration of old manufactures or who will propose new;

That we give orders to all our ambassadors, or residents among the princes our allies, to take in our name all convenient steps to render judgments on all complaints of merchants and to conserve the complete freedom of trade;

That we will house comfortably, at our court and household, all and each of the merchants who have business there, for all the time they will be obliged to stay, having ordered the grand Sergeant of our House to set aside a proper house for this purpose which will be called the *Maison du Commerce;*

That if the said merchants wish to depute someone among those at our court and household to take care of their affairs, we will lodge him at the said *Maison* and will grant him audience at all times;

That if they have trouble finding someone who can or will leave his family and his business for this position, we will appoint an intelligent and able person to whom we will give the means to live in the said *Maison,* there to receive all the merchants who have some business at our court and household, and to take their appeals and to forward them immediately with all the speed necessary, all without a single cost or expense;

That all the overseas merchants and traders who will purchase some vessels or who will build some new ones for their trade or commerce will receive from us some gratuities to help them with the said purchases or in the construction of the said (ships);

And that all those who will undertake long term voyages, in reporting for authentication in the form which will be prescribed by us, will also receive some gratuities for each ton of merchandise they will have carried or borne on the said voyages:

In all these matters we have asked you to give advice by this letter and say to you that, as soon as you have received it, you call together all the merchants and traders of our city of Marseilles, that you explain to them very carefully our intentions in regard to all the above, in order that, being informed of the favorable treatment which we desire to extend to them, they will be more especially invited to apply themselves to commerce. . . .

Proposal and Useful Advice Concerning the Commerce of Holland, 1668

All the world knows that the city of Amsterdam is beyond comparison the most rich and most flourishing city of Europe, and that it did not reach this degree of grandeur and wealth until, by means of the revolt of the United Provinces of the Low Country and with the aid of France, the Estates-General, after a long time of war, having been superior to the House of Spain, closed the passage to the sea at the city of Antwerp by the means of Zeeland[1] and of the naval forces which the said Estates have always had at sea in much greater strength than those of Spain. As a result the city of Amsterdam has found itself the best fitted to gather the entire commerce of the said city of Antwerp, not only has she profited, but more she has attracted to herself that which all the Dutch have established in the Indies, in the Baltic Sea, and all over the world. These are the means by which she has arrived at this degree of grandeur and of power so that she directs all the delibera-

[1] [Islands off the mouth of the Scheldt River on which Antwerp is located.—Ed.]

tions of the Estates and contributes only a seventh or an eighth of all costs.

All these reasons, and an infinity of others which are useless for the subject of this discourse, will require the said Estates to demand from the Spanish, (in accord with) the treaty of peace made with them in 1648, article 14, which follows:

"The Scheldt River, and the canals of the Sas, Zwyn, and other such waterways debouching there shall be kept closed by the Lords of the Estates-General."

By this article they thought to secure forever the commerce of the city of Amsterdam to the exclusion of that of Antwerp.

Now that peace is established between France and Spain,[2] and that the Estates-General are also at peace with these two crowns, it is undoubted that the Dutch, as a result of the above article, have the power to prevent the passage into Antwerp, either by the Scheldt or by the other canals, to all vessels of the King of Spain or of his subjects; but they do not have the same power in regard to French vessels which can enter without difficulty, and, by this method, the King is able to re-establish the commerce of Antwerp, since the subjects of His Majesty can carry all kinds of merchandise there.

If the King announces this plan and has it executed, since the city of Antwerp is, beyond comparison, more ample than that of Amsterdam, either for the berthing of ships or for the distribution of merchandise, it follows of necessity either the Dutch run the risk of seeing the commerce leave their hands and pass into those of the French and the Flemish or they come to an agreement with France on terms advantageous to the service of the king and proportionate to the importance of these advantages.

2 [Treaty of Aix-la-Chapelle, May 2, 1668.–Ed.]

ISAAC NEWTON

Isaac Newton (1642–1727) had formulated his theory of universal gravitation by the time he was twenty-four. Several years later, at the insistence of friends, he published it under the title, The Mathematical Principles of Natural Philosophy. *This triumph of scientific genius, which has been called "the greatest single monument of human learning," seems almost miraculous and its author somehow superhuman. And yet, without detracting from Newton's greatness, we must recognize that his theory of gravitation was the culmination of a scientific revival which had been in progress for well over a hundred years and had included such names as Copernicus, Kepler, and Galileo. But in an even broader sense Newton is the heir of the thinkers who had gone before. The selection from his* Optics *begins with a reaffirmation of the atomic theory of matter, which was first developed by the ancient Greek, Democritus; Newton, as a Christian, however, instead of regarding the atoms as eternal, argues that they were created by God. And in the second selection, from his* Mathematical Principles, *Rule I is Newton's restatement of a rule that was formulated at least as early as the fourteenth century, and Rule III clearly reveals the influence of Francis Bacon.*

During his long lifetime, Newton was widely honored, both in his own country and abroad. Yet toward the end of his life, he was able to make this modest assessment of his career: "I know not what the world will think of my labors, but to myself it seems that I have been but as a child playing on the seashore; now finding some pebble rather more polished, and now some shell rather more agreeably variegated than another, while the immense ocean of truth extended itself unexplored before me."

Optics

. . .

All these things being considered, it seems probable to me, that God in the beginning formed matter in solid, massy, hard, impenetrable, moveable particles, of such sizes and figures, and with such other properties, and in such proportion to space, as most conduced to the end for which he formed them; and that these primitive particles, being solids, are incomparably harder than any porous bodies compounded of them; even so very hard, as never to wear or break in pieces; no ordinary power being able to divide what God himself made one in the first creation. While the particles continue entire, they may compose bodies of one and the same nature and texture in all ages: But should they wear away, or break in pieces, the nature of things depending on them, would be changed. Water and earth, composed of old worn particles and fragments of particles, would not be of the same nature and texture now, with water and earth composed of entire particles in the beginning. And therefore, that nature may be lasting, the changes of corporeal things are to be placed only in the various separations and new associations and motions of these permanent particles; compound bodies being apt to break, not in the midst of solid particles, but where those particles are laid together, and only touch in a few points.

It seems to me farther, that these particles have not only a force of inertia accompanied with such passive laws of motion as naturally result from that force, but also that they are moved by certain active principles, such as is that of gravity, and that which causes fermentation, and the cohesion of bodies. These principles I consider, not as occult qualities, supposed to result from the specific forms of things, but as general laws of nature, by which the things themselves are formed; their truth appearing to us by phenomena, though their causes be not yet discovered. For these are manifest qualities, and their causes only are occult. And the *Aristotelians* gave the name of occult qualities, not to manifest qualities, but to such qualities only as they supposed to lie hid in bodies, and to be the unknown causes of manifest effects: Such as would be the causes of gravity, and of magnetic and electric attractions, and of fermentations, if we should suppose that these forces or actions arose from qualities unknown to us, and uncapable of being discovered and made manifest. Such occult qualities put a stop to the improvement of natural philosophy, and therefore of late years have been rejected. To tell us that every species of things is endowed with an

Isaac Newton, OPTICS, OR, A TREATISE OF THE REFLECTIONS, REFRACTIONS, INFLECTIONS AND COLOURS OF LIGHT, *4th ed. (London, 1730). [Capitalization and spelling have been modernized.—Ed.]*

occult specific quality by which it acts and produces manifest effects, is to tell us nothing: But to derive two or three general principles of motion from phenomena, and afterwards to tell us how the properties and actions of all corporeal things follow from those manifest principles, would be a very great step in philosophy, though the causes of those principles were not yet discovered: And therefore I scruple not to propose the principles of motion abovementioned, they being of very general extent, and leave their causes to be found out.

Now by the help of these principles, all material things seem to have been composed of the hard and solid particles above-mentioned, variously associated in the first creation by the counsel of an intelligent agent. For it became him who created them to set them in order. And if he did so, it's unphilosophical to seek for any other origin of the world, or to pretend that it might arise out of a chaos by the mere laws of nature; though being once formed, it may continue by those laws for many ages. For while comets move in very eccentric orbs in all manner of positions, blind fate could never make all the planets move one and the same way in orbs concentric, some inconsiderable irregularities excepted, which may have risen from the mutual actions of comets and planets upon one another, and which will be apt to increase, till this system wants a reformation. Such a wonderful uniformity in the planetary system must be allowed the effect of choice. And so much the uniformity in the bodies of animals, they having generally a right and a left side shaped alike, and on either side of their bodies two legs behind, and either two arms, or two legs, or two wings before upon their shoulders, and between their shoulders a neck running down into a back-bone, and a head upon it; and in the head two ears, two eyes, a nose, a mouth, and a tongue, alike situated. Also the first contrivance of those very artificial parts of animals, the eyes, ears, brain, muscles, heart, lungs, midriff, glands, larynx, hands, wings, swimming bladders, natural spectacles, and other organs of sense and motion; and the instinct of brutes and insects, can be the effect of nothing else than the wisdom and skill of a powerful ever-living agent, who being in all places, is more able by his will to move the bodies within his boundless uniform sensorium, and thereby to form and reform the parts of the universe, than we are by our will to move the parts of our own bodies. And yet we are not to consider the world as the body of God, or the several parts thereof, as the parts of God. He is a uniform being, void of organs, members or parts, and they are his creatures subordinate to him, and subservient to his will; and he is no more the soul of them, than the soul of man is the soul of the species of things carried through the organs of sense into the place of its sensation, where it perceives them by means of its immediate presence, without the intervention of any third thing. The organs of sense are not for enabling the soul to perceive the species of things in its sensorium, but only for conveying them thither; and God has no need of such organs, he being everywhere present to the things themselves. And since space is divisible *in infinitum,* and matter is not necessarily in all places, it may be also allowed that God is able to create particles of matter of several sizes and figures, and in several proportions to space, and perhaps of different densities and forces, and thereby to vary the laws of nature, and make worlds of several sorts in several parts of the universe. At least, I see nothing of contradiction in all this.

As in mathematics, so in natural philosophy, the investigation of difficult things by the method of analysis, ought ever to precede the method of composition. This analysis consists in making experiments and observations, and in drawing general conclusions from them by induction, and admitting of no objections against the conclusions, but such as are taken from experiments, or other certain truths. For hypotheses are not to be regarded in experimental philosophy. And although the arguing from experiments and observations by induction be no demonstration of general conclusions; yet it is the best way of arguing which the nature of things admits of, and may be looked upon as so much the stronger, by how much the induction is more general. And if no exception occur from phenomena, the conclusion may be pronounced generally. But if at any time afterwards any exception shall occur from experiments, it may then begin to be pronounced with such exceptions as occur. By this way of analysis we may proceed from compounds to ingredients, and from motions to the forces producing them; and in general, from effects to their causes, and from particular causes to more general ones, till the argument ends in the most general. This is the method of analysis: And the synthesis consists in assuming the causes discovered, and established as principles, and by them explaining the phenomena proceeding from them, and proving the explanations.

The Mathematical Principles of Natural Philosophy

THE RULES OF REASONING IN PHILOSOPHY

Rule I

We are to admit no more causes of natural things, than such as are both true and sufficient to explain their appearances.

To this purpose the philosophers say, that Nature does nothing in vain, and more is in vain, when less will serve; for Nature is pleased with simplicity, and affects not the pomp of superfluous causes.

Rule II

Therefore to the same natural effects we must, as far as possible, assign the same causes.

As to respiration in a man, and in a beast; the descent of stones in Europe and in America; the light of our culinary fire and of the sun; the reflection of light in the earth, and in the planets.

Rule III

The qualities of bodies, which admit neither intension nor remission of degrees, and which are found to belong to all bodies within the reach of our experiments, are to be esteemed the universal qualities of all bodies whatsoever.

For since the qualities of bodies are only known to us by experiments, we are to hold for universal, all such as universally agree with experiments; and such as are not liable to diminution, can never be quite taken away. We are certainly not to relinquish the evidence of experiments for the sake of dreams and vain fictions of our own devising; nor are we to recede from the analogy of Nature, which uses to be simple, and always consonant to itself. We no otherways know the extension of bodies, than by our senses, nor do these reach it in all bodies; but because we perceive ex-

Isaac Newton, THE MATHEMATICAL PRINCIPLES OF NATURAL PHILOSOPHY, *trans. A. Motte (London, 1729). [Capitalization and spelling have been modernized.—Ed.]*

tension in all that are sensible, therefore we ascribe it universally to all others also. That abundance of bodies are hard we learn by experience. And because the hardness of the whole arises from the hardness of the parts, we therefore justly infer the hardness of the undivided particles not only of the bodies we feel but of all others. That all bodies are impenetrable, we gather not from reason, but from sensation. The bodies which we handle we find impenetrable, and thence conclude impenetrability to be an universal property of all bodies whatsoever. That all bodies are moveable, and endowed with certain powers (which we call the forces of inertia) of persevering in their motion or in their rest, we only infer from the like properties observed in the bodies which we have seen. The extension, hardness, impenetrability, mobility, and force of inertia of the whole, result from the extension, hardness, impenetrability, mobility, and forces of inertia of the parts: and thence we conclude the least particles of all bodies to be also all extended, and hard, and impenetrable, and moveable, and endowed with their proper forces of inertia. And this is the foundation of all philosophy. Moreover, that the divided but contiguous particles of bodies may be separated from one another, is matter of observation; and, in the particles that remain undivided, our minds are able to distinguish yet lesser parts, as is mathematically demonstrated. But whether the parts so distinguished, and not yet divided, may, by the powers of nature, be actually divided and separated from one another, we cannot certainly determine. Yet had we the proof of but one experiment, that any undivided particle, in breaking a hard and solid body, suffered a division, we might by virtue of this rule, conclude, that the undivided as well as the divided particles, may be divided and actually separated to infinity.

Lastly, if it universally appears, by experiments and astronomical observations, that all bodies about the earth, gravitate toward the earth; and that in proportion to the quantity of matter which they severally contain; that the moon likewise, according to the quantity of its matter, gravitates toward the earth; that on the other hand our sea gravitates toward the moon; and all the planets mutually one toward another; and the comets in like manner towards the sun; we must, in consequence of this rule, universally allow, that all bodies whatsoever are endowed with a principle of mutual gravitation. For the argument from the appearances concludes with more force for the universal gravitation of all bodies, than for their impenetrability; of which among those in the celestial regions, we have no experiments, nor any manner of observation. Not that I affirm gravity to be essential to bodies. By their inherent force I mean nothing but their force of inertia. This is immutable. Their gravity is diminished as they recede from the earth.

Rule IV

In experimental philosophy we are to look upon propositions collected by general induction from phenomena as accurately or very nearly true, notwithstanding any contrary hypotheses that may be imagined, till such time as other phenomena occur, by which they may either be made more accurate, or liable to exceptions.

This rule we must follow that the argument of induction may not be evaded by hypotheses.

JOHN LOCKE

As the political philosophy of Thomas Hobbes was in part a reaction against the anarchy of the 1640's in England, so that of John Locke (1632–1704) represents a response to the Glorious Revolution of 1688. As Locke stated in the preface to his Of Civil Government, *he hoped "to establish the throne of our great restorer, our present King William; to make good his title, in the consent of the people . . . and to justify to the world the people of England, whose love of their just and natural rights, with their resolution to preserve them, saved the nation when it was on the very birth of slavery and ruin."*

Locke was personally involved in the crises that led up to the Revolution. As physician and secretary to the Earl of Shaftesbury, a prominent Whig politician and leader of the opposition against Charles II, he shared the political fortunes of his employer. When Shaftesbury, implicated in a plot to prevent the accession of James II, fled to Holland, Locke was forced to flee with him. It was during his exile in Holland that Locke wrote Of Civil Government, *which is divided into two treatises. The first treatise is a refutation of the doctrine of divine right, and the second (from which the first selection is taken) is a statement of his own political theory. Although Locke's second treatise, like Hobbes's* Leviathan, *grew out of the author's reaction to a particular political situation, both in its content and its influence it far transcended the local scene. It was the first philosophical statement of the modern position known as liberalism, a position that was to be reformulated by Jeremy Bentham in the eighteenth century, John Stuart Mill in the nineteenth, and John Dewey in the twentieth. The second treatise had its greatest practical effects during the eighteenth century when the leaders of the American and French revolutions found in it an intellectual justification for their cause. Many of the passages in the Declaration of Independence, for example, paraphrase the language of the second treatise.*

The second selection is from Locke's most important work, An Essay Concerning Human Understanding. *This book, a detailed analysis of the source, nature, and scope of human knowledge, exerted a subtle but profound influence on subsequent Western thought, particularly that of the Enlightenment. The eighteenth-century intellectuals hailed Locke for having accomplished, in the realm of human understanding, what Newton had achieved in the realm of physical nature. Just as Newton's law of universal gravitation, they felt, had eliminated the necessity for an appeal to divine Providence in explaining the operations of the physical world, so, they argued, Locke's denial of innate ideas undermined the whole doctrine of the absolute, revealed truths of religion. Hence both Newton and Locke were used as intellectual weapons in the battle that the leaders of the Enlightenment were waging on behalf of reason against what they conceived to be the obscurantism of the Church. Unfortunately, neither Locke nor his admirers were aware that the Lockian assumptions, when pushed to their ultimate conclusions, would undermine the very reason they were meant to support. It remained for his successor, David Hume, to demonstrate this point.*

Of Civil Government

BOOK II
Chapter I

. . .

I think it may not be amiss to set down what I take to be political power; that the power of a magistrate over a subject may be distinguished from that of a father over his children, a master over his servants, a husband over his wife, and a lord over his slave. All which distinct powers happening sometimes together in the same man, if he be considered under these different relations, it may help us to distinguish these powers one from another, and show the difference betwixt a ruler of a commonwealth, a father of a family, and a captain of a galley.

Political power, then, I take to be a right of making laws with penalties of death, and consequently all less penalties, for the regulating and preserving of property, and of employing the force of the community, in the execution of such laws, and in the defence of the commonwealth from foreign injury; and all this only for the public good.

Chapter II

OF THE STATE OF NATURE

To understand political power right, and derive it from its original, we must consider what state all men are naturally in, and that is, a state of perfect freedom to order their actions and dispose of their possessions and persons, as they think fit, within the bounds of the law of nature; without asking leave, or depending upon the will of any other man.

A state also of equality, wherein all the power and jurisdiction is reciprocal, no one having more than another; there being nothing more evident, than that creatures of the same species and rank, promiscuously born to all the same advantages of nature, and the use of the same faculties, should also be equal one amongst another without subordination or subjection; unless the lord and master of them all should, by any manifest declaration of his will, set one above another, and confer on him, by an evident and clear appointment, an undoubted right to dominion and sovereignty. . . .

But though this be a state of liberty, yet it is not a state of licence: though man in that state have an uncontrollable liberty to dispose of his person or possessions, yet he has not liberty to destroy himself, or so much as any creature in his possession, but where some nobler use than its bare preservation calls for it. The state of nature has a law of nature to govern it, which obliges every one: and reason, which is that law, teaches all mankind, who will but consult it, that being all equal and independent, no one ought to harm another in his life, health, liberty, or possessions: for men being all the workmanship of one omnipotent and infinitely wise Maker; all the servants of one sovereign master, sent into the world by his order, and about his business; they are his property, whose workmanship they are, made to last during his, not another's pleasure: and being furnished with like faculties, sharing all in one community of nature, there cannot be supposed any such subordination among us, that may authorize us to destroy another, as if we were made for one another's uses, as the inferior ranks of creatures are for

"Of Civil Government," in THE WORKS OF JOHN LOCKE, *12th ed., Vol. IV (London, 1824).*

ours. Every one, as he is bound to preserve himself, and not to quit his station wilfully, so by the like reason, when his own preservation comes not in competition, ought he, as much as he can, to preserve the rest of mankind, and may not, unless it be to do justice to an offender, take away or impair the life, or what tends to the preservation of life, the liberty, health, limb, or goods of another.

And that all men may be restrained from invading others' rights, and from doing hurt to one another, and the law of nature be observed, which willeth the peace and preservation of all mankind, the execution of the law of nature is, in that state, put into every man's hands, whereby every one has a right to punish the transgressors of that law to such a degree as may hinder its violation: for the law of nature would, as all other laws that concern men in this world, be in vain, if there were nobody that in the state of nature had a power to execute that law, and thereby preserve the innocent and restrain offenders. And if any one in the state of nature may punish another for any evil he has done, every one may do so: for in that state of perfect equality, where naturally there is no superiority or jurisdiction of one over another, what any may do in prosecution of that law, every one must needs have a right to do.

And thus, in the state of nature, "one man comes by a power over another"; but yet no absolute or arbitrary power, to use a criminal, when he has got him in his hands, according to the passionate heats, or boundless extravagancy of his own will; but only to retribute to him, so far as calm reason and conscience dictate, what is proportionate to his transgression; which is so much as may serve for reparation and restraint: for these two are the only reasons, why one man may lawfully do harm to another, which is that we call punishment. In transgressing the law of nature, the offender declares himself to live by another rule than that of reason and common equity, which is that measure God has set to the actions of men, for their mutual security; and so he becomes dangerous to mankind, the tie, which is to secure them from injury and violence, being slighted and broken by him. Which being a trespass against the whole species, and the peace and safety of it, provided for by the law of nature; every man upon this score, by the right he hath to preserve mankind in general, may restrain, or, where it is necessary, destroy things noxious to them, and so may bring such evil on any one, who hath transgressed that law, as may make him repent the doing of it, and thereby deter him, and by his example others, from doing the like mischief. And in this case, and upon this ground, "every man hath a right to punish the offender, and be executioner of the law of nature."

. . .

Chapter III

OF THE STATE OF WAR

The state of war is a state of enmity and destruction: and therefore declaring by word or action, not a passionate and hasty, but a sedate settled design upon another man's life, puts him in a state of war with him against whom he has declared such an intention, and so has exposed his life to the other's power to be taken away by him, or any one that joins with him in his defence, and espouses his quarrel; it being reasonable and just, I should have a right to destroy that which threatens me with destruction; for, by the fundamental law of nature, man being to be preserved as much as possible, when all cannot be preserved, the safety of the innocent is to be preferred: and one may destroy a man who makes war upon him, or has discovered an enmity to his being, for the same reason that he may kill a wolf or a lion; because such men are not under the ties of the common law of reason, have no other rule, than that of force and violence, and so may be treated as beasts of prey, those dangerous and noxious creatures, that will be sure to destroy him whenever he falls into their power.

And hence it is, that he who attempts to get another man into his absolute power, does thereby put himself into a state of war with him; it being to be understood as a declaration of a design upon his life: for I have reason to conclude, that he who would get me into his power without my consent, would use me as he pleased when he got me there, and destroy me too when he had a fancy to it; for nobody can desire to have me in his absolute power, unless it be to compel me by force to that which is against the right of my freedom, *i.e.*, make me a slave. To be free from such force is the only security of my preservation; and reason bids me look on him, as an enemy to my preservation, who would take away that freedom which is the fence to it; so that he who makes an attempt to enslave me, thereby puts himself into a state of war with me. He that, in the state of nature, would take away the freedom that belongs to any one in that state, must necessarily be supposed to have a design to take away every thing else, that freedom being the foundation of all the rest; as he that, in the state of society, would take away the freedom belonging to those of that society or commonwealth, must be supposed to design to take away from them every thing else, and so be looked on as in a state of war.

This makes it lawful for a man to kill a thief, who has not in the least hurt him, nor declared any design upon his life, any farther than, by the use of force, so to get him in his power, as to take away his money, or what he pleases, from him; because using force, where he has no right, to get me into his power, let his pretence be what it will, I have no reason to suppose, that he, who would take away my liberty, would not, when he had me in his power, take away every thing else. And therefore it is lawful for me to treat him as one who has put himself into a state of war with me, *i.e.*, kill him if I can; for to that hazard does he justly expose himself, whoever introduces a state of war, and is aggressor in it.

And here we have the plain "difference between the state of nature and the state of war," which however some men have confounded, are as far distant, as a state of peace, good-will, mutual assistance and preservation, and a state of enmity, malice, violence and mutual destruction, are one from another. Men living together according to reason, without a common superiour on earth, with authority to judge between them, is properly the state of nature. But force, or a declared design of force, upon the person of another, where there is no common superiour on earth to appeal to for relief, is the state of war: and it is the want of such an appeal gives a man the right of war even against an aggressor, though he be in society and a fellow-subject.

. . .

Chapter IV

OF SLAVERY

The natural liberty of man is to be free from any superior power on earth, and not to be under the will or legislative authority of man, but to have only the law of nature for his rule. The liberty of man, in society, is to be under no other legislative power, but that established, by consent, in the commonwealth; nor under the dominion of any will, or restraint of any law, but what that legislative shall enact, according to the trust put in it. Freedom then is not what Sir Robert Filmer tells us, "a liberty for every one to do what he lists, to live as he pleases, and not to be tied by any laws": but freedom of men under government is, to have a standing rule to live by, common to every one of that society, and made by the legislative power erected in it; a liberty to follow my own will in all things, where the rule prescribes not; and not to be subject to the inconstant, uncertain, unknown, arbitrary will of another man: as freedom of nature is, to be under no other restraint but the law of nature.

This freedom from absolute, arbitrary power, is so necessary to, and closely joined with a man's preservation, that he cannot part with it, but by what forfeits his preservation and life together.

. . .

Chapter V

OF PROPERTY

. . .

God, who hath given the world to men in common, hath also given them reason to make use of it to the best advantage of life, and convenience. The earth, and all that is therein, is given to men for the support and comfort of their being. And though all the fruits it naturally produces, and beasts it feeds, belong to mankind in common, as they are produced by the spontaneous hand of nature; and nobody has originally a private dominion, exclusive of the rest of mankind, in any of them, as they are thus in their natural state; yet being given for the use of men, there must of necessity be a means to appropriate them some way or other, before they can be of any use, or at all beneficial to any particular man. The fruit, or venison, which nourishes the wild Indian, who knows no enclosure, and is still a tenant in common, must be his, and so his, *i.e.*, a part of him, that another can no longer have any right to it, before it can do him any good for the support of his life.

Though the earth, and all inferior creatures, be common to all men, yet every man has a property in his own person: this nobody has any right to but himself. The labour of his body, and the work of his hands, we may say, are properly his. Whatsoever then he removes out of the state that nature hath provided, and left it in, he hath mixed his labour with, and joined to it something that is his own, and thereby makes it his property. It being by him removed from the common state nature hath placed it in, it hath by this labour something annexed to it, that excludes the common right of other men. For this labour being the unquestionable property of the labourer, no man but he can have a right to what that is once joined to, at least where there is enough, and as good, left in common for others.

He that is nourished by the acorns he picked up under an oak, or the apples he gathered from the trees in the wood, has certainly appropriated them to himself. Nobody can deny but the nourishment is his. I ask then, when did they begin to be his? when he digested? or when he eat? or when he boiled? or when he brought them home? or when he picked them up? and it is plain, if the first gathering made them not his, nothing else could. That labour put a distinction between them and common: that added something to them more than nature, the common mother of all, had done; and so they became his private right. And will any one say he had no right to those acorns or apples he thus appropriated, because he had not the consent of all mankind to make them his? was it a robbery thus to assume to himself what belonged to all in common? If such a consent as that was necessary, man had starved, notwithstanding the plenty God had given him. We see in commons, which remain so by compact, that it is the taking any part of what is common, and removing it out of the state nature leaves it in, which begins the property; without which the common is of no use. And the taking of this or that part does not depend on the express consent of all the commoners. Thus the grass my horse has bit; the turfs my servant has cut; and the ore I have digged in any place, where I have a right to them in common with others, become my property, without the assignation or consent of any body. The labour that was mine, removing them out of that common state they were in, hath fixed my property in them.

. . .

It will perhaps be objected to this, that "if gathering the acorns, or other fruits of the earth, &c. makes a right to them, then any one may engross as much as he will." To which I answer, Not so. The same law of nature, that does by this means give us property, does also bound that property too. "God has given us all things richly," I Tim. vi. 17, is the voice of reason confirmed by inspiration. But how far has he given it us? To enjoy. As much as any one can make use of to any advantage of life before it spoils, so much he may by his labour fix a property in: whatever is beyond this, is more than his share, and belongs to others. Nothing was made by God for man to spoil or destroy. And thus, considering the plenty of natural provisions there was a long time in the world, and the few spenders; and to how small a part of that provision the industry of one man could extend itself, and engross it to the prejudice of others; especially keeping within the bounds, set by reason, of what might serve for his use; there could be then little room for quarrels or contentions about property so established.

But the chief matter of property being now not the fruits of the earth, and the beasts that subsist on it, but the earth itself; as that which takes in, and carries with it all the rest; I think it is plain, that property in that too is acquired as the former. As much land as a man tills, plants, improves, cultivates, and can use the product of, so much is his property. He by his labour does, as it were, enclose it from the common. Nor will it invalidate his right, to say every body else has an equal title to it, and therefore he cannot appropriate, he cannot enclose, without the consent of all his fellow commoners, all mankind. God, when he gave the world in common to all mankind, commanded man also to labour, and the penury of his condition required it of him. God and his reason commanded him to subdue the earth, *i.e.*, improve it for the benefit of life, and therein lay out something upon it that was his own, his labour. He that, in obedience to this command of God, subdued, tilled, and sowed any part of it, thereby annexed to it something that was his property, which another had no title to, nor could without injury take from him.

. . .

Nor is it so strange, as perhaps before consideration it may appear, that the property of labour should be able to over-balance the community of land: for it is labour indeed that put the difference of value on every thing; and let any one consider what the difference is between an acre of land planted with tobacco or sugar, sown with wheat or barley, and an acre of the same land lying in common, without any husbandry upon it, and he will find, that the improvement of labour makes the far greater part of the value. I think it will be but a very modest computation to say, that of the products of the earth useful to the life of man, nine-tenths are the effects of labour: nay, if we will rightly estimate things as they come to our use, and cast up the several expenses about them, what in them is purely owing to nature, and what to labour, we shall find, that in most of them ninety-nine hundredths are wholly to be put on the account of labour.

. . .

Chapter VII

OF POLITICAL OR CIVIL SOCIETY

. . .

Whenever . . . any number of men are so united into one society, as to quit everyone his executive power of the law of nature, and to resign it to the public, there and there only is a political, or civil society. And this is done, wherever any number of men, in the state of nature, enter into society to make one people, one body politic, under one supreme government; or else when any one joins himself to, and incorporates with any government already made: for hereby he authorizes the society, or, which is all one, the legislative thereof, to make laws for him, as the public good of the society shall require; to the execution whereof, his own assistance (as to his own degrees) is due. And this puts men out of a state of nature into that of a commonwealth, by setting up a judge on earth, with authority to determine all the controversies, and redress the injuries that may happen to any member of the commonwealth: which judge is the legislative, or magistrate appointed by it. And wherever there are any number of men, however associated, that have no such decisive power to appeal to, there they are still in the state of nature.

Hence it is evident, that absolute monarchy, which by some men is counted the only government in the world, is indeed inconsistent with civil society, and so can be no form of civil government at all; for the end of civil society being to avoid and remedy these inconveniencies of the state of nature, which necessarily follow from every man being judge in his own case, by setting up a known authority, to which every one of that society may appeal upon any injury received, or controversy that may arise, and which every one of the society ought to obey; wherever any persons are, who have not such an authority to appeal to for the decision of any difference between them, there those persons are still in the state of nature; and so is every absolute prince, in respect of those who are under his dominion.

For he being supposed to have all, both legislative and executive power in himself alone, there is no judge to be found, no appeal lies open to any one, who may fairly and indifferently, and with authority decide, and from whose decision relief and redress may be expected of any injury or inconveniency that may be suffered from the prince, or by his order: so that such a man, however intitled, czar, or grand seignior, or how you please, is as much in the state of nature, with all under his dominion, as he is with the rest of mankind: for wherever any two men are, who have no standing rule, and common judge to appeal to on earth, for the determination of controversies of right betwixt them, there they are still in the state of nature, and under all the inconveniencies of it, with only this woeful difference to the subject, or rather slave of an absolute prince; that whereas in the ordinary state of nature he has a liberty to judge of his right, and, according to the best of his power, to maintain it; now whenever his property is invaded by the will and order of his monarch, he has not only no appeal, as those in society ought to have, but, as if he were degraded from the common state of rational creatures, is denied a liberty to judge of, or to defend his right; and so is exposed to all the misery and inconveniencies, that a man can fear from one, who being in the unrestrained state of nature, is yet corrupted with flattery, and armed with power.

For he that thinks absolute power purifies men's blood, and corrects the baseness of human nature, need read but the history of this or any other age, to be convinced of the contrary.

. . .

Chapter VIII

OF THE BEGINNING OF POLITICAL SOCIETIES

Men being, as has been said, by nature, all free, equal, and independent, no one can be put out of this estate, and subjected to the political power of another, without his own consent. The only way, whereby any one divests himself of his natural liberty, and puts on the bonds of civil society, is by agreeing with other men to join and unite into a community, for their comfortable, safe, and peaceable living one amongst another, in a secure enjoyment of their properties, and a greater security against any, that are not of it. This any number of men may do, because it injures not the freedom of the rest; they are left as they were in the liberty of the state of nature. When any number of men have so consented to make one community or government, they are thereby presently incorporated, and make one body politic, wherein the majority have a right to act and conclude the rest.

For when any number of men have, by the consent of every individual, made a community, they have thereby made that community one body, with a power to act as one body, which is only by the will and determination of the majority: for that which acts any community, being only the consent of the individuals of it, and it being necessary to that which is one body to move one way; it is necessary the body should move that way whither the greater force carries it, which is the consent of the majority: or else it is impossible it should act or continue one body, one community, which the consent of every individual that united into it, agreed that it should; and so every one is bound by that consent to be concluded by the majority. And therefore we see, that in assemblies, impowered to act by positive laws, where no number is set by that positive law which impowers them, the act of the majority passes for the act of the whole, and of course determines; as having, by the law of nature and reason, the power of the whole.

And thus every man, by consenting with others to make one body politic under one government, puts himself under an obligation, to every one of that society, to submit to the determination of the majority, and to be concluded by it; or else this original compact, whereby he with others incorporate into one society, would signify nothing, and be no compact, if he be left free, and under no other ties than he was in before in the state of nature.

. . .

Chapter IX

OF THE ENDS OF POLITICAL SOCIETY AND GOVERNMENT

If man in the state of nature be so free, as has been said; if he be absolute lord of his own person and possessions, equal to the greatest, and subject to nobody, why will he part with his freedom? why will he give up his empire, and subject himself to the dominion and control of any other power? To which it is obvious to answer, that though in the state of nature he hath such a right, yet the enjoyment of it is very uncertain, and constantly exposed to the invasion of others; for all being kings as much as he, every man his equal, and the greater part no strict observers of equity and justice, the enjoyment of the property he has in this state is very unsafe, very unsecure. This makes him willing to quit a condition, which, however free, is full of fears and continual dangers: and it is not without reason, that he seeks out, and is willing to join in society with others, who are already united, or have a mind to unite, for the mutual preservation of their lives, liberties, and estates, which I call by the general name, property.

The great and chief end, therefore, of men's uniting into commonwealths, and putting themselves under government, is the preservation of their property. To which in the state of nature there are many things wanting.

First, There wants an established, settled, known law, received and allowed by common consent to be the standard of right and wrong, and the common measure to decide all controversies between them: for though the law of nature be plain and intelligible to all rational creatures; yet men being biassed by their interest, as well as ignorant for want of studying it, are not apt to allow of it as a law binding to them in the application of it to their particular cases.

Secondly, In the state of nature there wants a known and indifferent judge, with authority to determine all differences according to the established law: for every one in that state being both judge and executioner of the law of nature, men being partial to themselves, passion and revenge is very apt to carry them too far, and with too much heat, in their own cases; as well as negligence, and unconcernedness, to make them too remiss in other men's.

Thirdly, In the state of nature, there often wants power to back and support the sentence when right, and to give it due execution. They who by any injustice offend, will seldom fail, where they are able, by force to make good their injustice; such resistance many times makes the punishment dangerous, and frequently destructive, to those who attempt it.

Thus mankind, notwithstanding all the privileges of the state of nature, being but in an ill condition, while they remain in it, are quickly driven into society. Hence it comes to pass that we seldom find any number of men live any time together in this state. The inconveniencies that they are therein exposed to, by the irregular and uncertain exercise of the power every man has of punishing the transgressions of others, make them take sanctuary under the established laws of government, and therein seek the preservation of their property. It is this makes them so willingly give up every one his single power of punishing, to be exercised by such alone, as shall be appointed to it amongst them; and by such rules as the community, or those authorized by them to that purpose, shall agree on. And in this we have the original right of both the legislative and executive power, as well as of the governments and societies themselves.

. . .

But though men, when they enter into society, give up the equality, liberty, and executive power they had in the state of nature, into the hands of the society, to be so far disposed of by the legislative, as the good of the society shall require; yet it being only with an intention in every one the better to preserve himself, his liberty and property; (for no rational creature can be supposed to change his condition with an intention to be worse) the power of the society, or legislative constituted by them, can never be supposed to extend farther, than the common good; but is obliged to secure every one's property, by providing against those three defects above mentioned, that made the state of nature so unsafe and uneasy. And so whoever has the legislative or supreme power of any commonwealth, is bound to govern by established standing laws, promulgated and known to the people, and not by extemporary decrees; by indifferent and upright judges, who are to decide controversies by those laws; and to employ the force of the community at home, only in the execution of such laws; or abroad to prevent or redress foreign injuries, and secure the community from inroads and invasion. And all this to be directed to no other end, but the peace, safety, and public good of the people.

. . .

Chapter XIII

OF THE SUBORDINATION OF THE POWERS OF THE COMMONWEALTH

Though in a constituted commonwealth, standing upon its own basis, and acting according to its own nature, that is, acting for the preservation of the community, there can be but one supreme power, which is the legislative, to which all the rest are and must be subordinate; yet the legislative being only a fiduciary power to act for certain ends, there remains still "in the people a supreme power to remove or alter the legislative," when they find the legislative act contrary to the trust reposed in them: for all power given with trust for the attaining an end, being limited by that end; whenever that end is manifestly neglected or opposed, the trust must necessarily be forfeited, and the power devolve into the hands of those that gave it, who may place it anew where they shall think best for their safety and security. And thus the community perpetually retains a supreme power of saving themselves from the attempts and designs of any body, even of their legislators, whenever they shall be so foolish, or so wicked, as to try and carry on designs against the liberties and properties of the subject: for no man, or society of men, having a power to deliver up their preservation, or consequently the means of it, to the absolute will and arbitrary dominion of another; whenever any one shall go about to bring them into such a slavish condition, they will always have a right to preserve what they have not a power to part with; and to rid themselves of those who invade this fundamental, sacred, and unalterable law of self-preservation, for which they entered into society. And thus the community may be said in this respect to be always the supreme power.

. . .

Chapter XIX

OF THE DISSOLUTION OF GOVERNMENT

. . .

The reason why men enter into society, is the preservation of their property; and the end why they choose and authorize a legislative, is, that there may be laws made, and rules set, as guards and fences to the properties of all the members of the society: to limit the power, and moderate the dominion, of every part and member of the society: for since it can never be supposed to be the will of the society, that the legislative should have a power to destroy that which every one designs to secure by entering into society, and for which the people submitted themselves to legislators of their own making; whenever the legislators endeavour to take away and destroy the property of the people, or to reduce them to slavery under arbitrary power, they put themselves into a state of war with the people, who are thereupon absolved from any farther obedience, and are left to the common refuge, which God hath provided for all men, against force and violence. Whensoever therefore the legislative shall transgress this fundamental rule of society; and either by ambition, fear, folly or corruption, endeavour to grasp themselves, or put into the hands of any other, an absolute power over the lives, liberties, and estates of the people; by this breach of trust they forfeit the power the people had put into their hands for quite contrary ends, and it devolves to the people, who have a right to resume their original liberty, and, by the establishment of a new legislative, (such as they shall think fit) provide for their own safety and security, which is the end for which they are in society. What I have said here, concerning the legislative in general, holds true also concerning the supreme executor, who having a double trust put in him, both to have a part in the legislative, and the supreme execution of the law, acts against both, when he goes about to set up his own arbitrary will as the law of the society. He acts also contrary to his trust, when he either employs the force, treasure, and offices of the society to corrupt the representatives, and gain them to his purposes; or openly pre-engages the electors, and prescribes to their choice, such, whom he has, by solicitations, threats, promises, or otherwise, won to his designs: and employs them to bring in such, who have promised beforehand what to vote, and what to enact. Thus to regulate candidates and electors, and new-model the ways of election, what is it but to cut up the government by the roots, and poison the very fountain of public security?

. . .

But it will be said, this hypothesis lays a ferment for frequent rebellion. To which I answer,

First, no more than any other hypothesis: for when the people are made miserable, and find themselves exposed to the ill-usage of arbitrary power, cry up their governors as much as you will, for sons of Jupiter; let them be sacred or divine, descended, or authorized from heaven; give them out for whom or what you please, the same will happen. The people generally ill-treated, and contrary to right, will be ready upon any occasion to ease themselves of a burden that sits heavy upon them. They will wish, and seek for the opportunity, which in the change, weakness, and accidents of human affairs, seldom delays long to offer itself. He must have lived but a little while in the world, who has not seen examples of this in his time; and he must have read very little, who cannot produce examples of it in all sorts of governments in the world.

Secondly, I answer, such revolutions happen not upon every little mismanagement in public affairs. Great mistakes in the ruling part, many wrong and inconvenient laws, and all the slips of human frailty, will be borne by the people without mutiny or murmur. But if a long train of abuses, prevarications and artifices, all tending the same way, make the design visible to the people, and they cannot but feel what they lie under, and see whither they are going; it is not to be wondered, that they should then rouse themselves, and endeavour to put the rule into such hands which may secure to them the ends for which government was at first erected; and without which, ancient names, and specious forms, are so far from being better, that they are much worse, than the state of nature, or pure anarchy; the inconveniencies being all as great and as near, but the remedy farther off and more difficult.

Thirdly, I answer, that this doctrine of a power in the people of providing for their safety anew, by a new legislative, when their legislators have acted contrary to their trust, by invading their property, is the best fence against rebellion, and the probablest means to hinder it: for rebellion being an opposition, not to persons, but authority, which is founded only in the constitutions and laws of the government; those, whoever they be, who by force break through, and by force justify their violation of them, are truly and properly rebels: for when men, by entering into society and civil government, have excluded force, and introduced laws for the preservation of property, peace, and unity amongst themselves; those who set up force again in opposition to the laws, do *rebellare,* that is, bring back again the state of war, and are properly rebels; which they who are in power, (by the pretence they have to authority, the temptation of force they have in their hands, and the flattery of those about them) being likeliest to do; the properest way to prevent the evil, is to show them the danger and injustice of it, who are under the greatest temptation to run into it.

In both the forementioned cases, when either the legislative is changed, or the legislators act contrary to the end for which they were constituted, those who are guilty are guilty of rebellion; for if any one by force takes away the established legislative of any society, and the laws by them made pursuant to their trust, he thereby takes away the umpirage, which every one had consented to, for a peaceable decision of all their controversies, and a bar to the state of war amongst them. They who remove, or change the legislative, take away this decisive power, which nobody can have but by the appointment and consent of the people; and so destroying the authority which the people did, and nobody else can set up, and introducing a power which the people hath not authorized, they actually introduce a state of war, which is that of force without authority; and thus by removing the legislative established by the society, (in whose decisions the people acquiesced and united, as to that of their own will) they untie the knot, and expose the people anew to the state of war. And if those, who by force take away the legislative, are rebels, the legislators themselves, as has been shown, can be no less esteemed so; when they, who were set up for the protection and preservation of the people, their liberties and properties, shall by force invade and endeavour to take them away; and so they putting themselves into a state of war with those who made them the protectors and guardians of their peace, are properly, and with the greatest aggravation, *rebellantes,* rebels.

But if they, who say, "it lays a foundation for rebellion," mean that it may occasion civil wars, or intestine broils, to tell the people they are absolved from obedience when illegal attempts are made upon their liberties or properties, and may oppose the unlawful violence of those who were their magistrates, when they invade their properties contrary to the trust put in them; and that therefore this doctrine is not to be allowed, being so destructive to the peace of the world: they may as well say, upon the same ground, that honest men may not oppose robbers or pirates, because this may occasion disorder or bloodshed. If any mischief come in such cases, it is not to be charged upon him who defends his own right, but on him that invades his neighbour's. If the innocent honest man must quietly quit all he has, for peace sake, to him who will lay violent hands upon it, I desire it may be considered, what a kind of peace there will be in the world, which consists only in violence and rapine; and which is to be maintained only for the benefit of robbers and oppressors.

. . .

Whosoever uses force without right, as every one does in society, who does it without law, puts himself into a state of war with those against whom he so used it; and in that state all former ties are cancelled, all other rights cease, and every one has a right to defend himself, and to resist the aggressor.

An Essay Concerning Human Understanding

. . .

NO INNATE PRINCIPLES IN THE MIND

It is an established opinion amongst some men, that there are in the understanding certain innate principles; some primary notions, characters, as it were, stamped upon the mind of man, which the soul receives in its very first being; and brings into the world with it. It would be sufficient to convince unprejudiced readers of the falseness of this supposition, if I should only shew (as I hope I shall in the following parts of this discourse) how men, barely by the use of their natural faculties, may attain to all the knowledge they have, without the help of any innate impressions; and may arrive at certainty, without any such original notions or principles. For I imagine any one will easily grant, that it would be impertinent to suppose, the ideas of colours innate in a creature, to whom God hath given sight, and a power to receive them by the eyes, from external objects: and no less unreasonable would it be to attribute several truths to the impressions of nature, and innate characters, when we may observe in ourselves faculties, fit to attain as easy and certain knowledge of them, as if they were originally imprinted on the mind.

But because a man is not permitted without censure to follow his own thoughts in the search of truth, when they lead him ever so little out of the common road; I shall set down the reasons, that made me doubt of the truth of that opinion, as an excuse for my mistake, if I be in one; which I leave to be considered by those, who, with me, dispose themselves to embrace truth, wherever they find it.

There is nothing more commonly taken for granted, than that there are certain principles, both speculative and practical (for they speak of both) universally agreed upon by all mankind: which therefore, they argue, must needs be constant impressions, which the souls of men receive in their first beings, and which they bring into the world with them, as necessarily and really as they do any of their inherent faculties.

This argument, drawn from universal consent, has this misfortune in it, that if it were true in matter of fact, that there were certain truths, wherein all mankind agreed, it would not prove them innate, if there can be any other way shewn, how men may come to that universal agreement, in the things they do consent in; which I presume may be done.

But, which is worse, this argument of universal consent, which is made use of to prove innate principles, seems to me a demonstration that there are none such; because there are none to which all mankind give an universal assent. I shall begin with the speculative, and instance in those magnified principles of demonstration; "whatsoever is, is"; and, "it is impossible for the same thing to be, and not to be"; which, of all others, I think have the most allowed title to innate. These have so settled a reputation of maxims universally received, that it will, no doubt, be thought strange, if any one should seem to question it. But yet I take liberty to say, that these propo-

John Locke, AN ESSAY CONCERNING HUMAN UNDERSTANDING, *21st ed. (London, 1805).*

sitions are so far from having an universal assent, that there are great part of mankind to whom they are not so much as known.

For, first, it is evident, that all children and idiots have not the least apprehension or thought of them; and the want of that is enough to destroy that universal assent, which must needs be the necessary concomitant of all innate truths: it seeming to me near a contradiction, to say, that there are truths imprinted on the soul, which it perceives or understands not: imprinting, if it signify any thing, being nothing else, but the making certain truths to be perceived. For to imprint any thing on the mind, without the mind's perceiving it, seems to me hardly intelligible. If therefore children and idiots have souls, have minds, with those impressions upon them, they must unavoidably perceive them, and necessarily know and assent to these truths; which since they do not, it is evident that there are no such impressions. For if they are not notions naturally imprinted, how can they be innate? and if they are notions imprinted, how can they be unknown? To say a notion is imprinted on the mind, and yet at the same time to say, that the mind is ignorant of it, and never yet took notice of it, is to make this impression nothing. No proposition can be said to be in the mind, which it never yet knew, which it was never yet conscious of. For if any one may, then, by the same reason, all propositions that are true, and the mind is capable of ever assenting to, may be said to be in the mind, and to be imprinted: since, if any one can be said to be in the mind, which it never yet knew, it must be only, because it is capable of knowing it, and so the mind is of all truths it ever shall know. Nay, thus truths may be imprinted on the mind, which it never did, nor ever shall know: for a man may live long, and die at last in ignorance of many truths, which his mind was capable of knowing, and that with certainty. So that if the capacity of knowing, be the natural impression contended for, all the truths a man ever comes to know, will, by this account, be every one of them innate; and this great point will amount to no more, but only to a very improper way of speaking; which, whilst it pretends to assert the contrary, says nothing different from those, who deny innate principles. For nobody, I think, ever denied that the mind was capable of knowing several truths. The capacity, they say, is innate, the knowledge acquired. But then to what end such contest for certain innate maxims? If truths can be imprinted on the understanding without being perceived, I can see no difference there can be, between any truths the mind is capable of knowing, in respect of their original: they must all be innate, or all adventitious: in vain shall a man go about to distinguish them. He therefore, that talks of innate notions of the understanding, cannot (if he intend thereby any distinct sort of truths) mean such truths to be in the understanding, as it never perceived, and is yet wholly ignorant of. For if these words (to be in the understanding) have any propriety, they signify to be understood: so that, to be in the understanding, and not to be understood; to be in the mind, and never to be perceived; is all one, as to say, any thing is, and is not, in the mind or understanding. If therefore these two propositions, "whatsoever is, is"; and "it is impossible for the same thing to be, and not to be," are by nature imprinted, children cannot be ignorant of them; infants, and all that have souls, must necessarily have them in their understandings, know the truth of them, and assent to it.

To avoid this, it is usually answered, That all men know and assent to them, when they come to the use of reason, and this is enough to prove them innate. I answer,

Doubtful expressions, that have scarce any signification, go for clear reasons, to those, who being prepossessed, take not the pains to examine, even what they themselves say. For to apply this answer with any tolerable sense to our present purpose, it must signify one of these two things; either, that, as soon as men come to the use of reason, these supposed native inscriptions come to be known, and observed by them: or else, that the use and exercise of men's reason assists them in the discovery of these principles, and certainly makes them known to them.

If they mean, that by the use of reason men may discover these principles; and that this is sufficient to prove them innate: their way of arguing will stand thus, *viz.*, that whatever truths reason can certainly discover to us, and make us firmly assent to, those are all naturally imprinted on the mind: since that universal assent, which is made the mark of them, amounts to no more but this; that by the use of reason, we are capable to come to a certain knowledge of, and assent to them; and, by this means, there will be no difference between the maxims of the mathematicians, and theorems they deduce from them. All must be equally allowed innate; they being all discoveries made by the use of reason, and truths that a rational creature may certainly come to know, if he apply his thoughts rightly that way.

But how can these men think the use of reason necessary, to discover principles that are supposed innate, when reason (if we may believe them) is nothing else but the faculty of deducing unknown truths from principles, or propositions, that are already known? That certainly can never be thought innate, which we have need of reason to discover; unless, as I have said, we will have all the certain truths, that reason ever teaches us, to be innate. We may as well think the use of reason necessary to make our eyes discover visible objects, as that there should be need of reason, or the exercise thereof, to make the understanding see what is originally engraven on it, and cannot be in the understanding before it be perceived by it. So that to make reason discover those truths thus imprinted, is to say, that the use of reason discovers to a man what he knew before: and if men have those innate impressed truths originally, and before the use of reason, and yet are always ignorant of them, till they come to the use of reason; it is in effect to say, that men know, and know them not, at the same time.

. . .

I

OF IDEALS IN GENERAL, AND THEIR ORIGIN

Every man being conscious to himself that he thinks, and that which his mind is applied about, whilst thinking, being the ideas that are there, it is past doubt, that men have in their minds several ideas, such as are those expressed by the words, Whiteness, Hardness, Sweetness, Thinking, Motion, Man, Elephant, Army, Drunkenness, and others. It is in the first place then to be inquired, how he comes by them. I know it is a received doctrine, that men have native ideas, and original characters, stamped upon their minds, in their very first being. This opinion I have, at large, examined already; and, I suppose, what I have said, in the foregoing book, will be much more easily admitted, when I have shown, whence the understanding may get all the ideas it has, and by what ways and degrees they may come into the mind; for which I shall appeal to every one's own observation and experience.

Let us then suppose the mind to be, as we say, white paper, void of all characters, without any ideas; how comes it to be furnished? Whence comes it by that vast store which the busy and boundless fancy of man has painted on it, with an almost endless variety? Whence has it all the materials of reason and knowledge? To this I answer, in one word, from experience; in that all our knowledge is founded, and from that it ultimately derives itself. Our observation employed either about external sensible objects, or about the internal operations of our minds, perceived and reflected on by ourselves, is that which supplies our understandings with all the materials of thinking. These two are the fountains of knowledge, from whence all the ideas we have, or can naturally have, do spring.

First, Our senses, conversant about particular sensible objects, do convey into the mind several distinct perceptions of things, according to those various ways wherein those objects do affect them: and thus we come by those ideas we have, of Yellow, White, Heat, Cold, Soft, Hard, Bitter, Sweet, and all those which we call sensible qualities; which when I say the senses convey into the mind, I mean, they from external objects convey into the mind what produces there those perceptions. This great source of most of the ideas we have, depending wholly upon our senses, and derived by them to the understanding, I call *sensation*.

Secondly, The other fountain, from which experience furnisheth the understanding with ideas, is the perception of the operations of our own mind within us, as it is employed about the ideas it has got; which operations when the soul comes to reflect on and consider, do furnish the understanding with another set of ideas, which could not be had from things without; and such are Perception, Thinking, Doubting, Believing, Reasoning, Knowing, Willing, and all the different actings of our own minds; which we being conscious of and observing in ourselves, do from these receive into our understandings as distinct ideas, as we do from bodies affecting our senses. This source of ideas every man has wholly in himself; and though it be not sense, as having nothing to do with external objects, yet it is very like it, and might properly enough be called internal sense. But as I call the other sensation, so I call this *reflection*, the ideas it affords being such only as the mind gets by reflecting on its own operations within itself. By reflection then, in the following part of this discourse, I would be understood to mean that notice which the mind takes of its own operations, and the manner of them; by reason whereof there come to be ideas of these operations in the understanding. These two, I say, *viz.*, external material things, as the objects of sensation; and the operations of our own minds within, as the objects of reflection; are to me the only originals from whence all our ideas take their beginnings. The term operations here I use in a large sense, as comprehending not barely the actions of the mind about its ideas, but some sort of passions arising sometimes from them, such as is the satisfaction or uneasiness arising from any thought.

The understanding seems to me not to have the least glimmering of any ideas, which it doth not receive from one of these two. External objects furnish the mind with the ideas of sensible qualities, which are all those different perceptions they produce in us: and the mind furnishes the understanding with ideas of its own operations.

These, when we have taken a full survey of them and their several modes, combinations, and relations, we shall find to contain all our whole stock of ideas; and that we have nothing in our minds which did not come in one of these two ways. Let any one examine his own thoughts, and thoroughly search into his understanding; and then let him tell me, whether all the original ideas he has there, are any other than of the objects of his senses, or of the operations of his mind, considered as objects of his reflection: and how great a mass of knowledge soever he imagines to be lodged there, he will, upon taking a strict view, see that he has not any idea in his mind, but what one of these two have imprinted; though perhaps, with infinite variety compounded and enlarged by the understanding, as we shall see hereafter.

. . .

OF OUR COMPLEX IDEAS OF SUBSTANCES

The mind being, as I have declared, furnished with a great number of the simple ideas, conveyed in by the senses, as they are found in exterior things, or by reflection on its own operations, takes notice also, that a certain number of these simple ideas go constantly together; which being presumed to belong to one thing, and words being suited to common apprehensions, and made use of for quick dispatch, are called, so united in one subject, by one name: which, by inadvertency, we are apt afterward to talk of, and consider as one simple idea, which indeed is a complication of many ideas together: because, as I have said, not imagining how these simple ideas can subsist by themselves, we accustom ourselves to suppose some substratum wherein they do subsist, and from which they do result; which therefore we call substance.

So that if any one will examine himself concerning his notion of pure substance in general, he will find he has no other idea of it at all, but only a supposition of he knows not what support of such qualities, which are capable of producing simple ideas in us; which qualities are commonly called accidents. If any one should be asked, what is the subject wherein colour or weight inheres, he would have nothing to say, but the solid extended parts: and if he were demanded, what is it that solidity and extension adhere in, he would not be in a much better case than the Indian before-mentioned, who, saying that the world was supported by a great elephant, was asked what the elephant rested on; to which his answer was, a great tortoise. But being again pressed to know what gave support to the broad-backed tortoise, replied, something, he knew not what. And thus here, as in all other cases where we use words without having clear and distinct ideas, we talk like children; who being questioned what such a thing is, which they know not, readily give this satisfactory answer, that it is something; which in truth signifies no more when so used either by children or men, but that they know not what; and that the thing they pretend to know and talk of, is what they have no distinct idea of at all, and so are perfectly ignorant of it, and in the dark. The idea then we have, to which we give the general name substance, being nothing but the supposed, but unknown support of those qualities we find existing, which we imagine cannot subsist, "sine re substante," without something to support them, we call that support substantia; which, according to the true import of the word, is in plain English, standing under or upholding.

An obscure and relative idea of substance in general being thus made, we come to have the ideas of particular sorts of substances, by collecting such combinations of simple ideas, as are by experience and observation of men's senses taken notice of to exist together, and are therefore supposed to flow from the particular internal constitution, or unknown essence of that substance. Thus we come to have the ideas of a man, horse, gold, water, etc., of which substances, whether any one has any other clear idea, farther than of certain simple ideas co-existent together, I appeal to every man's own experience. It is the ordinary qualities observable in iron, or a diamond, put together, that make the true complex idea of those substances, which a smith or a jeweller commonly knows better than a philosopher; who, whatever substantial forms he may talk of, has no other idea of those substances, than what is framed by a collection of those simple ideas which are to be found in them; only we must take notice, that our complex ideas of substances, besides all those simple ideas they are made up of, have always the confused idea of something to which they belong, and in which they subsist. And therefore when we speak of any sort of substance, we say it is a thing having such or such qualities; as body is a thing that is extended, figured, and capable of motion; spirit, a thing capable of thinking; and so hardness, friability, and power to draw iron, we say, are qualities to be found in a loadstone. These, and the like fashions of speaking, intimate, that the substance is supposed always something besides the extension, figure, solidity, motion, thinking, or other observable ideas, though we know not what it is.

Hence, when we talk or think of any particular sort of corporeal substances, as horse, stone, etc., though the idea we have of either of them be but the complication or collection of those several simple ideas of sensible qualities, which we used to find united in the thing called horse or stone; yet because we cannot conceive how they should subsist alone, or one in another, we suppose them existing in and supported by some common subject; which support we denote by the name substance, though it be certain we have no clear or distinct idea of that thing we suppose a support.

VOLTAIRE

"Ecrasez l'infâme," insisted Voltaire, in his ceaseless efforts to "crush the infamous thing" (the Church), which he felt was obstructing man's progress to a better world. Only when his pen was stilled by his death in 1778 at the age of eighty-three did he rest from his attack. An indefatigable and sparkling letter-writer, an inexhaustible but poor playwright, an indifferent but ardent poet, a devoted but unhistorical historian, and, above all, a superb and tireless propagandist, Voltaire used every method at his command to point up his conviction that the Church (or any organized religious body) had destroyed or was preventing the progress of mankind by hampering, through censorship and superstition, the activities of human reason. If left free to roam and investigate at will, human reason, Voltaire believed, could discover the natural laws of society, just as it had discerned the natural laws of the physical universe through the intellect and endeavors of Isaac Newton.

The first of the following selections is a rather random sampling from Voltaire's Philosophical Dictionary, *first published in 1764 and later expanded. The second is an excerpt from* Candide, *a sparkling, witty satire on the manners and mores of the Western world in the eighteenth century.*

Philosophical Dictionary

Atheism

. . .

MODERN ATHEISTS. ARGUMENTS OF THE WORSHIPPERS OF GOD

We are intelligent beings, and intelligent beings cannot have been formed by a blind, brute, insensible being; there is certainly some difference between a clod and the ideas of Newton. Newton's intelligence, then, came from some other intelligence.

When we see a fine machine, we say there is a good machinist, and that he has an excellent understanding. The world is assuredly an admirable machine; therefore there is in the world, somewhere or other, an admirable intelligence. This argument is old, but is not therefore the worse.

All animated bodies are composed of levers and pulleys, which act according to the laws of mechanics; of liquors, which are kept in perpetual circulation by the laws of hydrostatics; and the reflection that all these beings have sentiment which has no relation to their organization, fills us with wonder.

The motions of the stars, that of our little earth round the sun—all are operated according to the laws of the profoundest mathematics. How could it be that Plato, who knew not one of these laws—the eloquent but chimerical Plato, who said that the foundation of the earth was an equilateral triangle—the strange Plato, who said there could be but five worlds, because there were but five regular bodies—how, I say, was it that Plato, who was not even acquainted with spherical trigonometry, had nevertheless so fine a genius, so happy an instinct, as to call God the Eternal Geometrician—to feel that there exists a forming Intelligence? Spinoza himself confesses it. It is impossible to controvert this truth, which surrounds us and presses us on all sides.

ARGUMENT OF THE ATHEISTS

I have, however, known refractory individuals, who have said that there is no forming intelligence, and that motion alone has formed all that we see and all that we are. They say boldly that the combination of this universe was possible because it exists; therefore it was possible for motion of itself to arrange it. Take four planets only—Mars, Venus, Mercury, and the Earth; let us consider them solely in the situations in which they now are; and let us see how many probabilities we have that motion will bring them again to those respective places. There are but twenty-four chances in this combination; that is, it is only twenty-four to one that these planets will not be found in the same situations with respect to one another. To these four globes add that of Jupiter; and it is then only a hundred and twenty to one that Jupiter, Mars, Venus, Mercury, and our globe will not be placed in the same positions in which we now see them.

Lastly, add Saturn; and there will then be only seven hundred and twenty chances to one against putting these planets in their present arrangement, according to their given distances. It is, then, demonstrated that once, at least, in seven hun-

THE WORKS OF VOLTAIRE, *trans.* T. *Smollett (Paris, 1901).*

dred and twenty cases, chance might place these planets in their present order.

Then take all the secondary planets, all their motions, all the beings that vegetate, live, feel, think, act, on all these globes; you have only to increase the number of chances; multiply this number to all eternity—to what our weakness calls *infinity*—there will still be a unit in favor of the formation of the world, such as it is, by motion alone; therefore it is possible that, in all eternity, the motion of matter alone has produced the universe as it exists. Nay, this combination must, in eternity, of necessity happen. Thus, say they, not only it is possible that the world is as it is by motion alone, but it was impossible that it should not be so after infinite combinations.

Answer. All this supposition seems to me to be prodigiously chimerical, for two reasons: the first is, that in this universe there are intelligent beings, and you cannot prove it possible for motion alone to produce understanding. The second is, that, by your own confession, the chances are infinity to unity, that an intelligent forming cause produced the universe. Standing alone against infinity, a unit makes but a poor figure.

Again Spinoza himself admits this intelligence; it is the basis of his system. You have not read him, but you must read him. Why would you go further than he, and, through a foolish pride, plunge into the abyss where Spinoza dared not to descend? Are you not aware of the extreme folly of saying that it is owing to a blind cause that the square of the revolution of one planet is always to the squares of the others as the cube of its distance is to the cubes of the distances of the others from the common centre? Either the planets are great geometricians, or the Eternal Geometrician has arranged the planets.

But where is the Eternal Geometrician? Is He in one place, or in all places, without occupying space? I know not. Has He arranged all things of His own substance? I know not. Is He immense, without quantity and without quality? I know not. All I know is, that we must adore Him and be just.

NEW OBJECTION OF A MODERN ATHEIST

Can it be said that the conformation of animals is according to their necessities? What are those necessities? Self-preservation and propagation. Now, is it astonishing that, of the infinite combinations produced by chance, those only have survived which had organs adapted for their nourishment and the continuation of their species? Must not all others necessarily have perished?

Answer. This argument, taken from Lucretius, is sufficiently refuted by the sensation given to animals and the intelligence given to man. How, as has just been said in the preceding paragraph, should combinations produced by chance produce this sensation and this intelligence? Yes, doubtless, the members of animals are made for all their necessities with an incomprehensible art, and you have not the boldness to deny it. You do not mention it. You feel that you can say nothing in answer to this great argument which Nature brings against you. The disposition of the wing of a fly, or of the feelers of a snail, is sufficient to confound you.

AN OBJECTION OF MAUPERTUIS

The natural philosophers of modern times have done nothing more than extend these pretended arguments; this they have sometimes done even to minuteness and indecency. They have found God in the folds of a rhinoceros's hide; they might, with equal reason, have denied His existence on account of the tortoise's shell.

Answer. What reasoning! The tortoise and the rhinoceros, and all the different species, prove alike in their infinite varieties the same cause, the same design, the same end, which are preservation, generation, and death. Unity is found in this immense variety; the hide and the shell bear equal testimony. What! deny God, because a shell is not like a skin! And journalists have lavished upon this coxcombry praises which they have withheld from Newton and Locke, both worshippers of the Divinity from thorough examination and conviction!

ANOTHER OF MAUPERTUIS'S OBJECTIONS

Of what service are beauty and fitness in the construction of a serpent? Perhaps, you say, it has uses of which we are ignorant. Let us then, at least, be silent, and not admire an animal which we know only by the mischief it does.

Answer. Be you silent, also, since you know no more of its utility than myself; or acknowledge that, in reptiles, everything is admirably proportioned. Some of them are venomous; you have been so too. The only subject at present under consideration is the prodigious art which has formed serpents, quadrupeds, birds, fishes, and bipeds. This art is evident enough. You ask, Why is not the serpent harmless? And why have you not been harmless? Why have you been a persecutor? which, in a philosopher, is the greatest of crimes. This is quite another question; it is that of physical and moral evil. It has long been asked, Why are there so many serpents, and so many wicked men worse than serpents? If flies could reason, they would complain to God of the existence of spiders; but they would, at the same time, acknowledge what Minerva confessed to Arachne in the fable, that they arrange their webs in a wonderful manner.

We cannot, then, do otherwise than acknowledge an ineffable Intelligence, which Spinoza himself admitted. We must own that it is displayed as much in the meanest insect as in the planets. And with regard to moral and physical evil, what can be done or said? Let us console ourselves by the enjoyment of physical and moral good, and adore the Eternal Being, who has ordained the one and permitted the other.

One word more on this topic. Atheism is the vice of some intelligent men, and superstition is the vice of fools. And what is the vice of knaves?—Hypocrisy.

. . .

Chain or Generation of Events

The present, we say, is pregnant with the future; events are linked one with another by an invincible fatality. This is the fate which, in Homer, is superior to Jupiter himself. The master of gods and men expressly declares that he cannot prevent his son Sarpedon from dying at the time appointed. Sarpedon was born at the moment when it was necessary that he should be born, and could not be born at any other; he could not die elsewhere than before Troy; he could not be buried elsewhere than in Lycia; his body must, in the appointed time, produce vegetables, which must change into the substance of some of the Lycians; his heirs must establish a new order of things in his states; that new order must influence neighboring kingdoms, thence must result a new arrangement in war and in peace with the neighbors of Lycia. So that, from link to link, the destiny of the whole earth depended on the elopement of Helen, which had a necessary connection with the marriage of Hecuba, which, ascending to higher events, was connected with the origin of things.

Had any one of these occurrences been ordered otherwise, the result would have been a different universe. Now, it was not possible for the actual universe not to exist; therefore it was not possible for Jupiter, Jove as he was, to save the life of his son. We are told that this doctrine of necessity and fatality has been invented in our own times by Leibnitz, under the name of sufficing reason. It is, however, of great antiquity. It is no recent discovery that there is no effect without a cause and that often the smallest cause produces the greatest effects.

Lord Bolingbroke acknowledges that he was indebted to the petty quarrels between the duchess of Marlborough and Mrs. Masham for an opportunity of concluding the private treaty between Queen Anne and Louis XIV. This treaty led to the peace of Utrecht; the peace of Utrecht secured the throne of Spain to Philip V; Philip took Naples and Sicily from the house of Austria. Thus the Spanish prince, who is now king of Naples, evidently owes his kingdom to Mrs. Masham; he would not have had it, nor even have been born, if the duchess of Marlborough had been more complaisant toward the queen of England; his existence at Naples depended on one folly more or less at the court of London.

Examine the situations of every people upon earth; they are in like manner founded on a train of occurrences seemingly without connection, but all connected. In this immense machine all is wheel, pulley, cord, or spring. It is the same in physical order. A wind blowing from the southern seas and the remotest parts of Africa brings with it a portion of the African atmosphere, which, falling in showers in the valleys of the Alps, fertilizes our lands; on the other hand our north wind carries our vapors among the negroes; we do good to Guinea, and Guinea to us. The chain extends from one end of the universe to the other.

But the truth of this principle seems to me to be strangely abused; for it is thence concluded that there is no atom, however small, the movement of which has not influenced the actual arrangement of the whole world; that the most trivial accident, whether among men or animals, is an essential link in the great chain of destiny.

Let us understand one another. Every effect evidently has its cause, ascending from cause to cause, into the abyss of eternity; but every cause has not its effect, going down to the end of ages. I grant that the events are produced one by another; if the past was pregnant with the present, the present is pregnant with the future; everything is begotten, but everything does not beget. It is a genealogical tree; every house, we know, ascends to Adam, but many of the family have died without issue.

The events of this world form a genealogical tree. It is indisputable that the inhabitants of Spain and Gaul are descended from Gomer, and the Russians from his younger brother Magog, for in how many great books is this genealogy to be found! It cannot then be denied that the grand Turk, who is also descended from Magog, is obliged to him for the good beating given him in 1769 by the Empress Catherine II. This occurrence is evidently linked with other great events; but whether Magog spat to the right or to the left near Mount Caucasus—made two or three circles in a well—or whether he lay on his right side or his left, I do not see that it could have much influence on present affairs.

It must be remembered, because it is proved by Newton, that nature is not a plenum, and that motion is not communicated by collision until it has made the tour of the universe. Throw a body of a certain density into water, you easily calculate that at the end of such a time the movement of this body, and that which it has given to the water, will cease; the motion will be lost and rest will be restored. So the motion produced by Magog in spitting into a well cannot have influenced what is now passing in Moldavia and Wallachia. Present events, then, are not the offspring of all past events, they have their direct lines, but with a thousand small collateral lines they have nothing to do. Once more be it observed that every being has a parent but every one has not an offspring.

• • •

Prejudice

Prejudice is an opinion without judgment. Thus, throughout the world, children are inspired with opinions before they can judge. There are universal and necessary prejudices, and these even constitute virtue. In all countries, children are taught to acknowledge a rewarding and punishing God; to respect and love their fathers and mothers; to regard theft as a crime, and interested lying as a vice, before they can tell what is a virtue or a vice. Prejudice may, therefore, be very useful, and such as judgment will ratify when we reason.

Sentiment is not simply prejudice, it is something much stronger. A mother loves not her son because she is told that she must love him; she fortunately cherishes him in spite of herself. It is not through prejudice that you run to the aid of an unknown child nearly falling down a precipice, or being devoured by a beast.

But it is through prejudice that you will respect a man dressed in certain clothes, walking gravely, and talking at the same time. Your parents have told you that you must bend to this man; you respect him before you know whether he merits your respect; you grow in age and knowledge; you perceive that this man is a quack, made up of pride, interest, and artifice; you despise that which you revered, and prejudice yields to judgment. Through prejudice, you have believed the fables with which your infancy was lulled: you are told that the Titans made war against the gods, that Venus was amorous of Adonis; at twelve years of age you take these fables for truth; at twenty, you regard them as ingenious allegories.

Let us examine, in a few words, the different kinds of prejudices, in order to arrange our ideas. We shall perhaps be like those who, in the time of the scheme of Law, perceived that they had calculated upon imaginary riches.

PREJUDICES OF THE SENSES

Is it not an amusing thing, that our eyes always deceive us, even when we see very well, and that on the contrary our ears do not? When your properly-formed ear hears: "You are beautiful; I love you," it is very certain that the words are not: "I hate you; you are ugly;" but you see a smooth mirror—it is demonstrated that you are deceived; it is a very rough surface. You see the sun about two feet in diameter; it is demonstrated that it is a million times larger than the earth.

It seems that God has put truth into your ears, and error into your eyes; but study optics, and you will perceive that God has not deceived you, and that it was impossible for objects to appear to you otherwise than you see them in the present state of things.

PHYSICAL PREJUDICES

The sun rises, the moon also, the earth is immovable; these are natural physical prejudices. But that crabs are good for the blood, because when boiled they are of the same color; that eels cure paralysis, because they frisk about; that the moon influences our diseases, because an invalid was one day observed to have an increase of fever during the wane of the moon: these ideas and a thousand others were the errors of ancient charlatans, who judged without reason, and who, being themselves deceived, deceived others.

HISTORICAL PREJUDICES

The greater part of historians have believed without examining, and this confidence is a prejudice. Fabius Pictor relates, that, several ages before him, a vestal of the town of Alba, going to draw water in her pitcher, was violated, that she was delivered of Romulus and Remus, that they were nourished by a she-wolf. The Roman people believed this fable; they examined not whether at that time there were vestals at Latium; whether it was likely that the daughter of a king should go out of her convent with a pitcher, or whether it was probable that a she-wolf should suckle two children, instead of eating them: prejudice established it.

A monk writes that Clovis, being in great danger at the battle of Tolbiac, made a vow to become a Christian if he escaped; but is it natural that he should address a strange god on such an occasion? Would not the religion in which he was born have acted the most powerfully? Where is the Christian who, in a battle against the Turks, would not rather address himself to the holy Virgin Mary, than to Mahomet? He adds, that a pigeon brought the vial in his beak to anoint Clovis, and that an angel brought the oriflamme to conduct him: the prejudiced believed all the stories of this kind. Those who are acquainted with human nature well know, that the usurper Clovis, and the usurper Rollo, or Rol, became Christians to govern the Christians more securely as the Turkish usurpers became Mussulmans to govern the Mussulmans more securely.

RELIGIOUS PREJUDICES

If your nurse has told you, that Ceres presides over corn, or that Vishnu and Xac became men several times, or that Sammonocodom cut down a forest, or that Odin expects you in his hall near Jutland, or that Mahomet, or some other, made a journey to heaven; finally, if your preceptor afterwards thrusts into your brain what your nurse has engraven on it, you will possess it for life. If your judgment would rise above these prejudices, your neighbors, and above all, the ladies, exclaim "impiety!" and frighten you; your dervish, fearing to see his revenue diminished, accuses you before the cadi; and this cadi, if he can, causes you to be impaled, because he would command fools, and he believes that fools obey better than others; which state of things will last until your neighbors and the dervish and cadi begin to comprehend that folly is good for nothing, and that persecution is abominable.

Candide: or, the Optimist

Chapter I

HOW CANDIDE WAS BROUGHT UP IN A MAGNIFICENT CASTLE AND HOW HE WAS DRIVEN THENCE

In the country of Westphalia, in the castle of the most noble baron of Thunder-ten-tronckh, lived a youth whom nature had endowed with a most sweet disposition. His face was the true index of his mind. He had a solid judgment joined to the most unaffected simplicity; and hence, I presume, he had his name of Candide. The old servants of the house suspected him to have been the son of the baron's sister, by a very good sort of a gentleman of the neighborhood, whom that young lady refused to marry, because he could produce no more

THE WORKS OF VOLTAIRE, *trans.* T. *Smollett (Paris, 1901).*

than threescore and eleven quarterings in his arms; the rest of the genealogical tree belonging to the family having been lost through the injuries of time.

The baron was one of the most powerful lords in Westphalia; for his castle had not only a gate, but even windows; and his great hall was hung with tapestry. He used to hunt with his mastiffs and spaniels instead of greyhounds; his groom served him for huntsman; and the parson of the parish officiated as his grand almoner. He was called My Lord by all his people, and he never told a story but every one laughed at it.

My lady baroness weighed three hundred and fifty pounds, consequently was a person of no small consideration; and then she did the honors of the house with a dignity that commanded universal respect. Her daughter was about seventeen years of age, fresh colored, comely, plump, and desirable. The baron's son seemed to be a youth in every respect worthy of the father he sprung from. Pangloss, the preceptor, was the oracle of the family, and little Candide listened to his instructions with all the simplicity natural to his age and disposition.

Master Pangloss taught the metaphysico-theologo-cosmolo-nigology. He could prove to admiration that there is no effect without a cause; and that, in this best of all possible worlds, the baron's castle was the most magnificent of all castles, and my lady the best of all possible baronesses.

"It is demonstrable," said he, "that things cannot be otherwise than as they are; for as all things have been created for some end, they must necessarily be created for the best end. Observe, for instance, the nose is formed for spectacles, therefore we wear spectacles. The legs are visibly designed for stockings, accordingly we wear stockings. Stones were made to be hewn, and to construct castles, therefore My Lord has a magnificent castle; for the greatest baron in the province ought to be the best lodged. Swine were intended to be eaten, therefore we eat pork all the year round: and they, who assert that everything is *right,* do not express themselves correctly; they should say that everything is *best.*"

Candide listened attentively, and believed implicitly; for he thought Miss Cunegund excessively handsome, though he never had the courage to tell her so. He concluded that next to the happiness of being baron of Thunder-ten-tronckh, the next was that of being Miss Cunegund, the next that of seeing her every day, and the last that of hearing the doctrine of Master Pangloss, the greatest philosopher of the whole province, and consequently of the whole world.

One day when Miss Cunegund went to take a walk in a little neighboring wood which was called a park, she saw, through the bushes, the sage Doctor Pangloss giving a lecture in experimental philosophy to her mother's chambermaid, a little brown wench, very pretty, and very tractable. As Miss Cunegund had a great disposition for the sciences, she observed with the utmost attention the experiments, which were repeated before her eyes; she perfectly well understood the force of the doctor's reasoning upon causes and effects. She retired greatly flurried, quite pensive and filled with the desire of knowledge, imagining that she might be a *sufficing reason* for young Candide, and he for her.

On her way back she happened to meet the young man; she blushed, he blushed also; she wished him a good morning in a flattering tone, he returned the salute, without knowing what he said. The next day, as they were rising from dinner, Cunegund and Candide slipped behind the screen. The miss dropped her handkerchief, the young man picked it up. She innocently took hold of his hand, and he as innocently kissed hers with a warmth, a sensibility, a grace—all very particular; their lips met; their eyes sparkled; their knees trembled; their hands strayed. The baron chanced to come by; he beheld the cause and effect, and without hesitation, saluted Candide with some notable kicks on the breech, and drove him out of doors. The lovely Miss Cunegund fainted away, and, as soon as she came to herself, the baroness boxed her ears. Thus, general consternation was spread over this most magnificent and most agreeable of all possible castles.

Chapter II

WHAT BEFELL CANDIDE AMONG THE BULGARIANS

Candide, thus driven out of this terrestrial paradise, rambled a long time without knowing where he went; sometimes he raised his eyes, all bedewed with tears, toward heaven, and sometimes he cast a melancholy look towards the magnificent castle, where dwelt the fairest of young baronesses. He laid himself down to sleep in a furrow, heartbroken, and supperless. The snow fell in great flakes, and, in the morning when he awoke, he was almost frozen to death; however, he made shift to crawl to the next town, which was called Waldberghoff-trarbk-dikdorff, without a penny in his pocket, and half dead with hunger and fatigue. He took up his stand at the door of an inn. He had not been long there, before two men dressed in blue, fixed their eyes steadfastly upon him. "Faith, comrade," said one of them to the other, "yonder is a well-made young fellow, and of the right size." Upon which they made up to Candide, and with the greatest civility and politeness invited him to dine with them. "Gentlemen," replied Candide, with a most engaging modesty, "you do me much honor, but upon my word I have no money." "Money, sir!" said one of the blues to him, "young persons of your appearance and merit never pay anything; why, are not you five feet five inches high?" "Yes, gentlemen, that is really my size," replied he, with a low bow. "Come then, sir, sit down along with us; we will not only pay your reckoning, but will never suffer such a clever young fellow as you to want money. Men were born to assist one another." "You are perfectly right, gentlemen," said Candide, "this is precisely the doctrine of Master Pangloss; and I am convinced that everything is for the best." His generous companions next entreated him to accept of a few crowns, which he readily complied with, at the same time offering them his note for the payment, which they refused, and sat down to table. "Have you not a great affection for—" "Oh yes! I have a great affection for the lovely Miss Cunegund." "May be so," replied one of the blues, "but that is not the question! We ask you whether you have not a great affection for the king of the Bulgarians?" "For the king of the Bulgarians?" said Candide, "Oh Lord! not at all, why I never saw him in my life." "Is it possible! oh, he is a most charming king! Come, we must drink his health." "With all my heart, gentlemen," says Candide, and off he tossed his glass. "Bravo!" cried the blues; "you are now the support, the defender, the hero of the Bulgarians; your fortune is made; you are in the high road to glory." So saying, they handcuffed him, and carried him away to the regiment. There he was made to wheel about to the right, to the left, to draw his rammer, to return his rammer, to present, to fire, to march, and they gave him thirty blows with a cane; the next day he performed his exercise a little better, and they gave him but twenty; the day following he came off with ten, and was looked upon as a young fellow of surprising genius by all his comrades.

Candide was struck with amazement, and could not for the soul of him conceive how he came to be a hero. One fine spring morning, he took it into his head to take a walk, and he marched straight forward, conceiving it to be a privilege of the human species, as well as of the brute creation, to make use of their legs how and when they pleased. He had not gone above two leagues when he was overtaken by four other heroes, six feet high, who bound him neck and heels, and carried him to a dungeon. A court-martial sat upon him, and he was asked which he liked better, to run the gauntlet six and thirty times through the whole regiment, or to have his brains blown out with a dozen musket-balls? In vain did he remonstrate to them that the human will is free, and that he chose neither; they obliged him to make a choice, and he determined, in virtue of that divine gift called free will, to run the gauntlet six and thirty times. He had gone through his discipline twice, and the regiment being composed of two thousand men, they composed for him exactly four thousand strokes, which laid bare all his muscles and nerves from the nape of his neck to his rump. As they were preparing to make him set out the third time our young hero, unable to support it any longer, begged as a favor that they would be so obliging as to shoot him through the head; the favor being granted, a bandage was tied over his eyes, and he was made to kneel down. At that very instant, his Bulgarian majesty happening to pass by made a stop, and inquired into the delinquent's crime, and being a prince of great penetration, he found, from what he heard of Candide, that he was a young metaphysician, entirely ignorant of the world; and therefore, out of his great clemency, he condescended to pardon him, for which his name will be celebrated in every journal, and in every age. A skilful surgeon made a cure of the flagellated Candide in three weeks by means of emollient unguents prescribed by Dioscorides. His sores were now skinned over and he was able to march, when the king of the Bulgarians gave battle to the king of the Abares.

Chapter III

HOW CANDIDE ESCAPED FROM THE BULGARIANS AND WHAT BEFELL HIM AFTERWARDS

Never was anything so gallant, so well accoutred, so brilliant, and so finely disposed as the two armies. The trumpets, fifes, haut-boys, drums, and cannon made such harmony as never was heard in hell itself. The entertainment began by a discharge of cannon, which, in the twinkling of an eye, laid flat about six thousand men on each side. The musket bullets swept away, out of the best of all possible worlds, nine or ten thousand scoundrels that infested its surface. The bayonet was next the sufficient reason of the deaths of several thousands. The whole might amount to thirty thousand souls. Candide trembled like a philosopher, and concealed himself as well as he could during this heroic butchery.

At length, while the two kings were causing *Te Deums* to be sung in their camps, Candide took a resolution to go and reason somewhere else upon causes and effects. After passing over heaps of dead or dying men, the first place he came to was a neighboring village, in the Abarian territories, which had been burned to the ground by the Bulgarians, agreeably to the laws of war. Here lay a number of old men covered with wounds, who beheld their wives dying with their throats cut, and hugging their children to their breasts, all stained with blood. There several young virgins, whose bellies had been ripped open, after they had satisfied the natural necessities of the Bulgarian heroes, breathed their last; while others, half burned in the flames, begged to be despatched out of the world. The ground about them was covered with the brains, arms, and legs of dead men.

Candide made all the haste he could to another village, which belonged to the Bulgarians, and there he found the heroic Abares had enacted the same tragedy. Thence continuing to walk over palpitating limbs, or through ruined buildings, at length he arrived beyond the theatre of war, with a little provision in his budget, and Miss Cunegund's image in his heart. When he arrived in Holland his provision failed him; but having heard that the inhabitants of that country were all rich and Christians, he made himself sure of being treated by them in the same manner as at the baron's castle, before he had been driven thence through the power of Miss Cunegund's bright eyes.

He asked charity of several grave-looking people, who one and all answered him, that if he continued to follow this trade they would have him sent to the house of correction, where he should be taught to get his bread.

He next addressed himself to a person who had just come from haranguing a numerous assembly for a whole hour on the subject of charity. The orator, squinting at him under his broad-brimmed hat, asked him sternly, what brought him thither and whether he was for the good old cause? "Sir," said Candide, in a submissive manner, "I conceive there can be no effect without a cause; everything is necessarily concatenated and arranged for the best. It was necessary that I should be banished from the presence of Miss Cunegund; that I should afterwards run the gauntlet; and it is necessary I should beg my bread, till I am able to get it: all this could not have been otherwise." "Hark ye, friend," said the orator, "do you hold the pope to be Antichrist?" "Truly, I never heard anything about it," said Candide, "but whether he is or not, I am in want of something to eat." "Thou deservest not to eat or to drink," replied the orator, "wretch, monster, that thou art! hence! avoid my sight, nor ever come near me again while thou livest." The orator's wife happened to put her head out of the window at that instant, when, seeing a man who doubted whether the pope was Antichrist, she discharged upon his head a chamberpot full of ——. Good heavens, to what excess does religious zeal transport womankind!

A man who had never been christened, an honest anabaptist named James, was witness to the cruel and ignominious treatment showed to one of his brethren, to a rational, two-footed unfledged being. Moved with pity he carried him to his own house, caused him to be cleaned, gave him meat and drink, and made him a present of two florins, at the same time proposing to instruct him in his own trade of weaving Persian silks, which are fabricated in Holland. Candide, penetrated with so much goodness, threw himself at his feet, crying, "Now I am convinced that my Master Pangloss told me truth when he said that everything was for the best in this world; for I am infinitely more affected with your extraordinary generosity than with the inhumanity of that gentleman in the black cloak, and his wife." The next day, as Candide was walking out, he met a beggar all covered with scabs, his eyes sunk in his head, the end of his nose eaten off, his mouth drawn on one side, his teeth as black as a cloak, snuffling and coughing most violently, and every time he attempted to spit out dropped a tooth.

Chapter IV

HOW CANDIDE FOUND HIS OLD MASTER PANGLOSS AGAIN AND WHAT HAPPENED TO HIM

Candide, divided between compassion and horror, but giving way to the former, bestowed on this shocking figure the two florins which the honest anabaptist, James, had just before given to him. The spectre looked at him very earnestly, shed tears and threw his arms about his neck. Candide started back aghast. "Alas!" said the one wretch to the other, "don't you know your dear Pangloss?" "What do I hear? Is it you, my dear master! you I behold in this piteous plight? What dreadful misfortune has befallen you? What has made you leave the most magnificent and delightful of all castles? What has become of Miss Cunegund, the mirror of young ladies, and nature's masterpiece?" "Oh Lord!" cried Pangloss, "I am so weak I cannot stand," upon which Candide instantly led him to the anabaptist's stable, and procured him something to eat. As soon as Pangloss had a little refreshed himself, Candide began to repeat his inquiries concerning Miss Cunegund. "She is dead," replied the other. "Dead!" cried Candide, and immediately fainted away; his friend restored him by the help of a little bad vinegar, which he found by chance in the stable. Candide opened his eyes, and again repeated: "Dead! is Miss Cunegund dead? Ah, where is the best of worlds now? But of what illness did she die? Was it of grief on seeing her father kick me out of his magnificent castle?" "No," replied Pangloss, "her belly was ripped open by the Bulgarian soldiers, after they had ravished her as much as it was possible for a damsel to be ravished; they knocked the baron, her father, on the head for attempting to defend her; my lady, her mother, was cut in pieces; my poor pupil was served just in the same manner as his sister, and as for the castle, they have not left one stone upon another; they have destroyed all the ducks, and the sheep, the barns, and the trees; but we have had our revenge, for the Abares have done the very same thing in a neighboring barony, which belonged to a Bulgarian lord."

At hearing this, Candide fainted away a second time, but, having come to himself again, he said all that it became him to say; he inquired into the cause and effect, as well as into the sufficing reason that had reduced Pangloss to so miserable a condition. "Alas," replied the preceptor, "it was love; love, the comfort of the human species; love, the preserver of the universe; the soul of all sensible beings; love! tender love!" "Alas," cried Candide, "I have had some knowledge of love myself, this sovereign of hearts, this soul of souls; yet it never cost me more than a kiss and twenty kicks on the backside. But how could this beautiful cause produce in you so hideous an effect?"

Pangloss made answer in these terms: "O my dear Candide, you must remember Pacquette, that pretty wench, who waited on our noble baroness; in her arms I tasted the pleasures of paradise, which produced these hell-torments with which you see me devoured. She was infected with the disease, and perhaps has since died of it; she received this present of a learned cordelier, who derived it from the fountain head; he was indebted for it to an old countess, who had it of a captain of horse, who had it of a marchioness, who had it of a page, the page had it of a Jesuit, who, during his novitiate, had it in a direct line from one of the fellow-adventurers of Christopher Columbus; for my part I shall give it to nobody, I am a dying man."

"O sage Pangloss," cried Candide, "what a strange genealogy is this! Is not the devil the root of it?" "Not at all," replied the great man, "it was a thing unavoidable, a necessary ingredient in the best of worlds; for if Columbus had not caught in an island in America this disease, which contaminates the course of generation, and frequently impedes propagation itself, and is evidently opposed to the great end of nature, we should have had neither chocolate nor cochineal. It is also to be observed, that, even to the present time, in this continent of ours, this malady, like our religious controversies, is peculiar to ourselves. The Turks, the Indians, the Persians, the Chinese, the Siamese, and the Japanese are entirely unacquainted with it; but there is a sufficing reason for them to know it in a few centuries. In the meantime, it is making prodigious havoc among us, especially in those armies composed of well-disciplined hirelings, who determine the fate of nations; for we may safely affirm, that, when an army of thirty thousand men engages another equal in size, there are about twenty thousand infected with syphilis on each side."

"Very surprising, indeed," said Candide, "but you must get cured." "Lord help me, how can I?" said Pangloss; "my dear friend, I have not a penny in the world; and you know one cannot be bled or have a clyster without money."

This last speech had its effect on Candide; he flew to the charitable anabaptist, James; he flung himself at his feet, and gave him so striking a picture of the miserable condition of his friend that the good man without any further hesitation agreed to take Doctor Pangloss into his house, and to pay for his cure. The cure was effected with only the loss of one eye and an ear. As he wrote a good hand, and understood accounts tolerably well, the anabaptist made him his bookkeeper. At the expiration of two months, being obliged by some mercantile affairs to go to Lisbon he took the two philosophers with him in the same ship; Pangloss, during the course of the voyage, explained to him how everything was so constituted that it could not be better. James did not quite agree with him on this point: "Men," said he, "must, in some things, have deviated from their original innocence; for they were not born wolves, and yet they worry one another like those beasts of prey. God never gave them twenty-four pounders nor bayonets, and yet they have made cannons and bayonets to destroy one another. To this account I might add not only bankruptcies, but the law which seizes on the effects of bankrupts, only to cheat the creditors." "All this was indispensably necessary," replied the one-eyed doctor, "for private misfortunes are public benefits; so that the more private misfortunes there are, the greater is the general good." While he was arguing in this manner, the sky was overcast, the winds blew from the four quarters of the compass, and the ship was assailed by a most terrible tempest, within sight of the port of Lisbon.

. . .

[After a remarkable series of experiences and adventures, including two murders, an earthquake, and a touching reunion with Cunegund, Candide and his valet Cacambo are forced to flee from the Jesuit state of Paraguay into the wilds of South America. There they are seized by the Oreillon Indians, who release them when it is discovered they have been telling the truth. —Ed.]

Chapter XVII

CANDIDE AND HIS VALET ARRIVE IN THE COUNTRY OF EL DORADO—WHAT THEY SAW THERE

When they got to the frontiers of the Oreillons, "You see," said Cacambo to Candide, "this hemisphere is not better than the other; now take my advice and let us return to Europe by the shortest way possible."

"But how can we get back?" said Candide; "and whither shall we go? To my own country? The Bulgarians and the Abares are laying that waste with fire and sword; or shall we go to Portugal? There I shall be burned; and if we abide here we are every moment in danger of being spitted. But how can I bring myself to quit that part of the world where my dear Miss Cunegund has her residence?"

"Let us return towards Cayenne," said Cacambo; "there we shall meet with some Frenchmen; for you know those gentry ramble all over the world; perhaps they will assist us, and God will look with pity on our distress."

It was not so easy to get to Cayenne. They knew pretty nearly whereabouts it lay; but the mountains, rivers, precipices, robbers, savages, were dreadful obstacles in the way. Their horses died with fatigue and their provisions were at an end. They subsisted a whole month on wild fruit, till at length they came to a little river bordered with cocoa trees; the sight of which at once revived their drooping spirits and furnished nourishment for their enfeebled bodies.

Cacambo, who was always giving as good advice as the old woman herself, said to Candide: "You see there is no holding out any longer; we have travelled enough on foot. I spy an empty canoe near the river side; let us fill it with coconuts, get into it, and go down with the stream; a river always leads to some inhabited place. If we do not meet with agreeable things, we shall at least meet with something new."

"Agreed," replied Candide; "let us recommend ourselves to Providence."

They rowed a few leagues down the river, the banks of which were in some places covered with flowers; in others barren; in some parts smooth and level, and in others steep and rugged. The stream widened as they went further on, till at length it passed under one of the frightful rocks, whose summits seemed to reach the clouds. Here our two travellers had the courage to commit themselves to the stream, which, contracting in this part, hurried them along with a dreadful noise and rapidity. At the end of four-and-twenty hours they saw daylight again; but their canoe was dashed to pieces against the rocks. They were obliged to creep along, from rock to rock, for the space of a league, till at length a spacious plain presented itself to their sight. This place was bounded by a chain of inaccessible mountains. The country appeared cultivated equally for pleasure and to produce the necessaries of life. The useful and agreeable were here equally blended. The roads were covered, or rather adorned, with carriages formed of glittering materials, in which were men and women of a surprising beauty, drawn with great rapidity by red sheep of a very large size; which far surpassed the finest coursers of Andalusia, Tetuan, or Mecquinez.

"Here is a country, however," said Candide, "preferable to Westphalia."

He and Cacambo landed near the first village they saw, at the entrance of which they perceived some children covered with tattered garments of the richest brocade, playing at quoits. Our two inhabitants of the other hemisphere amused themselves greatly with what they saw. The quoits were large, round pieces, yellow, red, and green, which cast a most glorious lustre. Our travellers picked some of them up, and they proved to be gold, emeralds, rubies, and diamonds; the least of which would have been the greatest ornament to the superb throne of the Great Mogul.

"Without doubt," said Cacambo, "those children must be the king's sons that are playing at quoits." As he was uttering these words the schoolmaster of the village appeared, who came to call the children to school.

"There," said Candide, "is the preceptor of the royal family."

The little ragamuffins immediately quitted their diversion, leaving the quoits on the ground with all their other playthings. Candide gathered them up, ran to the schoolmaster, and, with a most respectful bow, presented them to him, giving him to understand by signs that their royal highnesses had forgot their gold and precious stones. The schoolmaster, with a smile, flung them upon the ground, then examining Candide from head to foot with an air of admiration, he turned his back and went on his way.

Our travellers took care, however, to gather up the gold, the rubies, and the emeralds.

"Where are we?" cried Candide. "The king's children in this country must have an excellent education, since they are taught to show such a contempt for gold and precious stones."

Cacambo was as much surprised as his master. They then drew near the first house in the village, which was built after the manner of a European palace. There was a crowd of people about the door, and a still greater number in the house. The sound of the most delightful instruments of music was heard, and the most agreeable smell came from the kitchen. Cacambo went up to the door and heard those within talking in the Peruvian language, which was his mother tongue; for every one knows that Cacambo was born in a village of Tucuman, where no other language is spoken.

"I will be your interpreter here," said he to Candide. "Let us go in; this is an eating-house."

Immediately two waiters and two servant-girls, dressed in cloth of gold, and their hair braided with ribbons of tissue, accosted the strangers and invited them to sit down to the ordinary. Their dinner consisted of four dishes of different soups, each garnished with two young paroquets, a large dish of bouille that weighed two hundred weight, two roasted monkeys of a delicious flavor, three hundred humming-birds in one dish, and six hundred fly-birds in another; some excellent ragouts, delicate tarts, and the whole served up in dishes of rock-crystal. Several sorts of liquors, extracted from the sugar-cane, were handed about by the servants who attended.

Most of the company were chapmen and wagoners, all extremely polite; they asked Cacambo a few questions with the utmost discretion and circumspection; and replied to his in a most obliging and satisfactory manner.

As soon as dinner was over, both Candide and Cacambo thought they should pay very handsomely for their entertainment by laying down two of those large gold pieces which they had picked off the ground; but the landlord and landlady burst into a fit of laughing and held their sides for some time. When the fit was over, "Gentlemen," said the landlord, "I plainly perceive you are strangers, and such we are not accustomed to charge; pardon us, therefore, for laughing when you offered us the common pebbles of our highways for payment of your reckoning. To be sure, you have none of the coin of this kingdom; but there is no necessity of having any money at all to dine in this house. All the inns, which are established for the convenience of those who carry on the trade of this nation, are maintained by the government. You have found but very indifferent entertainment here, because this is only a poor village; but in almost every other of these public houses you will meet with a reception worthy of persons of your merit." Cacambo explained the whole of this speech of the landlord to Candide, who listened to it with the same astonishment with which his friend communicated it.

"What sort of a country is this," said the one to the other, "that is unknown to all the world; and in which Nature has everywhere so different an appearance to what she has in ours? Possibly this is that part of the globe where everything is right, for there must certainly be some such place. And, for all that Master Pangloss could say, I often perceived that things went very ill in Westphalia."

Chapter XVIII

WHAT THEY SAW IN THE COUNTRY OF EL DORADO

Cacambo vented all his curiosity upon his landlord by a thousand different questions; the honest man answered him thus:

"I am very ignorant, sir, but I am contented with my ignorance; however, we have in this neighborhood an old man retired from court, who is the most learned and communicative person in the whole kingdom." He then conducted Cacambo to the old man; Candide acted now only a second character, and attended his valet. They entered a very plain house, for the door was nothing but silver, and the ceiling was only of beaten gold, but wrought in such elegant taste as to vie with the richest. The antechamber, indeed, was only incrusted with rubies and emeralds; but the order in which everything was disposed made amends for this great simplicity.

The old man received the strangers on his sofa, which was stuffed with hummingbirds' feathers; and ordered his servants to present them with liquors in golden goblets, after which he satisfied their curiosity in the following terms:

"I am now one hundred and seventy-two years old, and I learned of my late father, who was equerry to the king, the amazing revolutions of Peru, to which he had been an eye-witness. This kingdom is the ancient patrimony of the Incas, who very imprudently quitted it to conquer another part of the world, and were at length conquered and destroyed themselves by the Spaniards.

"Those princes of their family who remained in their native country acted more wisely. They ordained, with the consent of their whole nation, that none of the inhabitants of our little kingdom should ever quit it; and to this wise ordinance we owe the preservation of our innocence and happiness. The Spaniards had some confused notion of this country, to which they gave the name of *El Dorado;* and Sir Walter Raleigh, an Englishman, actually came very near it about three hundred years ago; but the inaccessible rocks and precipices with which our country is surrounded on all sides, has hitherto secured us from the rapacious fury of the people of Europe, who have an unaccountable fondness for the pebbles and dirt of our land, for the sack of which they would murder us all to the very last man."

The conversation lasted some time and turned chiefly on the form of government, their manners, their women, their public diversions, and the arts. At length, Candide, who had always had a taste for metaphysics, asked whether the people of that country had any religion.

The old man reddened a little at this question.

"Can you doubt it?" said he; "do you take us for wretches lost to all sense of gratitude?"

Cacambo asked in a respectful manner what was the established religion of El Dorado. The old man blushed again, and said: "Can there be two religions then? Ours, I apprehend, is the religion of the whole world; we worship God from morning till night."

"Do you worship but one God?" said Cacambo, who still acted as the interpreter of Candide's doubts.

"Certainly," said the old man; "there are not two, nor three, nor four Gods. I must confess the people of your world ask very extraordinary questions."

However Candide could not refrain from making many more inquiries of the old man; he wanted to know in what manner they prayed to God in El Dorado.

"We do not pray to him at all," said the reverend sage; "we have nothing to ask of Him, He has given us all we want, and we give Him thanks incessantly." Candide had a curiosity to see some of their priests, and desired Cacambo to ask the old man where they were. At which he smiling said:

"My friends, we are all of us priests; the king and all the heads of families sing solemn hymns of thanksgiving every morning, accompanied by five or six thousand musicians."

"What!" said Cacambo, "have you no

monks among you to dispute, to govern, to intrigue, and to burn people who are not of the same opinion with themselves?"

"Do you take us for fools?" said the old man. "Here we are all of one opinion, and know not what you mean by your monks."

During the whole of this discourse, Candide was in raptures, and he said to himself, "What a prodigious difference is there between this place and Westphalia; and this house and the baron's castle. Ah, Master Pangloss! had you ever seen El Dorado, you would no longer have maintained that the castle of Thunder-ten-tronckh was the finest of all possible edifices; there is nothing like seeing the world, that's certain."

This long conversation being ended, the old man ordered six sheep to be harnessed and put to the coach, and sent twelve of his servants to escort the travellers to court.

"Excuse me," said he, "for not waiting on you in person, my age deprives me of that honour. The king will receive you in such a manner that you will have no reason to complain; and doubtless you will make a proper allowance for the customs of the country if they should not happen altogether to please you."

Candide and Cacambo got into the coach, the six sheep flew, and, in less than a quarter of an hour, they arrived at the king's palace, which was situated at the further end of the capital. At the entrance was a portal two hundred and twenty feet high and one hundred wide; but it is impossible for words to express the materials of which it was built. The reader, however, will readily conceive that they must have a prodigious superiority over the pebbles and sand, which we call gold and precious stones.

Twenty beautiful young virgins in waiting received Candide and Cacambo on their alighting from the coach, conducted them to the bath and clad them in robes woven of the down of humming birds; after which they were introduced by the great officers of the crown of both sexes to the king's apartment, between two files of musicians, each file consisting of a thousand, agreeable to the custom of the country. When they drew near to the presence-chamber, Cacambo asked one of the officers in what manner they were to pay their obeisance to his majesty; whether it was the custom to fall upon their knees, or to prostrate themselves upon the ground; whether they were to put their hands upon their heads, or behind their backs; whether they were to lick the dust off the floor; in short, what was the ceremony usual on such occasions.

"The custom," said the great officer, "is to embrace the king and kiss him on each cheek."

Candide and Cacambo accordingly threw their arms around his majesty's neck, who received them in the most gracious manner imaginable, and very politely asked them to sup with him.

While supper was preparing orders were given to show them the city, where they saw public structures that reared their lofty heads to the clouds; the market-places decorated with a thousand columns; fountains of spring water, besides others of rose water, and of liquors drawn from the sugar-cane, incessantly flowing in the great squares; which were paved with a kind of precious stones that emitted an odor like that of cloves and cinnamon. Candide asked to see the high court of justice, the parliament; but was answered that they had none in that country, being utter strangers to lawsuits. He then inquired if they had any prisons; they replied none. But what gave him at once the greatest surprise and pleasure was the palace of sciences, where he saw a gallery two thousand feet long, filled with the various apparatus in mathematics and natural philosophy.

After having spent the whole afternoon in seeing only about the thousandth part of the city, they were brought back to the king's palace. Candide sat down at the table with his majesty, his valet Cacambo, and several ladies of the court. Never was entertainment more elegant, nor could any one possibly show more wit than his majesty displayed while they were at supper. Cacambo explained all the king's *bons mots* to Candide, and, although they were translated, they still appeared to be *bons mots*. Of all the things that surprised Candide, this was not the least. They spent a whole month in this hospitable place, during which time Candide was continually saying to Cacambo:

"I own, my friend, once more, that the castle where I was born is a mere nothing in comparison to the place where we now are; but still Miss Cunegund is not here, and you yourself have doubtless some fair one in Europe for whom you sigh. If we remain here we shall only be as others are; whereas, if we return to our own world with only a dozen of El Dorado sheep, loaded with the pebbles of this country, we shall be richer than all the kings in Europe; we shall no longer need to stand in awe of the inquisitors; and we may easily recover Miss Cunegund."

This speech was perfectly agreeable to Cacambo. A fondness for roving, for making a figure in their own country, and for boasting of what they had seen in their travels, was so powerful in our two wanderers that they resolved to be no longer happy; and demanded permission of the king to quit the country.

"You are about to do a rash and silly action," said the king. "I am sensible my kingdom is an inconsiderable spot; but when people are tolerably at their ease in any place, I should think it would be to their interest to remain there. Most assuredly, I have no right to detain you, or any strangers, against your wills; this is an act of tyranny to which our manners and our laws are equally repugnant; all men are by nature free; you have therefore an undoubted liberty to depart whenever you please, but you will have many and great difficulties to encounter in passing the frontiers. It is impossible to ascend that rapid river which runs under high and vaulted rocks, and by which you were conveyed hither by a kind of miracle. The mountains by which my kingdom are hemmed in on all sides, are ten thousand feet high, and perfectly perpendicular; they are above ten leagues across, and the descent from them is one continued precipice. However, since you are determined to leave us, I will immediately give orders to the superintendent of my carriages to cause one to be made that will convey you very safely. When they have conducted you to the back of the mountains, nobody can attend you farther; for my subjects have made a vow never to quit the kingdom, and they are too prudent to break it. Ask me whatever else you please."

"All we shall ask of your majesty," said Cacambo, "is only a few sheep laden with provisions, pebbles, and the clay of your country."

The king smiled at the request; and said: "I cannot imagine what pleasure you Europeans find in our yellow clay; but take away as much of it as you will, and much good may it do you."

He immediately gave orders to his engineers to make a machine to hoist these two extraordinary men out of the kingdom. Three thousand good machinists went to work and finished it in about fifteen days, and it did not cost more than twenty millions sterling of that country's money. Candide and Cacambo were placed on this machine, and they took with them two large red sheep, bridled and saddled, to ride upon when they got on the other side of the mountains; twenty others to serve as sumpters for carrying provisions; thirty laden with presents of whatever was most curious in the country, and fifty with gold, diamonds, and other precious stones. The king, at parting with our two adventurers, embraced them with the greatest cordiality.

It was a curious sight to behold the manner of their setting off, and the ingenious method by which they and their sheep were hoisted to the top of the mountains. The machinists and engineers took leave of them as soon as they had conveyed them to a place of safety, and Candide was wholly occupied with the thoughts of presenting his sheep to Miss Cunegund.

"Now," cried he, "thanks to heaven, we have more than sufficient to pay the governor of Buenos Ayres for Miss Cunegund, if she is redeemable. Let us make the best of our way to Cayenne, where we will take shipping and then we may at leisure think of what kingdom we shall purchase with our riches.

Chapter XIX

WHAT HAPPENED TO THEM AT SURINAM AND HOW CANDIDE BECAME ACQUAINTED WITH MARTIN

Our travellers' first day's journey was very pleasant; they were elated with the prospect of possessing more riches than were to be found in Europe, Asia, and Africa together. Candide, in amorous transports, cut the name of Miss Cunegund on almost every tree he came to. The second day two of their sheep sunk in a morass, and were swallowed up with their lading; two more died of fatigue; some few days afterwards seven or eight perished with hunger in a desert, and others, at different times, tumbled down precipices, or were otherwise lost, so that, after travelling about a hundred days they had only two sheep left of the hundred and two they brought with them from El Dorado. Said Candide to Cacambo:

"You see, my dear friend, how perishable the riches of this world are; there is nothing solid but virtue."

"Very true," said Cacambo, "but we have still two sheep remaining, with more treasure than ever the king of Spain will be possessed of; and I espy a town at a distance, which I take to be Surinam, a town belonging to the Dutch. We are now at the end of our troubles, and at the beginning of happiness."

As they drew near the town they saw a negro stretched on the ground with only one half of his habit, which was a kind of linen frock; for the poor man had lost his left leg and his right hand.

"Good God," said Candide in Dutch, "what dost thou here, friend, in this deplorable condition?"

"I am waiting for my master, Mynheer Vanderdendur, the famous trader," answered the negro.

"Was it Mynheer Vanderdendur that used you in this cruel manner?"

"Yes sir," said the negro; "it is the custom here. They give a linen garment twice a year, and that is all our covering. When we labor in the sugar works, and the mill happens to snatch hold of a finger, they instantly chop off our hand; and when we attempt to run away, they cut off a leg. Both these cases have happened to me, and it is at this expense that you eat sugar in Europe; and yet when my mother sold me for ten patacoons on the coast of Guinea, she said to me, 'My dear child, bless our fetiches; adore them forever; they will make thee live happy; thou hast the honor to be a slave to our lords the whites, by which thou wilt make the fortune of us thy parents.' Alas! I know not whether I have made their fortunes; but they have not made mine: dogs, monkeys, and parrots are a thousand times less wretched than I. The Dutch fetiches who converted me tell me every Sunday that the blacks and whites are all children of one father, whom they call Adam. As for me, I do not understand anything of genealogies; but if what these preachers say is true we are all second cousins; and you must allow that it is impossible to be worse treated by our relations than we are."

"O Pangloss!" cried out Candide, "such horrid doings never entered thy imagination. Here is an end of the matter; I find myself, after all, obliged to renounce thy Optimism."

"Optimism," said Cacambo, "what is that?"

"Alas!" replied Candide, "it is the obstinacy of maintaining that everything is best when it is worst." And so saying he turned his eyes towards the poor negro, and shed a flood of tears; and in this weeping mood he entered the town of Surinam.

Immediately upon their arrival our travellers inquired if there was any vessel in the harbor which they might send to Buenos Ayres. The person they addressed themselves to happened to be the master of a Spanish bark, who offered to agree with them on moderate terms, and appointed them a meeting at a public house. Thither Candide and his faithful Cacambo went to wait for him, taking with them their two sheep.

Candide, who was all frankness and sincerity, made an ingenuous recital of his adventures to the Spaniard, declaring to him at the same time his resolution of carrying off Miss Cunegund from the governor of Buenos Ayres.

"O ho!" said the shipmaster, "if that is the case, get whom you please to carry you to Buenos Ayres; for my part, I wash my hands of the affair. It would prove a hanging matter to us all. The fair Cunegund is the governor's favorite mistress." These words were like a clap of thunder to Candide; he wept bitterly for a long time, and, taking Cacambo aside, he said to him, "I'll tell you, my dear friend, what you must do. We have each of us in our pockets to the value of five or six millions in diamonds; you are cleverer at these matters than I; you must go to Buenos Ayres and bring off Miss Cunegund. If the governor makes any difficulty give him a million; if he holds out, give him two; as you have not killed an inquisitor, they will have no suspicion of you. I'll find out another ship and go to Venice, where I will wait for you. Venice is a free country, where we shall have nothing to fear from Bulgarians, Abares, Jews, or Inquisitors."

Cacambo greatly applauded this wise resolution. He was inconsolable at the thought of parting with so good a master, who treated him more like an intimate friend than a servant; but the pleasure of being able to do him a service soon got the better of his sorrow. They embraced each other with a flood of tears. Candide charged him not to forget the old woman. Cacambo set out the same day. This Cacambo was a very honest fellow.

Candide continued some days longer at Surinam, waiting for any captain to carry him and his two remaining sheep to Italy. He hired domestics, and purchased many things necessary for a long voyage; at length Mynheer Vanderdendur, skipper of a large Dutch vessel, came and offered his service.

"What will you have," said Candide, "to carry me, my servants, my baggage, and these two sheep you see here, directly to Venice?"

The skipper asked ten thousand piastres, and Candide agreed to his demand without hesitation.

"Ho, ho!" said the cunning Vanderdendur to himself, "this stranger must be very rich; he agrees to give me ten thousand piastres without hesitation." Returning a little while after he tells Candide that upon second consideration he could not undertake the voyage for less than twenty thousand. "Very well; you shall have them," said Candide.

"Zounds!" said the skipper to himself, "this man agrees to pay twenty thousand piastres with as much ease as ten." Accordingly he goes back again, and tells him roundly that he will not carry him to Venice for less than thirty thousand piastres.

"Then you shall have thirty thousand," said Candide.

"Odso!" said the Dutchman once more to himself, "thirty thousand piastres seem a trifle to this man. Those sheep must certainly be laden with an immense treasure. I'll e'en stop here and ask no more; but make him pay down the thirty thousand piastres, and then we may see what is to be done farther." Candide sold two small diamonds, the least of which was worth more than all the skipper asked. He paid him beforehand, the two sheep were put on board, and Candide followed in a small boat to join the vessel in the road. The skipper took advantage of his opportunity, hoisted sail, and put out to sea with a favorable wind. Candide, confounded and amazed, soon lost sight of the ship. "Alas!" said he, "this is a trick like those in our old world!"

He returned back to the shore overwhelmed with grief; and, indeed, he had lost what would have made the fortune of twenty monarchs.

Straightway upon his landing he applied to the Dutch magistrate; being transported with passion he thundered at the door, which being opened, he went in, told his case, and talked a little louder than was necessary. The magistrate began with fining him ten thousand piastres for his petulance, and then listened very patiently to what he had to say, promised to examine into the affair on the skipper's return, and ordered him to pay ten thousand piastres more for the fees of the court.

This treatment put Candide out of all patience; it is true, he had suffered misfortunes a thousand times more grievous, but the cool insolence of the judge, and the villainy of the skipper raised his choler and threw him into a deep melancholy. The villainy of mankind presented itself to his mind in all its deformity, and his soul was a prey to the most gloomy ideas. After some time, hearing that the captain of a French ship was ready to set sail for Bordeaux, as he had no more sheep loaded with diamonds to put on board, he hired the cabin at the usual price; and made it known in the town that he would pay the passage and board of any honest man who would give him his company during the voyage; besides making him a present of ten thousand piastres, on condition that such person was the most dissatisfied with his condition, and the most unfortunate in the whole province.

Upon this there appeared such a crowd of candidates that a large fleet could not have contained them. Candide, willing to choose from among those who appeared most likely to answer his intention, selected twenty, who seemed to him the most sociable, and who all pretended to merit the preference. He invited them to his inn, and promised to treat them with a supper, on condition that every man should bind himself by an oath to relate his own history; declaring at the same time, that he would make choice of that person who should appear to him the most deserving of compassion, and the most justly dissatisfied with his condition in life; and that he would make a present to the rest.

This extraordinary assembly continued sitting till four in the morning. Candide, while he was listening to their adventures, called to mind what the old woman had said to him in their voyage to Buenos Ayres, and the wager she had laid that there was not a person on board the ship but had met with great misfortunes. Every story he heard put him in mind of Pangloss.

"My old master," said he, "would be confoundedly put to it to demonstrate his favorite system. Would he were here! Certainly if everything is for the best, it is in El Dorado, and not in the other parts of the world."

At length he determined in favor of a poor scholar, who had labored ten years for the book-sellers at Amsterdam: being of opinion that no employment could be more detestable.

This scholar, who was in fact a very honest man, had been robbed by his wife, beaten by his son, and forsaken by his daughter, who had run away with a Portuguese. He had been likewise deprived of a small employment on which he subsisted, and he was persecuted by the clergy of Surinam, who took him for a Socinian. It must be acknowledged that the other competitors were, at least, as wretched as he; but Candide was in hopes that the company of a man of letters would relieve the tediousness of the voyage. All the other candidates complained that Candide had done them great injustice, but he stopped their mouths by a present of a hundred piastres to each.

ADAM SMITH

Although there had been many attacks on mercantilism both in England and on the Continent in the hundred years before Adam Smith, none was so sharply focused, so systematic, or so penetrating as An Inquiry into the Nature and Causes of the Wealth of Nations. *It is interesting to note (and is probably suggestive of the motives and orientation of the author) that this work, which became a* magnum opus, *was originally designed as simply an appendix to a larger study on moral philosophy. In any event,* The Wealth of Nations, *the first volume of which appeared in 1776 (the same year in which the first volume of Edward Gibbon's* The Decline and Fall of the Roman Empire *appeared), has taken its place among the truly significant and influential works of modern times.*

In analyzing the sources of the economic well-being of a nation, Smith concludes that specialization of labor and free enterprise are the most important. Here he reveals his acceptance of the intellectual movements of the eighteenth century. Although he refused to agree with the French physiocrats that agriculture alone was the source of a nation's wealth, Smith shared with the physiocrats the notion that each individual could best determine what was his own best interest. From this it followed logically that no one should be entitled to tell other people what sort of economic activity they should pursue. Thus, the government had no right to grant sole control over a market or an industry by patent or license, since such a grant violated the natural laws of political economy. That the free operation of the laws of supply and demand and the operations of the market economy should ever result in monopoly or monopsony Smith believed to be an impossibility, feeling instead that "enlightened self-interest" would always prevent such abuses.

Smith (1723–1790), a philosopher and a professor at the University of Edinburgh, would probably have been horrified at the crimes that were later committed under the sanction of his doctrines of laissez-faire, *free enterprise, economic individualism, and the pursuit of self-interest. For while he did argue for a minimum of governmental interference and a maximum of individual enterprise, he also, and most importantly, felt that each per-*

son should govern his actions by enlightened *self-interest. If one's self-interest is enlightened, Smith believed, he will realize that his own greatest good will be gained, not through the exploitation of his fellows, but through a recognition of his duties and obligations to the rest of society. Thus, to Smith, enlightened self-interest was a pursuit of what is best and most acceptable to the individual after, and only after, the concerns and interests of others have been satisfied.*

An Inquiry into the Nature and Causes of the Wealth of Nations

Introduction and Plan of the Work

The annual labour of every nation is the fund which originally supplies it with all the necessaries and conveniencies of life which it annually consumes, and which consist always either in the immediate produce of that labour, or in what is purchased with that produce from other nations.

According therefore, as this produce, or what is purchased with it, bears a greater or smaller proportion to the number of those who are to consume it, the nation will be better or worse supplied with all the necessaries and conveniencies for which it has occasion.

But this proportion must in every nation be regulated by two different circumstances; first, by the skill, dexterity, and judgment with which its labour is generally applied; and, secondly, by the proportion between the number of those who are employed in useful labour, and that of those who are not so employed. Whatever be the soil, climate, or extent of territory of any particular nation, the abundance or scantiness of its annual supply must, in that particular situation, depend upon those two circumstances.

Adam Smith, AN INQUIRY INTO THE NATURE AND CAUSES OF THE WEALTH OF NATIONS, *8th ed. (London, 1796).*

The abundance or scantiness of this supply too seems to depend more upon the former of those two circumstances than upon the latter. Among the savage nations of hunters and fishers, every individual who is able to work, is more or less employed in useful labour, and endeavours to provide, as well as he can, the necessaries and conveniencies of life, for himself, or such of his family or tribe as are either too old, or too young, or too infirm to go a hunting and fishing. Such nations, however, are so miserably poor, that from mere want, they are frequently reduced, or at least think themselves reduced, to the necessity sometimes of directly destroying, and sometimes of abandoning their infants, their old people, and those afflicted with lingering diseases, to perish with hunger, or to be devoured by wild beasts. Among civilized and thriving nations, on the contrary, though a great number of people do not labour at all, many of whom consume the produce of ten times, frequently of a hundred times more labour than the greater part of those who work; yet the produce of the whole labour of the society is so great, that all are often abundantly supplied, and a workman, even of the lowest and poorest order, if he is frugal and industrious, may enjoy a greater share of the necessaries and conveniencies of life than it is possible for any savage to acquire.

The causes of this improvement in the productive powers of labour, and the order, according to which its produce is naturally distributed among the different ranks and conditions of men in the society, make the subject of the First Book of this Inquiry.

Whatever be the actual state of the skill, dexterity, and judgment with which labour is applied in any nation, the abundance or scantiness of its annual supply must depend, during the continuance of that state, upon the proportion between the number of those who are annually employed in useful labour, and that of those who are not so employed. The number of useful and productive labourers, it will hereafter appear, is every where in proportion to the quantity of capital stock which is employed in setting them to work, and to the particular way in which it is so employed. The Second Book, therefore, treats of the nature of capital stock, of the manner in which it is gradually accumulated, and of the different quantities of labour which it puts into motion, according to the different ways in which it is employed.

Nations tolerably well advanced as to skill, dexterity, and judgment, in the application of labour, have followed very different plans in the general conduct or direction of it; and those plans have not all been equally favourable to the greatness of its produce. The policy of some nations has given extraordinary encouragement to the industry of the country; that of others to the industry of towns. Scarce any nation has dealt equally and impartially with every sort of industry. Since the downfall of the Roman empire, the policy of Europe has been more favourable to arts, manufactures, and commerce, the industry of towns; than to agriculture, the industry of the country. The circumstances which seem to have introduced and established this policy are explained in the Third Book.

Though those different plans were, perhaps, first introduced by the private interests and prejudices of particular orders of men, without any regard to, or foresight of, their consequences upon the general welfare of the society; yet they have given occasion to very different theories of political economy; of which some magnify the importance of that industry which is carried on in towns, others of that which is carried on in the country. Those theories have had a considerable influence, not only upon the opinions of men of learning, but upon the public conduct of princes and sovereign states. I have endeavoured in the Fourth Book, to explain, as fully and distinctly as I can, those different theories, and the principal effects which they have produced in different ages and nations.

To explain in what has consisted the revenue of the great body of the people, or what has been the nature of those funds, which, in different ages and nations, have supplied their annual consumption, is the object of these Four first Books. The Fifth and last Book treats of the revenue of the sovereignship, or commonwealth. In this Book I have endeavoured to show; first, what are the necessary expenses of the sovereign, or commonwealth; which of those expenses ought to be defrayed by the general contribution of the whole society; and which of them, by that of some particular part only, or of some particular members of it: secondly, what are the different methods in which the whole society may be made to contribute towards defraying the expenses incumbent on the whole society, and what are the principal advantages and inconveniencies of each of those methods: and, thirdly and lastly, what are the reasons and causes which have induced almost all modern governments to mortgage some part of this revenue, or to contract debts, and what have been the effects of those debts upon the real wealth, the annual produce of the land and labour of the society.

. . .

Book IV

CHAPTER II. OF RESTRAINTS UPON THE IMPORTATION FROM FOREIGN COUNTRIES OF SUCH GOODS AS CAN BE PRODUCED AT HOME

By restraining, either by high duties, or by absolute prohibitions, the importation of such goods from foreign countries as can be produced at home, the monopoly of the home-market is more or less secured to the domestic industry employed in producing them. Thus the prohibition of importing either live cattle or salt provisions from foreign countries secures to the graziers of Great Britain the monopoly of the home market for butchers'-meat. The high duties upon the importation of corn, which in times of moderate plenty amount to a prohibition, give a like advantage to the growers of that commodity. The prohibition of the importation of foreign woolens is equally favourable to the woolen manufactures. The silk manufacture, though altogether employed upon foreign materials, has lately obtained the same advantage. The linen manufacture has not yet obtained it, but is making great strides towards it. Many other sorts of manufactures have, in the same manner, obtained in Great Britain, either altogether, or very nearly a monopoly against their countrymen. The variety of goods of which the importation into Great Britain is prohibited, either absolutely, or under certain circumstances, greatly exceeds what can easily be suspected by those who are not well acquainted with the laws of the customs.

That this monopoly of the home-market frequently gives great encouragement to that particular species of industry which enjoys it, and frequently turns toward that employment a greater share of both the labour and stock of the society than would otherwise have gone to it, cannot be doubted. But whether it tends either to increase the general industry of the society, or to give it the most advantageous direction, is not, perhaps, altogether so evident.

The general industry of the society never can exceed what the capital of the society can employ. As the number of workmen that can be kept in employment by any particular person must bear a certain proportion to his capital, so the number of those that can be continually employed by all the members of a great society, must bear a certain proportion to the whole capital of that society, and never can exceed that proportion. No regulation of commerce can increase the quantity of industry in any society beyond what its capital can maintain. It can only divert a part of it into a direction into which it might not otherwise have gone; and it is by no means certain that this artificial direction is likely to be more advantageous to the society than that into which it would have gone of its own accord.

Every individual is continually exerting himself to find out the most advantageous employment for whatever capital he can command. It is his own advantage, indeed, and not that of the society, which he has in view. But the study of his own advantage naturally, or rather necessarily leads him to prefer that employment which is most advantageous to the society.

First, every individual endeavours to employ his capital as near home as he can, and consequently as much as he can in the support of domestic industry; provided always that he can thereby obtain the ordinary, or not a great deal less than the ordinary profits of stock.

Thus, upon equal or nearly equal profits,

every wholesale merchant naturally prefers the home-trade to the foreign trade of consumption, and the foreign trade of consumption to the carrying trade. In the home-trade his capital is never so long out of his sight as it frequently is in the foreign trade of consumption. He can know better the character and situation of the persons whom he trusts, and if he should happen to be deceived, he knows better the laws of the country from which he must seek redress. . . . Upon equal, or only nearly equal profits, therefore, every individual naturally inclines to employ his capital in the manner in which it is likely to afford the greatest support to domestic industry, and to give revenue and employment to the greatest number of people of his own country.

Secondly, every individual who employs his capital in the support of domestic industry, necessarily endeavours so to direct that industry, that its produce may be of the greatest possible value.

The produce of industry is what it adds to the subject or materials upon which it is employed. In proportion as the value of this produce is great or small, so will likewise be the profits of the employer. But it is only for the sake of profit that any man employs a capital in the support of industry; and he will always, therefore, endeavour to employ it in the support of that industry of which the produce is likely to be of the greatest value, or to exchange for the greatest quantity either of money or of other goods.

But the annual revenue of every society is always precisely equal to the exchangeable value of the whole annual produce of its industry, or rather is precisely the same thing with that exchangeable value. As every individual, therefore, endeavours as much as he can both to employ his capital in the support of domestic industry, and so to direct that industry that its produce may be of the greatest value; every individual necessarily labours to render the annual revenue of the society as great as he can. He generally, indeed, neither intends to promote the public interest, nor knows how much he is promoting it. By preferring the support of domestic to that of foreign industry, he intends only his own security; and by directing that industry in such a manner as its produce may be of the greatest value, he intends only his own gain, and he is in this, as in many other cases, led by an invisible hand to promote an end which was no part of his intention. Nor is it always the worse for the society that it was no part of it. By pursuing his own interest he frequently promotes that of the society more effectually than when he really intends to promote it. I have never known much good done by those who affected to trade for the public good. It is an affectation, indeed, not very common among merchants, and very few words need be employed in dissuading them from it.

What is the species of domestic industry which his capital can employ, and of which the produce is likely to be of the greatest value, every individual, it is evident, can, in his local situation, judge much better than any statesman or lawgiver can do for him. The statesman, who should attempt to direct private people in what manner they ought to employ their capitals, would not only load himself with a most unnecessary attention, but assume an authority which could safely be trusted, not only to no single person, but to no council or senate whatever, and which would nowhere be so dangerous as in the hands of a man who had folly and presumption enough to fancy himself fit to exercise it.

To give the monopoly of the home-market to the produce of domestic industry, in any particular art or manufacture, is in some measure to direct private people in what manner they ought to employ their capitals, and must, in almost all cases, be either a useless or a hurtful regulation. If the produce of domestic can be brought there as cheap as that of foreign industry, the regulation is evidently useless. If it cannot, it must generally be hurtful. It is the maxim of every prudent master of a family, never to attempt to make at home what it will cost him more to make than to buy. The taylor does not attempt to make his own shoes, but buys them of the shoemaker. The shoemaker does not attempt to make his own clothes, but employs a taylor. The farmer attempts to make neither the one nor the other, but employs those different artificers. All of them find it for their interest to employ their whole industry in a way in which they have some advantage over their neighbors, and to purchase with a part of its produce, or what is the same thing, with the price of a part of it, whatever else they have occasion for.

What is prudence in the conduct of every private family, can scarce be folly in that of a great kingdom. If a foreign country can supply us with a commodity cheaper than we ourselves can make it, better buy it of them with some part of the produce of our own industry, employed in a way in which we have some advantage. The general industry of the country, being always in proportion to the capital which employs it, will not thereby be diminished, no more than that of the abovementioned artificers; but only left to find out the way in which it can be employed with the greatest advantage. It is certainly not employed to the greatest advantage, when it is thus directed towards an object which it can buy cheaper than it can make. The value of its annual produce is certainly more or less diminished, when it is thus turned away from producing commodities evidently of more value than the commodity which it is directed to produce. According to the supposition, that commodity could be purchased from foreign countries cheaper than it can be made at home. It could, therefore, have been purchased with a part only of the commodities, or, what is the same thing, with a part only of the price of the commodities, which the industry employed by an equal capital would have produced at home, had it been left to follow its natural course. The industry of the country, therefore, is thus turned away from a more to a less advantageous employment, and the exchangeable value of its annual produce, instead of being increased, according to the intention of the lawgiver, must necessarily be diminished by every such regulation.

By means of such regulations, indeed, a particular manufacture may sometimes be acquired sooner than it could have been otherwise, and after a certain time may be made at home as cheap or cheaper than in the foreign country. But though the industry of the society may be thus carried with advantage into a particular channel sooner than it could have been otherwise, it will by no means follow that the sum total, either of its industry, or of its revenue, can ever be augmented by any such regulation. The industry of the society can augment only in proportion as its capital augments, and its capital can augment only in proportion to what can be gradually saved out of its revenue. But the immediate effect of every such regulation is to diminish its revenue, and what diminishes its revenue is certainly not very likely to augment its capital faster than it would have augmented of its own accord, had both capital and industry been left to find out their natural employments.

Though for want of such regulations the society should never acquire the proposed manufacture, it would not, upon that account, necessarily be the poorer in anv one period of its duration. In every period of its duration its whole capital and industry might still have been employed, though upon different objects, in the manner that was most advantageous at the time. In every period its revenue might have been the greatest which its capital could afford, and both capital and revenue might have been augmented with the greatest possible rapidity.

The natural advantages which one country has over another in producing particular commodities are sometimes so great, that it is acknowledged by all the world to be in vain to struggle with them. By means of glasses, hotbeds, and hotwalls, very good grapes can be raised in Scotland, and very good wine too can be made of them at about thirty times the expense for which at least equally good can be brought from foreign countries. Would it be a reasonable law to prohibit the importation of all foreign wines, merely to encourage the making of claret and burgundy in Scotland? But if there would be a manifest absurdity in turning towards any employment thirty times more of the capital and industry of the country, than would be necessary to purchase from foreign countries an equal quantity of the commodities wanted, there must be an absurdity, though not altogether so glaring, yet exactly of the same kind, in turning towards any such employment a thirtieth, or even a three hundreth part more of either. Whether the advantages which one country has over another be natural or acquired, is in this respect of no consequence. As long as the one country has those advantages, and the other wants them, it will always be more advantageous for the latter, rather to buy of the former than to make. It is an acquired advantage only, which one artificer has over his neighbour, who exercises another trade; and yet they both find it more advantageous to buy of one another, than to make what does not belong to their particular trades.

Merchants and manufacturers are the people who derive the greatest advantage from this monopoly of the home-market. The prohibition of the importation of foreign cattle, and of salt provisions, together with the high duties upon foreign corn, which in times of moderate plenty amount to a prohibition, are not near so advantageous to the graziers and farmers of Great Britain, as other regulations of the same kind are to its merchants and manufacturers. Manufactures, those of the finer kind especially, are more easily transported from one country to another than corn or cattle. It is in the fetching and carrying manufactures, accordingly, that foreign trade is chiefly employed. In manufactures, a very small advantage will enable foreigners to undersell our own workmen, even in the home-market. It will require a very great one to enable them to do so in the rude produce of the soil. If the free importation of foreign manufactures were permitted, several of the home manufactures would probably suffer, and some of them, perhaps, go to ruin altogether, and a considerable part of the stock and industry at present employed in them would be forced to find out some other employment. But the freest importation of the rude produce of the soil could have no such effect upon the agriculture of the country.

If the importation of foreign cattle, for example, were made ever so free, so few could be imported, that the grazing trade of Great Britain could be little affected by it. Live cattle are, perhaps, the only commodity of which the transportation is more expensive by sea than by land. By land they carry themselves to market. By sea, not only the cattle, but their food and their water too, must be carried at no small expense and inconveniency. The short sea between Ireland and Great Britain, indeed, renders the importation of Irish cattle more easy. But though the free importation of them, which was lately permitted only for a limited time, were rendered perpetual, it could have no considerable effect upon the interest of the graziers of Great Britain. Those parts of Great Britain which border upon the Irish sea are all grazing countries. Irish cattle could never be imported for their use, but must be drove through those very extensive countries, at no small expense and inconvenience, before they could arrive at the proper market. But cattle could not be drove so far. Lean cattle, therefore, only could be imported, and such importation could interfere, not with the interest of the feeding or fattening countries, to which, by reducing the price of lean cattle, it would rather be advantageous, but with that of the breeding countries only. The small number of Irish cattle imported since their importation was permitted, together with the good price at which lean cattle still continue to sell, seem to demonstrate that even the breeding countries of Great Britain are never likely to be much affected by the free importation of Irish cattle. The common people of Ireland, indeed, are said to have sometimes opposed with violence the exportation of their cattle. But if the exporters had found any great advantage in continuing the trade, they could easily, when the law was on their side, have conquered this mobbish opposition.

Feeding and fattening countries, besides, must always be highly improved, whereas breeding countries are generally uncultivated. The high price of lean cattle, by augmenting the value of uncultivated land, is like a bounty against improvement. To any country which was highly improved throughout, it would be more advantageous to import its lean cattle than to breed them. The province of Holland, accordingly is said to follow this maxim at present. The mountains of Scotland, Wales and Northumberland, indeed, are countries not capable of much improvement, and seem destined by nature to be the breeding countries of Great Britain. The freest importation of foreign cattle could have no other effect than to hinder those breeding countries from taking advantage of the increasing population and improvement of the rest of the kingdom, from raising their price to an exorbitant height, and from laying a real tax upon all the more improved and cultivated parts of the country.

. . .

Even the free importation of foreign corn could very little affect the interest of the farmers of Great Britain. Corn is a much more bulky commodity than butchers'-meat. A pound of wheat at a penny is as dear as a pound of butchers'-meat at fourpence. The small quantity of foreign corn imported even in times of the greatest scarcity, may satisfy our farmers that they can have nothing to fear from the freest importation. The average quantity imported one year with another, amounts only, according to the very well-informed author of the tracts upon the corn trade, to twenty-three thousand seven hundred and twenty-eight quarters of all sorts of grain, and does not exceed the five hundredth and seventy-one part of the annual consumption. But as the bounty upon corn occasions a greater exportation in years of plenty, so it must of consequence occasion a greater importation in years of scarcity, than in the actual state of tillage would otherwise take place. By means of it, the plenty of one year does not compensate the scarcity of another, and as the average quantity exported is necessarily augmented by it, so much likewise, in the actual state of tillage, the average quantity imported. If there were no bounty, as less corn would be exported, so it is probable that, one year with another, less would be imported than at present. The corn merchant, the fetchers and carriers of corn between Great Britain and foreign countries, would have much less employment, and might suffer considerably; but the country gentlemen and farmers could suffer very little. It is in the corn merchants accordingly, rather than in the country gentlemen and farmers, that I have observed the greatest anxiety for the renewal and continuation of the bounty.

Country gentlemen and farmers are, to their great honour, of all people, the least subject to the wretched spirit of monopoly. The undertaker of a great manufactory is sometimes alarmed if another work of the same kind is established within twenty miles of him. The Dutch undertaker of the woollen manufacture at Abbeville stipulated, that no work of the same kind should be established within thirty leagues of that city. Farmers and country gentlemen, on the contrary, are generally disposed rather to promote than to obstruct the cultivation and improvement of their neighbours' farms and estates. They have no secrets, such as those of the greater part of manufacturers, but are generally rather fond of communicating to their neighbours, and of extending as far as possible any new practice which they have found to be advantageous. . . . Country gentlemen and farmers, dispersed in different parts of the country, cannot so easily combine as merchants and manufacturers, who being collected into towns, and accustomed to that exclusive corporation spirit which prevails in them, naturally endeavour to obtain against all their countrymen, the same exclusive privilege which they generally possess against the inhabitants of their respective towns. They accordingly seem to have been the original inventors of those restraints upon the importation of foreign goods, which secure to them the monopoly of the home-market. It was probably in imitation of them, and to put themselves upon a level with those who, they found, were disposed to oppress them, that the country gentlemen and farmers of Great Britain so far forgot the generosity which is natural to their station, as to demand the exclusive privilege of supplying their countrymen with corn and butchers'-meat. They did not perhaps take time to consider, how much less their interest could be affected by the freedom of trade than that of the people whose example they followed.

To prohibit by a perpetual law the importation of foreign corn and cattle, is in reality to enact, that the population and industry of the country shall at no time exceed what the rude produce of its own soil can maintain.

There seem, however, to be two cases in which it will generally be advantageous to lay some burden upon foreign, for the encouragement of domestic industry.

The first is, when some particular sort of industry is necessary for the defense of the country. The defense of Great Britain, for example, depends very much upon the number of its sailors and shipping. The act of navigation, therefore, very properly endeavours to give the sailors and shipping of Great Britain the monopoly of the trade of their own country, in some cases, by absolute prohibitions, and in others by heavy burdens upon the shipping of foreign countries. The following are the principal dispositions of this act.

First, all ships, of which the owners, masters, and three-fourths of the mariners are not British subjects, are prohibited, upon pain of forfeiting ship and cargo, from trading to the British settlements and plantations, or from being employed in the coasting trade of Great Britain.

Secondly, a great variety of the most bulky articles of importation can be brought into Great Britain only, either in such ships as are above described, or in ships of the country where those goods are produced, and of which the owners, masters, and three-fourths of the mariners, are of that particular country; and when imported even in ships of this latter kind, they are subject to double aliens duty. If imported in ships of any other country, the penalty is forfeiture of ship and goods. When this act was made, the Dutch were, what they still are, the great carriers of Europe, and by this regulation they were entirely excluded from being carriers to Great Britain, or from importing to us the goods of any other European country.

Thirdly, a great variety of the most bulky articles of importation are prohibited from being imported, even in British ships, from any country but that in which they are produced; under pain of forfeiting ship and cargo. This regulation too was probably intended against the Dutch. Holland was then, as now, the great emporium for all European goods, and by this regulation, British ships were hindered from loading in Holland the goods of any other European country.

Fourthly, salt fish of all kinds, whale fins, whale-bone, oil, and blubber, not caught by and cured on board British vessels, when imported into Great Britain, are subjected to double aliens duty. The Dutch, as they are still the principal, were then the only fishers in Europe that attempted to supply foreign nations with fish. By this regulation, a very heavy burden was laid upon their supplying Great Britain.

When the act of navigation was made, though England and Holland were not actually at war, the most violent animosity subsisted between the two nations. It had begun during the government of the long parliament, which first framed this act, and it broke out soon after in the Dutch wars during that of the Protector and of Charles the second. It is not impossible, therefore, that some of the regulations of this famous act may have proceeded from national animosity. They are as wise, however, as if they had all been dictated by the most deliberate wisdom. National animosity at that particular time aimed at the very same object which the most deliberate wisdom would have recommended, the diminution of the naval power of Holland, the only naval power which could endanger the security of England.

The act of navigation is not favourable to foreign commerce or to the growth of that opulence which can arise from it. The interest of a nation in its commercial relations to foreign nations is, like that of a merchant with regard to the different people with whom he deals, to buy as cheap and to sell as dear as possible. But it will be most likely to buy cheap, when by the most perfect freedom of trade it encourages all nations to bring to it the goods which it has occasion to purchase; and, for the same reason, it will be most likely to sell dear, when its markets are thus filled with the greatest number of buyers. The act of navigation, it is true, lays no burden upon foreign ships that come to export the produce of British industry. Even the ancient aliens duty, which used to be paid upon all goods exported as well as imported, has, by several subsequent acts, been taken off from the greater part of the articles of exportation. But if foreigners, either by prohibitions or high duties, are hindered from coming to sell, they cannot always afford to come to buy; because coming without a cargo, they must lose the freight from their own country to Great Britain. By diminishing the number of sellers, therefore, we necessarily diminish that of buyers, and are thus likely not only to buy foreign goods dearer, but to sell our own cheaper, than if there was a more perfect freedom of trade. As defense, however, is of much more importance than opulence, the act of navigation is, perhaps, the wisest of all the commercial regulations of England.

The second case, in which it will generally be advantageous to lay some burden upon foreign for the encouragement of domestic industry, is, when some tax is imposed at home upon the produce of the latter. In this case, it seems reasonable that an equal tax should be imposed upon the like produce of the former. This would not give the monopoly of the home-market to domestic industry, nor turn towards a particular employment a greater share of the stock and labour of the country, than what would naturally go to it. It would only hinder any part of what would naturally go to it from being turned away by the tax, into a less natural direction, and would leave the competition between foreign and domestic industry, after the tax, as nearly as possible upon the same footing as before it. In Great Britain, when any such tax is laid upon the produce of domestic industry, it is usual at the same time, in order to stop the clamorous complaints of our merchants and manufacturers, that they will be undersold at home, to lay a much heavier duty upon the importation of all foreign goods of the same kind.

This second limitation of the freedom of trade according to some people should, upon some occasions, be extended much farther than to the precise foreign commodities which could come into competition with those which had been taxed at home. When the necessaries of life have been taxed in any country, it becomes proper, they pretend, to tax not only the like necessaries of life imported from other countries, but all sorts of foreign goods which can come into competition with any thing that is the produce of domestic industry. Subsistence, they say, becomes necessarily dearer in consequence of such taxes; and the price of labour must always rise with the price of the labourers subsistence. Every commodity, therefore, which is the produce of domestic industry, though not immediately taxed itself, becomes dearer in consequence of such taxes, because the labour which produces it becomes so. Such taxes, therefore, are really equivalent, they say, to a tax upon every particular commodity produced at home. In order to put domestic upon the same footing with foreign industry, therefore, it becomes necessary, they think, to lay some duty upon every foreign commodity, equal to this enhancement of the price of the home commodities with which it can come into competition.

Whether taxes upon the necessaries of life, such as those in Great Britain upon soap, salt, leather, candles, &c. necessarily raise the price of labour, and consequently that of all other commodities, I shall consider hereafter, when I come to treat of taxes. Supposing, however, in the mean time, that they have this effect, and they have it undoubtedly, this general enhancement of the price of all commodities, in consequence of that of labour, is a case which differs in the two following respects from that of a particular commodity, of which the price was enhanced by a particular tax immediately imposed upon it.

First, it might always be known with great exactness how far the price of such a commodity could be enhanced by such a tax: but how far the general enhancement of the price of labour might affect that of every different commodity about which labour was employed, could never be known with any tolerable exactness. It would be impossible, therefore, to proportion with any tolerable exactness the tax upon every foreign, to this enhancement of the price of every home commodity.

Secondly, taxes upon the necessaries of life have nearly the same effect upon the circumstances of the people as a poor soil and a bad climate. Provisions are thereby rendered dearer in the same manner as if it required extraordinary labour and expense to raise them. As in the natural scarcity arising from soil and climate, it would be absurd to direct the people in what manner they ought to employ their capitals and industry, so is it likewise in the artificial scarcity arising from such taxes. To be left to accommodate, as well as they could, their industry to their situation, and to find out those employments in which, notwithstanding their unfavourable circumstances, they might have some advantage either in the home or in the foreign market, is what in both cases would evidently be most for their advantage. To lay a new tax upon them, because they are already overburdened with taxes, and because they already pay too dear for the necessaries of life, to make them likewise pay too dear for the greater part of other commodities, is certainly a most absurd way of making amends.

Such taxes, when they have grown up to a certain height, are a curse equal to the barrenness of the earth and the inclemency of the heavens; and yet it is in the richest and most industrious countries that they have been most generally imposed. No other countries could support so great a disorder. As the strongest bodies only can live and enjoy health, under an unwholesome regimen; so the nations only, that in every sort of industry have the greatest natural and acquired advantages, can subsist and prosper under such taxes. Holland is the country in Europe in which they abound most, and which from peculiar circumstances continues to prosper, not by means of them, as has been most absurdly supposed, but in spite of them.

As there are two cases in which it will generally be advantageous to lay some burden upon foreign, for the encouragement of domestic industry; so there are two others in which it may sometimes be a matter of deliberation; in the one, how far it is proper to continue the free importation of certain foreign goods; and in the other, how far, or in what manner, it may be proper to restore that free importation after it has been for some time interrupted.

The case in which it may sometimes be a matter of deliberation how far it is proper to continue the free importation of certain foreign goods, is, when some foreign nation restrains by high duties or prohibitions the importation of some of our manufactures into their country. Revenge in this case naturally dictates retaliation, and that we should impose the like duties and prohibitions upon the importation of some or all of their manufactures into ours. Nations accordingly seldom fail to retaliate in this manner. The French have been particularly forward to favour their own manufactures by restraining the importation of such foreign goods as could come into competition with them. In this consisted a great part of the policy of Mr. Colbert, who, notwithstanding his great abilities, seems in this case to have been imposed upon by the sophistry of merchants and manufacturers, who are always demanding a monopoly against their countrymen. It is at present the opinion of the most intelligent men in France that his operations of this kind have not been beneficial to his country. That minister, by the tariff of 1667, imposed very high duties upon a great number of foreign manufactures. Upon his refusing to moderate them in favour of the Dutch, they in 1671 prohibited the importation of the wines, brandies, and manufactures of France. The war of 1672 seems to have been in part occasioned by this commercial dispute. The peace of Nimeguen put an end to it in 1678, by moderating some of those duties in favour of the Dutch, who in consequence took off their prohibition. It was about the same time that the French and English began mutually to oppress each other's industry, by the like duties and prohibitions, of which the French, however, seem to have set the first example. The spirit of hostility which has subsisted between the two nations ever since, has hitherto hindered them from being moderated on either side. In 1697 the English prohibited the importation of bonelace, the manufacture of Flanders. The government of that country, at that time under the dominion of Spain, prohibited in return the importation of English woollens. In 1700, the prohibition of importing bonelace into England was taken off upon condition that the importation of English woollens into Flanders should be put on the same footing as before.

There may be good policy in retaliations of this kind, when there is a probability that they will procure the repeal of the high duties or prohibitions complained of. The recovery of a great foreign market will generally more than compensate the transitory inconvenience of paying dearer during a short time for some sorts of goods. To judge whether such retaliations are likely to produce such an effect, does not, perhaps, belong so much to the science of a legislator, whose deliberations ought to be governed by general principles which are always the same, as to the skill of that insidious and crafty animal, vulgarly called a statesman or politician, whose councils are directed by the momentary fluctuations of affairs. When there is no probability that any such repeal can be procured, it seems a bad method of compensating the injury done to certain classes of our people, to do another injury ourselves, not only to those classes, but to almost all the other classes of them. When our neighbours prohibit some manufacture of ours, we generally prohibit, not only the same, for that alone would seldom affect them considerably, but some other manufacture of theirs. This may no doubt give encouragement to some particular class of workmen among ourselves, and by excluding some of their rivals, may enable them to raise their price in the home-market. Those workmen, however, who suffered by our neighbours' prohibition will not be benefited by ours. On the contrary, they and almost all the other classes of our citizens will thereby be obliged to pay dearer than before for certain goods. Every such law, therefore, imposes a real tax upon the whole country, not in favour of that particular class of workmen who were injured by our neighbours' prohibition, but of some other class.

The case in which it may sometimes be a matter of deliberation, how far, or in what manner, it is proper to restore the free importation of foreign goods, after it has been for some time interrupted, is, when particular manufactures, by means of high duties or prohibitions upon all foreign goods which can come into competition with them, have been so far extended as to employ a great multitude of hands. Humanity may in this case require that the freedom of trade should be restored only by slow gradations, and with a good deal of reserve and circumspection. Were those high duties and prohibitions taken away all at once, cheaper foreign goods of the same kind might be poured so fast into the home-market, as to deprive all at once many thousands of our people of their ordinary employment and means of subsistence. The disorder which this would occasion might no doubt be very considerable. It would in all probability, however, be much less than is commonly imagined, for the two following reasons:

First, all those manufactures, of which any part is commonly exported to other European countries without a bounty, could be very little affected by the freest importation of foreign goods. Such manufactures must be sold as cheap abroad as any other foreign goods of the same quality and kind, and consequently must be sold cheaper at home. They would still, therefore, keep possession of the home market, and though a capricious man of fashion might sometimes prefer foreign wares, merely because they were foreign, to cheaper and better goods of the same kind that were made at home, this folly could, from the nature of things, extend to so few, that it could make no sensible impression upon the general employment of the people. But a great part of all the different branches of our woollen manufacture, of our tanned leather, and of our hard-ware, are annually exported to other European countries without any bounty, and these are the manufactures which employ the greatest number of hands. The silk, perhaps, is the manufacture which would suffer the most by this freedom of trade, and after it the linen, though the latter much less than the former.

Secondly, though a great number of people should, by thus restoring the freedom of trade, be thrown all at once out of their ordinary employment and common method of subsistence, it would by no means follow that they would thereby be deprived either of employment or subsistence. By the reduction of the army and navy at the end of the late war, more than a hundred thousand soldiers and seamen, a number equal to what is employed in the greatest manufactures, were all at once thrown out of their ordinary employment; but, though they no doubt suffered some inconvenience, they were not thereby deprived of all employment and subsistence. The greater part of the seamen, it is probable, gradually betook themselves to the merchant-service as they could find occasion, and in the mean time both they and the soldiers were absorbed in the great mass of the people, and employed in a great variety of occupations. Not only no great convulsion, but no sensible disorder arose from so great a change in the situation of more than a hundred thousand men, all accustomed to the use of arms, and many of them to rapine and plunder. The number of vagrants was scarce anywhere sensibly increased by it, even the wages of labour were not reduced by it in any occupation, so far as I have been able to learn, except in that of seamen in the merchant-service. But if we compare together the habits of a soldier and of any sort of manufacturer, we shall find that those of the latter do not tend so much to disqualify him from being employed in a new trade, as those of the former from being employed in any. The manufacturer has always been accustomed to look for his subsistence from his labour only: the soldier to expect it from his pay. Application and industry have been familiar to the one; idleness and dissipation to the other. But it is surely much easier to change the direction of industry from one sort of labour to another, than to turn idleness and dissipation to any. To the greater part of manufactures besides, it has already been observed, there are other collateral manufactures of so similar a nature, that a workman can easily transfer his industry from one of them to another. The greater part of such workmen too are occasionally employed in country labour. The stock which employed them in a particular manufacture before, will still remain in the country to employ an equal number of people in some other way. The capital of the country remaining the same, the demand for labour will likewise be the same, or very nearly the same, though it may be exerted in different places and for different occupations. Soldiers and seamen, indeed, when discharged from the king's service, are at liberty to exercise any trade within any town or place of Great Britain or Ireland. Let the same natural liberty of exercising what species of industry they please, be restored to all his majesty's subjects, in the same manner as to soldiers and seamen; that is, break down the exclusive privileges of corporations, and repeal the statute of apprenticeship, both which are real encroachments upon natural liberty, and add to these the repeal of the law of settlements, so that a poor workman, when thrown out of employment either in one trade or in one place, may seek for it in another trade or in another place, without the fear either of a prosecution or of a removal, and neither the public nor the individuals will suffer much more from the occasional disbanding of some particular classes of manufacturers, than from that of soldiers. Our manufacturers have no doubt great merit with their country, but they cannot have more than those who defend it with their blood, nor deserve to be treated with more delicacy.

To expect, indeed, that the freedom of trade should ever be entirely restored in Great Britain, is as absurd as to expect that an Oceana or Utopia should ever be established in it. Not only the prejudices of the public, but what is much more unconquerable, the private interests of many individuals, irresistibly oppose it. Were the officers of the army to oppose with the same zeal and unanimity any reduction in the number of forces, with which master manufacturers set themselves against every law that is likely to increase the number of their rivals in the home-market; were the former to animate their soldiers, in the same manner as the latter inflame their workmen, to attack with violence and outrage the proposers of any such regulation; to attempt to reduce the army would be as dangerous as it has now become to attempt to diminish in any respect the monopoly which our manufacturers have obtained against us. This monopoly has so much increased the number of some particular tribes of them, that, like an overgrown standing army, they have become formidable to the government, and upon many occasions intimidate the legislature. The member of parliament who supports every proposal for strengthening this monopoly, is sure to acquire not only the reputation of understanding trade, but great popularity and influence with an order of men whose numbers and wealth render them of great importance. If he opposes them, on the contrary, and still more if he has authority enough to be able to thwart them, neither the most acknowledged probity, nor the highest rank, nor the greatest public services, can protect him from the most infamous abuse and detraction, from personal insults, nor sometimes from real danger, arising from the insolent outrage of furious and disappointed monopolists.

The undertaker of a great manufacture, who, by the home-markets being suddenly laid open to the competition of foreigners, should be obliged to abandon his trade, would no doubt suffer very considerably. That part of his capital which had usually been employed in purchasing materials and in paying his workmen, might, without much difficulty, perhaps, find another employment. But that part of it which was fixed in workhouses, and in the instruments of trade, could scarce be disposed of without considerable loss. The equitable regard, therefore, to his interest requires that changes of this kind should never be introduced suddenly, but slowly, gradually, and after a very long warning. The legislature, were it possible that its deliberations could be always directed, not by the clamorous importunity of partial interests, but by an extensive view of the general good, ought upon this very account, perhaps, to be particularly careful neither to establish any new monopolies of this kind, nor to extend further those which are already established. Every such regulation introduces some degree of real disorder into the constitution of the state, which it will be difficult afterwards to cure without occasioning another disorder.

How far it may be proper to impose taxes upon the importation of foreign goods, in order, not to prevent their importation, but to raise a revenue for government, I shall consider hereafter when I come to treat of taxes. Taxes imposed with a view to prevent or even to diminish importation, are evidently as destructive of the revenue of the customs as of the freedom of trade.

JEAN JACQUES ROUSSEAU

In Jean Jacques Rousseau (1712–1778), eighteenth-century society found its severest critic. Born in Geneva, Rousseau spent much of his career in intimate contact with the leaders of the French Enlightenment. But rather than sharing their ideas, he rejected them, vehemently and violently. To Rousseau, the major evils of contemporary society were political absolutism, over-intellectualism, and general artificiality. Nor were these evils separable; on the contrary, each fed on the others. Hence Rousseau could not agree with reformers who looked to reason to lead the way to liberty and equality. Society was rotten to the core, he contended, hence no solution short of total regeneration could cure its ills.

In The Social Contract *(1762), his most famous work, Rousseau attacked the problem of political despotism. Beginning with the provocative charge, "Man is born free; and everywhere he is in chains," he proposes a new social order in which freedom and equality will be the possession of all. How such a social order can be achieved in practice is the basic problem that he tries to solve in this book. How can we live under a government that, of necessity, exercises authority over us, and yet remain free men? This issue, with which Rousseau wrestled so earnestly in* The Social Contract, *still remains one of the fundamental political problems facing the Western world.*

In his other works Rousseau attacked with vigor and eloquence almost every facet of his society. Perhaps his most sweeping condemnation of the Enlightenment is his early work, the Discourse on the Arts and Sciences, *in which he offered up this prayer: "Almighty God! Thou who holdest in Thy hand the minds of men, deliver us from the fatal arts and sciences of our forefathers; give us back ignorance, innocence, and poverty which alone can make us happy and are precious in Thy sight." The opposition between this prayer and the ideals of the Enlightenment is obvious. To appreciate the extent of Rousseau's influence, we have only to realize that within about fifty years romanticism, a movement of which he was the chief prophet, was to sweep over Europe.*

The Social Contract

BOOK I

. . .

Chapter I

SUBJECT OF THE FIRST BOOK

Man is born free; and everywhere he is in chains. One thinks himself the master of others, and still remains a greater slave than they. How did this change come about? I do not know. What can make it legitimate? That question I think I can answer.

If I took into account only force, and the effects derived from it, I should say: "As long as a people is compelled to obey, and obeys, it does well; as soon as it can shake off the yoke, and shakes it off, it does still better; for, regaining its liberty by the same right as took it away, either it is justified in resuming it, or there was no justification for those who took it away." But the social order is a sacred right which is the basis of all rights. Nevertheless, this right does not come from nature, and must therefore be founded on conventions. Before coming to that, I have to prove what I have just asserted.

. . .

Chapter III

THE RIGHT OF THE STRONGEST

The strongest is never strong enough to be always the master, unless he transforms strength into right, and obedience into duty. Hence the right of the strongest, which, though to all seeming meant ironically, is really laid down as a fundamental principle. But are we never to have an explanation of this phrase? Force is a physical power, and I fail to see what moral effect it can have. To yield to force is an act of necessity, not of will—at the most, an act of prudence. In what sense can it be a duty?

Suppose for a moment that this so-called "right" exists. I maintain that the sole result is a mass of inexplicable nonsense. For, if force creates right, the effect changes with the cause: every force that is greater than the first succeeds to its right. As soon as it is possible to disobey with impunity, disobedience is legitimate; and, the strongest being always in the right, the only thing that matters is to act so as to become the strongest. But what kind of right is that which perishes when force fails? If we must obey perforce, there is no need to obey because we ought; and if we are not forced to obey, we are under no obligation to do so. Clearly, the word "right" adds nothing to force: in this connection, it means absolutely nothing.

Obey the powers that be. If this means yield to force, it is a good precept, but superfluous: I can answer for its never being violated. All power comes from God, I admit; but so does all sickness: does that mean that we are forbidden to call in the doctor? A brigand surprises me at the edge of a wood: must I not merely surrender my purse on compulsion; but, even if I could withhold it, am I in conscience bound to give it up? For certainly the pistol he holds is also a power.

Let us then admit that force does not create right, and that we are obligated to obey only legitimate powers. In that case, my original question recurs.

. . .

Jean Jacques Rousseau, THE SOCIAL CONTRACT AND DISCOURSES, *trans. G. D. H. Cole. Everyman's Library Edition. (New York: E. P. Dutton & Co., Inc.) Reprinted by permission of E. P. Dutton & Co., Inc.*

Chapter IV

SLAVERY

To renounce liberty is to renounce being a man, to surrender the rights of humanity and even its duties. For him who renounces everything no indemnity is possible. Such a renunciation is incompatible with man's nature; to remove all liberty from his will is to remove all morality from his acts. Finally, it is an empty and contradictory convention that sets up, on the one side, absolute authority, and, on the other, unlimited obedience. Is it not clear that we can be under no obligation to a person from whom we have the right to exact everything? Does not this condition alone, in the absence of equivalence or exchange, in itself involve the nullity of the act? For what right can my slave have against me, when all that he has belongs to me, and, his right being mine, this right of mine against myself is a phrase devoid of meaning?

. . .

So, from whatever aspect we regard the question, the right of slavery is null and void, not only as being illegitimate, but also because it is absurd and meaningless. The words *slave* and *right* contradict each other, and are mutually exclusive. It will always be equally foolish for a man to say to a man or to a people: "I make with you a convention wholly at your expense and wholly to my advantage; I shall keep it as long as I like, and you will keep it as long as I like."

Chapter V

THAT WE MUST ALWAYS GO BACK TO A FIRST CONVENTION

Even if I granted all that I have been refuting, the friends of despotism would be no better off. There will always be a great difference between subduing a multitude and ruling a society. Even if scattered individuals were successively enslaved by one man, however numerous they might be, I still see no more than a master and his slaves, and certainly not a people and its ruler; I see what may be termed an aggregation, but not an association; there is as yet neither public good nor body politic. The man in question, even if he has enslaved half the world, is still only an individual; his interest, apart from that of others, is still a purely private interest. If this same man comes to die, his empire, after him, remains scattered and without unity, as an oak falls and dissolves into a heap of ashes when the fire has consumed it.

"A people," says Grotius,[1] "can give itself to a king." Then according to Grotius, a people is a people before it gives itself. The gift is itself a civil act, and implies public deliberation. It would be better, before examining the act by which a people gives itself to a king, to examine that by which it has become a people; for this act, being necessarily prior to the other, is the true foundation of society.

Indeed, if there were no prior convention, where, unless the election were unanimous, would be the obligation on the minority to submit to the choice of the majority? How have a hundred men who wish for a master the right to vote on behalf of ten who do not? The law of majority voting is itself something established by convention, and presupposes unanimity, on one occasion at least.

Chapter VI

THE SOCIAL COMPACT

I suppose men to have reached the point at which the obstacles in the way of their preservation in the state of nature show their power of resistance to be greater than the resources at the disposal of each in-

[1] [A Dutch jurist (1583–1645).–Ed.]

dividual for his maintenance in that state. That primitive condition can then subsist no longer; and the human race would perish unless it change its manner of existence.

But, as men cannot engender new forces, but only unite and direct existing ones, they have no other means of preserving themselves than the formation, by aggregation, of a sum of forces great enough to overcome the resistance. These they have to bring into play by means of a single motive power, and cause to act in concert.

This sum of forces can arise only where several persons come together: but, as the force and liberty of each man are the chief instruments of his self-preservation, how can he pledge them without harming his own interests, and neglecting the care he owes to himself? This difficulty, in its bearing on my present subject, may be stated in the following terms:

"The problem is to find a form of association which will defend and protect with the whole common force the person and goods of each associate, and in which each, while uniting himself with all, may still obey himself alone, and remain as free as before." This is the fundamental problem of which the *Social Contract* provides the solution.

The clauses of this contract are so determined by the nature of the act that the slightest modification would make them vain and ineffective; so that, although they have perhaps never been formally set forth, they are everywhere the same and everywhere tacitly admitted and recognized, until, on the violation of the social compact, each regains his original rights and resumes his natural liberty, while losing the conventional liberty in favour of which he renounced it.

These clauses, properly understood, may be reduced to one—the total alienation of each associate, together with all his rights, to the whole community; for, in the first place, as each gives himself absolutely, the conditions are the same for all; and, this being so, no one has any interest in making them burdensome to others.

Moreover, the alienation being without reserve, the union is as perfect as it can be, and no associate has anything more to demand: for, if the individuals retained certain rights, as there would be no common superior to decide between them and the public, each, being on one point his own judge, would ask to be so on all; the state of nature would thus continue, and the association would necessarily become inoperative or tyrannical.

Finally, each man, in giving himself to all, gives himself to nobody; and as there is no associate over which he does not acquire the same right as he yields others over himself, he gains an equivalent for everything he loses, and an increase of force for the preservation of what he has.

If then we discard from the social compact what is not of its essence, we shall find that it reduces itself to the following terms:

"Each of us puts his person and all his power in common under the supreme direction of the general will, and, in our corporate capacity, we receive each member as an indivisible part of the whole."

At once, in place of the individual personality of each contracting party, this act of association creates a moral and collective body, composed of as many members as the assembly contains voters, and receiving from this act its unity, its common identity, its life, and its will. This public person, so formed by the union of all other persons, formerly took the name of *city,* and now takes that of *Republic* or *body politic;* it is called by its members *State* when passive, *Sovereign* when active, and *Power* when compared with others like itself. Those who are associated in it take collectively the name of *people,* and severally are called *citizens,* as sharing in the sovereign power, and *subjects,* as being under the laws of the State. But these terms are often confused and taken one for another: it is enough to know how to distinguish them when they are being used with precision.

Chapter VII

THE SOVEREIGN

This formula shows us that the act of association comprises a mutual undertaking between the public and the individuals, and that each individual, in making a contract, as we may say, with himself, is bound in a double capacity; as a member of the Sovereign he is bound to the individuals, and as a member of the State to the Sovereign. But the maxim of civil right, that no one is bound by undertakings made to himself, does not apply in this case; for there is a great difference between incurring an obligation to yourself and incurring one to a whole of which you form a part.

Attention must further be called to the fact that public deliberation, while competent to bind all the subjects to the Sovereign, because of the two different capacities in which each of them may be regarded, cannot, for the opposite reason, bind the Sovereign to itself; and that it is consequently against the nature of the body politic for the Sovereign to impose on itself a law which it cannot infringe. Being able to regard itself in only one capacity, it is in the position of an individual who makes a contract with himself; and this makes it clear that there neither is nor can be any kind of fundamental law binding on the body of the people—not even the social contract itself. This does not mean that the body politic cannot enter into undertakings with others, provided the contract is not infringed by them; for in relation to what is external to it, it becomes a simple being, an individual.

But the body politic, or the Sovereign, drawing its being wholly from the sanctity of the contract, can never bind itself, even to an outsider, to do anything derogatory to the original act, for instance, to alienate any part of itself, or to submit to another Sovereign. Violation of the act by which it exists would be self-annihilation; and that which is itself nothing can create nothing.

As soon as this multitude is so united in one body, it is impossible to offend against one of the members without attacking the body, and still more to offend against the body without the members resenting it. Duty and interest therefore equally oblige the two contracting parties to give each other help; and the same men should seek to combine, in their double capacity, all the advantages dependent upon that capacity.

Again, the Sovereign, being formed wholly of the individuals who compose it, neither has nor can have any interest contrary to theirs; and consequently the sovereign power need give no guarantee to its subjects, because it is impossible for the body to wish to hurt all its members. We shall also see later on that it cannot hurt any in particular. The Sovereign, merely by virtue of what it is, is always what it should be.

This, however, is not the case with the relation of the subjects to the Sovereign, which, despite the common interest, would have no security that they would fulfil their undertakings, unless it found means to assure itself of their fidelity.

In fact, each individual, as a man, may have a particular will contrary or dissimilar to the general will which he has as a citizen. His particular interest may speak to him quite differently from the common interest: his absolute and naturally independent existence may make him look upon what he owes to the common cause as a gratuitous contribution, the loss of which will do less harm to others than the payment of it is burdensome to himself; and, regarding the moral person which constitutes the State as a *persona ficta,* because not a man, he may not be an empty formula, it tacitly without being ready to fulfil the duties of a subject. The continuance of such an injustice could not but prove the undoing of the body politic.

In order then that the social compact may not be an empty formula, it tacitly includes the undertaking, which alone can give force to the rest, that whoever refuses to obey the general will shall be compelled to do so by the whole body. This means nothing less than that he will be forced to be free; for this is the condition which, by giving each citizen to his country, secures him against all personal dependence. In this lies the key to the working of the political machine; this alone legitimizes civil undertakings, which, without it, would be absurd, tyrannical, and liable to the most frightful abuses.

Chapter VIII

THE CIVIL STATE

The passage from the state of nature to the civil state produces a very remarkable change in man, by substituting justice for instinct in his conduct, and giving his actions the morality they had formerly lacked. Then only, when the voice of duty takes the place of physical impulses and right of appetite, does man, who so far had considered only himself, find that he is forced to act on different principles, and to consult his reason before listening to his inclinations. Although, in this state, he deprives himself of some advantages which he got from nature, he gains in return others so great, his faculties are so stimulated and developed, his ideas so extended, his feelings so ennobled, and his whole soul so uplifted, that, did not the abuses of this new condition often degrade him below that which he left, he would be bound to bless continually the happy moment which took him from it for ever, and, instead of a stupid and unimaginative animal, made him an intelligent being and a man.

Let us draw up the whole account in terms easily commensurable. What man loses by the social contract is his natural liberty and an unlimited right to everything he tries to get and succeeds in getting; what he gains is civil liberty and the proprietorship of all he possesses. If we are to avoid mistake in weighing one against the other, we must clearly distinguish natural liberty, which is bounded only by the strength of the individual, from civil liberty, which is limited by the general will; and possession, which is merely the effect of force or the right of the first occupier, from property, which can be founded only on a positive title.

We might, over and above all this, add, to what man acquires in the civil state, moral liberty, which alone makes him truly master of himself; for the mere impulse of appetite is slavery, while obedience to a law which we prescribe to ourselves is liberty.

. . .

BOOK II

Chapter I

THAT SOVEREIGNTY IS INALIENABLE

The first and most important deduction from the principles we have so far laid down is that the general will alone can direct the State according to the object for which it was instituted, *i.e.* the common good: for if the clashing of particular interests made the establishment of societies necessary, the agreement of these very interests made it possible. The common element in these different interests is what forms the social tie; and, were there no point of agreement between them all, no society could exist. It is solely on the basis of this common interest that every society should be governed.

I hold then that Sovereignty, being nothing less than the exercise of the general will, can never be alienated, and that the Sovereign, who is no less than a collective being, cannot be represented except by himself: the power indeed may be transmitted, but not the will.

In reality, if it is not impossible for a particular will to agree on some point with the general will, it is at least impossible for the agreement to be lasting and constant; for the particular will tends, by its very nature, to partiality, while the general will tends to equality. It is even more impossible to have any guarantee of this agreement; for even if it should always exist, it would be the effect not of art, but of chance. The Sovereign may indeed say: "I now will actually what this man wills, or at least what he says he wills"; but it cannot say: "What he wills to-morrow, I too shall will" because it is absurd for the will to bind itself for the future, nor is it incumbent on any will to consent to anything that is not for the good of the being who wills. If then the people promises simply to obey, by that very act it dissolves itself and loses what makes it a people; the moment a master exists, there is no longer a Sovereign, and from that moment the body politic has ceased to exist.

This does not mean that the commands of the rulers cannot pass for general wills, so long as the Sovereign, being free to oppose them, offers no opposition. In such a case, universal silence is taken to imply the consent of the people.

. . .

Chapter III

WHETHER THE GENERAL WILL IS FALLIBLE

It follows from what has gone before that the general will is always right and tends to the public advantage; but it does not follow that the deliberations of the people are always equally correct. Our will is always for our own good, but we do not always see what that is; the people is never corrupted, but it is often deceived, and on such occasions only does it seem to will what is bad.

There is often a great deal of difference between the will of all and the general will; the latter considers only the common interest, while the former takes private interest into account, and is no more than a sum of particular wills: but take away from these same wills the pluses and minuses that cancel one another, and the general will remains as the sum of the differences.

If, when the people, being furnished with adequate information, held its deliberations, the citizens had no communication one with another, the grand total of the small differences would always give the general will, and the decision would always be good. But when factions arise, and partial associations are formed at the expense of the great association, the will of each of these associations becomes general in relation to its members, while it remains particular in relation to the State: it may then be said that there are no longer as many votes as there are men, but only as many as there are associations. The differences become less numerous and give a less general result. Lastly, when one of these associations is so great as to prevail over all the rest, the result is no longer a sum of small differences, but a single difference; in this case there is no longer a general will, and the opinion which prevails is purely particular.

It is therefore essential, if the general will is to be able to express itself, that there should be no partial society within the State, and that each citizen should think only his own thoughts: which was indeed the sublime and unique system established by the great Lycurgus. But if there are partial societies, it is best to have as many as possible and to prevent them from being unequal, as was done by Solon, Numa, and Servius. These precautions are the only ones that can guarantee that the general will shall be always enlightened, and that the people shall in no way deceive itself.

. . .

BOOK III

. . .

Chapter I

GOVERNMENT IN GENERAL

I warn the reader that this chapter requires careful reading, and that I am unable to make myself clear to those who refuse to be attentive.

Every free action is produced by the concurrence of two causes; one moral, *i.e.* the will which determines the act; the other physical, *i.e.* the power which executes it. When I walk towards an object, it is necessary first that I should will to go there, and, in the second place, that my feet should carry me. If a paralytic wills to run and an active man wills not to, they will both stay where they are. The body politic has the same motive powers; here too force and will are distinguished, will under the name of legislative power and force under that of executive power. Without their concurrence, nothing is, or should be, done.

We have seen that the legislative power belongs to the people, and can belong to it alone. It may, on the other hand, readily be seen, from the principles laid down above, that the executive power cannot belong to the generality as legislature or Sovereign, because it consists wholly of particular acts which fall outside the competency of the law, and consequently of the Sovereign, whose acts must always be laws.

The public force therefore needs an agent of its own to bind it together and set it to work under the direction of the general will, to serve as a means of communication between the State and the Sovereign, and to do for the collective person more or less what the union of soul and body does for man. Here we have what is, in the State, the basis of government, often wrongly confused with the Sovereign, whose minister it is.

What then is government? An intermediate body set up between the subjects and the Sovereign, to secure their mutual correspondence, charged with the execution of the laws and the maintenance of liberty, both civil and political.

The members of this body are called magistrates or *kings,* that is to say *governors,* and the whole body bears the name *prince.* Thus those who hold that the act, by which a people puts itself under a prince, is not a contract, are certainly right. It is simply and solely a commission, an employment, in which the rulers, mere officials of the Sovereign, exercise in their own name the power of which it makes them depositaries. This power it can limit, modify, or recover at pleasure; for the alienation of such a right is incompatible with the nature of the social body, and contrary to the end of association.

I call then *government,* or supreme administration, the legitimate exercise of the executive power, and prince or magistrate the man or the body entrusted with that administration.

In government reside the intermediate forces whose relations make up that of the whole to the whole, or of the Sovereign to the State. This last relation may be represented as that between the extreme terms of a continuous proportion, which has government as its mean proportional. The government gets from the Sovereign the orders it gives the people, and, for the State to be properly balanced, there must, when everything is reckoned in, be equality between the product or power of the government taken in itself, and the product or power of the citizens, who are on the one hand sovereign and on the other subject.

Furthermore, none of these three terms can be altered without the equality being instantly destroyed. If the Sovereign desires to govern, or the magistrate to give laws, or if the subjects refuse to obey, disorder takes the place of regularity, force and will no longer act together, and the State is dissolved and falls into despotism or anarchy. Lastly, as there is also only one mean proportional between each relation, there is also only one good government possible for a State. But, as countless events may change the relations of a people, not only may different governments be good for different peoples, but also for the same people at different times.

. . .

Chapter X

THE ABUSE OF GOVERNMENT AND ITS TENDENCY TO DEGENERATE

As the particular will acts constantly in opposition to the general will, the government continually exerts itself against the Sovereignty. The greater this exertion becomes, the more the constitution changes; and, as there is in this case no other corporate will to create an equilibrium by resisting the will of the prince, sooner or later the prince must inevitably suppress the Sovereign and break the social treaty. This is the unavoidable and inherent defect which, from the very birth of the body politic, tends ceaselessly to destroy it, as age and death end by destroying the human body. . . .

The dissolution of the State may come about in either of two ways.

First, when the prince ceases to administer the State in accordance with the laws, and usurps the Sovereign power. A remarkable change then occurs: not the government, but the State, undergoes contraction; I mean that the great State is dissolved, and another is formed within it, composed solely of the members of the government, which becomes for the rest of the people merely master and tyrant. So that the moment the government usurps the Sovereignty, the social compact is broken, and all private citizens recover by right their natural liberty, and are forced, but not bound, to obey.

The same thing happens when the members of the government severally usurp the power they should exercise only as a body; this is as great an infraction of the laws, and results in even greater disorders. There are then, so to speak, as many princes as there are magistrates, and the State, no less divided than the government, either perishes or changes its form.

When the State is dissolved, the abuse of government, whatever it is, bears the common name of *anarchy*. To distinguish, democracy degenerates into *ochlocracy*, and aristocracy into *oligarchy;* and I would add that royalty degenerates into *tyranny;* but this last word is ambiguous and needs explanation.

In vulgar usage, a tyrant is a king who governs violently and without regard for justice and law. In the exact sense, a tyrant is an individual who arrogates to himself the royal authority without having a right to it. This is how the Greeks understood the word "tyrant": they applied it indifferently to good and bad princes whose authority was not legitimate. *Tyrant* and *usurper* are thus perfectly synonymous terms.

In order that I may give different things different names, I call him who usurps the royal authority a *tyrant,* and him who usurps the sovereign power a *despot.* The tyrant is he who thrusts himself in contrary to the laws to govern in accordance with the laws; the despot is he who sets himself above the laws themselves. Thus the tyrant cannot be a despot, but the despot is always a tyrant.

• • •

Chapter XV

DEPUTIES OR REPRESENTATIVES

As soon as public service ceases to be the chief business of the citizens and they would rather serve with their money than with their persons, the State is not far from its fall. When it is necessary to march out to war, they pay troops and stay at home: when it is necessary to meet in council, they name deputies and stay at home. By reason of idleness and money, they end by having soldiers to enslave their country and representatives to sell it.

It is through the hustle of commerce and the arts, through the greedy self-interest of profit, and through softness and love of amenities that personal services are replaced by money payments. Men surrender a part of their profits in order to have time to increase them at leisure. Make gifts of money, and you will not be long without chains. The word "finance" is a slavish word, unknown in the city-state. In a country that is truly free, the citizens do everything with their own arms and nothing by means of money; so far from paying to be exempted from their duties, they would even pay for the privilege of fulfilling them themselves. I am far from taking the common view: I hold enforced labour to be less opposed to liberty than taxes.

The better the constitution of a State is, the more do public affairs encroach on private in the minds of the citizens. Private affairs are even of much less importance, because the aggregate of the common happiness furnishes a greater proportion of that of each individual, so that there is less for him to seek in particular cares. In a well-ordered city every man flies to the assemblies: under a bad government no one cares to stir a step to get to them, because no one is interested in what happens there, because it is foreseen that the general will will not prevail, and lastly because domestic cares are all-absorbing. Good laws lead to the making of better ones; bad ones bring about worse. As soon as any man says of the affairs of the State *What does it matter to me?* the State may be given up for lost.

THOMAS PAINE

If ever there was a man who enjoyed a checkered career and yet lived a long, useful life to die peacefully, that man was Thomas Paine. Born, raised, educated, apprenticed, and employed in England, Paine left his native land at the age of 37 (1774) for the American colonies, after he had published an essay favoring raising the pay of tax collectors so that they would not be susceptible to bribery. Before leaving home Paine had struck up an acquaintanceship with the American colonial agent, Benjamin Franklin, so he sailed to the New World with letters of introduction that promptly moved him into influential circles.

Two years later he issued his pamphlet

Common Sense, *which immediately established his reputation as an inflammatory writer with a clear, logical mind and an incisive literary style. This essay, reproduced here, was one of the most persuasive and influential political writings ever penned and powerfully aided in the crystallization of opinion in America against the British monarchy.*

After a variety of employments in the United States, Paine returned to Europe to promote his idea for an iron bridge (an idea he is reputed to have acquired from observing a spider). While in England he wrote his second great essay, on the Rights of Man *(1790)—a reply to Edmund Burke and one so effective he was again obliged to depart England (1792). He fled to France where he was promptly elected to the National Convention by five different constituencies. His career in Revolutionary France was no different from the rest of his life; his strong opinions forced him to oppose the execution of Louis XVI, which in turn led him to the shadow of the guillotine (from which he was saved only by being desperately ill of a fever), and at last drove him into exile by the order of Napoleon. He returned to the United States where he died in 1809, aged 72, and still defending his religious heterodoxy and his political liberalism.*

Common Sense

OF THE ORIGIN AND DESIGN OF GOVERNMENT IN GENERAL; WITH CONCISE REMARKS ON THE ENGLISH CONSTITUTION

Some writers have so confounded Society with Government, as to leave little or no distinction between them: whereas they are not only different, but have different origins. Society is produced by our wants, and Government by our wickedness; the former promotes our happiness *positively*, by uniting our affections: the latter *negatively*, by restraining our vices. The one encourages intercourse, the other creates distinctions. The first is a patron, the last a punisher.

Society, in every state, is a blessing, but Government, even in its best state, is but a necessary evil; in its worst state, an intolerable one; for when we suffer, or are exposed to the same miseries *by a Government*, which we might expect in a country *without Government*, our calamity is heightened by reflecting, that we furnish the means by which we suffer. Government, like dress, is the badge of lost innocence; the palaces of Kings are built on the ruins of the bowers of Paradise. For, were the impulses of conscience clear, uniform, and irresistibly obeyed, man would need no other lawgiver; but that not being the case, he finds it necessary to surrender up a part of his property to furnish means for the protection of the rest; and this he is induced to do by the same prudence which, in every other case, advises him out of two evils to choose the least. *Wherefore*, security being the true design, and end of Government, it unanswerably follows, that whatever *form* thereof appears most likely to ensure it to us with the least expense and greatest benefit, is preferable to all others.

In order to gain a clear and just idea of the design and end of Government, let us suppose a small number of persons settled in some sequestered part of the earth, unconnected with the rest; they will then represent the first peopling of any country, or of the world. In this state of natural liberty, Society will be their first thought. A thousand motives will excite

THE POLITICAL AND MISCELLANEOUS WORKS OF THOMAS PAINE *(London, 1819).*

them thereto; the strength of one man is so unequal to his wants, and his mind so unfitted for perpetual solitude, that he is soon obliged to seek assistance and relief of another, who in his turn requires the same. Four or five united would be able to raise a tolerable dwelling in the midst of a wilderness: but *one* man might labour out the common period of his life without accomplishing any thing; when he had felled his timber he could not remove it, nor erect it after it was removed; hunger in the mean time would urge him from his work, and every different want call him a different way. Disease, nay even misfortune, would be death; for though neither might be mortal, yet either would disable him from living, and reduce him to a state in which he might be rather said to perish than to die.

Thus, necessity, like a gravitation power, would soon form our newly arrived emigrants into society, the reciprocal blessings of which would supersede and render the obligations of Law and Government unnecessary while they remained perfectly just to each other; but as nothing but Heaven is impregnable to vice, it will unavoidably happen, that in proportion as they surmount the first difficulties of emigration, which bound them together in a common cause, they will begin to relax in their duty and attachment to each other; and this remissness will point out the necessity of establishing some form of Government to supply the defect of moral virtue.

Some convenient tree will afford them a State-house, under the branches of which the whole colony may assemble to deliberate on public matters. It is more than probable that their first laws will have the title only of REGULATIONS, and be enforced by no other penalty than public disesteem. In this first Parliament every man by natural right will have a seat.

But as the colony increases, the public concerns will increase likewise, and the distance at which the members may be separated, will render it too inconvenient for all of them to meet on every occasion as at first, when their number was small, their habitations near, and the public concerns few and trifling. This will point out the convenience of their consenting to leave the legislative part to be managed by a select number chosen from the whole body, who are supposed to have the same concerns at stake which those have who appointed them, and who will act in the same manner as the whole body would act, were they present. If the colony continue increasing, it will become necessary to augment the number of the Representatives; and that the interest of every part of the colony may be attended to, it will be found best to divide the whole into convenient parts, each part sending its proper number; and that the *elected* might never form to themselves an interest separate from the *electors,* prudence will point out the necessity of having elections often; because, as the *elected* might by that means return and mix again with the general body of the *electors* in a few months, their fidelity to the public will be secured by the prudent reflection of not making a rod for themselves. And as this frequent interchange will establish a common interest with every part of the community, they will mutually and naturally support each other: and on this (not on the unmeaning name of King) depends the *strength of Government, and the happiness of the governed.*

Here, then, is the origin and rise of Government; namely, a mode rendered necessary by the inability of moral virtue to govern the world; here too is the design and end of Government, viz., Freedom and Security. And however our eyes may be dazzled with show, or our eyes deceived by sound; however prejudice may warp our wills, or interest darken our understanding, the simple voice of nature and of reason will say, it is right.

I draw my idea of the form of Government from a principle in nature, which no art can overturn, viz., that the more simple any thing is, the less liable it is to be disordered, and the easier repaired when disordered: and with this maximum in view, I offer a few remarks on the so-much-boasted Constitution of England. That it was noble for the dark and slavish times in which it was erected, is granted. When the world was over-run with tyranny, the least remove therefrom was a glorious risque. But that it is imperfect, subject to convulsions, and incapable of producing what it seems to promise, is easily demonstrated.

Absolute Governments, (though the disgrace of human nature) have this advantage with them, that they are simple; if the people suffer, they know the head from which their suffering springs, know likewise the remedy, and are not bewildered by a variety of causes and cures. But the Constitution of England is so exceedingly complex, that the Nation may suffer for years together without being able to discover in which part the fault lies; some will say in one, and some in another, and every political physician will advise a different medicine.

I know it is difficult to get over local or long standing prejudices; yet if we will suffer ourselves to examine the component parts of the English Constitution, we shall find them to be the base remains of two ancient tyrannies, compounded with some new republican materials.

First.—The remains of Monarchical Tyranny in the person of the King.

Secondly.—The remains of Aristocratical Tyranny in the persons of the Peers.

Thirdly.—The new Republican Materials in the persons of the Commons, on whose virtue depends the freedom of England.

The two first being hereditary, are independent of the People; wherefore, in a *constitutional sense,* they contribute nothing towards the Freedom of the State.

To say that the Constitution of England is a *union* of three powers, reciprocally *checking* each other, is farcical; either the words have no meaning, or they are flat contradictions.

To say that the Commons are a check upon the King, presupposes two things:

First.—That the King is not to be trusted without being looked after, or, in other words, that a thirst for absolute power is the natural disease of Monarchy.

Secondly.—That the Commons, by being appointed for that purpose, are either wiser or more worthy of confidence than the Crown.

But as the same Constitution which gives the Commons power to check the King, by withholding the Supplies, gives afterwards the King a power to check the Commons by empowering him to reject their other Bills, it again supposes that the King is wiser than those whom it has already supposed to be wiser than him. A mere absurdity!

There is something exceedingly ridiculous in the composition of Monarchy; it first excludes a man from the means of information, yet empowers him to act in cases where the highest judgment is required. The state of a King shuts him from the world, yet the business of a King requires him to know it thoroughly; wherefore the different parts, by unnaturally opposing and destroying each other, prove the whole character to be absurd and useless.

Some writers have explained the English Constitution thus: the King, they say, is one, the People another: the Peers are an House in behalf of the King, the Commons in behalf of the People; but this hath all the distinctions of an house divided against itself; and though the expressions be pleasantly arranged, yet when examined, they appear idle and ambiguous; and it will always happen, that the nicest construction that words are capable of, when applied to the description of something which either cannot exist, or is too incomprehensible to be within the compass of description, will be words of sound only, and though they may amuse the ear, they cannot inform the mind; for this explanation includes a previous question, viz., "How came the King by a power which the People are afraid to trust, and always obliged to check?" Such a power could not be the gift of a wise people, neither can any power *which needs checking* be from God; yet the provision which the Constitution makes supposes such a power to exist.

But the provision is unequal to the task; the means either cannot or will not accomplish the end, and the whole affair is a *felo de se;* for as the greater weight will always carry up the less, and as all the wheels of a machine are put in motion by one, it only remains to know which power in the Constitution, has the most weight, for that will govern; and though the others, or a part of them, may clog, or, as the phrase is, check the rapidity of its motion, yet so long as they cannot stop it, their endeavours will be ineffectual; the first moving power will at last have its way; and what it wants in speed, is supplied by time.

That the Crown is this overbearing part of the English Constitution, needs not be mentioned, and that it derives its whole consequence merely from being the giver of Places and Pensions is self-evident; wherefore, though we have been wise enough to shut and lock a door against absolute Monarchy, we at the same time have been foolish enough to put the Crown in possession of the key.

The prejudice of Englishmen in favour of their own Government, by King, Lords, and Commons, arises as much or more from national pride than reason. Individuals are, undoubtedly, safer in England than in some other countries, but the *will* of the King is as much the *law* of the land in Britain as in France, with this difference, that instead of proceeding directly from his mouth, it is handed to the People under the more formidable shape of an Act of Parliament. For the fate of Charles the First hath only made Kings more subtle—not more just.

Wherefore, laying aside all national pride and prejudice in favour of modes and forms, the plain truth is, that it is *wholly owing to the Constitution of the People, and not to the Constitution of the Government,* that the Crown is not as oppressive in England as in Turkey.

An inquiry into the *constitutional errors* in the English form of Government is at this time highly necessary: for as we are never in a proper condition of doing justice to others, while we continue under the influence of some leading partiality, so neither are we capable of doing it to ourselves while we remain fettered with an obstinate prejudice. And as a man who is attached to a prostitute, is unfitted to choose or judge a wife, so any prepossession in favour of a rotten Constitution of Government will disable us from discerning a good one.

OF MONARCHY AND HEREDITARY SUCCESSION

Mankind being originally equals in the order of creation, the equality could only be destroyed by some subsequent circumstances; the distinctions of rich and poor, may in a great measure be accounted for, and that without having recourse to the harsh and ill-sounding names of oppression and avarice. Oppression is often the *consequence,* but seldom the *means* of riches; and though avarice will preserve a man from being necessitously poor, it generally makes him too timorous to be wealthy.

But there is another and greater distinction, for which no truly natural or religious reason can be assigned, and that is, the distinction of men into KINGS and SUBJECTS. Male and female are the distinctions of Nature, good and bad, the distinctions of Heaven: but how a race of men came into the world so exalted above the rest, and distinguished like some new species, is worth inquiring into, and whether they are the means of happiness or of misery to mankind.

In the early ages of the world, according to the Scripture Chronology, there were no Kings; the consequence of which was, there were no Wars. It is the pride of Kings which throws mankind into confusion. Holland, without a King, hath enjoyed more peace for this last century than any of the Monarchical Governments in Europe. Antiquity favours the same remark; for the quiet and rural lives of the first patriarchs hath a happy something in them, which vanishes away when we come to the history of Jewish royalty.

Government by Kings was first introduced into the world by the Heathens, from whom the children of Israel copied the custom. It was the most prosperous invention the devil ever set on foot for the promotion of Idolatry. The Heathens paid divine honours to their deceased Kings, and the Christian world hath improved on the plan, by doing the same to their living ones. How impious is the title of sacred Majesty applied to a worm, who in the midst of his splendour is crumbling into dust!

As the exalting one man so greatly above the rest cannot be justified on the equal Rights of Nature, so neither can it be defended on the authority of Scripture; for the will of the Almighty has declared by Gideon and the prophet Samuel, expressly disapproves of Government by Kings. All anti-monarchical parts of the Scripture have been very smoothly glossed over in Monarchical Governments, but they undoubtedly merit the attention of countries which have their Governments yet to form. "Render unto Cæsar the things which are Cæsar's," is the Scripture doctrine of Courts, yet it is no support of Monarchical Government, for the Jews at that time were without a King, and in a state of vassalage to the Romans.

Near three thousand years passed away from the Mosaic account of the Creation, till the Jews, under a national delusion, requested a King. Till then, their form of Government (except in extraordinary cases, where the Almighty interposed) was a kind of Republic, administered by a Judge and the Elders of the Tribes. Kings they had none, and it was held sinful to acknowledge any being under that title but the Lord of Hosts. And when a man seriously reflects on the idolatrous homage which is paid to the persons of Kings, he need not wonder that the Almighty, ever jealous of his honour, should disapprove of a form of Government which so impiously invades the prerogative of Heaven.

Monarchy is ranked in Scripture as one of the sins of the Jews, for which a curse in reserve is denounced against them. The history of that transaction is worth attending to.

The children of Israel being oppressed by the Midianites, Gideon marched against them with a small army, and victory, through the Divine interposition, decided in his favour. The Jews, elated with success, and attributing it to the generalship of Gideon, proposed making him a King, saying, "Rule thou over us, thou and thy son, and thy son's son." Here was temptation in its fullest extent: not a kingdom only but an hereditary one. But Gideon, in the piety of his soul, replied, "I will not reign over you, neither shall my son rule over you; THE LORD SHALL RULE OVER YOU." Words need not be more explicit. Gideon doth not decline the honour, but denieth their right to give it; neither doth he compliment them with invented declarations of his thanks, but in the positive style of a prophet charges them with disaffection to their proper Sovereign, the King of Heaven.

About one hundred and thirty years after this, they fell again into the same error. The hankering which the Jews had for the idolatrous customs of the Heathens, is something exceedingly unaccountable; but so it was, that laying hold of the misconduct of Samuel's two sons, who were entrusted with some secular concerns, they came in an abrupt and clamourous manner to Samuel, saying, "Behold, thou art old, and thy sons walk not in thy ways; now make us a King to judge us, like all the other nations." And here we cannot but observe, that their motives were bad, viz., that they might be *like* unto other nations, *i.e.,* the Heathens; whereas their true glory laid in being as much *unlike* them as possible. "But the thing displeased Samuel, when they said, 'Give us a King to judge us'; and Samuel prayed unto the Lord, and the Lord said unto Samuel, 'Hearken unto the voice of the people in all they say unto thee, for they have not rejected thee, but they have rejected me, THAT I SHOULD NOT REIGN OVER THEM. According to all the works which they have done since the day that I brought them up out of Egypt, even unto this day: wherewith they have forsaken me and served other gods; so do they also unto thee. Now, therefore, hearken unto their voice, howbeit protest solemnly unto them, and shew the manner of a King that shall reign over them,' " (*i.e.,* not of any particular King, but the general manner of the Kings of the earth, whom Israel was so eagerly copying after. And notwithstanding the great difference of time and distance of manners, the character is still in fashion.) "And Samuel told all the words of the Lord unto the people, that asked of him a King. And he said, 'This shall be the manner of the King that shall reign over you; he will take your sons and appoint them for himself, for his chariots, and to be his horsemen, and some shall run before his chariots, (this description agrees with the present mode of impressing men) and he will appoint them captains over thousands, and captains over fifties, and will set them to ear his ground, and to reap his harvest, and to make his instruments of war, and instruments of his chariots: and he will take your daughters to be confectionaries, and to be cooks, and to be bakers, (this describes the expence and luxury, as well as the oppression of Kings) and he will take your fields and your olive yards, even the best of them, and give them to his servants; and he will take the tenth of your seed, and of your vineyards, and give them to his officers and to his servants, (by which we see that bribery, corruption, and favouritism, are the standing vices of Kings;) and he will take the tenth of your men servants, and your maid-servants, and your goodliest young men, and your asses, and put them to his work; and he will take the tenth of your sheep, and ye shall be his servants; and ye shall cry out in that day because of your King which ye shall have chosen, AND THE LORD WILL NOT HEAR YOU IN THAT DAY.' "

This accounts for the continuation of Monarchy; neither do the characters of the few good Kings which have lived since, either sanctify the title, or blot out the sinfulness of the origin; the high encomium given to David, takes no notice of him *official as a King,* but only as a *Man* after God's own heart. "Nevertheless the people refused to obey the voice of Samuel, and they said, 'Nay, but we will have a King over us, that we may be like all the Nations, and that our King may judge us, and go out before us, and fight our battles.' " Samuel continued to reason with them, but to no purpose: he set before them their ingratitude, but all would not avail; and seeing them fully bent on their folly, he cried out, " 'I will call unto the Lord, and he shall send thunder and rain (which then was a punishment, being in the time of wheat harvest) that ye may perceive and see that your wickedness is great which ye have done in the sight of the Lord, IN ASKING YOU A KING.' So Samuel called unto the Lord, and the Lord sent thunder and rain that day, and all the people greatly feared the Lord and Samuel. And all the people said unto Samuel, 'pray for thy servants unto the Lord thy God that we die not, for WE HAVE ADDED UNTO OUR SINS THIS EVIL, TO ASK A KING.' " These portions of Scripture are direct and positive. They admit of no equivocal construction. That the Almighty hath there entered his protest against Monarchical Government is true, or the Scripture is false. And a man hath good reason to believe that there is as much of king-craft as priestcraft, in withholding the Scripture from the public in Popish countries. For Monarchy in every instance is the Popery of Government.

To the evil of Monarchy we have added that of Hereditary Succession; and as the first is a degradation and lessening of ourselves, so the second, claimed as a matter of right, is an insult and imposition on posterity. For all men being originally equals, no *one* by *birth* could have a right to set up his own family in perpetual preference to all others for ever; and though himself might deserve *some* decent degree of honours of his contemporaries, yet his descendants might be far too unworthy to inherit them. One of the strongest *natural* proofs of the folly of Hereditary Right in Kings is, that nature disapproves it, otherwise she would not so frequently turn it into ridicule by giving mankind *an ass for a lion*.

Secondly, as no man at first could possess any other public honours than were bestowed upon him, so the givers of those honours could have no right to give away the right of posterity. And though they might say, "We choose you for our head," they could not, without manifest injustice to their children, say, "that your children, and your children's children shall reign over *ours* for ever," because such an unwise, unjust, unnatural compact might, perhaps, in the next succession, put them under the government of a rogue or a fool. Most wise men, in their private sentiments, have ever treated Hereditary Right with contempt; yet it is one of those evils which, when once established, is not easily removed; many submit from fear, others from superstition, and the most powerful part shares with the King the plunder of the rest.

This is supposing the present race of Kings in the world to have had an honourable origin; whereas it is more than probable, that could we take off the dark covering of antiquity, and trace them to their first rise, that we should find the first of them nothing better than the principal ruffian of some restless gang, whose savage manners, or pre-eminence in subtilty, obtained him the title of chief among plunderers; and who, by increasing in power, and extending his depredations, overawed the quiet and defenceless to purchase their safety by frequent contributions. Yet his electors could have no idea of giving Hereditary Right to his descendants, because such a perpetual exclusion of themselves was incompatible with the free and unrestrained principles they professed to live by. Wherefore hereditary succession in the early ages of Monarchy could not take place as a matter of claim, but as something casual or complimental: but as few or no records were extant in those days, and traditionary history stuffed with fables, it was very easy, after the lapse of a few generations, to trump up some superstitious tale, conveniently timed, Mahomet like, to cram Hereditary Right down the throats of the vulgar. Perhaps the disorders which threatened, or seemed to threaten, on the decease of a leader, and the choice of a new one (for elections among ruffians could not be very orderly) induced many at first to favour hereditary pretensions; by which means it happened, as it hath happened since, that what at first was submitted to as a convenience, was afterwards claimed as a right.

England, since the conquest, hath known some few good Monarchs, but groaned beneath a much larger number of bad ones, yet no man in his senses can say that their claim under William the Conqueror is a very honourable one. A French bastard landing with an armed banditti, and establishing himself King of England, against the consent of the natives, is, in plain terms, a very paltry, rascally original. It certainly hath no divinity in it. However, it is needless to spend much time in exposing the folly of Hereditary Right; if there are any so weak as to believe it, let them promiscuously worship the ass and the lion, and welcome; I shall neither copy their humility, nor disturb their devotion.

Yet I should be glad to ask, how they suppose Kings came at first? The question admits but of three answers, viz., either by lot, by election, or by usurpation. If the first King was taken by lot, it establishes a precedent for the next, which excludes hereditary succession. Saul was by lot, yet the succession was not hereditary, neither does it appear from that transaction, there was any intention it ever should. If the first King of any country was by election, that likewise establishes a precedent for the next; for to say that the right of all future generations is taken away by the act of the first electors, in their choice, not only of a King but of a family of Kings for ever, hath no parallel in or out of Scripture, but the doctrine of original sin, which supposes the free will of all men lost in Adam; and from such comparison (and it will admit of no other) hereditary succession can derive no glory. For as in Adam all sinned, and as in the first electors all men obeyed; as in the one all mankind are subjected to Satan, and the other to Sovereignty; as our innocence was lost in the first, and our authority in the last; and as both disable us from re-assuming some further state and privilege, it unanswerably follows, that original sin and hereditary succession are parallels. Dishonourable rank! Inglorious connection! Yet the most subtle sophist cannot produce a juster simile.

As to usurpation, no man will be so hardy as to defend it; and that William the Conqueror was an usurper, is a fact not to be contradicted. The plain truth is, that the antiquity of English Monarchy will not bear looking into.

But it is not so much the absurdity as the evil of hereditary succession which concerns mankind. Did it insure a race of good and wise men, it would have the seal of divine authority; but as it opens a door to the *foolish,* the *wicked,* and the *improper,* it hath in it the nature of oppression. Men who look upon themselves born to reign, and others to obey, soon grow insolent; selected from the rest of mankind, their minds are easily poisoned by importance, and the world they act in differs so materially from the world at large, that they have but little opportunity of knowing its true interests, and when they succeed to the Government, are frequently the most ignorant and unfit of any throughout the dominions.

Another evil which attends hereditary succession is, that the throne is liable to be possessed by a minor at any age; all which time the regency, acting under the cover of a King, have every opportunity and inducement to betray their trust. The same national misfortune happens, when a king, worn out with age and infirmity, enters the last stage of human weakness. In both these cases, the public becomes a prey to every miscreant, who can tamper with the follies either of age or infancy.

The most plausible plea which hath ever been offered in favour of hereditary succession, is that it preserves a nation from civil wars; and were this true, it would be weighty; whereas, it is the most barefaced falsity ever imposed upon mankind. The whole history of England disowns the fact. Thirty Kings and two minors have reigned in that distracted kingdom since the Conquest, in which time there have been (including the Revolution) no less than eight civil wars and nineteen rebellions. Wherefore, instead of making for peace, it makes against it, and destroys the very foundation it seems to stand on.

The contest for Monarchy and succession, between the houses of York and Lancaster, laid England in a scene of blood for many years. Twelve pitched battles, besides skirmishes and sieges, were fought between Henry and Edward. Twice was Henry prisoner to Edward, who in his turn was prisoner to Henry. And so uncertain is the fate of war, and temper of a nation, when nothing but personal matters are the ground of a quarrel, that Henry was taken in triumph from a prison to a palace, and Edward obliged to fly from a palace to a foreign land; yet, as sudden transitions of temper are seldom lasting, Henry in his turn was driven from the throne, and Edward recalled to succeed him: the Parliament always following the strongest side.

This contest began in the reign of Henry the Sixth, and was not entirely extinguished till Henry the Seventh: in whom the families were united; including a period of sixty-seven years, viz., from 1422 to 1489.

In short, Monarchy and succession have laid, not this or that kingdom only, but the world in blood and ashes. It is a form of Government which the word of God bears testimony against, and blood will attend it.

If we inquire into the business of a King, we shall find that in some countries they have none; and after sauntering away their lives without pleasure to themselves or advantage to the nation, withdraw from the scene, and leave their successors to tread the same idle ground. In absolute Monarchies the whole weight of business, civil and military, lies on the King; the children of Israel in their request for a King, urged this plea, "that he may judge us, and go out before us, and fight our battles." But in countries where he is neither a judge, nor a general, a man would be puzzled to know what *is* his business.

The nearer any Government approaches to a republic, the less business there is for a King. It is somewhat difficult to find a proper name for the Government of England. Sir William Meredith calls it a republic; but in its present state it is unworthy of the name, because the corrupt influence of the Crown, by having all the places in its disposal, hath so effectually swallowed up the power, and eaten out the virtue of the House of Commons (the republican part of the Constitution) that the Government of England is nearly as Monarchical as that of France or Spain. Men fall out with names without understanding them: for it is the republican, and not the monarchical part of the Constitution of England, which Englishmen glory in, viz., the liberty of choosing an House of Commons from out of their own body; and it is easy to see, that when republican virtue fails, slavery ensues. Why is the Constitution of England sickly, but because Monarchy hath poisoned the Republic, the Crown hath engrossed the Commons?

In England the King hath little more to do than to make war and give away places; which, in plain terms, is to impoverish the nation and set it together by the ears. A pretty business, indeed, for a man to be allowed eight hundred thousand sterling a year for, and worshipped into the bargain! Of more worth is one honest man to society, and in the sight of God, than all the crowned ruffians that ever lived.

GENERAL CAHIERS

The cahiers *were lists of grievances that each estate in each electoral division of France drew up for presentation to the king at the meeting of the Estates-General in 1789. Actually, there are two distinct types of* cahier: *the preliminary and the general. The preliminary* cahiers *were compiled at the first and second levels of election, and were submitted to the electoral body that actually chose the representatives sent to the Estates-General. The electoral body then compiled the general* cahiers *from the preliminary lists. This rather obscure method was followed by the first estate (the clergy) and the third estate (the commoners). The second estate (the nobility) developed only general* cahiers *which were sent directly to Versailles.*

This method of recording the grievances of the people and classes of France in 1789 is a great help to the modern historian. For instance, the general cahiers *tend to cite broad areas of needed reform, rather than specific abuses or corruptions within the system; moreover, they tend more clearly to reflect the political and economic philosophies that were occupying men's minds than any schedule of particulars would have.*

The following selections consist of three general cahiers, *one from each of the three estates of the* bailliage *of Dourdan in the* généralité *of Orléans. Although these* cahiers *are somewhat lengthy and repetitious, they give us a good picture of the contrasting aims, hopes, and desires of the major social and political groups of one community; and they indicate the degree to which current ideas on liberty and equality had penetrated each estate.*

The "August 4th Decrees" (which make up the last of the following selections) reflect both the grievances appearing in the cahiers *and the efforts of the National Assembly to remedy them.*

Cahier of the Clergy of Dourdan

27 March, 1789

. . .

When the King summons his subjects about him to consult them concerning the needs of the State, the ministers of religion are among the most eager to give him proof of their respectful gratitude. Their dual *rôle* as citizens and ecclesiastics entitles them to bring to the foot of the throne the most comprehensive wishes for the welfare of the monarchy and the main-

DOCUMENTARY SURVEY OF THE FRENCH REVOLUTION, *ed. John Hall Stewart (New York: The Macmillan Company, 1951).*

tenance of a religion that assures its tranquillity. Accordingly, His Majesty shall be humbly supplicated:

Chapter I: Religion

1. To preserve in its integrity the precious depository of the Catholic, Apostolic, and Roman religion, the most stable support of the fundamental laws of the State, to effect the enforcement of ordinances concerning the respect which is due churches, sanctification of feast days and Sundays, and, in general, whatever affects public worship.

2. To give consideration to the representations made by the last assembly of the clergy concerning the edict on non-Catholics, and not to permit any religion other than the Catholic to hold worship or give public instruction.

3. To permit the Church of France to hold provincial or national councils with a view to re-establishing and maintaining ecclesiastical discipline in all its vigor, so that convocation of the said councils may be effected, without great delay, upon the request and according to the needs of every metropolitan see.

4. To maintain the execution of all laws and ordinances recognized in the kingdom as constituting the public, ecclesiastical, and canonical law thereof, and which the kings, his august predecessors, have stamped with the seal of their authority.

5. Imbued with profound grief at the sight of the appalling deterioration of religion and the depravation of morals in the kingdom, we direct to His Majesty the most ardent and humble representations concerning the disastrous and widely acknowledged cause of this deplorable subversion of all principles. It obviously derives from the disgraceful excess of writings in which the spirit of libertinage, incredulity, and independence prevails, in which faith, modesty, reason, the throne, and the altar are attacked with equal audacity—impious and corrupting books circulated on all sides with the most revolting profusion and license, to which the strongest resistance could not be too promptly opposed.

6. Since diversity of religious opinions in the schools for French youth is the greatest danger in the world, His Majesty shall be humbly supplicated also to order all necessary precautions lest there be admitted into any of the universities and academic societies of the kingdom any teacher or member who has not previously given proofs of the greatest ability and of his respectful devotion to the Catholic religion.

7. Since national education is degenerating daily, the King will be willing to take into consideration a matter so pertinent to morals and to the glory of the kingdom and in his wisdom to provide resources for the talents of indigence by the endowment of the provincial *collèges,* almost all of which are insufficiently endowed, because a good education is the only means of assuring the State of good citizens, and religion of virtuous ministers.

8. Since the education of the rural population is valuable to the State, it is highly desirable that in every parish schoolteachers be established, whose stipends, added to the payments of those pupils who can afford to pay, would provide an income sufficient for them and their families; which teachers would be under the guidance and inspection of the *curé,* who would ascertain their religion and talents in advance, and would have the right to dismiss them if they did not fulfill expectations, reserving their right of appeal to the lord bishop.

9. We dare to solicit from the goodness and piety of the King a special protection for religious orders of either sex throughout the kingdom, under the happy auspices of his favor and authority; we hope that such holy institutions, useful to reli-

gion, to the good of the State, to needy families, and above all to the support of the poor in the rural districts, will flourish and vivify increasingly.

10. In provincial cities, and especially in this *bailliage,* there are numerous communities devoted to the education of indigent young girls for religion and for work; we supplicate His Majesty to regard such useful establishments with benevolence, and to facilitate access thereto in the bureaux established for the relief of religious houses.

Chapter II: Constitution

1. Since monarchical government is the steadfast constitution of the nation, the most conducive to its internal tranquillity and external security, the most suitable for the extent of its provinces, and the most consistent with the character of its people, who always have distinguished themselves by their love for and devotion to their sovereigns, we will never countenance anything that would tend to alter this form of government. We are inviolably attached to it by the most sacred duties of obedience, by ties of oath and fidelity, by love and respect for our masters, and by the happiness of being subject thereto.

2. We desire that in matters brought under deliberation in the Estates General relative to all orders, voting be by head; but in those concerning more especially one of the three orders, we request that voting be by order.

. . .

Cahier of the Nobles of Dourdan

29 March, 1789

. . .

Constitution

The citizens comprising the order of the nobility of the *bailliage* of Dourdan consider that, as soon as the Estates General is convened and the assembly constituted, an address should be voted to the King to thank him for the magnanimous act of justice he has just accorded the nation in restoring its rights, and to pledge to him, in the name of all Frenchmen, unlimited gratitude and love, inviolable submission and fidelity to his sacred person, his legitimate authority, and his august royal house. They would doubtless wish to use this liberty first in paying him new homage of their blood and fortune; but they wish more; they wish to contribute with all their power to the personal happiness of His Majesty, as well as to the general welfare of his people, by working in concert with him to bolster the tottering edifice of the French Constitution, by rendering his faithful commons happier through a just distribution of the taxes necessary to the State, by freeing him of the troubles and anxieties which extensive and absolute legislation necessarily entails; finally, by leaving to him only favors to grant and benefits to dispense throughout the free nation that he governs; thus the subjects of all orders, encompassing the Monarch with their liberty, their happiness, and their unlimited devotion, will render him, if possible, still more beloved throughout his realm, and assuredly more respected abroad.

Accordingly, the noble citizens of the *bailliage* of Dourdan request:

That the legislative power reside collectively in the hands of the King and the united nation.

That a formula for the drafting and publication of laws be established, and that it express both the right of the nation and that of the King, in these words, or similar ones:

The free and general Estates of France declare that the general will is ———. Accordingly, the said Estates most respectfully supplicate His Majesty to sanction the said articles by royal approbation ——— WE, KING OF FRANCE, upon the request of the Estates General, assembled at ———, have published and do publish ———, have ordered and do order ———. Thus, we inform all those whom it may concern that they are to take in hand and put into effect all articles above stated, according to their form, and tenor; FOR SUCH IS THE OUTCOME OF THE NATIONAL WILL, WHICH HAS RECEIVED THE SEAL OF OUR ROYAL AUTHORITY

Since the constitutional laws assure each and every one of his liberty, fortune, position, and property, the nobility requests:

That every arbitrary order prejudicial to the liberty of citizens be abolished entirely;

That individual liberty be assured and guaranteed, so that every citizen arrested may be placed in the prisons of the courts which are to take cognizance of his offence within twenty-four hours of the time of his arrest; that, immediately upon his detention, he be permitted to choose a counsel or advocate.

Liberty shall be understood to include the right to come, go, live, and reside wheresoever one pleases, inside or outside the kingdom, without need of permission; referring to the Estates General the determination of cases in which it is necessary to restrict such liberty with regard to leaving the kingdom.

That liberty of the press be granted, upon condition that author and printer are responsible; and the Estates General shall determine the most severe restrictions in order to prevent such liberty from degenerating into license.

The nobility of the *bailliage* of Dourdan requests, likewise, that, according to the formal wish of His Majesty, no tax be established and no loan be made without the concurrence of the legislative power.

That the administrator of finances be not permitted to make any anticipation or assignment other than on the annual income, under penalty for *lèse-patrie,* the lenders to forfeit all claim.

That any individual convicted of having collected any sum whatsoever in excess of that established by law be declared guilty of embezzlement and sentenced accordingly.

That no citizen be deprived of his rank, employment, or position, except according to a legal judgment.

That all property, whoever be the owner, be inviolable and sacred, property being whatever one owns on public faith and on the affirmation of the law; that no one be deprived thereof except for public interest, and that he then be compensated therefor without delay, and at the highest possible price.

Finally, that ministers henceforth be responsible and accountable to the Estates General.

But if it is magnanimous of the French Monarch to share the legislative power with free subjects, it is at the same time just and necessary that he be invested with all executive power, and that his person be ever sacred.

He must have command of the troops on land and sea, assign military positions, appoint generals and ministers, make peace or war, negotiate treaties of alliance or commerce with foreign powers, convoke, prorogue, and dissolve the Estates General, under the express condition, in case of dissolution, of effecting a new convocation immediately in the form and number approved by the assembled nation.

Finally, the King alone must preserve that right, so kind, so consoling, so worthy of a great monarch, that right to dispense benefits, to encourage virtue by dignities and marks of distinction, and, above all, the right to grant pardon.

The order of nobility desires further that the distinction of three orders in the Estates General be strengthened and regarded as inherent in the Constitution of the French monarchy, and that opinions be given therein only by order.

That in the event, however, that vote by order be absolutely rejected by the Estates General, and the deputy of the *bailliage* of Dourdan sees that further resistance to vote by head is useless, he then requests that vote by head be taken in the separate chamber of every order and not in the assembly of the three orders united.

That vote by head never take place on matters of particular interest to one of the three orders alone.

That the opposition of one order alone may not delay projects of the other two and result in *veto,* except by at least two-thirds of the votes.

That the Estates General be periodic; that it determine the time of its recurrence and the form of its convocation and composition; that it approve taxation only until its next assembly; and that if it be not convoked by the King at the established time, all taxes immediately cease to be valid throughout the entire extent of the kingdom.

That the Estates General may not concern itself with any deliberation until, in conjunction with the King, it has passed an act enunciating the Constitution and the rights above mentioned, and constituting henceforth, the fundamental law of the kingdom.

That, in the event of a new reign or a regency, the Estates General be convoked within two months by the King, or, in his name, by a warrant of the Great Seal drawn up by the Chancellor of France.

That there be no intermediate commission during the interval between Estates General.

That the powers of deputies be limited to a term of two years, dating from the opening of the next Estates General, and that the persons of the deputies be inviolable during the session of the Estates.

That since the custom of giving proxies to deputies of the *bailliages* is most disadvantageous, the Estates be requested to suppress them, or to place thereon whatever restrictions they deem advisable.

That provincial administrations, the form and power of which shall be determined by the Estates General, be established in all provinces of the kingdom.

Finally, that, in order to render these laws of Frenchmen more impressive, a uniform and invariable formula be drafted for the oath which kings must take at their coronation; by which oath they shall swear, in the presence of the Estates General, to observe the declaratory act, a duplicate of which shall be deposited in the treasury of the Church of Saint-Remi at Rheims, and shall be presented to them with as much pomp as the Holy Ampulla. By such oath the monarch shall be formally bound to protect the Christian, Catholic, Apostolic, and Roman religion, and likewise to use all his power and every means to maintain it in all its purity. Lastly, by said oath the constitution is to be fully guaranteed.

. . .

MORALS

That no citizen occupy civil or military positions before the age of twenty, because his life up to that time ought to be devoted to education.

That religion always be the basis of scholastic and moral education.

That in the cities there be public schools, presided over by citizens of distinguished personal attainments and of recognized enlightenment. That only the following subjects be taught therein: first, the principles of natural law, which illumine the rights and duties of man; second, the principles of civil law, which illumine the rights and duties of the citizen; third, the principles of public law, which illumine the rights and duties of the nation.

That only those fifteen years or over be admitted to the schools.

That since scholastic education is to prepare for moral education, the headmasters of the scholastic schools be required to render account of their conduct and their pupils to the headmasters of the schools of morality, and to receive their certificates in that essential subject.

That in rural parishes there be vicars or officiating ministers of religion to aid the *curés* in the work of their ministry, to increase the opportunities for attending divine worship, and to supervise and conduct free schools for youth on behalf of the needy; and that this be made possible through pensions for the benefices.

That, in order that no citizen be lost to the *Patrie,* religious orders be divided into two classes, one devoted to the education of youth, the other to visiting the sick to administer spiritual and temporal aid.

. . .

FINANCES

The nobles regard as decidedly advantageous and even necessary that the first declaration of the Estates General be that, since the nation has the right to consent to taxes, and since all existing taxes are of illegal origin and extension, the Estates General declares them all suppressed by law; that, nevertheless, because of the time required to reorganize this branch of national affairs, and also to avoid possible ill effects on future taxation from an absolute discontinuation of all relations between the taxpayers and the public treasury, the Estates General, desiring that there be no taxes other than those established by the present assembly before its first adjournment, enact provisionally that the present taxes, temporarily authorized, continue to be paid, but only during the present session.

. . .

Finally, the nobility declares that, in order to evince its sentiments of esteem, natural equity, and affection for its fellow citizens of the third estate, it wishes to share with them, in proportion to the property and possessions of all orders, whatever imposts and taxes are approved by the nation; claiming to reserve only the sacred rights of property, and prerogatives of rank, honor, and dignity which must appertain to it according to the constitutional principles of the French monarchy.

. . .

Cahier of the Third Estate of Dourdan

29 March, 1789

. . .

The order of the third estate of the City, *Bailliage,* and County of Dourdan, imbued with gratitude prompted by the paternal kindness of the King, who deigns to restore its former rights and its former constitution, forgets at this moment its misfortunes and impotence, to harken only to its foremost sentiment and its foremost duty, that of sacrificing everything to the glory of the *Patrie* and the service of His Majesty. It supplicates him to accept the grievances, complaints, and remonstrances which it is permitted to bring to the foot of the throne, and to see therein only the expression of its zeal and the homage of its obedience.

It wishes:

1. That his subjects of the third estate, equal by such status to all other citizens, present themselves before the common father without other distinction which might degrade them.

2. That all the orders, already united by duty and a common desire to contribute equally to the needs of the State, also deliberate in common concerning its needs.

3. That no citizen lose his liberty except according to law; that, consequently, no one be arrested by virtue of special orders, or, if imperative circumstances necessitate such orders, that the prisoner be handed over to the regular courts of justice within forty-eight hours at the latest.

4. That no letters or writings intercepted in the post be the cause of the detention of any citizen, or be produced in court against him, except in case of conspiracy or undertaking against the State.

5. That the property of all citizens be inviolable, and that no one be required to make sacrifice thereof for the public welfare, except upon assurance of indemnification based upon the statement of freely selected appraisers.

6. That, since the maintenance of the commonwealth necessitates an effective revenue, all taxes established since 1614, the year of the last meeting of the Estates General, be confirmed provisionally by His Majesty on the request of the Estates General, and the collection thereof ordered during a limited period of time, not to exceed one year, despite the fact that, owing to lack of consent of the nation, such taxes may be regarded as illegal.

7. That the customary and ordinary charges of the State be regulated; that the expenditure of every department [of the Government], the appointment of all who are employed therein, and the retirement pensions of same be established invariably.

8. That the taxes on land and on all real or nominal property, the domains of the Crown, and other branches of revenue deriving from establishments useful to the public, such as postal and messenger service, etc., be preferably assigned to the aforementioned primarily necessary charges.

9. That the national debt be verified; that the payment of arrears of said debt be assured by such indirect taxes as may not be injurious to the husbandry, industry, commerce, liberty, or tranquillity of the citizens.

10. That an annual reimbursement fund be established to liquidate the capital of the debt.

11. That as one part of the debt is liquidated, a corresponding part of the indirect tax also be liquidated.

12. That every tax, direct or indirect, be granted only for a limited time, and that every collection beyond such term be regarded as speculation, and punished as such.

13. That no loan be contracted, under any pretext or any security whatsoever, without the consent of the Estates General.

14. That every anticipation and every issuance of treasurer's notes or others on the account of the State, without public sanction, be regarded as a violation of public faith, and that the administrators ordering or authorizing them be punished.

15. That every personal tax be abolished; that thus the *capitation* and the *taille* and its accessories be merged with the *vingtièmes* in a tax on land and real or nominal property.

16. That such tax be borne equally, without distinction, by all classes of citi-

zens and by all kinds of property, even feudal and contingent rights.

17. That the tax substituted for the *corvée* be borne by all classes of citizens equally and without distinction. That said tax, at present beyond the capacity of those who pay it and the needs to which it is destined, be reduced by at least one-half.

18. That provincial Estates, subordinate to the Estates General, be established and charged with the assessment and levying of subsidies, with their deposit in the national treasury, with the administration of all public works, and with the examination of all projects conducive to the prosperity of lands situated within the limits of their jurisdiction.

19. That such Estates be composed of freely elected deputies of the three orders from the cities, boroughs, and parishes subject to their administration, and in the proportion established for the next session of the Estates General.

20. That district bureaux under said Estates be established in the chief towns of the *bailliages;* and that such jurisdictions be created for said bureaux that there may be prompt and convenient correspondence between the chief town and all points accountable thereto.

21. That in case of the death or retirement of deputies of the order of the third estate in the Estates General, or of any one among them, during the course of the next session, the present electors be authorized to reassemble to elect others in their place.

JUSTICE

1. That the administration of justice be reformed, either by restoring strict execution of ordinances, or by reforming the sections thereof that are contrary to the dispatch and welfare of justice.

. . .

7. That venality of offices be suppressed by successive reimbursement in proportion to their disestablishment; that, accordingly, a fund be constituted forthwith to effect such reimbursement.

8. That the excessive number of offices in the necessary courts be reduced in just measure, and that no one be given an office of magistracy if he is not at least twenty-five years of age, and until after a substantial public examination has verified his morality, integrity, and ability.

. . .

12. That deliberations of courts and companies of magistracy which tend to prevent entry of the third estate thereto be rescinded and annulled as injurious to the citizens of that order, in contempt of the authority of the King, whose choice they limit, and contrary to the welfare of justice, the administration of which would become the patrimony of those of noble birth instead of being entrusted to merit, enlightenment, and virtue.

13. That military ordinances which restrict entrance to the service to those possessing nobility be reformed.

That naval ordinances establishing a degrading distinction between officers born into the order of nobility and those born into that of the third estate be revoked, as thoroughly injurious to an order of citizens and destructive to the competition so necessary to the glory and prosperity of the State.

. . .

COMMERCE

1. That every regulation which tends to impede the business of citizens be revoked.

2. That the exportation and circulation of grain be directed by the provincial Estates, which shall correspond among themselves in order to prevent sudden and artificial increases in the price of provisions.

3. That when wheat reaches the price of

twenty-five *livres* per *septier* in the markets, all day laborers be forbidden to buy any, unless it be for their sustenance.

4. That if circumstances necessitate the revenue from certificates and letters of mastership in the arts and crafts, no member be admitted into corporations except upon condition of residing in the place of his establishment; that widows may carry on the profession of their husbands without new letters; that their children be admitted thereto at a moderate price; that all persons without an established and recognized domicile be forbidden to peddle.

5. That fraudulent bankruptcy be considered a public crime; that the public prosecutor be enjoined to prosecute it as such, and that privileged positions no longer serve as a refuge for bankrupts.

6. That all toll rights and other similar ones be suppressed throughout the interior of the Kingdom, that customhouses be moved back to the frontiers, and that rights of *traite* be entirely abolished.

7. That, within a given time, weights and measures be rendered uniform throughout the entire kingdom.

MORALS

1. That in the chief town of every *bailliage* a public school be established, where young citizens may be brought up in the principles of religion and provided with the necessary education by methods authorized by His Majesty on the request of the nation.

2. That in cities and villages schools be established where the poor will be admitted without cost, and instructed in whatever is necessary for them concerning either morals or their individual interests.

3. That livings and benefices for the care of souls henceforth be granted only by competitive examination.

4. That prelates and *curés* be subject to perpetual residence, under penalty of loss of the fruits of their benefices.

5. That, under the same penalty, beneficiaries without a charge be bound to residence during most of the year in the chief town of their benefice, if they have an annual income of one thousand *livres* or more.

6. That no ecclesiastic hold more than one benefice if such benefice is worth three thousand *livres* revenue or over; that those in excess of such revenue be declared vacant.

7. That every lottery, the effect of which is to corrupt public morals, every loan involving the element of chance, the effect of which is to encourage speculation and divert funds destined for agriculture and commerce, be proscribed forever.

8. That every community be required to provide for the maintenance of its invalid poor; that, accordingly, all private alms be strictly forbidden; that in every district a charity workshop be established, the funds for which shall be composed of voluntary contributions of individuals and sums which the provincial Estates shall designate therefor, in order to assure constant work for the able-bodied poor.

9. That within the limits of every principal administration a house of correction be established for the confinement of beggars and vagabonds.

10. That all charlatans, and those who have not completed the necessary studies and passed the required examinations, be forbidden to sell drugs or medicines or to practise medicine or surgery, and that the granting of any certificate, permission, or exemption for such purpose be forbidden.

11. That no woman may practise the art of midwifery until she has taken a course in it, has obtained a certificate of competence from a college of surgery, and has been received into the *bailliage*.

12. That the *maréchaussées* be enjoined

to obey the orders of the officials of the *bailliages* for the maintenance of public order; and that the municipalities of the several parishes be authorized to have internal police power therein, except in special cases which are to be reported to the public prosecutor of the *bailliage*.

13. That the sacraments be administered gratuitously, and contingent fees suppressed.

The August 4th Decrees

4–11 August, 1789

. . .

1. The National Assembly abolishes the feudal regime entirely, and decrees that both feudal and *censuel* rights and dues deriving from real or personal *mainmorte* and personal servitude, and those representative thereof, are abolished without indemnity, and all others declared redeemable; and that the price and manner of redemption shall be established by the National Assembly. Those of the said dues which are not suppressed by the present decree, however, shall continue to be collected until reimbursement has been made.

2. The exclusive right to *fuies* and *colombiers* is abolished; pigeons shall be confined at times determined by the communities; and during such periods they shall be regarded as game, and everyone shall have the right to kill them on his own land.

3. The exclusive right of hunting and open warrens is likewise abolished; and every proprietor has the right to destroy and to have destroyed, on his own property only, every kind of game, conditional upon conformity with police regulations relative to public security.

All *capitaineries,* even royal ones, and all hunting preserves, under whatever denomination, are likewise abolished; and provision shall be made, by means compatible with the respect due property and liberty, for the preservation of the personal diversions of the King.

The President shall be charged with requesting the King for the recall of persons exiled and consigned to the galleys simply for hunting, the release of prisoners now detained, and the cancellation of existing proceedings in that connection.

4. All seigneurial courts of justice are suppressed without any indemnity; nevertheless, the officials of such courts shall continue in office until the National Assembly has provided for the establishment of a new judicial organization.

5. Tithes of every kind and dues which take the place thereof, under whatever denomination they are known and collected, even by subscription, *possessed by secular and regular bodies,* by beneficed clergymen, *fabriques* and all persons in *mainmorte,* even by the Order of Malta and other religious and military orders, even those abandoned to laity in substitution for and option of *portion congruë,* are abolished, subject to the devising of means for providing in some other manner for the expenses of divine worship, the maintenance of ministers of religion, relief of the poor, repairs and rebuilding of churches and parsonages, and for all establishments, seminaries, schools, colleges, hospitals, communities and others, to the maintenance of which they are now assigned. Meanwhile, until such provision is made and the former possessors are furnished with their equivalent, the National Assembly orders that collection of the said tithes shall continue according to law and in the

usual manner. Other tithes, of whatever nature, shall be redeemable according to the regulations of the Assembly; and until such regulations are made, the National Assembly orders that the collection thereof also be continued.

6. All perpetual ground rents, either in kind or in money, of whatever species, whatever their origin, to whatever persons they are due . . . shall be redeemable; *champarts* of every kind and denomination likewise shall be redeemable at a rate established by the Assembly. No nonredeemable due may be created henceforth.

7. Venality of judicial and municipal offices is suppressed henceforth. Justice shall be rendered gratuitously; nevertheless, the incumbents of said offices shall continue to perform their duties and to collect the emoluments thereof until the Assembly has provided means of procuring their reimbursement.

8. The contingent fees of country *curés* are suppressed, and shall cease to be paid as soon as provision has been made for the increase of the *portions congruës* and for the payment of vicars, and a regulation determining the lot of the town *curés* shall be made.

9. Pecuniary privileges, personal or real, in matters of taxation are abolished forever. Collection shall be made from all citizens and on all property, in the same manner and in the same form: and means of effecting proportional payment of all taxes, even for the last six months of the current year, shall be considered.

10. Since a national constitution and public liberty are more advantageous to the provinces than the privileges which some of them enjoy, and the sacrifice of which is necessary for the close union of all parts of the realm, all special privileges of provinces, principalities, *pays*, cantons, cities, and communities of inhabitants, whether pecuniary or of any other kind, are declared abolished forever, and shall be absorbed into the law common to all Frenchmen.

11. All citizens may be admitted, without distinction of birth, to all ecclesiastical, civil, and military employments and offices, and no useful profession shall entail forfeiture.

12. In future no *deniers* for annates or for any other cause whatsoever shall be dispatched to the court of Rome, the vice-legation at Avignon, or the nunciature at Lucerne; diocesans shall address themselves to their bishops for all provisions of benefices and dispensations, which shall be granted gratuitously. . . .

13. The *déports,* rights of *côte-morte, dépouilles, vacat, censuel* dues, Peter's pence, and others of the same kind established in favor of bishops, archdeacons, archpriests, chapters, *curés primitifs,* and all others, under any name whatsoever, are abolished, subject to suitable provision for the endowment of insufficiently endowed archdeacons and archpriests.

14. Plurality of benefices shall no longer exist when the revenues of the benefice or benefices of an incumbent exceed the sum of three thousand *livres.* Possession of several pensions on a benefice, or a pension and a benefice, shall no longer be permitted if the revenue from those already held exceeds the said sum of three thousand *livres.*

15. On the basis of the account to be rendered concerning the state of pensions, favors, and stipends, the National Assembly, in concert with the King, shall undertake the suppression of those which are not merited, and the reduction of those which are excessive, subject to determining for the future a sum which the King may use for such purpose.

16. The National Assembly decrees that, in memory of the impressive and momentous deliberations just held for the welfare

of France, a medal shall be struck, and that, as an expression of gratitude, a *Te Deum* shall be sung in all parishes and churches of the kingdom.

17. The National Assembly solemnly proclaims King Louis XVI *Restorer of French Liberty*.

18. The National Assembly shall repair *en masse* to the King to present to His Majesty the decree just pronounced, to bear him the homage of its most respectful gratitude, and to supplicate him to permit the *Te Deum* to be sung in his chapel, and to be present there himself.

19. Immediately after the Constitution, the National Assembly shall undertake the drafting of laws necessary for the development of the principles established by the present decree, which, with the decree of the tenth of this month, shall be dispatched immediately by the deputies into all the provinces, there to be printed, proclaimed also at the parish sermons, and posted wherever necessary.

THE NINETEENTH CENTURY

THE HISTORY OF THE NINETEENTH CENTURY was molded in great part by two quite different but related events, the French Revolution and the Industrial Revolution. We can speak without ambiguity of the French Revolution as an event, for it can be dated with precision, from the spring of 1789 to the Battle of Waterloo in 1815. But the Industrial Revolution had neither a precise beginning nor an ending. The best we can say is that it had got underway, certainly in England, by the last quarter of the eighteenth century, that it transformed Europe's economy and society during the nineteenth, and that it has continued into the twentieth.

Although one of these revolutions was primarily political and the other economic, they were not without influence on each other. For it is now generally agreed, as Karl Marx first clearly pointed out, that the French Revolution was a bourgeois or middle-class upheaval. It was the rising capitalist class in France that led the revolution, profited most from it, and then assumed the initiative in the industrial expansion that followed. In England, too, the French Revolution had important economic consequences. For the difficulties caused by the Napoleonic Wars, including the effects on England of the Continental System and the necessity for a vast increase in military and naval power to defeat the French, led to a rapid expansion of English industrial production.

The nineteenth-century reaction to these two great revolutions can best be seen in the host of new doctrines and movements that appeared on the European scene, particularly in the years following 1815. Although most of these doctrines differed widely from one another, they all had one feature in common: the suffix "ism." That most of the major nineteenth-century "isms," particularly those that were primarily political or economic in emphasis, were responses to the revolutions can be seen by an examination of some of them. Both conservatism and nationalism, for example, were directly inspired by the events of the French Revolution and the Napoleonic era.

Conservatism rejected the French Revolution, not only for its effects but also for its methods. Revolution, conservatives like the Englishman Burke argued, necessarily destroys its ideals in its very attempt to achieve them. Social and political progress cannot be brought about through violence and destruction, but only through the conservation and enrichment of the traditions of the past. Although conservatism, in the able diplomatic hands of the Austrian foreign minister Metternich, exerted a considerable influence on European politics until mid-century, it rapidly lost ground after that. Its emphasis was on the past, but Europe's eyes in the nineteenth century were on the future.

Considerably more influential in the long term was nationalism. This doctrine, first espoused by the French during the Revolution, later spread across Europe in the reaction to the Napoleonic Empire. Across the Continent, peoples who had been conquered by the armies of Napoleon came to equate French culture with French imperialism. To assert their cultural independence from France, they searched their history and traditions for the foundations of a national culture which would equal or even surpass that of France. This cultural nationalism almost always had political implications. And political nationalism expressed itself in a variety of ways. With the German philosopher, Hegel, it led to a worship of the state; with the Italian patriot, Mazzini, it became the basis for a humanitarian crusade against political oppression. In practical politics, nationalism led to movements for independence in many areas of Europe, resulting, for example, in the liberation of Greece from the Turks, and of Belgium from the Dutch. Perhaps the most important result of nineteenth-century nationalism was the unification of Italy and Germany.

Three other nineteenth-century "isms," all of them both political and economic in nature, merit attention. The first of these was liberalism. Although liberalism eventually spread over most of Europe, its homeland was England and its greatest spokesman was John Stuart Mill. The liberals tried to adapt the ideals of the Enlightenment to the era of industrialism. Believing firmly in the rationality of man, they held that each individual must be given a maximum of freedom to develop his highest potentialities. The liberals were defenders of constitutional government and of lawful rather than violent political change. They believed, also, that government interference in the activities of citizens should be held to a minimum. In economics, this meant that they generally advocated *laissez-faire*. The history of liberalism in the past hundred years has centered around a growing conflict between the humanitarian ideals of the liberals, on the one hand, and their belief in government non-interference, on the other.

A second movement, more radical than liberalism, was republicanism. The republicans considered themselves the heirs of the French Revolution and the Republic of 1793. Republicanism, which spread from France over the entire Continent, was suppressed by the police of reactionary governments everywhere. But the republicans fought back by forming secret societies and by agitating for the revival of the revolutionary spirit in Europe. They were leaders in the many revolutions that rocked Europe during the century, particularly in 1848.

Most radical of the major "isms" was socialism, particularly as developed by Karl Marx. The socialists differed from the liberals and the republicans in one important respect. Both the liberals and the republicans rejected the pre-revolutionary social structure of Europe, but they accepted the new bourgeois society that grew out of industrialism. The socialists, however, rejected bourgeois society as well, and championed the cause of a new class, the industrial proletariat, also a product of the Industrial Revolution. Although Marx was the most important of the socialists, he had been preceded by several other socialist writers, mainly in France, and he was followed by a variety of socialistic groups that showed his influence. Among these groups were the British Fabian socialists, who helped found the Labor Party in Britain. The Fabian socialists differed from Marx mainly in their belief that the social goals of the laboring class could be attained through constitutional means without recourse either to class warfare or to the elimination of the bourgeoisie.

Perhaps the most pervasive "ism" of nineteenth-century society was optimism. With few exceptions the intellectual leaders of the period were firm believers in progress. For Hegel, progress was a metaphysical necessity; for Marx, it was a historical necessity; and even Darwin seemed to accept it as a biological necessity. The general optimism of nineteenth-century thought found a firm basis in the undeniable fact that progress was actually being made. For it was clear, even to the casual observer, that through industrialization man was rapidly conquering nature and bending her to serve his every material need. The prophets of progress looked forward to an era in which the economic, political, and social advances achieved by Europeans might be shared by all the world.

Such hopes plus, unfortunately, others less lofty, led to still another characteristic nineteenth-century "ism": imperialism. Even the United States, for a brief period at the end of the century, joined the imperialistic movement. As President Theodore Roosevelt proclaimed, "Nations that expand and nations that do not may both ultimately go down, but the one leaves heirs and a glorious memory, and the other leaves neither."

Another source for the optimism of the nineteenth century lay in the freedom from general warfare that lasted for an entire century, from Waterloo to 1914. No such era of peace had been known in the West since the *Pax Romana*. This is not to imply, however, that the period was without violence. For, in addition to several limited wars, the century witnessed a series of revolutions that were symptomatic of the underlying flaws in European society. The most serious flaw was the failure of society to keep pace with the rapid progress that was being made in politics and economics. The political developments leading to democracy, and the economic developments leading to industrial urbanization, combined to produce the modern "mass man," a man who could not be assimilated into the pattern of traditional European civilization. With the tremendous growth of population which almost all countries have experienced since the Industrial Revolution, this new type of man has become an increasingly influential force in society. The consequences of the appearance of this new social force on the European scene, though partially revealed in certain of the "isms" as well as in the revolutions of the nineteenth century, did not become fully apparent until our own century, on whose turbulent history they have had a profound effect.

In summary, the nineteenth century marked the climax of European civilization. By the end of the century, developments that had been in progress for hundreds of years came to final fruition, to make Western Europe—and, to a lesser extent, the United States—the leader and very nearly the master of the entire world. The supremacy of Western Europe exhibited itself in a variety of ways. In the first place, the nations of Western Europe were supreme in military power. Their armies could defeat any non-European foe. Secondly, these nations served as the center of the world's economy. Capital poured out from the great banking institutions of London and Paris to finance the economic exploitation of the most remote areas of the globe. Economic supremacy, in turn, contributed to a high standard of living. The people of Western Europe were able to enjoy the material comforts of life on a scale never before equaled. Politically, the Western European nations were highly progressive. Although none of these nations was yet a full democracy, all seemed to be moving in that direction. At the least, all had governments based on constitutions and governed by law. In this respect alone, they were far in advance of much of the rest of mankind. Finally, Western Europe was generally acknowledged to be the cultural center of the world. Here were to be found the greatest universities, libraries, art galleries, and museums. No one who contemplated an intellectual or artistic career could count his education complete until he had made a pilgrimage to the shrines of European culture.

EDMUND BURKE

The French Revolution was greeted in many different ways, but most people felt that a new and better society would quickly emerge from the reform of the French monarchy. Conservatives had their moments of doubt and hesitation, of course, but the majority of people were more inclined to agree with Samuel Coleridge:

Shall France alone a Despot spurn?
  Shall she alone, O Freedom, boast thy care?
Lo, round thy standard Belgia's heroes burn,
  Tho' Power's blood-stain'd streamers fire the air,
    And wider yet thy influence spread,
    Nor e'er recline thy weary head,
    Till every land from pole to pole
    Shall boast one independent soul!
And still, as erst, let favour'd Britain be
First ever of the first and freest of the free! [1]

William Wordsworth, in later years, was to recall his own reaction to the stirring events of 1789:

But Europe at that time was thrilled with joy,
France standing on the top of golden hours,
And human nature seeming born again.[2]

These flowerings of hope rapidly faded, however, to be replaced by fear, distrust, and contempt when it was discovered that the Golden Age had not arrived. A leading spirit in the rejection of the French Revolution was Edmund Burke (1729–1797), whose influence in Britain and elsewhere became greater as the Revolution ran its violent course. In 1790, Burke published his Reflections on the Revolution in France, *in which he insisted that men cannot create a totally new government and code of laws through the use of reason alone. Such reforms can come about only through the workings of history, through the gradual adaptation of the old and the traditional to serve the best interests of the new. Violence and revolution bring only more violence to a society and finally lead to the destruction of the society itself. Burke's* Reflections *were very widely read (the tenth edi-*

[1] Samuel Coleridge, "Destruction of the Bastile," stanza VI.

[2] William Wordsworth, "The Prelude," Book VI, lines 339–341.

tion was exhausted less than a year after the original publication) and aroused in England and on the Continent a deep suspicion of anyone who seemed to advocate reform or who argued for the application of rational principles to political questions.

Burke wrote the Reflections *ostensibly as a letter to a young Frenchman, but in reality he was replying to a sermon delivered before the Revolution Society (which was dedicated to the commemoration of the "Glorious Revolution" of 1688) in which the Reverend Richard Price had hailed the events in France and had exhorted England to follow along.*

Reflections on the Revolution in France

. . .

Kings, in one sense, are undoubtedly the servants of the people, because their power has no other rational end than that of the general advantage; but it is not true that they are, in the ordinary sense, (by our constitution at least), anything like servants; the essence of whose situation is to obey the commands of some other, and to be removable at pleasure. But the king of Great Britain obeys no other person; all other persons are individually, and collectively too, under him, and owe to him a legal obedience. The law, which knows neither to flatter nor to insult, calls this high magistrate, not our servant, as this humble divine calls him, but *"our sovereign Lord the king"*; and we, on our parts, have learned to speak only the primitive language of the law, and not the confused jargon of their Babylonian pulpits.

As he is not to obey us, but as we are to obey the law in him, our constitution has made no sort of provision towards rendering him, as a servant, in any degree responsible. Our constitution knows nothing of a magistrate like the *Justicia* of Arragon; nor of any court legally appointed, nor of any process legally settled, for submitting the king to the responsibility belonging to all servants. In this he is not distinguished from the Commons and the Lords; who, in their several public capacities, can never be called to an account for their conduct; although the Revolution Society chooses to assert in direct opposition to one of the wisest and most beautiful parts of our constitution, that "a king is no more than the first servant of the public, created by it, *and responsible to it."*

Ill would our ancestors at the Revolution have deserved their fame for wisdom, if they had found no security for their freedom, but in rendering their government feeble in its operations and precarious in its tenure; if they had been able to contrive no better remedy against arbitrary power than civil confusion. Let these gentlemen state who that *representative* public is to whom they will affirm the king, as a servant, to be responsible. It will be then time enough for me to produce to them the positive statute law which affirms that he is not.

The ceremony of cashiering kings, of which these gentlemen talk so much at their ease, can rarely, if ever, be performed without force. It then becomes a case of war, and not of constitution. Laws are commanded to hold their tongues amongst arms; and tribunals fall to the ground with the peace they are no longer able to uphold. The Revolution of 1688 was obtained by a just war, in the only case in which any war, and much more a civil war, can be just. "Justa bella quibus *necessaria."* [1] The question of dethroning, or, if these

Edmund Burke, WORKS *(London, 1867).*

[1] ["Wars are just to those to whom they are necessary."—Ed.]

gentlemen like the phrase better, "cashiering kings," will always be, as it has always been an extraordinary question of state, and wholly out of the law; a question (like all other questions of state) of dispositions, and of means, and of probable consequences, rather than of positive rights. As it was not made for common abuses, so it is not to be agitated by common minds. The speculative line of demarcation, where obedience ought to end, and resistance must begin, is faint, obscure, and not easily definable. It is not a single act, or a single event, which determines it. Governments must be abused and deranged indeed, before it can be thought of; and the prospect of the future must be as bad as the experience of the past. When things are in that lamentable condition, the nature of the disease is to indicate the remedy to those whom nature has qualified to administer in extremities this critical, ambiguous, bitter potion to a distempered state. Times, and occasions, and provocations, will teach their own lessons. The wise will determine from the gravity of the case; the irritable, from sensibility to oppression; the high-minded, from disdain and indignation at abusive power in unworthy hands; the brave and bold, from the love of honourable danger in a generous cause: but, with or without right, a revolution will be the very last resource of the thinking and the good.

The third head of right, asserted by the pulpit of the Old Jewry, namely, the "right to form a government for ourselves," has, at least, as little countenance from anything done at the Revolution [*of 1688*], either in precedent or principle, as the two first of their claims. The Revolution was made to preserve our *ancient,* indisputable laws and liberties, and that *ancient* constitution of government which is our only security for law and liberty. If you are desirous of knowing the spirit of our constitution, and the policy which predominated in that great period which has secured it to this hour, pray look for both in our histories, in our records, in our acts of parliament, and journals of parliament, and not in the sermons of the Old Jewry, and the after-dinner toasts of the Revolution Society. In the former you will find other ideas and another language. Such a claim is as ill-suited to our temper and wishes as it is unsupported by any appearance of authority. The very idea of the fabrication of a new government is enough to fill us with disgust and horror. We wished at the period of the Revolution, and do now wish, to derive all we possess as *an inheritance from our forefathers.* Upon that body and stock of inheritance we have taken care not to inoculate any scion alien to the nature of the original plant. All the reformations we have hitherto made have proceeded upon the principle of reverence to antiquity: and I hope, nay I am persuaded, that all those which possibly may be made hereafter, will be carefully formed upon analogical precedent, authority, and example.

Our oldest reformation is that of Magna Charta. You will see that Sir Edward Coke, that great oracle of our law, and indeed all the great men who follow him, to Blackstone, are industrious to prove the pedigree of our liberties. They endeavour to prove, that the ancient charter, the Magna Charta of King John, was connected with another positive charter from Henry I, and that both the one and the other were nothing more than a re-affirmance of the still more ancient standing law of the kingdom. In the matter of fact, for the greater part, these authors appear to be in the right; perhaps not always; but if the lawyers mistake in some particulars, it proves my position still the more strongly; because it demonstrates the powerful prepossession towards antiquity, with which the minds of all our lawyers and legislators, and of all the people whom they wish to influence, have been always filled; and the stationary policy of this kingdom in considering their most sacred rights and franchises as an *inheritance.*

In the famous law of the 3rd of Charles I, called the *Petition of Right,* the parliament says to the king, "Your subjects have *inherited* this freedom," claiming their franchises not on abstract principles "as the rights of men," but as the rights of Englishmen, and as a patrimony derived from their forefathers. Selden, and the other profoundly learned men, who drew this Petition of Right, were as well acquainted, at least, with all the general theories concerning the "rights of men," as any of the discourses in our pulpits, or on your tribune; full as well as Dr. Price, or as the Abbé Siéyès. But, for reasons worthy of that practical wisdom which superseded their theoretic science, they preferred this positive, recorded, *hereditary* title to all which can be dear to the man and the citizen, to that vague speculative right, which exposed their sure inheritance to be scrambled for and torn to pieces by every wild, litigious spirit.

The same policy pervades all the laws which have since been made for the preservation of our liberties. In the 1st of William and Mary, in the famous statute, called the Declaration of Right, the two Houses utter not a syllable of "a right to frame a government for themselves." You will see, that their whole care was to secure the religion, laws, and liberties that had been long possessed, and had been lately endangered. "Taking into their most serious consideration the *best* means for making such an establishment, that their religion, laws, and liberties might not be in danger of being again subverted," they auspicate all their proceedings, by stating as some of those *best* means, "in the *first place*" to do "as their *ancestors in like cases have usually* done for vindicating their *ancient* rights and liberties, to *declare*";—and then they pray the king and queen, "that it may be *declared* and enacted, that *all and singular* the rights and liberties *asserted and declared,* are the true *ancient* and indubitable rights and liberties of the people of this kingdom."

You will observe that from Magna Charta to the Declaration of Right, it has been the uniform policy of our constitution to claim and assert our liberties, as an *entailed inheritance* derived to us from our forefathers, and to be transmitted to our posterity; as an estate specially belonging to the people of this kingdom, without any reference whatever to any other more general or prior right. By this means our constitution preserves a unity in so great a diversity of its parts. We have an inheritable crown; an inheritable peerage; and a House of Commons and a people inheriting privileges, franchises, and liberties, from a long line of ancestors.

This policy appears to me to be the result of profound reflection; or rather the happy effect of following nature, which is wisdom without reflection, and above it. A spirit of innovation is generally the result of a selfish temper, and confined views. People will not look forward to posterity, who never look backward to their ancestors. Besides, the people of England well know, that the idea of inheritance furnishes a sure principle of conservation, and a sure principle of transmission; without at all excluding a principle of improvement. It leaves acquisition free; but it secures what it acquires. Whatever advantages are obtained by a state proceeding on these maxims, are locked fast as in a sort of family settlement; grasped as in a kind of mortmain for ever. By a constitutional policy, working after the pattern of nature, we receive, we hold, we transmit our government and our privileges, in the same manner in which we enjoy and transmit our property and our lives. The institutions of policy, the goods of fortune, the gifts of providence, are handed down to us, and from us, in the same course and order. Our political system is placed in a just correspondence and symmetry with the order of the world, and with the mode of existence decreed to a permanent body composed of transitory parts; wherein, by the disposition of a stupendous wisdom, moulding together the great mysterious incorporation of the human race, the whole, at one time, is never old, or middleaged, or young, but, in a condition of unchangeable constancy, moves on through the varied tenor of perpetual decay, fall, renovation, and progression. Thus, by preserving the method of nature in the conduct of the state, in what we improve, we are never wholly new; in what we retain, we are never wholly obsolete. By adhering in this manner and on those principles to our forefathers, we are guided not by the superstition of antiquarians, but by the spirit of philosophic analogy. In this choice of inheritance we have given to our frame of polity the image of a relation in blood; binding up the constitution of our country with our dearest domestic ties; adopting our fundamental laws into the bosom of our family affections; keeping inseparable, and cherishing with the warmth of all their combined and mutually reflected charities, our state, our hearths, our sepulchres, and our altars.

Through the same plan of a conformity to nature in our artificial institutions, and by calling in the aid of her unerring and powerful instincts, to fortify the fallible and feeble contrivances of our reason, we have derived several others, and those no small benefits, from considering our liberties in the light of an inheritance. Always acting as if in the presence of canonized forefathers, the spirit of freedom, leading in itself to misrule and excess, is tempered with an awful gravity. This idea of a liberal descent inspires us with a sense of habitual native dignity, which prevents that upstart insolence almost inevitably adhering to and disgracing those who are the first acquirers of any distinction. By this means our liberty becomes a noble freedom. It carries an imposing and majestic aspect. It has a pedigree and illustrating ancestors. It has its bearings and its ensigns armorial. It has its gallery of portraits; its monumental inscriptions; its records, evidences, and titles. We procure reverence to our civil institutions on the principle upon which nature teaches us to revere individual men; on account of their age, and on account of those from whom they are descended. All your sophisters cannot produce anything better adapted to preserve a rational and manly freedom than the course that we have pursued, who have chosen our nature rather than our speculations, our breasts rather than our inventions, for the great conservatories and magazines of our rights and privileges.

You [*in France*] might, if you pleased, have profited of our example, and have given to your recovered freedom a correspondent dignity. Your privileges, though discontinued, were not lost to memory. Your constitution, it is true, whilst you were out of possession, suffered waste and dilapidation; but you possessed in some parts the walls, and, in all, the foundations, of a noble and venerable castle. You might have repaired those walls; you might have built on those old foundations. Your constitution was suspended before it was perfected; but you had the elements of a constitution very nearly as good as could be wished. In your old states you possessed that variety of parts corresponding with the various descriptions of which your community was happily composed; you had all that combination, and all that opposition of interests, you had that action and counteraction, which, in the natural and in the political world, from the reciprocal struggle of discordant powers, draws out the harmony of the universe. These opposed and conflicting interests, which you considered as so great a blemish in your old and in our present constitution, interpose a salutary check to all precipitate resolutions. They render deliberation a matter not of choice, but of necessity; they make all change a subject of *compromise,* which naturally begets moderation; they produce *temperaments* preventing the sore evil of harsh, crude, unqualified reformations; and rendering all the headlong exertions of arbitrary power, in the few or in the many, for ever impracticable. Through that diversity of members and interests, general liberty had as many securities as there were separate views in the several orders; whilst by pressing down the whole by the weight of a real monarchy, the separate parts would have been prevented from warping, and starting from their allotted places.

You had all these advantages in your ancient states; but you chose to act as if you had never been moulded into civil society, and had everything to begin anew. You began ill, because you began by despising everything that belonged to you. You set up your trade without a capital. If the last generations of your country appeared without much lustre in your eyes, you might have passed them by, and derived your claims from a more early race of ancestors. Under a pious predilection for those ancestors, your imaginations would have realized in them a standard of virtue and wisdom, beyond the vulgar practice of the hour: and you would have risen with the example to whose imitation you aspired. Respecting your forefathers, you would have been taught to respect yourselves. You would not have chosen to consider the French as a people of yesterday, as a nation of low-born servile wretches until the emancipating year of 1789. In order to furnish, at the expense of your honour, an excuse to your apologists here for several enormities of yours, you would not have been content to be represented as a gang of Maroon slaves, suddenly broke loose from the house of bondage, and therefore to be pardoned for your abuse of the liberty to which you were not accustomed, and ill fitted. Would it not, my worthy friend, have been wiser to have you thought, what I, for one, always thought you, a generous and gallant nation, long misled to your disadvantage by your high and romantic sentiments of fidelity, honour, and loyalty; that events had been unfavourable to you, but that you were not enslaved through any illiberal or servile disposition; that in your most devoted submission, you were actuated by a principle of public spirit, and that it was your country you worshipped, in the person of your king? Had you made it to be understood, that in the delusion of this amiable error you had gone further than your wise ancestors; that you were resolved to resume your ancient privileges, whilst you preserved the spirit of your ancient and your recent loyalty and honour; or if, diffident of yourselves, and not clearly discerning the almost obliterated constitution of your ancestors, you had looked to your neighbours in this land, who had kept alive the ancient principles and models of the old common law of Europe meliorated and adapted to its present state—by following wise examples you would have given new examples of wisdom to the world. You would have rendered the cause of liberty venerable in the eyes of every worthy mind in every nation. You would have shamed despotism from the earth, by showing that freedom was not only reconcilable, but, as when well disciplined it is, auxiliary to law. You would have had an unoppressive but a productive revenue. You would have had a flourishing commerce to feed it. You would have had a free constitution; a potent monarchy; a disciplined army; a reformed and venerated clergy; a mitigated but spirited nobility, to lead your virtue, not to overlay it; you would have had a liberal order of commons, to emulate and to recruit that nobility; you would have had a protected, satisfied, laborious, and obedient people, taught to seek and to recognise the happiness that is to be found by virtue in all conditions; in which consists the true moral equality of mankind, and not in that monstrous fiction, which, by inspiring false ideas and vain expectations into men destined to travel in the obscure walk of laborious life, serves only to aggravate and embitter that real inequality, which it never can remove; and which the order of civil life establishes as much for the benefit of those whom it must leave in an humble state, as those whom it is able to exalt to a condition more splendid, but not more happy. You had a smooth and easy career of felicity and glory laid open to you, beyond anything recorded in the history of the world; but you have shown that difficulty is good for men.

Compute your gains: see what is got by those extravagant and presumptuous speculations which have taught your leaders to despise all their predecessors, and all their contemporaries, and even to despise themselves, until the moment in which they became truly despicable. By following those false lights, France has bought undisguised calamities at a higher price than any nation has purchased the most unequivocal blessings! France has bought poverty by crime! France has not sacrificed her virtue to her interest, but she has abandoned her interest, that she might prostitute her virtue. All other nations, have begun the fabric of a new government, or the reformation of an old, by establishing originally, or by enforcing with greater exactness, some rites or other of religion. All other people have laid the foundations of civil freedom in severer manners, and a system of a more austere and masculine morality. France, when she let loose the reins of regal authority, doubled the license of a ferocious dissoluteness in manners, and of an insolent irreligion in opinions and practices; and has extended through all ranks of life, as if she were communicating some privilege, or laying open some secluded benefit, all the unhappy corruptions that usually were the disease of wealth and power. This is one of the new principles of equality in France.

France, by the perfidy of her leaders, has utterly disgraced the tone of lenient council in the cabinets of princes, and disarmed it of its most potent topics. She has sanctified the dark, suspicious maxims of tyrannous distrust; and taught kings to tremble at (what will hereafter be called) the delusive plausibilities of moral politicians. Sovereigns will consider those, who advise them to place an unlimited confidence in their people, as subverters of their thrones; as traitors who aim at their destruction, by leading their easy good-nature, under specious pretences, to admit combinations of bold and faithless men into a participation of their power. This alone (if there were nothing else) is an irreparable calamity to you and to mankind. Remember that your parliament of Paris told your king, that, in calling the states together, he had nothing to fear but the prodigal excess of their zeal in providing for the support of the throne. It is right that these men should hide their heads. It is right that they should bear their part in the ruin which their counsel has brought on their sovereign and their country. Such sanguine declarations tend to lull authority asleep; to encourage it rashly to engage in perilous adventures of untried policy; to neglect those provisions, preparations, and precautions, which distinguish benevolence from imbecility; and without which no man can answer for the salutary effect of any abstract plan of government or of freedom. For want of these, they have seen the medicine of the state corrupted into its poison. They have seen the French rebel against a mild and lawful monarch, with more fury, outrage, and insult, than ever any people has been known to rise against the most illegal usurper, or the most sanguinary tyrant. Their resistance was made to concession; their revolt was from protection; their blow was aimed at a hand holding out graces, favours, and immunities.

This was unnatural. The rest is in order. They have found their punishment in their success. Laws overturned; tribunals subverted; industry without vigour; commerce expiring; the revenue unpaid, yet the people impoverished; a church pillaged, and a state not relieved; civil and military anarchy made the constitution of the kingdom; everything human and divine sacrificed to the idol of public credit, and national bankruptcy the consequence; and, to crown all, the paper securities of new, precarious, tottering power, the discredited paper securities of impoverished fraud and beggared rapine, held out as a currency for the support of an empire, in lieu of the two great recognised species that represent the lasting, conventional credit of mankind, which disappeared and hid themselves in the earth from whence they came, when the principle of property, whose creatures and representatives they are, was systematically subverted.

Were all these dreadful things necessary? Were they the inevitable results of the desperate struggle of determined patriots, compelled to wade through blood and tumult, to the quiet shore of a tranquil and prosperous liberty? No! nothing like it. The fresh ruins of France, which shock our feelings wherever we can turn our eyes, are not the devastation of civil war; they are the sad but instructive monuments of rash and ignorant counsel in time of profound peace. They are the display of inconsiderate and presumptuous, because unresisted and irresistible, authority. The persons who have thus squandered away the precious treasure of their crimes, the persons who have made this prodigal and wild waste of public evils, (the last stage reserved for the ultimate ransom of the state), have met in their progress with little, or rather with no opposition at all. Their whole march was more like a triumphal procession, than the progress of a war. Their pioneers have gone before them, and demolished and laid everything level at their feet. Not one drop of *their* blood have they shed in the cause of the country they have ruined. They have made no sacrifices to their projects of greater consequence than their shoe-buckles, whilst they were imprisoning their king, murdering their fellow-citizens, and bathing in tears, and plunging in poverty and distress, thousands of worthy men and worthy families. Their cruelty has not even been the base result of fear. It has been the effect of their sense of perfect safety, in authorizing treasons, robberies, rapes, assassinations, slaughters, and burnings, throughout their harassed land. But the cause of all was plain from the beginning.

This unforced choice, this fond election of evil, would appear perfectly unaccountable, if we did not consider the composition of the National Assembly: I do not mean its formal constitution, which, as it now stands, is exceptional enough, but the materials of which, in a great measure, it is composed, which is of ten thousand times greater consequence than all the formalities in the world. If we were to know nothing of this assembly but by its title and function, no colours could paint to the imagination anything more venerable. In that light the mind of an inquirer, subdued by such an awful image as that of the virtue and wisdom of a whole people collected into a focus, would pause and hesitate in condemning things even of the very worst aspect. Instead of blameable, they would appear only mysterious. But no name, no power, no function, no artificial institution whatsoever, can make the men of whom any system of authority is composed, any other than God, and nature, and education, and their habits of life have made them. Capacities beyond these the people have not to give. Virtue and wisdom may be the objects of their choice; but their choice confers neither the one nor the other on those upon whom they lay their ordaining hands. They have not the engagement of nature, they have not the promise of revelation, for any such powers.

After I had read over the list of the persons and descriptions elected into the *Tiers Etat,* nothing which they afterwards did could appear astonishing. Among them, indeed, I saw some of known rank; some of shining talents; but of any practical experience in the state, not one man was to be found. The best were only men of theory. But whatever the distinguished few may have been, it is the substance the mass of the body which constitutes its character, and must finally determine its direction. In all bodies, those who will lead, must also, in a considerable degree, follow. They must conform their propositions to the taste, talent, and disposition, of those whom they wish to conduct: therefore, if an assembly is viciously or feebly composed in a very great part of it, nothing but such a supreme degree of virtue as very rarely appears in the world, and for that reason cannot enter into calculation, will prevent the men of talent disseminated through it from becoming only the expert instruments of absurd projects! If, what is the more likely event, instead of that unusual degree of virtue, they should be actuated by sinister ambition, and a lust of meretricious glory, then the feeble part of the assembly, to whom at first they conform, becomes in its turn the dupe and instrument of their designs. In this political traffic, the leaders will be obliged to bow to the ignorance of their followers, and the followers to become subservient to the worst designs of their leaders.

To secure any degree of sobriety in the propositions made by the leaders in any public assembly, they ought to respect, in some degree perhaps to fear, those whom they conduct. To be led any otherwise than blindly, the followers must be qualified, if not for actors, at least for judges; they must also be judges of natural weight and authority. Nothing can secure a steady and moderate conduct in such assemblies, but that the body of them should be respectably composed, in point of condition in life, of permanent property, of education, and of such habits as enlarge and liberalize the understanding.

In the calling of the Estates-General of France, the first thing that struck me, was a great departure from the ancient course. I found the representation for the third estate composed of six hundred persons. They were equal in number to the representatives of both the other orders. If the orders were to act separately, the number would not, beyond the consideration of the expense, be of much moment. But when it became apparent that the three orders were to be melted down into one, the policy and necessary effect of this numerous representation became obvious. A very small desertion from either of the other two orders must throw the power of both into the hands of the third. In fact, the whole power of the state was soon resolved into that body. Its due composition became therefore of infinitely the greater importance.

Judge, Sir, of my surprise, when I found that a very great proportion of the assembly (a majority, I believe, of the members who attended) was composed of practitioners in the law. It was composed, not of distinguished magistrates, who had given pledges to their country of their science, prudence, and integrity; not of leading advocates, the glory of the bar; not of renowned professors in universities;—but for the far greater part, as it must in such a number, of the inferior, unlearned, mechanical, merely instrumental members of the profession. There were distinguished exceptions; but the general composition was of obscure provincial advocates, of stewards of petty local jurisdictions, country attorneys, notaries, and the whole train of the ministers of municipal litigation, the fomenters and conductors of the petty war of village vexation. From the moment I read the list, I saw distinctly, and very nearly as it has happened, all that was to follow.

The degree of estimation in which any profession is held becomes the standard of the estimation in which the professors hold themselves. Whatever the personal merits of many individual lawyers might have been, and in many it was undoubtedly very considerable, in that military kingdom no part of the profession had been much regarded, except the highest of all, who often united to their professional offices great family splendour, and were invested with great power and authority. These certainly were highly respected, and even with no small degree of awe. The next rank was not much esteemed; the mechanical part was in a very low degree of repute.

Whenever the supreme authority is vested in a body so composed, it must evidently produce the consequences of supreme authority placed in the hands of men not taught habitually to respect themselves; who had no previous fortune in character at stake; who could not be expected to bear with moderation, or to conduct with discretion, a power, which they themselves, more than any others, must be surprised to find in their hands. Who could flatter himself that these men, suddenly, and, as it were, by enchantment, snatched from the humblest rank of subordination, would not be intoxicated with their unprepared greatness? Who could conceive that men, who are habitually meddling, daring, subtle, active, of litigious dispositions and unquiet minds would easily fall back into their old condition of obscure contention, and laborious, low, and unprofitable chicane? Who could doubt but that, at any expense to the state, of which they understood nothing, they must pursue their private interests which they understood but too well? It was not an event depending on chance, or contingency. It was inevitable; it was necessary; it was planted in the nature of things. They must *join* (if their capacity did not permit them to *lead*) in any project which could procure them those innumerable lucrative jobs, which follow in the train of all great convulsions and revolutions in the state, and particularly in all great and violent permutations of property. Was it to be expected that they would attend to the stability of property, whose existence had always depended upon whatever rendered property questionable, ambiguous, and insecure? Their objects would be enlarged with their elevation, but their disposition and habits, and mode of accomplishing their designs, must remain the same.

Well! but these men were to be tempered and restrained by other descriptions, of more sober and more enlarged understandings. Were they then to be awed by the supereminent authority and awful dignity of a handful of country clowns, who have seats in that assembly, some of whom are said not to be able to read and write? and by not a great number of traders, who, though somewhat more instructed, and more conspicuous in the order of society, had never known anything beyond their counting-house. No! both these descriptions were more formed to be overborne and swayed by the intrigues and artifices of lawyers, than to become their counterpoise. With such a dangerous disproportion, the whole must needs be governed by them. To the faculty of law was joined a pretty considerable proportion of the faculty of medicine. This faculty had not, any more than that of the law, possessed in France its just estimation. Its professors, therefore, must have the qualities of men not habituated to sentiments of dignity. But supposing they had ranked as they ought to do, and as with us they do actually, the sides of sick beds are not the academies for forming statesmen and legislators. Then came the dealers in stocks and funds, who must be eager, at any expense to change their ideal paper wealth for the more solid substance of land. To these were joined men of other descriptions, from whom as little knowledge of, or attention to, the interests of a great state was to be expected, and as little regard to the stability of any institution; men formed to be instruments, not controls. Such in general was the composition of the *Tiers Etat* in the National Assembly; in which was scarcely to be perceived the slightest traces of what we call the natural landed interest of the country.

We know that the British House of Commons, without shutting its doors to any merit in any class, is, by the sure operation of adequate causes, filled with everything illustrious in rank, in descent, in hereditary and in acquired opulence, in cultivated talents, in military, civil, naval, and politic distinction, that the country can afford. But supposing, what hardly can be supposed, as a case, that the House of Commons should be composed in the same manner with the *Tiers Etat* in France, would this dominion of chicane be borne with patience, or even conceived without horror? God forbid I should insinuate anything derogatory to that profession, which is another priesthood, administrating the rights of sacred justice. But whilst I revere men in the functions which belong to them, and would do as much as one man can do to prevent their exclusion from any, I cannot, to flatter them, give the lie to nature. They are good and useful in the composition; they must be mischievous if they preponderate so as virtually to become the whole. Their very excellence in their peculiar functions may be far from a qualification for others. It cannot escape observation, that when men are too much confined to professional and faculty habits, and as it were inveterate in the recurrent employment of that narrow circle, they are rather disabled than qualified for whatever depends on the knowledge of mankind, on experience in mixed affairs, on a comprehensive, connected view of the various, complicated, external and internal interests, which go to the formation of that multifarious thing called a state.

After all, if the House of Commons were to have a wholly professional and faculty composition, what is the power of the House of Commons, circumscribed and shut in by the immoveable barriers of laws, usages, positive rules of doctrine and practice, counterpoised by the House of Lords, and every moment of its existence at the discretion of the crown to continue, prorogue, or dissolve us? The power of the House of Commons, direct or indirect, is indeed great; and long may it be able to preserve its greatness, and the spirit belonging to true greatness, at the full; and it will do so, as long as it can keep the breakers of law in India from becoming the makers of law for England. The power, however, of the House of Commons, when least diminished, is as a drop of water in the ocean, compared to that residing in a settled majority of your National Assembly. That assembly, since the destruction of the orders, has no fundamental law, no strict convention, no respected usage to restrain it. Instead of finding themselves obliged to conform to a fixed constitution, they have a power to make a constitution which shall conform to their designs. Nothing in heaven or upon earth can serve as a control on them. What ought to be the heads, the hearts, the dispositions, that are qualified, or that dare, not only to make laws under a fixed constitution, but at one heat to strike out a totally new constitution for a great kingdom, and in every part of it, from the monarch on the throne to the vestry of a parish? But—"fools rush in where angels fear to tread." In such a state of unbounded power for undefined and undefinable purposes, the evil of a moral and almost physical inaptitude of the man to the function must be the greatest we can conceive to happen in the management of human affairs.

Having considered the composition of the third estate as it stood in its original frame, I took a view of the representatives of the clergy. There too it appeared, that full as little regard was had to the general security of property, or to the aptitude of the deputies for their public purposes, in the principles of their election. That election was so contrived, as to send a very large proportion of mere country curates to the great and arduous work of new-modelling a state; men who never had seen the state so much as in a picture; men who knew nothing of the world beyond the bounds of an obscure village; who, immersed in hopeless poverty, could regard all property, whether secular or ecclesiastical, with no other eye than that of envy; among whom must be many who, for the smallest hope of the meanest dividend in plunder, would readily join in any attempts upon a body of wealth, in which they could hardly look to have any share, except in a general scramble. Instead of balancing the power of the active chicaners in the other assembly, these curates must necessarily become the active coadjutors, or at best the passive instruments, of those by whom they had been habitually guided in their petty village concerns. They too could hardly be the most conscientious of their kind, who presuming upon their incompetent understanding, could intrigue for a trust which led them from their natural relation to their flocks, and their natural spheres of action, to undertake the regeneration of kingdoms. This preponderating weight, being added to the force of the body of chicane in the *Tiers Etat*, completed that momentum of ignorance, rashness, presumption, and lust of plunder, which nothing has been able to resist.

To observing men it must have appeared from the beginning, that the majority of the Third Estate, in conjunction with such a deputation from the clergy as I have described, whilst it pursued the destruction of the nobility, would inevitably become subservient to the worst designs of individuals in that class. In the spoil and humiliation of their own order these individuals would possess a sure fund for the pay of their new followers. To squander away the objects which made the happiness of their fellows, would be to them no sacrifice at all. Turbulent, discontented men of quality, in proportion as they are puffed up with personal pride and arrogance, generally despise their own order. One of the first symptoms they discover of a selfish and mischievous ambition, is a profligate disregard of a dignity which they partake with others. To be attached to the subdivision, to love the little platoon we belong to in society is the first principle (the germ as it were) of public affections. It is the first link in the series by which we proceed towards a love to our country, and to mankind. The interest of that portion of social arrangement is a trust in the hands of all those who compose it; and as none but bad men would justify it in abuse, none but traitors would barter it away for their own personal advantage.

ROMANTICISM

It is often said that Romanticism was a reaction against the rationalism of the Enlightenment. And yet this interpretation does not provide a complete explanation of the movement. For Romanticism was more than an anti-intellectual outburst; it was a general rebellion against the whole civilization of late eighteenth-century Europe. Although the positive views of the Romantics were often quite divergent and sometimes even contradictory, almost without exception the Romantics shared a desire to escape from the immediate historical situation in which they found themselves. The escape routes varied. Some Romantics, like the novelists Hugo and Scott, immersed themselves in the medieval past; some, like the philosopher Hegel, identified themselves with a supernatural Reality transcending the vicissitudes of time and space; some, like the political theorist De Maistre, found refuge in the traditions and authority of the Church; some, like the poet Wordsworth, sought communion with an idyllic Nature, itself soon to be despoiled by the mills and factories of the Industrial Revolution.

The first of the selections that follow is taken from the writings of the English poet Thomas Gray (1716–1771), who is most famous as the author of the "Elegy Written in a Country Churchyard." Although Gray is actually a pre-Romantic figure, the excerpts (selected from his journal and letters) reveal many typically Romantic attitudes and values.

The short poems that conclude the selection illustrate respectively two major Romantic themes: the rebellion of the individual against the gods and the worship of Nature. The first, "Prometheus" (1774), is by the German writer, Johann Wolfgang von Goethe (1749–1832). Goethe was too broad in his interests and attitudes to be classified simply as a Romantic; indeed he has been called the last uomo-universale *in Western civilization. The second poem, "Tintern Abbey" (1798) is by the English Romantic poet, William Wordsworth (1770–1850).*

Gray: Selections

From Journal in France *(1739)*

Journey to Geneva. The road runs over a mountain, which gives you the first taste of the Alps, in its magnificant rudeness, and steep precipices. Set out from Echelles on horseback to see the Grande Chartreuse; the way to it up a vast mountain, in many places the road not two yards broad; on one side the rock hanging over you, and on the other side a monstrous precipice. In the bottom runs a torrent, called *Les Guiers morts,* that works its way among the rocks with a mighty noise, and frequent falls. You here meet with all the beauties so savage and horrid a place can present you with; rocks of various and uncouth figures, cascades pouring down from an immense height out of hanging groves of pine trees, and the solemn sound of the stream that roars below, all concur to form one of the most poetical scenes imaginable.

From The Letters *(1739)* [1]

It is now almost five weeks since I left Dijon, one of the gayest and most agreeable little cities of France, for Lyons, its reverse in all these particulars. It is the second in the kingdom in bigness and rank, the streets excessively narrow and nasty; the houses immensely high and large. . . . It swarms with inhabitants like Paris itself, but chiefly a mercantile people, too much given up to commerce, to think of their own, much less of a stranger's diversions. We have no acquaintance in the town, but such English as happen to be passing through here, on their way to Italy and the south, which at present happen to be near thirty in number. It is a fortnight since we set out from hence upon a little excursion to Geneva. We took the longest road, which lies through Savoy, on purpose to see a famous monastery, called the Grande Chartreuse, and had no reason to think our time lost. After having travelled seven days very slow (for we did not change horses, it being impossible for a chaise to go post in these roads), we arrived at a little village, among the mountains of Savoy, called Echelles; from thence we proceeded on horses, who are used to the way, to the mountains of the Chartreuse. It is six miles to the top; the road runs winding up it, commonly not six feet broad; on one hand is the rock, with woods of pine-trees hanging over head; on the other, a monstrous precipice, almost perpendicular, at the bottom of which rolls a torrent, that sometimes tumbling among the fragments of stone that have fallen from on high, and sometimes precipitating itself down vast descents with a noise like thunder, which is still made greater by the echo from the mountains on each side, concurs to form one of the most solemn, the most romantic, and the most astonishing scenes I ever beheld. Add to this the strange views made by the crags and cliffs on the other hand; the cascades that in many places throw themselves from the very summit down into the vale, and the river below; and many other particulars impossible to describe; you will conclude we had no occasion to repent our pains. This place St. Bruno chose to retire to, and upon its very top founded the aforesaid convent, which is the superior of the whole order. When we came there, the two fathers, who are commissioned to entertain strangers (for the rest must neither speak one to another, nor to any one else), received us very kindly; and set before us a repast of dried fish, eggs, butter, and fruits, all excellent in their kind, and extremely neat. They pressed us to spend the night there, and to stay some days with them; but this we could not do, so they led us about their house, which is, you must think, like a little city; for there are one hundred fathers, besides three hundred servants, that make their clothes, grind their corn, press their wine, and do everything among themselves. The whole is quiet, orderly, and simple; nothing of finery, but the wonderful decency, and the strange situation, more than supply the place of it. In the evening we descended by the same way, passing through many clouds that were then forming themselves on the mountain's side. Next day we continued our journey by Chamberry, which, though the chief city of the Dutchy [sic.], and residence of the King of Sardinia, when he comes into this part of his dominions, makes but a very mean and insignificant appearance; we lay at Aix, once famous for its hot baths, and the next night at Annecy; the day after, by noon,

[1] [To Mrs. Dorothy Gray.—Ed.]

we got to Geneva. I have not time to say anything about it, nor of our solitary journey back again.

. . .

From The Letters *(1739)* [2]

After eight days' journey through Greenland, we arrived at Turin. You approach it by a handsome avenue of nine miles long, and quite strait. The entrance is guarded by certain vigilant dragons, called Douâniers, who mumbled at us for some time. The city is not large, as being a place of strength, and consequently confined within its fortifications; it has many beauties and some faults; among the first are streets all laid out by the line, regular uniform buildings, fine walks that surround the whole, and in general a good lively clean appearance. But the houses are of brick plastered, which is apt to want repairing; the windows of oiled paper, which is apt to be torn; and everything very slight, which is apt to tumble down. There is an excellent opera, but it is only in the carnival; balls every night, but only in the carnival; masquerades too, but only in the carnival. This carnival lasts only from Christmas to Lent; one half of the remaining part of the year is passed to remembering the last, the other in expecting the future carnival. We cannot well subsist upon such slender diet, no more than upon an execrable Italian comedy, and a puppet-show . . . which, I think, are all the present diversions of the place; except the Marquise de Cavaillac's Conversazione, where one goes to see people play at ombre and taroc, a game with seventy-two cards all painted with suns and moons and devils and monks. Mr. Walpole has been at court; the family are at present at a country palace, called La Venerie. The palace here in town is the very quintessence of gilding and looking-glass; inlaid floors, carved panels, and painting, wherever they could stick a brush. I own I have not, as yet, anywhere met with those grand and simple works of art that are to amaze one, and whose sight one is to be the better for; but those of Nature have astonished me beyond expression. In our little journey up to the Grande Chartreuse, I do not remember to have gone ten paces without an exclamation, that there was no restraining: not a precipice, not a torrent, not a cliff, but is pregnant with religion and poetry. There are certain scenes that would awe an atheist into belief, without the help of other argument. One need not have a very fantastic imagination to see spirits there at noon-day. You have Death perpetually before your eyes, only so far removed as to compose the mind without frighting it. I am well persuaded St. Bruno was a man of no common genius to choose such a situation for his retirement, and perhaps should have been a disciple of his, had I been born in his time. You may believe Abelard and Heloise were not forgot upon this occasion. If I do not mistake, I saw you too every now and then at a distance along the trees; . . . You seemed to call to me from the other side of the precipice, but the noise of the river below was so great, that I really could not distinguish what you said; it seemed to have a cadence like verse. In your next you will be so good to let me know what it was. The week we have since passed among the Alps has not equalled the single day upon that mountain, because the winter was rather too far advanced, and the weather a little foggy. However, it did not want its beauties; the savage rudeness of the view is inconceivable without seeing it. I reckoned in one day thirteen cascades, the least of which was, I dare say, one hundred feet in height. . . . Mont Cenis, I confess, carries the permission mountains have of being fright-

[2] [To Richard West.–Ed.]

ful rather too far; and its horrors were accompanied with too much danger to give one time to reflect upon their beauties. There is a family of the Alpine monsters I have mentioned, upon its very top, that in the middle of winter calmly lay in their stock of provisions and firing, and so are buried in their hut for a month or two under the snow. . . .

From The Letters *(1760)* [3]

I am so charmed with the two specimens of Erse [Gaelic] poetry, that I cannot help giving you the trouble to enquire a little farther about them, and should wish to see a few lines of the original, that I may form some slight idea of the language, the measures, and the rhythm.

Is there anything known of the author or authors, and of what antiquity are they supposed to be? Is there any more to be had of equal beauty, or at all approaching to it? I have been often told that the poem called *Hardicanute* (which I always admired and still admire) was the work of somebody that lived a few years ago. This I do not at all believe, though it has evidently been retouched in places by some modern hand: but however, I am authorized by this report to ask whether the two poems in question are certainly antique and genuine. I make this enquiry in quality of an antiquary, and am not otherwise concerned about it: for, if I were sure that any one now living in Scotland had written them to divert himself, and laugh at the credulity of the world, I would undertake a journey into the Highlands only for the pleasure of seeing him.

[3] [To Horace Walpole.—Ed.]

Prometheus

Cover your heavens
In cloud-mists, Zeus,
And like a boy
Beheading thistles, go practice
On oaks and mountain tops!
Still you'll have to
Leave me my earth,
The hut you did not build,
And the hearth,
Whose fire
You envy me.

I know nothing under the sun
Less enviable than you gods!
Your majesty,
Wretchedly nourished
On exacted sacrifice
And breath of prayer,
Would famish were not
Children and beggars
Hopeful fools.

While yet a child,
Knowing no other way,
Lost, I turned my face
To the sun, as if up there
Some ear might hear my lamentation,
Some heart like mine
Pity my affliction.

Who helped me
Resist Titanic arrogance?
Who rescued me from death,
From slavery?
Didn't you accomplish it yourself,
High impassioned heart?
And yet, youthfully passionate and good,
You gave deluded thanks for rescue
To the slumberer above.

Johann Wolfgang von Goethe, PROMETHEUS, *trans. Milton Miller of the University of California, Riverside.*

Why should I honor you?
Did you ever soothe the pain
Of the oppressed?
Or still the tears
Of anguish, ever?
Wasn't I forged a man
By everlasting fate
And time omnipotent,
My lords and yours?

Did you suppose
I'd come to hate life,
Escape to deserts,
Because not all
Dreams blossomed?

Here I sit and create men
After my own image,
A race like myself,
To suffer, to weep,
To relish, to rejoice,
And to ignore you,
As do I!

Tintern Abbey

LINES COMPOSED A FEW MILES ABOVE TINTERN ABBEY, ON REVISITING THE BANKS OF THE WYE DURING A TOUR

July 13, 1798

Five years have past; five summers, with the length
Of five long winters! and again I hear
These waters, rolling from their mountain-springs
With a soft inland murmur.—Once again
Do I behold these steep and lofty cliffs,
That on a wild secluded scene impress
Thoughts of more deep seclusion; and connect
The landscape with the quiet of the sky.
The day is come when I again repose
Here, under this dark sycamore, and view
These plots of cottage-ground, these orchard-tufts,
Which at this season, with their unripe fruits,
Are clad in one green hue, and lose themselves
'Mid groves and copses. Once again I see
These hedge-rows, hardly hedge-rows, little lines
Of sportive wood run wild: these pastoral farms,
Green to the very door; and wreaths of smoke
Sent up, in silence, from among the trees!
With some uncertain notice, as might seem
Of vagrant dwellers in the houseless woods,
Or of some Hermit's cave, where by his fire
The Hermit sits alone.

These beauteous forms,
Through a long absence, have not been to me
As is a landscape to blind man's eye:
But oft, in lonely rooms, and 'mid the din
Of towns and cities, I have owed to them
In hours of weariness, sensations sweet,
Felt in the blood, and felt along the heart;
And passing even into my purer mind,
With tranquil restoration:—feelings too
Of unremembered pleasure: such, perhaps,
As have no slight or trivial influence
On that best portion of a good man's life,
His little, nameless, unremembered, acts
Of kindness and of love. Nor less, I trust,
To them I may have owed another gift,
Of aspect more sublime; that blessed mood,
In which the burthen of the mystery,
In which the heavy and the weary weight
Of all this unintelligible world,

"Lines Composed a Few Miles Above Tintern Abbey," in THE POETICAL WORKS OF WORDSWORTH *(London, 1889).*

Is lightened:—that serene and blessed mood,
In which the affections gently lead us on,—
Until, the breath of this corporeal frame
And even the motion of our human blood
Almost suspended, we are laid asleep
In body, and become a living soul:
While with an eye made quiet by the power
Of harmony, and the deep power of joy,
We see into the life of things.

If this
Be but a vain belief, yet, oh! how oft—
In darkness and amid the many shapes
Of joyless daylight; when the fretful stir
Unprofitable, and the fever of the world,
Have hung upon the beatings of my heart—
How oft, in spirit, have I turned to thee,
O sylvan Wye! thou wanderer thro' the woods,
How often has my spirit turned to thee!
And now, with gleams of half-extinguished thought,
With many recognitions dim and faint,
And somewhat of a sad perplexity,
The picture of the mind revives again:
While here I stand, not only with the sense
Of present pleasure, but with pleasing thoughts
That in this moment there is life and food
For future years. And so I dare to hope,
Though changed, no doubt, from what I was when first
I came among these hills; when like a roe
I bounded o'er the mountains, by the sides
Of the deep rivers, and the lonely streams,
Wherever nature led: more like a man
Flying from something that he dreads, than one
Who sought the thing he loved. For nature then
(The coarser pleasures of my boyish days,
And their glad animal movements all gone by)
To me was all in all.—I cannot paint
What then I was. The sounding cataract
Haunted me like a passion: the tall rock,
The mountain, and the deep and gloomy wood,
Their colours and their forms, were then to me
An appetite; a feeling and a love,
That had no need of a remoter charm,
By thought supplied, nor any interest
Unborrowed from the eye.—That time is past,
And all its aching joys are now no more,
And all its dizzy raptures. Not for this
Faint I, nor mourn nor murmur; other gifts
Have followed; for such loss, I would believe,
Abundant recompense. For I have learned
To look on nature, not as in the hour
Of thoughtless youth; but hearing oftentimes
The still, sad music of humanity,
Nor harsh nor grating, though of ample power
To chasten and subdue. And I have felt
A presence that disturbs me with the joy
Of elevated thoughts; a sense sublime
Of something far more deeply interfused,
Whose dwelling is the light of setting suns,
And the round ocean and the living air,
And the blue sky, and in the mind of man;
A motion and a spirit, that impels
All thinking things, all objects of all thought,
And rolls through all things. Therefore am I still
A lover of the meadows and the woods,
And mountains; and of all that we behold
From this green earth; of all the mighty world
Of eye, and ear,—both what they half create,
And what perceive; well pleased to recognise
In nature and the language of the sense,
The anchor of my purest thoughts, the nurse,
The guide, the guardian of my heart, and soul
Of all my moral being.

Nor perchance,
If I were not thus taught, should I the more
Suffer my genial spirits to decay:
For thou art with me here upon the banks
Of this fair river; thou my dearest Friend,
My dear, dear Friend;[1] and in thy voice I catch
The language of my former heart, and read
My former pleasures in the shooting lights
Of thy wild eyes. Oh! yet a little while
May I behold in thee what I was once,
My dear, dear Sister! and this prayer I make,
Knowing that Nature never did betray
The heart that loved her; 'tis her privilege,
Through all the years of this our life, to lead
From joy to joy: for she can so inform
The mind that is within us, so impress
With quietness and beauty, and so feed
With lofty thoughts, that neither evil tongues,
Rash judgments, nor the sneers of selfish men,
Nor greetings where no kindness is, nor all
The dreary intercourse of daily life,
Shall e'er prevail against us, or disturb
Our cheerful faith, that all which we behold
Is full of blessings. Therefore let the moon
Shine on thee in thy solitary walk;
And let the misty mountain-winds be free
To blow against thee: and, in after years,
When these wild ecstasies shall be matured
Into a sober pleasure; when thy mind
Shall be a mansion for all lovely forms,
Thy memory be as a dwelling-place
For all sweet sounds and harmonies; oh! then,
If solitude, or fear, or pain, or grief,
Should be thy portion, with what healing thoughts
Of tender joy wilt thou remember me,
And these my exhortations! Nor, perchance—
If I should be where I no more can hear
Thy voice, nor catch from thy wild eyes these gleams
Of past existence—wilt thou then forget
That on the banks of this delightful stream
We stood together; and that I, so long
A worshipper of Nature, hither came
Unwearied in that service; rather say
With warmer love—oh! with far deeper zeal
Of holier love. Nor wilt thou then forget,
That after many wanderings, many years
Of absence, these steep woods and lofty cliffs,
And this green pastoral landscape, were to me
More dear, both for themselves and for thy sake!

[1] [Wordsworth is here addressing his sister Dorothy.—Ed.]

THOMAS MALTHUS

After a tranquil youth, Thomas Malthus (1766–1834) entered Cambridge University and received his Master of Arts degree in 1797. The same year he took orders in the Church of England. Most of his intellectual interests were centered on the problems of history and political economy, subjects that he taught at both Cambridge and Haileybury College (which trained candidates for service with the East India Company). His life in general was quiet and scholarly, though it was enlivened by a circle of distinguished friends, such as James Mill and David Ricardo, and spiced by the periodic outbursts of abuse and vilification that he suffered after his great study on population had been published. This work was denounced as unholy, atheistic, and subversive, but it was admired by such men as William Pitt and Archdeacon William Paley, and by such noted periodicals as the Edinburgh Review *and the* Quarterly Review.

The book that caused all this furor was An Essay on the Principle of Population, *which first appeared in 1798. The first edition, however, was premature, for Malthus lacked sufficient evidence to support his thesis strongly, and he chose to write in an excessively rhetorical style. But as the years passed, he assembled more and more factual support, eliminated errors in interpretation, and excised some of the more polemical passages. At last, in 1826, he released the sixth and final edition. It is from this edition that the following selection has been taken. Some of the flavor—and the dogmatism—of the Malthusian argument is suggested by the full title of the work:* An Essay on the Principle of Population, or a View of its Past and Present Effects on Human Happiness with an Inquiry into Our Prospects Respecting the Future Removal or Mitigation of the Evils which it Occasions.

An Essay on the Principle of Population

BOOK I

Of the Checks to Population in the Less Civilized Parts of the World and in Past Times

Chapter I

STATEMENT OF THE SUBJECT. RATIOS OF THE INCREASE OF POPULATION AND FOOD

In an inquiry concerning the improvement of society, the mode of conducting the subject which naturally presents itself, is,

1. To investigate the causes that have hitherto impeded the progress of mankind towards happiness; and,
2. To examine the probability of the total or partial removal of these causes in future.

To enter fully into this question, and to enumerate all the causes that have hitherto influenced human improvement, would be much beyond the power of an individual.

Thomas Robert Malthus, AN ESSAY ON THE PRINCIPLE OF POPULATION *(London, 1890).*

The principal object of the present essay is to examine the effects of the one great cause intimately united with the very nature of man; which, though it has been constantly and powerfully operating since the commencement of society, has been little noticed by the writers who have treated this subject. The facts which establish the existence of this cause have, indeed, been repeatedly stated and acknowledged; but its natural and necessary effects have been almost totally overlooked; though probably among these effects may be reckoned a very considerable portion of that vice and misery, and of that unequal distribution of the bounties of nature, which it has been the unceasing object of the enlightened philanthropist in all ages to correct.

The cause to which I allude, is the constant tendency in all animated life to increase beyond the nourishment prepared for it.

It is observed by Dr. Franklin that there is no bound to the prolific nature of plants or animals, but what is made by their crowding or interfering with each other's means of subsistence. Were the face of the earth, he says, vacant of other plants, it might gradually be sowed and overspread with one kind only, as for instance with fennel: and were it empty of other inhabitants, it might in a few ages be replenished from one nation only, as for instance with Englishmen.

This is incontrovertibly true. Through the animal and vegetable kingdoms Nature has scattered the seeds of life abroad with the most profuse and liberal hand; but has been comparatively sparing in the room and the nourishment necessary to rear them. The germs of existence contained in this earth, if they could freely develop themselves, would fill millions of worlds in the course of a few thousand years. Necessity, that imperious, all-pervading law of nature, restrains them within the prescribed bounds. The race of plants and the race of animals shrink under this great restrictive law; and man cannot by any efforts of reason escape from it.

In plants and irrational animals, the view of the subject is simple. They are all impelled by a powerful instinct to the increase of their species; and this instinct is interrupted by no doubts about providing for their offspring. Wherever, therefore there is liberty, the power of increase is exerted; and the super-abundant effects are repressed afterwards by want of room and nourishment.

The effects of this check on man are more complicated. Impelled to the increase of his species by an equally powerful instinct, reason interrupts his career, and asks him whether he may not bring beings into the world, for whom he cannot provide the means of support. If he attend to this natural suggestion, the restriction too frequently produces vice. If he hear it not, the human race will be constantly endeavouring to increase beyond the means of subsistence. But as, by that law of our nature which makes food necessary to the life of man, population can never actually increase beyond the lowest nourishment capable of supporting it, a strong check on population, from the difficulty of acquiring food, must be constantly in operation. This difficulty must fall somewhere, and must necessarily be severely felt in some or other of the various forms of misery, or the fear of misery, by a large portion of mankind.

That population has this constant tendency to increase beyond the means of subsistence, and that it is kept to its necessary level by these causes, will sufficiently appear from a review of the different states of society in which man has existed. But, before we proceed to this review, the subject will, perhaps, be seen in a clearer light, if we endeavour to ascertain what would be the natural increase of population, if left to exert itself with perfect freedom, and what might be expected to be the rate of increase in the productions of the earth, under the most favourable circumstances of human industry.

It will be allowed that no country has hitherto been known, where the manners were so pure and simple, and the means of subsistence so abundant, that no check whatever has existed to early marriages from the difficulty of providing for a family, and that no waste of the human species has been occasioned by vicious customs, by towns, by unhealthy occupations, or too severe labour. Consequently in no state that we have yet known, has the power of population been left to exert itself with perfect freedom.

Whether the law of marriage be instituted, or not, the dictate of nature and virtue seems to be an early attachment to one woman; and where there were no impediments of any kind in the way of a union to which such an attachment would lead, and no causes of depopulation afterwards, the increase of the human species would be evidently much greater than any increase which has been hitherto known.

In the northern states of America, where the means of subsistence have been more ample, the manners of the people more pure, and the checks to early marriages fewer, than in any of the modern states of Europe, the population has been found to double itself, for above a century and a half successively, in less than twenty-five years. Yet, even during these periods, in some of the towns, the deaths exceed the births, a circumstance which clearly proves that, in those parts of the country which supplied this deficiency, the increase must have been much more rapid than the general average.

In the back settlements, where the sole employment is agriculture, and vicious customs and unwholesome occupations are little known, the population has been found to double itself in fifteen years. Even this extraordinary rate of increase is probably short of the utmost power of population. Very severe labour is requisite to clear a fresh country; such situations are not in general considered as particularly healthy; and the inhabitants, probably, are occasionally subject to the incursions of the Indians, which may destroy some lives, or at any rate diminish the fruits of industry.

According to a table of Euler, calculated on a mortality of 1 in 36, if the births be to the deaths in the proportion of 3 to 1, the period of doubling will be only 12 years and 4/5ths. And this proportion is not only a possible supposition, but has actually occurred for short periods in more countries than one.

Sir William Petty supposes a doubling possible in so short a time as ten years.

But, to be perfectly sure that we are far within the truth, we will take the slowest of these rates of increase, a rate in which all concurring testimonies agree, and which has been repeatedly ascertained to be from procreation only.

It may safely be pronounced, therefore, that population, when unchecked, goes on doubling itself every twenty-five years, or increases in a geometrical ratio.

The rate according to which the productions of the earth may be supposed to increase, it will not be so easy to determine. Of this, however, we may be perfectly certain, that the ratio of their increase in a limited territory must be of a totally different nature from the ratio of the increase of population. A thousand millions are just as easily doubled every twenty-five years by the power of population as a thousand. But the food to support the increase from the greater number will by no means be obtained with the same facility. Man is necessarily confined in room. When acre has been added to acre till all the fertile land is occupied, the yearly increase of food must depend upon the melioration of the land already in possession. This is a fund, which, from the nature of all soils, instead of increasing, must be gradually diminishing. But population, could it be supplied with food, would go on with unexhausted vigour; and the increase of one period would furnish the power of a greater increase the next, and this without any limit.

From the accounts we have of China and Japan, it may be fairly doubted, whether the best-directed efforts of human industry could double the produce of these countries even once in any number of years. There are many parts of the globe, indeed, hitherto uncultivated, and almost unoccupied; but the right of exterminating, or driving into a corner where they must starve, even the inhabitants of these thinly-peopled regions, will be questioned in a moral view. The process of improving their minds and directing their industry would necessarily be slow; and during this time, as population would regularly keep pace with the increasing produce, it would rarely happen that a great degree of knowledge and industry would have to operate at once upon rich unappropriated soil. Even where this might take place, as it does sometimes in new colonies, a geometrical ratio increases with such extraordinary rapidity, that the advantage could not last long. If the United States of America continue increasing, which they certainly will do, though not with the same rapidity as formerly, the Indians will be driven further and further back into the country, till the whole race is ultimately exterminated, and the territory is incapable of further extension.

These observations are, in a degree, applicable to all the parts of the earth, where the soil is imperfectly cultivated. To exterminate the inhabitants of the greatest part of Asia and Africa, is a thought that could not be admitted for a moment. To civilise and direct the industry of the various tribes of Tartars and Negroes, would certainly be a work of considerable time, and of variable and uncertain success.

Europe is by no means so fully peopled as it might be. In Europe there is the fairest chance that human industry may receive its best direction. The science of agriculture has been much studied in England and Scotland; and there is still a great portion of uncultivated land in these countries. Let us consider at what rate the produce of this island might be supposed to increase under circumstances the most favourable to improvement.

If it be allowed that by the best possible policy, and great encouragements to agriculture, the average produce of the island could be doubled in the first twenty-five years, it will be allowing, probably, a greater increase than could with reason be expected.

In the next twenty-five years, it is impossible to suppose that the produce could be quadrupled. It would be contrary to all our knowledge of the properties of land. The improvement of the barren parts would be a work of time and labour; and it must be evident to those who have the slightest acquaintance with agricultural subjects that in proportion as cultivation extended, the additions that could yearly be made to the former average produce must be gradually and regularly diminishing. That we may be the better able to compare the increase of population and food, let us make a supposition, which, without pretending to accuracy, is clearly more favourable to the power of production in the earth, than any experience we have had of its qualities will warrant.

Let us suppose that the yearly additions which might be made to the former average produce, instead of decreasing, which they certainly would do, were to remain the same; and that the produce of this island might be increased every twenty-five years, by a quantity equal to what it at present produces. The most enthusiastic speculator cannot suppose a greater increase than this. In a few centuries it would make every acre of land in the island like a garden.

If this supposition be applied to the whole earth, and if it be allowed that the subsistence for man which the earth affords might be increased every twenty-five years by a quantity equal to what it at present produces, this will be supposing a rate of increase much greater than we can imagine that any possible exertions of mankind could make it.

It may be fairly pronounced, therefore, that, considering the present average state of the earth, the means of subsistence, under circumstances the most favourable to human industry, could not possibly be made to increase faster than in an arithmetical ratio.

The necessary effects of these two different rates of increase, when brought together, will be very striking. Let us call the population of this island eleven millions; and suppose the present produce equal to the easy support of such a number. In the first twenty-five years the population would be twenty-two millions, and the food also being doubled, the means of subsistence would be equal to this increase. In the next twenty-five years, the population would be forty-four millions, and the means of subsistence only equal to the support of thirty-three millions. In the next period the population would be eighty-eight millions, and the means of subsistence just equal to the support of half that number. And, at the conclusion of the first century, the population would be a hundred and seventy-six millions, and the means of subsistence only equal to the support of fifty-five millions, leaving a population of a hundred and twenty-one millions totally unprovided for.

Taking the whole earth, instead of this island, emigration would of course be excluded; and, supposing the present population equal to a thousand millions, the human species would increase as the numbers 1, 2, 4, 8, 16, 32, 64, 128, 256, and subsistence as 1, 2, 3, 4, 5, 6, 7, 8, 9. In two centuries the population would be to the means of subsistence as 256 to 9; in three centuries as 4096 to 13, and in two thousand years the difference would be almost incalculable.

In this supposition no limits whatever are placed to the produce of the earth. It may increase for ever and be greater than any assignable quantity; yet still the power of population being in every period so much superior, the increase of the human species can only be kept down to the level of the means of subsistence by the constant operation of the strong law of necessity, acting as a check upon the greater power.

Chapter II

OF THE GENERAL CHECKS TO POPULATION AND THE MODE OF THEIR OPERATION

The ultimate check to population appears then to be a want of food, arising necessarily from the different ratios according to which population and food increase. But this ultimate check is never the immediate check, except in cases of actual famine.

The immediate check may be stated to consist in all those customs, and all those diseases, which seem to be generated by a scarcity of the means of subsistence; and all those causes, independent of this scarcity, whether of a moral or physical nature, which tend prematurely to weaken and destroy the human frame.

These checks to population, which are constantly operating with more or less force in every society, and keep down the number to the level of the means of subsistence, may be classed under two general heads—the preventive, and the positive checks.

The preventive check, as far as it is voluntary, is peculiar to man, and arises from that distinctive superiority in his reasoning faculties, which enables him to calculate distant consequences. The checks to the indefinite increase of plants and irrational animals are all either positive, or, if preventive, involuntary. But man cannot look around him, and see the distress which frequently presses upon those who have large families; he cannot contemplate his present possessions or earnings, which he now nearly consumes himself, and calculate the amount of each share, when with very little addition they must be divided, perhaps, among seven or eight, without feeling a doubt whether, if he follow the bent of his inclinations, he may be able to support the offspring which he will probably bring into the world. In a state of equality, if such can exist, this would be the simple question. In the present state of society other considerations occur. Will he not lower his rank in life, and be obliged to give up in great measure his former habits? Does any mode of employment present itself by which he may reasonably hope to maintain a family? Will he not at any rate subject himself to greater difficulties, and more severe labour, than in his single state? Will he not be unable to transmit to his children the same advantages of education and improvement that he had himself possessed? Does he even feel secure that, should he have a large family, his utmost exertions can save them from rags and squalid poverty, and their consequent degradation from the community? And may he not be reduced to the grating necessity of forfeiting his independence, and of being obliged to the sparing hand of Charity for support?

These considerations are calculated to prevent, and certainly do prevent, a great number of persons in all civilised nations from pursuing the dictate of nature in an early attachment to one woman.

If this restraint does not produce vice, it is undoubtedly the least evil that can arise from the principle of population. Considered as a restraint on a strong natural inclination, it must be allowed to produce a certain degree of temporary unhappiness; but evidently slight, compared with the evils which result from any of the other checks to population; and merely of the same nature as many other sacrifices of temporary to permanent gratification, which it is the business of a moral agent continually to make.

When this restraint produces vice, the evils which follow are but too conspicuous. A promiscuous intercourse to such a degree as to prevent the birth of children, seems to lower, in the most marked manner, the dignity of human nature. It cannot be without its effect on men, and nothing can be more obvious than its tendency to degrade the female character, and to destroy all its most amiable and distinguishing characteristics. Add to which, that among those unfortunate females, with which all great towns abound, more real distress and aggravated misery are, perhaps, to be found, than in any other department of human life.

When a general corruption of morals with regard to the sex, pervades all the classes of society, its effects must necessarily be, to poison the springs of domestic happiness, to weaken conjugal and parental affection, and to lessen the united exertions and ardour of parents in the care and education of their children:—effects which cannot take place without a decided diminution of the general happiness and virtue of the society; particularly as the necessity of art in the accomplishment and conduct of intrigues, and in the concealment of their consequences necessarily leads to many other vices.

The positive checks to population are extremely various, and include every cause, whether arising from vice or misery, which in any degree contributes to shorten the natural duration of human life. Under this head, therefore, may be enumerated all unwholesome occupations, severe labour and exposure to the seasons, extreme poverty, bad nursing of children, great towns, excesses of all kinds, the whole train of common diseases and epidemics, wars, plagues, and famine.

On examining these obstacles to the increase of population which I have classed under the heads of preventive and positive checks, it will appear that they are all resolvable into moral restraint, vice, and misery.

Of the preventive checks, the restraint from marriage which is not followed by irregular gratifications may properly be termed moral restraint.[1]

Promiscuous intercourse, unnatural passions, violations of the marriage bed, and improper arts to conceal the consequences of irregular connexions, are preventive checks that clearly come under the head of vice.

Of the positive checks, those which appear to arise unavoidably from the laws of nature, may be called exclusively misery; and those which we obviously bring upon ourselves, such as wars, excesses, and many others which it would be in our power to avoid, are of a mixed nature. They are brought upon us by vice, and their consequences are misery.[2]

The sum of all these preventive and positive checks, taken together, forms the immediate check to population; and it is evident that, in every country where the whole of the procreative power cannot be called into action, the preventive and the positive checks must vary inversely as each other; that is, in countries either naturally unhealthy, or subject to a great mortality, from whatever cause it may arise, the preventive check will prevail very little. In those countries, on the contrary, which are naturally healthy, and where the preventive check is found to prevail with considerable force, the positive check will prevail very little, or the mortality be very small.

In every country some of these checks are, with more or less force, in constant operation; yet notwithstanding their general prevalence, there are few states in which there is not a constant effort in the population to increase beyond the means of subsistence. This constant effort as constantly

[1] It will be observed, that I here use the term *moral* in its most confined sense. By moral restraint I would be understood to mean a restraint from marriage, from prudential motives, with a conduct strictly moral during the period of this restraint; and I have never intentionally deviated from this sense. When I have wished to consider the restraint from marriage connected with its consequences, I have either called it prudential restraint, or a part of the preventive check, of which indeed it forms the principal branch.

In my review of the different stages of society, I have been accused of not allowing sufficient weight in the prevention of population to moral restraint; but when the confined sense of the term, which I have here explained, is adverted to, I am fearful that I shall not be found to have erred much in this respect. I should be very glad to believe myself mistaken.

[2] As the general consequence of vice is misery, and as this consequence is the precise reason why an action is termed vicious, it may appear that the term misery alone would be here sufficient, and that it is superfluous to use both. But the rejection of the term vice would introduce a considerable confusion into our language and ideas. We want it particularly to distinguish those actions, the general tendency of which is to produce misery, and which are therefore prohibited by the commands of the Creator, and the precepts of the moralist, although, in their immediate or individual effects, they may produce perhaps exactly the contrary. The gratification of all our passions in its immediate effect is happiness, not misery; and, in individual instances, even the remote consequences (at least in this life) may possibly come under the same denomination. There may have been some irregular connexions with women, which have added to the happiness of both parties, and have injured no one. These individual actions, therefore, cannot come under the head of misery. But they are still evidently vicious, because an action is so denominated, which violates an express precept, founded upon its general tendency to produce misery, whatever may be its individual effect; and no person can doubt the general tendency of an illicit intercourse between the sexes, to injure the happiness of society.

tends to subject the lower classes of society to distress, and to prevent any great permanent melioration of their condition.

These effects, in the present state of society, seem to be produced in the following manner. We will suppose the means of subsistence in any country just equal to the easy support of the inhabitants. The constant effort towards population, which is found to act even in the most vicious societies, increases the number of people before the means of subsistence are increased. The food, therefore, which before supported eleven millions, must now be divided among eleven millions and a half. The poor consequently must live much worse, and many of them be reduced to severe distress. The number of labourers also being above the proportion of work in the market, the price of labour must tend to fall, while the price of provisions would at the same time tend to rise. The labourer therefore must do more work, to earn the same as he did before. During this season of distress, the discouragements to marriage and the difficulty of rearing a family are so great, that the progress of population is retarded. In the mean time, the cheapness of labour, the plenty of labourers, and the necessity of an increased industry among them, encourage cultivators to employ more labour upon their land, to turn up fresh soil, and to manure and improve more completely what is already in tillage, till ultimately the means of subsistence may become in the same proportion to the population, as at the period from which we set out. The situation of the labourer being then again tolerably comfortable, the restraints to population are in some degree loosened; and, after a short period, the same retrograde and progressive movements, with respect to happiness, are repeated.

This sort of oscillation will not probably be obvious to common view; and it may be difficult even for the most attentive observer to calculate its periods. Yet that, in the generality of old states, some alternation of this kind does exist though in a much less marked, and in a much more irregular manner, than I have described it, no reflecting man, who considers the subject deeply, can well doubt.

One principal reason why this oscillation has been less remarked, and less decidedly confirmed by experience than might naturally be expected, is, that the histories of mankind which we possess are, in general, histories only of the higher classes. We have not many accounts that can be depended upon, of the manners and customs of that part of mankind, where these retrograde and progressive movements chiefly take place. A satisfactory history of this kind, of one people and of one period, would require the constant and minute attention of many observing minds in local and general remarks on the state of the lower classes of society, and the causes that influenced it; and to draw accurate inferences upon this subject, a succession of such historians for some centuries would be necessary. This branch of statistical knowledge has, of late years, been attended to in some countries, and we may promise ourselves a clearer insight into the internal structure of human society from the progress of these inquiries. But the science may be said yet to be in its infancy, and many of the objects, on which it would be desirable to have information, have been either omitted or not stated with sufficient accuracy. Among these, perhaps, may be reckoned the proportion of the number of adults to the number of marriages; the extent to which vicious customs have prevailed in consequence of the restraints upon matrimony; the comparative mortality among the children of the most distressed part of the community, and of those who live rather more at their ease; the variations in the real price of labour; the observable differences in the state of the lower classes of society, with respect to ease and happiness, at different times during a certain period; and very accurate registers of births, deaths, and marriages, which are of the utmost importance in this subject.

A faithful history, including such particulars, would tend greatly to elucidate the manner in which the constant check upon population acts; and would probably prove that existence of the retrograde and progressive movements that have been mentioned; though the times of their vibration must necessarily be rendered irregular from the operation of many interrupting causes; such as, the introduction or failure of certain manufactures; a greater or less prevalent spirit of agricultural enterprise; years of plenty, or years of scarcity; wars, sickly seasons, poor-laws, emigrations and other causes of a similar nature.

A circumstance which has, perhaps, more than any other, contributed to conceal this oscillation from common view, is the difference between the nominal and real price of labour. It very rarely happens that the nominal price of labour universally falls; but we well know that it frequently remains the same, while the nominal price of provisions has been gradually rising. This, indeed, will generally be the case, if the increase of manufactures and commerce be sufficient to employ the new labourers that are thrown into the market, and to prevent the increased supply from lowering the money-price. But an increased number of labourers receiving the same money-wages will necessarily, by their competition, increase the money-price of corn. This is, in fact, a real fall in the price of labour; and, during this period, the condition of the lower classes of the community must be gradually growing worse. But the farmers and capitalists are growing rich from the real cheapness of labour. Their increasing capitals enable them to employ a greater number of men; and, as the population had probably suffered some check from the greater difficulty of supporting a family, the demand for labour, after a certain period, would be great in proportion to the supply, and its price would of course rise, if left to find its natural level; and thus the wages of labour, and consequently the condition of the lower classes of society, might have progressive and retrograde movements, though the price of labour might never nominally fall.

In savage life, where there is no regular price of labour, it is little to be doubted that similar oscillations took place. When population has increased nearly to the utmost limits of the food, all the preventive and the positive checks will naturally operate with increased force. Vicious habits with respect to the sex will be more general, the exposing of children more frequent, and both the probability and fatality of wars and epidemics will be considerably greater; and these causes will probably continue their operation till the population is sunk below the level of the food; and then the return to comparative plenty will again produce an increase, and, after a certain period, its further progress will again be checked by the same causes.

But without attempting to establish these progressive and retrograde movements in different countries, which would evidently require more minute histories than we possess, and which the progress of civilisation naturally tends to counteract, the following propositions are intended to be proved:—

1. Population is necessarily limited by the means of subsistence.

2. Population invariably increases when the means of subsistence increase, unless prevented by some very powerful and obvious checks.

3. These checks, and the checks which

repress the superior power of population, and keep its effects on a level with the means of subsistence, are all resolvable into moral restraint, vice, and misery.

The first of these propositions scarcely needs illustration. The second and third will be sufficiently established by a review of the immediate checks to population in the past and present state of society.

PRINCE KLEMENS VON METTERNICH

One of the most powerful and influential figures at the glittering Congress of Vienna of both 1814 and 1815 was Prince Klemens von Metternich. His power was based on the fact that he spoke for a great empire that had been most often opposed to Napoleonic France and, likewise, most often been defeated by it; his influence can be attributed to his highly developed rhetorical skills, his intellectual brilliance in the political arena, and his fundamentally realistic approach to the reconciliation of means and ends.

These qualities were aptly summarized by Metternich himself when he said that his primary function politically was to "prop up the moldering edifice" of the Austrian Empire. The figure of speech is Churchillian in its clarity; the political insight reveals a hardness of view and an assessment of situation worthy of a Machiavellian prince. The following selection from his Memoirs *can stand as evidence of his methods and skills for accomplishing his goal—the preservation of a European state-system uninfluenced by the corrupt ideas of "Liberty, Equality, and Fraternity."*

Metternich was born in 1773, the scion of a noble Rhenish family. During the French Revolution he was being educated at the University of Strasbourg where he developed a profound distaste for the revolutionary activities and excesses that he witnessed there. Between 1797 and 1809 he held a variety of diplomatic appointments in the Austrian government, and finally (1809) was elevated to the post of Minister of Foreign Affairs. It was in that capacity that he played a successful part in the negotiations leading to the marriage of the daughter of the Austrian Emperor, Marie Louise, to Napoleon. Sometimes the years 1815–1848 are called the "Age of Metternich" because of the pre-eminent role the Prince assumed in European politics during the first half of the nineteenth century. Metternich devoted his energies to the maintenance of a European state-system based on the principles of legitimacy and conservatism and, reciprocally, profoundly antagonistic to liberalism and nationalism. His system collapsed in the wave of liberal-national revolutionary movements of 1848.

Confession of Faith

Secret Memorandum
to the Emperor Alexander

"L'Europe," a celebrated writer has recently said, *"fait aujourd'hui pitié à l'homme d'esprit et horreur à l'homme vertueux."*

It would be difficult to comprise in a few words a more exact picture of the situation at the time we are writing these lines!

Kings have to calculate the chances of their very existence in the immediate future; passions are let loose, and league together to overthrow everything which society respects as the basis of its existence; religion, public morality, laws, customs, rights, and duties, all are attacked, confounded, overthrown, or called in question. The great mass of the people are tranquil spectators of these attacks and revolutions, and of the absolute want of all means of defence. A few are carried off by the torrent, but the wishes of the immense majority are to maintain a repose which exists no longer, and of which even the first elements seem to be lost.

What is the cause of all these evils? By what methods has this evil established itself, and how is it that it penetrates into every vein of the social body?

Do remedies still exist to arrest the progress of this evil, and what are they?

These are doubtless questions worthy of the solicitude of every good man who is a true friend to order and public peace—two elements inseparable in principle and which are at once the first needs and the first blessings of humanity.

MEMOIRS OF PRINCE METTERNICH, *trans. Mrs. A. Napier (London, 1881).*

Has there never been offered to the world an institution really worthy of the name? Has truth been always confounded with error ever since society has believed itself able to distinguish one from the other? Have the experiences bought at the price of so many sacrifices and repeated at intervals, and in so many different places, been all in error? Will a flood of light be shed upon society at one stroke? Will knowledge come by inspiration? If one could believe in such phenomena it would not be the less necessary, first of all, to assure oneself of their reality. Of all things, nothing is so fatal as error; and it is neither our wish nor our intention ever to give ourselves up to it. Let us examine the matter!

THE SOURCE OF THE EVIL

Man's nature is immutable. The first needs of society are and remain the same, and the differences which they seem to offer find their explanation in the diversity of influences, acting on the different races by natural causes, such as the diversity of climate, barrenness or richness of soil, insular or continental position, &c., &c. These local differences no doubt produce effects which extend far beyond purely physical necessities; they create and determine particular needs in a more elevated sphere; finally, they determine the laws, and exercise an influence even on religions.

It is, on the other hand, with institutions as with everything else. Vague in their origin, they pass through periods of development and perfection, to arrive in time at their decadence; and, conforming to the laws of man's nature, they have, like him, their infancy, their youth, their age of strength and reason, and their age of decay.

Two elements alone remain in all their strength, and never cease to exercise their indestructible influence with equal power. These are the precepts of morality, religious as well as social, and the necessities created by locality. From the time that men attempt to swerve from these bases, to become rebels against these sovereign arbiters of their destinies, society suffers from a *malaise* which sooner or later will lead to a state of convulsion. The history of every country, in relating the consequences of such errors, contains many pages stained with blood; but we dare to say, without fear of contradiction, one seeks in vain for an epoch when an evil of this nature has extended its ravages over such a vast area as it has done at the present time. The causes are natural.

History embraces but a very limited space of time. It did not begin to deserve the name of history until long after the fall of great empires. There, where it seems to conduct us to the cradle of civilisation, it really conducts us to ruins. We see republics arise and prosper, struggle, and then submit to the rule of one fortunate soldier. We see one of these republics pass through all the phases common to society, and end in an almost universal monarchy—that is to say, subjugating the scattered portions of the then civilised world. We see this monarchy suffer the fate of all political bodies: we see its first springs become enfeebled, and finally decay.

Centuries of darkness followed the irruption of the barbarians. The world, however, could not return to barbarism. The Christian religion had appeared; imperishable in its essence, its very existence was sufficient to disperse the darkness and establish civilisation on new foundations, applicable to all times and all places, satisfying all needs, and establishing the most important of all on the basis of a pure and eternal law! To the formation of new Christian States succeeded the Crusades, a curious mixture of good and evil.

A decisive influence was shortly exercised on the progress of civilisation by three discoveries—the invention of printing, that of gunpowder, and the discovery of the New World. Still later came the Reformation—another event which had incalculable effects, on account of its influence on the moral world. From that time the face of the world was changed.

The facilitation of the communication of thoughts by printing; the total change in the means of attack and defence brought about by the invention of gunpowder; the difference suddenly produced in the value of property by the quantity of metals which the discovery of America put in circulation; the spirit of adventure provoked by the chances of fortune opened in a new hemisphere; the modifications in the relations of society caused by so many and such important changes, all became more developed, and were in some sort crowned by the revolution which the Reformation worked in the moral world.

The progress of the human mind has been extremely rapid in the course of the last three centuries. This progress having been accelerated more rapidly than the growth of wisdom (the only counterpoise to passions and to error); a revolution prepared by the false systems, the fatal errors into which many of the most illustrious sovereigns of the last half of the eighteenth century fell, has at last broken out in a country advanced in knowledge, and enervated by pleasure, in a country inhabited by a people whom one can only regard as frivolous, from the facility with which they comprehend and the difficulty they experience in judging calmly.

Having now thrown a rapid glance over the first causes of the present state of society, it is necessary to point out in a more particular manner the evil which threatens to deprive it, at one blow, of the real blessings, the fruits of genuine civilisation, and to disturb it in the midst of its enjoyments. This evil may be described in one word—presumption; the natural effect of the rapid progression of the human mind towards the perfecting of so many things. This it is which at the present day leads so many individuals astray, for it has become an almost universal sentiment.

Religion, morality, legislation, economy, politics, administration, all have become common and accessible to everyone. Knowledge seems to come by inspiration; experience has no value for the presumptuous man; faith is nothing to him; he substitutes for it a pretended individual conviction, and to arrive at this conviction dispenses with all inquiry and with all study; for these means appear too trivial to a mind which believes itself strong enough to embrace at one glance all questions and all facts. Laws have no value for him, because he has not contributed to make them, and it would be beneath a man of his parts to recognise the limits traced by rude and ignorant generations. Power resides in himself; why should he submit himself to that which was only useful for the man deprived of light and knowledge? That which, according to him, was required in an age of weakness cannot be suitable in an age of reason and vigour, amounting to universal perfection, which the German innovators designate by the idea, absurd in itself, of the Emancipation of the People! Morality itself he does not attack openly, for without it he could not be sure for a single instant of his own existence; but he interprets its essence after his own fashion, and allows every other person to do so likewise, provided that other person neither kills nor robs him.

In thus tracing the character of the presumptuous man, we believe we have traced that of the society of the day, composed of like elements, if the denomination of society is applicable to an order of things which only tends in principle towards individualising all the elements of which society is composed. Presumption makes every man the guide of his own belief, the arbiter of laws according to which he is pleased to govern himself, or to allow some one else to govern him and his neighbours; it makes him, in short, the sole judge of his own faith, his own actions, and the principles according to which he guides them.

Is it necessary to give a proof of this last fact? We think we have furnished it in remarking that one of the sentiments most natural to man, that of nationality, is erased from the Liberal catechism, and that where the word is still employed, it is used by the heads of the party as a pretext to enchain Governments, or as a lever to bring about destruction. The real aim of the idealists of the party is religious and political fusion, and this being analysed is nothing else but creating in favour of each individual an existence entirely independent of all authority, or of any other will than his own, an idea absurd and contrary to the nature of man, and incompatible with the needs of human society.

THE COURSE WHICH THE EVIL HAS FOLLOWED AND STILL FOLLOWS

The causes of the deplorable intensity with which this evil weighs on society appear to us to be of two kinds. The first are so connected with the nature of things that no human foresight could have prevented them. The second should be subdivided into two classes, however similar they may appear in their effects.

Of these causes, the first are negative, the others positive. We will place among the first the feebleness and the inertia of Governments.

It is sufficient to cast a glance on the course which the Governments followed during the eighteenth century, to be convinced that not one among them was ignorant of the evil or of the crisis towards which the social body was tending. There were, however, some men, unhappily endowed with great talents, who felt their own strength, and were not slow to appraise the progressive course of their influence, taking into account the weakness or the inertia of their adversaries; and who had the art to prepare and conduct men's minds to the triumph of their detestable enterprise —an enterprise all the more odious as it was pursued without regard to results, simply abandoning themselves to the one feeling of hatred of God and of His immutable moral laws.

France had the misfortune to produce the greatest number of these men. It is in her midst that religion and all that she holds sacred, that morality and authority, and all connected with them, have been attacked with a steady and systematic animosity, and it is there that the weapon of ridicule has been used with the most ease and success.

Drag through the mud the name of God and the powers instituted by His divine decrees, and the revolution will be prepared! Speak of a social contract, and the revolution is accomplished! The revolution was already completed in the palaces of Kings, in the drawing-rooms and boudoirs of certain cities, while among the great mass of the people it was still only in a state of preparation.

It would be difficult not to pause here to consider the influence which the example of England had for a long time exercised on France. England is herself placed in such a peculiar situation that we believe we may safely say that not one of the forms possible to that State, not one of its customs or institutions, would suit any Continental State, and that where we might wish to take them for models, we should only obtain inconvenience and danger, without securing a single one of the advantages which accompany them.

According to the best minds in France, at the time of the convocation of the *notables,* and in consequence of the direction which public opinion had received for more than fifty years—a direction which, latterly, had been strengthened and in some sort adapted to France by the imprudent help which her Government had given to the American revolution—all reform in France touching the very foundations of the monarchy was soon transformed into a revolution. What might have been foreseen, and what had been foretold by everybody, the Government alone excepted, was realised but too soon. The French Revolution broke out, and has gone through a complete revolutionary cycle in a very short period, which could only have appeared long to its victims and to its contemporaries.

The scenes of horror which accompanied the first phases of the French Revolution prevented the rapid propagation of its subversive principles beyond the frontiers of France, and the wars of conquest which succeeded them gave to the public mind a direction little favourable to revolutionary principles. Thus the Jacobin propaganda failed entirely to realise criminal hopes.

Nevertheless the revolutionary seed had penetrated into every country and spread more or less. It was greatly developed under the *régime* of the military despotism of Bonaparte. His conquests displaced a number of laws, institutions, and customs; broke through bonds sacred among all nations, strong enough to resist time itself; which is more than can be said of certain benefits conferred by these innovators. From these perturbations it followed that the revolutionary spirit could in Germany, Italy, and later on in Spain, easily hide itself under the veil of patriotism.

Prussia committed a grave fault in calling to her aid such dangerous weapons as secret associations always will be: a fault which could not be justified even by the deplorable situation in which that Power then found itself. This it was that first gave a strong impulse to the revolutionary spirit in her States, and this spirit made rapid progress, supported as it was in the rest of Germany by the system of foreign despotism which since 1806 has been there developed. Many Princes of the Rhenish Confederation were secretly auxiliaries and accomplices of this system, to which they sacrificed the institutions which in their country from time immemorial had served as a protection against despotism and democracy.

The war of the Allies, by putting bounds to the predominance of France, was vigorously supported in Germany by the same men whose hatred of France was in reality nothing but hatred of the military despotism of Bonaparte, and also of the legitimate power of their own masters. With wisdom in the Governments and firmness in principles, the end of the war in 1814 might nevertheless have insured to the world the most peaceful and happy future. Great experiences had been gained and great lessons, which might have been usefully applied. But fate had decided otherwise.

The return of the usurper to France, and the completely false steps taken by the French Government from 1815 to 1820, accumulated a mass of new dangers and great calamities for the whole civilised world. It is to the first of these misfortunes that is partly due the critical state in which France and the whole social body is placed. Bonaparte destroyed in a hundred days the work of the fourteen years during which he had exercised his authority. He set free the revolution which he came to France to subdue; he brought back men's minds, not to the epoch of the 18th Brumaire, but to the principles which the National Assembly had adopted in its deplorable blindness.

What Bonaparte had thus done to the detriment of France and Europe, the grave errors which the French Government have since committed, and to which other Governments have yielded—all these unhappy influences weigh heavily on the world of to-day; they threaten with total ruin the work of restoration, the fruit of so many glorious efforts, and of a harmony between the greatest monarchs unparalleled in the records of history, and they give rise to fears of indescribable calamities to society.

In this memoir we have not yet touched on one of the most active and at the same time most dangerous instruments used by the revolutionists of all countries, with a success which is no longer doubtful. I refer to the secret societies, a real power, all the more dangerous as it works in the dark, undermining all parts of the social body, and depositing everywhere the seeds of a moral gangrene which is not slow to develop and increase. This plague is one of the worst which those Governments who are lovers of peace and of their people have to watch and fight against.

DO REMEDIES FOR THIS EVIL EXIST, AND WHAT ARE THEY?

We look upon it as a fundamental truth, that for every disease there is a remedy, and that the knowledge of the real nature of the one should lead to the discovery of the other. Few men, however, stop thoroughly to examine a disease which they intend to combat. There are hardly any who are not subject to the influence of passion, or held under the yoke of prejudice; there are a great many who err in a way more perilous still, on account of its flattering and often brilliant appearance: we speak of *l'esprit de système*; that spirit always false, but indefatigable, audacious and irrepressible, is satisfactory to men imbued with it (for they live in and govern a world created by themselves), but it is so much the more dangerous for the inhabitants of the real world, so different from that created by *l'esprit de système*.

There is another class of men who, judging of a disease by its outward appearance, confound the accessory manifestations with the root of the disease, and, instead of directing their efforts to the source of the evil, content themselves with subduing some passing symptoms.

It is our duty to try and avoid both of these dangers.

The evil exists and it is enormous. We do not think we can better define it and its cause at all times and in all places than we have already done by the word "presumption," that inseparable companion of the half-educated, that spring of an unmeasured ambition, and yet easy to satisfy in times of trouble and confusion.

It is principally the middle classes of society which this moral gangrene has affected, and it is only among them that the real heads of the party are found.

For the great mass of the people it has no attraction and can have none. The labours to which this class—the real people—are obliged to devote themselves, are too continuous and too positive to allow them to throw themselves into vague abstractions and ambitions. The people know what is the happiest thing for them: namely, to be able to count on the morrow, for it is the morrow which will repay them for the cares and sorrows of to-day. The laws which afford a just protection to individuals, to families, and to property, are quite simple in their essence. The people dread any movement which injures industry and brings new burdens in its train.

Men in the higher classes of society who join the revolution are either falsely ambitious men or, in the widest acceptation of the word, lost spirits. Their career, moreover, is generally short! They are the first victims of political reforms, and the part played by the small number among them who survive is mostly that of courtiers despised by upstarts, their inferiors, promoted to the first dignities of the State; and of this France, Germany, Italy, and Spain furnish a number of living examples.

We do not believe that fresh disorders with a directly revolutionary end—not even revolutions in the palace and the highest places in the Government—are to be feared at present in France, because of the decided aversion of the people to anything which might disturb the peace they are now enjoying after so many troubles and disasters.

In Germany, as in Spain and Italy, the people ask only for peace and quiet.

In all four countries the agitated classes are principally composed of wealthy men—real cosmopolitans, securing their personal advantage at the expense of any order of things whatever—paid State officials, men of letters, lawyers, and the individuals charged with the public education.

To these classes may be added that of the falsely ambitious, whose number is never considerable among the lower orders, but is larger in the higher ranks of society.

There is besides scarcely any epoch which does not offer a rallying cry to some particular faction. This cry, since 1815, has been *Constitution*. But do not let us deceive ourselves: this word, susceptible of great latitude of interpretation, would be but imperfectly understood if we supposed that the factions attached quite the same meaning to it under the different *régimes*. Such is certainly not the case. In pure monarchies it is qualified by the name of "national representation." In countries which have lately been brought under the representative *régime* it is called "development," and promises charters and fundamental laws. In the only State which possesses an ancient national representation it takes "reform" as its object. Everywhere it means change and trouble.

In pure monarchies it may be paraphrased thus:—"The level of equality shall pass over your heads; your fortunes shall pass into other hands; your ambitions, which have been satisfied for centuries, shall now give place to our ambitions, which have been hitherto repressed."

In the States under a new *régime* they say:—"The ambitions satisfied yesterday must give place to those of the morrow, and this is the morrow for us."

Lastly, in England, the only place in the third class, the rallying cry—that of Reform—combines the two meanings.

Europe thus presents itself to the impartial observer under an aspect at the same time deplorable and peculiar. We find everywhere the people praying for the maintenance of peace and tranquillity, faithful to God and their Princes, remaining proof against the efforts and seductions of the factious who call themselves friends of the people and wish to lead them to an agitation which the people themselves do not desire!

The Governments, having lost their balance, are frightened, intimidated, and thrown into confusion by the cries of the intermediary class of society, which, placed between the Kings and their subjects, breaks the sceptre of the monarch, and usurps the cry of the people—that class so often disowned by the people, and nevertheless too much listened to, caressed, and feared by those who could with one word reduce it again to nothingness.

We see this intermediary class abandon itself with a blind fury and animosity which proves much more its own fears than any confidence in the success of its enterprises, to all the means which seem proper to assuage its thirst for power, applying itself to the task of persuading Kings that their rights are confined to sitting upon a throne, while those of the people are to govern, and to attack all that centuries have bequeathed as holy and worthy of man's respect—denying, in fact, the value of the past, and declaring themselves the masters of the future. We see this class take all sorts of disguises, uniting and subdividing as occasion offers, helping each other in the hour of danger, and the next day depriving each other of all their conquests. It takes possession of the press, and employs it to promote impiety, disobedience to the laws of religion and the State, and goes so far as to preach murder as a duty for those who desire what is good.

One of its leaders in Germany defined public opinion as "the will of the strong man in the spirit of the party"—a maxim too often put in practice, and too seldom understood by those whose right and duty it is to save society from its own errors, its own weaknesses, and the crimes which the factious commit while pretending to act in its interests.

The evil is plain; the means used by the faction which causes these disorders are so blameable in principle, so criminal in their application, and expose the faction itself to so many dangers, that what men of narrow views (whose head and heart are broken by circumstances stronger than their calculations or their courage) regard as the end of society may become the first step towards a better order of things. These weak men would be right unless men stronger than they are come forward to close their ranks and determine the victory.

We are convinced that society can no longer be saved without strong and vigorous resolutions on the part of the Governments still free in their opinions and actions.

We are also convinced that this may yet be, if the Governments face the truth, if they free themselves from all illusion, if they join their ranks and take their stand on a line of correct, unambiguous, and frankly announced principles.

By this course the monarchs will fulfil the duties imposed upon them by Him who, by entrusting them with power, has charged them to watch over the maintenance of justice, and the rights of all, to avoid the paths of error, and tread firmly in the way of truth. Placed beyond the passions which agitate society, it is in days of trial chiefly that they are called upon to despoil realities of their false appearances, and to show themselves as they are, fathers invested with the authority belonging by right to the heads of families, to prove that, in days of mourning, they know how to be just, wise, and therefore strong, and that they will not abandon the people whom they ought to govern to be the sport of factions, to error and its consequences, which must involve the loss of society. The moment in which we are putting our thoughts on paper is one of those critical moments. The crisis is great; it will be decisive according to the part we take or do not take.

There is a rule of conduct common to individuals and to States, established by the experience of centuries as by that of every-day life. This rule declares "that one must not dream of reformation while agitated by passion; wisdom directs that at such moments we should limit ourselves to maintaining."

Let the monarchs vigorously adopt this principle; let all their resolutions bear the impression of it. Let their actions, their measures, and even their words announce and prove to the world this determination—they will find allies everywhere. The Governments, in establishing the principle of *stability,* will in no wise exclude the development of what is good, for stability is not immobility. But it is for those who are burdened with the heavy task of government to augment the well-being of their people! It is for Governments to regulate it according to necessity and to suit the times. It is not by concessions, which the factious strive to force from legitimate power, and which they have neither the right to claim nor the faculty of keeping within just bounds, that wise reforms can be carried out. That all the good possible should be done is our most ardent wish; but that which is not good must never be confounded with that which is, and even real good should be done only by those who unite to the right of authority the means of enforcing it. Such should be also the sincere wish of the people, who know by sad experience the value of certain phrases and the nature of certain caresses.

Respect for all that is; liberty for every Government to watch over the well-being of its own people; a league between all Governments against factions in all States; contempt for the meaningless words which have become the rallying cry of the factious; respect for the progressive development of institutions in lawful ways; refusal on the part of every monarch to aid or succour partisans under any mask whatever—such are happily the ideas of the great monarchs: the world will be saved if they bring them into action—it is lost if they do not.

Union between the monarchs is the basis of the policy which must now be followed to save society from total ruin.

What is the particular object towards which this policy should be directed? The more important this question is, the more necessary it is to solve it. A principle is something, but it acquires real value only in its application.

The first sources of the evil which is crushing the world have been indicated by us in a paper which has no pretension to be anything more than a mere sketch. Its further causes have also there been pointed out: if, with respect to individuals, it may be defined by the word *presumption,* in applying it to society, taken as a whole, we believe we can best describe the existing evil as the *confusion of ideas,* to which too much generalisation constantly leads. This is what now troubles society. Everything which up to this time has been considered as fixed in principle is attacked and overthrown.

In religious matters criticism and inquiry are to take the place of faith, Christian morality is to replace the Law of Christ as it is interpreted by Christian authorities.

In the Catholic Church, the Jansenists and a number of isolated sectarians, who wish for a religion without a Church, have devoted themselves to this enterprise with ardent zeal: among the Protestant sects, the Methodists, subdivided into almost as many sects as there are individuals; then the enlightened promoters of the Bible Societies and the Unitarians—the promoters of the fusion of Lutherans and Calvinists in one Evangelical community—all pursue the same end.

The object which these men have in common, to whatever religion they may ostensibly belong, is simply to overthrow all authority. Put on moral grounds, they wish *to enfranchise souls* in the same way as some of the political revolutionists who were not actuated by motives of personal ambition wished *to enfranchise the people*.

If the same elements of destruction which are now throwing society into convulsion have existed in all ages—for every age has seen immoral and ambitious men, hypocrites, men of heated imaginations, wrong motives, and wild projects—yet ours, by the single fact of the liberty of the press, possesses more than any preceding age the means of contact, seduction, and attraction whereby to act on these different classes of men.

We are certainly not alone in questioning if society can exist with the liberty of the press, a scourge unknown to the world before the latter half of the seventeenth century, and restrained until the end of the eighteenth, with scarcely any exceptions but England—a part of Europe separated from the continent by the sea, as well as by her language and by her peculiar manners.

The first principle to be followed by the monarchs, united as they are by the coincidence of their desires and opinions, should be that of maintaining the stability of political institutions against the disorganised excitement which has taken possession of men's minds; the immutability of principles against the madness of their interpretation; and respect for laws actually in force against a desire for their destruction.

The hostile faction is divided into two very distinct parties. One is that of the Levellers; the other, that of the Doctrinaires. United in times of confusion, these men are divided in times of inaction. It is for the Governments to understand and estimate them at their just value.

In the class of Levellers there are found men of strong will and determination. The Doctrinaires can count none such among their ranks. If the first are more to be feared in action, the second are more dangerous in that time of deceitful calm which precedes it; as with physical storms, so with those of social order. Given up to abstract ideas inapplicable to real wants, and generally in contradiction to those very wants, men of this class unceasingly agitate the people by their imaginary or simulated fears, and disturb Governments in order to make them deviate from the right path. The world desires to be governed by facts and according to justice, not by phrases and theories; the first need of society is to be maintained by strong authority (no authority without real strength deserves the name) and not to govern itself. In comparing the number of contests between parties in mixed Governments, and that of just complaints caused by aberrations of power in a Christian State, the comparison would not be in favour of the new doctrines. The first and greatest concern for the immense majority of every nation is the stability of the laws, and their uninterrupted action—never their change. Therefore let the Governments govern, let them maintain the groundwork of their institutions, both ancient and modern; for if it is at all times dangerous to touch them, it certainly would not now, in the general confusion, be wise to do so.

Let them announce this determination to their people, and demonstrate it by facts. Let them reduce the Doctrinaires to silence within their States, and show their contempt for them abroad. Let them not encourage by their attitude or actions the suspicions of being favourable or indifferent to error: let them not allow it to be believed that experience has lost all its rights to make way for experiments which at the least are dangerous. Let them be precise and clear in all their words, and not seek by concessions to gain over those parties who aim at the destruction of all power but their own, whom concessions will never gain over, but only further embolden in their pretensions to power.

Let them in these troublous times be more than usually cautious in attempting real ameliorations, not imperatively claimed by the needs of the moment, to the end that good itself may not turn against them—which is the case whenever a Government measure seems to be inspired by fear.

Let them not confound concessions made to parties with the good they ought to do for their people, in modifying, according to their recognised needs, such branches of the administration as require it.

Let them give minute attention to the financial state of their kingdoms, so that their people may enjoy, by the reduction of public burdens, the real, not imaginary, benefits of a state of peace.

Let them be just, but strong; beneficent, but strict.

Let them maintain religious principles in all their purity, and not allow the faith to be attacked and morality interpreted according to the *social contract* or the visions of foolish sectarians.

Let them suppress Secret Societies, that gangrene of society.

In short, let the great monarchs strengthen their union, and prove to the world that if it exists, it is beneficent, and ensures the political peace of Europe: that it is powerful only for the maintenance of tranquillity at a time when so many attacks are directed against it; that the principles which they profess are paternal and protective, menacing only the disturbers of private tranquillity.

The Governments of the second order will see in such a union the anchor of their salvation, and they will be anxious to connect themselves with it. The people will take confidence and courage, and the most profound and salutary peace which the history of any time can show will have been effected. This peace will first act on countries still in a good state, but will not be without a very decided influence on the fate of those threatened with destruction, and even assist the restoration of those which have already passed under the scourge of revolution.

To every great State determined to survive the storm there still remain many chances of salvation, and a strong union between the States on the principles we have announced will overcome the storm itself.

THE SADLER REPORT

In the early nineteenth century, the Industrial Revolution had spread from England and was beginning to transform Europe from a rural to an urbanized society. In England, this transformation often depressed the living standards of workers to depths even lower than those that had characterized life under the cottage manufacturing system. In doing so, however, it paved the way for its own reform. For it laid bare to the public eye in an aggravated form conditions that had long existed but that had passed relatively unnoticed. Poverty and misery could be overlooked so long as the workers remained scattered about the countryside, but once they were congregated in the hideous slums of the Midlands industrial centers their plight became too obvious to remain unheeded. Consequently, social reform became the order of the day.

Among the most prominent of the English reformers was the seventh Earl of Shaftesbury (1801–1885), who concentrated his attention on working conditions in the factories. At Shaftesbury's instigation, another reformer, Michael Sadler, introduced a bill into Parliament in 1831 that would regulate the working conditions of children in textile mills. The bill was referred to a committee, with Sadler as chairman. The selection that follows is an excerpt from the evidence presented before that committee. The committee's investigations resulted in the enactment of the Factory Act of 1833, which limited the working hours of children and set up a system of inspection which would insure that its regulations were being carried out.

The Sadler Report *requires no comment; it speaks for itself. The selection included here was picked almost at random from a bulky volume of testimony provided by literally hundreds of witnesses, each one presenting, with slight variations, the same picture of factory life in early nineteenth-century England.*

The Sadler Report

Veneris, 18° die Maii, 1832

MICHAEL THOMAS SADLER, ESQUIRE, IN THE CHAIR

. . .

MR. MATTHEW CRABTREE, *called in; and Examined.*

THE SADLER REPORT, REPORT FROM THE COMMITTEE ON THE BILL TO REGULATE THE LABOUR OF CHILDREN IN THE MILLS AND FACTORIES OF THE UNITED KINGDOM *(London: The House of Commons, 1832).*

What age are you?——Twenty-two.

What is your occupation?——A blanket manufacturer.

Have you ever been employed in a factory?——Yes.

At what age did you first go to work in one?——Eight.

How long did you continue in that occupation?——Four years.

Will you state the hours of labour at the period when you first went to the factory, in ordinary times?——From 6 in the morning to 8 at night.

Fourteen hours?——Yes.

With what intervals for refreshment and rest?——An hour at noon.

Then you had no resting time allowed in which to take your breakfast, or what is in Yorkshire called your "drinking"?——No.

When trade was brisk what were your hours?——From 5 in the morning to 9 in the evening.

Sixteen hours?——Yes.

With what intervals at dinner?——An hour.

How far did you live from the mill?——About two miles.

Was there any time allowed for you to get your breakfast in the mill?——No.

Did you take it before you left your home?——Generally.

During those long hours of labour could you be punctual; how did you awake?——I seldom did awake spontaneously; I was most generally awoke or lifted out of bed, sometimes asleep, by my parents.

Were you always in time?——No.

What was the consequence if you had been too late?——I was most commonly beaten.

Severely?——Very severely, I thought.

In whose factory was this?——Messrs. Hague & Cook's, of Dewsbury.

Will you state the effect that those long hours had upon the state of your health and feelings?——I was, when working those long hours, commonly very much fatigued at night, when I left my work; so much so that I sometimes should have slept as I walked if I had not stumbled and started awake again; and so sick often that I could not eat, and what I did eat I vomited.

Did this labour destroy your appetite?——It did.

In what situation were you in that mill?——I was a piecener.

Will you state to this Committee whether piecening is a very laborious employment for children, or not?——It is a very laborious employment. Pieceners are continually running to and fro, and on their feet the whole day.

The duty of the piecener is to take the cardings from one part of the machinery, and to place them on another?——Yes.

So that the labour is not only continual, but it is unabated to the last?——It is unabated to the last.

Do you not think, from your own experience, that the speed of the machinery is so calculated as to demand the utmost exertions of a child, supposing the hours were moderate?——It is as much as they could do at the best; they are always upon the stretch, and it is commonly very difficult to keep up with their work.

State the condition of the children toward the latter part of the day, who have thus to keep up with the machinery.——It is as much as they can do when they are not very much fatigued to keep up with their work, and toward the close of the day, when they come to be more fatigued, they cannot keep up with it very well, and the consequence is that they are beaten to spur them on.

Were you beaten under those circumstances?——Yes.

Frequently?——Very frequently.

And principally at the latter end of the day?——Yes.

And is it your belief that if you had not been so beaten, you should not have got through the work?——I should not if I had not been kept up to it by some means.

Does beating then principally occur at the latter end of the day, when the children are exceedingly fatigued?——It does at the latter end of the day, and in the morning sometimes, when they are very drowsy, and have not got rid of the fatigue of the day before.

What were you beaten with principally?——A strap.

Any thing else?——Yes, a stick sometimes; and there is a kind of roller which runs on the top of the machine called a billy, perhaps two or three yards in length, and perhaps an inch and a half, or more, in diameter; the circumference would be four or five inches; I cannot speak exactly.

Were you beaten with that instrument?——Yes.

Have you yourself been beaten, and have you seen other children struck severely with that roller?——I have been struck very severely with it myself, so much so as to knock me down, and I have seen other children have their heads broken with it.

You think that it is a general practice to beat the children with the roller?——It is.

You do not think then that you were worse treated than other children in the mill?——No, I was not, perhaps not so bad as some were.

In those mills is chastisement towards the latter part of the day going on perpetually?——Perpetually.

So that you can hardly be in a mill without hearing constant crying?——Never an hour, I believe.

Do you think that if the overlooker were naturally a humane person it would be still found necessary for him to beat the children, in order to keep up their attention and vigilance at the termination of those extraordinary days of labour?——Yes; the machine turns off a regular quantity of cardings, and of course they must keep as regularly to their work the whole of the day; they must keep with the machine, and therefore however humane the slubber may be, as he must keep up with the machine or be found fault with, he spurs the children to keep up also by various means but that which he commonly resorts to is to strap them when they become drowsy.

At the time when you were beaten for not keeping up with your work, were you anxious to have done it if you possibly could?——Yes; the dread of being beaten if we could not keep up with our work was a sufficient impulse to keep us to it if we could.

When you got home at night after this labour, did you feel much fatigued?——Very much so.

Had you any time to be with your parents, and to receive instruction from them?——No.

What did you do?——All that we did when we got home was to get the little bit of supper that was provided for us and go to bed immediately. If the supper had not been ready directly, we should have gone to sleep while it was preparing.

Did you not, as a child, feel it a very grievous hardship to be roused so soon in the morning?——I did.

Were the rest of the children similarly circumstanced?——Yes, all of them; but they were not all of them so far from their work as I was.

And if you had been too late you were under the apprehension of being cruelly beaten?——I generally was beaten when I happened to be too late; and when I got up in the morning the apprehension of that was so great, that I used to run, and cry all the way as I went to the mill.

That was the way by which your punctual attendance was secured?——Yes.

And you do not think it could have been secured by any other means?——No.

Then it is your impression from what you have seen, and from your own experience, that those long hours of labour have the effect of rendering young persons who are subject to them exceedingly unhappy?——Yes.

You have already said it had a considerable effect upon your health?——Yes.

Do you conceive that it diminished your growth?——I did not pay much attention to that; but I have been examined by some persons who said they thought I was rather stunted, and that I should have been taller if I had not worked at the mill.

What were your wages at that time?——Three shillings [per week].

And how much a day had you for overwork when you were worked so exceedingly long?——A halfpenny a day.

Did you frequently forfeit that if you were not always there to a moment?——Yes; I most frequently forfeited what was allowed for those long hours.

You took your food to the mill; was it in your mill, as is the case in cotton mills, much spoiled by being laid aside?——It was very frequently covered by flues from the wool; and in that case they had to be blown off with the mouth, and picked off with the fingers before it could be eaten.

So that not giving you a little leisure for eating your food, but obliging you to take it at the mill, spoiled your food when you did get it?——Yes, very commonly.

And that at the same time that this overlabour injured your appetite?——Yes.

Could you eat when you got home?——Not always.

What is the effect of this piecening upon the hands?——It makes them bleed; the skin is completely rubbed off, and in that case they bleed in perhaps a dozen parts.

The prominent parts of the hand?——Yes, all the prominent parts of the hand are rubbed down till they bleed; every day they are rubbed in that way.

All the time you continue at work?——All the time we are working. The hands never can be hardened in that work, for the grease keeps them soft in the first instance, and long and continual rubbing is always wearing them down, so that if they were hard they would be sure to bleed.

Is it attended with much pain?——Very much.

Do they allow you to make use of the back of the hand?——No; the work cannot be so well done with the back of the hand, or I should have made use of that.

Is the work done as well when you are so many hours engaged in it, as it would be if you were at it a less time?——I believe it is not done so well in those long hours; toward the latter end of the day the children become completely bewildered, and know not what they are doing, so that they spoil their work without knowing.

Then you do not think that the masters gain much by the continuance of the work to so great a length of time?——I believe not.

Were there girls as well as boys employed in this manner?——Yes.

Were they more tenderly treated by the overlookers, or were they worked and beaten in the same manner?——There was no difference in their treatment.

Were they beaten by the overlookers, or by the slubber?——By the slubber.

But the overlooker must have been perfectly aware of the treatment that the children endured at the mill?——Yes; and sometimes the overlooker beat them himself; but the man that they wrought under had generally the management of them.

Did he pay them their wages?——No; their wages were paid by the master.

But the overlooker of the mill was perfectly well aware that they could not have performed the duty exacted from them in the mill without being thus beaten?——I believe he was.

You seem to say that this beating is absolutely necessary, in order to keep the children up to their work; is it universal throughout all factories?——I have been in several other factories, and I have witnessed the same cruelty in them all.

Did you say that you were beaten for being too late?——Yes.

Is it not the custom in many of the factories to impose fines upon children for being too late, instead of beating them?——It was not in that factory.

What then were the fines by which you lost the money you gained by your long hours?——The spinner could not get on so fast with his work when we happened to be too late; he could not begin his work so soon, and therefore it was taken by him.

Did the slubber pay you your wages? ——No, the master paid our wages.

And the slubber took your fines from you?——Yes.

Then you were fined as well as beaten? ——There was nothing deducted from the ordinary scale of wages, but only from that received for over-hours, and I had only that taken when I was too late, so that the fine was not regular.

When you were not working over-hours, were you so often late as when you were working over-hours?——Yes.

You were not very often late whilst you were not working over-hours?——Yes, I was often late when I was not working over-hours; I had to go at six o'clock in the morning, and consequently had to get up at five to eat my breakfast and go to the mill, and if I failed to get up by five I was too late; and it was nine o'clock before we could get home, and then we went to bed; in the best times I could not be much above eight hours at home, reckoning dressing and eating my meals, and every thing.

Was it a blanket-mill in which you worked?——Yes.

Did you ever know that the beatings to which you allude inflicted a serious injury upon the children?——I do not recollect any very serious injury, more than that they had their heads broken, if that may be called a serious injury; that has often happened; I, myself, had no more serious injury than that.

You say that the girls as well as the boys were employed as you have described, and you observed no difference in their treatment?——No difference.

The girls were beat in this unmerciful manner?——They were.

They were subject, of course, to the same bad effects from this over-working? ——Yes.

Could you attend an evening-school during the time you were employed in the mill?——No, that was completely impossible.

Did you attend the Sunday-school?——Not very frequently when I work at the mill.

How then were you engaged during the Sunday?——I very often slept till it was too late for school time or for divine worship, and the rest of the day I spent in walking out and taking a little fresh air.

Did your parents think that it was necessary for you to enjoy a little fresh air?——I believe they did; they never said anything against it; before I went to the mill I used to go to the Sunday-school.

Did you frequently sleep nearly the whole of the day on Sunday?——Very often.

At what age did you leave that employment?——I was about 12 years old.

Why did you leave that place?——I went very late one morning, about seven o'clock, and I got severely beaten by the spinner, and he turned me out of the mill, and I went home, and never went any more.

Was your attendance as good as the other children?——Being at rather a greater distance than some of them, I was generally one of the latest.

Where was your next work?——I worked as bobbin-winder in another part of the works of the same firm.

How long were you a bobbin-winder? ——About two years, I believe.

What did you become after that?——A weaver.

How long were you a weaver?——I was a weaver till March in last year.

A weaver of what?——A blanket-weaver.

With the same firm?——With the same firm.

Did you leave them?——No; I was dismissed from my work for a reason which I am willing and anxious to explain.

Have you had opportunities of observing the way in which the children are treated in factories up to a late period?——Yes.

You conceive that their treatment still remains as you first found it, and that the system is in great want of regulation?——It does.

Children you still observe to be very much fatigued and injured by the hours of labour?——Yes.

From your own experience, what is your opinion as to the utmost labour that a child in piecening could safely undergo?——If I were appealed to from my own feelings to fix a limit, I should fix it at ten hours, or less.

And you attribute to longer hours all the cruelties that you describe?——A good deal of them.

Are the children sleepy in mills?——Very.

Are they more liable to accidents in the latter part of the day than in the other part?——I believe they are; I believe a greater number of accidents happen in the latter part of the day than in any other. I have known them so sleepy that in the short interval while the others have been going out, some of them have fallen asleep, and have been left there.

Is it an uncommon case for children to fall asleep in the mill, and remain there all night?——Not to remain there all night; but I have known a case the other day, of a child whom the overlooker found when he went to lock the door, that had been left there.

So that you think there has been no change for the better in the treatment of those children; is it your opinion that there will be none, except Parliament interfere in their behalf?——It is my decided conviction.

Have you recently seen any cruelties in mills?——Yes; not long since I was in a mill and I saw a girl severely beaten; at a mill called Hick-lane Mill, in Batley; I happened to be in at the other end of the room, talking; and I heard the blows, and I looked that way, and saw the spinner beating one of the girls severely with a large stick. Hearing the sound, led me to look round, and to ask what was the matter, and they said it was "Nothing but——paying [beating] 'his ligger-on.' "

What age was the girl?——About 12 years.

Was she very violently beaten?——She was.

Was this when she was over-fatigued?——It was in the afternoon.

Can you speak as to the effect of this labour in the mills and factories on the morals of the children, as far as you have observed?——As far as I have observed with regard to morals in the mills, there is every thing about them that is disgusting to every one conscious of correct morality.

Do you find that the children, the females especially, are very early demoralized in them?——They are.

Is their language indecent?——Very indecent; and both sexes take great familiarities with each other in the mills, without at all being ashamed of their conduct.

Do you connect their immorality of language and conduct with their excessive labour?——It may be somewhat connected with it, for it is to be observed that most of that goes on toward night, when they begin to be drowsy; it is a kind of stimulus which they use to keep them awake; they say some pert thing or other to keep themselves from drowsiness, and it generally happens to be some obscene language.

Have not a considerable number of the females employed in mills illegitimate children very early in life?——I believe there are; I have known some of them have illegitimate children when they were between 16 and 17 years of age.

How many grown-up females had you in the mill?——I cannot speak to the exact number that were grown up; perhaps there might be thirty-four or so that worked in the mill at that time.

How many of those had illegitimate children?——A great many of them; eighteen or nineteen of them, I think.

Did they generally marry the men by whom they had the children?——No; it sometimes happens that young women have children by married men, and I have known an instance, a few weeks since, where one of the young women had a child by a married man.

Is it your opinion that those who have the charge of mills very often avail themselves of the opportunity they have to debauch the young women?——No, not generally; most of the improper conduct takes place among the younger part of those that work in the mill.

Do you find that the children and young persons in those mills are moral in other respects, or does their want of education tend to encourage them in a breach of the law?——I believe it does, for there are very few of them that can know anything about it; few of them can either read or write.

Are criminal offences then very frequent?——Yes, theft is very common; it is practised a great deal in the mills, stealing their bits of dinner, or something of that sort. Some of them have not so much to eat as they ought to have, and if they can fall in with the dinner of some of their partners they steal it. The first day my brother and I went to the mill we had our dinner stolen, because we were not up to the tricks; we were more careful in future, but still we did not always escape.

Was there any correction going on at the mills for indecent language or improper conduct?——No, I never knew of any.

From what you have seen and known of those mills, would you prefer that the hours of labour should be so long with larger wages, or that they should be shortened with a diminution of wages?——If I were working at the mill now, I would rather have less labour and receive a trifle less, than so much labour and receive a trifle more.

Is that the general impression of individuals engaged in mills with whom you are acquainted?——I believe it is.

What is the impression in the country from which you come with respect to the effect of this Bill upon wages?——They do not anticipate that it will affect wages at all.

They think it will not lower wages?——They do.

Do you mean that it will not lower wages by the hour, or that you will receive the same wages per day?——They anticipate that it may perhaps lower their wages at a certain time of the year when they are working hard, but not at other times, so that they will have their wages more regular.

Does not their wish for this Bill mainly rest upon their anxiety to protect their children from the consequences of this excessive labour, and to have some opportunity of affording them a decent education?——Yes; such are the wishes of every humane father that I have heard speak about the thing.

Have they not some feeling of having the labour equalized?——That is the feeling of some that I have heard speak of it.

Did your parents work in the same factories?——No.

Were any of the slubbers' children working there?——Yes.

Under what slubber did you work in that mill?——Under a person of the name of Thomas Bennett, in the first place; and I was changed from him to another of the name of James Webster.

Did the treatment depend very much upon the slubber under whom you were?——No, it did not depend directly upon him, for he was obliged to do a certain quantity of work, and therefore to make us keep up with that.

Were the children of the slubbers strapped in the same way?——Yes, except that it is very natural for a father to spare his own child.

Did it depend upon the feelings of a slubber toward his children?——Very little.

Did the slubbers fine their own spinners? ——I believe not.

You said that the piecening was very hard labour; what labour is there besides moving about; have you anything heavy to carry or to lift?——We have nothing heavy to carry, but we are kept upon our feet in brisk times from 5 o'clock in the morning to 9 at night.

How soon does the hand get sore in piecening?——How soon mine became sore I cannot speak to exactly; but they get a little hard on the Sunday, when we are not working, and they will get sore again very soon on the Monday.

Is it always the case in piecening that the hand bleeds, whether you work short or long hours?——They bleed more when we work more.

Do they always bleed when you are working?——Yes.

Do you think that the children would not be more competent to this task, and their hands far less hurt, if the hours were fewer every day, especially when their hands had become seasoned to the labour? ——I believe it would have an effect, for the longer they are worked the more their hands are worn, and the longer it takes to heal them, and they do not get hard enough after a day's rest to be long without bleeding again; if they were not so much worn down, they might heal sooner, and not bleed so often or so soon.

After a short day's work, have you found your hands hard the next morning?——They do not bleed much after we have ceased work; they then get hard; they will bleed soon in the morning when in regular work.

Do you think if the work of the children were confined to about ten hours a day, that after they were accustomed to it, they would not be able to perform this piecening without making their hands bleed?——I believe they would.

So that it is your opinion, from your experience, that if the hours were mitigated, their hands would not be so much worn, and would not bleed by the business of piecening?——Yes.

Do you mean to say that their hands would not bleed at all?——I cannot say exactly, for I always wrought long hours, and therefore my hands always did bleed.

Have you any experience of mills where they only work ten hours?——I have never wrought at such mills, and in most of the mills I have seen their hands bleed.

At a slack time, when you were working only a few hours, did your hands bleed? ——No, they did not for three or four days, after we had been standing still for a week; the mill stood still sometimes for a week together, but when we did work we worked the common number of hours.

Were all the mills in the neighbourhood working the same number of hours in brisk times?——Yes.

So that if any parent found it necessary to send his children to the mill for the sake of being able to maintain them, and wished to take them from any mill where they were excessively worked, he could not have found any other place where they would have been less worked?——No, he could not; for myself, I had no desire to change, because I thought I was as well off as I could be at any other mill.

And if the parent, to save his child, had taken him from the mill, and had applied to the parish for relief, would the parish, knowing that he had withdrawn his child from its work, have relieved him?——No.

So that the long labour which you have described, or actual starvation, was, practically, the only alternative that was presented to the parent under such circumstances?——It was; they must either work at the mill they were at or some other, and there was no choice in the mills in that respect.

What, in your opinion, would be the effect of limiting the hours of labour upon the happiness, and the health, and the intelligence of the rising generation?——If the hours are shortened, the children may, perhaps, have a chance of attending some evening-school, and learning to read and write; and those that I know who have been to school and learned to read and write, have much more comfort than those who have not. For myself, I went to a school when I was six years old, and I learned to read and write a little then.

At a free-school?——Yes, at a free-school in Dewsbury; but I left school when I was six years old. The fact is, that my father was a small manufacturer, and in comfortable circumstances, and he got into debt with Mr. Cook for a wool bill, and as he had no other means of paying him, he came and agreed with my father, that my brother and I should go to work at his mill till that debt was paid; so that the whole of the time that we wrought at the mill we had no wages.

THOMAS BENNETT, *called in; and Examined.*

Where do you reside?——At Dewsbury.

What is your business?——A slubber.

What age are you?——About 48.

Have you had much experience regarding the working of children in factories? ——Yes, about twenty-seven years.

Have you a family?——Yes, eight children.

Have any of them gone to factories?—— All.

At what age?——The first went at six years of age.

To whose mill?——To Mr. Halliley's, to piece for myself.

What hours did you work at that mill? ——We have wrought from 4 to 9, from 4 to 10, and from 5 to 9, and from 5 to 10.

What sort of a mill was it?——It was a blanket-mill; we sometimes altered the time, according as the days increased and decreased.

What were your regular hours?——Our regular hours when we were not so throng, was from 6 to 7.

And when you were the throngest, what were your hours then?——From 5 to 9, and from 5 to 10, and from 4 to 9.

Seventeen hours?——Yes.

What intervals for meals had the children at that period?——Two hours; an hour for breakfast, and an hour for dinner.

Did they always allow two hours for meals at Mr. Halliley's?——Yes, it was allowed, but the children did not get it, for they had business to do at that time, such as fettling and cleaning the machinery.

But they did not all stop in at that time, did they?——They all had their share of the cleaning and other work to do.

That is, they were cleaning the machinery?——Cleaning the machinery at the time of dinner.

How long a time together have you known those excessive hours to continue? ——I have wrought so myself very nearly two years together.

Were your children working under you then?——Yes, two of them.

State the effect upon your children.—— Of a morning when they had to get up, they have been so fast asleep that I have had to go up stairs and lift them out of bed, and have heard them crying with the feelings of a parent; I have been much affected by it.

Were not they much fatigued at the termination of such a day's labour as that? ——Yes; many a time I have seen their hands moving while they have been nodding, almost asleep; they have been doing their business almost mechanically.

While they have been almost asleep, they have attempted to work?——Yes; and they have missed the carding and spoiled the thread, when we have had to beat them for it.

Could they have done their work towards the termination of such a long day's labour, if they had not been chastised to it? ——No.

You do not think that they could have kept awake or up to their work till the seventeenth hour, without being chastised? ——No.

Will you state what effect it had upon your children at the end of their day's work? ——At the end of their day's work, when they have come home, instead of taking their victuals, they have dropped asleep with the victuals in their hands; and sometimes when we have sent them to bed with a little bread or something to eat in their hand, I have found it in their bed the next morning.

Has it affected their health?——I cannot say much of that; they were very hearty children.

Do you live at a distance from the mill? ——Half a mile.

Did your children feel a difficulty in getting home?——Yes, I have had to carry the lesser child on my back, and it has been asleep when I got home.

Did these hours of labour fatigue you? ——Yes; they fatigued me to that excess, that in divine worship I have not been able to stand according to order; I have sat to worship.

So that even during the Sunday you have felt fatigue from your labour in the week?——Yes, we felt it, and always took as much rest as we could.

Were you compelled to beat your own children, in order to make them keep up with the machine?——Yes, that was forced upon us, or we could not have done the work; I have struck them often, though I felt as a parent.

If the children had not been your own, you would have chastised them still more severely?——Yes.

What did you beat them with?——A strap sometimes; and when I have seen my work spoiled, with the roller.

Was the work always worse done at the end of the day?——That was the greatest danger.

Do you conceive it possible that the children could do their work well at the end of such a day's labour as that?——No.

Matthew Crabtree, the last Witness examined by this Committee, I think mentioned you as one of the slubbers under whom he worked?——Yes.

He states that he was chastised and beaten at the mill?——Yes, I have had to chastise him.

You can confirm then what he has stated as to the length of time he had to work as a child, and the cruel treatment that he received?——Yes, I have had to chastise him in the evening, and often in the morning for being too late; when I had one out of the three wanting I could not keep up with the machine, and I was getting behindhand compared with what another man was doing; and therefore I should have been called to account on Saturday night if the work was not done.

Was he worse than others?——No.

Was it the constant practice to chastise the children?——Yes.

It was necessary in order to keep up your work?——Yes.

And you would have lost your place if you had not done so?——Yes; when I was working at Mr. Wood's mill, at Dewsbury, which at present is burnt down, but where I slubbed for him until it was, while we were taking our meals he used to come up and put the machine agoing; and I used to say, "You do not give us time to eat"; he used to reply, "Chew it at your work"; and

I often replied to him, "I have not yet become debased like a brute, I do not chew my cud." Often has that man done that, and then gone below to see if a strap were off, which would have shown if the machinery was not working, and then he would come up again.

Was this at the drinking time?——Yes, at breakfast and at drinking.

Was this where the children were working?——Yes, my own children and others.

Were your own children obliged to employ most of their time at breakfast and at the drinking in cleansing the machine, and in fettling the spindles?——I have seen at that mill, and I have experienced and mentioned it with grief, that the English children were enslaved worse than the Africans. Once when Mr. Wood was saying to the carrier who brought his work in and out, "How long has that horse of mine been at work?" and the carrier told him the time, and he said, "Loose him directly, he has been in too long," I made this reply to him, "You have more mercy and pity for your horse than you have for your men."

Did not this beating go on principally at the latter part of the day?——Yes.

Was it not also dangerous for the children to move about those mills when they became so drowsy and fatigued?——Yes, especially by lamp-light.

Do the accidents principally occur at the latter end of those long days of labour?——Yes, I believe mostly so.

Do you know of any that have happened?——I know of one; it was at Mr. Wood's mill; part of the machinery caught a lass who had been drowsy and asleep, and the strap which ran close by her catched her at about her middle, and bore her to the ceiling, and down she came, and her neck appeared broken, and the slubber ran up to her and pulled her neck, and I carried her to the doctor myself.

Did she get well?——Yes, she came about again.

What time was that?——In the evening.

You say that you have eight children who have gone to the factories?——Yes.

There has been no opportunity for you to send them to a day-school?——No; one boy had about twelve months' schooling.

Have they gone to Sunday-schools?——Yes.

Can any of them write?——Not one.

They do not teach writing at Sunday-schools?——No; it is objected to, I believe.

So that none of your children can write?——No.

What would be the effect of a proper limitation of the hours of labour upon the conduct of the rising generation?——I believe it would have a very happy effect in regard to correcting their morals; for I believe there is a deal of evil that takes place in one way or other in consequence of those long hours.

Is it your opinion that they would then have an opportunity of attending night-schools?——Yes; I have often regretted, while working those long hours, that I could not get my children there.

Is it your belief that if they were better instructed, they would be happier and better members of society?——Yes, I believe so.

KARL MARX AND FRIEDRICH ENGELS

According to Lenin, Marxism was derived from three sources: German philosophy, English political economy, and French socialism. The German philosophy was the Idealism of Hegel, which Marx had imbibed while a student at the University of Berlin. Central to this philosophy was the notion of dialectic, *the theory that history is a series of struggles between opposing forces, with each successive struggle occurring on a higher level than the one that preceded it. For Hegel, the struggles took place between opposing ideas embodied in distinct national cultures. But Marx shifted the struggles from the ideational plane to the economic or material plane, and transformed the antagonists from nations to classes. In other words, he replaced Hegel's dialectical idealism with his own dialectical materialism; or, as he put it, he turned the dialectic, which Hegel had stood on its head, back on its feet again.*

The English political economy that Lenin referred to consisted of the writings of the classical economists, Smith and Ricardo, whose labor theory of value provided Marx with the basic assumption underlying his greatest work, Capital. *But Marx reversed the argument of the classical economists; where they found in the labor theory of value a defense of capitalism, he found a weapon to attack it.*

Finally, in his reference to French socialism Lenin had in mind the works of a group of writers, including Saint-Simon, Fourier, Proudhon, and Blanc, whose views on the elimination of capitalism and the establishment of the ideal society greatly influenced Marx—even though later he scornfully brushed their theories aside as "utopian" socialism, while claiming that his own were "scientific."

Although Lenin and most other orthodox Marxists would vehemently deny it, Marxism owes a debt to a fourth source. This is the moral tradition of Western thought, stretching back all the way to Socrates and the Old Testament prophets. For Marx, the philosopher, historian, and economist, was above all else a moral reformer. Though he clothed his critique of capitalism in an elaborate intellectual framework, at heart it was a moral protest against the human misery and degradation resulting from early nineteenth-century industrialism. And though he assiduously repeated that his socialism was scientific, the new era of human happiness that he envisioned in the classless society following the revolution was an ideal as utopian as that of Plato's Republic.

The Communist Manifesto, *the joint production of Marx (1818–1883) and his lifelong friend and collaborator, Friedrich Engels (1820–1895), contains in capsule form most of the major Marxist doctrines. It was composed in 1848 as a platform for the Communist League, a small organization of radical workmen. The* Manifesto *is here reproduced complete except for Part III, in which the authors criticize other forms of socialism.*

Manifesto of the Communist Party

A specter is haunting Europe—the specter of Communism. All the powers of Old Europe have entered into a holy alliance to exorcise this specter; Pope and Czar, Metternich and Guizot, French Radicals and German police-spies.

Where is the party in opposition that has not been decried as communistic by its opponents in power? Where the opposition that has not hurled back the branding reproach of Communism, against the more advanced opposition parties, as well as against its reactionary adversaries?

Two things result from this fact.

I. Communism is already acknowledged by all European powers to be in itself a power.

II. It is high time that Communists should openly, in the face of the whole world, publish their views, their aims, their tendencies, and meet this nursery tale of the specter of Communism with a Manifesto of the party itself.

To this end Communists of various nationalities have assembled in London, and sketched the following Manifesto to be published in the English, French, German, Italian, Flemish, and Danish languages.

I

BOURGEOIS AND PROLETARIANS [1]

The history of all hitherto existing society is the history of class struggles.

[1] By bourgeoisie is meant the class of modern Capitalists, owners of the means of social production and employers of wage-labor. By proletariat the class of modern wage-laborers who, having no means of production of their own, are reduced to selling their labor-power in order to live.

Karl Marx and Friedrich Engels, MANIFESTO OF THE COMMUNIST PARTY, *trans. S. Moore (New York, 1888).*

Freeman and slave, patrician and plebeian, lord and serf, guild-master and journeyman, in a word, oppressor and oppressed, stood in constant opposition to one another, carried on an uninterrupted, now hidden, now open fight, that each time ended, either in a revolutionary reconstitution of society at large, or in the common ruin of the contending classes.

In the earlier epochs of history we find almost everywhere a complicated arrangement of society into various orders, a manifold gradation of social rank. In ancient Rome we have patricians, knights, plebeians, slaves; in the Middle Ages, feudal lords, vassals, guild-masters, journeymen, apprentices, serfs; in almost all of these classes, again, subordinate gradations.

The modern bourgeois society that has sprouted from the ruins of feudal society, has not done away with class antagonisms. It has but established new classes, new conditions of oppression, new forms of struggle in place of the old ones.

Our epoch, the epoch of the bourgeoisie, possesses, however, this distinctive feature; it has simplified the class antagonisms. Society as a whole is more and more splitting up into two great hostile camps, into two great classes directly facing each other: Bourgeoisie and Proletariat.

From the serfs of the middle ages sprang the chartered burghers of the earliest towns. From these burgesses the first elements of the bourgeoisie were developed.

The discovery of America, the rounding of the Cape, opened up fresh ground for the rising bourgeoisie. The East-Indian and Chinese markets, the colonization of America, trade with the colonies, the increase in the means of exchange and in commodities generally, gave to commerce, to navigation, to industry, an impulse never before known, and thereby, to the revolutionary element in the tottering feudal society, a rapid development.

The feudal system of industry, under which industrial production was monopolized by closed guilds, now no longer sufficed for the growing wants of the new market. The manufacturing system took its place. The guild-masters were pushed on one side by the manufacturing middle class; division of labor between the different corporate guilds vanished in the face of division of labor in each single workshop.

Meantime the markets kept ever growing, the demand ever rising. Even manufacture no longer sufficed. Thereupon steam and machinery revolutionized industrial production. The place of manufacture was taken by the giant, Modern Industry, the place of the industrial middle class, by industrial millionaires, the leaders of whole industrial armies, the modern bourgeois.

Modern Industry has established the world's market, for which the discovery of America paved the way. This market has given an immense development to commerce, to navigation, to communication by land. This development has, in its turn, reacted on the extension of industry; and in proportion as industry, commerce, navigation, railways extended, in the same proportion, the bourgeoisie developed, increased its capital, and pushed into the background every class handed down from the Middle Ages.

We see, therefore, how the modern bourgeoisie is itself the product of a long course of development, of a series of revolutions in the modes of production and of exchange.

Each step in the development of the bourgeoisie was accompanied by a corresponding political advance of that class. An oppressed class under the sway of the feudal nobility, an armed and self-governing association in the mediaeval commune, here independent urban republic (as in Italy and Germany), here taxable "third estate" of the monarchy (as in France), afterwards, in the period of manufacture proper, serving either the semi-feudal or the absolute monarchy as a counterpoise against the nobility, and, in fact, corner-stone of the great monarchies in general, the bourgeoisie has at last, since the establishment of Modern Industry and of the world's market, conquered for itself, in the modern representative State, exclusive political sway. The executive of the modern State is but a committee for managing the common affairs of the whole bourgeoisie.

The bourgeoisie, historically, has played a most revolutionary part.

The bourgeoisie, wherever it has got the upper hand, has put an end to all feudal, patriarchal, idyllic relations. It has pitilessly torn asunder the motley feudal ties that bound man to his "natural superiors," and has left remaining no other nexus between man and man than naked self-interest, than callous "cash payment." It has drowned the most heavenly ecstasies of religious fervor, of chivalrous enthusiasm, of Philistine sentimentalism, in the icy water of egotistical calculation. It has resolved personal worth into exchange value, and in place of the numberless indefeasible chartered freedoms, has set up that single, unconscionable freedom—Free Trade. In one word, for exploitation, veiled by religious and political illusions, it has substituted naked, shameless, direct, brutal exploitation.

The bourgeoisie has stripped of its halo every occupation hitherto honored and looked up to with reverent awe. It has converted the physician, the lawyer, the priest, the poet, the man of science, into its paid wage-laborers.

The bourgeoisie has torn away from the family its sentimental veil, and has reduced the family relation to a mere money relation.

The bourgeoisie has disclosed how it

came to pass that the brutal display of vigor in the Middle Ages, which reactionists so much admire, found its fitting complement in the most slothful indolence. It has been the first to show what man's activity can bring about. It has accomplished wonders far surpassing Egyptian pyramids, Roman aqueducts, and Gothic cathedrals; it has conducted expeditions that put in the shade all former Exoduses of nations and crusades.

The bourgeoisie cannot exist without constantly revolutionizing the instruments of production, and thereby the relations of production, and with them the whole relations of society. Conservation of the old modes of production in unaltered form, was, on the contrary, the first condition of existence for all earlier industrial classes. Constant revolutionizing of production, uninterrupted disturbance of all social conditions, everlasting uncertainty and agitation, distinguish the bourgeois epoch from all earlier ones. All fixed, fast-frozen relations, with their train of ancient and venerable prejudices and opinions, are swept away; all new-formed ones become antiquated before they can ossify. All that is solid melts into air, all that is holy is profaned, and man is at last compelled to face with sober senses his real conditions of life, and his relations with his kind.

The need of a constantly expanding market for its products chases the bourgeoisie over the whole surface of the globe. It must nestle everywhere, settle everywhere, establish connections everywhere.

The bourgeoisie has through its exploitation of the world's market given a cosmopolitan character to production and consumption in every country. To the great chagrin of reactionists, it has drawn from under the feet of industry the national ground on which it stood. All old established national industries have been destroyed or are daily being destroyed. They are dislodged by new industries, whose introduction becomes a life and death question for all civilized nations, by industries that no longer work up indigenous raw material, but raw material drawn from the remotest zones, industries whose products are consumed, not only at home, but in every quarter of the globe. In place of the old wants, satisfied by the productions of the country, we find new wants, requiring for their satisfaction the products of distant lands and climes. In place of the old local and national seclusion and self-sufficiency we have had intercourse in every direction, universal interdependence of nations. And as in material, so also in intellectual production. The intellectual creations of individual nations become common property. National onesidedness and narrowmindedness become more and more impossible, and from the numerous national and local literatures, there arises a world-literature.

The bourgeoisie, by the rapid improvement of all instruments of production, by the immensely facilitated means of communication, draws all, even the most barbarian, nations into civilization. The cheap prices of its commodities are the heavy artillery with which it batters down all Chinese walls, with which it forces the barbarians' intensely obstinate hatred of foreigners to capitulate. It compels all nations, on pain of extinction, to adopt the bourgeois mode of production; it compels them to introduce what it calls civilization into their midst, *i.e.*, to become bourgeois themselves. In one word, it creates a world after its own image.

The bourgeoisie has subjected the country to the rule of the towns. It has created enormous cities, has greatly increased the urban population as compared with the rural, and has thus rescued a considerable part of the population from the idiocy of rural life. Just as it has made the country dependent on the towns, so it has made barbarian and semi-barbarian countries dependent on the civilized ones, nations of peasants on nations of bourgeois, the East on the West.

The bourgeoisie keeps more and more doing away with the scattered state of the population, of the means of production, and of property. It has agglomerated population, centralized means of production, and has concentrated property in a few hands. The necessary consequence of this was political centralization. Independent, or but loosely connected provinces, with separate interests, laws, governments, and systems of taxation, became lumped together into one nation, with one government, one code of laws, one national class interest, one frontier, and one customs tariff.

The bourgeoisie, during its rule of scarce one hundred years, has created more massive and more colossal productive forces than have all preceding generations together. Subjection of Nature's forces to man, machinery, application of chemistry to industry and agriculture, steam-navigation, railways, electric telegraphs, clearing of whole continents for cultivation, canalization of rivers, whole populations conjured out of the ground—what earlier century had even a presentiment that such productive forces slumbered in the lap of social labor?

We see then: the means of production and of exchange on whose foundation the bourgeoisie built itself up, were generated in feudal society. At a certain stage in the development of these means of production and of exchange, the conditions under which feudal society produced and exchanged, the feudal organization of agriculture and manufacturing industry, in one word, the feudal relations of property, became no longer compatible with the already developed productive forces; they became so many fetters. They had to burst asunder; they were burst asunder.

Into their places stepped free competition, accompanied by a social and political constitution adapted to it, and by the economical and political sway of the bourgeois class.

A similar movement is going on before our own eyes. Modern bourgeois society with its relations of production, of exchange, and of property, a society that has conjured up such gigantic means of production and of exchange, is like the sorcerer, who is no longer able to control the powers of the nether world whom he has called up by his spells. For many a decade past the history of industry and commerce is but the history of the revolt of modern productive forces against modern conditions of production, against the property relations that are the conditions for the existence of the bourgeoisie and of its rule. It is enough to mention the commercial crises that by their periodical return put on its trial, each time more threateningly, the existence of the bourgeois society. In these crises a great part not only of the existing products, but also of the previously created productive forces, is periodically destroyed. In these crises there breaks out an epidemic that, in all earlier epochs, would have seemed an absurdity—the epidemic of overproduction. Society suddenly finds itself put back into a state of momentary barbarism; it appears as if a famine, a universal war of devastation, had cut off the supply of every means of subsistence; industry and commerce seem to be destroyed; and why? because there is too much civilization, too much means of subsistence, too much industry, too much commerce. The productive forces at the disposal of society no longer tend to further the development of the conditions of bourgeois property; on the contrary, they have become too powerful for these conditions, by which they are fettered, and as soon as they overcome these fetters, they bring disorder into the whole of bourgeois society, endanger the existence of bourgeois property. The conditions of bourgeois society are too narrow to comprise the wealth created by them.

And how does the bourgeoisie get over these crises? On the one hand by enforced destruction of a mass of productive forces; on the other, by the conquest of new markets, and by the more thorough exploitation of the old ones. That is to say, by paving the way for more extensive and more destructive crises, and by diminishing the means whereby crises are prevented.

The weapons with which the bourgeoisie felled feudalism to the ground are now turned against the bourgeoisie itself.

But not only has the bourgeoisie forged the weapons that bring death to itself; it has also called into existence the men who are to wield those weapons—the modern working class—the proletarians.

In proportion as the bourgeoisie, *i.e.*, capital, is developed, in the same proportion is the proletariat, the modern working class, developed; a class of laborers, who live only so long as they find work, and who find work only so long as their labor increases capital. These laborers, who must sell themselves piecemeal, are a commodity, like every other article of commerce, and are consequently exposed to all the vicissitudes of competition, to all the fluctuations of the market.

Owing to the extensive use of machinery and to division of labor, the work of the proletarians has lost all individual character, and, consequently, all charm for the workman. He becomes an appendage of the machine, and it is only the most simple, most monotonous, and most easily acquired knack, that is required of him. Hence, the cost of production of a workman is restricted almost entirely to the means of subsistence that he requires for his maintenance, and for the propagation of his race. But the price of a commodity, and therefore also of labor, is equal to its cost of production. In proportion, therefore, as the repulsiveness of the work increases, the wage decreases. Nay, more, in proportion as the use of machinery and division of labor increases, in the same proportion the burden of toil also increases, whether by prolongation of the working hours, by increase of the work enacted in a given time, or by increased speed of the machinery, etc.

Modern industry has converted the little workshop of the patriarchal master into the great factory of the industrial capitalist. Masses of laborers, crowded into factories, are organized like soldiers. As privates of the industrial army they are placed under the command of a perfect hierarchy of officers and sergeants. Not only are they the slaves of the bourgeois class, and of the bourgeois State, they are daily and hourly enslaved by the machine, by the overlooker, and, above all, by the individual bourgeois manufacturer himself. The more openly this despotism proclaims gain to be its end and aim, the more petty, the more hateful and the more embittering it is.

The less skill and exertion of strength implied in manual labor, in other words, the more modern industry becomes developed, the more is the labor of men superseded by that of women. Differences of age and sex have no longer any distinctive social validity for the working class. All are instruments of labor, more or less expensive to use, according to age and sex.

No sooner is the exploitation of the laborer by the manufacturer, so far at an end, that he receives his wages in cash, than he is set upon by the other portions of the bourgeoisie, the landlord, the shopkeeper, and pawnbroker, etc.

The lower strata of the middle class—the small tradespeople, shopkeepers, and retired tradesmen generally, the handicraftsmen and peasant—all these sink gradually into the proletariat, partly because their diminutive capital does not suffice for the scale on which modern industry is carried on, and is swamped in the competition with the large capitalists, partly because their specialized skill is rendered worthless by new methods of production. Thus the proletariat is recruited from all classes of the population.

The proletariat goes through various stages of development. With its birth begins its struggle with the bourgeoisie. At first the contest is carried on by individual laborers, then by the workpeople of a factory, then by the operatives of one trade, in one locality, against the individual bourgeois who directly exploits them. They direct their attacks not against the bourgeois conditions of production, but against the instruments of production themselves; they destroy imported wares that compete with their labor, they smash to pieces machinery, they set factories ablaze, they seek to restore by force the vanished status of the workman of the Middle Ages.

At this stage the laborers still form an incoherent mass scattered over the whole country, and broken up by their mutual competition. If anywhere they unite to form more compact bodies, this is not yet the consequence of their own active union, but of the union of the bourgeoisie, which class, in order to attain its own political ends, is compelled to set the whole proletariat in motion, and is moreover yet, for a time, able to do so. At this stage, therefore, the proletarians do not fight their enemies, but the enemies of their enemies, the remnants of absolute monarchy, the landowners, the non-industrial bourgeois, the petty bourgeoisie. Thus the whole historical movement is concentrated in the hands of the bourgeoisie; every victory so obtained is a victory for the bourgeoisie.

But with the development of industry the proletariat not only increases in number; it becomes concentrated in greater masses, its strength grows and it feels that strength more. The various interests and conditions of life within the ranks of the proletariat are more and more equalized, in proportion as machinery obliterates all distinctions of labor, and nearly everywhere reduces wages to the same low level. The growing competition among the bourgeois, and the resulting commercial crises, make the wages of the workers even more fluctuating. The unceasing improvement of machinery, ever more rapidly developing, makes their livelihood more and more precarious; the collisions between individual workmen and individual bourgeois take more and more the character of collisions between two classes. Thereupon the workers begin to form combinations (Trades' Unions) against the bourgeois; they club together in order to keep up the rate of wages; they found permanent associations in order to make provision beforehand for these occasional revolts. Here and there the contest breaks out into riots.

Now and then the workers are victorious, but only for a time. The real fruit of their battles lies not in the immediate results but in the ever-improved means of communication that are created by modern industry, and that place the workers of different localities in contact with one another. It was just this contact that was needed to centralize the numerous local struggles, all of the same character, into one national struggle between classes. But every class struggle is a political struggle. And that union, to attain which the burghers of the Middle Ages, with their miserable highways, required centuries, the modern proletarians, thanks to railways, achieve in a few years.

This organization of the proletarians into a class, and consequently into a political party, is continually being upset again by the competition between the workers themselves. But it ever rises up again; stronger, firmer, mightier. It compels legislative recognition of particular interests of the workers, by taking advantage of the divisions among the bourgeoisie itself. Thus the ten-hours' bill in England was carried.

Altogether collisions between the classes of the old society further, in many ways, the course of development of the proletariat. The bourgeoisie finds itself involved in a constant battle. At first with the aristocracy; later on, with those portions of the bourgeoisie itself, whose interests have become antagonistic to the progress of industry; at all times with the bourgeoisie of foreign countries. In all these countries it sees itself compelled to appeal to the proletariat, to ask for its help, and thus to drag it into the political arena. The bourgeoisie itself, therefore, supplies the proletariat with weapons for fighting the bourgeoisie.

Further, as we have already seen, entire sections of the ruling classes are, by the advance of industry, precipitated into the proletariat, or are at least threatened in their conditions of existence. These also supply the proletariat with fresh elements of enlightenment and progress.

Finally, in times when the class struggle nears the decisive hour, the process of dissolution going on within the ruling class, in fact, within the whole range of an old society, assumes such a violent, glaring character, that a small section of the ruling class cuts itself adrift, and joins the revolutionary class, the class that holds the future in its hands. Just as, therefore, at an earlier period, a section of the nobility went over to the bourgeoisie, so now a portion of the bourgeoisie goes over to the proletariat, and in particular, a portion of the bourgeois ideologists, who have raised themselves to the level of comprehending theoretically the historical movement as a whole.

Of all the classes that stand face to face with the bourgeoisie today the proletariat alone is a really revolutionary class. The other classes decay and finally disappear in the face of modern industry; the proletariat is its special and essential product.

The lower middle class, the small manufacturer, the shopkeeper, the artisan, the peasant, all these fight against the bourgeoisie to save from extinction their existence as fractions of the middle class. They are therefore not revolutionary, but conservative. Nay, more, they are reactionary, for they try to roll back the wheel of history. If by chance they are revolutionary, they are so only in view of their impending transfer into the proletariat; they thus defend not their present, but their future interests, they desert their own standpoint to place themselves at that of the proletariat.

The "dangerous class," the social scum, that passively rotting class thrown off by the lowest layers of old society, may, here and there, be swept into the movement by a proletarian revolution; its conditions of life, however, prepare it far more for the part of a bribed tool of reactionary intrigue.

In the conditions of the proletariat, those of the old society at large are already virtually swamped. The proletarian is without property; his relation to his wife and children has no longer anything in common with the bourgeois family relations; modern industrial labor, modern subjection to capital, the same in England as in France, in America as in Germany, has stripped him of every trace of national character. Law, morality, religion, are to him so many bourgeois prejudices, behind which lurk in ambush just as many bourgeois interests.

All the preceding classes that got the upper hand sought to fortify their already acquired status by subjecting society at large to their conditions of appropriation. The proletarians cannot become masters of the productive forces of society, except by abolishing their own previous mode of appropriation, and thereby also every other previous mode of appropriation. They have nothing of their own to secure and to fortify; their mission is to destroy all previous securities for, and insurances of, individual property.

All previous historical movements were movements of minorities, or in the interest of minorities. The proletarian movement is the self-conscious, independent movement of the immense majority, in the interest of the immense majority. The proletariat, the lowest stratum of our present society, cannot stir, cannot raise itself up, without the whole super-incumbent strata of official society being sprung into the air.

Though not in substance, yet in form, the struggle of the proletariat with the bourgeoisie is at first a national struggle. The proletariat of each country must, of course, first of all settle matters with its own bourgeoisie.

In depicting the most general phases of the development of the proletariat, we traced the more or less veiled civil war, raging within existing society, up to the point where that war breaks out into open revolution, and where the violent overthrow of the bourgeoisie lays the foundation for the sway of the proletariat.

Hitherto every form of society has been based, as we have already seen, on the antagonism of oppressing and oppressed classes. But in order to oppress a class certain conditions must be assured to it under which it can, at least, continue its slavish existence. The serf, in the period of serfdom, raised himself to membership in the commune, just as the petty bourgeois, under the yoke of feudal absolutism, managed to develop into a bourgeois. The modern laborer, on the contrary, instead of rising with the progress of industry, sinks deeper and deeper below the conditions of existence of his own class. He becomes a pauper, and pauperism develops more rapidly than population and wealth. And here it becomes evident that the bourgeoisie is unfit any longer to be the ruling class in society and to impose its conditions of existence upon society as an over-riding law. It is unfit to rule because it is incompetent to assure an existence to its slave within his slavery, because it cannot help letting him sink into such a state that it has to feed him instead of being fed by him. Society can no longer live under this bourgeoisie, in other words its existence is no longer compatible with society.

The essential condition for the existence and for the sway of the bourgeois class, is the formation and augmentation of capital; the condition for capital is wage-labor. Wage-labor rests exclusively on competition between the laborers. The advance of industry, whose involuntary promoter is the bourgeoisie, replaces the isolation of the laborers, due to competition, by their revolutionary combination, due to association. The development of modern industry, therefore, cuts from under its feet the very foundation on which the bourgeoisie produces and appropriates products. What the bourgeoisie therefore produces, above all, are its own grave-diggers. Its fall and the victory of the proletariat are equally inevitable.

II

PROLETARIANS AND COMMUNISTS

In what relation do the Communists stand to the proletarians as a whole?

The Communists do not form a separate party opposed to other working class parties.

They have no interests separate and apart from those of the proletariat as a whole.

They do not set up any sectarian principles of their own by which to shape and mould the proletarian movement.

The Communists are distinguished from the other working class parties by this only: 1. In the national struggles of the proletarians of the different countries, they point out and bring to the front the common interests of the entire proletariat, independently of all nationality. 2. In the various stages of development which the struggle of the working class against the bourgeoisie has to pass through, they always and everywhere represent the interests of the movement as a whole.

The Communists, therefore, are on the one hand, practically, the most advanced and resolute section of the working class parties of every country, that section which pushes forward all others; on the other hand, theoretically, they have over the great mass of the proletariat the advantage of clearly understanding the line of march, the conditions, and the ultimate general results of the proletarian movement.

The immediate aim of the Communists is the same as that of all the other proletarian parties: formation of the proletariat into a class, overthrow of the bourgeois supremacy, conquest of political power by the proletariat.

The theoretical conclusions of the Communists are in no way based on ideas or principles that have been invented, or discovered, by this or that would-be universal reformer.

They merely express, in general terms, actual relations springing from an existing class struggle, from a historical movement going on under our very eyes. The abolition of existing property relations is not at all a distinctive feature of Communism.

All property relations in the past have continually been subject to historical change, consequent upon the change in historical conditions.

The French Revolution, for example, abolished feudal property in favor of bourgeois property.

The distinguishing feature of Communism is not the abolition of property generally, but the abolition of bourgeois property. But modern bourgeois private property is the final and most complete expression of the system of producing and appropriating products, that is based on class antagonisms, on the exploitation of the many by the few.

In this sense the theory of the Communists may be summed up in the single sentence: Abolition of private property.

We Communists have been reproached with the desire of abolishing the right of personally acquiring property as the fruit of a man's own labor, which property is alleged to be the groundwork of all personal freedom, activity, and independence.

Hard-won, self-acquired, self-earned property! Do you mean the property of the petty artisan and of the small peasant, a form of property that preceded the bourgeois form? There is no need to abolish that; the development of industry has to a great extent already destroyed it, and is still destroying it daily.

Or do you mean modern bourgeois private property?

But does wage-labor create any property for the laborer? Not a bit. It creates capital, *i.e.,* that kind of property which exploits wage-labor, and which cannot increase except upon condition of begetting a new supply of wage-labor for fresh exploitation. Property, in its present form, is based on the antagonism of capital and wage-labor. Let us examine both sides of this antagonism.

To be a capitalist, is to have not only a purely personal, but a social *status* in production. Capital is a collective product, and only by the united action of many members, nay, in the last resort, only by the united action of all members of society, can it be set in motion.

Capital is therefore not a personal, it is a social power.

When, therefore, capital is converted into common property, into the property of all members of society, personal property is not thereby transformed into social property. It is only the social character of the property that is changed. It loses its class character.

Let us now take wage-labor.

The average price of wage-labor is the minimum wage, *i.e.*, that quantum of the means of subsistence, which is absolutely requisite to keep the laborer in bare existence as a laborer. What, therefore, the wage-laborer appropriates by means of his labor, merely suffices to prolong and reproduce a bare existence. We by no means intend to abolish this personal appropriation of the products of labor, an appropriation that is made for the maintenance and reproduction of human life, and that leaves no surplus wherewith to command the labor of others. All that we want to do away with, is the miserable character of this appropriation, under which the laborer lives merely to increase capital, and is allowed to live only in so far as the interest of the ruling class requires it.

In bourgeois society living labor is but a means to increase accumulated labor. In Communist society accumulated labor is but a means to widen, to enrich, to promote the existence of the laborer.

In bourgeois society, therefore, the past dominates the present; in Communist society, the present dominates the past. In bourgeois society capital is independent and has individuality, while the living person is dependent and has no individuality.

And the abolition of this state of things is called by the bourgeois: abolition of individuality and freedom! And rightly so. The abolition of bourgeois individuality, bourgeois independence, and bourgeois freedom is undoubtedly aimed at.

By freedom is meant, under the present bourgeois conditions of production, free trade, free selling, and buying.

But if selling and buying disappears, free selling and buying disappears also. This talk about free selling and buying, and all the other "brave words" of our bourgeoisie about freedom in general, have a meaning, if any, only in contrast with restricted selling and buying, with the fettered traders of the Middle Ages, but have no meaning when opposed to the Communistic abolition of buying and selling, of the bourgeois conditions of production, and of the bourgeoisie itself.

You are horrified at our intending to do away with private property. But in your existing society private property is already done away with for nine-tenths of the population; its existence for the few is solely due to its non-existence in the hands of those nine-tenths. You reproach us, therefore, with intending to do away with a form of property, the necessary condition for whose existence is, the non-existence of any property for the immense majority of society.

In one word, you reproach us with intending to do away with your property. Precisely so: that is just what we intend.

From the moment when labor can no longer be converted into capital, money, or rent, into a social power capable of being monopolized, *i.e.*, from the moment when individual property can no longer be transformed into bourgeois property, into capital, from that moment, you say, individuality vanishes!

You must, therefore, confess that by "individual" you mean no other person than the bourgeois, than the middle-class owner of property. This person must, indeed, be swept out of the way, and made impossible.

Communism deprives no man of the power to appropriate the products of society: all that it does is to deprive him of the power to subjugate the labor of others by means of such appropriation.

It has been objected, that upon the abolition of private property all work will cease, and universal laziness will overtake us.

According to this, bourgeois society ought long ago to have gone to the dogs through sheer idleness; for those of its members who work, acquire nothing, and those who acquire anything, do not work.

The whole of this objection is but another expression of the tautology: that there can no longer be any wage-labor when there is no longer any capital.

All objections against the communistic mode of producing and appropriating material products, have, in the same way, been urged against the communistic modes by producing and appropriating intellectual products. Just as, to the bourgeois, the disappearance of class property is the disappearance of production itself, so the disappearance of class culture is to him identical with the disappearance of all culture.

That culture, the loss of which he laments, is, for the enormous majority, a mere training to act as a machine.

But don't wrangle with us so long as you apply to our intended abolition of bourgeois property, the standard of your bourgeois notions of freedom, culture, law, etc. Your very ideas are but the outgrowth of the conditions of your bourgeois production and bourgeois property, just as your jurisprudence is but the will of your class made into a law for all, a will, whose essential character and direction are determined by the economical conditions of existence of your class.

The selfish misconception that induces you to transform into eternal laws of nature and of reason, the social forms springing from your present mode of production and form of property—historical relations that rise and disappear in the progress of production—this misconception you share with every ruling class that has preceded you. What you see clearly in the case of ancient property, what you admit in the case of feudal property, you are of course forbidden to admit in the case of your own bourgeois form of property.

Abolition of the family! Even the most radical flare up at this infamous proposal of the Communists.

On what foundation is the present family, the bourgeois family, based? On capital, on private gain. In its completely developed form this family exists only among the bourgeoisie. But this state of things finds its complement in the practical absence of the family among the proletarians, and in public prostitution.

The bourgeois family will vanish as a matter of course when its complement vanishes, and both will vanish with the vanishing of capital.

Do you charge us with wanting to stop the exploitation of children by their parents? To this crime we plead guilty.

But, you will say, we destroy the most hallowed of relations, when we replace home education by social.

And your education! Is not that also social, and determined by the social conditions under which you educate, by the intervention, direct or indirect, of society by means of schools, etc.? The Communists have not invented the intervention of society in education; they do but seek to alter the character of that intervention, and to rescue education from the influence of the ruling class.

The bourgeois clap-trap about the family and education, about the hallowed co-relation of parent and child becomes all the more disgusting, as, by the action of modern industry, all family ties among the proletarians are torn asunder and their children transformed into simple articles of commerce and instruments of labor.

But you Communists would introduce community of women, screams the whole bourgeoisie in chorus.

The bourgeois sees in his wife a mere instrument of production. He hears that the instruments of production are to be exploited in common, and, naturally, can come to no other conclusion then that the lot of being common to all will likewise fall to the women.

He has not even a suspicion that the real point aimed at is to do away with the status of women as mere instruments of production.

For the rest nothing is more ridiculous than the virtuous indignation of our bourgeois at the community of women which, they pretend, is to be openly and officially established by the Communists. The Communists have no need to introduce community of women; it has existed almost from time immemorial.

Our bourgeois, not content with having the wives and daughters of their proletarians at their disposal, not to speak of common prostitutes, take the greatest pleasure in seducing each other's wives.

Bourgeois marriage is in reality a system of wives in common and thus, at the most, what the Communists might possibly be reproached with, is that they desire to introduce, in substitution for a hypocritically concealed, an openly legalized community of women. For the rest it is self-evident that the abolition of the present system of production must bring with it the abolition of the community of woman springing from that system, *i.e.,* of prostitution both public and private.

The Communists are further reproached with desiring to abolish countries and nationality.

The workingmen have no country. We cannot take from them what they have not got. Since the proletariat must first of all acquire political supremacy, must rise to be the leading class of the nation, must constitute itself *the* nation, it is, so far, itself national, though not in the bourgeois sense of the word.

National differences and antagonisms between peoples are daily more and more vanishing, owing to the development of the bourgeoisie, to freedom of commerce, to the world's market, to uniformity in the mode of production and in the conditions of life corresponding thereto.

The supremacy of the proletariat will cause them to vanish still faster. United action, of the leading civilized countries at least, is one of the first conditions for the emancipation of the proletariat.

In proportion as the exploitation of one individual by another is put an end to, the exploitation of one nation by another will also be put an end to. In proportion as the antagonism between classes within the nation vanishes, the hostility of one nation to another will come to an end.

The charges against Communism made from a religious, a philosophical, and, generally, from an ideological standpoint, are not deserving of serious examination.

Does it require deep intuition to comprehend that man's ideas, views, and conceptions, in one word, man's consciousness changes with every change in the conditions of his material existence, in his social relations and in his social life?

What else does the history of ideas prove than that intellectual production changes its character in proportion as material production is changed? The ruling ideas of each age have ever been the ideas of its ruling class.

When people speak of ideas that revolutionize society they do but express the fact that within the old society the elements of a new one have been created, and that the dissolution of the old ideas keeps even pace with the dissolution of the old conditions of existence.

When the ancient world was in its last throes, the ancient religions were overcome by Christianity. When Christian ideas succumbed in the eighteenth century to rationalist ideas, feudal society fought its death-battle with the then revolutionary bourgeoisie. The ideas of religious liberty and freedom of conscience merely gave expression to the sway of free competition within the domain of knowledge.

"Undoubtedly," it will be said, "religious, moral, philosophical, and juridical ideas have been modified in the course of historical development. But religion, morality, philosophy, political science, and law, constantly survived this change.

"There are besides, eternal truths, such as Freedom, Justice, etc., that are common to all states of society. But Communism abolishes eternal truths, it abolishes all religion and all morality, instead of constituting them on a new basis; it therefore acts as a contradiction to all past historical experience."

What does this accusation reduce itself to? The history of all past society has consisted in the development of class antagonisms, antagonisms that assumed different forms at different epochs.

But whatever form they may have taken, one fact is common to all past ages, *viz.*, the exploitation of one part of society by the other. No wonder, then, that the social consciousness of past ages, despite all the multiplicity and variety it displays, moves within certain common forms, or general ideas, which cannot completely vanish except with the total disappearance of class antagonisms.

The Communist revolution is the most radical rupture with traditional property relations; no wonder that its development involves the most radical rupture with traditional ideas.

But let us have done with the bourgeois objections to Communism.

We have seen above that the first step in the revolution by the working class is to raise the proletariat to the position of the ruling class, to win the battle of democracy.

The proletariat will use its political supremacy to wrest, by degrees, all capital from the bourgeoisie; to centralize all instruments of production in the hands of the State, *i.e.*, of the proletariat organized as the ruling class; and to increase the total of productive forces as rapidly as possible.

Of course, in the beginning this cannot be effected except by means of despotic inroads on the rights of property and on the conditions of bourgeois production; by means of measures, therefore, which appear economically insufficient and untenable, but which, in the course of the movement, outstrip themselves, necessitate further inroads upon the old social order and are unavoidable as a means of entirely revolutionizing the mode of production.

These measures will of course be different in different countries.

Nevertheless in the most advanced countries the following will be pretty generally applicable:

1. Abolition of property in land and application of all rents of land to public purposes.
2. A heavy progressive or graduated income tax.
3. Abolition of all rights of inheritance.
4. Confiscation of the property of all emigrants and rebels.
5. Centralization of credit in the hands of the State, by means of a national bank with State capital and an exclusive monopoly.
6. Centralization of the means of communication and transport in the hands of the State.
7. Extension of factories and instruments of production owned by the State; the bringing into cultivation of waste lands, and the improvement of the soil generally in accordance with a common plan.
8. Equal liability of all to labor. Establishment of industrial armies, especially for agriculture.
9. Combination of agriculture with manufacturing industries: gradual abolition of the distinction between town and country, by a more equable distribution of the population over the country.
10. Free education for all children in public schools. Abolition of children's factory labor in its present form. Combination of education with industrial production, etc., etc.

When, in the course of development,

class distinctions have disappeared and all production has been concentrated in the hands of a vast association of the whole nation, the public power will lose its political character. Political power, properly so called, is merely the organized power of one class for oppressing another. If the proletariat during its contest with the bourgeoisie is compelled, by the force of circumstances, to organize itself as a class, if, by means of a revolution, it makes itself the ruling class, and, as such, sweeps away by force the old conditions of production, then it will, along with these conditions, have swept away the conditions for the existence of class antagonism, and of classes generally, and will thereby have abolished its own supremacy as a class.

In place of the old bourgeois society with its classes and class antagonisms we shall have an association in which the free development of each is the condition for the free development of all.

• • •

IV

POSITION OF THE COMMUNISTS IN RELATION TO THE VARIOUS EXISTING OPPOSITION PARTIES

Section II has made clear the relations of the Communist to the existing working class parties, such as the Chartists in England and the Agrarian Reformers in America.

The Communists fight for the attainment of the immediate aims, for the enforcement of the momentary interests of the working class; but in the movement of the present they also represent and take care of the future of that movement. In France the Communists ally themselves with the Social-Democrats, against the conservative and radical bourgeoisie, reserving, however, the right to take up a critical position in regard to phrases and illusions traditionally handed down from the great Revolution.

In Switzerland they support the Radicals, without losing sight of the fact that this party consists of antagonistic elements, partly of Democratic Socialists, in the French sense, partly of radical bourgeois.

In Poland they support the party that insists on an agrarian revolution, as the prime condition for national emancipation, that party which fomented the insurrection of Cracow in 1846.

In Germany they fight with the bourgeoisie whenever it acts in a revolutionary way against the absolute monarchy, the feudal squirearchy, and the petty bourgeoisie.

But they never cease, for a single instant, to instill into the working class the clearest possible recognition of the hostile antagonism between bourgeoisie and proletariat, in order that the German workers may straightway use, as so many weapons against the bourgeoisie the social and political conditions that the bourgeoisie must necessarily introduce along with its supremacy, and in order that, after the fall of the reactionary classes in Germany, the fight against the bourgeoisie itself may immediately begin.

The Communists turn their attention chiefly to Germany, because that country is on the eve of a bourgeois revolution that is bound to be carried out under more advanced conditions of European civilization, and with a much more developed proletariat, than that of England was in the seventeenth, and of France in the eighteenth century, and because the bourgeois revolution in Germany will be but the prelude to an immediately following proletarian revolution.

In short, the Communists everywhere support every revolutionary movement against the existing social and political order of things.

In all these movements they bring to the front, as the leading question in each, the property question, no matter what its degree of development at the time.

Finally, they labor everywhere for the union and agreement of the democratic parties of all countries.

The Communists disdain to conceal their views and aims. They openly declare that their ends can be attained only by the forcible overthrow of all existing social conditions. Let the ruling classes tremble at a communistic revolution. The proletarians have nothing to lose but their chains. They have a world to win.

Working men of all countries, unite!

JOHN STUART MILL

If John Stuart Mill (1806–1873) had been able to look ahead from his childhood to the years that followed, he would have found the entire course of his life laid out for him in advance. Educated at home by his father and by Jeremy Bentham, both of whom were leaders in an influential group of English intellectuals known as the "Philosophical Radicals," he was carefully groomed by his tutors to take over the leadership of the movement. The social program of the Radicals (later called Liberals) was based on Bentham's dictum that the goal of society must be to promote "the greatest happiness [pleasure] of the greatest number." Assuming with Hobbes that all men are innately selfish, Bentham argued that this very selfishness would produce the desired goal. For, if each person is free to seek his own happiness, the end result is bound to be the greatest happiness of all. Hence, all restraints upon the action of individuals, especially restraints exercised by government, must be eliminated. This freedom was regarded as particularly important in the economic realm, where the liberals, following Smith and Ricardo, advocated a policy of strict laissez-faire.

Young Mill seems to have learned his lessons well, for almost all his writings (including his essay On Liberty*) commence with a reaffirmation of the principles of his elders. Yet the more we study his works the more apparent it becomes that he is often paying little more than lip-service to the doctrines instilled in him, while the real tenor of his views often represents a significant departure from the original Liberal position.*

There were at least two reasons for Mill's defection. The first was personal. A man of great perceptiveness, warm sympathies, and intellectual breadth, he could no more contain himself within the doctrinaire limitations of the Benthamite position than he could accept its assumption of universal selfishness or its identification of happiness with pleasure. The second reason was theoretical. While still a youth Mill had become acquainted, through reading the English poet-philosopher Coleridge, with the philosophy of the German idealists, Kant and Hegel, a philosophy that ran counter to the views of the Liberals. Man, the idealists argued, is not an atom, who can separate himself from the rest of society to pursue his own selfish ends. When anyone attempts to live this way, rather than attaining freedom and happiness, he destroys himself as a human being. On the contrary, man is, as Aristotle said, made for society; the true realization of his own selfhood, hence his freedom and happiness, can be achieved only through identifying his interests with those of his social group. Such a view, translated into practice, leads to some form of collectivism, the exact antithesis of the individualism of the Liberals.

The tension between these contrasting views of man's relationship to society is apparent throughout Mill's writings; in fact, it created a problem that he never succeeded in solving. And since his time it has occupied the attention of all social thinkers who have called themselves liberals, including, in our own century, the great American philosopher, John Dewey.

The selection that follows, from Mill's essay On Liberty, *reveals not only the author's basic liberal position but also some of his qualifications of that position. But more than this, the essay stands as one of the most inspired defenses of human freedom to be found in Western literature.*

On Liberty

Chapter I

INTRODUCTORY

The subject of this Essay is not the so-called Liberty of the Will, so unfortunately opposed to the misnamed doctrine of Philosophical Necessity; but Civil, or Social Liberty: the nature and limits of the power which can be legitimately exercised by society over the individual. A question seldom stated, and hardly ever discussed, in general terms but which profoundly influences the practical controversies of the age by its latent presence, and is likely soon to make itself recognized as the vital question of the future. It is so far from being new, that, in a certain sense, it has divided mankind, almost from the remotest ages; but in the stage of progress into which the more civilized portions of the species have now entered, it presents itself under new conditions, and requires a different and more fundamental treatment.

The struggle between Liberty and Authority is the most conspicuous feature in the portions of history with which we are earliest familiar, particularly in that of Greece, Rome, and England. But in old times this contest was between subjects, or some classes of subjects, and the Government. By liberty, was meant protection against the tyranny of the political rulers. The rulers were conceived (except in some of the popular governments of Greece) as in a necessarily antagonistic position to the people whom they ruled. They consisted of a governing One, or a governing tribe or caste, who derived their authority from inheritance or conquest, who, at all events, did not hold it at the pleasure of the governed, and whose supremacy men did not venture, perhaps did not desire, to contest, whatever precautions might be taken against its oppressive exercise. Their power was regarded as necessary, but also as highly dangerous; as a weapon which they would attempt to use against their subjects, no less than against external enemies. To prevent the weaker members of the community from being preyed upon by innumerable vultures, it was needful that there should be an animal of prey stronger than the rest, commissioned to keep them down. But as the king of the vultures would be no less bent upon preying on the flock than any of the minor harpies, it was indispensable to be in a perpetual attitude of defence against his beak and claws. The aim, therefore, of patriots was to set limits to the power which the ruler should be suf-

John Stuart Mill, ON LIBERTY *(New York, 1885).*

fered to exercise over the community; and this limitation was what they meant by liberty. It was attempted in two ways. First, by obtaining a recognition of certain immunities, called political liberties or rights, which it was to be regarded as a breach of duty in the ruler to infringe, and which if he did infringe, specific resistance, or general rebellion, was held to be justifiable. A second, and generally a later expedient, was the establishment of constitutional checks, by which the consent of the community, or of a body of some sort, supposed to represent its interests, was made a necessary condition to some of the more important acts of the governing power. To the first of these modes of limitation, the ruling power, in most European countries, was compelled, more or less, to submit. It was not so with the second; and, to attain this, or when already in some degree possessed, to attain it more completely, became everywhere the principal object of the lovers of liberty. And so long as mankind were content to combat one enemy by another, and to be ruled by a master, on condition of being guaranteed more or less efficaciously against his tyranny, they did not carry their aspirations beyond this point.

A time, however, came, in the progress of human affairs, when men ceased to think it a necessity of nature that their governors should be an independent power, opposed in interest to themselves. It appeared to them much better that the various magistrates of the State should be their tenants or delegates, revocable at their pleasure. In that way alone, it seemed, they could have complete security that the powers of government would never be abused to their disadvantage. By degrees this new demand for elective and temporary rulers became the prominent object of the exertions of the popular party, wherever any such party existed; and superseded, to a considerable extent, the previous efforts to limit the power of rulers. As the struggle proceeded for making the ruling power emanate from the periodical choice of the ruled, some persons began to think that too much importance had been attached to the limitation of the power itself. *That* (it might seem) was a resource against rulers whose interests were habitually opposed to those of the people. What was now wanted was, that the rulers should be identified with the people; that their interest and will should be the interest and will of the nation. The nation did not need to be protected against its own will. There was no fear of its tyrannizing over itself. Let the rulers be effectually responsible to it, promptly removable by it, and it could afford to trust them with power of which it could itself dictate the use to be made. Their power was but the nation's own power, concentrated, and in a form convenient for exercise. This mode of thought, or rather perhaps of feeling, was common among the last generation of European liberalism, in the Continental section of which it still apparently predominates. Those who admit any limit to what a government may do, except in the case of such governments as they think ought not to exist, stand out as brilliant exceptions among the political thinkers of the Continent. A similar tone of sentiment might by this time have been prevalent in our own country, if the circumstances which for a time encouraged it, had continued unaltered.

But, in political and philosophical theories, as well as in persons, success discloses faults and infirmities which failure might have concealed from observation. The notion, that the people have no need to limit their power over themselves, might seem axiomatic, when popular government was a thing only dreamed about, or read of as having existed at some distant period of the past. Neither was that notion necessarily disturbed by such temporary aberrations as those of the French Revolution, the worst of which were the work of an usurping few, and which, in any case, belonged, not to the permanent working of popular institutions, but to a sudden and convulsive outbreak against monarchical and aristocratic despotism. In time, however, a democratic republic came to occupy a large portion of the earth's surface, and made itself felt as one of the most powerful members of the community of nations; and elective and responsible government became subject to the observations and criticisms which wait upon a great existing fact. It was now perceived that such phrases as "self-government," and "the power of the people over themselves," do not express the true state of the case. The "people" who exercise the power are not always the same people with those over whom it is exercised; and the "self-government" spoken of is not the government of each by himself, but of each by all the rest. The will of the people, moreover, practically means the will of the most numerous or the most active *part* of the people, the majority, or those who succeed in making themselves accepted as the majority; the people, consequently, *may* desire to oppress a part of their number; and precautions are as much needed against this as against any other abuse of power. The limitation, therefore, of the power of government over individuals loses none of its importance when the holders of power are regularly accountable to the community, that is, to the strongest party therein. This view of things, recommending itself equally to the intelligence of thinkers and to the inclination of those important classes in European society to whose real or supposed interests democracy is adverse, has had no difficulty in establishing itself; and in political speculations "the tyranny of the majority" is now generally included among the evils against which society requires to be on its guard.

. . .

The object of this Essay is to assert one very simple principle, as entitled to govern absolutely the dealings of society with the individual in the way of compulsion and control, whether the means used be physical force in the form of legal penalties, or the moral coercion of public opinion. That principle is, that the sole end for which mankind are warranted, individually or collectively, in interfering with the liberty of action of any of their number, is self-protection. That the only purpose for which power can be rightfully exercised over any member of a civilized community, against his will, is to prevent harm to others. His own good, either physical or moral, is not a sufficient warrant. He cannot rightfully be compelled to do or forebear because it will be better for him to do so, because it will make him happier, because, in the opinions of others, to do so would be wise, or even right. These are good reasons for remonstrating with him, or reasoning with him, or persuading him, or entreating him, but not for compelling him, or visiting him with any evil in case he do otherwise. To justify that, the conduct from which it is desired to deter him, must be calculated to produce evil to some one else. The only part of the conduct of any one, for which he is amenable to society, is that which concerns others. In the part which merely concerns himself, his independence is, of right, absolute. Over himself, over his own body and mind, the individual is sovereign.

It is, perhaps, hardly necessary to say that this doctrine is meant to apply only to human beings in the maturity of their faculties. We are not speaking of children, or of young persons below the age which the law may fix as that of manhood or womanhood. Those who are still in a state to require being taken care of by others, must be protected against their own actions as well as against external injury. For the same reason, we may leave out of consideration those backward states of society in which the race itself may be considered as in its nonage. The early difficulties in the way of spontaneous progress are so great, that there is seldom any choice of means for overcoming them; and a ruler full of the spirit of improvement is warranted in the use of any expedients that will attain an end, perhaps otherwise unattainable. Despotism is a legitimate mode of government in dealing with barbarians, provided the end be their improvement, and the means justified by actually effecting that end. Liberty, as a principle, has no application to any state of things anterior to the time when mankind have become capable of being improved by free and equal discussion. Until then, there is nothing for them but implicit obedience to an Akbar or a Charlemagne, if they are so fortunate as to find one. But as soon as mankind have attained the capacity of being guided to their own improvement by conviction or persuasion (a period long since reached in all nations with whom we need here concern ourselves), compulsion, either in the direct form or in that of pains and penalties for non-compliance, is no longer admissible as a means to their own good, and justifiable only for the security of others.

It is proper to state that I forego any advantage which could be derived to my argument from the idea of abstract right, as a thing independent of utility. I regard utility as the ultimate appeal on all ethical questions: but it must be utility in the largest sense, grounded on the permanent interests of a man as a progressive being. Those interests, I contend, authorize the subjection of individual spontaneity to external control, only in respect to those actions of each, which concern the interest of other people. If any one does an act hurtful to others, there is a *prima facie* case for punishing him, by law, or, where legal penalties are not safely applicable, by general disapprobation. There are also many positive acts for the benefit of others, which he may rightfully be compelled to perform; such as to give evidence in a court of justice; to bear his fair share in the common defence, or in any other joint work necessary to the interest of the society of which he enjoys the protection; and to perform certain acts of individual beneficence, such as saving a fellow-creature's life, or interposing to protect the defenceless against ill-usage, things which whenever it is obviously a man's duty to do, he may rightfully be made responsible to society for not doing. A person may cause evil to others not only by his actions but by his inaction, and in either case he is justly accountable to them for the injury. The latter case, it is true, requires a much more cautious exercise of compulsion than the former. To make any one answerable for doing evil to others, is the rule; to make him answerable for not preventing evil, is, comparatively speaking, the exception. Yet there are many cases clear enough and grave enough to justify that exception. In all things which regard the external relations of the individual, he is *de jure* amenable to those whose interests are concerned, and if need be, to society as their protector. There are often good reasons for not holding him to the responsibility; but these reasons must arise from the special expediences of the case: either because it is a kind of case in which he is on the whole likely to act better, when left to his own discretion, than when controlled in any way in which society have it in their power to control him; or because the attempt to exercise control would produce other evils, greater than those which it would prevent. When such reasons as these preclude the enforcement of responsibility, the conscience of the agent himself should step into the vacant judgment seat, and protect those interests of others which have no external protection; judging himself all the more rigidly, because the case does not admit of his being made accountable to the judgment of his fellow-creatures.

But there is a sphere of action in which society, as distinguished from the individual, has, if any, only an indirect interest; comprehending all that portion of a person's life and conduct which affects only himself, or if it also affects others, only with their free, voluntary, and undeceived consent and participation. When I say only himself, I mean directly and in the first instance; for whatever affects himself, may affect others through himself; and the objection which may be grounded on this contingency, will receive consideration in the sequel. This, then, is the appropriate region of human liberty. It comprises, first, the inward domain of consciousness; demanding liberty of conscience, in the most comprehensive sense; liberty of thought and feeling; absolute freedom of opinion and sentiment on all subjects, practical or speculative, scientific, moral or theological. The liberty of expressing and publishing opinions may seem to fall under a different principle, since it belongs to that part of the conduct of an individual which concerns other people; but, being almost of as much importance as the liberty of thought itself, and resting in great part on the same reasons, is practically inseparable from it. Secondly, the principle requires liberty of tastes and pursuits; of framing the plan of our life to suit our own character; of doing as we like, subject to such consequences as may follow: without impediment from our fellow-creatures, so long as what we do does not harm them, even though they should think our conduct foolish, perverse, or wrong. Thirdly, from this liberty of each individual, follows the liberty, within the same limits, of combination among individuals; freedom to unite, for any purpose not involving harm to others: the persons combining being supposed to be of full age, and not forced or deceived.

No society in which these liberties are not, on the whole, respected, is free, whatever may be its form of government; and none is completely free in which they do not exist absolutely and unqualified. The only freedom which deserves the name, is that of pursuing our own good in our own way, so long as we do not attempt to deprive others of theirs, or impede their efforts to obtain it. Each is the proper guardian of his own health, whether bodily, or mental and spiritual. Mankind are greater gainers by suffering each other to live as seems good to themselves, than by compelling each to live as seems good to the rest.

. . .

Chapter II

OF THE LIBERTY OF THOUGHT AND DISCUSSION

The time, it is to be hoped, is gone by, when any defence would be necessary of the "liberty of the press" as one of the securities against corrupt or tyrannical government. No argument, we may suppose, can now be needed, against permitting a legislature or an executive, not identified in interest with the people, to prescribe opinions to them, and determine what doctrines or what arguments they shall be allowed to hear. This aspect of the question, besides, has been so often and so triumphantly enforced by preceding writers, that it needs not be specially insisted on in this place. Though the law of England on the subject of the press, is as servile to this day as it was in the time of the Tudors, there is little danger of its being actually put in force against political discussion, except during some temporary panic, when fear of insurrection drives ministers and judges from their propriety; and, speaking generally, it is not, in constitutional countries, to be apprehended, that the government, whether completely responsible to the people or not, will often attempt to control the expression of opinion, except when in doing so it makes itself the organ of the general intolerance of the public. Let us suppose, therefore, that the government is entirely at one with the people, and never thinks of exerting any power of coercion unless in agreement with what it conceives to be their voice. But I deny the right of the people to exercise such coercion, either by themselves, or by their government. The power itself is illegitimate. The best government has no more title to it than the worst. It is as noxious, or more noxious, when exerted in accordance with public opinion, than when in opposition to it. If all mankind minus one, were of one opinion, and only one person were of the contrary opinion, mankind would be no more justified in silencing that one person, than he, if he had the power, would be justified in silencing mankind. Were an opinion a personal possession of no value except to the owner; if to be obstructed in the enjoyment of it were simply a private injury, it would make some difference whether the injury was inflicted only on a few persons or on many. But the peculiar evil of silencing the expression of an opinion is, that it is robbing the human race, posterity as well as the existing generation; those who dissent from the opinion, still more than those who hold it. If the opinion is right, they are deprived of the opportunity of exchanging error for truth: if wrong, they lose, what is almost as great a benefit, the clearer perception and livelier impression of truth, produced by its collision with error.

It is necessary to consider separately these two hypotheses, each of which has a distinct branch of the argument corresponding to it. We can never be sure that the opinion we are endeavoring to stifle is a false opinion; and if we were sure, stifling it would be an evil still.

. . .

Mankind can hardly be too often reminded, that there was once a man named Socrates, between whom and the legal authorities and public opinion of his time, there took place a memorable collision. Born in an age and country abounding in individual greatness, this man has been handed down to us by those who best knew both him and the age, as the most virtuous man in it; while *we* know him as the head and prototype of all subsequent teachers of virtue, the source equally of the lofty inspiration of Plato and the judicious utilitarianism of Aristotle, *"i maestri di color che sanno,"* [1] the two headsprings of ethical as of all other philosophy. This acknowledged master of all the eminent thinkers who have since lived—whose fame, still growing after more than two thousand years, all but outweighs the whole remainder of the names which make his native city illustrious—was put to death by his countrymen, after a judicial conviction, for impiety and immorality. Impiety, in denying the gods recognized by the State; indeed his accuser asserted (see the "Apologia") that he believed in no gods at all. Immorality, in being, by his doctrines and instructions, a "corrupter of youth." Of these charges the tribunal, there is every ground for believing, honestly found him guilty, and condemned the man who probably of all then born had deserved best of mankind, to be put to death as a criminal.

To pass from this to the only other instance of judicial iniquity, the mention of which, after the condemnation of Socrates, would not be an anti-climax: the event which took place on Calvary rather more than eighteen hundred years ago. The man who left on the memory of those who witnessed his life and conversation, such an impression of his moral grandeur, that

[1] ["the masters of those who know."—Ed.]

eighteen subsequent centuries have done homage to him as the Almighty in person, was ignominiously put to death, as what? As a blasphemer. Men did not merely mistake their benefactor; they mistook him for the exact contrary of what he was, and treated him as that prodigy of impiety, which they themselves are now held to be, for their treatment of him. The feelings with which mankind now regard these lamentable transactions, especially the later of the two, render them extremely unjust in their judgment of the unhappy actors. These were, to all appearance, not bad men —not worse than men commonly are, but rather the contrary; men who possessed in a full, or somewhat more than a full measure, the religious, moral, and patriotic feelings of their time and people: the very kind of men who, in all times, our own included, have every chance of passing through life blameless and respected. The high-priest who rent his garments when the words were pronounced, which according to all the ideas of his country, constituted the blackest guilt, was in all probability quite as sincere in his horror and indignation, as the generality of respectable and pious men now are in the religious and moral sentiments they profess; and most of those who now shudder at his conduct, if they had lived in his time, and been born Jews, would have acted precisely as he did. Orthodox Christians who are tempted to think that those who stoned to death the first martyrs must have been worse men than they themselves are, ought to remember that one of those persecutors was Saint Paul.

. . .

Before quitting the subject of freedom of opinion, it is fit to take some notice of those who say, that the free expression of all opinions should be permitted, on condition that the manner be temperate, and do not pass the bounds of fair discussion. Much might be said on the impossibility of fixing where these supposed bounds are to be placed; for if the test be offence to those whose opinions are attacked, I think experience testifies that this offence is given whenever the attack is telling and powerful, and that every opponent who pushes them hard, and whom they find it difficult to answer, appears to them, if he shows any strong feeling on the subject, an intemperate opponent. But this, though an important consideration in a practical point of view, merges in a more fundamental objection. Undoubtedly the manner of asserting an opinion, even though it be a true one, may be very objectionable, and may justly incur severe censure. But the principal offences of the kind are such as it is mostly impossible, unless by accidental self-betrayal, to bring home to conviction. The gravest of them is, to argue sophistically, to suppress facts or arguments, to misstate the elements of the case, or misrepresent the opposite opinion. But all this, even to the most aggravated degree, is so continually done in perfect good faith, by persons who are not considered, and in many other respects may not deserve to be considered, ignorant or incompetent, that it is rarely possible, on adequate grounds, conscientiously to stamp the misrepresentation as morally culpable; and still less could law presume to interfere with this kind of controversial misconduct. With regard to what is commonly meant by intemperate discussion, namely, invective, sarcasm, personality, and the like, the denunciation of these weapons would deserve more sympathy if it were ever proposed to interdict them equally to both sides; but it is only desired to restrain the employment of them against the prevailing opinion: against the unprevailing they may not only be used without general disapproval, but will be likely to obtain for him who uses them the praise of honest zeal and righteous indignation. Yet whatever mischief arises from their use, is greatest when they are employed against the comparatively defenceless; and whatever unfair advantage can be derived by an opinion from this mode of asserting it, accrues almost exclusively to received opinions. The worst offence of this kind which can be committed by a polemic, is to stigmatize those who hold the contrary opinion as bad and immoral men. To calumny of this sort, those who hold any unpopular opinion are peculiarly exposed, because they are in general few and uninfluential, and nobody but themselves feels much interested in seeing justice done them; but this weapon is, from the nature of the case, denied to those who attack a prevailing opinion: they can neither use it with safety to themselves, nor, if they could, would it do anything but recoil on their own cause. In general, opinions contrary to those commonly received can only obtain a hearing by studied moderation of language, and the most cautious avoidance of unnecessary offence, from which they hardly ever deviate even in a slight degree without losing ground: while unmeasured vituperation employed on the side of the prevailing opinion, really does deter people from professing contrary opinions, and from listening to those who profess them. For the interest, therefore, of truth and justice, it is far more important to restrain this employment of vituperative language than the other; and, for example, if it were necessary to choose, there would be much more need to discourage offensive attacks on infidelity than on religion. It is, however, obvious that law and authority have no business with restraining either, while opinion ought, in every instance, to determine its verdict by the circumstances of the individual case; condemning every one, on whichever side of the argument he places himself, in whose mode of advocacy either want of candor, or malignity, bigotry, or intolerance of feeling manifest themselves; but not inferring these vices from the side which a person takes, though it be the contrary side of the question to our own: and giving merited honor to every one, whatever opinion he may hold, who has calmness to see and honesty to state what his opponents and their opinions really are, exaggerating nothing to their discredit, keeping nothing back which tells, or can be supposed to tell, in their favor. This is the real morality of public discussion: and if often violated, I am happy to think that there are many controversialists who to a great extent observe it, and a still greater number who conscientiously strive towards it.

Chapter III

OF INDIVIDUALITY, AS ONE OF THE ELEMENTS OF WELL-BEING

Such being the reasons which make it imperative that human beings should be free to form opinions, and to express their opinions without reserve; and such the baneful consequences to the intellectual, and through that to the moral nature of man, unless this liberty is either conceded, or asserted in spite of prohibition; let us next examine whether the same reasons do not require that men should be free to act upon their opinions—to carry these out in their lives, without hindrance, either physical or moral, from their fellow-men, so long as it is at their own risk and peril. This last proviso is of course indispensable. No one pretends that actions should be as free as opinions. On the contrary, even opinions lose their immunity, when the circumstances in which they are expressed are such as to constitute their expression a positive instigation to some mischievous act. An opinion that corn-dealers are starvers of the poor, or that private property is robbery, ought to be unmolested when simply circulated through the press, but may justly incur punishment when delivered orally to an excited mob, assembled before the house of a corn-dealer, or when handed about among the same mob in the form of a placard. Acts, of whatever kind, which, without justifiable cause, do harm to others, may be, and in the more important cases absolutely require to be, controlled by the unfavorable sentiments, and, when needful, by the active interference of mankind. The liberty of the individual must be thus far limited; he must not make himself a nuisance to other people. But if he refrains from molesting others in what concerns them, and merely acts according to his own inclination and judgment in things which concern himself, the same reasons which show that opinion should be free, prove also that he should be allowed, without molestation, to carry his opinions into practice at his own cost. That mankind are not infallible; that their truths, for the most part, are only half-truths; that unity of opinion, unless resulting from the fullest and freest comparison of opposite opinions, is not desirable, and diversity not an evil, but a good, until mankind are much more capable than at present of recognizing all sides of the truth, are principles applicable to men's modes of action, not less than to their opinions. As it is useful that while mankind are imperfect there should be different opinions, so it is that there should be different experiments of living; that free scope should be given to varieties of character short of injury to others; and that the worth of different modes of life should be proved practically, when any one thinks fit to try them. It is desirable, in short, that in things which do not primarily concern others, individuality should assert itself. Where, not the person's own character, but the traditions or customs of other people are the rule of conduct, there is wanting one of the principal ingredients of human happiness, and quite the chief ingredient of individual and social progress.

In maintaining this principle, the greatest difficulty to be encountered does not lie in the appreciation of means towards an acknowledged end, but in the indifference of persons in general to the end itself. If it were felt that the free development of individuality is one of the leading essentials of well-being; that it is not only a co-ordinate element with all that is designated by the terms civilization, instruction, education, culture, but is itself a necessary part and condition of all those things; there would be no danger that liberty should be under-valued, and the adjustment of the boundaries between it and social control would present no extraordinary difficulty. But the evil is, that individual spontaneity is hardly recognized by the common modes of thinking, as having any intrinsic worth, or deserving any regard on its own account. The majority, being satisfied with the ways of mankind as they now are (for it is they who make them what they are), cannot comprehend why those ways should not be good enough for everybody; and what is more, spontaneity forms no part of the ideal of the majority of moral and social reformers, but is rather looked on with jealousy, as a troublesome and perhaps rebellious obstruction to the general acceptance of what these reformers, in their own judgment, think would be best for mankind. Few persons, out of Germany, even comprehend the meaning of the doctrine which Wilhelm von Humboldt, so eminent both as a *savant* and as a politician, made the text of a treatise—that "the end of man, or that which is prescribed by the eternal or immutable dictates of reason, and not suggested by vague and transient desires, is the highest and most harmonious development of his powers to a complete and consistent whole"; that, therefore, the object "towards which every human being must ceaselessly direct his efforts, and on which especially those who design to influence their fellow-men must ever keep their eyes, is the individuality of power and development," that for this there are two requisites, "freedom, and variety of situations"; and that from the union of these arise "individual vigor and manifold diversity," which combine themselves in "originality."

Little, however, as people are accustomed to a doctrine like that of Von Humboldt and surprising as it may be to them to find so high a value attached to individuality, the question one must nevertheless think, can only be one of degree. No one's idea of excellence in conduct is that people should do absolutely nothing but copy one another. No one would assert that people ought not to put into their mode of life, and into the conduct of their concerns, any impress whatever of their own judgment, or of their own individual character. On the other hand, it would be absurd to pretend that people ought to live as if nothing whatever had been known in the world before they came into it; as if experience had as yet done nothing towards showing that one mode of existence, or of conduct, is preferable to another. Nobody denies that people should be so taught and trained in youth, as to know and benefit by the ascertained results of human experience. But it is the privilege and proper condition of a human being, arrived at the maturity of his faculties, to use and interpret experience in his own way. It is for him to find out what part of recorded experience is properly applicable to his own circumstances and character. The traditions and customs of other people are, to a certain extent, evidence of what their experience has taught *them;* presumptive evidence, and as such, have a claim to his deference: but, in the first place, their experience may be too narrow; or they may not have interpreted it rightly. Secondly, their interpretation of experience may be correct, but unsuitable to him. Customs are made for customary circumstances, and customary characters; and his circumstances or his character may be uncustomary. Thirdly, though the customs be both good as customs, and suitable to him yet to conform to custom, merely *as* custom, does not educate or develop in him any of the qualities which are the distinctive endowment of a human being. The human faculties of perception, judgment, discriminative feeling, mental activity, and even moral preference, are exercised only in making a choice. He who does anything because it is the custom, makes no choice. He gains no practice either in discerning or in desiring what is best. The mental and moral, like the muscular powers, are improved only by being used. The faculties are called into no exercise by doing a thing merely because others do it, no more than by believing a thing only because others believe it. If the grounds of an opinion are not conclusive to the person's own reason, his reason cannot be strengthened, but is likely to be weakened, by his adopting it: and if the inducements to an act are not such as are consentaneous to his own feelings and character (where affection, or the rights of others, are not concerned) it is so much done towards rendering his feelings and character inert and torpid, instead of active and energetic.

He who lets the world, or his own portion of it, choose his plan of life for him, has no need of any other faculty than the ape-like one of imitation. He who chooses his plan for himself, employs all his faculties. He must use observation to see, reasoning and judgment to foresee, activity to gather materials for decision, discrimination to decide, and when he has decided, firmness and self-control to hold to his deliberate decision. And these qualities he requires and exercises exactly in proportion as the part of his conduct which he determines according to his own judgment and feelings is a large one. It is possible that he might be guided in some good path, and kept out of harm's way, without any of these things. But what will be his comparative worth as a human being? It really is of importance, not only what men do, but also what manner of men they are that do it. Among the works of man, which human life is rightly employed in perfecting and beautifying, the first in importance surely is man himself. Supposing it were possible to get houses built, corn grown, battles fought, causes tried, and even churches erected and prayers said, by machinery—by automatons in human form—it would be a considerable loss to exchange for these automatons even the men and women who at present inhabit the more civilized parts of the world, and who assuredly are but starved specimens of what nature can and will produce. Human nature is not a machine to be built after a model, and set to do exactly the work prescribed for it, but a tree, which requires to grow and develop itself on all sides, according to the tendency of the inward forces which make it a living thing.

It will probably be conceded that it is desirable people should exercise their understandings, and that an intelligent following of custom, or even occasionally an intelligent deviation from custom, is better than a blind and simply mechanical adhesion to it. To a certain extent it is admitted, that our understanding should be our own: but there is not the same willingness to admit that our desires and impulses should be our own likewise; or that to possess impulses of our own, and of any strength, is anything but a peril and a snare. Yet desires and impulses are as much a part of a perfect human being, as beliefs and restraints: and strong impulses are only perilous when not properly balanced; when one set of aims and inclinations is developed into strength, while others, which ought to co-exist with them, remain weak and inactive. It is not because men's desires are strong that they are ill; it is because their consciences are weak. There is no natural connection between strong impulses and a weak conscience. The natural connection is the other way. To say that one person's desires and feelings are stronger and more various than those of another, is merely to say that he has more of the raw material of human nature, and is therefore capable, perhaps of more evil, but certainly of more good. Strong impulses are but another name for energy. Energy may be turned to bad uses; but more good may always be made of an energetic nature, than of an indolent and impassive one. Those who have most natural feeling, are always those whose cultivated feelings may be made the strongest. The same strong susceptibilities which make the personal impulses vivid and powerful, are also the source from whence are generated the most passionate love of virtue, and the sternest self-control. It is through the cultivation of these, that society both does its duty and protects its interests: not by rejecting the stuff of which heroes are made, because it knows not how to make them. A person whose desires and impulses are his own—are the expression of his own nature, as it has been developed and modified by his own culture—is said to have a character. One whose desires and impulses are not his own, has no character, no more than a steam-engine has a character. If, in addition to being his own, his impulses are strong, and are under the government of a strong will, he has an energetic character. Whoever thinks that individuality of desires and impulses should not be encouraged to unfold itself, must maintain that society has no need of strong natures—is not the better for containing many persons who have much character—and that a high general average of energy is not desirable.

In some early states of society, these forces might be, and were, too much ahead of the power which society then possessed of disciplining and controlling them. There has been a time when the element of spontaneity and individuality was in excess and the social principle had a hard struggle with it. The difficulty then was, to induce men of strong bodies or minds to pay obedience to any rules which required them to control their impulses. To overcome this difficulty, law and discipline, like the Popes struggling against the Emperors, asserted a power over the whole man, claiming to control all his life in order to control his character—which society had not found any other sufficient means of binding. But society has now fairly got the better of individuality; and the danger which threatens human nature is not the excess, but the deficiency, of personal impulses and preferences. Things are vastly changed, since the passions of those who were strong by station or by personal endowment were in a state of habitual rebellion against laws and ordinances, and required to be rigorously chained up to enable the persons within their reach to enjoy any particle of security. In our times, from the highest class of society down to the lowest, every one lives as under the eye of a hostile and dreaded censorship. Not only in what concerns others, but in what concerns only themselves, the individual or the family do not ask themselves—what do I prefer? or, what would suit my character and disposition? or, what would allow the best and highest in me to have fair play, and enable it to grow and thrive? They ask themselves, what is suitable to my position? what is usually done by persons of my station and pecuniary circumstances? or (worse still) what is usually done by persons of a station and circumstances superior to mine? I do not mean that they choose what is customary, in preference to what suits their own inclination. It does not occur to them to have any inclination, except for what is customary. Thus the mind itself is bowed to the yoke: even in what people do for pleasure, conformity is the first thing thought of; they like in crowds; they exercise choice only among things commonly done: peculiarity of taste, eccentricity of conduct, are shunned equally with crimes: until by dint of not following their own nature, they have no nature to follow: their human capacities are withered and starved: they become incapable of any strong wishes or native pleasures, and are generally without either opinions or feelings of home growth, or properly their own. Now is this, or is it not, the desirable condition of human nature?

It is so, on the Calvinistic theory. According to that, the one great offence of man is self-will. All the good of which humanity is capable, is comprised in obedience. You have no choice; thus you must do, and no otherwise: "whatever is not a duty, is a sin." Human nature being radically corrupt, there is no redemption for any one until human nature is killed within him. To one holding this theory of life, crushing out any of the human faculties, capacities, and susceptibilities, is no evil: man needs no capacity, but that of surrendering himself to the will of God: and if he uses any of his faculties for any other purpose but to do that supposed will more effectually, he is better without them. This is the theory of Calvinism; and it is held, in a mitigated form by many who do not consider themselves Calvinists; the mitigation consisting in giving a less ascetic interpretation to the alleged will of God; asserting it to be his will that mankind should gratify some of their inclinations; of course not in the manner they themselves prefer, but in the way of obedience, that is, in a way prescribed to them by authority; and, therefore, by the necessary condition of the case, the same for all.

In some such insidious form, there is at present a strong tendency to this narrow theory of life, and to the pinched and hidebound type of human character which it patronizes. Many persons, no doubt, sincerely think that human beings thus cramped and dwarfed, are as their Maker designed them to be; just as many have thought that trees are a much finer thing when clipped into pollards, or cut out into figures of animals, than as nature made them. But if it be any part of religion to believe that man was made by a good Being, it is more consistent with that faith to believe, that this Being gave all human faculties that they might be cultivated and unfolded, not rooted out and consumed, and that he takes delight in every nearer approach made by his creatures to the ideal conception embodied in them, every increase in any of their capabilities of comprehension, of action, or of enjoyment. There is a different type of human excellence from the Calvinistic: a conception of humanity as having its nature bestowed on it for other purposes than merely to be abnegated. "Pagan self-assertion" is one of the elements of human worth, as well as "Christian self-denial." There is a Greek ideal of self-development, which the Platonic and Christian ideal of self-government blends with, but does not supersede. It may be better to be a John Knox than an Alcibiades, but it is better to be a Pericles than either; nor would a Pericles, if we had one in these days, be without anything good which belonged to John Knox.

It is not by wearing down into uniformity all that is individual in themselves, but by cultivating it, and calling it forth, within the limits imposed by the rights and interests of others, that human beings become a noble and beautiful object of contemplation; and as the works partake the character of those who do them, by the same process human life also becomes rich, diversified, and animating, furnishing more abundant aliment to high thoughts and elevating feelings, and strengthening the tie which binds every individual to the race, by making the race infinitely better worth belonging to. In proportion to the development of his individuality, each person becomes more valuable to himself, and is therefore capable of being more valuable to others. There is a great fullness of life about his own existence, and when there is more life in the units there is more in the mass which is composed of them. As much compression as is necessary to prevent the stronger specimens of human nature from encroaching on the rights of others, cannot be dispensed with; but for this there is ample compensation even in the point of view of human development. The means of development which the individual loses by being prevented from gratifying his inclinations to the injury of others, are chiefly obtained at the expense of the development of other people. And even to himself there is a full equivalent in the better development of the social part of his nature, rendered possible by the restraint put upon the selfish part. To be held to rigid rules of justice for the sake of others, develops the feelings and capacities which have the good of others for their object. But to be restrained in things not affecting their good by their mere displeasure, develops nothing valuable, except such force of character as may unfold itself in resisting the restraint. If acquiesced in, it dulls and blunts the whole nature. To give any fair play to the nature of each, it is essential that different persons should be allowed to lead different lives. In proportion as this latitude has been exercised in any age, has that age been noteworthy to posterity. Even despotism does not produce its worst effects, so long as individuality exists under it; and whatever crushes individuality is despotism, by whatever name it may be called, and whether it professes to be enforcing the will of God or the injunctions of men.

CHARLES DARWIN

In 1831, having graduated from Cambridge University where he had been a theology student, Charles Darwin (1809–1882) accepted the position of naturalist aboard the ship Beagle, *which was setting sail on an extended surveying expedition to South America and the Pacific. During the voyage, which lasted five years, Darwin observed plant and animal life in widely scattered areas of the earth, gathering the evidence on which he was later to base his theory of biological evolution. To render the theory of evolution plausible, however, Darwin had to overcome two obstacles: First, he had to find evidence that the earth was old enough to provide time for the evolutionary process to have taken place, and, second, he had to provide an explanation of this process.*

His first problem was solved by the geologist, Sir Charles Lyell, whose Principles of Geology *(published in 1830) established the fact that the earth had existed through vast periods of geological time. The clue to the solution of his second problem came from Malthus's* Essay on Population, *with its view that organic beings multiply faster than their food supply. Starting from Malthus's assumption, Darwin undertook in The* Origin of Species *to deduce the process by which biological evolution is accomplished and to provide empirical evidence to support his deduction. Darwin's theory of evolution, in its assumption that new species evolve from older ones, repudiated the doctrine, which had stemmed from Aristotle and had been defended on theological grounds from the time of the Middle Ages, of the immutability of species. Thus it marked a major revolution in the history of thought.*

The selections that follow are taken from Darwin's two great works, The Origin of Species *and* The Descent of Man. *The first book, which was published in 1859, contains Darwin's statement of the theory of biological evolution, along with the evidence on which it rests. In the second, published in 1871, Darwin completes his theory by including man within the evolutionary process.*

The Origin of Species

. . .

Nothing is easier than to admit in words the truth of the universal struggle for life, or more difficult—at least I have found it so—than constantly to bear this conclusion in mind. Yet unless it be thoroughly engrained in the mind, the whole economy of nature, with every fact on distribution, rarity, abundance, extinction, and variation, will be dimly seen or quite misunderstood. We behold the face of nature bright with gladness, we often see superabundance of food; we do not see or we forget, that the birds which are idly singing round us

Charles Darwin, THE ORIGIN OF SPECIES, BY MEANS OF NATURAL SELECTION OR THE PRESERVATION OF FAVOURED RACES IN THE STRUGGLE FOR LIFE, *6th ed. (London, 1900).*

mostly live on insects or seeds, and are thus constantly destroying life; or we forget how largely these songsters, or their eggs, or their nestlings, are destroyed by birds and beasts of prey; we do not always bear in mind, that, though food may be now superabundant, it is not so at all seasons of each recurring year.

. . .

A struggle for existence inevitably follows from the high rate at which all organic beings tend to increase. Every being, which during its natural lifetime produces several eggs or seeds, must suffer destruction during some period of its life, and during some season or occasional year, otherwise, on the principle of geometrical increase, its numbers would quickly become so inordinately great that no country could support the product. Hence, as more individuals are produced than can possibly survive, there must in every case be a struggle for existence, either one individual with another of the same species, or with the individuals of distinct species, or with the physical conditions of life. It is the doctrine of Malthus applied with manifold force to the whole animal and vegetable kingdoms; for in this case there can be no artificial increase of food, and no prudential restraint from marriage. Although some species may be now increasing, more or less rapidly, in numbers, all cannot do so, for the world would not hold them.

There is no exception to the rule that every organic being naturally increases at so high a rate, that, if not destroyed, the earth would soon be covered by the progeny of a single pair. Even slow-breeding man has doubled in twenty-five years, and at this rate, in less than a thousand years, there would literally not be standing-room for his progeny. Linneaus has calculated that if an annual plant produced only two seeds—and there is no plant so unproductive as this—and their seedlings next year produced two, and so on, then in twenty years there would be a million plants. The elephant is reckoned the slowest breeder of all known animals, and I have taken some pains to estimate its probable minimum rate of natural increase; it will be safest to assume that it begins breeding when thirty years old, and goes on breeding till ninety years old, bringing forth six young in the interval, and surviving till one hundred years old; if this be so, after a period of from 740 to 750 years there would be nearly nineteen million elephants alive, descended from the first pair.

But we have better evidence on this subject than mere theoretical calculations, namely, the numerous recorded cases of the astonishingly rapid increase of various animals in a state of nature, when circumstances have been favourable to them during two or three following seasons. Still more striking is the evidence from our domestic animals of many kinds which have run wild in several parts of the world; if the statements of the rate of increase of slow-breeding cattle and horses in South America, and latterly in Australia, had not been well authenticated, they would have been incredible. So it is with plants; cases could be given of introduced plants which have become common throughout whole islands in a period of less than ten years. Several of the plants, such as the cardoon and a tall thistle, which are now the commonest over the wide plains of La Plata, clothing square leagues of surface almost to the exclusion of every other plant, have been introduced from Europe; and there are plants which now range in India, as I hear from Dr. Falconer, from Cape Comorin to the Himalaya, which have been imported from America since its discovery. In such cases, and endless others could be given, no one supposes, that the fertility of the animals or plants has been suddenly and temporarily increased in any sensible degree. The obvious explanation is that the conditions of life have been highly favourable, and that there has consequently been less destruction of the old and young, and that nearly all the young have been enabled to breed. Their geometrical ratio of increase, the result of which never fails to be surprising, simply explains their extraordinarily rapid increase and wide diffusion in their new homes.

In a state of nature almost every full-grown plant annually produces seeds, and amongst animals there are very few which do not annually pair. Hence we may confidently assert, that all plants and animals are tending to increase at a geometrical ratio,—that all would rapidly stock every station in which they could anyhow exist, —and that this geometrical tendency to increase must be checked by destruction at some period of life. Our familiarity with the larger domestic animals tends, I think, to mislead us: we see no great destruction falling on them, but we do not keep in mind that thousands are annually slaughtered for food, and that in a state of nature an equal number would have somehow to be disposed of.

The only difference between organisms which annually produce eggs or seeds by the thousand, and those which produce extremely few, is, that the slow-breeders would require a few more years to people, under favourable conditions, a whole district, let it be ever so large. The condor lays a couple of eggs and the ostrich a score, and yet in the same country the condor may be the more numerous of the two; the Fulmar petrel lays but one egg, yet it is believed to be the most numerous bird in the world. One fly deposits hundreds of eggs, and another, like the hippobosca, a single one; but this difference does not determine how many individuals of the two species can be supported in a district. A large number of eggs is of some importance to those species which depend on a fluctuating amount of food, for it allows them rapidly to increase in number. But the real importance of a large number of eggs or seeds is to make up for much destruction at some period of life; and this period in the great majority of cases is an early one. If an animal can in any way protect its own eggs or young, a small number may be produced, and yet the average stock be fully kept up; but if many eggs or young are destroyed, many must be produced, or the species will become extinct. It would suffice to keep up the full number of a tree, which lived on an average for a thousand years, if a single seed were produced once in a thousand years, supposing that this seed were never destroyed, and could be ensured to germinate in a fitting place. So that, in all cases, the average number of any animal or plant depends only indirectly on the number of its eggs or seeds.

In looking at Nature, it is most necessary to keep the foregoing considerations always in mind—never to forget that every single organic being may be said to be striving to the utmost to increase in numbers; that each lives by a struggle at some period of its life; that heavy destruction inevitably falls either on the young or old, during each generation or at recurrent intervals. Lighten any check, mitigate the destruction ever so little, and the number of the species will almost instantaneously increase to any amount.

The causes which check the natural tendency of each species to increase are most obscure. Look at the most vigorous species; by as much as it swarms in numbers, by so much will it tend to increase still further. We know not exactly what the checks are even in a single instance. Nor will this surprise any one who reflects how ignorant we are on this head, even in regard to mankind, although so incomparably better known than any other animal. This subject of the checks to increase has been ably treated by several authors, and I hope in a future work to discuss it at considerable length, more especially in regard to the feral animals of South America. Here I will make only a few remarks, just to recall to the reader's mind some of the chief points. Eggs or very young animals seem generally to suffer most, but this is not invariably the case. With plants there is a vast destruction of seeds, but, from some observations which I have made it appears that the seedlings suffer most from germinating in ground already thickly stocked with other plants. Seedlings, also, are destroyed in vast numbers by various enemies; for instance, on a piece of ground three feet long and two wide, dug and cleared, and where there could be no choking from other plants, I marked all the seedlings of our native weeds as they came up, and out of 357 no less than 295 were destroyed, chiefly by slugs and insects. If turf which has long been mown, and the case would be the same with turf closely browsed by quadrupeds, be let to grow, the more vigorous plants gradually kill the less vigorous, though fully grown plants; thus out of twenty species growing on a little plot of mown turf (three feet by four) nine species perished, from the other species being allowed to grow up freely.

The amount of food for each species of course gives the extreme limit to which each can increase; but very frequently it is not the obtaining food, but the serving as prey to other animals, which determines the average number of a species. Thus, there seems to be little doubt that the stock of partridges, grouse, and hares on any large estate depends chiefly on the destruction of vermin. If not one head of game were shot during the next twenty years in England, and, at the same time, if no vermin were destroyed, there would, in all probability, be less game than at present, although hundreds of thousands of game animals are now annually shot. On the other hand, in some cases, as with the elephant, none are destroyed by beasts of prey; for even the tiger in India most rarely dares to attack a young elephant protected by its dam.

. . .

Many cases are on record showing how complex and unexpected are the checks and relations between organic beings, which have to struggle together in the same country.

. . .

[*I give an*] instance showing how plants and animals, remote in the scale of nature, are bound together by a web of complex relations. I shall hereafter have occasion to show that the exotic Lobelia fulgens is never visited in my garden by insects, and consequently, from its peculiar structure, never sets a seed. Nearly all our orchidaceous plants absolutely require the visits of insects to remove their pollen-masses and thus to fertilise them. I find from experiments that humble-bees are almost indispensable to the fertilisation of the heartsease (Violo tricolor), for other bees do not visit this flower. I have also found that the visits of bees are necessary for the fertilisation of some kinds of clover; for instance, 20 heads of Dutch clover (Trifolium repens) yielded 2,290 seeds, but 20 other heads protected from bees produced not one. Again, 100 heads of red clover (T. pratense) produced 2,700 seeds, but the same number of protected heads produced not a single seed. Humble-bees alone visit red clover, as other bees cannot reach the nectar. It has been suggested that moths may fertilise the clovers; but I doubt whether they could do so in the case of the red clover, from their weight not being sufficient to depress the wing petals. Hence we may infer as highly probable that, if the whole genus of humble-bees became extinct or very rare in England, the heartsease and red clover would become very rare, or wholly disappear. The number of humble-bees in any district depends in a great measure upon the number of field-mice, which destroy their combs and nests; and Col. Newman, who has long attended to the habits of humble-bees, believes that "more than two-thirds of them are thus destroyed all over England." Now the number of mice is largely dependent, as every one knows, on the number of cats; and Col. Newman says, "Near villages and small towns I have found the nests of humble-bees more numerous than elsewhere, which I attribute to the number of cats that destroy the mice." Hence it is quite credible that the presence of a feline animal in large numbers in a district might determine, through the intervention first of mice and then of bees, the frequency of certain flowers in that district!

. . .

If under changing conditions of life organic beings present individual differences in almost every part of their structure, and this cannot be disputed; if there be, owing to their geometrical rate of increase, a severe struggle for life at some age, season, or year, and this certainly cannot be disputed; then, considering the infinite complexity of the relations of all organic beings to each other and to their conditions of life, causing an infinite diversity in structure, constitution, and habits, to be advantageous to them, it would be a most extraordinary fact if no variations had ever occurred useful to each being's own welfare, in the same manner as so many variations have occurred useful to man. But if variations useful to any organic being ever do occur, assuredly individuals thus characterised will have the best chance of being preserved in the struggle for life; and from the strong principle of inheritance, these will tend to produce offspring similarly characterised. This principle of preservation, or the survival of the fittest, I have called Natural Selection. It leads to the improvement of each creature in relation to its organic and inorganic conditions of life; and consequently, in most cases, to what must be regarded as an advance in organisation. Nevertheless, low and simple forms will long endure if well fitted for their simple conditions of life.

Natural selection, on the principle of qualities being inherited at corresponding ages, can modify the egg, seed, or young, as easily as the adult. Amongst many animals, sexual selection will have given its aid to ordinary selection, by assuring to the most vigorous and best adapted males the greatest number of offspring. Sexual selection will also give characters useful to the males alone, in their struggles or rivalry with other males; and these characters will be transmitted to one sex or to both sexes, according to the form of inheritance which prevails.

Whether natural selection has really thus acted in adapting the various forms of life to their several conditions and stations, must be judged by the general tenor and balance of evidence given in the following chapters. But we have already seen how it entails extinction; and how largely extinction has acted in the world's history, geology plainly declares. Natural selection, also, leads to divergence of character; for the more organic beings diverge in structure, habits, and constitution, by so much the more can a large number be supported on the area,—of which we see proof by looking to the inhabitants of any small spot, and to the productions naturalised in foreign lands. Therefore, during the modification of the descendants of any one species, and during the incessant struggle of all species to increase in numbers, the more diversified the descendants become, the better will be their chance of success in the battle for life. Thus the small differences distinguishing varieties of the same species, steadily tend to increase, till they equal the greater differences between species of the same genus, or even of distinct genera.

We have seen that it is the common, the widely-diffused and widely-ranging species, belonging to the larger genera within each class, which vary most; and these tend to transmit to their modified offspring that superiority which now makes them dominant in their own countries. Natural selection, as has just been remarked, leads to divergence of character and to much extinction of the less improved and intermediate forms of life. On these principles, the nature of the affinities, and the generally well-defined distinctions between the innumerable organic beings in each class throughout the world, may be explained. It is a truly wonderful fact—the wonder of which we are apt to overlook from familiarity—that all animals and all plants throughout all time and space should be related to each other in groups, subordinate to groups, in the manner which we everywhere behold—namely, varieties of the same species most closely related, species of the same genus less closely and unequally related, forming sections and sub-genera, species of distinct genera much less closely related, and genera related in different degrees, forming sub-families, families, orders, sub-classes and classes. The several subordinate groups in any class cannot be ranked in a single file, but seem clustered round points, and these round other points, and so on in almost endless cycles. If species had been independently created, no explanation would have been possible of this kind of classification; but it is explained through inheritance and the complex action of natural selection, entailing extinction and divergence of character, as we have seen illustrated in the diagram.

The affinities of all the beings of the same class have sometimes been represented by a great tree. I believe this simile largely speaks the truth. The green and budding twigs may represent existing species; and those produced during former years may represent the long succession of extinct species. At each period of growth all the growing twigs have tried to branch out on all sides, and to overtop and kill the surrounding twigs and branches, in the same manner as species and groups of species have at all times overmastered other species in the great battle for life. The limbs divided into great branches, and these into lesser and lesser branches, were themselves once, when the tree was young, budding twigs; and this connection of the former and present buds by ramifying branches may well represent the classification of all extinct and living species in groups subordinate to groups. Of the many twigs which flourished when the tree was a mere bush, only two or three, now grown into great branches, yet survive and bear the other branches; so with the species which lived during long-past geological periods, very few have left living and modified descendants. From the first growth of the tree, many a limb and branch has decayed and dropped off; and these fallen branches of various sizes may represent those whole orders, families, and genera which have now no living representatives, and which are known to us only in a fossil state. As we here and there see a thin straggling branch springing from a fork low down in a tree, and which by some chance has been favoured and is still alive on its summit, so we occasionally see an animal like the Ornithorhynchus or Lepidosiren, which in some small degree connects by its affinities two large branches of life, and which has apparently been saved from fatal competition by having inhabited a protected station. As buds give rise by growth to fresh buds, and these, if vigorous, branch out and overtop on all sides many a feebler branch, so by generation I believe it has been with the great Tree of Life, which fills with its dead and broken branches the crust of the earth, and covers the surface with its ever-branching and beautiful ramifications.

. . .

I have now recapitulated the facts and considerations which have thoroughly convinced me that species have been modified, during a long course of descent. This has been effected chiefly through the natural selection of numerous successive, slight, favourable variations; aided in an important manner by the inherited effects of the use and disuse of parts; and in an unimportant manner, that is in relation to adaptive structures, whether past or present, by the direct action of external conditions, and by variations which seem to us in our ignorance to rise spontaneously. It appears that I formerly underrated the frequency and value of these latter forms of variation, as leading to permanent modifications of structure independently of natural selection. But as my conclusions have lately been much misrepresented, and it has been stated that I attribute the modification of species exclusively to natural selection, I may be permitted to remark that in the first edition of this work, and subsequently, I placed in a most conspicuous position—namely, at the close of the Introduction—the following words: "I am convinced that natural selection has been the main but not the exclusive means of modification." This has been of no avail. Great is the power of steady misrepresentation; but the history of science shows that fortunately this power does not long endure.

It can hardly be supposed that a false theory would explain, in so satisfactory a manner as does the theory of natural selection, the several large classes of facts above specified. It has recently been objected that this is an unsafe method of arguing; but it is a method used in judging of the common events of life, and has often been used by the greatest natural philosophers. The undulatory theory of light has thus been arrived at, and the belief in the revolution of the earth on its own axis was until lately supported by hardly any direct evidence. It is no valid objection that science as yet throws no light on the far higher problem of the essence or origin of life. Who can explain what is the essence of the attraction of gravity? No one now objects to following out the results consequent on this unknown element of attraction; notwithstanding that Leibnitz formerly accused Newton of introducing "occult qualities and miracles into philosophy."

I see no good reason why the views given in this volume should shock the religious feelings of any one. It is satisfactory, as showing how transient such impressions are, to remember that the greatest discovery ever made by man, namely, the law of the attraction of gravity, was also attacked by Leibnitz, "as subversive of natural, and inferentially of revealed, religion." A celebrated author and divine has written to me that "he has gradually learnt to see that it is just as noble a conception of the Deity to believe that He created a few original forms capable of self-development into other and needful forms, as to believe that He required a fresh act of creation to supply the voids caused by the action of His laws."

Why, it may be asked, until recently did nearly all the most eminent living naturalists and geologists disbelieve in the mutability of species. It cannot be asserted that organic beings in a state of nature are subject to no variation; it cannot be proved that the amount of variation in the course of long ages is a limited quantity; no clear distinction has been, or can be, drawn between species and well-marked varieties. It cannot be maintained that species when intercrossed are invariably sterile, and varieties invariably fertile; or that sterility is a special endowment and sign of creation. The belief that species were immutable productions was almost unavoidable as long as the history of the world was thought to be of short duration; and now that we have acquired some idea of the lapse of time, we are too apt to assume, without proof, that the geological record is so perfect that it would have afforded us plain evidence of the mutation of species, if they had undergone mutation.

But the chief cause of our natural unwillingness to admit that one species has given birth to other and distinct species, is that we are always slow in admitting great changes of which we do not see the steps. The difficulty is the same as that felt by so many geologists, when Lyell first insisted that long lines of inland cliffs had been formed, and great valleys excavated, by the agencies which we see still at work. The mind cannot possibly grasp the full meaning of the term of even a million years; it cannot add up and perceive the full effects of many slight variations, accumulated during an almost infinite number of generations.

Although I am fully convinced of the truth of the views given in this volume under the form of an abstract, I by no means expect to convince experienced naturalists whose minds are stocked with a multitude of facts all viewed, during a long course of years, from a point of view directly opposite to mine. It is so easy to hide our ignorance under such expressions as the "plan of creation," "unity of design," &c., and to think that we give an explanation when we only re-state a fact. Any one whose disposition leads him to attach more weight to unexplained difficulties than to the explanation of a certain number of facts will certainly reject the theory. A few naturalists, endowed with much flexibility of mind, and who have already begun to doubt the immutability of species, may be influenced by this volume; but I look with confidence to the future,—to young and rising naturalists, who will be able to view both sides of the question with impartiality. Whoever is led to believe that species are mutable will do good service by conscientiously expressing his conviction; for thus only can the load of prejudice by which this subject is overwhelmed be removed.

Several eminent naturalists have of late published their belief that a multitude of reputed species in each genus are not real species; but that other species are real, that is, have been independently created. This seems to me a strange conclusion to arrive at. They admit that a multitude of forms, which till lately they themselves thought were special creations, and which are still thus looked at by the majority of naturalists, and which consequently have all the external characteristic features of true species,—they admit that these have been produced by variation, but they refuse to extend the same view to other and slightly different forms. Nevertheless they do not pretend that they can define, or even conjecture, which are the created forms of life, and which are those produced by secondary laws. They admit variation as a *vera causa* in one case, they arbitrarily reject it in another, without assigning any distinction in the two cases. The day will come when this will be given as a curious illustration of the blindness of preconceived opinion. These authors seem no more startled at a miraculous act of creation than at an ordinary birth. But do they really believe that at innumerable periods in the earth's history certain elemental atoms have been commanded suddenly to flash into living tissues? Do they believe that at each supposed act of creation one individual or many were produced? Were all the infinitely numerous kinds of animals and plants created as eggs or seed, or as full grown? and in the case of mammals, were they created bearing the false marks of nourishment from the mother's womb? Undoubtedly some of these same questions cannot be answered by those who believe in the appearance or creation of only a few forms of life, or of some one form alone. It has been maintained by several authors that it is as easy to believe in the creation of a million beings as of one; but Maupertuis' philosophical axiom "of least action" leads the mind more willingly to admit the smaller number; and certainly we ought not to believe that innumerable beings within each great class have been created with plain, but deceptive, marks of descent from a single parent.

As a record of a former state of things, I have retained in the foregoing paragraphs, and elsewhere, several sentences which imply that naturalists believe in the separate creation of each species; and I have been much censured for having thus expressed myself. But undoubtedly this was the general belief when the first edition of the present work appeared. I formerly spoke to very many naturalists on the subject of evolution, and never once met with any sympathetic agreement. It is probable that some did then believe in evolution, but they were either silent, or expressed themselves so ambiguously that it was not easy to understand their meaning. Now things are wholly changed, and almost every naturalist admits the great principle of evolution. There are, however, some who still think that species have suddenly given birth, through quite unexplained means, to new and totally different forms: but, as I have attempted to show, weighty evidence can be opposed to the admission of great and abrupt modifications. Under a scientific point of view, and as leading to further investigation, but little advantage is gained by believing that new forms are suddenly developed in an inexplicable manner from old and widely different forms, over the old belief in the creation of species from the dust of the earth.

It may be asked how far I extend the doctrine of the modification of species. The question is difficult to answer, because the more distinct the forms are which we consider, by so much the arguments in favour of community of descent become fewer in number and less in force. But some arguments of the greatest weight extend very far. All the members of whole classes are connected together by a chain of affinities, and all can be classed on the same principle, in groups subordinate to groups. Fossil remains sometimes tend to fill up very wide intervals between existing orders.

Organs in a rudimentary condition plainly show that an early progenitor had the organ in a fully developed condition; and this in some cases implies an enormous amount of modification in the descendants. Throughout whole classes various structures are formed on the same pattern, and at a very early age the embryos closely resemble each other. Therefore I cannot doubt that the theory of descent with modification embraces all the members of the same great class or kingdom. I believe that animals are descended from at most only four or five progenitors, and plants from an equal or lesser number.

Analogy would lead me one step farther, namely, to the belief that all animals and plants are descended from some one prototype. But analogy may be a deceitful guide. Nevertheless all living things have much in common, in their chemical composition, their cellular structure, their laws of growth, and their liability to injurious influences. We see this even in so trifling a fact as that the same poison often similarly affects plants and animals; or that the poison secreted by the gall-fly produces monstrous growths on the wild rose or oak-tree. With all organic beings, excepting perhaps some of the very lowest, sexual reproduction seems to be essentially similar. With all, as far as is at present known, the germinal vesicle is the same; so that all organisms start from a common origin. If we look even to the two main divisions

—namely, to the animal and vegetable kingdoms—certain low forms are so far intermediate in character that naturalists have disputed to which kingdom they should be referred. As Professor Asa Gray has remarked, "the spores and other reproductive bodies of many of the lower algae may claim to have first a characteristically animal, and then an unequivocally vegetable existence." Therefore, on the principle of natural selection with divergence of character, it does not seem incredible that, from such low and intermediate form, both animals and plants may have been developed; and, if we admit this, we must likewise admit that all the organic beings which have ever lived on this earth may be descended from some one primordial form. But this inference is chiefly grounded on analogy, and it is immaterial whether or not it be accepted. No doubt it is possible, as Mr. G. H. Lewes has urged, that at the first commencement of life many different forms were evolved; but if so, we may conclude that only a very few have left modified descendants. For, as I have recently remarked in regard to the members of each great kingdom, such as the Vertebrata, Articulata, &c., we have distinct evidence in their embryological, homologous, and rudimentary structures, that within each kingdom all the members are descended from a single progenitor.

When the views advanced by me in this volume, and by Mr. Wallace, or when analogous views on the origin of species are generally admitted, we can dimly foresee that there will be a considerable revolution in natural history. Systematists will be able to pursue their labours as at present; but they will not be incessantly haunted by the shadowy doubt whether this or that form be a true species. This, I feel sure and I speak after experience, will be no slight relief. The endless disputes whether or not some fifty species of British brambles are good species will cease. Systematists will have only to decide (not that this will be easy) whether any form be sufficiently constant and distinct from other forms, to be capable of definition; and if definable, whether the differences be sufficiently important to deserve a specific name. This latter point will become a far more essential consideration than it is at present; for differences, however slight, between any two forms, if not blended by intermediate gradations, are looked at by most naturalists as sufficient to raise both forms to the rank of species.

Hereafter we shall be compelled to acknowledge that the only distinction between species and well-marked varieties is, that the latter are known, or believed, to be connected at the present day by intermediate gradations whereas species were formerly thus connected. Hence, without rejecting the consideration of the present existence of intermediate gradations between any two forms, we shall be led to weigh more carefully and to value higher the actual amount of difference between them. It is quite possible that forms now generally acknowledged to be merely varieties may hereafter be thought worthy of specific names; and in this case scientific and common language will come into accordance. In short, we shall have to treat species in the same manner as those naturalists treat genera, who admit that genera are merely artificial combinations made for convenience. This may not be a cheering prospect; but we shall at least be freed from the vain search for the undiscovered and undiscoverable essence of the term species.

The other and more general departments of natural history will rise greatly in interest. The terms used by naturalists, of affinity, relationship, community of type, paternity, morphology, adaptive characters, rudimentary and aborted organs, &c., will cease to be metaphorical, and will have a plain signification. When we no longer look at an organic being as a savage looks at a ship, as something wholly beyond his comprehension; when we regard every production of nature as one which has had a long history; when we contemplate every complex structure and instinct as the summing up of many contrivances, each useful to the possessor, in the same way as any great mechanical invention is the summing up of the labour, the experience, the reason, and even the blunders of numerous workmen; when we thus view each organic being, how far more interesting—I speak from experience—does the study of natural history become!

A grand and almost untrodden field of inquiry will be opened, on the causes and laws of variation, on correlation, on the effects of use and disuse, on the direct action of external conditions, and so forth. The study of domestic productions will rise immensely in value. A new variety raised by man will be a more important and interesting subject for study than one more species added to the infinitude of already recorded species. Our classifications will come to be, as far as they can be so made, genealogies; and will then truly give what may be called the plan of creation. The rules for classifying will no doubt become simpler when we have a definite object in view. We possess no pedigrees or armorial bearings; and we have to discover and trace the many diverging lines of descent in our natural genealogies, by characters of any kind which have long been inherited. Rudimentary organs will speak infallibly with respect to the nature of long-lost structures. Species and groups of species which are called aberrant, and which may fancifully be called living fossils, will aid us in forming a picture of the ancient forms of life. Embryology will often reveal to us the structure, in some degree obscured, of the prototypes of each great class.

When we can feel assured that all the individuals of the same species, and all the closely allied species of most genera, have within a not very remote period descended from one parent, and have migrated from some one birth-place; and when we better know the many means of migration, then, by the light which geology now throws, and will continue to throw, on former changes of climate and of the level of the land, we shall surely be enabled to trace in an admirable manner the former migrations of the inhabitants of the whole world. Even at present, by comparing the differences between the inhabitants of the sea on the opposite sides of a continent, and the nature of the various inhabitants on that continent in relation to their apparent means of immigration, some light can be thrown on ancient geography.

The noble science of Geology loses glory from the extreme imperfection of the record. The crust of the earth with its imbedded remains must not be looked at as a well-filled museum, but as a poor collection made at hazard and at rare intervals. The accumulation of each great fossiliferous formation will be recognised as having depended on an unusual concurrence of favourable circumstances, and the blank intervals between the successive stages as having been of vast duration. But we shall be able to gauge with some security the duration of these intervals by a comparison of the preceding and succeeding organic forms. We must be cautious in attempting to correlate as strictly contemporaneous two formations, which do not include many identical species, by the general succession of the forms of life. As species are produced and exterminated by slowly acting and still existing causes, and not by miraculous acts of creation; and as the most important of all causes of organic change is one which is almost independent of altered and perhaps suddenly altered physical conditions, namely, the mutual relation of organism to organism,

—the improvement of one organism entailing the improvement or the extermination of others; it follows, that the amount of organic change in the fossils of consecutive formations probably serves as a fair measure of the relative, though not actual lapse of time. A number of species, however, keeping in a body might remain for a long period unchanged, whilst within the same period several of these species by migrating into new countries and coming into competition with foreign associates, might become modified; so that we must not overrate the accuracy of organic change as a measure of time.

In the future I see open fields for far more important researches. Psychology will be securely based on the foundation already well laid by Mr. Herbert Spencer, that of the necessary acquirement of each mental power and capacity by gradation. Much light will be thrown on the origin of man and his history.

Authors of the highest eminence seem to be fully satisfied with the view that each species has been independently created. To my mind it accords better with what we know of the laws impressed on matter by the Creator, that the production and extinction of the past and present inhabitants of the world should have been due to secondary causes, like those determining the birth and death of the individual. When I view all beings not as special creations, but as the lineal descendants of some few beings which lived long before the first bed of the Cambrian system was deposited, they seem to me to become ennobled. Judging from the past, we may safely infer that not one living species will transmit its unaltered likeness to a distant futurity. And of the species now living very few will transmit progeny of any kind to a far distant futurity; for the manner in which all organic beings are grouped, shows that the greater number of species in each genus, and all the species in many genera, have left no descendants, but have become utterly extinct. We can so far take a prophetic glance into futurity as to foretell that it will be the common and widely-spread species, belonging to the larger and dominant groups within each class, which will ultimately prevail and procreate new and dominant species. As all the living forms of life are the lineal descendants of those which lived long before the Cambrian epoch, we may feel certain that the ordinary succession by generation has never once been broken, and that no cataclysm has desolated the whole world. Hence we may look with some confidence to a secure future of great length. And as natural selection works solely by and for the good of each being, all corporeal and mental endowments will tend to progress towards perfection.

It is interesting to contemplate a tangled bank, clothed with many plants of many kinds, with birds singing on the bushes, with various insects flitting about, and with worms crawling through the damp earth, and to reflect that these elaborately constructed forms, so different from each other, and dependent upon each other in so complex a manner, have all been produced by laws acting around us. These laws, taken in the largest sense, being Growth with Reproduction; Inheritance which is almost implied by reproduction; Variability from the indirect and direct action of the conditions of life, and from use and disuse: a Ratio of Increase so high as to lead to a Struggle for Life, and as a consequence to Natural Selection, entailing Divergence of Character and the Extinction of less-improved forms. Thus, from the war of nature, from famine and death, the most exalted object which we are capable of conceiving, namely, the production of the higher animals, directly follows. There is grandeur in this view of life, with its several powers, having been originally breathed by the Creator into a few forms or into one; and that, whilst this planet has gone cycling on according to the fixed law of gravity, from so simple a beginning endless forms most beautiful and most wonderful have been, and are being evolved.

The Descent of Man

Chapter XXI

GENERAL SUMMARY AND CONCLUSION

. . .

The main conclusion arrived at in this work, and now held by many naturalists who are well competent to form a sound judgment, is that man is descended from some less highly-organized form. The grounds upon which this conclusion rests will never be shaken, for the close similarity between man and the lower animals in embryonic development, as well as in innumerable points of structure and constitution, both of high and of the most trifling importance—the rudiments which he retains, and the abnormal reversions to which he is occasionally liable—are facts which cannot be disputed. They have long been known, but until recently they told us nothing with respect to the origin of man. Now, when viewed by the light of our knowledge of the whole organic world, their meaning is unmistakable. The great principle of evolution stands up clear and firm, when these groups of facts are considered in connection with others, such as the mutual affinities of the members of the same group, their geographical distribution in past and present times, and their geological succession. It is incredible that all these facts should speak falsely. He who is not content to look, like a savage, at the phenomena of Nature as disconnected, cannot any longer believe that man is the work of a separate act of creation. He will be forced to admit that the close resemblance of the embryo of man to that, for instance, of a dog—the construction of his skull, limbs, and whole frame, independently of the uses to which the parts may be put, on the same plan with that of other mammals—the occasional reappearance of various structures, for instance, of several distinct muscles, which man does not normally possess, but which are common to the Quadrumana—and a crowd of analogous facts—all point in the plainest manner to the conclusion that man is the co-descendant with other mammals of a common progenitor.

[*This*] conclusion . . . that man is descended from some lowly-organized form, will, I regret to think, be highly distasteful to many persons. But there can hardly be a doubt that we are descended from barbarians. The astonishment which I felt on first seeing a party of Fuegians on a wild and broken shore will never be forgotten by me, for the reflection at once rushed into my mind—such were our ancestors. These men were absolutely naked and bedaubed with paint, their long hair was tangled, their mouths frothed with excitement, and their expression was wild, startled, and distrustful. They possessed hardly any arts, and, like wild animals, lived on what they could catch; they had no government, and were merciless to every one not of their own small tribe. He who has seen a savage in his native land will not feel much shame, if forced to acknowledge

Charles Darwin, THE DESCENT OF MAN, AND SELECTION IN RELATION TO SEX *(New York, 1872).*

that the blood of some more humble creature flows in his veins. For my own part, I would as soon be descended from that heroic little monkey, who braved his dreaded enemy in order to save the life of his keeper; or from that old baboon, who, descending from the mountains, carried away in triumph his young comrade from a crowd of astonished dogs—as from a savage who delights to torture his enemies, offers up bloody sacrifices, practises infanticide without remorse, treats his wives like slaves, knows no decency, and is haunted by the grossest superstitions.

Man may be excused for feeling some pride at having risen, though not through his own exertions, to the very summit of the organic scale; and the fact of his having thus risen, instead of having been aboriginally placed there, may give him hopes for a still higher destiny in the distant future. But we are not here concerned with hopes or fears, only with the truth as far as our reason allows us to discover it. I have given the evidence to the best of my ability; and we must acknowledge, as it seems to me, that man with all his noble qualities, with sympathy which feels for the most debased, with benevolence which extends not only to other men but to the humblest living creature, with his godlike intellect which has penetrated into the movements and constitution of the solar system—with all these exalted powers—Man still bears in his bodily frame the indelible stamp of his lowly origin.

ANDREW CARNEGIE

To many the life of Andrew Carnegie is proof-positive that the great American dream can be a reality; the poverty-ridden immigrant rising to immense wealth and power has been a favored theme in Western thought and literature ever since there has been a New World. And such indeed was the life of this Scottish immigrant. Born in 1835 in Dunfermline, Scotland, he and his family arrived in the United States in 1848 where the next year young Carnegie went to work in a cotton mill in Pennsylvania. A year later he got a job as a messenger with a telegraph company and two years later (at the age of sixteen) he was one of the best telegraphers in the country.

This talent led him rapidly up the promotional ladder to the point where he performed important organizational services for the Union Army during the Civil War. From these he gained an interest in another branch of industry and so in 1865 he abandoned his railway-telegraph interests to concentrate on steel. By 1900 he had so succeeded that he virtually controlled steel production in the United States, which by that time had surpassed the output of the British industry. The following year he sold all his holdings to a financial group that had formed the United States Steel Corporation for several hundred million dollars.

It is easy to criticize tycoons like Carnegie, Rockefeller, and Morgan harshly, to challenge their motives and to question their methods of acquiring their huge fortunes. One can also be smartly cynical and describe their immense philanthropies as "conscience" payments designed to redeem themselves in the sight and smell of man and God. But while these posi-

tions are probably tenable, they are also too simple, for they tend to ignore the very real genius such individuals and the world in which they operated shared. All of these outstanding men had genuine insight into the management of men and things; they had true organizational ability and the talents that could convert a moribund business into a thriving enterprise; they exhibited astounding industry working toward their economic ends; and finally they generally shared the views toward their own wealth that Andrew Carnegie expressed in the following essay, written in 1889.

The Gospel of Wealth

THE PROBLEM OF THE ADMINISTRATION OF WEALTH

The problem of our age is the proper administration of wealth, that the ties of brotherhood may still bind together the rich and poor in harmonious relationship. The conditions of human life have not only been changed, but revolutionized, within the past few hundred years. In former days there was little difference between the dwelling, dress, food, and environment of the chief and those of his retainers. The Indians are to-day where civilized man then was. When visiting the Sioux, I was led to the wigwam of the chief. It was like the others in external appearance, and even within the difference was trifling between it and those of the poorest of his braves. The contrast between the palace of the millionaire and the cottage of the laborer with us to-day measures the change which has come with civilization. This change, however, is not to be deplored, but welcomed as highly beneficial. It is well, nay, essential, for the progress of the race that the houses of some should be homes for all that is highest and best in literature and the arts, and for all the refinements of civilization, rather than that none should be so. Much better this great irregularity than universal squalor. Without wealth there can be no Maecenas. The "good old times" were not good old times. Neither master nor servant was as well situated then as to-day. A relapse to old conditions would be disastrous to both—not the least so to him who serves—and would sweep away civilization with it. But whether the change be for good or ill, it is upon us, beyond our power to alter, and, therefore, to be accepted and made the best of. It is a waste of time to criticize the inevitable.

It is easy to see how the change has come. One illustration will serve for almost every phase of the cause. In the manufacture of products we have the whole story. It applies to all combinations of human industry, as stimulated and enlarged by the inventions of this scientific age. Formerly, articles were manufactured at the domestic hearth, or in small shops which formed part of the household. The master and his apprentices worked side by side, the latter living with the master, and therefore subject to the same conditions. When these apprentices rose to be masters, there was little or no change in their mode of life, and they in turn, educated succeeding apprentices in the same routine. There was, substantially, social equality, and even political equality, for those engaged in industrial pursuits had then little or no voice in the State.

The inevitable result of such a mode of manufacture was crude articles at high prices. To-day the world obtains commodi-

NORTH AMERICAN REVIEW *(December, 1889).*

ties of excellent quality at prices which even the preceding generation would have deemed incredible. In the commercial world similar causes have produced similar results, and the race is benefited thereby. The poor enjoy what the rich could not before afford. What were the luxuries have become the necessaries of life. The laborer has now more comforts than the farmer had a few generations ago. The farmer has more luxuries than the landlord had, and is more richly clad and better housed. The landlord has books and pictures rarer and appointments more artistic than the king could then obtain.

The price we pay for this salutary change is, no doubt, great. We assemble thousands of operatives in the factory, and in the mine, of whom the employer can know little or nothing, and to whom he is little better than a myth. All intercourse between them is at an end. Rigid castes are formed, and, as usual, mutual ignorance breeds mutual distrust. Each caste is without sympathy with the other, and ready to credit anything disparaging in regard to it. Under the law of competition, the employer of thousands is forced into the strictest economies, among which the rates paid to labor figure prominently, and often there is friction between the employer and the employed, between capital and labor, between rich and poor. Human society loses homogeneity.

The price which society pays for the law of competition, like the price it pays for cheap comforts and luxuries, is also great; but the advantages of this law are also greater still than its cost—for it is to this law that we owe our wonderful material development, which brings improved conditions in its train. But, whether the law be benign or not, we must say of it, as we say of the change in the conditions of men to which we have referred: It is here; we cannot evade it; no substitutes for it have been found; and while the law may be some times hard for the individual, it is best for the race, because it insures the survival of the fittest in every department. We accept and welcome, therefore, as conditions to which we must accommodate ourselves, great inequality of environment; the concentration of business, industrial and commercial, in the hands of a few; and the law of competition between these, as being not only beneficial, but essential to the future progress of the race. Having accepted these, it follows that there must be great scope for the exercise of special ability in the merchant and in the manufacturer who has to conduct affairs upon a great scale. That this talent for organization and management is rare among men is proved by the fact that it invariably secures enormous rewards for its possessor, no matter where or under what laws or conditions. The experienced in affairs always rate the man whose services can be obtained as a partner as not only the first consideration, but such as render the question of his capital scarcely worth considering: for able men soon create capital; in the hands of those without the special talent required, capital soon takes wings. Such men become interested in firms or corporations using millions; and, estimating only simple interests to be made upon the capital invested, it is inevitable that their income must exceed their expenditure and that they must, therefore, accumulate wealth. Nor is there any middle ground which such men can occupy, because the great manufacturing or commercial concern which does not earn at least interest upon its capital soon becomes bankrupt. It must either go forward or fall behind; to stand still is impossible. It is a condition essential to its successful operation that it should be thus far profitable, and even that, in addition to interest on capital, it should make profit. It is a law, as certain as any of the others named, that men possessed of this peculiar talent for affairs, under the free play of economic forces must, of necessity, soon be in receipt of more revenue than can be judiciously expended upon themselves; and this law is as beneficial for the race as the others.

Objections to the foundations upon which society is based are not in order, because the condition of the race is better with these than it has been with any other which has been tried. Of the effect of any new substitutes proposed we cannot be sure. The Socialist or Anarchist who seeks to overturn present conditions is to be regarded as attacking the foundation upon which civilization itself rests, for civilization took its start from the day when the capable, industrious workman said to his incompetent and lazy fellow, "If thou dost not sow, that shalt not reap," and thus ended primitive Communism by separating the drones from the bees. One who studies this subject will soon be brought face to face with the conclusion that upon the sacredness of property civilization itself depends—the right of the laborer to his hundred dollars in the savings bank, and equally the legal right of the millionaire to his millions. Every man must be allowed "to sit under his own vine and fig-tree, with none to make afraid," if human society is to advance, or even to remain so far advanced as it is. To those who propose to substitute Communism for this intense Individualism, the answer therefore is: The race has tried that. All progress from that barbarous day to the present time has resulted from its displacement. Not evil, but good, has come to the race from the accumulation of wealth by those who have had the ability and energy to produce it. But even if we admit for a moment that it might be better for the race to discard its present foundation, Individualism,—that it is a nobler ideal that man should labor, not for himself alone, but in and for a brotherhood of his fellows, and share with them all in common, realizing Swedenborg's idea of heaven, where, as he says, the angels derive their happiness, not from laboring for self, but for each other,—even admit all this, and a sufficient answer is, This is not evolution, but revolution. It necessitates the changing of human nature itself—a work of eons, even if it were good to change it, which we cannot know.

It is not practicable in our day or in our age. Even if desirable theoretically, it belongs to another and long-succeeding sociological stratum. Our duty is with what is practicable now—with the next step possible in our day and generation. It is criminal to waste our energies in endeavoring to uproot, when all we can profitably accomplish is to bend the universal tree of humanity a little in the direction most favorable to the production of good fruit under existing circumstances. We might as well urge the destruction of the highest existing type of man because he failed to reach our ideal as to favor the destruction of Individualism, Private Property, the Law of Accumulation of Wealth, and the Law of Competition; for these are the highest result of human experience, the soil in which society, so far, has produced the best fruit. Unequally or unjustly, perhaps, as these laws sometimes operate, and imperfect as they appear to the Idealist, they are, nevertheless, like the highest type of man, the best and the most valuable of all that humanity has yet accomplished.

We start, then, with a condition of affairs under which the best interests of the race are promoted, but which inevitably gives wealth to the few. Thus far, accepting conditions as they exist, the situation can be surveyed and pronounced good. The question then arises,—and if the foregoing be correct, it is the only question with which we have to deal,—What is the proper mode of administering wealth after the laws upon which civilization is founded have thrown it into the hands of the few? And it is of this great question that I believe I offer the true solution. It will be understood that fortunes are here spoken of, not moderate sums saved by many years of effort, the returns from which are required for the comfortable maintenance and education of families. This is not wealth, but only competence, which it should be the aim of all to acquire, and which for the best interests of society should be acquired.

There are but three modes in which surplus wealth can be disposed of. It can be left to the families of the decedents; or it can be bequeathed for public purposes; or finally, it can be administered by its possessors during their lives. Under the first and second modes most of the wealth of the world that has reached the few has hitherto been applied. Let us in turn consider each of these modes. The first is the most injudicious. In monarchial countries, the estates and the greatest portion of the wealth are left to the first son, that the vanity of the parent may be gratified by the thought that his name and title are to descend unimpaired to succeeding generations. The condition of this class in Europe to-day teaches the failure of such hopes or ambitions. The successors have become impoverished through their follies, or from the fall in the value of land. Even in Great Britain the strict law of entail has been found inadequate to maintain an hereditary class. Its soil is rapidly passing into the hands of the stranger. Under republican institutions the division of property among the children is much fairer; but the question which forces itself upon thoughtful men in all lands is, Why should men leave great fortunes to their children? If this is done from affection, is it not misguided affection? Observation teaches that, generally speaking, it is not well for the children that they should be so burdened. Neither is it well for the State. Beyond providing for the wife and daughters moderate sources of income, and very moderate allowances indeed, if any, for the sons, men may well hesitate; for it is no longer questionable that great sums bequeathed often work more for the injury than for the good of the recipients. Wise men will soon conclude that, for the best interests of the members of their families, and of the State, such bequests are an improper use of their means.

It is not suggested that men who have failed to educate their sons to earn a livelihood shall cast them adrift in poverty. If any man has seen fit to rear his sons with a view to their living idle lives, or, what is highly commendable, has instilled in them the sentiment that they are in a position to labor for public ends without reference to pecuniary considerations, then, of course, the duty of the parent is to see that such are provided for in moderation. There are instances of millionaires' sons unspoiled by wealth, who, being rich, still perform great services to the community. Such are the very salt of the earth, as valuable as, unfortunately, they are rare. It is not the exception, however, but the rule, that men must regard; and, looking at the usual result of enormous sums conferred upon legatees, the thoughtful man must shortly say, "I would as soon leave to my son a curse as the almighty dollar," and admit to himself that it is not the welfare of the children, but family pride, which inspires these legacies.

As to the second mode, that of leaving wealth at death for public uses, it may be said that this is only a means for the disposal of wealth, provided a man is content to wait until he is dead before he becomes of much good in the world. Knowledge of the results of legacies bequeathed is not calculated to inspire the brightest hopes of much posthumous good being accomplished by them. The cases are not few in which the real object sought by the testator is not attained, nor are they few in which his real wishes are thwarted. In many cases the bequests are so used as to become only monuments of his folly. It is well to remember that it requires the exercise of not less ability than that which acquires it, to use wealth so as to be really beneficial to the community. Besides this, it may fairly be said that no man is to be extolled for doing what he cannot help doing, nor is he to be thanked by the community to which he only leaves wealth at death. Men who leave vast sums in this way may fairly be thought men who would not have left it at all had they been able to take it with them. The memories of such cannot be held in grateful remembrance, for there is no grace in their gifts. It is not to be wondered at that such bequests seem so generally to lack the blessing.

The growing disposition to tax more and more heavily large estates left at death is a cheering indication of the growth of a salutary change in public opinion. The State of Pennsylvania now takes—subject to some exceptions—one-tenth of the property left by its citizens. The budget presented in the British Parliament the other day proposes to increase the death duties; and, most significant of all, the new tax is to be a graduated one. Of all forms of taxation this seems the wisest. Men who continue hoarding great sums all their lives, the proper use of which for public ends would work good to the community from which it chiefly came, should be made to feel that the community, in the form of the State, cannot thus be deprived of its proper share. By taxing estates heavily at death the State marks its condemnation of the selfish millionaire's unworthy life.

It is desirable that nations should go much further in this direction. Indeed, it is difficult to set bounds to the share of a rich man's estate which should go at his death to the public through the agency of the State, and by all means such taxes should be graduated, beginning at nothing upon moderate sums to dependents, and increasing rapidly as the amounts swell, until of the millionaire's hoard, as of Shylock's, at least "the other half comes to the privy coffer of the State." This policy would work powerfully to induce the rich man to attend to the administration of wealth during his life, which is the end that society should always have in view, as being by far the most fruitful for the people. Nor need it be feared that this policy would sap the root of enterprise and render men less anxious to accumulate, for, to the class whose ambition it is to leave great fortunes and be talked about after their death, it will attract even more attention, and, indeed, be a somewhat nobler ambition, to have enormous sums paid over to the State from their fortunes.

There remains, then, only one mode of using great fortunes; but in this we have the true antidote for the temporary unequal distribution of wealth, the reconciliation of the rich and the poor—a reign of harmony, another ideal, differing, indeed, from that of the Communist in requiring only the further evolution of existing conditions, not the total overthrow of our civilization. It is founded upon the present most intense Individualism, and the race is prepared to put it in practice by degrees whenever it pleases. Under its sway we shall have an ideal State, in which the surplus wealth of the few will become, in the best sense, the property of the many, because administered for the common good; and this wealth, passing through the hands of the few, can be made a much more potent force for the elevation of our race than if distributed in small sums to the people themselves. Even the poorest can be made to see this, and to agree that great sums gathered by some of their fellow-citizens and spent for public purposes, from which the masses reap the principal benefit, are more valuable to them than if scattered among themselves in trifling amounts through the course of many years.

If we consider the results which flow from the Cooper Institute, for instance, to the best portion of the race in New York not possessed of means, and compare these with those which would have ensued for the good of the masses from an equal sum distributed by Mr. Cooper in his lifetime in the form of wages, which is the highest form of distribution, being for work done and not for charity, we can form some estimate of the possibilities for the improvement of the race which lie embedded in the present law of the accumulation of wealth. Much of this sum, if distributed in small quantities among the people, would have been wasted in the indulgence of appetite, some of it in excess, and it may be doubted whether even the part put to the best use, that of adding to the comforts of the home, would have yielded results for the race, as a race, at all comparable to those which are flowing and are to flow from the Cooper Institute from generation to generation. Let the advocate of violent or radical change ponder well this thought.

We might even go so far as to take another instance—that of Mr. Tilden's bequest of five millions of dollars for a free library in the city of New York; but in referring to this one cannot help saying involuntarily: How much better if Mr. Tilden had devoted the last years of his own life to the proper administration of this immense sum; in which case neither legal contest nor any other case of delay could have interfered with his aims. But let us assume that Mr. Tilden's millions finally become the means of giving to this city a noble public library, where the treasures of the world contained in books will be open to all forever, without money and without price. Considering the good of that part of the race which congregates in and around Manhattan Island, would its permanent benefit have been better promoted had these millions been allowed to circulate in small sums through the hands of the masses? Even the most strenuous advocate of Communism must entertain a doubt upon this subject. Most of those who think will probably entertain no doubt whatever.

Poor and restricted are our opportunities in this life, narrow our horizon, our best work most imperfect; but rich men should be thankful for one inestimable boon. They have it in their power during their lives to busy themselves in organizing benefactions from which the masses of their fellows will derive lasting advantage, and thus dignify their own lives. The highest life is probably to be reached, not by such imitation of the life of Christ as Count Tolstoi gives us, but, while animated by Christ's spirit, by recognizing the changed conditions of this age, and adopting modes of expressing this spirit suitable to the changed conditions under which we live, still laboring for the good of our fellows, which was the essence of his life and teaching, but laboring in a different manner.

This, then, is held to be the duty of the man of wealth: To set an example of modest, unostentatious living, shunning display or extravagance; to provide moderately for the legitimate wants of those dependent upon him; and, after doing so, to consider all surplus revenues which come to him simply as trust funds, which he is called upon to administer, and strictly bound as a matter of duty to administer in the manner which, in his judgment, is best calculated to produce the most beneficial results for the community —the man of wealth thus becoming the mere trustee and agent for his poorer brethren, bringing to their service his superior wisdom, experience, and ability to administer, doing for them better than they would or could do for themselves.

We are met here with the difficulty of determining what are moderate sums to leave to members of the family; what is modest, unostentatious living; what is the test of extravagance. There must be different standards for different conditions. The answer is that it is as impossible to name exact amounts or actions as it is to define good manners, good taste, or the rules of propriety; but, nevertheless, these are verities, well-known, although indefinable. Public sentiment is quick to know and to feel what offends these. So in the case of wealth. The rule in regard to good taste in the dress of men or women applies here. Whatever makes one conspicuous offends the canon. If any family be chiefly known for display, for extravagance in home, table, or equipage, for enormous sums ostentatiously spent in any form upon itself —if these be its chief distinctions, we have no difficulty in estimating its nature or culture. So likewise in regard to the use or abuse of its surplus wealth, or to generous, free-handed cooperation in good public uses, or to unabated efforts to accumulate and hoard to the last, or whether they administer or bequeath. The verdict rests with the best and most enlightened public sentiment. The community will surely judge, and its judgments will not often be wrong.

The best uses to which surplus wealth can be put have already been indicated. Those who would administer wisely must, indeed, be wise; for one of the serious obstacles to the improvement of our race is indiscriminate charity. It were better for mankind that the millions of the rich were thrown into the sea than so spent as to encourage the slothful, the drunken, the unworthy. Of every thousand dollars spent in so-called charity to-day, it is probable that nine hundred and fifty dollars is unwisely spent—so spent, indeed, as to produce the very evils which it hopes to mitigate or cure. A well-known writer of philosophic books admitted the other day that he had given a quarter of a dollar to a man who approached him as he was coming to visit the house of his friend. He knew nothing of the habits of this beggar, knew not the use that would be made of this money, although he had every reason to suspect that it would be spent improperly. This man professed to be a disciple of Herbert Spencer; yet the quarter-dollar given that night will probably work more injury than all the money will do good which its thoughtless donor will ever be able to give in true charity. He only gratified his own feelings, saved himself from annoyance—and this was probably one of the most selfish and very worst actions of his life, for in all respects he is most worthy.

In bestowing charity, the main consideration should be to help those who will help themselves; to provide part of the means by which those who desire to improve may do so; to give those who desire to rise the aids by which they may rise; to assist, but rarely or never to do all. Neither the individual nor the race is improved by almsgiving. Those worthy of assistance, except in rare cases, seldom require assistance. The really valuable men of the race never do, except in case of accident or sudden change. Every one has, of course, cases of individuals brought to his own knowledge where temporary assistance can do genuine good, and these he will not overlook. But the amount which can be wisely given by the individual for individuals is necessarily limited by his lack of knowledge of the circumstances connected with each. He is the only true reformer who is as careful and as anxious not to aid the unworthy as he is to aid the worthy, and, perhaps, even more so, for in almsgiving more injury is probably done by rewarding vice than by relieving virtue.

The rich man is thus almost restricted to following the examples of Peter Cooper, Enoch Pratt of Baltimore, Mr. Pratt of Brooklyn, Senator Stanford, and others, who know that the best means of benefiting the community is to place within its reach the ladders upon which the aspiring can rise—free libraries, parks, and means of recreation, by which men are helped in body and mind; works of art, certain to give pleasure and improve the public taste; and public institutions of various kinds, which will improve the general condition of the people; in this manner returning their surplus wealth to the mass of their fellows in the forms best calculated to do them lasting good.

Thus is the problem of rich and poor to be solved. The laws of accumulation will be left free, the laws of distribution free. Individualism will continue, but the millionaire will be but a trustee for the poor, intrusted for a season with a great part of the increased wealth of the community, but administering it for the community far better than it could or would have done for itself. The best minds will thus have reached a stage in the development of the race in which it is clearly seen that there is no mode of disposing of surplus wealth creditable to thoughtful and earnest men into whose hands it flows, save by using it year by year for the general good. This day already dawns. Men may die without incurring the pity of their fellows, still sharers in great business enterprises from which their capital cannot be or has not been withdrawn, and which is left chiefly at death for public uses; yet the day is not far distant when the man who dies leaving behind him millions of available wealth, which was free for him to administer during life, will pass away "unwept, unhonored, and unsung," no matter to what uses he leaves the dross which he cannot take with him. Of such as these the public verdict will then be: "The man who dies thus rich dies disgraced."

Such, in my opinion, is the true gospel concerning wealth, obedience to which is destined some day to solve the problem of the rich and the poor, and bring "Peace on earth, among men good will."

FRIEDRICH NIETZSCHE

To most readers, Friedrich Nietzsche is a profoundly shocking writer. He meant to be. To read him with profit, therefore, requires both imagination and sympathy. If the reader is willing to make the necessary effort, he may be surprised (and somewhat disconcerted) to find himself agreeing with the author from time to time. Like Marx, Nietzsche (1844–1900) rejected wholesale the economic, political, social, and intellectual ideas of the nineteenth century. But unlike Marx, he did so in the interest, not of an ideal classless society, but of a society in which class distinctions would be hardened into caste barriers. To most of us, who are committed to the ideals of democratic society, such an ideal is repugnant, both politically and morally. It is a simple task, too, to draw a line from Nietzsche to Hitler, especially when we remember Nietzsche's use of such terms as "Supermen" and "the great blonde beasts." Nevertheless, whatever the similarities between them—and there can be no doubt that Hitler borrowed from Nietzsche—to reduce Nietzsche to nothing more than a proto-Nazi would be to miss the complexities and subtleties of his thinking that make him worth our consideration. In fact, a good case could be made for the thesis that, had he been living under the Nazis, he would have turned his back with contempt and disgust on Hitler and all his works. Rather than dismiss Nietzsche without a hearing, then, we may be able to discern in his writings the reaction of a highly sensitive and intelligent, though arrogant, personality to the far-from-ideal realities of nineteenth-century industrial civilization.

The following is from Nietzsche's unfinished The Will to Power. *The order of sections has been altered slightly.*

The Will to Power

854. In the era of "universal suffrage," meaning that everyone is able to sit in judgment upon everyone and everything, I am constrained to re-establish the *order of rank.*

855. Power-quanta and nothing but power-quanta determine and distinguish rank.

. . .

857. I make a distinction between two types, one representative of life in ascendancy, the other of life in decline, decay, debilitude. Is it to be believed that the order of rank between these two types can even be questioned seriously?

. . .

859. There is an advantage in standing at a distance from one's time, i.e., in standing at a distance from both movements, individualistic as well as collectivistic morality—for indeed the former also refuses to acknowledge the order of rank, and means to give to one the same freedom it would give to all. My thoughts do not revolve around the degree of freedom to be granted to one or another or all, but around the degree of *power* that ought to be exercised by one or another over some or all;—in particular I ask to what extent a sacrifice of freedom, even enslavement, might be the basis for the nurture of a *higher type.* Most crudely put: *how might one sacrifice the evolution of mankind* for the sake of ushering into being a species higher than man?

Friedrich Nietzche, DER WILLE ZUR MACHT, *trans. Peter Fuss of the University of California, Riverside.*

. . .

861. A declaration of war on the part of *higher men* against the masses is necessary! Everywhere mediocrity is gathering forces in order to make itself master! Everything that enervates, that eases, that enhances "the People" or "the Womanly" works to the advantage of universal suffrage, i.e., to the rulership of the *lower* men. But we are determined to retaliate and to bring the entire business (which began in Europe with the onset of Christianity) into the light of day and before the bar of judgment.

862. What is needed is a doctrine strong enough to work *selectively:* fortifying for the strong, crippling and disintegrating for the world-weary.

—The annihilation of decadent races. The decline of Europe. The annihilation of slave-oriented value appraisals. Mastery over the earth as means to the engendering of a higher type. The annihilation of the twaddle that passes for "morality" (Christianity as a hysterical sort of honesty included: Augustine, Bunyan). The annihilation of universal suffrage, i.e., the system by virtue of which the lowest natures set themselves up as law for the higher. The annihilation of mediocrity and its wide currency.

. . .

866. It is imperative to set forth a counterdirection to the ever-increasing economic exploitation of man and mankind, to the ever more tightly interlocked "machinery" of interests and output. I designate this counterdirection *the extraction of man's luxury-surplus:* through it shall be brought to light a stronger kind, a higher type, whose conditions of origin and maintenance shall be other than those of the average man. My concept, my *image* for this type is, as one knows, the word "Overman."[1]

The first direction, which is now fully in view, is marked by conformity, levelling, higher Orientalism, modesty of instinct, contentment with the diminution of man—a kind of *human standstill-level.* Once we achieve, as is unavoidably imminent, the collective economic management of the earth, mankind *can* find its meaning as machinery in such service—as a colossal gearbox consisting of ever smaller and ever more finely "adaptable" wheels, characterized by an ever-increasing superfluousness of dominating and ruling elements; as an enormously powerful whole whose component parts represent *minutiae* of power and of value.

To counteract this shrinkage and adaptation of men to a specialized utility, one must go in the opposite direction: the production of the *synoptic,* the *all-encompassing,* the *vindicating* man, for whom the mechanization of mankind is a precondition, a foundation upon which he can erect his *higher form of being.*

He needs the *antagonism* of the mass, of the "be-levelled"—the feeling of distance that comes from comparing himself with them. He stands on them, he lives off them. This higher form of *aristocratism* is that of the future. Morally speaking, the machine-collectivity, the solidarity of all wheels, represents a maximum of *human exploitation;* but it presupposes those for whose sake such exploitation would *make sense.* Otherwise it would indeed be nothing but the collective diminution, the *value*-diminution of the human type—a *retrogression* in high style.

It should be apparent that what I am fighting is *economic* optimism: as though the increasing sacrifice of each were necessarily accompanied by an increasing advantage for all. To me just the contrary seems the case: *the sacrifice of each aggregates into a collective loss;* man is diminished, in such a way that one no longer knows *what end* this stupendous process was meant to subserve. A what-for? A *new* what-for? *That's* what mankind requires.

. . .

881. *With reference to the order of rank:* What is mediocre about the typical man?—That he fails to comprehend that things necessarily have a *reverse side;* that he combats evils as though they could be dispensed with; that he refuses to take the one with the other,—that he would blur and efface the *typical character* of a thing, a state of affairs, a period, a person by sanctioning only part of their qualities and *dismissing* the rest. The "wishfulness" of the mediocre is what we others contend with: the *Ideal* conceived as something devoid of anything injurious, evil, dangerous, dubious, or destructive. Our conception is quite the contrary: that with man's every growth his reverse side must also grow,

[1] [Most translators have rendered Nietzsche's *Übermensch* as "Superman" in English; a more accurate and less misleading rendering is "Overman."—Tr.]

that the *highest* man (granted such a concept is permitted) would be that man who would exhibit *the antithetical character of existence* most vigorously, as his glory and sole vindication. Ordinary men can allow themselves to exhibit this quality of nature only to the smallest degree: increase the many-sidedness of the elements and the tension among antitheses—the preconditions of man's *greatness*—and they soon perish. That man must become better *and* worse: that is my formula for this inevitability.

Most men constitute mere bits and pieces of men; only when they are added together does a man emerge. In this sense there is something fragmentary about whole ages, whole peoples; perhaps it is inherent in the economy of human evolution that man develops only piecemeal. Precisely for this reason we must not fail to recognize that the emergence of the comprehensive man is all that matters, and that the inferior men, the vast majority, are nothing but preludes and rehearsals—an ensemble out of which here and there the *whole man* emerges, the milestone-man, the measure of how far mankind has thus far advanced. It does *not* advance in a straight line; frequently the already achieved type is lost again (for example, notwithstanding three hundred years' exertion, we have failed to measure up to the men of the Renaissance—and Renaissance man in turn fell short of the men of Antiquity).

. . .

874. The deterioration of the rulers and the ruling classes has brought about the greatest mischief in history! Without the Roman Caesars and Roman society the madness of Christianity would never have come to the fore.

When inferior men come to doubt *whether* there are higher men, then there is great danger! Ultimately one discovers that even the inferior, the subjugated, the spiritually impoverished have *virtues*, and that *before God* all men are equal: than which no greater nonsense has ever existed on earth! For eventually the higher men themselves accept as their measure the slaves' standard of virtue—find themselves "prideful," etc., find all their *higher* qualities to be reprehensible.

It was when Nero and Caracalla sat on high that the paradox arose, "the lowest man is *worth more* than the one on high!" And an *image of God* became prevalent which was as *remote* as possible from the image of the All-mighty—God on the Cross!

. . .

871. It is the ghastly barbarism of morality which, notably in the Middle Ages, forced through a veritable "federation of virtue"—alongside equally ghastly exaggerations of what constitutes man's *value*. A militant "civilization" (domestication) needs all sorts of weapons and tortures to preserve itself against the terrifying and the beast of prey.

Here a confusion arises quite naturally, although it has the most pernicious effect: whatever men of power and will are able to exact from themselves becomes the criterion as well for what they may allow themselves. Such natures are the *antitheses* of the vicious and the licentious, although in certain circumstances they may do things for which an inferior man would be convicted of wickedness and excess.

In this context the notion of the "equality of men before God" does enormous damage; actions and dispositions were forbidden which, as such, are among the prerogatives of the strong—as though they were in themselves unworthy of man. The entire thrust of the strong was discredited by establishing the defense-mechanisms of the weakest (including the weakest *vis-à-vis* themselves) as standards of value.

This confusion was carried to such an extent that just the greatest *virtuosi* of life (whose authoritarian character provides the sharpest contrast to the vicious and the licentious) were branded with the most infamous names. Even now one finds it necessary to condemn a Caesar Borgia, which is ridiculous. German emperors have been anathematized by the Church on grounds of their depravity: as if a monk or a priest were competent to speak on what Frederick the Second should demand of himself. A Don Juan is dispatched to hell: that's very naive. Has it been noted that heaven is devoid of all interesting men? (A hint to the girls concerning where their salvation is best found.) All one need do is think a bit consistently and with a deepened insight into what a "great man" is, and no doubt remains that the Church consigns all "great men" to hell,—she wars *against* all human greatness.

. . .

877. The Revolution made possible Napoleon: that is its justification. For a comparable prize one should long for the anarchic collapse of our entire civilization. Napoleon made possible nationalism: that is his excuse.

The value of a man (leaving aside, and rightly so, morality and immorality, since these concepts do not even begin to touch a man's *worth*) is not to be found in his usefulness; for it persists even if there were no one to whom he could be useful. And why couldn't precisely the man who engenders the most destructive consequences be the summit of the entire human species—so grand, so superior that confronted by him everything would die of envy?

. . .

373. *The origin of moral values.*—Egoism has as much value as the physiological worth of its bearer.

Each individual constitutes the entire evolutionary lineage (he is not, contrary to the moralistic conception of him, merely something that begins with his birth). Should he represent the *ascendancy* of the human lineage, then his value is, in fact, exceptional, and great may be the concern over the maintenance and encouragement of his growth. (It is the concern over the promise of the future which he embodies that gives the fortunate individual so extraordinary a right to egoism). But should he represent the *descending* lineage, that of degeneration and chronic sickness, then little value accrues to him; and it is a matter of elementary justice that he takes from the fortunate as little space, strength, and sunlight as possible. In this instance society's task is the *suppression of egoism* (it occasionally expresses itself in absurd, pathological, and rebellious forms), be it a question of individuals or of entire degenerated, vestigial strata of mankind. Among such strata, a dogma or religion of "love," of *suppression* of self-affirmation, of patience, suffering, and service, of mutuality in word and deed can be of highest value, even from the point of view of their rulers. For it suppresses feelings of rivalry, resentment, and envy, —the all-too-natural feelings of the ill-begotten; it even deifies them by idealizing slavish humility and obedience, subordination, poverty, infirmity, and lowliness. Accordingly, we see why ruling classes (or races) and individuals have always supported the cult of unselfishness, the slave-gospel of the "God on the Cross."

The predominance of an altruistic mode of valuing is the consequence of an instinct-to-failure. At bottom, this value judgment affirms: "I am not worth much,"—a mere physiological value judgment; plainer yet: the feeling of impotence, the dearth of great yea-saying surges of power (in the muscles, nerves, limbs). In accordance with the particular culture of these strata, this value judgment translates itself into a moral or religious judgment (the pre-eminence of religious or moral judgments is always a mark of an inferior culture); it seeks to establish itself out of contexts in which the concept of "value" is already familiar. The interpretation by which the Christian sinner seeks to understand himself is an attempt to *justify* his lack of power and self-assurance: he would rather find himself guilty than feel himself to be bad for no reason; to have need of such interpretations in the first place is already a symptom of decadence. In other instances the misbegotten seeks the reason for it not in his own "guilt" (like the Christian does), but in society (the socialist, the anarchist, the nihilist). Insofar as he feels his condition to be one for which someone *ought* to be guilty, however, he remains the next-of-kin of the Christian, who also believes that he can better endure his negative self-discovery and misbegottenness if he has found someone he can hold *responsible* for it. In both instances, the instinct for *revenge* and *resentment* appears as a means of bearing it, as an instinct of self-preservation,—much the same as the predilection for *altruistic* theory and practice. The *hatred of egoism,* be it directed against self (as with the Christian) or other (as with the socialist), reveals itself thereby as a value judgment under the aegis of revenge; yet at the same time as the cunning of self-preservation on the part of the suffering, through an enhancing of their feelings of cooperation and solidarity. Basically, as already indicated, this discharge of resentment in the form of judging, condemning, and punishing egoism (one's own or another's) is nothing but an instinct of self-preservation on the part of the misbegotten. In sum: the cult of altruism is a special form of egoism which, given certain physiological conditions, regularly appears.

When, in righteous indignation, the socialist demands "justice," "equality," "equal rights," he is under pressure of a substandard culture which cannot help him comprehend why he suffers; otherwise regarded, he is amusing himself,—were he better off, he would not dream of making such outcries: he would amuse himself in some other way. Likewise for the Christian: he condemns, calumniates, curses the world —and himself in the bargain. But that is no reason to take his clamor seriously. In both instances we are in the midst of invalids whom crying *benefits,* for whom calumny affords relief.

. . .

753. I am averse to (1) socialism, because it dreams naively of "the Good, the True, the Beautiful" and "equal rights" (anarchism too pursues similar ideals, only in a more brutal way); (2) parliamentarianism and the cult of the newspaper, because they are the means by which the herd-animal becomes master.

. . .

755. How absurd are the socialists, with their silly optimism over the "good man," whose emergence awaits only the overthrow of the hitherto existing "order" and the releasing of all "natural impulses." And the opposition is equally absurd, because it refuses to countenance the violence inherent in law, the hardness and egoism inseparable from every sort of authority. "I and my kind will rule and endure; whoever defects will be driven out or liquidated" is the sentiment underlying all traditional lawmaking.

The notion of a *higher kind* of man is detested much more than are monarchs. Anti-aristocracy uses hatred of monarchy only as its mask.

. . .

926. *Against John Stuart Mill.*—I abhor his vulgarity, which maintains, "What is right for one is right for all," "What you don't wish done to you, don't do to others," etc., which would ground all human intercourse on *reciprocity of output,* so that every action would appear as a sort of cash payment for a service rendered us. Here is an hypothesis vulgar in the crudest sense; here actions are assumed to

have *equivalent value* irrespective of mine and yours; here the uniquely personal worth of an action (namely, that for which there is no equivalent and for which there is no return) is simply annulled. This "reciprocity" is a stupendous vulgarity; that what *I* do *should not* and *cannot* be done by another, that there must be no equivalence (except in those most select circles of genuine equals, *inter pares*), that in the deepest sense one never pays back, since one is *unique* and *acts* only uniquely, —this root conviction contains the source of the aristocratic differentiation from the mass, since it is the mass which believes in "equality" and consequently in equivalence and in "reciprocity."

. . .

728. It is part of the very concept of life that it must grow,—that it must extend its power and consequently absorb alien forces. Befogged by the narcotic called morality, one speaks of the right of the individual to *defend* himself. By the same token, one ought to speak of the individual's right to *attack,* for *both*—and the second more than the first—are necessities for every living thing: aggressive and defensive egoism are not matters of choice (not to speak of "free will") but the *fatality* of life itself.

In this context it makes no difference whether an individual or a living organism, an aspiring "society," is held in view. At bottom, the right to punish (society's self-defense) was arrived at only through a misuse of the word "right": a right is obtained only by contract, whereas self-defense and self-protection do not rest on a contractual basis. At the very least, and with just as much show of reason, a people should describe its passion for conquest, its lust for power, be it by force of arms, trade, commerce, or colonization, as a right —say a growth-right. A society which, definitively and in accordance with its instinct, foreswears war and conquest, is in a state of decline: it is ripe for democracy and rule by shopkeepers.

. . .

898. *The strong of the future.*—The conditions for the achievement of a *stronger* species, heretofore attained here and there, in part through necessity, in part through chance: these conditions we are now able to understand and consciously to *will.* We can create the conditions that make possible such an advance.

Heretofore "education" had the good of society in view: *not* the greatest possible good of the future, but the good of the currently existing society. For this, "tools" were demanded. Supposing that power resources were greater, one might consider drawing on them in the interests *not* of society's welfare, but of future good.

Such a task would be in order, the more one realized to what extent a current form of society were in a state of transition so that sooner or later it would be *no longer able to exist for its own sake*—but only as *means* in the hands of a stronger race.

The increasing diminution of man is the very force impelling one to think of the cultivation of a stronger race, whose overflow of strength would consist in precisely the respect in which the dwarfed species was weak and becoming weaker (will, responsibility, self-assurance, and self-postulation of goals).

The equalization of European man is the great process which should not be interfered with: it should, in fact, be accelerated. The need for an opening of chasms, for distance, for ordering of rank is thereby postulated—*not* the need for retarding this process.

The equalized species requires, as soon as it is attained, a *justification*: it is to be found in the service of a higher, sovereign species standing on it and, by virtue of this position, able for the first time to rise to its proper destiny. Not merely a race of masters whose task would be fulfilled in ruling, but a race having its *own life-realm,* with an overflow of vitality for beauty, gallantry, culture, and style to the point of holiness; a *yea-saying* race able to permit itself every great luxury—strong enough to have no need of the tyranny of moral imperatives, rich enough to have no need for thrift and pedantry, *beyond* good and evil; a hothouse for rare and exotic plants.

. . .

957. It draws near, inexorable, trembling, as frightening as fate—the great task and question, How shall the earth as a whole be administered? And *toward what end* shall mankind as a whole—no longer a mere people, a race—be trained and cultivated?

Legislated morals are the chief means whereby one can cull from man what is suitable to a creative and profound will: provided that such a high order artist-will has power in hand and is able to impose itself over long periods in the form of law-giving, religions, and moralities. To my mind, such men of great achievement, such authentically great men, will be pursued in vain today and probably for a long time to come. They are *lacking,* and will be, until finally, after much disappointment, one begins to understand *why* they are lacking, and that now and for a long time to come nothing impedes their genesis and development with greater hostility than what passes in Europe for "*the* morality"—as though there were and could be no other—the one heretofore described as herd morality, the one which strives with all its might for that common green pasture-land happiness on earth, i.e., security, absence of danger, coziness, ease of life, and, last but not least, "if all goes well," the pious hope of dispensing with all manner of shepherds and bell-wethers. Its two most broadly preached doctrines are called "equality of rights" and "compassion for all suffering"—and suffering itself is thought to be something which must by all means be *got rid of.* That such ideas can still be modern inclines one to a low opinion of modernity. But whoever ponders thoroughly the question where and how the plant Man has hitherto grown up most vigorously cannot help but suppose that this occurred under quite the *contrary* conditions: that the danger of its habitat must be magnified to frightful proportions, its powers of sensation and locomotion must struggle against long hardship and constriction, its will to life must be intensified into an unconditioned will to power and predominance, and that danger, harshness, violence, peril in the street as in the heart, inequality of rights, concealment, stoicism, the art of seduction, deviltry of every kind—in short, that the elevation of the species Man demands the very antithesis of all herdlike wish-fulfillment. A morality with such opposite intentions, seeking to nurture man upwards instead of into the cozy and the mediocre, a morality seeking to nurture a ruling caste—the future *lords of the earth*—must, before it can be promulgated, introduce itself as though in league with prevalent moral law and in the guise of the latter's words and shapes. But that accordingly a number of provisional and diversionary tactics need be discovered and that, whereas the life-span of a man means next to nothing in face of the fulfillment of such protracted tasks and aims, above all else *a new species* must be nurtured, in which the appropriate wills and instincts will be guaranteed duration through many generations—a new ruling species and caste: to envision all this is no easier than to comprehend the lengthy and hard-to-articulate *Etcetera* of its underlying thought. To prepare a *transvaluation of values* for a certain powerful species of men, endowed with the highest intellect and will-power, and to this end liberate him slowly and carefully from a host of repressed and villified instincts: who ponders this belongs to us, the free spirits. . . .

. . .

464. . . . But where might I look with any hope at all for my kind of philosophers, or at the very least for *my kind of yearning for new philosophers?* Only where there prevails a *noble* turn of mind, one that believes in slavery and in many gradations of serfdom as being the preconditions of any higher culture; where there prevails a *creative* turn of mind, one that does not postulate the bliss of eternal repose, the "Sabbath of Sabbaths" as the world's destiny, but honors, even in peacetime, the means to new wars; a turn of mind that prescribes laws to the future, one that for the future's sake deals harshly and tyrannically with itself and its time; an unscrupulous, "immoral" turn of mind, determined to nourish towards greatness man's good and evil qualities in equal measure, entrusting itself with the power to give each its proper due,—proper in so far as each requires the other. But he who goes in quest of philosophers today, what are his prospects of finding what he seeks? Isn't it likely that even with the best lamp-of-Diogenes to hand, he wanders about day and night in vain? This age has the *contrary* instincts: first and foremost, it wants comfort; secondly, it wants publicity, the bustle and din of the theatre and the dancehall, so congenial to its county-fair tastes; thirdly, it wants everybody to crawl on his belly in abject submission before the greatest of all lies—its name is "equality of mankind"—and pay homage exclusively to the *equalizing*, the *levelling* virtues. But therewith the advent of the philosopher, as I understand him, is utterly precluded, even though in all innocence this age imagines itself to be conducive to him. Indeed, all the world presently bemoans the evils *earlier* philosophers had to endure, caught as they were between the stake, their guilty conscience, and the presumptuous wisdom of the Church Fathers. But the truth is that just these circumstances afforded far more *favorable* conditions for a powerful, comprehensive, subtle, and audacious mentality than do the circumstances of present-day life. Today, conditions favor the appearance of another kind of spirit, that of the demagogue, the actor, perhaps that of the beaver-like, ant-like scholar as well. The superior artists, on the other hand, are already in a bad way: aren't nearly all of them being ruined for want of inner discipline? They are no longer being tyrannized from without by Church- or Court-imposed tablets of absolute value; accordingly, they no longer learn to cultivate their "inner tyrant," their *will*. And what holds true for artists holds true in a higher and more ominous sense for philosophers. Where *are* the free spirits today? Show me a free spirit today!

. . .

997. I teach that there are higher and lower men, and that in some cases the existence of entire millennia may be justified by a single individual—that is, a fuller, richer, greater, more whole man, in contrast with countless incomplete, fragmentary men.

998. The highest men live beyond rulers, free of all bonds; and in the rulers they find their instruments.

999. *Order of rank:* he who *determines* values and directs the will of millennia by directing the highest natures, is the *highest man*.

1000. I think I have fathomed something of what goes on in the soul of the highest man;—perhaps anyone who fathoms him entire is doomed: but whoever has glimpsed him must help to make him *possible*.

Fundamental idea: we must take the future as the criterion for all our value appraisals—and not look *behind* us for the laws of our action.

1001. Not "mankind" but the *Overman* is the goal!

THEODORE ROOSEVELT

At the Mount Rushmore National Memorial in South Dakota the chief attraction for sightseers is the mountainside converted into portraits of four American presidents. Presumably these four were the greatest chief executives of the United States—at least if this was not the criterion, one can wonder what the standards might have been. Certainly cragginess of physiognomy could hardly have swayed the final decision, for it would have been impossible to ignore Andrew Jackson. In any event, there at Rushmore are the four gigantic heads—Washington, Jefferson, Lincoln, and Theodore Roosevelt.

At the time the following essay was first published (1899), Theodore Roosevelt (1858–1919) was Governor of the state of New York and was soon to become Vice-president of the United States and then, with the assassination of William McKinley (1901), President. At other points in his career he was a successful Police Commissioner of New York City and Assistant Secretary of the Navy. He resigned the latter post to head the cavalry unit known as the Roosevelt Roughriders (even though they left their horses in the United States when they sailed to Cuba during the Spanish-American War). During World War I, he bedeviled Woodrow Wilson for permission to raise and command his own division of troops. At one point, he even recommended himself for the Congressional Medal of Honor.

A prolific writer, Theodore Roosevelt published many volumes of history, travel, big-game hunting, memoirs, and general reflections, of which the essay, Expansion and Peace, *is one. While the views that Roosevelt expresses in the essay may seem naive as well as distasteful to the reader of today, we must remember that he was far from alone in his advocacy of a righteous war, a morally justified conquest of "primitive" people. The latter part of the nineteenth century is replete with discussions of the "white man's burden," to use Rudyard Kipling's phrase, in defense of imperialism. Kipling and Joseph Chamberlain in England, Jules Ferry in France, Leopold II in Belgium, and many others were all convinced that it was their duty to carry their civilization to the backward peoples of the world.*

In the essay that follows, Roosevelt reveals a belligerency of character that is perhaps expressed best in his famous "big-stick" policy. Nevertheless, it should not be forgotten that, for his efforts in bringing to an end the Russo-Japanese War of 1904–1905, Roosevelt was awarded the Nobel Peace Prize in 1906.

Expansion and Peace

It was the gentlest of our poets who wrote:

"Be bolde! Be bolde! and everywhere, Be bolde";
Be not too bold! Yet better the excess
Than the defect; better the more than less.

Longfellow's love of peace was profound; but he was a man, and a wise man, and he knew that cowardice does not promote peace, and that even the great evil of war may be a less evil than cringing to iniquity.

Captain Mahan, than whom there is not in the country a man whom we can more appropriately designate by the fine and high phrase, "a Christian gentleman," and who is incapable of advocating wrongdoing of any kind, national or individual, gives utterance to the feeling of the great majority of manly and thoughtful men when he denounces the great danger of indiscriminate advocacy of peace at any price, because "it may lead men to tamper with iniquity, to compromise with unrighteousness, soothing their conscience with the belief that war is so entirely wrong that beside it no other tolerated evil is wrong. Witness Armenia and witness Crete. War has been avoided; but what of the national consciences that beheld such iniquity and withheld the hand?"

Peace is a great good; and doubly harmful, therefore, is the attitude of those who advocate it in terms that would make it synonymous with selfish and cowardly shrinking from warring against the existence of evil. The wisest and most far-seeing champions of peace will ever remember that, in the first place, to be good it must be righteous, for unrighteous and cowardly peace may be worse than any war; and, in the second place, that it can often be obtained only at the cost of war. Let me take two illustrations:

THE WORKS OF THEODORE ROOSEVELT *(New York, 1900).*

The great blot upon European international morality in the closing decade of this century has been not a war, but the infamous peace kept by the joint action of the great powers, while Turkey inflicted the last horrors of butchery, torture, and outrage upon the men, women, and children of despairing Armenia. War was avoided; peace was kept; but what a peace! Infinitely greater human misery was inflicted during this peace than in the late wars of Germany with France, of Russia with Turkey; and this misery fell, not on armed men, but upon defenceless women and children, upon the gray-beard and the stripling no less than upon the head of the family; and it came, not in the mere form of death or imprisonment, but of tortures upon men, and, above all, upon women, too horrible to relate—tortures of which it is too terrible even to think. Moreover, no good resulted from the bloodshed and misery. Often this is the case in a war, but often it is not the case. The result of the last Turko-Russian war was an immense and permanent increase of happiness for Bulgaria, Servia, Bosnia, and Herzegovina. These provinces became independent or passed under the dominion of Austria, and the advantage that accrued to them because of this expansion of the domain of civilization at the expense of barbarism has been simply incalculable. This expansion produced peace, and put a stop to the ceaseless, grinding, bloody tyranny that had desolated the Balkans for so many centuries. There are many excellent people who have praised Tolstoi's fantastic religious doctrines, his fantastic advocacy of peace. The same quality that makes the debauchee and the devotee alternate in certain decadent families, the hysterical development which leads to violent emotional reaction in a morbid nature from vice to virtue, also leads to the creation of Tolstoi's "Kreutzer Sonata" on the one hand, and of his unhealthy peace-mysticism on the other. A sane and healthy mind would be as incapable of the moral degradation of the novel as of the decadent morality of the philosophy. If Tolstoi's countrymen had acted according to his moral theories they would now be extinct, and savages would have taken their place. Unjust war is a terrible sin. It does not nowadays in the aggregate cause anything like the misery that is caused in the aggregate by unjust dealing toward one's neighbors in the commercial and social world; and to condemn all war is just as logical as to condemn all business and all social relations, as to condemn love and marriage because of the frightful misery caused by brutal and unregulated passion. If Russia had acted upon Tolstoi's philosophy, all its people would long ago have disappeared from the face of the earth, and the country would now be occupied by wandering tribes of Tartar barbarians. The Armenian massacres are simply illustrations on a small scale of what would take place on the very largest scale if Tolstoi's principles became universal among civilized people. It is not necessary to point out that the teaching which would produce such a condition of things is fundamentally immoral.

Again, peace may come only through war. There are men in our country who seemingly forget that at the outbreak of the Civil War the great cry raised by the opponents of the war was the cry for peace. One of the most amusing and most biting satires written by the friends of union and liberty during the Civil War was called the "New Gospel of Peace," in derision of this attitude. The men in our own country who, in the name of peace, have been encouraging Aguinaldo and his people to shoot down our soldiers in the Philippines might profit not a little if they would look back to the days of the bloody draft riots, which were deliberately incited in the name of peace and free speech, when the mob killed men and women in the streets and burned orphan children in the asylums as a protest against the war. Four years of bloody struggle with an armed foe, who was helped at every turn by the self-styled advocates of peace, were needed in order to restore the Union; but the result has been that the peace of this continent has been effectually assured. Had the shortsighted advocates of peace for the moment had their way, and secession become an actual fact, nothing could have prevented a repetition in North America of the devastating anarchic warfare that obtained for three quarters of a century in South America after the yoke of Spain was thrown off. We escaped generations of anarchy and bloodshed, because our fathers who upheld Lincoln and followed Grant were men in every sense of the term, with too much common sense to be misled by those who preached that war was always wrong, and with a fund of stern virtue deep in their souls which enabled them to do deeds from which men of oversoft natures would have shrunk appalled.

Wars between civilized communities are very dreadful, and as nations grow more and more civilized we have every reason, not merely to hope, but to believe that they will grow rarer and rarer. Even with civilized peoples, as was shown by our own experience in 1861, it may be necessary at last to draw the sword rather than to submit to wrong-doing. But a very marked feature in the world-history of the present century has been the growing infrequency of wars between great civilized nations. The Peace Conference at The Hague is but one of the signs of this growth. I am among those who believe that much was accomplished at that conference, and I am proud of the leading position taken in the conference by our delegates. Incidentally I may mention that the testimony is unanimous that they were able to take this leading position chiefly because we had just emerged victorious from our most righteous war with Spain. Scant attention is paid to the weakling or the coward who babbles of peace; but due heed is given to the strong man with the sword girt on thigh who preaches peace, not from ignoble motives, not from fear or distrust of his own powers, but from a deep sense of moral obligation.

The growth of peacefulness between nations, however, has been confined strictly to those that are civilized. It can only come when both parties to a possible quarrel feel the same spirit. With a barbarous nation peace is the exceptional condition. On the border between civilization and barbarism war is generally normal because it must be under the conditions of barbarism. Whether the barbarian be the Red Indian on the frontier of the United States, the Afghan on the border of British India, or the Turkoman who confronts the Siberian Cossack, the result is the same. In the long run civilized man finds he can keep the peace only by subduing his barbarian neighbor; for the barbarian will yield only to force, save in instances so exceptional that they may be disregarded. Back of the force must come fair dealing, if the peace is to be permanent. But without force fair dealing usually amounts to nothing. In our history we have had more trouble from the Indian tribes whom we pampered and petted than from those we wronged; and this has been true in Siberia, Hindustan, and Africa.

Every expansion of civilization makes for peace. In other words, every expansion of a great civilized power means a victory for law, order, and righteousness. This has been the case in every instance of expansion during the present century, whether the expanding power were France or England, Russia or America. In every instance the expansion has been of benefit, not so much to the power nominally benefited as to the whole world. In every instance the result proved that the expanding power was doing a duty to civilization far greater and more important than could have been done by any stationary power. Take the case of France and Algiers. During the early decades of the present century, piracy of the most dreadful description was rife on the Mediterranean, and thousands of civilized men were yearly dragged into slavery by the Moorish pirates. A degrading peace was purchased by the civilized powers by the payment of tribute. Our own country was one among the tributary nations which thus paid blood-money to the Moslem bandits of the sea. We fought occasional battles with them; and so, on a larger scale, did the English. But peace did not follow, because the country was not occupied. Our last payment was made in 1830, and the reason it was the last was because in that year the French conquest of Algiers began. Foolish sentimentalists, like those who wrote little poems in favor of the Mahdists against the English, and who now write little essays in favor of Aguinaldo against the Americans, celebrated the Algerian freebooters as heroes who were striving for liberty against the invading French. But the French continued to do their work; France expanded over Algiers, and the result was that piracy on the Mediterranean came to an end, and Algiers has thriven as never before in its history. On an even larger scale the same thing is true of England and the Soudan. The expansion of England throughout the Nile valley has been an incalculable gain for civilization. Any one who reads the writings of the Austrian priests and laymen who were prisoners in the Soudan under the Mahdi will realize that when England crushed him and conquered the Soudan she conferred a priceless boon upon humanity and made the civilized world her debtor. Again, the same thing is true of the Russian advance in Asia. As in the Soudan the English conquest was followed by peace, and the endless massacres of the Mahdi are stopped forever, so the Russian conquest of the khanates of central Asia meant the cessation of the barbarous warfare under which Asian civilization had steadily withered away since the days of Genghis Khan, and the substitution in its place of the reign of peace and order. All civilization has been the gainer by the advance of France in North Africa; as it has been the gainer by the advance of England in both Asia and Africa, both Canada and Australia. Above all, there has been the greatest possible gain in peace. The rule of law and of order has succeeded to the rule of barbarous and bloody violence. Until the great civilized nations stepped in there was no chance for anything but such bloody violence.

So it has been in the history of our own country. Of course our whole national history has been one of expansion. Under Washington and Adams we expanded westward to the Mississippi; under Jefferson we expanded across the continent to the mouth of the Columbia; under Monroe we expanded into Florida; and then into Texas and California; and finally, largely through the instrumentality of Seward, into Alaska; while under every administration the process of expansion in the great plains and the Rockies has continued with growing rapidity. While we had a frontier the chief feature of frontier life was the endless war between the settlers and the red men. Sometimes the immediate occasion for the war was to be found in the conduct of the whites and sometimes in that of the reds, but the ultimate cause was simply that we were in contact with a country held by savages or half-savages.

Where we abut on Canada there is no danger of war, nor is there any danger where we abut on the well-settled regions of Mexico. But elsewhere war had to continue until we expanded over the country. Then it was succeeded at once by a peace which has remained unbroken to the present day. In North America, as elsewhere throughout the entire world, the expansion of a civilized nation has invariably meant the growth of the area in which peace is normal throughout the world.

The same will be true of the Philippines. If the men who have counseled national degradation, national dishonor, by urging us to leave the Philippines and put the Aguinaldan oligarchy in control of those islands, could have their way, we should merely turn them over to rapine and bloodshed until some stronger, manlier power stepped in to do the task we had shown ourselves fearful of performing. But, as it is, this country will keep the islands and will establish therein a stable and orderly government, so that one more fair spot of the world's surface shall have been snatched from the forces of darkness. Fundamentally the cause of expansion is the cause of peace.

With civilized powers there is but little danger of our getting into war. In the Pacific, for instance, the great progressive, colonizing nations are England and Germany. With England we have recently begun to feel ties of kindness as well as of kinship, and with her our relations are better than ever before; and so they ought to be with Germany. Recently affairs in Samoa have been straightened out, although there we suffered from the worst of all types of government, one in which three powers had a joint responsibility (the type, by the way, which some of the anti-imperialists actually advocated our introducing in the Philippines, under the pretence of rendering them neutral). This was accomplished very largely because the three nations set good-humoredly to work to come to an agreement which would do justice to all. In the preliminary negotiations the agents of America and Germany were Mr. Tripp and Baron Sternburg. No difficulty can ever arise between Germany and the United States which will not be settled with satisfaction to both, if the negotiations are conducted by such representatives of the two powers as these two men. What is necessary is to approach the subject, not with a desire to get ahead of one another, but to do even and exact justice, and to put into operation a scheme which will work, while scrupulously conserving the honor and interest of all concerned.

Nations that expand and nations that do not expand may both ultimately go down, but the one leaves heirs and a glorious memory, and the other leaves neither. The Roman expanded, and he has left a memory which has profoundly influenced the history of mankind, and he has further left as the heirs of his body, and, above all, of his tongue and culture, the so-called Latin peoples of Europe and America. Similarly to-day it is the great expanding peoples who bequeath to the future ages the great memories and material results of their achievements, and the nations which shall have sprung from their loins, England standing as the archetype and best exemplar of all such mighty nations. But the peoples that do not expand leave, and can leave, nothing behind them.

It is only the warlike power of a civilized people that can give peace to the world. The Arab wrecked the civilization of the Mediterranean coasts, the Turk wrecked the civilization of southeastern Europe, and the Tartar desolated from China to Russia and to Persia, setting back the progress of the world for centuries, solely because the civilized nations opposed to them had lost the great fighting qualities, and, in becoming overpeaceful, had lost the power of keeping peace with a strong hand. Their passing away marked the beginning of a period of chaotic barbarian warfare. Those whose memories are not so short as to have forgotten the defeat of the Greeks by the Turks, of the Italians by the Abyssinians, and the feeble campaigns waged by Spain against feeble Morocco, must realize that at the present moment the Mediterranean coasts would be overrun either by the Turks or by the Soudan Mahdists if these warlike barbarians had only to fear those southern European powers which have lost the fighting edge. Such a barbarian conquest would mean endless war; and the fact that nowadays the reverse takes place, and that the barbarians recede or are conquered, with the attendant fact that peace follows their retrogression or conquest, is due solely to the power of the mighty civilized races which have not lost the fighting instinct, and which by their expansion are gradually bringing peace into the red wastes where the barbarian peoples of the world hold sway.

SIDNEY WEBB

Throughout the nineteenth century there were many voices of discontent and protest. Men sensed that something had gone wrong with the economic and industrial system in which Adam Smith had foreseen the wealth of nations. A few, like William Morris, inventor and social reformer, and Thomas Carlyle, novelist, historian, and biographer, advocated a return to a bygone age when craftsmen had produced useful goods that were aesthetically appealing to the consumer and psychologically satisfying to the workman. Karl Marx protested against "bourgeois capitalism," insisting that workers should (and ultimately would) reap the full rewards of their efforts by displacing those who had exploited them. But many thinkers felt that Marxian economics was inadequate, largely because of its philosophical anarchism. Georges Sorel, for example, turned to syndicalism, which provided an organizational principle and a system of production and distribution that were more acceptable to the logical mind. Various forms of socialism—democratic, fascist, utopian, national, Christian—were also suggested.

The form of socialism most acceptable to the democratic tradition was developed in England by a group of young intellectuals. They named their association the Fabian Society, after the Roman general, Fabius, who frustrated Hannibal by avoiding battle until Hannibal's resources were virtually exhausted. These young social reformers dedicated themselves to the cause of evolutionary social control over the means of production. They rejected the need for force and violence in achieving this goal, insisting that it could be attained by gradual means, by operating within the framework of contemporary legal institutions.

George Bernard Shaw, playwright, H. G. Wells, novelist, and Sidney and Beatrice Webb, historians, were among the most persistent and persuasive of the Fabians. The Webbs (who later became Lord and Lady Passfield) were particularly tireless in their efforts to sway people to their beliefs. The following selection is from one of many socialist tracts written by Sidney Webb (1859–1947). Here he expresses the Fabians' objections to revolution and their conviction that a new and better world can be achieved naturally, without recourse to violence.

Socialism: True and False

I do not know whether many of those here present are aware that we celebrate to-night what may be regarded as the tenth anniversary of the foundation of this Society. It was on the 4th of January, 1884, that the little group which had been for some months discussing the Regeneration of the World and a Fellowship of

Sidney Webb, SOCIALISM: TRUE AND FALSE, *Fabian Tract No. 51 (London: The Fabian Society, 1894), pp. 3–10. Courtesy of the Fabian Society.*

the New Life, formally adopted the title of the Fabian Society—thereby indicating, as I take it, an underlying suspicion that the Devil of Individualism was not to be driven out by any short and sharp encounter, but that it behoved all true believers to watch and wait and diligently equip themselves for a warfare which must necessarily be harassing and protracted. But though we took the title of the Fabian Society in January, 1884, it was two or three years before we had quite found out what our instinctive choice of a title really portended. In 1884 the Fabian Society, like the other Socialist organizations, had its enthusiastic young members—aye, and old ones, too—who placed all their hopes on a sudden tumultuous uprising of a united proletariat, before whose mighty onrush, kings, landlords, and capitalists would go down like ninepins, leaving society quietly to re-sort itself into Utopia. The date for this Social Revolution was sometimes actually fixed for 1889, the centenary of the opening of the French Revolution. I remember myself that one of our friends, in his zeal that the rural districts might not be forgotten, printed and circulated a proposal that a few Socialist missionaries should buy a gipsy caravan and live in it "until the Revolution," an event evidently to be expected before the ensuing winter!

It was against all thinking and teaching of this catastrophic kind that the Society gradually came to set its face—not, as I believe, because we were any less in earnest in our warfare against existing evils, or less extreme in our remedies, but because we were sadly and sorrowfully driven to the conclusion that no sudden or simultaneous transformation of society from an Individualist to a Collectivist basis was possible, or even thinkable.

On the other hand we had but little sympathy with schemes for the regeneration of mankind by the establishment of local Utopias, whether in Cumberland or in Chili. To turn our back on the Unearned Increment and the Machine Industry seemed a poor way of conquering them. We had no faith in the recuperative qualities of spade husbandry or in any devices for dodging the Law of Rent. In short, we repudiated the common assumption that Socialism was necessarily bound up with Insurrectionism on the one hand or Utopianism on the other, and we set to work to discover for ourselves and to teach to others how practically to transform England into a Social Democratic Commonwealth.

Well, we have I hope, all learnt a great deal since 1884, but everything that has happened during these ten years has strengthened our faith in the fundamental principles of our association. If I might speak in the name of our members, I should say that we are more than ever convinced of the utter impossibility of what may be called Catastrophic Socialism, and all its attendant heresies. Nor have we seen reason to alter our distrust of separate Socialist communities, in whatever specious new form the old idea may clothe itself. For ten years we have held on our course, turning neither to Insurrectionism on the one hand nor to Utopianism on the other.

If now I briefly recall to your mind some instances of the progress of Collectivist ideas during these years, I trust that no one will imagine that I am attempting to claim that progress as the work of the Fabian Society, or indeed of any society whatever. Nothing is more futile than to endeavor to ascribe the exact cause and origin of a general intellectual movement, of which we are, indeed, ourselves a product. The seeds of the Socialist harvest of the last few years were sown by the great thinkers and teachers of the last two generations; and it would be idle to attempt to measure the exact influence of any one of them in the transformation of ideas amid which we are now living.

I take as a starting point, not 1884, but the year 1880, which as I conceive, approximately marks the turning of thought.

Fourteen years ago we may almost say that an unsystematic and empirical Individualism reigned supreme. Not in one political party alone, or in one class of society, but in all alike, we find the assumption that the functions of government ought to be reduced to the barest minimum; that free competition, leading as it was supposed to the survival of the fittest, was the only sure foundation of a prosperous State; and that the incessant private "war which leads each man to strive to place himself on another's shoulders and to remain there," was, on the whole, a benevolent dispensation of Providence, and part of the "Laws of Nature," not impiously to be interfered with.

The Liberal Party, at that time almost exclusively dominated by the manufacturers and the Whig families, was living on the remnants of the political reputation of the Manchester School. A vague belief in the saving grace of non-intervention abroad and *laisser faire* at home, was vitalised only by a practical programme of the extension of household franchise to the counties. To the rising desire for social reform it presented no more hopeful solution than the economic negations of Nassau Senior and Fawcett. The object of all social reforms, authorized or unauthorized, was to enable the artisan to become a small capitalist, and the laborer a small landowner. "Three acres and a cow" in the country had its analogue in schemes of leasehold enfranchisement in the towns. As an alternative to the existing order of squires and captains of industry, we had offered to us a millennium of peasant proprietors and small masters. It is needless to enlarge upon the self-complacency with which both Liberal and Conservative capitalists delighted in reminding the working-men of all the future possibilities of self-advancement, when land should be "free," food cheap, and industrial competition unrestricted. The epics of this faith have been written by that unconscious corrupter of youth, Mr. Samuel Smiles, and are still fresh in the memories of most of us.

In 1880, Mr. Gladstone came into power on a wave of popular indignation against atrocities in Bulgaria, which dispensed with the necessity for any programme of social reforms in England. The political Radicals, swept along by the same wave, were too busy denouncing international aggression to be effective even on fiscal reform and political democracy, beyond which they had practically no vision. The Conservatives, less traditionally bound to Administrative Nihilism, had just consolidated the Factory Acts, but their leaders had been so far perverted as deliberately to leave the whole range of sweated trades outside the effective scope of the law and to give up all attempts to shorten the hours of labor. Even the working-men had been permeated by the same policy. The Trade Union leaders could think of only four trivial amendments to propose to the Factory Bill of 1878. The Trade Union Congress of those years asked for practically nothing but an Employers' Liability Bill. In 1879 there were a great many more unemployed than there have ever been since, but no responsible authority thought of anything but charity or poor relief for them. Free Education, Extension of the Factory Acts, Limitation of the Hours of Labor, Expansion of Municipal Activity, though all proposed long before, seem, in 1880, scarcely to have entered the heads of any of those who were leading either the Conservative, the Liberal, the Radical, or the Trade Union forces. But more striking even than this barrenness of programme was the total absence of any systematic view of politics as a whole. In this respect the most advanced statesmen of fourteen years ago stood in marked contrast with the Philosophic

Radicals of the first half of the century. I will quote the significant comment of a shrewd critic of Mr. Gladstone's Cabinet:

> James Mill and his school had two characteristics which have not always marked energetic types of Liberalism, and perhaps do not mark them in our own day. The advanced Liberals of his time were systematic, and they were constructive. They surveyed society and institutions as a whole; they connected their advocacy of political and legal changes with theories of human nature; they considered the great art of government in connection with the character of man, his proper education, his potential capacities. They could explain in the large dialect of a definite scheme what were their aims and whither they were going. . . . Is there any such approach to a body of systematic political thought in our own day? We cannot say that there is.[1]

Now, in estimating the progress of Collectivism between 1880 and 1894, I do not propose to make any parade of the membership and influence of the various Socialist societies, which seem to me to be, at the present time, far greater than at any previous period. Nor will I recite a long list of bills which have been passed during the last fourteen years, and claim these as more or less triumphs of Collectivism. It would be easy to argue that the multiplication of municipal gasworks is an unconscious adoption of the principle of Socialism, just as the freeing of schools and the building of gratuitous libraries is of that of Communism. But what we Socialists are aiming at is not to secure this or that reform, still less to put this or that party into power, but to convert the great mass of the English people to our own views. We are trying to satisfy the ordinary man, not merely that most of the existing arrangements of society are fundamentally defective—for on that point the great majority have always been most painfully convinced—but also that the main principle of reform must be the substitution of Collective Ownership and Control for Individual Private Property in the means of production. In short, the Socialist task is to contribute to this generation the "body of systematic political thought," of which Mr. John Morley was in 1882 deploring the lack. Though we cannot count among our ranks any men of the calibre of Bentham and James Mill, though we have neither the wealth nor the position of the Philosophic Radicals of the first part of the century, yet I take it that the work set before us is analogous to theirs. The Socialists are the Benthamites of this generation. And if I had to sum up the effect upon the public mind of the Socialist propaganda of the past fourteen years, I could find no better description than that given of the work of the Benthamites.

"They produced," says a very competent observer,

> a much more serious effect on public opinion than superficial inquirers perceived, or interested ones would acknowledge. The important practical effect was not made evident by converting and bringing over large numbers of political partisans from one banner or class to another, or by making them renounce one appellation and adopt another; but it was shown by affecting the conclusions of all classes, and inducing them, while they retained their old distinctive names, to reason after a new fashion, and according to principles wholly different from those to which they had been previously accustomed.[2]

It is, of course, especially in the economic and industrial field that we find this reasoning "after a new fashion, and according to principles wholly different from those to which they had been previously accustomed." It has become more and more plain

[1] Mr. John Morley, in a review of Bain's "Life of James Mill," *Fortnightly Review*, Vol. XXXI (April, 1882), 503.

[2] J. A. Roebuck.

that the facts of industrial life are "dead against" the realization of the individualist ideal of each man becoming his own master. The Industrial Revolution, with its aggregation of production into fewer larger enterprises, has rendered it practically impossible for five-sixths of the population to be anything but hired servants, dependent on the owners of land and capital for leave to earn a living. At the same time the spread of economic knowledge has made it clear that even the most virtuous artizan cannot dodge the law of rent; and he is therefore left face to face with the grim fact of a colossal tribute levied by ownership upon industry without any obligation on the part of the receivers to render social service in return. It is especially the growing understanding of this Ricardian law of rent which has revolutionized London politics, and has caused the hostile indifference with which the artizan in other centres is coming to regard both the great political parties. The outcome of this new ferment is the formation of an incipient Collectivist body of opinion among the great bulk of the younger men, the rising London party, and the new-born Labor Movement.

The political effect of this change of opinion is seen in the gradual transformation of party programmes, especially on the Land question. In the Liberal party the new Collectivist section is in direct antagonism to the "old gang." Its aim is not the subdivision of property, whether capital or land, but the control and administration of it by the representatives of the community. It has no desire to see the Duke of Bedford replaced by five hundred little Dukes of Bedford under the guise of enfranchised leaseholders, but prefers to assert the claim of the whole community to the land, and especially to that "unearned increment" of value which the whole community creates. It has no vain dream of converting the agricultural laborer into a freeholder, farming his own land, but looks to the creation of parish councils empowered to acquire land for communal ownership, and to build cottages for the laborers to rent. The path to its town Utopia is that of Mr. Chamberlain's early career, though not of his political programme—unlimited municipalization of local public services and a wide extension of corporate activity. London in particular has caught up the old Birmingham cry of "High rates and a healthy city," but with a significant difference. Our modern economists tell us that the first source of public revenue for a rising city is the growing rental value of its site, which at present falls into private hands. Hence the new demand for the gradual municipalization by taxation of urban land values—a demand still so little understood by most of our statesmen that they fondly imagine it to have something to do with a division of rates between house-owner and occupier. It is coming to be remembered, in short, that Bentham himself, the great father of Political Radicalism, urged that taxation need not be limited to the supply of funds for the bare administrative expenses of the State, but that, wisely handled, it also supplied a means of gradually securing the great end of equality of opportunity to every citizen.

The typical young politician, who twenty years ago was a convinced Individualist quoting Mr. Herbert Spencer, is nowadays an empirical Collectivist of a practical kind. His face is turned away from the Individualist ideal of his fathers towards a period of ever-increasing collective action. Happily, however, he is no Utopian, and realizes that it is impossible all at once to take over the administration of the land and capital of the community. Where direct public administration is still impracticable, the public interest can only be secured by collective regulation of the conditions of labor, in order to prevent the Standard of Life of the workers from being degraded by private greed. And hence it is that the extremely valuable mantle shared by Robert Owen and Lord Shaftesbury, and despised by the older Liberals, is now the joint heritage of the Labor party and the Collectivist Radicals; Eight Hours Bills, practicable and impracticable, are the order of the day, and drastic proposals for the annihilation of "Sweating" excite the undisguised horror of the older members of both Liberal and Conservative parties. And since all this regulation and supervision of private enterprises is burdensome and expensive, the presumption of the younger politicians is distinctly against individual profit-making where it is possible to dispense with it. The best Government is no longer "that which governs least," but "that which can safely and advantageously administer most."

All this is encouraging progress for so short a period as fourteen years. But it amounts, of course, to no more than the preliminary steps in the conversion of England. Public opinion, in fact, is in "a fine state to begin on." Adhesion to Socialism is no longer a disqualification for a candidate. Politicians lend a willing ear to Socialist proposals. Now is the time to bring to bear a body of systematic and constructive political thought such as that with which the Philosophic Radicals won their great triumphs. The greatest need of the English Socialist Party at this moment is men and women of brains who will deliberately set themselves, by serious study, to work out the detailed application of Collectivist principles to the actual problems of modern life. We need to do a great deal more hard thinking in almost every department of our Socialist programme. I am appalled when I realize how little attention we have yet been able to pay to what I may call the Unsettled Questions of Democratic Administration.

To take, for instance, the pressing problem of the Unemployed. In my humble judgment no plan has yet been devised by which the fluctuations of work could be entirely prevented, or safe and profitable employment found for those rendered idle by no fault of their own. It is easy enough to demand that something should be done, and I entirely agree with agitating the subject; but something more than agitation is required. It is of no use urging remedies which can be demonstrably proved to be worse for the patient than the disease itself. I fear that if we were given full power to-morrow to deal with the unemployed all over England we should find ourselves hard put to it how to solve the problem. Or to turn to another field, in which practically nothing has yet been done. Have we any clear and decided view as to the relation between central and local authorities? How far do we wish to increase the power of the national administration at the expense of local governing bodies—to what extent, that is, will our Social-Democracy be consistent with local Home Rule? The Glasgow Town Council, for instance, is at this moment quarrelling with the Postmaster-General as to whether the telephone shall fall within the sphere of municipal or of national Socialism. It is evident that some departments of public administration can be best managed from one central office. It is, I suppose, equally evident that others must be administered locally, under some kind of central control. But which subjects should be local and which should be central—upon what principle the division should be made, and in what form and to what extent there should be a central control—these are problems to which, as far as I know, no solution has been found and very little serious thought been given.

I do not suggest that we Socialists are more ignorant than other people: on the contrary, the two puzzles that I have chosen are at present puzzles to the whole world. But the whole world is not equally interested with ourselves in getting a solution of them. Those who believe that nothing ought to be done for the unemployed are not likely to succeed in finding anything; and we can hardly expect those who object to any extension of Democracy to help us to solve the problems which it presents. It is we who must discover the answers to our own conundrums; and I do most seriously suggest that there is no more valuable field of work for any group of Socialists, no more fruitful service to the Socialist cause, than for them earnestly and persistently to study, in the light of the ascertained facts, some one of the many social problems to which we have to apply our Socialist faith. Depend upon it, the first step to getting what we want is a very clear and precise knowledge of what it is that we want.

But this want of precision in our thinking may easily do worse than merely delay our progress; there is, as it seems to me, a good deal of danger of its leading us positively astray from the Socialist goal. The circumstances of modern life are so complicated, the problems to be dealt with are so difficult, the need for prompt action is often so great that we may easily be led to take up schemes of reform which promise some immediate improvement on the present state of things, but which are not really in the line of advance towards a genuine Collectivism.

Here I venture on dangerous ground. But if we are to clear up our ideas, and apply our Socialist principles to the practical problems of life, we must definitely make up our mind between contrary ideals. If our aim is the transformation of England into a Social-Democracy, we must frankly accept the changes brought about by the Industrial Revolution, the factory system, the massing of population in great cities, the elaborate differentiation and complication of modern civilization, the subordination of the worker to the citizen, and of the individual to the community. We must rid ourselves resolutely of those schemes and projects of byegone Socialisms which have now passed out of date, as well as from the specious devices of Individualism in a new dress. All these I class together as Spurious Collectivism, making, in my view, not for social progress, but for reaction.

THE CONTEMPORARY WORLD

Any historian who tries to generalize about twentieth-century civilization faces two serious obstacles: lack of perspective and complexity of detail. Inevitably caught up in the events that he wishes to analyze, he must somehow free himself from them, stand back, and view them objectively and dispassionately. To achieve such detachment is not an easy task. The second obstacle is the tremendous complexity of his subject matter. Both in scope and detail, the data on which the historian of contemporary civilization must base his generalizations vastly exceed those of any earlier time. And yet it is possible at least to indicate the most significant features of our twentieth-century world.

When we glance at the history of our century so far, the events which first strike our eye are probably the two world wars, a fact that may lead us to conclude that we live in a period of almost constant warfare. But this is not a peculiarity of our own time, for the Western world has seldom been without war. What sets our time apart is not the *fact* of war so much as the *nature* of war. Twentieth-century warfare has tended to become total both in scope and intensity. While earlier wars were usually limited in geographical extent, our two, particularly the second, have been conducted on virtually a world-wide scale. Nor, like earlier conflicts, have their effects been limited primarily to a professional military class. Rather, the brunt of the devastation has often fallen directly upon civilians.

Although these two great wars have undoubtedly been the most dramatic episodes of the twentieth century, they have not been the most significant ones. Less obvious, but of more lasting effect on our civilization, are certain basic changes that have been in process constantly throughout the century, and even before. The details of these changes are almost infinitely complex, but the changes themselves can be divided into three major types—political, economic, and scientific-technological.

The most important political change of the twentieth century has been a shift of the center of power away from Western Europe. After hundreds of years of supremacy, Western Europe is no longer the political center of the world. Political power has moved in three main directions: to the United States, to Russia, and to Asia. Of these shifts of power, that to the United States appears least likely to cause either abrupt or major changes in the future course of world history and civilization. For we are basically a cultural extension of Western Europe, the direct heirs of her civilization. Russia, though closer geographically to Western Europe, is separated by greater cultural barriers. In all its historical contacts with the West, Russia has remained half-alien. Even in periods when their leaders have deliberately copied the ways of the West, the Russians have retained their own, non-European point of view. The rapid growth of Russia's power is even now causing changes in the lives of people in Europe, America, and elsewhere. The future will undoubtedly witness an increase in these changes. The twentieth century, finally, has witnessed a remarkable increase in the political power of Asia, primarily in Japan, China, and India. Although these countries do not equal either the United States or Russia in power today, it would be hazardous to predict either the limit of their potential or the effects that their increasing power will have on the future of our civilization.

We are in the midst, then, of a period of fundamental political change. This is an exciting time in which to live, and it is a time of uncertainty. The shifts in power that have already taken place have aroused concern in many Europeans, as well as Americans, who fear that the political ascendancy of non-Western peoples may mean the destruction of our civilization.

In economics, as in politics, the world today is undergoing basic and sometimes violent change. The capitalist system, which was developed in the West over several hundred years, and which reached its climax only in the late nineteenth century, seems now to be on the decline. Although capitalism has been under attack by its opponents from before the time of Marx, the most serious blow it has yet suffered was self-inflicted—the great depression of the thirties. While it has not been wholly rejected by any of the Western countries, as it has been by some of the non-Western nations, still capitalism has, particularly since the depression, been compromised and supplemented by non-capitalistic forms of economic organization. The current decline of capitalism poses serious problems: Has capitalism had its day, or will it recover? If the former, what kind of economic organization will replace it, and can the transition be accomplished without social cataclysm?

Finally, we are in the midst of a scientific-technological revolution. Although this revolution began as far back as the time of Copernicus, its pace has been greatly accelerated in recent years. It holds forth great promise for man's future, but it poses great dangers as well. And it is the dangers, symbolized by the term "ultimate weapon"—whether this be an intercontinental ballistics missile with a nuclear warhead or some even more fantastic creation of modern science and technology—that occupy our attention. The fact that man's greatest achievements in science, which have done so much to enrich human life, may be used as a means for extinguishing human life is a clear indication of the grave problems facing us today. These problems have not been created by science and technology; rather, they have sprung from the underlying political, economic, and social dislocations that plague our world.

None of the three changes that are in process in today's world, taken in itself, *need* be a cause for great concern. The shifts in political power could well lead to the end of an old era of national rivalries and the effective development of a new world-wide political organization. As for the decline of capitalism, it is far from complete, and in nations like Britain and the Scandinavian countries, non-capitalistic economic systems have been developed without either revolution or war. Turning to the achievements in science and technology, it is not even necessary to list the benefits that we have received from them. Why, then, do men today fear for the future of the human race? The answer lies mainly in the relationships among the three changes we have been discussing. Starting with the fact that the shifts in political power have generally benefited the non-Western at the expense of the Western world, adding to this the fact that the most powerful of these non-Western nations are anti-capitalistic, and concluding with the fact that weapons of great destructive force have been perfected and are now in production, we can easily understand why men are apprehensive of the future.

Our century is often called "the age of anxiety." With the experience of two world wars behind us and the threat of a third hanging over our heads, there is just cause for anxiety. What is perhaps more important than our emotional reactions to world events, however, is the way in which we attempt to deal with the problems these events raise. On this score the record of twentieth-century civilization has been far from encouraging. The growth of totalitarianism, in Germany, Italy, and elsewhere, revealed a serious breakdown in the morale of Western Europe. The peoples of these countries, finding themselves unable to cope with the problems facing them, proved willing to give up their freedom and responsibility and to accept the authority of a dictator, provided he would insure their security. The quest for security is not a phenomenon peculiar to the twentieth century. Neither is absolute government. What is most disturbing in the recent history of Europe is the fact that people, instead of proving more jealous of their freedom than did those of the past, have too often shown themselves to be just the opposite. Although earlier forms of absolute government exercised virtually complete control over limited areas of social life, modern totalitarianism implies total control over all. In theory at least, every act that an individual performs and even every thought that he thinks are prescribed by the political leaders. And, though fascistic totalitarianism was almost completely destroyed by World War II, the communistic variety today dominates an even greater proportion of the world and its inhabitants.

What, then, of the future? What chance does our civilization have to survive? In the opinion of many sober analysts, our prospects are dim. Even without considering the possibility of annihilation in a third world war, these men see little hope for the survival of those ideals and institutions we have developed in the West since the time of the Greeks. On the other hand, there are those who believe that man can survive the crises he faces and at the same time preserve the basic values he has developed in his historical past. Among the optimists are two twentieth-century philosophers, John Dewey and A.N. Whitehead, both of whom insist that we can solve the problems that lie ahead through the active and practical employment of our intelligence or reason. To develop the individual's intellectual potentialities, however, both agree on the necessity for education. But what kind of education? To this question everyone seems to have a different answer. Without attempting to give the final answer here, we merely suggest that one area of education that can contribute to man's ability to preserve his civilization for future generations is a knowledge and appreciation of that civilization's past.

SIGMUND FREUD

It is tempting to describe Sigmund Freud (1856–1939) as one of the last of the great eighteenth-century rationalists, for there are striking similarities between his thought and that of the philosophes. *First, there is the assumption common to both that "knowledge is power," that once man knows the* why *of an event or relationship he can exercise rational control over it. In his lectures on the origin and development of psychoanalysis, Freud often concluded his descriptions of case histories with remarks such as, "When the memory of this scene was revived in hypnosis, the paralysis of the right arm, which had existed since the beginning of the illness, was cured and the treatment ended"; or "She remembered it during the treatment, reproduced the pathogenic moment with every sign of intense emotional excitement, and was cured by this treatment. . . ." Second, both Freud and the eighteenth-century* philosophes *accept John Locke's* tabula rasa, *his denial that men are born with innate ideas, although Freud put heavier emphasis on the nature and function of instincts, particularly biological, than did the earlier writers.*

But to suggest such parallels tends to minimize the extraordinary contributions made by this Viennese physician. Freud first became interested in the problems of mental health in Vienna and later pursued the study of hysteria and hysterical symptoms in Paris. In 1893 he persuaded Dr. Joseph Breuer to collaborate on a work that later appeared as Studien über Hysterie *(1895). From then until 1906, Freud worked on alone, perfecting his psychoanalytic techniques and substituting for hypnosis the major element of the new psychology—the technique of free association of ideas. After 1906, Freud was joined by an enthusiastic band of followers and disciples, including A. A. Brill, Carl Jung, Alfred Adler, and Ernest Jones. To the end of his long life Freud continued his studies, although they occasionally were impaired by profound disagreements with some of his younger colleagues. Freud retained his conviction that the most basic instinct in man was the desire to achieve sensory (sexual) pleasure, an instinct that automatically brought the individual into conflict with society. This particular emphasis was minimized by Jung and Adler, who, though disagreeing with each other, agreed that Freud had oversimplified and overstated his case.*

The selection that follows is taken from the unfinished An Outline of Psychoanalysis, *Freud's last major work.*

An Outline of Psychoanalysis

Chapter One

THE PSYCHICAL APPARATUS

Psychoanalysis makes a basic assumption,[1] the discussion of which falls within the sphere of philosophical thought, but the justification of which lies in its results. We know two things concerning what we call our psyche or mental life: firstly, its bodily organ and scene of action, the brain (or nervous system), and secondly, our acts of consciousness, which are immediate data and cannot be more fully explained by any kind of description. Everything that lies between these two terminal points is unknown to us and, so far as we are aware, there is no direct relation between them. If it existed, it would at the most afford an exact localization of the processes of consciousness and would give us no help toward understanding them.

Our two hypotheses start out from these ends or beginnings of our knowledge. The first is concerned with localization. We assume that mental life is the function of an apparatus to which we ascribe the characteristics of being extended in space and of being made up of several portions—which we imagine, that is, as being like a telescope or microscope or something of the sort. The consistent carrying through of a conception of this kind is a scientific novelty, even though some attempts in that direction have been made previously.

We have arrived at our knowledge of this psychical apparatus by studying the individual development of human beings. To the oldest of these mental provinces or agencies we give the name of *id*. It contains everything that is inherited, that is present at birth, that is fixed in the constitution—above all, therefore, the instincts, which originate in the somatic organization and which find their first mental expression in the id in forms unknown to us.[2]

Under the influence of the real external world which surrounds us, one portion of the id has undergone a special development. From what was originally a cortical layer, provided with organs for receiving stimuli and with apparatus for protection against excessive stimulation, a special organization has arisen which henceforward acts as an intermediary between the id and the external world. This region of our mental life has been given the name of *ego*.

The principal characteristics of the ego are these. In consequence of the relation which was already established between sensory perception and muscular action, the ego is in control of voluntary movement. It has the task of self-preservation. As regards *external* events, it performs that task by becoming aware of the stimuli from without, by storing up experiences of them (in the memory), by avoiding excessive stimuli (through flight), by dealing with moderate stimuli (through adaptation) and, fi-

[1] [It will be seen that this basic assumption is a double-barrelled one and is sometimes referred to by the author as two separate hypotheses.—Trans.]

Sigmund Freud, AN OUTLINE OF PSYCHOANALYSIS, *trans. James Strachey (New York: W. W. Norton & Company, Inc., 1949; London: The Hogarth Press, Ltd.).*

[2] This oldest portion of the mental apparatus remains the most important throughout life, and it was the first subject of the investigations of psychoanalysis. [Throughout this book the English word "instinct" is, with some misgivings, used to render the German "*Trieb*." The sense in which Freud uses the term is, in any case, made clear in the following pages.—Trans.]

nally, by learning to bring about appropriate modifications in the external world to its own advantage (through activity). As regards *internal* events, in relation to the id, it performs that task by gaining control over the demands of the instincts, by deciding whether they shall be allowed to obtain satisfaction, by postponing that satisfaction to times and circumstances favorable in the external world or by suppressing their excitations completely. Its activities are governed by consideration of the tensions produced by stimuli present within it or introduced into it. The raising of these tensions is in general felt as *unpleasure* and their lowering as *pleasure.* It is probable, however, that what is felt as pleasure or unpleasure is not the *absolute* degree of the tensions but something in the rhythm of their changes. The ego pursues pleasure and seeks to avoid unpleasure. An increase in unpleasure which is expected and foreseen is met by a *signal of anxiety;* the occasion of this increase, whether it threatens from without or within, is called a *danger.* From time to time the ego gives up its connection with the external world and withdraws into the state of sleep, in which its organization undergoes far-reaching changes. It may be inferred from the state of sleep that that organization consists in a particular distribution of mental energy.

The long period of childhood, during which the growing human being lives in dependence upon his parents, leaves behind it a precipitate, which forms within his ego a special agency in which this parental influence is prolonged. It has received the name of *superego.* In so far as the superego is differentiated from the ego or opposed to it, it constitutes a third force which the ego must take into account.

Thus, an action by the ego is as it should be if it satisfies simultaneously the demands of the id, of the superego, and of reality, that is to say if it is able to reconcile their demands with one another. The details of the relation between the ego and the superego become completely intelligible if they are carried back to the child's attitude toward his parents. The parents' influence naturally includes not merely the personalities of the parents themselves but also the racial, national, and family traditions handed on through them as well as the demands of the immediate social *milieu* which they represent. In the same way, an individual's superego in the course of his development takes over contributions from later successors and substitutes of his parents, such as teachers, admired figures in public life, or high social ideals. It will be seen that, in spite of their fundamental difference, the id and the superego have one thing in common: they both represent the influences of the past (the id the influence of heredity, the superego essentially the influence of what is taken over from other people), whereas the ego is principally determined by the individual's own experience, that is to say by accidental and current events.

This general pattern of a psychical apparatus may be supposed to apply equally to the higher animals which resemble man mentally. A superego must be presumed to be present wherever, as in the case of man, there is a long period of dependence in childhood. The assumption of a distinction between ego and id cannot be avoided.

Animal psychology has not yet taken in hand the interesting problem which is here presented.

Chapter Two

THE THEORY OF THE INSTINCTS

The power of the id expresses the true purpose of the individual organism's life. This consists in the satisfaction of its innate needs. No such purpose as that of keeping itself alive or of protecting itself from dangers by means of anxiety can be attributed to the id. That is the business of the ego, which is also concerned with discovering the most favorable and least perilous method of obtaining satisfaction, taking the external world into account. The superego may bring fresh needs to the fore, but its chief function remains the *limitation* of satisfactions.

The forces which we assume to exist behind the tensions caused by the needs of the id are called *instincts*. They represent the somatic demands upon mental life. Though they are the ultimate cause of all activity, they are by nature conservative; the state, whatever it may be, which a living thing has reached, gives rise to a tendency to re-establish that state so soon as it has been abandoned. It is possible to distinguish an indeterminate number of instincts and in common practice this is in fact done. For us, however, the important question arises whether we may not be able to derive all of these various instincts from a few fundamental ones. We have found that instincts can change their aim (by displacement) and also that they can replace one another—the energy of one instinct passing over to another. This latter process is still insufficiently understood. After long doubts and vacillations we have decided to assume the existence of only two basic instincts, *Eros* and *the destructive instinct*. (The contrast between the instincts of self-preservation and of the preservation of the species, as well as the contrast between ego-love and object-love, fall within the bounds of Eros.) The aim of the first of these basic instincts is to establish ever greater unities and to preserve them thus—in short, to bind together; the aim of the second, on the contrary, is to undo connections and so to destroy things. We may suppose that the final aim of the destructive instinct is to reduce living things to an inorganic state. For this reason we also call it the *death instinct*. If we suppose that living things appeared later than inanimate ones and arose out of them, then the death instinct agrees with the formula that we have stated, to the effect that instincts tend toward a return to an earlier state. We are unable to apply the formula to Eros (the love instinct). That would be to imply that living substance had once been a unity but had subsequently been torn apart and was now tending toward reunion.[3]

In biological functions the two basic instincts work against each other or combine with each other. Thus, the act of eating is a destruction of the object with the final aim of incorporating it, and the sexual act is an act of aggression having as its purpose the most intimate union. This interaction of the two basic instincts with and against each other gives rise to the whole variegation of the phenomena of life. The analogy of our two basic instincts extends from the region of animate things to the pair of opposing forces—attraction and repulsion—which rule in the inorganic world.[4]

. . .

Chapter Six

THE TECHNIQUE OF PSYCHOANALYSIS

A dream, then, is a psychosis, with all the absurdities, delusions, and illusions of a psychosis. No doubt it is a psychosis which has only a short duration, which is harmless and even performs a useful function, which is brought about with the subject's consent and is ended by an act of his will. Nevertheless it *is* a psychosis, and we learn from it that even so deep-going a modification of mental life as this can be undone and can give place to normal func-

[3] Something of the sort has been imagined by poets, but nothing like it is known to us from the actual history of living substance.

[4] This picture of the basic forces or instincts, which still arouses much opposition among analysts, was already a familiar one to the philosopher Empedocles of Acragas.

tioning. Is it too bold, then, to hope that it must also be possible to submit the dreaded spontaneous illnesses of the mind to our control and bring about their cure?

We already possess much knowledge preliminary to such an undertaking. We have postulated that it is the ego's task to meet the demands of the three forces upon which it is dependent—reality, the id, and the superego—and meanwhile to preserve its own organization and maintain its own autonomy. The necessary condition for the pathological states we have mentioned can only be a relative or absolute weakening of the ego which prevents it from performing its tasks. The severest demand upon the ego is probably the keeping down of the instinctual claims of the id, and for this end the ego is obliged to maintain great expenditures of energy upon anti-cathexes. But the claims made by the superego, too, may become so powerful and so remorseless that the ego may be crippled, as it were, for its other tasks. We may suspect that, in the economic conflicts which now arise, the id and the superego often make common cause against the hardpressed ego, which, in order to retain its normal state, clings on to reality. But if the other two are too strong, they may succeed in loosening the organization of the ego and altering it so that its proper relation to reality is disturbed or even abolished. We have seen it happen in dreams: when the ego is detached from the reality of the external world, then, under the influence of the internal world, it slips down into psychosis.

Our plan of cure is based upon these views. The ego has been weakened by the internal conflict; we must come to its aid. The position is like a civil war which can only be decided by the help of an ally from without. The analytical physician and the weakened ego of the patient, basing themselves upon the real external world, are to combine against the enemies, the instinctual demands of the id, and the moral demands of the superego. We form a pact with each other. The patient's sick ego promises us the most complete candor, promises, that is, to put at our disposal all of the material which his self-perception provides; we, on the other hand, assure him of the strictest discretion and put at his service our experience in interpreting material that has been influenced by the unconscious. Our knowledge shall compensate for his ignorance and shall give his ego once more mastery over the lost provinces of his mental life. This pact constitutes the analytic situation.

No sooner have we taken this step than we meet with a first disappointment, a first warning against complacency. If the patient's ego is to be a useful ally in our common work, it must, however hard it may be pressed by the hostile powers, have retained a certain degree of coherence, a fragment at least of understanding for the demands of reality. But this is not to be expected from the ego of a psychotic; it cannot carry out a pact of this sort, indeed it can scarcely engage in it. It will very soon toss us away and the help we offer it, to join the portions of the external world that no longer mean anything to it. Thus we learn that we must renounce the idea of trying our plan of cure upon psychotics—renounce it forever, perhaps, or only for the moment, until we have discovered some other plan better suited for that purpose.

But there is another class of psychological patients who evidently resemble the psychotics very closely, the immense number of sufferers from severe neuroses. The causes as well as the pathogenic mechanisms of their illness must be the same or at least very similar. Their ego, however, has proved more resistant and has become less disorganized. Many of them, in spite of their troubles and of their consequent inadequacy, are none the less able to maintain their position in real life. It may be that these neurotics will show themselves ready to accept our help. We will confine our interest to them and see how far and by what means we can "cure" them.

We conclude our pact then with the neurotics: complete candor on one side, strict discretion on the other. This looks as though we were aiming at the post of a secular father confessor. But there is a great difference, for what we want to hear from our patient is not only what he knows and conceals from other people, but what he does *not* know. With this end in view we give him a more detailed definition of what we mean by candor. We impose upon him the *fundamental rule* of analysis, which is henceforward to govern his behavior to us. He must tell us not only what he can say intentionally and willingly, what will give him relief like a confession, but everything else besides that his self-observation presents him with—everything that comes into his head, even if it is *disagreeable* to say it, even if it seems *unimportant* or positively *meaningless.* If he can succeed after this injunction in putting his self-criticism out of action, he will provide us with a mass of material—thoughts, ideas, recollections—which already lie under the influence of the unconscious, which are often its direct derivatives, and which thus put us in a position to conjecture the nature of his repressed unconscious material and to extend, by the information we give him, his ego's knowledge of his unconscious.

VLADIMIR ILYICH LENIN

The history of communism presents one of the major anomalies of the modern world. In their writings, Marx and Engels always assumed that the revolution and the consequent ushering in of the classless society would occur first in the most advanced industrial countries of Europe—England, France, and Germany. Russia, still slumbering in a state of semi-barbaric feudalism, was almost the last place in the world in which they expected their ideas to bear fruit. Nevertheless, it has been Russia, rather than Western Europe, that has become communistic. The reasons for this unforeseen historical development obviously are numerous and highly complex. Yet, important among them is the personal carrer of Vladimir Ilyich Lenin[1] *(1870–1924). For it was Lenin who revised the Marxist theory to fit conditions in Russia, and then led the bitter struggle, both against the existing regime and against rival revolutionaries and reformers, that resulted in 1917 in the victory of his version of Marxism in Russia. As critics have often pointed out, however, Lenin so modified Marx's doctrines in the process that the result ought to be labeled, as one writer has put it, "inverted Marxism."*

The first of the two following selections, taken from a pamphlet entitled What Is To Be Done? *written in 1902, contains Lenin's most complete and significant departure from Marx—namely, his views on the nature and function of the "Party." Leon Trotsky, Lenin's famous brother-revolutionary, made the following prophecy about Lenin's views on the Party: "The organization of the Party takes*

[1] Born Vladimir Ilyich Ulyanov.

the place of the Party itself; the Central Committee takes the place of the organization; and finally the dictator takes the place of the Central Committee." The subsequent history of Russia has amply justified this prophecy. The second selection is from Lenin's most important work, State and Revolution, *written during the revolution of 1917 in Russia. Ostensibly a commentary on Marxist doctrine, it became a detailed statement of Lenin's own views, often quite un-Marxian, regarding the political and social organization that was to follow the revolution.*

What Is To Be Done?

. . .

The history of all countries shows that the working class, exclusively by its own effort, is able to develop only trade union consciousness, *i.e.*, it may itself realise the necessity for combining in unions, for fighting against the employers and for striving to compel the government to pass necessary labour legislation, etc. The theory of socialism, however, grew out of the philosophic, historical and economic theories that were elaborated by the educated representatives of the propertied classes, the intellectuals. According to their social status, the founders of modern scientific socialism, Marx and Engels, themselves belonged to the bourgeois intelligentsia. Similarly, in Russia, the theoretical doctrine of Social-Democracy arose quite independently of the spontaneous growth of the labour movement; it arose as a natural and inevitable outcome of the development of ideas among the revolutionary socialist intelligentsia. At the time of which we are speaking, *i.e.*, the middle of the 'nineties, this doctrine not only represented the completely formulated programme of the Emancipation of Labour group, but had already won the adherence of the majority of the revolutionary youth in Russia.

. . .

V. I. Lenin, "What Is To Be Done?" LENIN COLLECTED WORKS, *Vol. 5 (London: Lawrence and Wishart Ltd., 1961), pp. 375–76, 451–53, 464–67.*

It is only natural that a Social-Democrat, who conceives the political struggle as being identical with the "economic struggle against the employers and the government," should conceive of an "organisation of revolutionaries" as being more or less identical with an "organisation of workers." And this, in fact, is what actually happens; so that when we talk about organisation, we literally talk in different tongues. I recall a conversation I once had with a fairly consistent Economist, with whom I had not been previously acquainted. We were discussing the pamphlet *Who Will Make the Political Revolution?* and we were very soon agreed that the principal defect in that brochure was that it ignored the question of organisation. We were beginning to think that we were in complete agreement with each other—but as the conversation proceeded, it became clear that we were talking of different things. My interlocutor accused the author of the brochure just mentioned of ignoring strike funds, mutual aid societies, etc.; whereas I had in mind an organisation of revolutionaries as an essential factor in "making" the political revolution. After that became clear, I hardly remember a single question of importance upon which I was in agreement with that Economist!

What was the source of our disagreement? The fact that on questions of organisation and politics the Economists are forever lapsing from Social-Democracy into trade unionism. The political struggle carried on by the Social-Democrats is far more extensive and complex than the economic struggle the workers carry on against the employers and the government. Similarly (and indeed for that reason), the organisation of a revolutionary Social-Democratic Party must inevitably *differ* from the organisations of the workers designed for the latter struggle. A workers' organisation must in the first place be a trade organisation; secondly, it must be as wide as possible; and thirdly, it must be as public as conditions will allow (here, and further on, of course, I have only autocratic Russia in mind). On the other hand, the organisations of revolutionaries must consist first and foremost of people whose profession is that of a revolutionary (that is why I speak of organisations of *revolutionaries,* meaning revolutionary Social-Democrats). In view of this common feature of the members of such an organisation, *all distinctions as between workers and intellectuals,* and certainly distinctions of trade and profession, must be obliterated. Such an organisation must of necessity be not too extensive and as secret as possible.

• • •

I assert: (1) that no movement can be durable without a stable organisation of leaders to maintain continuity; (2) that the more widely the masses are spontaneously drawn into the struggle and form the basis of the movement and participate in it, the more necessary is it to have such an organisation, and the more stable must it be (for it is much easier for demagogues to sidetrack the more backward sections of the masses); (3) that the organisation must consist chiefly of persons engaged in revolutionary activities as a profession; (4) that in a country with an autocratic government, the more we *restrict* the membership of this organisation to persons who are engaged in revolutionary activities as a profession and who have been professionally trained in the art of combating the political police, the more difficult will it be to catch the organisation, and (5) the *wider* will be the circle of men and women of the working class or of other classes of society able to join the movement and perform active work in it. . . .

The active and widespread participation of the masses will not suffer; on the contrary, it will benefit by the fact that a "dozen" experienced revolutionaries, no less professionally trained than the police, will centralise all the secret side of the work—prepare leaflets, work out approximate plans and appoint bodies of leaders for each urban district, for each factory district and to each educational institution, etc. (I know that exception will be taken to my "undemocratic" views, but I shall reply to this altogether unintelligent objection later on.) The centralisation of the more secret functions in an organisation of revolutionaries will not diminish, but rather increase the extent and the quality of the activity of a large number of other organisations intended for wide membership and which, therefore, can be as loose and as public as possible, for example, trade unions, workers' circles for self-education and the reading of illegal literature, and socialist and also democratic circles for *all other sections of the population,* etc., etc. We must have *as large a number as possible* of such organisations having the widest possible variety of functions, but it is absurd and dangerous to *confuse these with organisations of revolutionaries,* to erase the line of demarcation between them, to dim still more the masses' already incredibly hazy appreciation of the fact that in order to "serve" the mass movement we must have people who will devote themselves exclusively to Social-Democratic activities, and that such people must *train* themselves patiently and steadfastly to be professional revolutionaries.

Aye, this appreciation has become incredibly dim. The most grievous sin we have committed in regard to organisation is that *by our primitiveness we have lowered the prestige of revolutionaries in Russia.* A man who is weak and vacillating on theoretical questions, who has a narrow outlook, who makes excuses for his own slackness on the ground that the masses are awakening spontaneously, who resembles a trade union secretary more than a people's tribune, who is unable to conceive of a broad and bold plan, who is incapable of inspiring even his opponents with respect for himself, and who is inexperienced and clumsy in his own professional art—the art of combating the political police—such a man is not a revolutionary but a wretched amateur!

Let no active worker take offense at these frank remarks, for as far as insufficient training is concerned, I apply them first and foremost to myself. I used to work in a circle that set itself great and all-embracing tasks; and every member of that circle suffered to the point of torture from the realisation that we were proving ourselves to be amateurs at a moment in history when we might have been able to say, paraphrasing a well-known epigram: "Give us an organisation of revolutionaries, and we shall overturn the whole of Russia!"

State and Revolution

Chapter I

CLASS SOCIETY AND THE STATE

. . .

4. *The "Withering Away" of the State and Violent Revolution.* Engels' words regarding the "withering away" of the state enjoy such popularity, they are so often quoted, and they show so clearly the essence of the usual adulteration by means of which Marxism is made to look like opportunism, that we must dwell on them in detail. Let us quote the whole passage from which they are taken.

The proletariat seizes state power, and then transforms the means of production into state property. But in doing this, it puts an end to itself as the proletariat, it puts an end to all class differences and class antagonisms, it puts an end also to the state as the state. Former society, moving in class antagonisms, had need of the state, that is, an organisation of the exploiting class at each period for the maintenance of its external conditions of production; therefore, in particular, for the forcible holding down of the exploited class in the conditions of oppression (slavery, bondage or serfdom, wage-labour) determined by the existing mode of production. The state was the official representative of society as a whole, its embodiment in a visible corporate body; but it was this only in so far as it was the state of that class which itself, in its epoch, represented society as a whole: in ancient times, the state of the slave-owning citizens; in the Middle Ages, of the feudal nobility; in our epoch, of the bourgeoisie. When ultimately it becomes really representative of society as a whole, it makes itself superfluous. As soon as there is no longer any class of society to be held in subjection; as soon as, along with class domination and the struggle for individual existence based on the former anarchy of production, the collisions and excesses arising from these have also been abolished, there is nothing more to be repressed, and a special repressive force, a state, is no longer necessary. The first act in which the state really comes forward as the representative of society as a whole—

V. I. Lenin, STATE AND REVOLUTION *(New York: International Publishers Co., Inc., 1932), pp. 15–17, 20, 70–75, 78–85. By permission of International Publishers Co., Inc.*

the seizure of the means of production in the name of society—is at the same time its last independent act as a state. The interference of a state power in social relations becomes superfluous in one sphere after another, and then becomes dormant of itself. Government over persons is replaced by the administration of things and the direction of the processes of production. The state is not "abolished," *it withers away*. It is from this standpoint that we must appraise the phrase "people's free state"—both its justification at times for agitational purposes, and its ultimate scientific inadequacy—and also the demand of the so-called Anarchists that the state should be abolished overnight.

Without fear of committing an error, it may be said that of this argument by Engels so singularly rich in ideas, only one point has become an integral part of Socialist thought among modern Socialist parties, namely, that, unlike the Anarchist doctrine of the "abolition" of the state, according to Marx the state "withers away." To emasculate Marxism in such a manner is to reduce it to opportunism, for such an "interpretation" only leaves the hazy conception of a slow, even, gradual change, free from leaps and storms, free from revolution. The current popular conception, if one may say so, of the "withering away" of the state undoubtedly means a slurring over, if not a negation, of revolution.

Yet, such an "interpretation" is the crudest distortion of Marxism, which is advantageous only to the bourgeoisie; in point of theory, it is based on a disregard for the most important circumstances and considerations pointed out in the very passage summarising Engels' ideas, which we have just quoted in full.

In the first place, Engels at the very outset of his argument says that, in assuming state power, the proletariat by that very act "puts an end to the state as the state." One is "not accustomed" to reflect on what this really means. Generally, it is either ignored altogether, or it is considered as a piece of "Hegelian weakness" on Engels' part. As a matter of fact, however, these words express succinctly the experience of one of the greatest proletarian revolutions—the Paris Commune of 1871, of which we shall speak in greater detail in its proper place. As a matter of fact, Engels speaks here of the destruction of the bourgeois state by the proletarian revolution, while the words about its withering away refer to the remains of *proletarian* statehood *after* the Socialist revolution. The bourgeois state does not "wither away," according to Engels, but is "put an end to" by the proletariat in the course of the revolution. What withers away after the revolution is the proletarian state or semi-state.

Secondly, the state is a "special repressive force." This splendid and extremely profound definition of Engels' is given by him here with complete lucidity. It follows from this that the "special repressive force" of the bourgeoisie for the suppression of the proletariat, of the millions of workers by a handful of the rich, must be replaced by a "special repressive force" of the proletariat for the suppression of the bourgeoisie (the dictatorship of the proletariat). It is just this that constitutes the destruction of "the state as the state." It is just this that constitutes the "act" of "the seizure of the means of production in the name of society." And it is obvious that such a substitution of one (proletarian) "special repressive force" for another (bourgeois) "special repressive force" can in no way take place in the form of a "withering away."

Thirdly, as to the "withering away" or, more expressively and colourfully, as to the state "becoming dormant," Engels refers quite clearly and definitely to the period *after* "the seizure of the means of production [by the state] in the name of society," that is, *after* the Socialist revolution. We all know that the political form of the "state" at that time is complete democracy. But it never enters the head of any of the opportunists who shamelessly distort Marx that when Engels speaks here of the state "withering away," or "becoming dormant," he speaks of *democracy*. At first sight this seems very strange. But it is "unintelligible" only to one who has not reflected on the fact that democracy is *also* a state and that, consequently, democracy will *also* disappear when the state disappears. The bourgeois state can only be "put an end to" by a revolution. The state in general, *i.e.*, most complete democracy, can only "wither away."

. . .

The replacement of the bourgeois by the proletarian state is impossible without a violent revolution. The abolition of the proletarian state, *i.e.*, of all states, is only possible through "withering away."

. . .

Chapter V

THE ECONOMIC BASE OF THE WITHERING AWAY OF THE STATE

1. Formulation of the Question by Marx.

. . .

The whole theory of Marx is an application of the theory of evolution—in its most consistent, complete, well-considered and fruitful form—to modern capitalism. It was natural for Marx to raise the question of applying this theory both to the *coming* collapse of capitalism and to the *future* evolution of *future* Communism.

On the basis of what *data* can the future evolution of future Communism be considered?

On the basis of the fact that *it has its origin* in capitalism, that it develops historically from capitalism, that it is the result of the action of a social force to which capitalism *has given birth*. There is no shadow of an attempt on Marx's part to conjure up a Utopia, to make idle guesses about that which cannot be known. Marx treats the question of Communism in the same way as a naturalist would treat the question of the evolution of, say, a new biological species, if he knew that such and such was its origin, and such and such the direction in which it changed.

. . .

The first fact that has been established with complete exactness by the whole theory of evolution, by science as a whole—a fact which the Utopians forgot, and which is forgotten by the present-day opportunists who are afraid of the Socialist revolution—is that, historically, there must undoubtedly be a special stage or epoch of *transition* from capitalism to Communism.

2. *Transition from Capitalism to Communism.* Marx continues:

> Between capitalist and Communist society lies the period of the revolutionary transformation of the former into the latter. To this also corresponds a political transition period, in which the state can be no other than the *revolutionary dictatorship of the proletariat.*

This conclusion Marx bases on an analysis of the role played by the proletariat in modern capitalist society, on the data concerning the evolution of this society, and on the irreconcilability of the opposing interests of the proletariat and the bourgeoisie.

Earlier the question was put thus: to attain its emancipation, the proletariat must overthrow the bourgeoisie, conquer political power and establish its own revolutionary dictatorship.

Now the question is put somewhat differently: the transition from capitalist society, developing towards Communism, towards a Communist society, is impossible without a "political transition period," and the state in this period can only be the revolutionary dictatorship of the proletariat.

What, then, is the relation of this dictatorship to democracy?

We have seen that the *Communist Manifesto* simply places side by side the two ideas: the "transformation of the proletariat into the ruling class" and the "establishment of democracy." On the basis of all that has been said above, one can define more exactly how democracy changes in the transition from capitalism to Communism.

In capitalist society, under the conditions most favourable to its development, we have more or less complete democracy in the democratic republic. But this democracy is always bound by the narrow framework of capitalist exploitation, and consequently always remains, in reality, a democracy for the minority, only for the possessing classes, only for the rich. Freedom in capitalist society always remains just about the same as it was in the ancient Greek republics: freedom for the slave-owners. The modern wage-slaves, owing to the conditions of capitalist exploitation, are so much crushed by want and poverty that "democracy is nothing to them," "politics is nothing to them"; that, in the ordinary peaceful course of events, the majority of the population is debarred from participating in social and political life.

The correctness of this statement is perhaps most clearly proved by Germany, just because in this state constitutional legality lasted and remained stable for a remarkably long time—for nearly half a century (1871–1914)—and because Social-Democracy in Germany during that time was able to achieve far more than in other countries in "utilising legality," and was able to organise into a political party a larger proportion of the working class than anywhere else in the world.

What, then, is this largest proportion of politically conscious and active wage-slaves that has so far been observed in capitalist society? One million members of the Social-Democratic party—out of fifteen million wage-workers! Three million organized in trade unions—out of fifteen million.

Democracy for an insignificant minority, democracy for the rich—that is the democracy of capitalist society. If we look more closely into the mechanism of capitalist democracy, everywhere, both in the "petty"—so-called petty—details of the suffrage (residential qualification, exclusion of women, etc.), and in the technique of the representative institutions, in the actual obstacles to the right of assembly (public buildings are not for "beggars"!), in the purely capitalist organisation of the daily press, etc., etc.—on all sides we see restriction after restriction upon democracy. These restrictions, exceptions, exclusions, obstacles for the poor, seem slight, especially in the eyes of one who has himself never known want and has never been in close contact with the oppressed classes in their mass life (and nine-tenths, if not ninety-nine hundredths, of the bourgeois publicists and politicians are of this class), but in their sum total these restrictions exclude and squeeze out the poor from politics and from an active share in democracy.

Marx splendidly grasped this *essence* of capitalist democracy, when, in analysing the experience of the Commune, he said that the oppressed were allowed, once every few years, to decide which particular representatives of the oppressing class should be in parliament to represent and repress them!

But from this capitalist democracy—inevitably narrow, subtly rejecting the poor, and therefore hypocritical and false to the core—progress does not march onward, simply, smoothly and directly, to "greater and greater democracy," as the liberal professors and petty-bourgeois opportunists would have us believe. No, progress marches onward, *i.e.*, towards Communism, through the dictatorship of the proletariat; it cannot do otherwise, for there is no one else and no other way to *break the resistance* of the capitalist exploiters.

But the dictatorship of the proletariat—*i.e.,* the organisation of the vanguard of the oppressed as the ruling class for the purpose of crushing the oppressors—cannot produce merely an expansion of democracy. *Together* with an immense expansion of democracy which *for the first time* becomes democracy for the poor, democracy for the people, and not democracy for the rich folk, the dictatorship of the proletariat produces a series of restrictions of liberty in the case of the oppressors, the exploiters, the capitalists. We must crush them in order to free humanity from wage-slavery; their resistance must be broken by force; it is clear that where there is suppression there is also violence, there is no liberty, no democracy.

Engels expressed this splendidly in his letter to Bebel when he said, as the reader will remember, that "as long as the proletariat still *needs* the state, it needs it not in the interests of freedom, but for the purpose of crushing its antagonists; and as soon as it becomes possible to speak of freedom, then the state, as such, ceases to exist."

Democracy for the vast majority of the people, and suppression by force, *i.e.,* exclusion from democracy, of the exploiters and oppressors of the people—this is the modification of democracy during the *transition* from capitalism to Communism.

Only in Communist society, when the resistance of the capitalists has been completely broken, when the capitalists have disappeared, when there are no classes (*i.e.,* there is no difference between the members of society in their relation to the social means of production), *only then* "the state ceases to exist," and *"it becomes possible to speak of freedom."* Only then a really full democracy, a democracy without any exceptions, will be possible and will be realised. And only then will democracy itself begin to *wither away* due to the simple fact that, freed from capitalist slavery, from the untold horrors, savagery, absurdities, and infamies of capitalist exploitation, people will gradually *become accustomed* to the observance of the elementary rules of social life that have been known for centuries and repeated for thousands of years in all school books; they will become accustomed to observing them without force, without compulsion, without subordination, without the *special apparatus* for compulsion which is called the state.

The expression "the state *withers away,*" is very well chosen, for it indicates both the gradual and the elemental nature of the process. Only habit can, and undoubtedly will, have such an effect; for we see around us millions of times how readily people get accustomed to observe the necessary rules of life in common, if there is no exploitation, if there is nothing that causes indignation, that calls forth protest and revolt and has to be *suppressed.*

Thus, in capitalist society, we have a democracy that is curtailed, poor, false; a democracy only for the rich, for the minority. The dictatorship of the proletariat, the period of transition to Communism, will, for the first time, produce democracy for the people, for the majority, side by side with the necessary suppression of the minority—the exploiters. Communism alone is capable of giving a really complete democracy, and the more complete it is the more quickly will it become unnecessary and wither away of itself.

In other words: under capitalism we have a state in the proper sense of the word, that is, special machinery for the suppression of one class by another, and of the majority by the minority at that. Naturally, for the successful discharge of such a task as the systematic suppression by the exploiting minority of the exploited majority, the greatest ferocity and savagery of suppression are required, seas of blood are required, through which mankind is marching in slavery, serfdom, and wage-labor.

Again, during the *transition* from capitalism to Communism, suppression is *still* necessary; but it is the suppression of the minority of exploiters by the majority of exploited. A special apparatus, special machinery for suppression, the "state," is *still* necessary, but this is now a transitional state, no longer a state in the usual sense, for the suppression of the minority of exploiters, by the majority of the wage slaves of *yesterday,* is a matter comparatively so easy, simple and natural that it will cost far less bloodshed than the suppression of the risings of slaves, serfs or wage laborers, and will cost mankind far less. This is compatible with the diffusion of democracy among such an overwhelming majority of the population, that the need for *special machinery* of suppression will begin to disappear. The exploiters are, naturally, unable to suppress the people without a most complex machinery for performing this task; but *the people* can suppress the exploiters even with very simple "machinery," almost without any "machinery," without any special apparatus, by the simple *organisation of the armed masses* (such as the Soviets of Workers' and Soldiers' Deputies, we may remark, anticipating a little).

Finally, only Communism renders the state absolutely unnecessary, for there is *no one* to be suppressed—"no one" in the sense of a *class,* in the sense of a systematic struggle with a definite section of the population. We are not Utopians, and we do not in the least deny the possibility and inevitability of excesses on the part of *individual persons,* nor the need to suppress *such* excesses. But, in the first place, no special machinery, no special apparatus of repression is needed for this; this will be done by the armed people itself, as simply and as readily as any crowd of civilised people, even in modern society, parts a pair of combatants or does not allow a woman to be outraged. And, secondly, we know that the fundamental social cause of excesses which consist in violating the rules of social life is the exploitation of the masses, their want and their poverty. With the removal of this chief cause, excesses will inevitably begin to *"wither away."* We do not know how quickly and in what succession, but we know that they will wither away. With their withering away, the state will also *wither away.*

Without going into Utopias, Marx defined more fully what can *now* be defined regarding this future, namely, the difference between the lower and higher phases (degrees, stages) of Communist society.

. . .

4. Higher Phase of Communist Society. Marx continues:

> In a higher phase of Communist society, when the enslaving subordination of individuals in the division of labour has disappeared, and with it also the antagonism between mental and physical labour; when labour has become not only a means of living, but itself the first necessity of life; when, along with the all-round development of individuals, the productive forces too have grown, and all the springs of social wealth are flowing more freely—it is only at that stage that it will be possible to pass completely beyond the narrow horizon of bourgeois rights, and for society to inscribe on its banners: from each according to his ability; to each according to his needs!

Only now can we appreciate the full correctness of Engels' remarks in which he mercilessly ridiculed all the absurdity of combining the words "freedom" and "state." While the state exists there is no freedom. When there is freedom, there will be no state.

The economic basis for the complete withering away of the state is that high stage of development of Communism when the antagonism between mental and physical labour disappears, that is to say, when one of the principal sources of modern *social* inequality disappears—a source, moreover, which it is impossible to remove immediately by the mere conversion of the means of production into public property, by the mere expropriation of the capitalists.

This expropriation will make a gigantic development of the productive forces *possible.* And seeing how incredibly, even now, capitalism *retards* this development, how much progress could be made even on the basis of modern technique at the level it has reached, we have a right to say, with the fullest confidence, that the expropriation of the capitalists will inevitably result in a gigantic development of the productive forces of human society. But how rapidly this development will go forward, how soon it will reach the point of breaking away from the division of labour, of removing the antagonism between mental and physical labour, of transforming work into the "first necessity of life"—this we do not and *cannot* know.

Consequently, we have a right to speak solely of the inevitable withering away of the state, emphasising the protracted nature of this process and its dependence upon the rapidity of development of the *higher phase* of Communism; leaving quite open the question of lengths of time, or the concrete forms of withering away, since material for the solution of such questions is *not available.*

The state will be able to wither away completely when society has realised the rule: "From each according to his ability; to each according to his needs," *i.e.,* when people have become accustomed to observe the fundamental rules of social life, and their labour is so productive, that they voluntarily work *according to their ability.* "The narrow horizon of bourgeois rights," which compels one to calculate, with the hard-heartedness of a Shylock, whether he has not worked half an hour more than another, whether he is not getting less pay than another—this narrow horizon will then be left behind. There will then be no need for any exact calculation by society of the quantity of products to be distributed to each of its members; each will take freely "according to his needs."

. . .

What is generally called Socialism was termed by Marx the "first" or lower phase of Communist society. In so far as the means of production become *public* property, the word "Communism" is also applicable here, providing we do not forget that it is *not* full Communism. The great significance of Marx's elucidations consist in this: that here, too, he consistently applied materialist dialectics, the doctrine of evolution, looking upon Communism as something which evolves *out of* capitalism. Instead of artificial, "elaborate," scholastic definitions and profitless disquisitions on the meaning of words (what Socialism is, what Communism is), Marx gives an analysis of what may be called stages in the economic ripeness of Communism.

In its first phase or first stage Communism *cannot* as yet be economically ripe and entirely free of all tradition and of all taint of capitalism. Hence the interesting phenomenon of Communism retaining, in its first phase, "the narrow horizon of bourgeois rights." Bourgeois rights, with respect to distribution of articles of *consumption,* inevitably presupposes, of course, the existence of the *bourgeois state,* for rights are nothing without an apparatus capable of *enforcing* the observance of the rights.

Consequently, for a certain time not only bourgeois rights, but even the bourgeois state remains under Communism, without the bourgeoisie!

This may look like a paradox, or simply a dialectical puzzle for which Marxism is often blamed by people who would not make the least effort to study its extraordinarily profound content.

But, as a matter of fact, the old surviving in the new confronts us in life at every step, in nature as well as in society. Marx did not smuggle a scrap of "bourgeois" rights into Communism of his own accord; he indicated what is economically and politically inevitable in a society issuing *from the womb* of capitalism.

Democracy is of great importance for the working class in its struggle for freedom against the capitalists. But democracy is by no means a limit one may not overstep; it is only one of the stages in the course of development from feudalism to capitalism, and from capitalism to Communism.

Democracy means equality. The great significance of the struggle of the proletariat for equality, and the significance of equality as a slogan, are apparent, if we correctly interpret it as meaning the abolition of *classes*. But democracy means only *formal* equality. Immediately after the attainment of equality for all members of society *in respect of* the ownership of the means of production, that is, of equality of labour and equality of wages, there will inevitably arise before humanity the question of going further from formal equality to real equality, *i.e.*, to realising the rule, "From each according to his ability; to each according to his needs." By what stages, by means of what practical measures humanity will proceed to this higher aim—this we do not and cannot know. But it is important to realise how infinitely mendacious is the usual bourgeois presentation of Socialism as something lifeless, petrified, fixed once for all, whereas in reality, it is *only* with Socialism that there will commence a rapid, genuine, real mass advance, in which first the *majority* and then the whole of the population will take part—an advance in all domains of social and individual life.

Democracy is a form of the state—one of its varieties. Consequently, like every state, it consists in organised, systematic application of force against human beings. This on the one hand. On the other hand, however, it signifies the formal recognition of the equality of all citizens, the equal right of all to determine the structure and administration of the state. This, in turn, is connected with the fact that, at a certain stage in the development of democracy, it first rallies the proletariat as a revolutionary class against capitalism, and gives it an opportunity to crush, to smash to bits, to wipe off the face of the earth the bourgeois state machinery—even its republican variety: the standing army, the police, and bureaucracy; then it substitutes for all this a *more* democratic, but still a state machinery in the shape of armed masses of workers, which becomes transformed into universal participation of the people in the militia.

Here "quantity turns into quality": *such* a degree of democracy is bound up with the abandonment of the framework of bourgeois society, and the beginning of its Socialist reconstruction. If *every one* really takes part in the administration of the state, capitalism cannot retain its hold. In its turn, capitalism, as it develops, itself creates *prerequisites* for "every one" *to be able* really to take part in the administration of the state. Among such prerequisites are: universal literacy, already realised in most of the advanced capitalist countries, then the "training and disciplining" of millions of workers by the huge, complex, and socialised apparatus of the post-office, the railways, the big factories, large-scale commerce, banking, etc., etc.

With such *economic* prerequisites it is perfectly possible, immediately, within twenty-four hours after the overthrow of the capitalists and bureaucrats, to replace them, in the control of production and distribution, in the business of *control* of labour and products, by the armed workers, by the whole people in arms. (The question of control and accounting must not be confused with the question of the scientifically educated staff of engineers, agronomists, and so on. These gentlemen work today, obeying the capitalists; they will work even better tomorrow, obeying the armed workers.)

Accounting and control—these are the *chief* things necessary for the organising and correct functioning of the *first phase* of Communist society. *All* citizens are here transformed into hired employees of the state, which is made up of the armed workers. *All* citizens become employees and workers of *one* national state "syndicate." All that is required is that they should work equally, should regularly do their share of work, and should receive equal pay. The accounting and control necessary for this have been *simplified* by capitalism to the utmost, till they have become the extraordinarily simple operations of watching, recording and issuing receipts, within the reach of anybody who can read and write and knows the first four rules of arithmetic.[1]

When the *majority* of the people begin everywhere to keep such accounts and maintain such control over the capitalists (now converted into employees) and over the intellectual gentry, who still retain capitalist habits, this control will really become universal, general, national; and there will be no way of getting away from it, there will be "nowhere to go."

The whole of society will have become one office and one factory, with equal work and equal pay.

But this "factory" discipline, which the proletariat will extend to the whole of society after the defeat of the capitalists and the overthrow of the exploiters, is by no means our ideal, or our final aim. It is but a *foothold* necessary for the radical cleansing of society of all the hideousness and foulness of capitalist exploitation, *in order to advance further*.

From the moment when all members of society, or even only the overwhelming majority, have learned how to govern the state *themselves,* have taken this business into their own hands, have "established" control over the insignificant minority of capitalists, over the gentry with capitalist leanings, and the workers thoroughly demoralised by capitalism—from this moment the need for any government begins to disappear. The more complete the democracy, the nearer the moment when it begins to be unnecessary. The more democratic the "state" consisting of armed workers, which is "no longer a state in the proper sense of the word," the more rapidly does *every* state begin to wither away.

For when *all* have learned to manage, and independently are actually managing by themselves social production, keeping accounts, controlling the idlers, the gentlefolk, the swindlers and similar "guardians of capitalist traditions," then the escape from this national accounting and control will inevitably become so increasingly difficult, such a rare exception, and will probably be accompanied by such swift and severe punishment (for the armed workers are men of practical life, not sentimental intellectuals, and they will scarcely allow any one to trifle with them), that very soon the *necessity* of observing the simple, fundamental rules of every-day social life in common will have become a *habit*.

The door will then be wide open for the transition from the first phase of Communist society to its higher phase, and along with it to the complete withering away of the state.

[1] When most of the functions of the state are reduced to this accounting and control by the workers themselves, then it ceases to be a "political state," and the "public functions will lose their political character and be transformed into simple administrative functions."

THE GREAT DEPRESSION

The Wall Street stock market crash on "Black Thursday" (October 24, 1929) marked a major turning point in American history. An era—the "roaring twenties"—came to an abrupt and dramatic end and a new era—the "great depression"—was ushered in. Although the depression lasted approximately a decade and engulfed the entire world, its worst years in the United States coincided with the administration of President Herbert Hoover (1929–1933). The magnitude of the world-wide economic collapse is clearly revealed in the statistics: Between 1929 and 1932, it is estimated that total world production decreased by 38 per cent and international trade fell by two-thirds. During the same years the national income of the United States declined from 85 to 37 billion dollars. Although everyone was affected to some extent, those who suffered most were the "little people," particularly small farmers and working men. Unemployment became massive and chronic; during the depths of the depression in the United States alone 13 million workers out of a total labor force of approximately 50 million were without jobs. Worse still, the unemployed remained without work not simply for weeks or months but in many cases for several years. In our great cities the bread line and the soup kitchen became familiar sights.

Estimates of the total economic loss caused by the depression have ranged as high as 200 billion dollars. Less easily calculable but more lastingly important was the harm caused by way of human suffering, loss of self-respect, and increasing disillusionment with democratic institutions. Although democracy survived the depression in America, in Europe it was not so fortunate. Of crucial importance was the collapse of the Weimar Republic in Germany and the rise to power of Hitler and the Nazis, which in turn set in motion a series of events that culminated in World War II.

To illustrate the great depression we have chosen speeches made by the two American presidents most closely associated with it—Herbert Hoover and Franklin D. Roosevelt—the first delivered just a year before the Wall Street cataclysm and the second at the depths of the depression that followed. In reading the Hoover speech, one should avoid the temptation to interpret it simply in partisan terms. Although he spoke as a Republican campaigning for the presidency, Hoover was enunciating a set of beliefs enthusiastically embraced by the vast majority of Americans during the twenties. Roosevelt's inaugural address reveals the enormous change in political thought and in the direction of our national life that had been brought about by three years of depression, years in which most Americans lost their faith both in the traditional system of "free enterprise" and in its philosophy of "rugged individualism."

Herbert Hoover: New York City

October 22, 1928

This campaign now draws near a close. The platforms of the two parties defining principles and offering solutions of various national problems have been presented and are being earnestly considered by our people.

After four months' debate it is not the Republican Party which finds reason for abandonment of any of the principles it has laid down or of the views it has expressed for solution of the problems before the country. The principles to which it adheres are rooted deeply in the foundations of our national life. The solutions which it proposes are based on experience with government and on a consciousness that it may have the responsibility for placing those solutions in action.

In my acceptance speech I endeavored to outline the spirit and ideals by which I would be guided in carrying that platform into administration. Tonight, I will not deal with the multitude of issues which have been already well canvassed. I intend rather to discuss some of those more fundamental principles and ideals upon which I believe the government of the United States should be conducted. . . .

After the war, when the Republican Party assumed administration of the country, we were faced with the problem of determination of the very nature of our national life. During one hundred and fifty years we have builded up a form of self-government and a social system which is peculiarly our own. It differs essentially from all others in the world. It is the American system. It is just as definite and positive a political and social system as has ever been developed on earth. It is founded upon a particular conception of self-government in which decentralized local responsibility is the very base. Further than this, it is founded upon the conception that only through ordered liberty, freedom, and equal opportunity to the individual will his initiative and enterprise spur on the march of progress. And in our insistence upon equality of opportunity has our system advanced beyond all the world.

During the war we necessarily turned to the government to solve every difficult economic problem. The government having absorbed every energy of our people for war, there was no other solution. For the preservation of the state the federal government became a centralized despotism which undertook unprecedented responsibilities, assumed autocratic powers, and took over the business of citizens. To a large degree we regimented our whole people temporarily into a socialistic state. However justified in time of war, if continued in peacetime it would destroy not only our American system but with it our progress and freedom as well.

When the war closed, the most vital of all issues both in our own country and throughout the world was whether governments should continue their war-time ownership and operation of many instrumentalities of production and distribution. We were challenged with a peacetime choice between the American system of rugged individualism and a European philosophy

Herbert Hoover, THE NEW DAY, *2nd ed. (Stanford: Stanford University Press, 1929). Courtesy of Stanford University Press.*

of diametrically opposed doctrines—doctrines of paternalism and state socialism. The acceptance of these ideas would have meant the destruction of self-government through centralization of government. It would have meant the undermining of the individual initiative and enterprise through which our people have grown to unparalleled greatness.

The Republican Party from the beginning resolutely turned its face away from these ideas and these war practices. A Republican Congress co-operated with the Democratic administration to demobilize many of our war activities. At that time the two parties were in accord upon that point. When the Republican Party came into full power it went at once resolutely back to our fundamental conception of the state and the rights and responsibilities of the individual. Thereby it restored confidence and hope in the American people, it freed and stimulated enterprise, it restored the government to its position as an umpire instead of a player in the economic game. For these reasons the American people have gone forward in progress while the rest of the world has halted, and some countries have even gone backward. If anyone will study the causes of retarded recuperation in Europe, he will find much of it due to stifling of private initiative on one hand, and overloading of the government with business on the other.

There has been revived in this campaign, however, a series of proposals which, if adopted, would be a long step toward the abandonment of our American system and a surrender to the destructive operation of governmental conduct of commercial business. Because the country is faced with difficulty and doubt over certain national problems—that is, prohibition, farm relief, and electrical power—our opponents propose that we must thrust government a long way into the businesses which give rise to these problems. In effect, they abandon the tenets of their own party and turn to state socialism as a solution for the difficulties presented by all three. It is proposed that we shall change from prohibition to the state purchase and sale of liquor. If their agricultural relief program means anything, it means that the government shall directly or indirectly buy and sell and fix prices of agricultural products. And we are to go into the hydro-electric power business. In other words, we are confronted with a huge program of government in business.

There is, therefore, submitted to the American people a question of fundamental principle. That is: shall we depart from the principles of our American political and economic system, upon which we have advanced beyond all the rest of the world, in order to adopt methods based on principles destructive of its very foundations? And I wish to emphasize the seriousness of these proposals. I wish to make my position clear; for this goes to the very roots of American life and progress.

I should like to state to you the effect that this projection of government in business would have upon our system of self-government and our economic system. That effect would reach to the daily life of every man and woman. It would impair the very basis of liberty and freedom not only for those left outside the fold of expanded bureaucracy but for those embraced within it.

Let us first see the effect upon self-government. When the federal government undertakes to go into commerical business it must at once set up the organization and administration of that business, and it immediately finds itself in a labyrinth, every alley of which leads to the destruction of self-government.

Commercial business requires a concentration of responsibility. Self-government requires decentralization and many checks and balances to safeguard liberty. Our government to succeed in business would need become in effect a despotism. There at once begins the destruction of self-government.

The first problem of the government about to adventure in commercial business is to determine a method of administration. It must secure leadership and direction. Shall this leadership be chosen by political agencies or shall we make it elective? The hard practical fact is that leadership in business must come through the sheer rise in ability and character. That rise can only take place in the free atmosphere of competition. Competition is closed by bureaucracy. Political agencies are feeble channels through which to select able leaders to conduct commercial business.

Government, in order to avoid the possible incompetence, corruption, and tyranny of too great authority in individuals entrusted with commercial business, inevitably turns to boards and commissions. To make sure that there are checks and balances, each member of such boards and commissions must have equal authority. Each has his separate responsibility to the public, and at once we have the conflict of ideas and the lack of decision which would ruin any commercial business. It has contributed greatly to the demoralization of our shipping business. Moreover, these commissions must be representative of different sections and different political parties, so that at once we have an entire blight upon coordinated action within their ranks which destroys any possibility of effective administration.

Moreover, our legislative bodies cannot in fact delegate their full authority to commissions or to individuals for the conduct of matters vital to the American people; for if we would preserve government by the people we must preserve the authority of our legislators in the activities of our government.

Thus every time the federal government goes into a commercial business, five hundred and thirty-one Senators and Congressmen become the actual board of directors of that business. Every time a state government goes into business one or two hundred state senators and legislators become the actual directors of that business. Even if they were supermen and if there were no politics in the United States, no body of such numbers could competently direct commercial activities; for that requires initiative, instant decision, and action. It took Congress six years of constant discussion to even decide what the method of administration of Muscle Shoals should be.

When the federal government undertakes to go into business, the state governments are at once deprived of control and taxation of that business; when a state government undertakes to go into business, it at once deprives the municipalities of taxation and control of that business. Municipalities, being local and close to the people, can, at times, succeed in business where federal and state governments must fail. We have trouble enough with log-rolling in legislative bodies today. It originates naturally from desires of citizens to advance their particular section or to secure some necessary service. It would be multiplied a thousandfold were the federal and state governments in these businesses.

The effect upon our economic progress would be even worse. Business progressiveness is dependent on competition. New methods and new ideas are the outgrowth of the spirit of adventure, of individual initiative, and of individual enterprise. Without adventure there is no progress. No government administration can rightly take chances with taxpayers' money. . . .

The government in commercial business does not tolerate amongst its customers the freedom of competitive reprisals to which private business is subject. Bureaucracy does not tolerate the spirit of independence; it spreads the spirit of submission into our daily life and penetrates the temper of our people not with the habit of powerful resistance to wrong but with the habit of timid acceptance of irresistible might.

Bureaucracy is ever desirous of spreading its influence and its power. You cannot extend the mastery of the government over the daily working life of a people without at the same time making it the master of the people's souls and thoughts. Every expansion of government in business means that government in order to protect itself from the political consequences of its errors and wrongs is driven irresistibly without peace to greater and greater control of the nation's press and platform. Free speech does not live many hours after free industry and free commerce die.

It is a false liberalism that interprets itself into the government operation of commercial business. Every step of bureaucratizing of the business of our country poisons the very roots of liberalism—that is, political equality, free speech, free assembly, free press, and equality of opportunity. It is the road not to more liberty, but to less liberty. Liberalism should be found not striving to spread bureaucracy but striving to set bounds to it. True liberalism seeks all legitimate freedom first in the confident belief that without such freedom the pursuit of all other blessings and benefits is vain. That belief is the foundation of all American progress, political as well as economic.

Liberalism is a force truly of the spirit, a force proceeding from the deep realization that economic freedom cannot be sacrificed if political freedom is to be preserved. Even if governmental conduct of business could give us more efficiency instead of less efficiency, the fundamental objection to it would remain unaltered and unabated. It would stifle initiative and invention. It would undermine the development of leadership. It would cramp and cripple the mental and spiritual energies of our people. It would extinguish equality and opportunity. It would dry up the spirit of liberty and progress. For these reasons primarily it must be resisted. For a hundred and fifty years liberalism has found its true spirit in the American system, not in the European systems.

I do not wish to be misunderstood in this statement. I am defining a general policy. It does not mean that our government is to part with one iota of its national resources without complete protection to the public interest. I have already stated that where the government is engaged in public works for purposes of flood control, of navigation, of irrigation, of scientific research or national defense, or in pioneering a new art, it will at times necessarily produce power or commodities as a by-product. But they must be a by-product of the major purpose, not the major purpose itself.

Nor do I wish to be misinterpreted as believing that the United States is free-for-all and devil-take-the-hindmost. The very essence of equality of opportunity and of American individualism is that there shall be no domination by any group or combination in this republic, whether it be business or political. On the contrary, it demands economic justice as well as political and social justice. It is no system of laissez faire. . . .

And what have been the results of our American system? Our country has become the land of opportunity to those born without inheritance, not merely because of the wealth of its resources and industry but because of this freedom of initiative and enterprise. Russia has natural resources equal to ours. Her people are equally industrious, but she has not had the blessings of one hundred and fifty years of our form of government and of our social system.

By adherence to the principles of decentralized self-government, ordered liberty, equal opportunity, and freedom to the individual, our American experiment in human welfare has yielded a degree of well-being unparalleled in all the world. It has come nearer to the abolition of poverty, to the abolition of fear of want, than humanity has ever reached before. Progress of the past seven years is the proof of it. This alone furnishes the answer to our opponents, who ask us to introduce destructive elements into the system by which this has been accomplished.

Let us see what this system has done for us in our recent years of difficult and trying reconstruction and then solemnly ask ourselves if we now wish to abandon it.

As a nation we came out of the war with great losses. We made no profits from it. The apparent increases in wages were at that time fictitious. We were poorer as a nation when we emerged from the war. Yet during these last eight years we have recovered from these losses and increased our national income by over one-third, even if we discount the inflation of the dollar. That there has been a wide diffusion of our gain in wealth and income is marked by a hundred proofs. I know of no better test of the improved conditions of the average family than the combined increase in assets of life and industrial insurance, building and loan associations, and savings deposits. These are the savings banks of the average man. These agencies alone have in seven years increased by nearly 100 per cent to the gigantic sum of over fifty billions of dollars, or nearly one-sixth of our whole national wealth. We have increased in home ownership, we have expanded the investments of the average man.

In addition to these evidences of larger savings, our people are steadily increasing their spending for higher standards of living. Today there are almost nine automobiles for each ten families, where seven and one-half years ago only enough automobiles were running to average less than four for each ten families. The slogan of progress is changing from the full dinner pail to the full garage. Our people have more to eat, better things to wear, and better homes. We have even gained in elbow room, for the increase of residential floor space is over 25 per cent, with less than 10 per cent increase in our number of people. Wages have increased, the cost of living has decreased. The job of every man and woman has been made more secure. We have in this short period decreased the fear of poverty, the fear of unemployment, the fear of old age; and these are fears that are the greatest calamities of humankind.

All this progress means far more than increased creature comforts. It finds a thousand interpretations into a greater and fuller life. A score of new helps save the drudgery of the home. In seven years we have added 70 per cent to the electric power at the elbows of our workers and further promoted them from carriers of burdens to directors of machines. We have steadily reduced the sweat in human labor. Our hours of labor are lessened; our leisure has increased. We have expanded our parks and playgrounds. We have nearly doubled our attendance at games. We pour into outdoor recreation in every direction. The visitors at our national parks have trebled and we have so increased the number of sportsmen fishing in our streams and lakes that the longer time between bites is becoming a political issue. In these seven and one-half years the radio has brought music and laughter, education, and political discussion to almost every fireside.

Springing from our prosperity with its greater freedom, its vast endowment of scientific research, and the greater resources with which to care for public health, we have according to our insurance actuaries during this short period since the war lengthened the average span of life by nearly eight years. We have reduced infant mortality, we have vastly decreased the days of illness and suffering in the life of every man and woman. We have improved the facilities for the care of the crippled and helpless and deranged.

From our increasing resources we have expanded our educational system in eight years from an outlay of twelve hundred millions to twenty-seven hundred millions of dollars. The education of our youth has become almost our largest and certainly our most important activity. From our greater income and thus our ability to free youth from toil we have increased the attendance in our grade schools by 14 per cent, in our high schools by 80 per cent, and in our institutions of higher learning by 95 per cent. Today we have more youth in these institutions of higher learning twice over than all the rest of the world put together. We have made notable progress in literature, in art, and in public taste.

We have made progress in the leadership of every branch of American life. Never in our history was the leadership in our economic life more distinguished in its abilities than today, and it has grown greatly in its consciousness of public responsibility. Leadership in our professions and in moral and spiritual affairs of our country was never of a higher order. And our magnificent educational system is bringing forward a host of recruits for the succession to this leadership. . . .

I have endeavored to present to you that the greatness of America has grown out of a political and social system and a method of control of economic forces distinctly its own—our American system—which has carried this great experiment in human welfare farther than ever before in all history. We are nearer today to the ideal of the abolition of poverty and fear from the lives of men and women than ever before in any land. And I again repeat that the departure from our American system by injecting principles destructive to it which our opponents propose will jeopardize the very liberty and freedom of our people, will destroy equality of opportunity not alone to ourselves but to our children. . . .

Franklin D. Roosevelt: First Inaugural Address

I am certain that my fellow Americans expect that on my induction into the Presidency I will address them with a candor and a decision which the present situation of our Nation impels. This is preeminently the time to speak the truth, the whole truth, frankly and boldly. Nor need we shrink from honestly facing conditions in our country today. This great Nation will endure as it has endured, will revive, and will prosper. So, first of all, let me assert my firm belief that the only thing we have to fear is fear itself—nameless, unreasoning, unjustified terror which paralyzes needed efforts to convert retreat into advance. In every dark hour of our national life a leadership of frankness and vigor has met with that understanding and support of the people themselves which is essential to victory. I am convinced that you will again give that support to leadership in these critical days.

In such a spirit on my part and on yours we face our common difficulties. They con-

[Delivered March 4, 1933.]

cern, thank God, only material things. Values have shrunken to fantastic levels; taxes have risen; our ability to pay has fallen; government of all kinds is faced by serious curtailment of income; the means of exchange are frozen in the currents of trade; the withered leaves of industrial enterprise lie on every side; farmers find no markets for their produce; the savings of many years in thousands of families are gone.

More important, a host of unemployed citizens face the grim problem of existence, and an equally great number toil with little return. Only a foolish optimist can deny the dark realities of the moment.

Yet our distress comes from no failure of substance. We are stricken by no plague of locusts. Compared with the perils which our forefathers conquered because they believed and were not afraid, we have still much to be thankful for. Nature still offers her bounty and human efforts have multiplied it. Plenty is at our doorstep, but a generous use of it languishes in the very sight of the supply. Primarily this is because rulers of the exchange of mankind's goods have failed through their own stubbornness and their own incompetence, have admitted their failure, and have abdicated. Practices of the unscrupulous money changers stand indicted in the court of public opinion, rejected by the hearts and minds of men.

True they have tried, but their efforts have been cast in the pattern of an outworn tradition. Faced by failure of credit they have proposed only the lending of more money. Stripped of the lure of profit by which to induce our people to follow their false leadership, they have resorted to exhortations, pleading tearfully for restored confidence. They know only the rules of a generation of self-seekers. They have no vision, and when there is no vision the people perish.

The money changers have fled from their high seats in the temple of our civilization. We may now restore that temple to the ancient truths. The measure of the restoration lies in the extent to which we apply social values more noble than mere monetary profit.

Happiness lies not in the mere possession of money; it lies in the joy of achievement, in the thrill of creative effort. The joy and moral stimulation of work no longer must be forgotten in the mad chase of evanescent profits. These dark days will be worth all they cost us if they teach us that our true destiny is not to be ministered unto but to minister to ourselves and to our fellow men.

Recognition of the falsity of material wealth as the standard of success goes hand in hand with the abandonment of the false belief that public office and high political position are to be valued only by the standards of pride of place and personal profit; and there must be an end to a conduct in banking and in business which too often has given to a sacred trust the likeness of callous and selfish wrongdoing. Small wonder that confidence languishes, for it thrives only on honesty, on honor, on the sacredness of obligations, on faithful protection, on unselfish performance; without them it cannot live.

Restoration calls, however, not for changes in ethics alone. This Nation asks for action, and action now.

Our greatest primary task is to put people to work. This is no unsolvable problem if we face it wisely and courageously. It can be accomplished in part by direct recruiting by the government itself, treating the task as we would treat the emergency of a war, but at the same time, through this employment, accomplishing greatly needed projects to stimulate and reorganize the use of our national resources.

Hand in hand with this we must frankly recognize the overbalance of population in our industrial centers and, by engaging on a national scale in a redistribution, endeavor to provide a better use of the land for those best fitted for the land. The task can be helped by definite efforts to raise the values of agricultural products and with this the power to purchase the output of our cities. It can be helped by preventing realistically the tragedy of the growing loss through foreclosure of our small homes and our farms. It can be helped by insistence that the federal, state, and local governments act forthwith on the demand that their cost be drastically reduced. It can be helped by the unifying of relief activities which today are often scattered, uneconomical, and unequal. It can be helped by national planning for and supervision of all forms of transportation and of communications and other utilities which have a definitely public character. There are many ways in which it can be helped, but it can never be helped merely by talking about it. We must act and act quickly.

Finally, in our progress toward a resumption of work we require two safeguards against a return of the evils of the old order: there must be a strict supervision of all banking and credits and investments, so that there will be an end to speculation with other people's money; and there must be provision for an adequate but sound currency.

These are the lines of attack. I shall presently urge upon a new Congress, in special session, detailed measures for their fulfillment, and I shall seek the immediate assistance of the several states.

Through this program of action we address ourselves to putting our own national house in order and making income balance outgo. Our international trade relations, though vastly important, are in point of time and necessity secondary to the establishment of a sound national economy. I favor as a practical policy the putting of first things first. I shall spare no effort to restore world trade by international economic readjustment, but the emergency at home cannot wait on that accomplishment.

The basic thought that guides these specific means of national recovery is not narrowly nationalistic. It is the insistence, as a first consideration, upon the interdependence of the various elements in and parts of the United States—a recognition of the old and permanently important manifestation of the American spirit of the pioneer. It is the way to recovery. It is the immediate way. It is the strongest assurance that the recovery will endure.

In the field of world policy I would dedicate this Nation to the policy of the good neighbor—the neighbor who resolutely respects himself and, because he does so, respects the rights of others—the neighbor who respects his obligations and respects the sanctity of his agreements in and with a world of neighbors.

If I read the temper of our people correctly, we now realize as we have never realized before our interdependence on each other; that we cannot merely take but we must give as well; that if we are to go forward, we must move as a trained and loyal army willing to sacrifice for the good of a common discipline, because without such discipline no progress is made, no leadership becomes effective. We are, I know, ready and willing to submit our lives and property to such discipline, because it makes possible a leadership which aims at a larger good. This I propose to offer, pledging that the larger purposes will bind upon us all as a sacred obligation with a unity of duty hitherto evoked only in time of armed strife.

With this pledge taken, I assume unhesitatingly the leadership of this great army of our people dedicated to a disciplined attack upon our common problems.

Action in this image and to this end is feasible under the form of government which we have inherited from our ancestors. Our Constitution is so simple and practical that it is possible always to meet extraordinary needs by changes in emphasis and arrangement without loss of essential form. That is why our constitutional system has proved itself the most superbly enduring political mechanism the modern world has produced. It has met every stress of vast expansion of territory, of foreign wars, of bitter internal strife, of world relations.

It is to be hoped that the normal balance of executive and legislative authority may be wholly adequate to meet the unprecedented task before us. But it may be that an unprecedented demand and need for undelayed action may call for temporary departure from that normal balance of public procedure.

I am prepared under my constitutional duty to recommend the measures that a stricken Nation in the midst of a stricken world may require. These measures, or such other measures as the Congress may build out of its experience and wisdom, I shall seek, within my constitutional authority, to bring to speedy adoption.

But in the event that the Congress shall fail to take one of these two courses, and in the event that the national emergency is still critical, I shall not evade the clear course of duty that will then confront me. I shall ask the Congress for the one remaining instrument to meet the crisis—broad executive power to wage a war against the emergency, as great as the power that would be given to me if we were in fact invaded by a foreign foe.

For the trust reposed in me I will return the courage and the devotion that befit the time. I can do no less.

We face the arduous days that lie before us in the warm courage of national unity; with the clear consciousness of seeking old and precious moral values; with the clean satisfaction that comes from the stern performance of duty by old and young alike. We aim at the assurance of a rounded and permanent national life.

We do not distrust the future of essential democracy. The people of the United States have not failed. In their need they have registered a mandate that they want direct, vigorous action. They have asked for discipline and direction under leadership. They have made me the present instrument of their wishes. In the spirit of the gift I take it.

In this dedication of a Nation we humbly ask the blessing of God. May He protect each and every one of us. May He guide me in the days to come.

FASCISM

Strictly speaking, the term fascism applies to the party and the regime that Mussolini led in Italy during the years from World War I to World War II. In general usage, however, the term has come to designate any non-communistic authoritarian movement or government in the contemporary Western world. The most important of these was the National Socialist (or Nazi) government of Hitler in Germany. In addition to Germany and Italy, however, there have been lesser fascist regimes, some of which are still with us, in other countries. The tendency to identify modern fascism with earlier tyrannies, though it has some validity, overlooks features of the modern movement that are genuinely novel. Among the most important of these, as Mussolini points out, is the fascist conception of totalitarianism, *the view that the state must dominate and, in fact, permeate the lives and activities of all its members. As the fascist motto puts it: "Everything for the state; nothing against the state; nothing outside the state."*

The two selections that follow are from the main works of Adolf Hitler (1889–1945) and Benito Mussolini (1883–1945), respectively. The first comes from Chapter XI of the first volume of Hitler's Mein Kampf *("My Battle"), written while Hitler was in prison following his unsuccessful "beer hall"* putsch *in 1923. The passage provides insight not only into the beliefs Hitler held on the vital topic of racism but also into the character of the man himself.*

The second selection, The Doctrine of Fascism *(which is presented in its entirety) was written by Mussolini with the aid of the Italian philosopher, Giovanni Gentile, and first appeared in the* Enciclopedia Italiana *(1932). In it, Mussolini touches on most of the major strains in fascist philosophy and practice. A striking feature of the article, particularly when it is viewed from the perspective of subsequent history, is the lofty, idealistic tone in which most of it is written.*

Mein Kampf

XI Nation and Race

There are some truths which are so obvious that for this very reason they are not seen or at least not recognized by ordinary people. They sometimes pass by such truisms as though blind and are most astonished when someone suddenly discovers what everyone really ought to know. Columbus's eggs lie around by the hundreds of thousands, but Columbuses are met with less frequently.

Thus men without exception wander about in the garden of Nature; they imagine that they know practically everything and yet with few exceptions pass blindly by one of the most patent principles of Nature's rule: the inner segregation of the species of all living beings on this earth.

Even the most superficial observation shows that Nature's restricted form of propagation and increase is an almost rigid basic law of all the innumerable forms of expression of her vital urge. Every animal mates only with a member of the same species. The titmouse seeks the titmouse, the finch the finch, the stork the stork, the field mouse the field mouse, the dormouse the dormouse, the wolf the she-wolf, etc.

Only unusual circumstances can change this, primarily the compulsion of captivity or any other cause that makes it impossible to mate within the same species. But then Nature begins to resist this with all possible means, and her most visible protest consists either in refusing further capacity for propagation to bastards or in limiting the fertility of later offspring; in most cases, however, she takes away the power of resistance to disease or hostile attacks.

This is only too natural.

Any crossing of two beings not at exactly the same level produces a medium between the level of the two parents. This means: the offspring will probably stand higher than the racially lower parent, but not as high as the higher one. Consequently, it will later succumb in the struggle against the higher level. Such mating is contrary to the will of Nature for a higher breeding of all life. The precondition for this does not lie in associating superior and inferior, but in the total victory of the former. The stronger must dominate and not blend with the weaker, thus sacrificing his own greatness. Only the born weakling can view this as cruel, but he after all is only a weak and limited man; for if this law did not prevail, any conceivable higher development of organic living beings would be unthinkable.

The consequence of this racial purity, universally valid in Nature, is not only the sharp outward delimitation of the various races, but their uniform character in themselves. The fox is always a fox, the goose a goose, the tiger a tiger, etc., and the difference can lie at most in the varying measure of force, strength, intelligence, dexterity, endurance, etc., of the individual specimens. But you will never find a fox who in his inner attitude might, for example, show humanitarian tendencies toward geese, as similarly there is no cat with a friendly inclination toward mice.

Therefore, here, too, the struggle among themselves arises less from inner aversion than from hunger and love. In both cases, Nature looks on calmly, with satisfaction, in fact. In the struggle for daily bread all those who are weak and sickly or less determined succumb, while the struggle of the males for the female grants the right or opportunity to propagate only to the healthiest. And struggle is always a means for improving a species' health and power of resistance and, therefore, a cause of its higher development.

If the process were different, all further and higher development would cease and the opposite would occur. For, since the inferior always predominates numerically over the best, if both had the same possibility of preserving life and propagating, the inferior would multiply so much more rapidly that in the end the best would inevitably be driven into the background, unless a correction of this state of affairs were undertaken. Nature does just this by subjecting the weaker part to such severe living conditions that by them alone the number is limited, and by not permitting the remainder to increase promiscuously, but making a new and ruthless choice according to strength and health.

No more than Nature desires the mating of weaker with stronger individuals, even less does she desire the blending of a higher with a lower race, since, if she did, her whole work of higher breeding, over perhaps hundreds of thousands of years, might be ruined with one blow.

Historical experience offers countless proofs of this. It shows with terrifying clarity that in every mingling of Aryan blood with that of lower peoples the result was the end of the cultured people. North America, whose population consists in by far the largest part of Germanic elements who mixed but little with the lower colored peoples, shows a different humanity and culture from Central and South America, where the predominantly Latin immigrants often mixed with the aborigines on a large scale. By this one example, we can clearly and distinctly recognize the effect of racial mixture. The Germanic inhabitant of the American continent, who has remained racially pure and unmixed, rose to be master of the continent; he will remain the master as long as he does not fall a victim to defilement of the blood.

The result of all racial crossing is therefore in brief always the following:

(a) Lowering of the level of the higher race;

(b) Physical and intellectual regression

and hence the beginning of a slowly but surely progressing sickness.

To bring about such a development is, then, nothing else but to sin against the will of the eternal creator. . . .

Everything we admire on this earth today—science and art, technology and inventions—is only the creative product of a few peoples and originally perhaps of one race. On them depends the existence of this whole culture. If they perish, the beauty of this earth will sink into the grave with them.

However much the soil, for example, can influence men, the result of the influence will always be different depending on the races in question. The low fertility of a living space may spur the one race to the highest achievements; in others it will only be the cause of bitterest poverty and final undernourishment with all its consequences. The inner nature of peoples is always determining for the manner in which outward influences will be effective. What leads the one to starvation trains the other to hard work.

All great cultures of the past perished only because the originally creative race died out from blood poisoning.

The ultimate cause of such a decline was their forgetting that all culture depends on men and not conversely; hence that to preserve a certain culture the man who creates it must be preserved. This preservation is bound up with the rigid law of necessity and the right to victory of the best and stronger in this world.

Those who want to live, let them fight, and those who do not want to fight in this world of eternal struggle do not deserve to live.

Even if this were hard—that is how it is! Assuredly, however, by far the harder fate is that which strikes the man who thinks he can overcome Nature, but in the last analysis only mocks her. Distress, misfortune, and diseases are her answer.

The man who misjudges and disregards the racial laws actually forfeits the happiness that seems destined to be his. He thwarts the triumphal march of the best race and hence also the precondition for all human progress, and remains, in consequence, burdened with all the sensibility of man, in the animal realm of helpless misery.

It is idle to argue which race or races were the original representative of human culture and hence the real founders of all that we sum up under the word "humanity." It is simpler to raise this question with regard to the present, and here an easy, clear answer results. All the human culture, all the results of art, science, and technology that we see before us today, are almost exclusively the creative product of the Aryan. This very fact admits of the not unfounded inference that he alone was the founder of all higher humanity, therefore representing the prototype of all that we understand by the word "man." He is the Prometheus of mankind from whose bright forehead the divine spark of genius has sprung at all times, forever kindling anew that fire of knowledge which illumined the night of silent mysteries and thus caused man to climb the path to mastery over the other beings of this earth. Exclude him—and perhaps after a thousand years darkness will again descend on the earth, human culture will pass, and the world turn to a desert.

If we were to divide mankind into three groups, the founders of culture, the bearers of culture, the destroyers of culture, only the Aryan could be considered as the representative of the first group. From him originate the foundations and walls of all human creation, and only the outward form and color are determined by the changing traits of character of the various peoples. He provides the mightiest building stones and plans for all human progress and only the execution corresponds to the nature of the varying men and races. . . .

The question of the inner causes of the Aryan's importance can be answered to the effect that they are to be sought less in a natural instinct of self-preservation than in the special type of its expression. The will to live, subjectively viewed, is everywhere equal and different only in the form of its actual expression. In the most primitive living creatures the instinct of self-preservation does not go beyond concern for their own ego. Egoism, as we designate this urge, goes so far that it even embraces time; the moment itself claims everything, granting nothing to the coming hours. In this condition the animal lives only for himself, seeks food only for his present hunger, and fights only for his own life. As long as the instinct of self-preservation expresses itself in this way, every basis is lacking for the formation of a group, even the most primitive form of family. Even a community between male and female beyond pure mating, demands an extension of the instinct of self-preservation, since concern and struggle for the ego are now directed toward the second party; the male sometimes seeks food for the female, too, but for the most part both seek nourishment for the young. Nearly always one comes to the defense of the other, and thus the first, though infinitely simple, forms of a sense of sacrifice result. As soon as this sense extends beyond the narrow limits of the family, the basis for the formation of larger organisms and finally formal states is created.

In the lowest peoples of the earth this quality is present only to a very slight extent, so that often they do not go beyond the formation of the family. The greater the readiness to subordinate purely personal interests, the higher rises the ability to establish comprehensive communities.

This self-sacrificing will to give one's personal labor and if necessary one's own life for others is most strongly developed in the Aryan. The Aryan is not greatest in his mental qualities as such, but in the extent of his willingness to put all his abilities in the service of the community. In him the instinct of self-preservation has reached the noblest form, since he willingly subordinates his own ego to the life of the community and, if the hour demands, even sacrifices it.

Not in his intellectual gifts lies the source of the Aryan's capacity for creating and building culture. If he had just this alone, he could only act destructively, in no case could he organize; for the innermost essence of all organization requires that the individual renounce putting forward his personal opinion and interests and sacrifice both in favor of a larger group. Only by way of this general community does he again recover his share. Now, for example, he no longer works directly for himself, but with his activity articulates himself with the community, not only for his own advantage, but for the advantage of all. The most wonderful elucidation of this attitude is provided by his word "work," by which he does not mean an activity for maintaining life in itself, but exclusively a creative effort that does not conflict with the interests of the community. Otherwise he designates human activity, in so far as it serves the instinct of self-preservation without consideration for his fellow men, as theft, usury, robbery, burglary, etc.

This state of mind, which subordinates the interests of the ego to the conservation of the community, is really the first premise for every truly human culture. From it alone can arise all the great works of mankind, which bring the founder little reward, but the richest blessings to posterity. Yes from it alone can we understand how so many are able to bear up faithfully under a scanty life which imposes on them nothing but poverty and frugality, but gives the community the foundations of its existence. Every worker, every peasant, every inventor, official, etc., who works without ever being able to achieve any happiness or prosperity for himself, is a representative of this lofty idea, even if the deeper meaning of his activity remains hidden in him.

What applies to work as the foundation of human sustenance and all human progress is true to an even greater degree for the defense of man and his culture. In giving one's own life for the existence of the community lies the crown of all sense of sacrifice. It is this alone that prevents what human hands have built from being overthrown by human hands or destroyed by Nature.

Our own German language possesses a word which magnificently designates this kind of activity: *Pflichterfüllung* (fulfillment of duty); it means not to be self-sufficient but to serve the community.

The basic attitude from which such activity arises, we call—to distinguish it from egoism and selfishness—idealism. By this we understand only the individual's capacity to make sacrifices for the community, for his fellow men.

How necessary it is to keep realizing that idealism does not represent a superfluous expression of emotion, but that in truth it has been, is, and will be, the premise for what we designate as human culture, yes, that it alone created the concept of "man." It is to this inner attitude that the Aryan owes his position in this world, and to it the world owes man; for it alone formed from pure spirit the creative force which, by a unique pairing of the brutal fist and the intellectual genius, created the monuments of human culture.

Without his idealistic attitude all, even the most dazzling faculties of the intellect, would remain mere intellect as such—outward appearance without inner value, and never creative force.

But, since true idealism is nothing but the subordination of the interests and life of the individual to the community, and this in turn is the precondition for the creation of organizational forms of all kinds, it corresponds in its innermost depths to the ultimate will of Nature. It alone leads men to voluntary recognition of the privilege of force and strength, and thus makes them into a dust particle of that order which shapes and forms the whole universe.

The purest idealism is unconsciously equivalent to the deepest knowledge.

How correct this is, and how little true idealism has to do with playful flights of the imagination, can be seen at once if we let the unspoiled child, a healthy boy, for example, judge. The same boy who feels like throwing up when he hears the tirades of a pacifist "idealist" is ready to give his young life for the ideal of his nationality.

Here the instinct of knowledge unconsciously obeys the deeper necessity of the preservation of the species, if necessary at the cost of the individual, and protests against the visions of the pacifist windbag who in reality is nothing but a cowardly, though camouflaged, egoist, transgressing the laws of development; for development requires willingness on the part of the individual to sacrifice himself for the community, and not the sickly imaginings of cowardly know-it-alls and critics of Nature.

Especially, therefore, at times when the ideal attitude threatens to disappear, we can at once recognize a diminution of that force which forms the community and thus creates the premises of culture. As soon as egoism becomes the ruler of a people, the bands of order are loosened and in the chase after their own happiness men fall from heaven into a real hell.

Yes, even posterity forgets the men who have only served their own advantage and praises the heroes who have renounced their own happiness.

The mightiest counterpart to the Aryan is represented by the Jew. In hardly any people in the world is the instinct of self-preservation developed more strongly than in the so-called "chosen." Of this, the mere fact of the survival of this race may be considered the best proof. Where is the people which in the last two thousand years has been exposed to so slight changes of inner disposition, character, etc., as the Jewish people? What people, finally, has gone through greater upheavals than this one—and nevertheless issued from the mightiest catastrophes of mankind unchanged? What an infinitely tough will to live and preserve the species speaks from these facts!

The mental qualities of the Jew have been schooled in the course of many centuries. Today he passes as "smart," and this in a certain sense he has been at all times. But his intelligence is not the result of his own development, but of visual instruction through foreigners. For the human mind cannot climb to the top without steps; for every step upward he needs the foundation of the past, and this in the comprehensive sense in which it can be revealed only in general culture. All thinking is based only in small part on man's own knowledge, and mostly on the experience of the time that has preceded. The general cultural level provides the individual man, without his noticing it as a rule, with such a profusion of preliminary knowledge that, thus armed, he can more easily take further steps of his own. The boy of today, for example, grows up among a truly vast number of technical acquisitions of the last centuries, so that he takes for granted and no longer pays attention to much that a hundred years ago was a riddle to even the greatest minds, although for following and understanding our progress in the field in question it is of decisive importance to him. If a very genius from the twenties of the past century should suddenly leave his grave today, it would be harder for him even intellectually to find his way in the present era than for an average boy of fifteen today. For he would lack all the infinite preliminary education which our present contemporary unconsciously, so to speak, assimilates while growing up amidst the manifestations of our present general civilization.

Since the Jew—for reasons which will at once become apparent—was never in possession of a culture of his own, the foundations of his intellectual work were always provided by others. His intellect at all times developed through the cultural world surrounding him.

The reverse process never took place.

For if the Jewish people's instinct of self-preservation is not smaller but larger than that of other peoples, if his intellectual faculties can easily arouse the impression that they are equal to the intellectual gifts of other races, he lacks completely the most essential requirement for a cultured people, the idealistic attitude.

In the Jewish people the will to self-sacrifice does not go beyond the individual's naked instinct of self-preservation. Their apparently great sense of solidarity is based on the very primitive herd instinct that is seen in many other living creatures in this world. It is a noteworthy fact that the herd instinct leads to mutual support only as long as a common danger makes this seem useful or inevitable. The same pack of wolves which has just fallen on its prey together disintegrates when hunger abates into its individual beasts. The same is true of horses which try to defend themselves against an assailant in a body, but scatter again as soon as the danger is past.

It is similar with the Jew. His sense of sacrifice is only apparent. It exists only as long as the existence of the individual makes it absolutely necessary. However, as soon as the common enemy is conquered, the danger threatening all averted and the booty hidden, the apparent harmony of the Jews among themselves ceases, again making way for their old causal tendencies. The Jew is only united when a common danger forces him to be or a common booty entices him; if these two grounds are lacking, the qualities of the crassest egoism come into their own, and in the twinkling of an eye the united people turns into a horde of rats, fighting bloodily among themselves.

If the Jews were alone in this world, they would stifle in filth and offal; they would try to get ahead of one another in hate-filled struggle and exterminate one another, in so far as the absolute absence of all sense of self-sacrifice, expressing itself in their cowardice, did not turn battle into comedy here too.

So it is absolutely wrong to infer any ideal sense of sacrifice in the Jews from the fact that they stand together in struggle, or, better expressed, in the plundering of their fellow men.

Here again the Jew is led by nothing but the naked egoism of the individual.

That is why the Jewish state—which should be the living organism for preserving and increasing a race—is completely unlimited as to territory. For a state formation to have a definite spatial setting always presupposes an idealistic attitude on the part of the state-race, and especially a correct interpretation of the concept of work. In the exact measure in which this attitude is lacking, any attempt at forming, even of preserving, a spatially delimited state fails. And thus the basis on which alone culture can arise is lacking.

Hence the Jewish people, despite all apparent intellectual qualities, is without any true culture, and especially without any culture of its own. For what sham culture the Jew today possesses is the property of other peoples, and for the most part it is ruined in his hands.

In judging the Jewish people's attitude on the question of human culture, the most essential characteristic we must always bear in mind is that there has never been a Jewish art and accordingly there is none today either; that above all the two queens of all the arts, architecture and music, owe nothing original to the Jews. What they do accomplish in the field of art is either patchwork or intellectual theft. Thus, the Jew lacks those qualities which distinguish the races that are creative and hence culturally blessed.

To what an extent the Jew takes over foreign culture, imitating or rather ruining it, can be seen from the fact that he is mostly found in the art which seems to require least original invention, the art of acting. But even here, in reality, he is only a "juggler," or rather an ape; for even here he lacks the last touch that is required for real greatness; even here he is not the creative genius, but a superficial imitator, and all the twists and tricks that he uses are powerless to conceal the inner lifelessness of his creative gift. Here the Jewish press most lovingly helps him along by raising such a roar of hosannahs about even the most mediocre bungler, just so long as he is a Jew, that the rest of the world actually ends up by thinking that they have an artist before them, while in truth it is only a pitiful comedian.

No, the Jew possesses no culture-creating force of any sort, since the idealism, without which there is no true higher development of man, is not present in him and never was present. Hence his intellect will never have a constructive effect, but will be destructive, and in very rare cases perhaps will at most be stimulating, but then as the prototype of the "force which always wants evil and nevertheless creates good." [1] Not through him does any progress of mankind occur, but in spite of him.

[1] Goethe's *Faust,* lines 1336–37: Mephistopheles to Faust.

The Doctrine of Fascism

FUNDAMENTAL IDEAS

1. Like every sound political conception, Fascism is both practice and thought; action in which a doctrine is immanent, and a doctrine which, arising out of a given system of historical forces, remains embedded in them and works there from within. Hence it has a form correlative to the contingencies of place and time, but it has also a content of thought which raises it to a formula of truth in the higher level of the history of thought. In the world one does not act spiritually as a human will dominating other wills without a conception of the transient and particular reality under which it is necessary to act, and of the permanent and universal reality in which the first has its being and its life. In order to know men it is necessary to know man; and in order to know man it is necessary to know reality and its laws. There is no concept of the State which is not fundamentally a concept of life: philosophy or intuition, a system of ideas which develops logically or is gathered up into a vision or into a faith, but which is always, at least virtually, an organic conception of the world.

2. Thus Fascism could not be understood in many of its practical manifestations as a party organization, as a system of education, as a discipline, if it were not always looked at in the light of its whole way of conceiving life, a spiritualized way. The world seen through Fascism is not this material world which appears on the surface, in which man is an individual separated from all others and standing by himself, and in which he is governed by a natural law that makes him instinctively live a life of selfish and momentary pleasure. The man of Fascism is an individual who is nation and fatherland, which is a moral law, binding together individuals and the generations into a tradition and a mission, suppressing the instinct for a life enclosed within the brief round of pleasure in order to restore within duty a higher life free from the limits of time and space: a life in which the individual, through the denial of himself, through the sacrifice of his own private interests, through death itself, realizes that completely spiritual existence in which his value as a man lies.

3. Therefore it is a spiritualized conception, itself the result of the general reaction of modern times against the flabby materialistic positivism of the nineteenth century. Anti-positivistic, but positive: not sceptical, nor agnostic, nor pessimistic, nor passively optimistic, as are, in general, the doctrines (all negative) that put the centre of life outside man, who with his free will can and must create his own world. Fascism desires an active man, one engaged in activity with all his energies: it desires a

Benito Mussolini, "The Doctrine of Fascism," ed. and trans. M. Oakeshott, in THE SOCIAL AND POLITICAL DOCTRINES OF CONTEMPORARY EUROPE *(London: Cambridge University Press, 1953), pp. 164–79. Courtesy of Cambridge University Press.*

man virilely conscious of the difficulties that exist in action and ready to face them. It conceives of life as a struggle, considering that it behoves man to conquer for himself that life truly worthy of him, creating first of all in himself the instrument (physical, moral, intellectual) in order to construct it. Thus for the single individual, thus for the nation, thus for humanity. Hence the high value of culture in all its forms (arts, religion, science), and the enormous importance of education. Hence also the essential value of work, with which man conquers nature and creates the human world (economic, political, moral, intellectual).

4. This positive conception of life is clearly an ethical conception. It covers the whole of reality, not merely the human activity which controls it. No action can be divorced from moral judgment; there is nothing in the world which can be deprived of the value which belongs to everything in its relation to moral ends. Life, therefore, as conceived by the Fascist, is serious, austere, religious: the whole of it is poised in a world supported by the moral and responsible forces of the spirit. The Fascist disdains the "comfortable" life.

5. Fascism is a religious conception in which man is seen in his immanent relationship with a superior law and with an objective Will that transcends the particular individual and raises him to conscious membership of a spiritual society. Whoever has seen in the religious politics of the Fascist regime nothing but mere opportunism has not understood that Fascism besides being a system of government is also, above all, a system of thought.

6. Fascism is an historical conception, in which man is what he is only in so far as he works with the spiritual process in which he finds himself, in the family or social group, in the nation, and in the history in which all nations collaborate. From this follows the great value of tradition, in memories, in language, in customs, in the standards of social life. Outside history man is nothing. Consequently Fascism is opposed to all the individualistic abstractions of a materialistic nature like those of the eighteenth century; and it is opposed to all Jacobin utopias and innovations. It does not consider that "happiness" is possible upon earth, as it appeared to be in the desire of the economic literature of the eighteenth century, and hence it rejects all teleological theories according to which mankind would reach a definitive stabilized condition at a certain period in history. This implies putting oneself outside history and life, which is a continual change and coming to be. Politically, Fascism wishes to be a realistic doctrine; practically, it aspires to solve only the problems which arise historically of themselves and that of themselves find or suggest their own solution. To act among men, as to act in the natural world, it is necessary to enter into the process of reality and to master the already operating forces.

7. Against individualism, the Fascist conception is for the State; and it is for the individual in so far as he coincides with the State, which is the conscience and universal will of man in his historical existence. It is opposed to classical Liberalism, which arose from the necessity of reacting against absolutism, and which brought its historical purpose to an end when the State was transformed into the conscience and will of the people. Liberalism denied the State in the interests of the particular individual; Fascism reaffirms the State as the true reality of the individual. And if liberty is to be the attribute of the real man, and not of that abstract puppet envisaged by individualistic Liberalism, Fascism is for liberty. And for the only liberty which can be a real thing, the liberty of the State and of the individual within the State. Therefore, for the Fascist, everything is in the State, and nothing human or spiritual ex-

ists, much less has value, outside the State. In this sense Fascism is totalitarian, and the Fascist State, the synthesis and unity of all values, interprets, develops and gives strength to the whole life of the people.

8. Outside the State there can be neither individuals nor groups (political parties, associations, syndicates, classes). Therefore Fascism is opposed to Socialism, which confines the movement of history within the class struggle and ignores the unity of classes established in one economic and moral reality in the State; and analogously it is opposed to class syndicalism. Fascism recognizes the real exigencies for which the socialist and syndicalist movement arose, but while recognizing them wishes to bring them under the control of the State and give them a purpose within the corporative system of interests reconciled within the unity of the State.

9. Individuals form classes according to the similarity of their interests, they form syndicates according to differentiated economic activities within these interests; but they form first, and above all, the State, which is not to be thought of numerically as the sum-total of individuals forming the majority of a nation. And consequently Fascism is opposed to Democracy, which equates the nation to the majority, lowering it to the level of that majority; nevertheless it is the purest form of democracy if the nation is conceived, as it should be, qualitatively and not quantitatively, as the most powerful idea (most powerful because most moral, most coherent, most true) which acts within the nation as the conscience and the will of a few, even of One, which ideal tends to become active within the conscience and the will of all those who rightly constitute a nation by reason of nature, history or race, and have set out upon the same line of development and spiritual formation as one conscience and one sole will. Not a race, nor a geographically determined region, but as a community historically perpetuating itself, a multitude unified by a single idea, which is the will to existence and to power: consciousness of itself, personality.

10. This higher personality is truly the nation in so far as it is the State. It is not the nation that generates the State, as according to the old naturalistic concept which served as the basis of the political theories of the national States of the nineteenth century. Rather the nation is created by the State, which gives to the people, conscious of its own moral unity, a will and therefore an effective existence. The right of a nation to independence derives not from a literary and ideal consciousness of its own being, still less from a more or less unconscious and inert acceptance of a *de facto* situation, but from an active consciousness, from a political will in action and ready to demonstrate its own rights: that is to say, from a state already coming into being. The State, in fact, as the universal ethical will, is the creator of right.

11. The nation as the State is an ethical reality which exists and lives in so far as it develops. To arrest its development is to kill it. Therefore the State is not only the authority which governs and gives the form of laws and the value of spiritual life to the wills of individuals, but it is also a power that makes its will felt abroad, making it known and respected, in other words, demonstrating the fact of its universality in all the necessary directions of its development. It is consequently organization and expansion, at least virtually. Thus it can be likened to the human will which knows no limits to its development and realizes itself in testing its own limitlessness.

12. The Fascist State, the highest and most powerful form of personality, is a force, but a spiritual force, which takes over all the forms of the moral and intellectual life of man. It cannot therefore confine itself simply to the functions of order

and supervision as Liberalism desired. It is not simply a mechanism which limits the sphere of the supposed liberties of the individual. It is the form, the inner standard and the discipline of the whole person; it saturates the will as well as the intelligence. Its principle, the central inspiration of the human personality living in the civil community, pierces into the depths and makes its home in the heart of the man of action as well as of the thinker, of the artist as well as of the scientist: it is the soul of the soul.

13. Fascism, in short, is not only the giver of laws and the founder of institutions, but the educator and promoter of spiritual life. It wants to remake, not the forms of human life, but its content, man, character, faith. And to this end it requires discipline and authority that can enter into the spirits of men and there govern unopposed. Its sign, therefore, is the Lictors' rods, the symbol of unity, of strength and justice.

POLITICAL AND SOCIAL DOCTRINE

1. When in the now distant March of 1919 I summoned to Milan, through the columns of the *Popolo d'Italia,* my surviving supporters who had followed me since the constitution of the Fasces of Revolutionary Action, founded in January 1915, there was no specific doctrinal plan in my mind. I had known and lived through only one doctrine, that of the Socialism of 1903–4 up to the winter of 1914, almost ten years. My experience in this had been that of a follower and of a leader, but not that of a theoretician. My doctrine, even in that period, had been a doctrine of action. An unequivocal Socialism, universally accepted, did not exist after 1905, when the Revisionist Movement began in Germany under Bernstein and there was formed in opposition to that, in the seesaw of tendencies, an extreme revolutionary movement, which in Italy never emerged from the condition of mere words, whilst in Russian Socialism it was the prelude to Bolshevism. Reform, Revolution, Centralization—even the echoes of the terminology are now spent; whilst in the great river of Fascism are to be found the streams which had their source in Sorel, Peguy, in the Lagardelle of the *Mouvement Socialiste* and the groups of Italian Syndicalists, who between 1904 and 1914 brought a note of novelty into Italian Socialism, which by that time had been devitalized and drugged by fornication with Giolitti, in *Pagine Libere* of Olivetti, *La Lupa* of Orano, and *Divenire Sociale* of Enrico Leone.

In 1919, at the end of the War, Socialism as a doctrine was already dead: it existed only as hatred, it had still only one possibility, especially in Italy, that of revenge against those who had wished for the War and who should be made to expiate it. The *Popolo d'Italia* expressed it in its sub-title —"The Newspaper of Combatants and Producers." The word "producers" was already the expression of a tendency. Fascism was not given out to the wet nurse of a doctrine elaborated beforehand round a table: it was born of the need for action; it was not a party, but in its first two years it was a movement against all parties. The name which I gave to the organization defined its characteristics. Nevertheless, whoever rereads, in the now crumpled pages of the time, the account of the constituent assembly of the *Fasci italiani di Combattimento* will not find a doctrine, but a series of suggestions, of anticipations, of admonitions, which when freed from the inevitable vein of contingency, were destined later, after a few years, to develop into a series of doctrinal attitudes which made of Fascism a self-sufficient political doctrine able to face all others, both past and present. "If the bourgeoisie," I said at that time, "thinks to find in us a lightning-conductor, it is mistaken. We must go forward in opposition to Labour. . . . We want to accustom the working classes to being under a leader, to convince them also that it is not easy to direct an industry or a commercial undertaking successfully. . . . We shall fight against technical and spiritual retrogression. . . . The successors of the present regime still being undecided, we must not be unwilling to fight for it. We must hasten; when the present regime is superseded, we must be the ones to take its place. The right of succession belongs to us because we pushed the country into the War and we lead it to victory. The present method of political representation cannot be sufficient for us, we wish for a direct representation of individual interests. . . . It might be said against this programme that it is return to the corporations. It doesn't matter! . . . I should like, nevertheless, the Assembly to accept the claims of national syndicalism from the point of view of economics. . . ."

Is it not surprising that from the first day in the Piazza San Sepolcro there should resound the word "Corporation" which was destined in the course of the revolution to signify one of the legislative and social creations at the base of the regime?

2. The years preceding the March on Rome were years during which the necessity of action did not tolerate enquiries or complete elaborations of doctrine. Battles were being fought in the cities and villages. There were discussions, but—and this is more sacred and important—there were deaths. People knew how to die. The doctrine—beautiful, well-formed, divided into chapters and paragraphs and surrounded by a commentary—might be missing; but there was present something more decisive to supplant it—Faith. Nevertheless, he who recalls the past with the aid of books, articles, votes in Parliament, the major and the minor speeches, he who knows how to investigate and weigh evidence, will find that the foundations of the doctrine were laid while the battle was raging. It was precisely in these years that Fascist thought armed itself, refined itself, moving towards one organization of its own. The problems of the individual and the State; the problems of authority and liberty; political and social problems and those more specifically national; the struggle against liberal, democratic, socialist, Masonic, demagogic doctrines was carried on at the same time as the "punitive expeditions." But since the "system" was lacking, adversaries ingenuously denied that Fascism had any power to make a doctrine of its own, while the doctrine rose up, even though tumultuously, at first under the aspect of a violent and dogmatic negation, as happens to all ideas that break new ground, then under the positive aspect of a constructive policy which, during the years 1926, 1927, 1928, was realized in the laws and institutions of the regime.

Fascism is to-day clearly defined not only as a regime but as a doctrine. And I mean by this that Fascism to-day, self-critical as well as critical of other movements, has an unequivocal point of view of its own, a criterion, and hence an aim, in face of all the material and intellectual problems which oppress the people of the world.

3. Above all, Fascism, in so far as it considers and observes the future and the development of humanity quite apart from the political considerations of the moment, believes neither in the possibility nor in the utility of perpetual peace. It thus repudiates the doctrine of Pacifism—born of a renunciation of the struggle and an act of cowardice in the face of sacrifice. War alone brings up to their highest tension all human energies and puts the stamp of nobility upon the peoples who have the courage to meet it. All other trials are substitutes, which never really put a man in front of himself in the alternative of life and death. A doctrine, therefore, which begins with a prejudice in favour of peace is foreign to

Fascism; as are foreign to the spirit of Fascism, even though acceptable by reason of the utility which they might have in given political situations, all internationalistic and socialistic systems which, as history proves, can be blown to the winds when emotional, idealistic and practical movements storm the hearts of peoples. Fascism carries over this antipacifist spirit even into the lives of individuals. The proud motto of the *Squadrista,* "Me ne frego," written on the bandages of a wound is an act of philosophy which is not only stoical, it is the epitome of a doctrine that is not only political: it is education for combat, the acceptance of the risks which it brings; it is a new way of life for Italy. Thus the Fascist accepts and loves life, he knows nothing of suicide and despises it; he looks on life as duty, ascent, conquest: life which must be noble and full: lived for oneself, but above all for those others near and far away, present and future.

4. The "demographic" policy of the regime follows from these premises. Even the Fascist does in fact love his neighbour, but this "neighbour" is not for him a vague and ill-defined concept; love for one's neighbour does not exclude necessary educational severities, and still less differentiations and distances. Fascism rejects universal concord, and, since it lives in the community of civilized peoples, it keeps them vigilantly and suspiciously before its eyes, it follows their states of mind and the changes in their interests and it does not let itself be deceived by temporary and fallacious appearances.

5. Such a conception of life makes Fascism the precise negation of that doctrine which formed the basis of the so-called Scientific or Marxian Socialism: the doctrine of historical Materialism, according to which the history of human civilizations can be explained only as the struggle of interest between the different social groups and as arising out of change in the means and instruments of production. That economic improvements—discoveries of raw materials, new methods of work, scientific inventions—should have an importance of their own, no one denies, but that they should suffice to explain human history to the exclusion of all other factors is absurd: Fascism believes, now and always, in holiness and in heroism, that is in acts in which no economic motive—remote or immediate—plays a part. With this negation of historical materialism, according to which men would be only by-products of history, who appear and disappear on the surface of the waves while in the depths the real directive forces are at work, there is also denied the immutable and irreparable "class struggle" which is the natural product of this economic conception of history, and above all it is denied that the class struggle can be the primary agent of social changes. Socialism, being thus wounded in these two primary tenets of its doctrine, nothing of it is left save the sentimental aspiration—old as humanity—toward a social order in which the sufferings and the pains of the humblest folk could be alleviated. But here Fascism rejects the concept of an economic "happiness" which would be realized socialistically and almost automatically at a given moment of economic evolution by assuring to all a maximum prosperity. Fascism denies the possibility of the materialistic conception of "happiness" and leaves it to the economists of the first half of the eighteenth century; it denies, that is, the equation of prosperity with happiness, which would transform men into animals with one sole preoccupation: that of being well-fed and fat, degraded in consequence to a merely physical existence.

6. After Socialism, Fascism attacks the whole complex of democratic ideologies and rejects them both in their theoretical premises and in their applications or practical manifestations. Fascism denies that the majority, through the mere fact of be-

ing a majority, can rule human societies; it denies that this majority can govern by means of a periodical consultation; it affirms the irremediable, fruitful, and beneficent inequality of men, who cannot be levelled by such a mechanical and extrinsic fact as universal suffrage. By democratic regimes we mean those in which from time to time the people is given the illusion of being sovereign, while true effective sovereignty lies in other, perhaps irresponsible and secret, forces. Democracy is a regime without a king, but with very many kings, perhaps more exclusive, tyrannical, and violent than one king even though a tyrant. This explains why Fascism, although before 1922 for reasons of expediency it made a gesture of republicanism, renounced it before the March on Rome, convinced that the question of the political forms of a State is not pre-eminent to-day, and that studying past and present monarchies, past and present Republics it becomes clear that monarchy and republic are not to be judged *sub specie aeternitatis,* but represent forms in which the political evolution, the history, the tradition, the psychology of a given country are manifested. Now Fascism overcomes the antithesis between monarchy and republic which retarded the movements of democracy, burdening the former with every defect and defending the latter as the regime of perfection. Now it has been seen that there are inherently reactionary and absolutistic republics, and monarchies that welcome the most daring political and social innovations.

7. "Reason, Science," said Renan (who was inspired before Fascism existed) in one of his philosophical Meditations, "are products of humanity, but to expect reason directly from the people and through the people is a chimera. It is not necessary for the existence of reason that everybody should know it. In any case, if such an initiation should be made, it would not be made by means of base democracy, which apparently must lead to the extinction of every difficult culture, and every higher discipline. The principle that society exists only for the prosperity and the liberty of the individuals who compose it does not seem to conform with the plans of nature, plans in which the species alone is taken into consideration and the individual seems to be sacrificed. It is strongly to be feared lest the last word of democracy thus understood (I hasten to say that it can also be understood in other ways) would be a social state in which a degenerate mass would have no other care than to enjoy the ignoble pleasures of vulgar men."

Thus far Renan. Fascism rejects in democracy the absurd conventional lie of political equalitarianism clothed in the dress of collective irresponsibility and the myth of happiness and indefinite progress. But if democracy can be understood in other ways, that is, if democracy means not to relegate the people to the periphery of the State, then Fascism could be defined as an "organized, centralized, authoritarian democracy."

8. In face of Liberal doctrines, Fascism takes up an attitude of absolute opposition both in the field of politics and in that of economics. It is not necessary to exaggerate—merely for the purpose of present controversies—the importance of Liberalism in the past century, and to make of that which was one of the numerous doctrines sketched in that century a religion of humanity for all times, present and future. Liberalism flourished for no more than some fifteen years. It was born in 1830, as a reaction against the Holy Alliance that wished to drag Europe back to what it had been before 1789, and it had its year of splendour in 1848 when even Pius IX was a Liberal. Immediately afterwards the decay set in. If 1848 was a year of light and of poetry, 1849 was a year of darkness and of tragedy. The Republic of Rome was destroyed by another Republic, that of France. In the same

year Marx launched the gospel of the religion of Socialism with the famous *Communist Manifesto*. In 1851 Napoleon III carried out his unliberal *coup d'état* and ruled over France until 1870, when he was dethroned by a popular revolt, but as a consequence of a military defeat which ranks among the most resounding that history can relate. The victor was Bismarck, who never knew the home of the religion of liberty or who were its prophets. It is symptomatic that a people of high culture like the Germans should have been completely ignorant of the religion of liberty during the whole of the nineteenth century. It was, there, no more than a parenthesis, represented by what has been called the "ridiculous Parliament of Frankfort" which lasted only a season. Germany has achieved her national unity outside the doctrines of Liberalism, against Liberalism, a doctrine which seems foreign to the German soul, a soul essentially monarchial, whilst Liberalism is the historical and logical beginning of anarchism. The stages of German unity are the three wars of 1864, 1866, and 1870, conducted by "Liberals" like Moltke and Bismarck. As for Italian unity, Liberalism has had in it a part absolutely inferior to the share of Mazzini and of Garibaldi, who were not Liberals. Without the intervention of the unliberal Napoleon we should not have gained Lombardy, and without the help of the unliberal Bismarck at Sadowa and Sedan, very probably we should not have gained Venice in 1866; and in 1870 we should not have entered Rome. From 1870–1915 there occurs the period in which the very priests of the new creed had to confess the twilight of their religion, defeated as it was by decadence in literature, by activism in practice. Activism: that is to say, Nationalism, Futurism, Fascism. The "Liberal" century, after having accumulated an infinity of Gordian knots, tried to untie them by the hecatomb of the World War. Never before has any religion imposed such a cruel sacrifice. Were the gods of Liberalism thirsty for blood? Now Liberalism is about to close the doors of its deserted temples because the peoples feel that its agnosticism in economics, its indifferentism in politics and in morals, would lead, as they have led, the States to certain ruin. In this way one can understand why all the political experiences of the contemporary world are anti-Liberal, and it is supremely ridiculous to wish on that account to class them outside of history; as if history were a hunting ground reserved to Liberalism and its professors, as if Liberalism were the definitive and no longer surpassable message of civilization.

9. But the Fascist repudiations of Socialism, Democracy, Liberalism must not make one think that Fascism wishes to make the world return to what it was before 1789, the year which has been indicated as the year of the beginning of the liberal-democratic age. One does not go backwards. The Fascist doctrine has not chosen De Maistre as its prophet. Monarchical absolutism is a thing of the past and so also is every theocracy. So also feudal privileges and division into impenetrable and isolated castes have had their day. The theory of Fascist authority has nothing to do with the police State. A party that governs a nation in a totalitarian way is a new fact in history. References and comparisons are not possible. Fascism takes over from the ruins of Liberal Socialistic democratic doctrines those elements which still have a living value. It preserves those that can be called the established facts of history, it rejects all the rest, that is to say the idea of a doctrine which holds good for all times and all peoples. If it is admitted that the nineteenth century has been the century of Socialism, Liberalism, and Democracy, it does not follow that the twentieth must also be the century of Liberalism, Socialism, and Democracy. Political doctrines pass; peoples remain. It is to be expected that

this century may be that of authority, a century of the "Right," a Fascist century. If the nineteenth was the century of the individual (Liberalism means individualism), it may be expected that this one may be the century of "collectivism" and therefore the century of the State. That a new doctrine should use the still vital elements of other doctrines is perfectly logical. No doctrine is born quite new, shining, never beforé seen. No doctrine can boast of an absolute "originality." It is bound, even if only historically, to other doctrines that have been, and to develop into other doctrines that will be. Thus the scientific socialism of Marx is bound to the Utopian Socialism of the Fouriers, the Owens, and the Saint-Simons; thus the Liberalism of the nineteenth century is connected with the whole "Enlightenment" of the eighteenth century. Thus the doctrines of democracy are bound to the *Encyclopedie*. Every doctrine tends to direct the activity of men towards a determined objective; but the activity of man reacts upon the doctrine, transforms it, adapts it to new necessities or transcends it. The doctrine itself, therefore, must be, not words, but an act of life. Hence, the pragmatic veins in Fascism, its will to power, its will to be, its attitude in the face of the fact of "violence" and of its own courage.

10. The keystone of Fascist doctrine is the conception of the State, of its essence, of its tasks, of its ends. For Fascism the State is an absolute before which individuals and groups are relative. Individuals and groups are "thinkable" in so far as they are within the State. The Liberal State does not direct the interplay and the material and spiritual development of the groups, but limits itself to registering the results; the Fascist State has a consciousness of its own, a will of its own, on this account it is called an "ethical" State. In 1929, at the first quinquennial assembly of the regime, I said: "For Fascism, the State is not the night-watchman who is concerned only with the personal security of the citizens; nor is it an organization for purely material ends, such as that of guaranteeing a certain degree of prosperity and a relatively peaceful social order, to achieve which a council of administration would be sufficient, nor is it a creation of mere politics with no contact with the material and complex reality of the lives of individuals and the life of peoples. The State, as conceived by Fascism and as it acts, is a spiritual and moral fact because it makes concrete the political, juridical, economic organization of the nation and such an organization is, in its origin and in its development, a manifestation of the spirit. The State is the guarantor of internal and external security, but it is also the guardian and the transmitter of the spirit of the people as it has been elaborated through the centuries in language, custom, faith. The State is not only present, it is also past, and above all future. It is the State which, transcending the brief limit of individual lives, represents the immanent conscience of the nation. The forms in which States express themselves change, but the necessity of the State remains. It is the State which educates citizens for civic virtue, makes them conscious of their mission, calls them to unity; harmonizes their interests in justice; hands on the achievements of thought in the sciences, the arts, in law, in human solidarity; it carries men from the elementary life of the tribe to the highest human expression of power which is Empire; it entrusts to the ages the names of those who died for its integrity or in obedience to its laws; it puts forward as an example and recommends to the generations that are to come the leaders who increased its territory and the men of genius who gave it glory. When the sense of the State declines and the disintegrat-

ing and centrifugal tendencies of individuals and groups prevail, national societies move to their decline."

11. From 1929 up to the present day these doctrinal positions have been strengthened by the whole economico-political evolution of the world. It is the State alone that grows in size, in power. It is the State alone that can solve the dramatic contradictions of capitalism. What is called the crisis cannot be overcome except by the State, within the State. Where are the shades of the Jules Simons who, at the dawn of liberalism, proclaimed that "the State must strive to render itself unnecessary and to prepare for its demise"; of the MacCullochs who, in the second half of the last century, affirmed that the State must abstain from too much governing? And faced with the continual, necessary, and inevitable interventions of the State in economic affairs what would the Englishman Bentham now say, according to whom industry should have asked of the State only to be left in peace? Or the German Humbolt, according to whom the "idle" State must be considered the best? It is true that the second generation of liberal economists was less extremist than the first, and already Smith himself opened, even though cautiously, the door to State intervention in economics. But when one says Liberalism, one says the individual; when one says Fascism, one says the State. But the Fascist State is unique; it is an original creation. It is not reactionary, but revolutionary in that it anticipates the solutions of certain universal problems. These problems are no longer seen in the same light: in the sphere of politics they are removed from party rivalries, from the supreme power of parliament, from the irresponsibility of assemblies; in the sphere of economics they are removed from the sphere of the syndicates' activities—activities that were ever widening their scope and increasing their power both on the workers' side and on the employers'—removed from their struggles and their designs; in the moral sphere they are divorced from ideas of the need for order, discipline and obedience, and lifted into the plane of the moral commandments of the fatherland. Fascism desires the State to be strong, organic and at the same time founded on a wide popular basis. The Fascist State has also claimed for itself the field of economics and, through the corporative, social and educational institutions which it has created, the meaning of the State reaches out to and includes the farthest off-shoots; and within the State, framed in their respective organizations, there revolve all the political, economic and spiritual forces of the nation. A State founded on millions of individuals who recognize it, feel it, are ready to serve it, is not the tyrannical State of the medieval lord. It has nothing in common with the absolutist States that existed either before or after 1789. In the Fascist State the individual is not suppressed, but rather multiplied, just as in a regiment a soldier is not weakened but multiplied by the number of his comrades. The Fascist State organizes the nation, but it leaves sufficient scope to individuals; it has limited useless or harmful liberties and has preserved those that are essential. It cannot be the individual who decides in this matter, but only the State.

12. The Fascist State does not remain indifferent to the fact of religion in general and to that particular positive religion which is Italian Catholicism. The State has no theology, but it has an ethic. In the Fascist State religion is looked upon as one of the deepest manifestations of the spirit; it is, therefore, not only respected, but defended and protected. The Fascist State does not create a "God" of its own, as Robespierre once, at the height of the Convention's foolishness, wished to do; nor

does it vainly seek, like Bolshevism, to expel religion from the minds of men; Fascism respects the God of the ascetics, of the saints, of the heroes, and also God as seen and prayed to by the simple and primitive heart of the people.

13. The Fascist State is a will to power and to government. In it the tradition of Rome is an idea that has force. In the doctrine of Fascism Empire is not only a territorial, military, or mercantile expression, but spiritual or moral. One can think of an empire, that is to say a nation that directly or indirectly leads other nations, without needing to conquer a single square kilometre of territory. For Fascism the tendency to Empire, that is to say, to the expansion of nations, is a manifestation of vitality; its opposite, staying at home, is a sign of decadence: peoples who rise or rerise are imperialist, peoples who die are renunciatory. Fascism is the doctrine that is most fitted to represent the aims, the states of mind, of a people, like the Italian people, rising again after many centuries of abandonment or slavery to foreigners. But Empire calls for discipline, co-ordination of forces, duty and sacrifice; this explains many aspects of the practical working of the regime and the direction of many of the forces of the State and the necessary severity shown to those who would wish to oppose this spontaneous and destined impulse of the Italy of the twentieth century, to oppose it in the name of the superseded ideologies of the nineteenth, repudiated wherever great experiments of political and social transformation have been courageously attempted: especially where, as now, peoples thirst for authority, for leadership, for order. If every age has its own doctrine, it is apparent from a thousand signs that the doctrine of the present age is Fascism. That it is a doctrine of life is shown by the fact that it has resuscitated a faith. That this faith has conquered minds is proved by the fact that Fascism has had its dead and its martyrs.

Fascism henceforward has in the world the universality of all those doctrines which, by fulfilling themselves, have significance in the history of the human spirit.

JOHN DEWEY

For the first half of the twentieth century, the American intellectual scene was dominated by the figure of John Dewey (1859–1952). Born of a family whose roots reached back to the early colonial days of New England, Dewey became interested in philosophy while he was attending the University of Vermont. After finishing college he entered graduate school at Johns Hopkins University to study for his doctorate in philosophy. There, as almost everywhere else in late nineteenth-century America, the philosophy that was taught was the absolute idealism of Hegel. Though Dewey accepted Hegelian idealism for a time, he gave it up before long in favor of the pragmatic philosophy of the great American philosopher, William James (1842–1910).

Pragmatism, as developed first by James and later more fully by Dewey, was an at-

tempt to find a basis for philosophy in the experimental methods employed by the empirical sciences. During the preceding three hundred years scientists had achieved phenomenal results through the method of experimentation. And Dewey believed that the use of this same method could lead to similar advances in every field of intellectual endeavor. This conviction became the basis for Dewey's pragmatic philosophy, which rested on two basic theses: (1) that the truth or validity of any hypothesis depended on the results it produced when it was put into practice, and, therefore, (2) that experimental verification was the ideal method for attaining truth and, hence, for solving man's problems in all areas of life and thought.

In the selection that follows, Dewey uses the pragmatic theory to attack one of the great problems of contemporary politics. The problem with which he is concerned is evident from the title of the book from which the selection is taken, Liberalism and Social Action. *Historically, the liberal movement (particularly with such writers as Locke and Bentham) had stood for a minimum of social action by government agencies. Even Mill, though he had begun to have doubts, still believed that the liberty of the individual must be preserved from the encroachments of government. But Dewey, writing in the middle of the great depression of the thirties, could see that the policy of* laissez-faire *could no longer be defended. So the problem, as he saw it, was this: How can one preserve the human liberty in which liberals believe, and yet admit the need for society to act in behalf of its members? His answer, which he gives in the final chapter of the book, is reproduced in the selection that follows.*

Liberalism and Social Action

. . .

RENASCENT LIBERALISM

Nothing is blinder than the supposition that we live in a society and world so static that either nothing new will happen or else it will happen because of the use of violence. Social change is here as a fact, a fact having multifarious forms and marked in intensity. Changes that are revolutionary in effect are in process in every phase of life. Transformations in the family, the church, the school, in science and art, in economic and political relations, are occurring so swiftly that imagination is baffled in attempt to lay hold of them. Flux does not have to be created. But it does have to be directed. It has to be so controlled that it will move to some end in accordance with the principles of life, since life itself is development. Liberalism is committed to an end that is at once enduring and flexible: the liberation of individuals so that realization of their capacities may be the law of their life. It is committed to the use of freed intelligence as the method of directing change. In any case, civilization is faced with the problem of uniting the changes that are going on into a coherent pattern of social organization. The liberal spirit is marked by its own picture of the pattern that is required: a social organization that will make possible effective liberty and opportunity for personal growth in mind and spirit in all individuals. Its present need is recognition that established material security is a prerequisite of the ends which it cherishes, so that, the basis of life being secure, individuals may actively share in the wealth of cultural resources that now exist and may contribute, each in his own way, to their further enrichment.

John Dewey, LIBERALISM AND SOCIAL ACTION *(New York: G. P. Putnam's Sons, 1935).*

The fact of change has been so continual and so intense that it overwhelms our minds. We are bewildered by the spectacle of its rapidity, scope and intensity. It is not surprising that men have protected themselves from the impact of such vast change by resorting to what psychoanalysis has taught us to call rationalizations, in other words, protective fantasies. The Victorian idea that change is a part of an evolution that necessarily leads through successive stages to some preordained divine far-off event is one rationalization. The conception of a sudden, complete, almost catastrophic, transformation, to be brought about by the victory of the proletariat over the class now dominant, is a similar rationalization. But men have met the impact of change in the realm of actuality, mostly by drift and by temporary, usually incoherent, improvisations. Liberalism, like every other theory of life, has suffered from the state of confused uncertainty that is the lot of a world suffering from rapid and varied change for which there is no intellectual and moral preparation.

Because of this lack of mental and moral preparation the impact of swiftly moving changes produced, as I have just said, confusion, uncertainty and drift. Change in patterns of belief, desire and purpose has lagged behind the modification of the external conditions under which men associate. Industrial habits have changed most rapidly; there has followed at considerable distance, change in political relations; alterations in legal relations and methods have lagged even more, while changes in the institutions that deal most directly with patterns of thought and belief have taken place to the least extent. This fact defines the primary, though not by any means the ultimate, responsibility of a liberalism that intends to be a vital force. Its work is first of all education, in the broadest sense of that term. Schooling is a part of the work of education, but education in its full meaning includes all the influences that go to form the attitudes and dispositions (of desire as well as of belief), which constitute dominant habits of mind and character.

Let me mention three changes that have taken place in one of the institutions in which immense shifts have occurred, but that are still relatively external—external in the sense that the pattern of intelligent purpose and emotion has not been correspondingly modified. Civilization existed for most of human history in a state of scarcity in the material basis for a humane life. Our ways of thinking, planning and working have been attuned to this fact. Thanks to science and technology we now live in an age of potential plenty. The immediate effect of the emergence of the new possibility was simply to stimulate, to a point of incredible exaggeration, the striving for the material resources, called wealth, opened to men in the new vista. It is a characteristic of all development, physiological and mental, that when a new force and factor appears, it is first pushed to an extreme. Only when its possibilities have been exhausted (at least relatively) does it take its place in the life perspective. The economic-material phase of life, which belongs in the basal ganglia of society, has usurped for more than a century the cortex of the social body. The habits of desire and effort that were bred in the age of scarcity do not readily subordinate themselves and take the place of the matter-of-course routine that becomes appropriate to them when machines and impersonal power have the capacity to liberate man from bondage to the strivings that were once needed to make secure his physical basis. Even now when there is a vision of an age of abundance and when the vision is supported by hard fact, it is material security as an end that appeals to most rather than the way of living which this security makes possible. Men's minds are still pathetically held in the clutch of old habits and haunted by old memories.

For, in the second place, insecurity is the natural child and the foster child, too, of scarcity. Early liberalism emphasized the importance of insecurity as a fundamentally necessary economic motive, holding that without this goad men would not work, abstain, or accumulate. Formulation of this conception was new. But the fact that was formulated was nothing new. It was deeply rooted in the habits that were formed in the long struggle against material scarcity. The system that goes by the name of capitalism is a systematic manifestation of desires and purposes built up in an age of ever threatening want and now carried over into a time of ever increasing potential plenty. The conditions that generate insecurity for the many no longer spring from nature. They are found in institutions and arrangements that are within deliberate human control. Surely this change marks one of the greatest revolutions that has taken place in all human history. Because of it, insecurity is not now the motive to work and sacrifice but to despair. It is not an instigation to put forth energy but to an impotency that can be converted from death into endurance only by charity. But the habits of mind and action that modify institutions to make potential abundance an actuality are still so inchoate that most of us discuss labels like individualism, socialism and communism instead of even perceiving the possibility, much less the necessity for realizing what can and should be.

In the third place, the patterns of belief and purpose that still dominate economic institutions were formed when individuals produced with their hands, alone or in small groups. The notion that society in general is served by the unplanned coincidence of the consequences of a vast multitude of efforts put forth by isolated individuals without reference to any social end, was also something new as a formulation. But it also formulated the working principle of an epoch which the advent of new forces of production was to bring to an end. It demands no great power of intelligence to see that under present conditions the isolated individual is well-nigh helpless. Concentration and corporate organization are the rule. But the concentration and corporate organization are still controlled in their operation by ideas that were institutionalized in eons of separate individual effort. The attempts at cooperation for mutual benefit that are put forth are precious as experimental moves. But that society itself should see to it that a cooperative industrial order be instituted, one that is consonant with the realities of production enforced by an era of machinery and power, is so novel an idea to the general mind that its mere suggestion is hailed with abusive epithets—sometimes with imprisonment.

When, then, I say that the first object of a renascent liberalism is education, I mean that its task is to aid in producing the habits of mind and character, the intellectual and moral patterns, that are somewhere near even with the actual movements of events. It is, I repeat, the split between the latter as they have externally occurred and the ways of desiring, thinking, and of putting emotion and purpose into execution that is the basic cause of present confusion in mind and paralysis in action. The educational task cannot be accomplished merely by working upon men's minds, without action that effects actual change in institutions. The idea that dispositions and attitudes can be altered by merely "moral" means conceived of as something that goes on wholly inside of persons is itself one of the old patterns that has to be changed. Thought, desire and purpose exist in a constant give and take of interaction with environing conditions. But resolute thought is the first step in that change of action that will itself carry further the needed change in patterns of mind and character.

In short, liberalism must now become radical, meaning by "radical" perception of the necessity of thoroughgoing changes in the set-up of institutions and corresponding activity to bring the changes to pass. For the gulf between what the actual situation makes possible and the actual state itself is so great that it cannot be bridged by piecemeal policies undertaken *ad hoc*. The process of producing the changes will be, in any case, a gradual one. But "reforms" that deal now with this abuse and now with that without having a social goal based upon an inclusive plan, differ entirely from effort at re-forming, in its literal sense, the institutional scheme of things. The liberals of more than a century ago were denounced in their time as subversive radicals, and only when the new economic order was established did they become apologists for the *status quo* or else content with social patchwork. If radicalism be defined as perception of need for radical change, then today any liberalism which is not also radicalism is irrelevant and doomed.

But radicalism also means, in the minds of many, both supporters and opponents, dependence upon use of violence as the main method of effecting drastic changes. Here the liberal parts company. For he is committed to the organization of intelligent action as the chief method. Any frank discussion of the issue must recognize the extent to which those who decry the use of any violence are themselves willing to resort to violence and are ready to put their will into operation. Their fundamental objection is to change in the economic institution that now exists, and for its maintenance they resort to the use of the force that is placed in their hands by this very institution. They do not need to advocate the use of force; their only need is to employ it. Force, rather than intelligence, is built into the procedures of the existing social system, regularly as coercion, in times of crisis as overt violence. The legal system, conspicuously in its penal aspect, more subtly in civil practice, rests upon coercion. Wars are the methods recurrently used in settlement of disputes between nations. One school of radicals dwells upon the fact that in the past the transfer of power in one society has either been accomplished by or attended with violence. But what we need to realize is that physical force is used, at least in the form of coercion, in the very set-up of our society. That the competitive system, which was thought of by early liberals as the means by which the latent abilities of individuals were to be evoked and directed into socially useful channels, is now in fact a state of scarcely disguised battle hardly needs to be dwelt upon. That the control of the means of production by the few in legal possession operates as a standing agency of coercion of the many, may need emphasis in statement, but is surely evident to one who is willing to observe and honestly report the existing scene. It is foolish to regard the political state as the only agency now endowed with coercive power. Its exercise of this power is pale in contrast with that exercised by concentrated and organized property interests.

It is not surprising in view of our standing dependence upon the use of coercive force that at every time of crisis coercion breaks out into open violence. In this country, with its tradition of violence fostered by frontier conditions and by the conditions under which immigration went on during the greater part of our history, resort to violence is especially recurrent on the part of those who are in power. In times of imminent change, our verbal and sentimental worship of the Constitution, with its guarantees of civil liberties of expression, publication and assemblage, readily goes overboard. Often the officials of the law are the worst offenders, acting as agents of some power that rules the economic life of a community. What is said about the value of free speech as a safety valve is then forgotten with the utmost of ease: a comment, perhaps, upon the weakness of the defense of freedom of expression that values it simply as a means of blowing-off steam.

It is not pleasant to face the extent to which, as matter of fact, coercive and violent force is relied upon in the present social system as a means of social control. It is much more agreeable to evade the fact. But unless the fact is acknowledged as a fact in its full depth and breadth, the meaning of dependence upon intelligence as the alternative method of social direction will not be grasped. Failure in acknowledgment signifies, among other things, failure to realize that those who propagate the dogma of dependence upon force have the sanction of much that is already entrenched in the existing system. They would but turn the use of it to opposite ends. The assumption that the method of intelligence already rules and that those who urge the use of violence are introducing a new element into the social picture may not be hypocritical but it is unintelligently unaware of what is actually involved in intelligence as an alternative method of social action.

I begin with an example of what is really involved in the issue. Why is it, apart from our tradition of violence, that liberty of expression is tolerated and even lauded when social affairs seem to be going in a quiet fashion, and yet is so readily destroyed whenever matters grow critical? The general answer, of course, is that at bottom social institutions have habituated us to the use of force in some veiled form. But a part of the answer is found in our ingrained habit of regarding intelligence as an individual possession and its exercise as an individual right. It is false that freedom of inquiry and of expression are not modes of action. They are exceedingly potent modes of action. The reactionary grasps this fact, in practice if not in express idea, more quickly than the liberal, who is too much given to holding that this freedom is innocent of consequences, as well as being a merely individual right. The result is that this liberty is tolerated as long as it does not seem to menace in any way the *status quo* of society. When it does, every effort is put forth to identify the established order with the public good. When this identification is established, it follows that any merely individual right must yield to the general welfare. As long as freedom of thought and speech is claimed as a merely individual right, it will give way, as do other merely personal claims, when it is, or is successively represented to be, in opposition to the general welfare.

I would not in the least disparage the noble fight waged by early liberals in behalf of individual freedom of thought and expression. We owe more to them than it is possible to record in words. No more eloquent words have ever come from any one than those of Justice Brandeis in the case of a legislative act that in fact restrained freedom of political expression. He said: "Those who won our independence believed that the final end of the State was to make men free to develop their faculties, and that in its government the deliberative faculties should prevail over the arbitrary. They valued liberty both as an end and as a means. They believed liberty to be the secret of happiness and courage to be the secret of liberty. They believed that freedom to think as you will and to speak as you think are means indispensable to the discovery and spread of political truth; that without free speech and assembly discussion would be futile; that with them, discussion affords ordinary adequate protection against the dissemination of noxious doctrines; that the greatest menace to freedom is an inert people; that public discussion is a political duty; and that this should be a fundamental principle of the American government." This is the creed of a fighting liberalism. But the issue I am raising is connected with the fact that these words are found in a dissenting, a minority opinion of the Supreme Court of the United States. The public function of free individual thought and speech is clearly recognized in the words quoted. But the reception of the truth of the words is met by an obstacle: the old habit of defending liberty of thought and expression as something inhering in individuals apart from and even in opposition to social claims.

Liberalism has to assume the responsibility for making it clear that intelligence is a social asset and is clothed with a function as public as is its origin, in the concrete, in social cooperation. It was Comte who, in reaction against the purely individualistic ideas that seemed to him to underlie the French Revolution, said that in mathematics, physics and astronomy there is no right of private conscience. If we remove the statement from the context of actual scientific procedure, it is dangerous because it is false. The individual inquirer has not only the right but the duty to criticize the ideas, theories and "laws" that are current in science. But if we take the statement in the context of scientific method, it indicates that he carries on this criticism in virtue of a socially generated body of knowledge and by means of methods that are not of private origin and possession. He uses a method that retains public validity even when innovations are introduced in its use and application.

Henry George, speaking of ships that ply the ocean with a velocity of five or six hundred miles a day, remarked, "There is nothing whatever to show that the men who today build and navigate and use such ships are one whit superior in any physical or mental quality to their ancestors, whose best vessel was a coracle of wicker and hide. The enormous improvement which these ships show is not an improvement of human nature; it is an improvement of society—it is due to a wider and fuller union of individual efforts in accomplishment of common ends." This single instance, duly pondered, gives a better idea of the nature of intelligence and its social office than would a volume of abstract dissertation. Consider merely two of the factors that enter in and their social consequences. Consider what is involved in the production of steel, from the first use of fire and then the crude smelting of ore, to the processes that now effect the mass production of steel. Consider also the development of the power of guiding ships across trackless wastes from the day when they hugged the shore, steering by visible sun and stars, to the appliances that now enable a sure course to be taken. It would require a heavy tome to describe the advances in science, in mathematics, astronomy, physics, chemistry, that have made these two things possible. The record would be an account of a vast multitude of cooperative efforts, in which one individual uses the results provided for him by a countless number of other individuals, and uses them so as to add to the common and public store. A survey of such facts brings home the actual social character of intelligence as it actually develops and makes its way. Survey of the consequences upon the ways of living of individuals and upon the terms on which men associate together, due to the new method of transportation would take us to the wheat farmer of the prairies, the cattle raiser of the plains, the cotton grower of the South; into a multitude of mills and factories, and to the counting-room of banks, and what would be seen in this country would be repeated in every country of the globe.

It is to such things as these, rather than to abstract and formal psychology that we must go if we would learn the nature of intelligence: in itself, in its origin and development, and its uses and consequences. At this point, I should like to recur to an idea put forward in the preceding chapter. I then referred to the contempt often expressed for reliance upon intelligence as a social method, and I said this scorn is due to the identification of intelligence with native endowments of individuals. In contrast to this notion, I spoke of the power of individuals to appropriate and respond to the intelligence, the knowledge, ideas and purposes that have been integrated in the medium in which individuals live. Each of us knows, for example, some mechanic of ordinary native capacity who is intelligent with the matters of his calling. He has lived in an environment in which the cumulative intelligence of a multitude of cooperating individuals is embodied, and by the use of his native capacities he makes some phase of this intelligence his own. Given a social medium in whose institutions the available knowledge, ideas and art of humanity were incarnate, and the average individual would rise to undreamed heights of social and political intelligence.

The rub, the problem, is found in the proviso. Can the intelligence actually existent and potentially available be embodied in that institutional medium in which an individual thinks, desires and acts? Before dealing directly with this question, I wish to say something about the operation of intelligence in our present political institutions, as exemplified by current practices of democratic government. I would not minimize the advance scored in substitution of methods of discussion and conference for the method of arbitrary rule. But the better is too often the enemy of the still better. Discussion, as the manifestation of intelligence in political life, stimulates publicity; by its means sore spots are brought to light that would otherwise remain hidden. It affords opportunity for promulgation of new ideas. Compared with despotic rule, it is an invitation to individuals to concern themselves with public affairs. But discussion and dialectic, however indispensable they are to the elaboration of ideas and policies after ideas are once put forth, are weak reeds to depend upon for systematic origination of comprehensive plans, the plans that are required if the problem of social organization is to be met. There was a time when discussion, the comparison of ideas already current so as to purify and clarify them, was thought to be sufficient in discovery of the structure and laws of physical nature. In the latter field, the method was displaced by that of experimental observation guided by comprehensive working hypotheses, and using all the resources made available by mathematics.

But we still depend upon the method of discussion, with only incidental scientific control, in politics. Our system of popular suffrage, immensely valuable as it is in comparison with what preceded it, exhibits the idea that intelligence is an individualistic possession, at best enlarged by public discussion. Existing political practice, with its complete ignoring of occupational groups and the organized knowledge and purposes that are involved in the existence of such groups, manifests a dependence upon a summation of individuals quantitatively, similar to Bentham's purely quantitative formula of the greatest sum of pleasures of the greatest possible number. The formation of parties or, as the eighteenth-century writers called them, factions, and the system of party government is the practically necessary counterweight to a numerical and atomistic individualism. The idea that the conflict of parties will, by means of public discussion, bring out necessary public truths is a kind of political watered-down version of the Hegelian dialectic, with its synthesis arrived at by a union of antithetical conceptions. The method has nothing in common with the procedure of organized cooperative inquiry which has won the triumphs of science in the field of physical nature.

Intelligence in politics when it is identified with discussion means reliance upon symbols. The invention of language is probably the greatest single invention achieved by humanity. The development of political forms that promote the use of symbols in place of arbitrary power was another great invention. The nineteenth-century establishment of parliamentary institutions, written constitutions and the suffrage as means of political rule, is a tribute to the power of symbols. But symbols are significant only in connection with realities behind them. No intelligent observer can deny, I think, that they are often used in party politics as a substitute for realities instead of as means of contact with them. Popular literacy, in connection with the telegraph, cheap postage and the printing press, has enormously multiplied the number of those influenced. That which we term education has done a good deal to generate habits that put symbols in the place of realities. The forms of popular government make necessary the elaborate use of words to influence political action. "Propaganda" is the inevitable consequence of the combination of these influences and it extends to every area of life. Words not only take the place of realities but are themselves debauched. Decline in the prestige of suffrage and of parliamentary government are intimately associated with the belief, manifest in practice even if not expressed in words, that intelligence is an individual possession to be reached by means of verbal persuasion.

This fact suggests, by way of contrast, the genuine meaning of intelligence in connection with public opinion, sentiment and action. The crisis in democracy demands the substitution of the intelligence that is exemplified in scientific procedure for the kind of intelligence that is now accepted. The need for this change is not exhausted in the demand for greater honesty and impartiality, even though these qualities be now corrupted by discussion carried on mainly for purposes of party supremacy and for imposition of some special but concealed interest. These qualities need to be restored. But the need goes further. The social use of intelligence would remain deficient even if these moral traits were exalted, and yet intelligence continued to be identified simply with discussion and persuasion, necessary as are these things. Approximation to use of scientific method in investigation and of the engineering mind in the invention and projection of far-reaching social plans is demanded. The habit of considering social realities in terms of cause and effect and social policies in terms of means and consequences is still inchoate. The contrast between the state of intelligence in politics and in the physical control of nature is to be taken literally. What has happened in this latter is the outstanding demonstration of the meaning of organized intelligence. The combined effect of science and technology has released more productive energies in a bare hundred years than stands to the credit of prior human history in its entirety. Productively it has multiplied nine million times in the last generation alone. The prophetic vision of Francis Bacon of subjugation of the energies of nature through change in methods of inquiry has well-nigh been realized. The stationary engine, the locomotive, the dynamo, the motor car, turbine, telegraph, telephone, radio and moving picture are not the products of either isolated individual minds nor of the particular economic regime called capitalism. They are the fruit of methods that first penetrated to the working causalities of nature and then utilized the resulting knowledge in bold imaginative ventures of invention and construction.

We hear a great deal in these days about class conflict. The past history of man is held up to us as almost exclusively a record of struggles between classes, ending in the victory of a class that had been oppressed and the transfer of power to it. It is difficult to avoid reading the past in terms of the contemporary scene. Indeed, fundamentally it is impossible to avoid this course. With a certain proviso, it is highly important that we are compelled to follow this path. For the past as past is gone, save for esthetic enjoyment and refreshment, while the present is with us. Knowledge of the past is significant only as it deepens and extends our understanding of the present. Yet there is a proviso. We must grasp the things that are most important in the present when we turn to the past and not allow ourselves to be misled by secondary phenomena no matter how intense and immediately urgent they are. Viewed from this standpoint, the rise of scientific method and of technology based upon it is the genuinely active force in producing the vast complex of changes the world is now undergoing, not the class struggle whose spirit and method are opposed to science. If we lay hold upon the causal force exercised by this embodiment of intelligence we shall know where to turn for the means of directing further change.

When I say that scientific method and technology have been the active force in producing the revolutionary transformations society is undergoing, I do not imply no other forces have been at work to arrest, deflect and corrupt their operation. Rather this fact is positively implied. At this point, indeed, is located the conflict that underlies the confusions and uncertainties of the present scene. The conflict is between institutions and habits originating in the pre-scientific and pre-technological age and the new forces generated by science and technology. The application of science, to a considerable degree, even its own growth, has been conditioned by the system to which the name of capitalism is given, a rough designation of a complex of political and legal arrangements centering about a particular mode of economic relations. Because of the conditioning of science and technology by this setting, the second and humanly most important part of Bacon's prediction has so far largely missed realization. The conquest of natural energies has not accrued to the betterment of the common human estate in anything like the degree he anticipated.

Because of conditions that were set by the legal institutions and the moral ideas existing when the scientific and industrial revolutions came into being, the chief usufruct of the latter has been appropriated by a relatively small class. Industrial entrepreneurs have reaped out of all proportion to what they sowed. By obtaining private ownership of the means of production and exchange they deflected a considerable share of the results of increased productivity to their private pockets. This appropriation was not the fruit of criminal conspiracy or of sinister intent. It was sanctioned not only by legal institutions of age-long standing but by the entire prevailing moral code. The institution of private property long antedated feudal times. It is the institution with which men have lived, with few exceptions, since the dawn of civilization. Its existence has deeply impressed itself upon mankind's moral conceptions. Moreover, the new industrial forces tended to break down many of the rigid class barriers that had been in force, and to give to millions a new outlook and inspire a new hope;—especially in this country with no feudal background and no fixed class system.

Since the legal institutions and the patterns of mind characteristic of ages of civilization still endure, there exists the conflict that brings confusion into every phase of present life. The problem of bringing into being a new social orientation and organization is, when reduced to its ultimates, the problem of using the new resources of production, made possible by the advance of physical science, for social ends, for what Bentham called the greatest good of the greatest number. Institutional relationships fixed in the pre-scientific age stand in the way of accomplishing this great transformation. Lag in mental and moral patterns provides the bulwark of the older institutions; in expressing the past they still express present beliefs, outlooks and purposes. Here is the place where the problem of liberalism centers today.

The argument drawn from past history that radical change must be effected by means of class struggle, culminating in open war, fails to discriminate between the two forces, one active, the other resistant and deflecting, that have produced the social scene in which we live. The active force is, as I have said, scientific method and technological application. The opposite force is that of older institutions and the habits that have grown up around them. Instead of discrimination between forces and distribution of their consequences, we find the two things lumped together. The compound is labeled the capitalistic or the bourgeois class, and to this class as a class is imputed all the important features of present industrialized society—much as the defenders of the regime of economic liberty exercised for private property are accustomed to attribute every improvement made in the last century and a half to the same capitalistic regime. Thus in orthodox communist literature, from the Communist Manifesto of 1848 to the present day, we are told that the bourgeoisie, the name for a distinctive class, has done this and that. It has, so it is said, given a cosmopolitan character to production and consumption; has destroyed the national basis of industry; has agglomerated population in urban centers; has transferred power from the country to the city, in the process of creating colossal productive force, its chief achievement. In addition, it has created crises of ever renewed intensity; has created imperialism of a new type in frantic effort to control raw materials and markets. Finally, it has created a new class, the proletariat, and has created it as a class having a common interest opposed to that of the bourgeoisie, and is giving an irresistible stimulus to its organization, first as a class and then as a political power. According to the economic version of the Hegelian dialectic, the bourgeois class is thus creating its own complete and polar opposite, and this in time will end the old power and rule. The class struggle of veiled civil war will finally burst into open revolution and the result will be either the common ruin of the contending parties or a revolutionary reconstitution of society at large through a transfer of power from one class to another.

The position thus sketched unites vast sweep with great simplicity. I am concerned with it here only as far as it emphasizes the idea of a struggle between classes, culminating in open and violent warfare as being the method for production of radical social change. For, be it noted, the issue is not whether some amount of violence will accompany the effectuation of radical change of institutions. The question is whether force or intelligence is to be the method upon which we consistently rely and to whose promotion we devote our energies. Insistence that the use of violent force is *inevitable* limits the use of available intelligence, for wherever the inevitable reigns intelligence cannot be used. Commitment to inevitability is always the fruit of dogma; intelligence does not pretend to *know* save as a result of experimentation, the opposite of preconceived dogma. Moreover, acceptance in advance of the inevitability of violence tends to produce the use of violence in cases where peaceful methods might otherwise avail. The curious fact is that while it is generally admitted that this and that particular social problem, say of the family, or railroads or banking, must be solved, if at all, by the method of intelligence, yet there is supposed to be some one all-inclusive social problem which can be solved only by the use of violence. This fact would be inexplicable were it not a conclusion from dogma as its premise.

It is frequently asserted that the method of experimental intelligence can be applied to physical facts because physical nature does not present conflicts of class interests, while it is inapplicable to society because the latter is so deeply marked by incompatible interests. It is then assumed that the "experimentalist" is one who has chosen to ignore the uncomfortable fact of conflicting interests. Of course, there *are* conflicting interests; otherwise there would be no social problems. The problem under discussion is precisely *how* conflicting claims are to be settled in the interest of the widest possible contribution to the interests of all—or at least of the great majority. The method of democracy—inasfar as it is that of organized intelligence—is to bring these conflicts out into the open where their special claims can be seen and appraised, where they can be discussed and judged in the light of more inclusive interests than are represented by either of them separately. There is, for example, a clash of interests between munition manufacturers and most of the rest of the population. The more the respective claims of the two are publicly and scientifically weighed, the more likely it is that the public interest will be disclosed and be made effective. There is an undoubted objective clash of interests between finance-capitalism that controls the means of production and whose profit is served by maintaining relative scarcity, and idle workers and hungry consumers. But what generates violent strife is failure to bring the conflict into the light of intelligence where the conflicting interests can be adjudicated in behalf of the interest of the great majority. Those most committed to the dogma of inevitable force recognize the need for intelligently discovering and expressing the dominant social interest up to a certain point and then draw back. The "experimentalist" is one who would see to it that the method depended upon by all in some degree in every democratic community be followed through to completion.

In spite of the existence of class conflicts, amounting at times to veiled civil war, any one habituated to the use of the method of science will view with considerable suspicion the erection of actual human beings into fixed entities called classes, having no overlapping interests and so internally unified and externally separated that they are made the protagonists of history—itself hypothetical. Such an idea of classes is a survival of a rigid logic that once prevailed in the sciences of nature, but that no longer has any place there. This conversion of abstractions into entities smells more of a dialectic of concepts than of a realistic examination of facts, even though it makes more of an emotional appeal to many than do the results of the latter. To say that all past historic social progress has been the result of cooperation and not of conflict would be also an exaggeration. But exaggeration against exaggeration, it is the more reasonable of the two. And it is no exaggeration to say that the measure of civilization is the degree in which the method of cooperative intelligence replaces the method of brute conflict.

But the point I am especially concerned with just here is the indiscriminate lumping together as a single force of two different things—the results of scientific technology and of a legal system of property relations. It is science and technology that have had the revolutionary social effect while the legal system has been the relatively static element. According to the Marxians themselves, the economic foundations of society consist of two things, the forces of production on one side and, on the other side, the social relations of production, that is, the legal property system under which the former operates. The latter lags behind, and "revolutions" are produced by the power of the forces of production to change the system of institutional relations. But what are the modern forces of production save those of scientific technology? And what is scientific technology save a large-scale demonstration of organized intelligence in action?

It is quite true that what is happening socially is the result of the combination of the two factors, one dynamic, the other relatively static. If we choose to call the combination by the name of capitalism, then it is true, or a truism, that capitalism is the "cause" of all the important social changes that have occurred—an argument that the representatives of capitalism are eager to put forward whenever the increase of productivity is in question. But if we want to *understand,* and not just to paste labels, unfavorable or favorable as the case may be, we shall certainly begin and end with discrimination. Colossal increase in productivity, the bringing of men together in cities and large factories, the elimination of distance, the accumulation of capital, fixed and liquid—these things would have come about, at a certain stage, no matter what the established institutional system. They are the consequence of the new means of technological production. Certain other things have happened because of inherited institutions and the habits of belief and character that accompany and support them. If we begin at this point, we shall see that the release of productivity is the product of cooperatively organized intelligence, and shall also see that the institutional framework is precisely that which is not subjected as yet, in any considerable measure, to the impact of inventive and constructive intelligence. That coercion and oppression on a large scale exists, no honest person can deny. But these things are not the product of science and technology but of the perpetuation of old institutions and patterns untouched by scientific method. The inference to be drawn is clear.

The argument, drawn from history, that great social changes have been effected only by violent means, needs considerable qualification, in view of the vast scope of changes that are taking place without the use of violence. But even if it be admitted to hold of the past, the conclusion that violence is the method now to be depended upon does not follow—unless one is committed to a dogmatic philosophy of history. The radical who insists that the future method of change must be like that of the past has much in common with the hidebound reactionary who holds to the past as an ultimate fact. Both overlook the *fact that history in being a process of change generates change not only in details but also in the method of directing social change.* I recur to what I said at the beginning of this chapter. It is true that the social order is largely conditioned by the use of coercive force, bursting at times into open violence. But what is also true is that mankind now has in its possession a new method, that of cooperative and experimental science which expresses the method of intelligence. I should be meeting dogmatism with dogmatism if I asserted that the existence of this historically new factor completely invalidates all arguments drawn from the effect of force in the past. But it is within the bounds of reason to assert that the presence of this social factor demands that the present situation be analyzed on its own terms, and not be rigidly subsumed under fixed conceptions drawn from the past.

Any analysis made in terms of the present situation will not fail to note one fact that militates powerfully against arguments drawn from past use of violence. Modern warfare is destructive beyond anything known in older times. This increased destructiveness is due primarily, of course, to the fact that science has raised to a new pitch of destructive power all the agencies of armed hostility. But it is also due to the much greater interdependence of all the elements of society. The bonds that hold modern communities and states together are as delicate as they are numerous. The self-sufficiency and independence of a local community, characteristic of more primitive societies, have disappeared in every highly industrialized country. The gulf that once separated the civilian population from the military has virtually gone. War involves paralysis of all normal social activities, and not merely the meeting of armed forces in the field. The *Communist Manifesto* presented two alternatives: *either* the revolutionary change and transfer of power to the proletariat, *or* the common ruin of the contending parties. Today, the civil war that would be adequate to effect transfer of power and a reconstitution of society at large, as understood by official Communists, would seem to present but one possible consequence: the ruin of all parties and the destruction of civilized life. This fact alone is enough to lead us to consider the potentialities of the method of intelligence.

The argument for putting chief dependence upon violence as the method of effecting radical change is, moreover, usually put in a way that proves altogether too much for its own case. It is said that the dominant economic class has all the agencies of power in its hands, directly the army, militia, and police; indirectly, the courts, schools, press, and radio. I shall not stop to analyze this statement. But if one admits it to be valid, the conclusion to be drawn is surely the folly of resorting to a use of force against force that is so well intrenched. The positive conclusion that emerges is that conditions that would promise success in the case of use of force are such as to make possible great change without any great recourse to such a method.

Those who uphold the necessity of dependence upon violence usually much oversimplify the case by setting up a disjunction they regard as self-evident. They say that the sole alternative is putting our trust in parliamentary procedures as they now exist. This isolation of law-making from other social forces and agencies that are constantly operative is wholly unrealistic. Legislatures and congresses do not exist in a vacuum—not even the judges on the bench live in completely secluded sound-proof chambers. The assumption that it is possible for the constitution and activities of law-making bodies to persist unchanged while society itself is undergoing great change is an exercise in verbal formal logic.

It is true that in this country, because of the interpretations made by courts of a written constitution, our political institutions are unusually inflexible. It is also true, as well as even more important (because it is a factor in causing this rigidity) that our institutions, democratic in form, tend to favor in substance a privileged plutocracy. Nevertheless, it is sheer defeatism to assume in advance of actual trial that democratic political institutions are incapable either of further development or of constructive social application. Even as they now exist, the forms of representative government are potentially capable of expressing the public will when that assumes anything like unification. And there is nothing inherent in them that forbids their supplementation by political agencies that represent definitely economic social interests, like those of producers and consumers.

The final argument in behalf of the use of intelligence is that as are the means used so are the actual ends achieved—that is, the consequences. I know of no greater fallacy than the claim of those who hold to the dogma of the necessity of brute force that this use will be the method of calling genuine democracy into existence—of which they profess themselves the simon-pure adherents. It requires an unusually credulous faith in the Hegelian dialectic of opposites to think that all of a sudden the use of force by a class will be transmuted into a democratic classless society. Force breeds counterforce; the Newtonian law of action and reaction still holds in physics, and violence is physical. To profess democracy as an ultimate ideal and the supression of democracy as a means to the ideal may be possible in a country that has never known even rudimentary democracy, but when professed in a country that has anything of a genuine democratic spirit in its traditions, it signifies desire for possession and retention of power by a class, whether that class be called Fascist or Proletarian. In the light of what happens in non-democratic countries, it is pertinent to ask whether the rule of a class signifies the dictatorship of the majority, or dictatorship over the chosen class by a minority party; whether dissenters are allowed even within the class the party claims to represent; and whether the development of literature and the other arts proceeds according to a formula prescribed by a party in conformity with a doctrinaire dogma of history and of infallible leadership, or whether artists are free from regimentation? Until these questions are satisfactorily answered, it is permissible to look with considerable suspicion upon those who assert that suppression of democracy is the road to the adequate establishment of genuine democracy. The one exception—and that apparent rather than real—to dependence upon organized intelligence as the method for directing social change is found when society through an authorized majority has entered upon the path of social experimentation leading to great social change, and a minority refuses by force to permit the method of intelligent action to go into effect. Then force may be intelligently employed to subdue and disarm the recalcitrant minority.

There may be some who think I am unduly dignifying a position held by a comparatively small group by taking their arguments as seriously as I have done. But their position serves to bring into strong relief the alternatives before us. It makes clear the meaning of renascent liberalism. The alternatives are continuation of drift with attendant improvisations to meet special emergencies; dependence upon violence; dependence upon socially organized intelligence. The first two alternatives, however, are not mutually exclusive, for if things are allowed to drift, the result may be some sort of social change effected by the use of force, whether so planned or not. Upon the whole, the recent policy of liberalism has been to further "social legislation"; that is, measures which add performance of social services to the older functions of government. The value of this addition is not to be despised. It marks a decided move away from *laissez faire* liberalism, and has considerable importance in educating the public mind to a realization of the possibilities of organized social control. It has helped to develop some of the techniques that in any case will be needed in a socialized economy. But the cause of liberalism will be lost for a considerable period if it is not prepared to go further and socialize the forces of production, now at hand, so that the liberty of individuals will be supported by the very structure of economic organization.

The ultimate place of economic organization in human life is to assure the secure basis for an ordered expression of individual capacity and for the satisfaction of the needs of man in non-economic directions. The effort of mankind in connection with material production belongs, as I said earlier, among interests and activities that are, relatively speaking, routine in character, "routine" being defined as that which, without absorbing attention and energy, provides a constant basis for liberation of the values of intellectual, esthetic and companionship life. Every significant religious and moral teacher and prophet has asserted that the material is instrumental to the good life. Nominally at least, this idea is accepted by every civilized community. The transfer of the burden of material production from human muscles and brain to steam, electricity and chemical processes now makes possible the effective actualization of this idea. Needs, wants and desires are always the moving force in generating creative action. When these wants are compelled by force of conditions to be directed for the most part, among the mass of mankind, into obtaining the means of subsistence, what should be a means becomes perforce an end in itself. Up to the present the new mechanical forces of production, which are the means of emancipation from this state of affairs, have been employed to intensify and exaggerate the reversal of the true relation between means and ends. Humanly speaking, I do not see how it would have been possible to avoid an epoch having this character. But its perpetuation is the cause of the continually growing social chaos and strife. Its termination cannot be effected by preaching to individuals that they should place spiritual ends above material means. It can be brought about by organized social reconstruction that puts the results of the mechanism of abundance at the free disposal of individuals. The actual corrosive "materialism" of our times does not proceed from science. It springs from the notion, sedulously cultivated by the class in power, that the creative capacities of individuals can be evoked and developed only in a struggle for material possessions and material gain. We either should surrender our professed belief in the supremacy of ideal and spiritual values and accommodate our beliefs to the predominant material orientation, or we should through organized endeavor institute the socialized economy of material security and plenty that will release human energy for pursuit of higher values.

Since liberation of the capacities of individuals for free, self-initiated expression is an essential part of the creed of liberalism, liberalism that is sincere must will the means that condition the achieving of its ends. Regimentation of material and mechanical forces is the only way by which the mass of individuals can be released from regimentation and consequent suppression of their cultural possibilities. The eclipse of liberalism is due to the fact that it has not faced the alternatives and adopted the means upon which realization of its professed aims depends. Liberalism can be true to its ideals only as it takes the course that leads to their attainment. The notion that organized social control of economic forces lies outside the historic path of liberalism shows that liberalism is still impeded by remnants of its earlier *laissez faire* phase, with its opposition of society and the individual. The thing which now dampens liberal ardor and paralyzes its efforts is the conception that liberty and development of individuality as ends exclude the use of organized social effort as means. Earlier liberalism regarded the separate and competing economic action of individuals as the means of social well-being as the end. We must reverse the perspective and see that socialized economy is the means of free individual development as the end.

That liberals are divided in outlook and endeavor while reactionaries are held together by community of interests and the ties of custom is well-nigh a commonplace. Organization of standpoint and belief among liberals can be achieved only in and by unity of endeavor. Organized unity of action attended by consensus of beliefs will come about in the degree in which social control of economic forces is made the goal of liberal action. The greatest educational power, the greatest force in shaping the dispositions and attitudes of individuals, is the social medium in which they live. The medium that now lies closest to us is that of unified action for the inclusive end of a socialized economy. The attainment of a state of society in which a basis of material security will release the powers of individuals for cultural expression is not the work of a day. But by concentrating upon the task of securing a socialized economy as the ground and medium for release of the impulses and capacities men agree to call ideal, the now scattered and often conflicting activities of liberals can be brought to effective unity.

It is no part of my task to outline in detail a program for renascent liberalism. But the question of "what is to be done" cannot be ignored. Ideas must be organized, and this organization implies an organization of individuals who hold these ideas and whose faith is ready to translate itself into action. Translation into action signifies that the general creed of liberalism be formulated as a concrete program of action. It is in organization for action that liberals are weak, and without this organization there is danger that democratic ideals may go by default. Democracy has been a fighting faith. When its ideals are reenforced by those of scientific method and experimental intelligence, it cannot be that it is incapable of evoking discipline, ardor and organization. To narrow the issue for the future to a struggle between Fascism and Communism is to invite a catastrophe that may carry civilization down in the struggle. Vital and courageous democratic liberalism is the one force that can surely avoid such a disastrous narrowing of the issue. I for one do not believe that Americans living in the tradition of Jefferson and Lincoln will weaken and give up without a whole-hearted effort to make democracy a living reality. This, I repeat, involves organization.

The question cannot be answered by argument. Experimental method means experiment, and the question can be answered only by trying, by organized effort. The reasons for making the trial are not abstract or recondite. They are found in the confusion, uncertainty and conflict that mark the modern world. The reasons for thinking that the effort if made will be successful are also not abstract and remote. They lie in what the method of experimental and cooperative intelligence has already accomplished in subduing to potential human use the energies of physical nature. In material production, the method of intelligence is now the established rule; to abandon it would be to revert to savagery. The task is to go on, and not backward, until the method of intelligence and experimental control is the rule in social relations and social direction. Either we take this road or we admit that the problem of social organization in behalf of human liberty and the flowering of human capacities is insoluble.

It would be fantastic folly to ignore or to belittle the obstacles that stand in the way. But what has taken place, also against great odds, in the scientific and industrial revolutions, is an accomplished fact; the way is marked out. It may be that the way will remain untrodden. If so, the future holds the menace of confusion moving into chaos, a chaos that will be externally masked for a time by an organization of force, coercive and violent, in which the liberties of men will all but disappear. Even so, the cause of the liberty of the human spirit, the cause of opportunity of human beings for full development of their powers, the cause for which liberalism enduringly stands, is too precious and too ingrained in the human constitution to be forever obscured. Intelligence after millions of years of errancy has found itself as a method, and it will not be lost forever in the blackness of night. The business of liberalism is to bend every energy and exhibit every courage so that these precious goods may not even be temporarily lost but be intensified and expanded here and now.

BERTRAND RUSSELL

In his most famous aphorism Friedrich Nietzsche proclaimed, "God is dead." Hidden behind its shocking surface this statement contains a profound truth. During the last hundred years people in increasing numbers have found themselves unable any longer to accept a world view based on a belief in the existence of God. Thus, some writers, putting Nietzsche's point in more prosaic terms, have asserted that the twentieth century may well mark the end of "the Christian era." Although many causes have contributed to the decline of traditional religious faith in the contemporary world, the most important has been modern science, and, in particular, the theory of evolution, which, in its account of man's origin through descent from other species, renders God, the creator, superfluous. In the half-century following Darwin, scientists and philosophers developed the evolutionary thesis to the logical conclusion of a complete materialism, in which there was no need to postulate any God at all.

But if God is banished from the universe, what becomes of religion? Can there be any meaning or value in a universe of blind matter? Any significance in the life of man, brief and powerless, and soon to be "seized by the silent orders of omnipotent Death"? Can one accept the world view of contemporary science and still find any reason for worship? These are the questions that Bertrand Russell attempts to answer in his essay, which some have termed atheistic and others profoundly religious—"A Free Man's Worship."

Bertrand Russell, one of the most eminent intellectual leaders of the twentieth century, was born in Wales in 1872. His family was prominent in politics, his grandfather, Lord John Russell, having served as Prime Minister early in the reign of Queen Victoria. Russell's first scholarly interest was in mathematics and led to the publication in 1910 of Principia Mathematica *(written in collaboration with A. N. Whitehead), one of the most important books of the century. In the years that have followed, Russell has written more than forty additional books, mainly on philosophy and social and political issues. During World War I he was imprisoned for his outspoken opposition to the war and in recent years he has received considerable notoriety as a result of his leadership in the movement to ban nuclear weapons. He was awarded the Nobel prize in literature in 1950, in recognition of his long and influential career "as a defender of humanity and freedom of thought."*

A Free Man's Worship

To Dr. Faustus in his study Mephistopheles told the history of the Creation, saying:

"The endless praises of the choirs of angels had begun to grow wearisome; for, after all, did he not deserve their praise? Had he not given them endless joy? Would it not be more amusing to obtain undeserved praise, to be worshipped by beings whom he tortured? He smiled inwardly, and resolved that the great drama should be performed.

"For countless ages the hot nebula whirled aimlessly through space. At length it began to take shape, the central mass threw off planets, the planets cooled, boiling seas and burning mountains heaved and tossed, from black masses of cloud hot sheets of rain deluged the barely solid crust. And now the first germ of life grew in the depths of the ocean, and developed rapidly in the fructifying warmth into vast forest trees, huge ferns springing from the damp mould, sea monsters breeding, fighting, devouring, and passing away. And from the monsters, as the play unfolded itself, Man was born, with the power of thought, the knowledge of good and evil, and the cruel thirst for worship. And Man saw that all is passing in this mad, monstrous world, that all is struggling to snatch, at any cost, a few brief moments of life before Death's inexorable decree. And Man said: 'There is a hidden purpose, could we but fathom it, and the purpose is good; for we must reverence something, and in the visible world there is nothing worthy of reverence.' And Man stood aside from the struggle, resolving that God intended harmony to come out of chaos by human efforts. And when he followed the instincts which God had transmitted to him from his ancestry of beasts of prey, he called it Sin, and asked God to forgive him. But he doubted whether he could be justly forgiven, until he invented a divine Plan by which God's wrath was to have been appeased. And seeing the present was bad, he made it yet worse, that thereby the future might be better. And he gave God thanks for the strength that enabled him to forgo even the joys that were possible. And God smiled; and when he saw that Man had become perfect in renunciation and worship, he sent another sun through the sky, which crashed into Man's sun; and all returned again to nebula.

" 'Yes,' he murmured, 'it was a good play; I will have it performed again.' "

Such, in outline, but even more purposeless, more void of meaning, is the world which Science presents for our belief. Amid such a world, if anywhere, our ideals henceforward must find a home. That Man is the product of causes which had no prevision of the end they were achieving; that his origin, his growth, his hopes and fears, his loves and his beliefs, are but the outcome of accidental collocations of atoms; that no fire, no heroism, no intensity of thought and feeling, can preserve an individual life beyond the grave; that all the labours of the ages, all the devotion, all the inspiration, all the noonday brightness of human genius, are destined to extinction in the vast death of the solar system, and that the whole temple of Man's achievement must inevitably be buried

Bertrand Russell, "A Free Man's Worship," from MYSTICISM AND LOGIC *(London: George Allen & Unwin, Ltd., 1917). Courtesy of George Allen & Unwin, Ltd.*

beneath the débris of a universe in ruins—all these things, if not quite beyond dispute, are yet so nearly certain, that no philosophy which rejects them can hope to stand. Only within the scaffolding of these truths, only on the firm foundation of unyielding despair, can the soul's habitation henceforth be safely built.

How, in such an alien and inhuman world, can so powerless a creature as Man preserve his aspirations untarnished? A strange mystery it is that Nature, omnipotent but blind, in the revolutions of her secular hurryings through the abysses of space, has brought forth at last a child, subject still to her power, but gifted with sight, with knowledge of good and evil, with the capacity of judging all the works of his unthinking Mother. In spite of Death, the mark and seal of the parental control, Man is yet free, during his brief years, to examine, to criticise, to know, and in imagination to create. To him alone, in the world with which he is acquainted, this freedom belongs; and in this lies his superiority to the resistless forces that control his outward life.

The savage, like ourselves, feels the oppression of his impotence before the powers of Nature; but having in himself nothing that he respects more than Power, he is willing to prostrate himself before his gods, without inquiring whether they are worthy of his worship. Pathetic and very terrible is the long history of cruelty and torture, of degradation and human sacrifice, endured in the hope of placating the jealous gods: surely, the trembling believer thinks, when what is most precious has been freely given, their lust for blood must be appeased, and more will not be required. The religion of Moloch—as such creeds may be generically called—is in essence the cringing submission of the slave, who dare not, even in his heart, allow the thought that his master deserves no adulation. Since the independence of ideals is not yet acknowledged, Power may be freely worshipped, and receive an unlimited respect, despite its wanton infliction of pain.

But gradually, as morality grows bolder, the claim of the ideal world begins to be felt; and worship, if it is not to cease, must be given to gods of another kind than those created by the savage. Some, though they feel the demands of the ideal, will still consciously reject them, still urging that naked Power is worthy of worship. Such is the attitude inculcated in God's answer to Job out of the whirlwind: the divine power and knowledge are paraded, but of the divine goodness there is no hint. Such also is the attitude of those who, in our own day, base their morality upon the struggle for survival, maintaining that the survivors are necessarily the fittest. But others, not content with an answer so repugnant to the moral sense, will adopt the position which we have become accustomed to regard as specially religious, maintaining that, in some hidden manner, the world of fact is really harmonious with the world of ideals. Thus Man creates God, all-powerful and all-good, the mystic unity of what is and what should be.

But the world of fact, after all, is not good; and, in submitting our judgment to it, there is an element of slavishness from which our thoughts must be purged. For in all things it is well to exalt the dignity of Man, by freeing him as far as possible from the tyranny of non-human Power. When we have realised that Power is largely bad, that man, with his knowledge of good and evil, is but a helpless atom in a world which has no such knowledge, the choice is again presented to us: Shall we worship Force, or shall we worship Goodness? Shall our God exist and be evil, or shall he be recognised as the creation of our own conscience?

The answer to this question is very

momentous, and affects profoundly our whole morality. The worship of Force, to which Carlyle and Nietzsche and the creed of Militarism have accustomed us, is the result of failure to maintain our own ideals against a hostile universe: it is itself a prostrate submission to evil, a sacrifice of our best to Moloch. If strength indeed is to be respected, let us respect rather the strength of those who refuse that false "recognition of facts" which fails to recognise that facts are often bad. Let us admit that, in the world we know, there are many things that would be better otherwise, and that the ideals to which we do and must adhere are not realised in the realm of matter. Let us preserve our respect for truth, for beauty, for the ideal of perfection which life does not permit us to attain, though none of these things meet with the approval of the unconscious universe. If Power is bad, as it seems to be, let us reject it from our hearts. In this lies Man's true freedom: in determination to worship only the God created by our own love of the good, to respect only the heaven which inspires the insight of our best moments. In action, in desire, we must submit perpetually to the tyranny of outside forces; but in thought, in aspiration, we are free, free from our fellow-men, free from the petty planet on which our bodies impotently crawl, free even, while we live, from the tyranny of death. Let us learn, then, that energy of faith which enables us to live constantly in the vision of the good; and let us descend, in action, into the world of fact, with that vision always before us.

When first the opposition of fact and ideal grows fully visible, a spirit of fiery revolt, of fierce hatred of the gods, seems necessary to the assertion of freedom. To defy with Promethean constancy a hostile universe, to keep its evil always in view, always actively hated, to refuse no pain that the malice of Power can invent, appears to be the duty of all who will not bow before the inevitable. But indignation is still a bondage, for it compels our thoughts to be occupied with an evil world; and in the fierceness of desire from which rebellion springs there is a kind of self-assertion which it is necessary for the wise to overcome. Indignation is a submission of our thoughts, but not of our desires; the Stoic freedom in which wisdom consists is found in the submission of our desires, but not of our thoughts. From the submission of our desires springs the virtue of resignation; from the freedom of our thoughts springs the whole world of art and philosophy, and the vision of beauty by which, at last, we half reconquer the reluctant world. But the vision of beauty is possible only to unfettered contemplation, to thoughts not weighted by the load of eager wishes; and thus Freedom comes only to those who no longer ask of life that it shall yield them any of those personal goods that are subject to the mutations of Time.

Although the necessity of renunciation is evidence of the existence of evil, yet Christianity, in preaching it, has shown a wisdom exceeding that of the Promethean philosophy of rebellion. It must be admitted that, of the things we desire, some, though they prove impossible, are yet real goods; others, however, as ardently longed for, do not form part of a fully purified ideal. The belief that what must be renounced is bad, though sometimes false, is far less often false than untamed passion supposes; and the creed of religion, by providing a reason for proving that it is never false, has been the means of purifying our hopes by the discovery of many austere truths.

But there is in resignation a further good element: even real goods, when they are unattainable, ought not to be fretfully desired. To every man comes, sooner or later, the great renunciation. For the young, there is nothing unattainable; a good thing desired with the whole force of a passionate will, and yet impossible, is to them not credible. Yet, by death, by illness, by poverty, or by the voice of duty, we must learn, each one of us, that the world was not made for us, and that, however beautiful may be the things we crave, Fate may nevertheless forbid them. It is the part of courage, when misfortune comes, to bear without repining the ruin of our hopes, to turn away our thoughts from vain regrets. This degree of submission to Power is not only just and right: it is the very gate of wisdom.

But passive renunciation is not the whole of wisdom; for not by renunciation alone can we build a temple for the worship of our own ideals. Haunting foreshadowings of the temple appear in the realm of imagination, in music, in architecture, in the untroubled kingdom of reason, and in the golden sunset magic of lyrics, where beauty shines and glows, remote from the touch of sorrow, remote from the fear of change, remote from the failures and disenchantments of the world of fact. In the contemplation of these things the vision of heaven will shape itself in our hearts, giving at once a touchstone to judge the world about us, and an inspiration by which to fashion to our needs whatever is not incapable of serving as a stone in the sacred temple.

Except for those rare spirits that are born without sin, there is a cavern of darkness to be traversed before that temple can be entered. The gate of the cavern is despair, and its floor is paved with the gravestones of abandoned hopes. There Self must die; there the eagerness, the greed of untamed desire must be slain, for only so can the soul be freed from the empire of Fate. But out of the cavern the Gate of Renunciation leads again to the daylight of wisdom, by whose radiance a new insight, a new joy, a new tenderness, shine forth to gladden the pilgrim's heart.

When, without the bitterness of impotent rebellion, we have learnt both to resign ourselves to the outward rule of Fate and to recognise that the non-human world is unworthy of our worship, it becomes possible at last so to transform and refashion the unconscious universe, so to transmute it in the crucible of imagination, that a new image of shining gold replaces the old idol of clay. In all the multiform facts of the world—in the visual shapes of trees and mountains and clouds, in the events of the life of man, even in the very omnipotence of Death—the insight of creative idealism can find the reflection of a beauty which its own thoughts first made. In this way mind asserts its subtle mastery over the thoughtless forces of Nature. The more evil the material with which it deals, the more thwarting to untrained desire, the greater is its achievement in inducing the reluctant rock to yield up its hidden treasures, the prouder its victory in compelling the opposing forces to swell the pageant of its triumph. Of all the arts, Tragedy is the proudest, the most triumphant; for it builds its shining citadel in the very centre of the enemy's country, on the very summit of his highest mountain; from its impregnable watchtowers, his camps and arsenals, his columns and forts, are all revealed; within its walls the free life continues, while the legions of Death and Pain and Despair, and all the servile captains of tyrant Fate, afford the burghers of that dauntless city new spectacles of beauty. Happy those sacred ramparts, thrice happy the dwellers on that all-seeing eminence. Honour to those brave warriors who, through countless ages of warfare, have preserved for us the priceless heritage of liberty, and have kept undefiled by sacrilegious invaders the home of the unsubdued.

But the beauty of Tragedy does but make visible a quality which, in more or less obvious shapes, is present always and everywhere in life. In the spectacle of Death, in the endurance of intolerable pain, and in the irrevocableness of a vanished past, there is a sacredness, an overpowering awe, a feeling of the vastness, the depth, the inexhaustible mystery of existence, in which, as by some strange marriage of pain, the sufferer is bound to the world by bonds of sorrow. In these moments of insight, we lose all eagerness of temporary desire, all struggling and striving for petty ends, all care for the little trivial things that, to a superficial view, make up the common life of day by day; we see, surrounding the narrow raft illumined by the flickering light of human comradeship, the dark ocean on whose rolling waves we toss for a brief hour; from the great night without, a chill blast breaks in upon our refuge; all the loneliness of humanity amid hostile forces is concentrated upon the individual soul, which must struggle alone, with what of courage it can command, against the whole weight of a universe that cares nothing for its hopes and fears. Victory, in this struggle with the powers of darkness, is the true baptism into the glorious company of heroes, the true initiation into the overmastering beauty of human existence. From that awful encounter of the soul with the outer world, enunciation, wisdom, and charity are born; and with their birth a new life begins. To take into the inmost shrine of the soul the irresistible forces whose puppets we seem to be—Death and change, the irrevocableness of the past, and the powerlessness of man before the blind hurry of the universe from vanity to vanity—to feel these things and know them is to conquer them.

This is the reason why the Past has such magical power. The beauty of its motionless and silent pictures is like the enchanted purity of late autumn, when the leaves, though one breath would make them fall, still glow against the sky in golden glory. The Past does not change or strive; like Duncan, after life's fitful fever it sleeps well; what was eager and grasping, what was petty and transitory, has faded away, the things that were beautiful and eternal shine out of it like stars in the night. Its beauty, to a soul not worthy of it, is unendurable; but to a soul which has conquered Fate it is the key of religion.

The life of Man, viewed outwardly, is but a small thing in comparison with the forces of Nature. The slave is doomed to worship Time and Fate and Death, because they are greater than anything he finds in himself, and because all his thoughts are of things which they devour. But, great as they are, to think of them greatly, to feel their passionless splendour, is greater still. And such thought makes us free men; we no longer bow before the inevitable in Oriental subjection, but we absorb it, and make it a part of ourselves. To abandon the struggle for private happiness, to expel all eagerness of temporary desire, to burn with passion for eternal things—this is emancipation, and this is the free man's worship. And this liberation is effected by a contemplation of Fate; for Fate itself is subdued by the mind which leaves nothing to be purged by the purifying fire of Time.

United with his fellow-men by the strongest of all ties, the tie of a common doom, the free man finds that a new vision is with him always, shedding over every daily task the light of love. The life of Man is a long march through the night, surrounded by invisible foes, tortured by weariness and pain, towards a goal that few can hope to reach, and where none may tarry long. One by one, as they march, our comrades vanish from our sight, seized by the silent orders of omnipotent Death. Very brief is the time in which we can help them, in which their happiness or misery is decided. Be it ours to shed sunshine on their path, to lighten their sorrows by the balm of sympathy, to give them the pure joy of a never-tiring affection, to strengthen failing courage, to instil faith in hours of despair. Let us not weigh in grudging scales their merits and demerits, but let us think only of their need—of the sorrows, the difficulties, perhaps the blindnesses, that make the misery of their lives; let us remember that they are fellow-sufferers in the same darkness, actors in the same tragedy with ourselves. And so, when their day is over, when their good and their evil have become eternal by the immortality of the past, be it ours to feel that, where they suffered, where they failed, no deed of ours was the cause; but wherever a spark of the divine fire kindled in their hearts, we were ready with encouragement, with sympathy, with brave words in which high courage glowed.

Brief and powerless is Man's life; on him and all his race the slow, sure doom falls pitiless and dark. Blind to good and evil, reckless of destruction, omnipotent matter rolls on its relentless way; for Man, condemned to-day to lose his dearest, to-morrow himself to pass through the gate of darkness, it remains only to cherish, ere yet the blow falls, the lofty thoughts that ennoble his little day; disdaining the coward terrors of the slave of Fate, to worship at the shrine that his own hands have built; undismayed by the empire of chance, to preserve a mind free from the wanton tyranny that rules his outward life; proudly defiant of the irresistible forces that tolerate, for a moment, his knowledge and his condemnation, to sustain alone, a weary but unyielding Atlas, the world that his own ideals have fashioned despite the trampling march of unconscious power.

ALFRED NORTH WHITEHEAD

In his long and active life, Alfred North Whitehead (1861–1947) pursued two distinct, and highly distinguished, careers. The first was in mathematics, a subject that he taught for nearly forty years at Cambridge University and the University of London. This career was capped by the publication of Principia Mathematica *(1910), a three-volume work written in collaboration with Bertrand Russell, in which logic and mathematics are combined into one theoretical discipline.*

Toward the end of his career at the University of London, Whitehead became interested in philosophy. On his retirement, at the age of sixty-three, he accepted an offer to come to Harvard University as professor of philosophy. Thus began his second career, which lasted until his death at the age of eighty-six and which established him as one of the eminent philosophical thinkers of our era. Science and the Modern World *(1926) was the first of ten books on philosophy that Whitehead wrote during these years. In it he analyzes modern science and its effects upon our civilization. Then, in the last chapter (which is given in the following selection) he states what he believes to be the requisites for the future progress of our society. It is interesting to compare Whitehead's conclusions regarding the future of man with those of*

Bertrand Russell in "A Free Man's Worship." Although both recognize the enormous impact of science on contemporary civilization, each presents a quite different picture of the ultimate significance of scientific knowledge for human life.

Science and the Modern World

REQUISITES FOR SOCIAL PROGRESS

It has been the purpose of these lectures to analyse the reactions of science in forming that background of instinctive ideas which control the activities of successive generations. Such a background takes the form of a certain vague philosophy as to the last word about things, when all is said. The three centuries, which form the epoch of modern science, have revolved round the ideas of *God, mind, matter,* and also of *space* and *time* in their characters of expressing *simple location* for matter. Philosophy has on the whole emphasised *mind,* and has thus been out of touch with science during the two latter centuries. But it is creeping back into its old importance owing to the rise of psychology and its alliance with physiology. Also, this rehabilitation of philosophy has been facilitated by the recent breakdown of the seventeenth century settlement of the principles of physical science. But, until that collapse, science seated itself securely upon the concepts of matter, space, time, and latterly, of energy. Also there were arbitrary laws of nature determining locomotion. They were empirically observed, but for some obscure reason were known to be universal. Anyone who in practice or theory disregarded them was denounced with unsparing vigour. This position on the part of scientists was pure bluff, if one may credit them with believing their own statements. For their current philosophy completely failed to justify the assumption that the immediate knowledge inherent in any present occasion throws any light either on its past, or its future.

I have also sketched an alternative philosophy of science in which *organism* takes the place of *matter.* For this purpose, the mind involved in the materialist theory dissolves into a function of organism. The psychological field then exhibits what an event is in itself. Our bodily event is an unusually complex type of organism and consequently includes cognition. Further, space and time, in their most concrete signification, become the locus of events. An organism is the realisation of a definite shape of value. The emergence of some actual value depends on limitation which excludes neutralising cross-lights. Thus an event is a matter of fact which by reason of its limitation is a value for itself; but by reason of its very nature it also requires the whole universe in order to be itself.

Importance depends on endurance. Endurance is the retention through time of an achievement of value. What endures is identity of pattern, self-inherited. Endurance requires the favourable environment. The whole of science revolves round this question of enduring organisms.

The general influence of science at the present moment can be analysed under the headings: General Conceptions Respecting the Universe, Technological Applications, Professionalism in Knowledge, Influence of

A. N. Whitehead, SCIENCE AND THE MODERN WORLD *(New York: The Macmillan Company, 1926; New York: Cambridge University Press, 1926), pp. 277–300. Courtesy of The Macmillan Company and Cambridge University Press.*

Biological Doctrines on the Motives of Conduct. I have endeavoured in the preceding lectures to give a glimpse of these points. It lies within the scope of this concluding lecture to consider the reaction of science upon some problems confronting civilised societies.

The general conceptions introduced by science into modern thought cannot be separated from the philosophical situation as expressed by Descartes. I mean the assumption of bodies and minds as independent individual substances, each existing in its own right apart from any necessary reference to each other. Such a conception was very concordant with the individualism which had issued from the moral discipline of the Middle Ages. But, though the easy reception of the idea is thus explained, the derivation in itself rests upon a confusion, very natural but none the less unfortunate. The moral discipline had emphasised the intrinsic value of the individual entity. This emphasis had put the notions of the individual and of its experiences into the foreground of thought. At this point the confusion commences. The emergent individual value of each entity is transformed into the independent substantial existence of each entity, which is a very different notion.

I do not mean to say that Descartes made this logical, or rather illogical transition, in the form of explicit reasoning. Far from it. What he did, was first to concentrate upon his own conscious experiences, as being facts within the independent world of his own mentality. He was led to speculate in this way by the current emphasis upon the individual value of his total self. He implicitly transformed this emergent individual value, inherent in the very fact of his own reality, into a private world of passions, or modes, of independent substance.

Also the independence ascribed to bodily substances carried them away from the realm of values altogether. They degenerated into a mechanism entirely valueless, except as suggestive of an external ingenuity. The heavens had lost the glory of God. This state of mind is illustrated in the recoil of Protestantism from aesthetic effects dependent upon a material medium. It was taken to lead to an ascription of value to what is in itself valueless. This recoil was already in full strength antecedently to Descartes. Accordingly, the Cartesian scientific doctrine of bits of matter, bare of intrinsic value, was merely a formulation, in explicit terms, of a doctrine which was current before its entrance into scientific thought or Cartesian philosophy. Probably this doctrine was latent in the scholastic philosophy, but it did not lead to its consequences till it met with the mentality of northern Europe in the sixteenth century. But science, as equipped by Descartes, gave stability and intellectual status to a point of view which has had very mixed effects upon the moral presuppositions of modern communities. Its good effects arose from its efficiency as a method for scientific researches within those limited regions which were then best suited for exploration. The result was a general clearing of the European mind away from the stains left upon it by the hysteria of remote barbaric ages. This was all to the good, and was most completely exemplified in the eighteenth century.

But in the nineteenth century, when society was undergoing transformation into the manufacturing system, the bad effects of these doctrines have been very fatal. The doctrine of minds, as independent substances, leads directly not merely to private worlds of experience, but also to private worlds of morals. The moral intuitions can be held to apply only to the strictly private world of psychological experience. Accordingly, self-respect, and the making the most of your own individual opportunities, together constituted the efficient morality of the leaders among the industrialists of that period. The western world is now suffering from the limited moral outlook of the three previous generations.

Also the assumption of the bare valuelessness of mere matter led to a lack of reverence in the treatment of natural or artistic beauty. Just when the urbanisation of the western world was entering upon its state of rapid development, and when the most delicate, anxious consideration of the aesthetic qualities of the new material environment was requisite, the doctrine of the irrelevance of such ideas was at its height. In the most advanced industrial countries, art was treated as a frivolity. A striking example of this state of mind in the middle of the nineteenth century is to be seen in London where the marvellous beauty of the estuary of the Thames, as it curves through the city, is wantonly defaced by the Charing Cross railway bridge, constructed apart from any reference to aesthetic values.

The two evils are: one, the ignoration of the true relation of each organism to its environment; and the other, the habit of ignoring the intrinsic worth of the environment which must be allowed its weight in any consideration of final ends.

Another great fact confronting the modern world is the discovery of the method of training professionals, who specialise in particular regions of thought and thereby progressively add to the sum of knowledge within their respective limitations of subject. In consequence of the success of this professionalising of knowledge, there are two points to be kept in mind, which differentiate our present age from the past. In the first place, the rate of progress is such that an individual human being, of ordinary length of life, will be called upon to face novel situations which find no parallel in his past. The fixed person for the fixed duties, who in older societies was such a godsend, in the future will be a public danger. In the second place, the modern professionalism in knowledge works in the opposite direction so far as the intellectual sphere is concerned. The modern chemist is likely to be weak in zoology, weaker still in his general knowledge of the Elizabethan drama, and completely ignorant of the principles of rhythm in English versification. It is probably safe to ignore his knowledge of ancient history. Of course I am speaking of general tendencies; for chemists are no worse than engineers, or mathematicians, or classical scholars. Effective knowledge is professionalised knowledge, supported by a restricted acquaintance with useful subjects subservient to it.

This situation has its dangers. It produces minds in a groove. Each profession makes progress, but it is progress in its own groove. Now to be mentally in a groove is to live in contemplating a given set of abstractions. The groove prevents straying across country, and the abstraction abstracts from something to which no further attention is paid. But there is no groove of abstractions which is adequate for the comprehension of human life. Thus in the modern world, the celibacy of the medieval learned class has been replaced by a celibacy of the intellect which is divorced from the concrete contemplation of the complete facts. Of course, no one is merely a mathematician, or merely a lawyer. People have lives outside their professions or their businesses. But the point is the restraint of serious thought within a groove. The remainder of life is treated superficially, with the imperfect categories of thought derived from one profession.

The dangers arising from this aspect of professionalism are great, particularly in our democratic societies. The directive force of reason is weakened. The leading intellects lack balance. They see this set of circumstances, or that set; but not both sets together. The task of coordination is left to those who lack either the force or the character to succeed in some definite career. In short, the specialised functions of the community are performed better and more progressively, but the generalised direction lacks vision. The progressiveness in detail only adds to the danger produced by the feebleness of coordination.

This criticism of modern life applies throughout, in whatever sense you construe the meaning of a community. It holds if you apply it to a nation, a city, a district, an institution, a family, or even to an individual. There is a development of particular abstractions, and a contraction of concrete appreciation. The whole is lost in one of its aspects. It is not necessary for my point that I should maintain that our directive wisdom, either as individuals or as communities, is less now than in the past. Perhaps it has slightly improved. But the novel pace of progress requires a greater force of direction if disasters are to be avoided. The point is that the discoveries of the nineteenth century were in the direction of professionalism, so that we are left with no expansion of wisdom and with greater need of it.

Wisdom is the fruit of a balanced development. It is this balanced growth of individuality which it should be the aim of education to secure. The most useful discoveries for the immediate future would concern the furtherance of this aim without detriment to the necessary intellectual professionalism.

My own criticism of our traditional educational methods is that they are far too much occupied with intellectual analysis, and with the acquirement of formularised information. What I mean is, that we neglect to strengthen habits of concrete appreciation of the individual facts in their full interplay of emergent values, and that we merely emphasise abstract formulations which ignore this aspect of the interplay of diverse values.

In every country the problem of the balance of the general and specialist education is under consideration. I cannot speak with first-hand knowledge of any country but my own. I know that there, among practical educationalists, there is considerable dissatisfaction with the existing practice. Also, the adaptation of the whole system to the needs of a democratic community is very far from being solved. I do not think that the secret of the solution lies in terms of the antithesis between thoroughness in special knowledge and general knowledge of a slighter character. The make-weight which balances the thoroughness of the specialist intellectual training should be of a radically different kind from purely intellectual analytical knowledge. At present our education combines a thorough study of a few abstractions, with a slighter study of a larger number of abstractions. We are too exclusively bookish in our scholastic routine. The general training should aim at eliciting our concrete apprehensions, and should satisfy the itch of youth to be doing something. There should be some analysis even here, but only just enough to illustrate the ways of thinking in diverse spheres. In the Garden of Eden Adam saw the animals before he named them; in the traditional system, children named the animals before they saw them.

There is no easy single solution of the practical difficulties of education. We can, however, guide ourselves by a certain simplicity in its general theory. The student should concentrate within a limited field. Such concentration should include all practical and intellectual acquirements requisite for that concentration. This is the ordinary procedure; and, in respect to it, I should be inclined even to increase the facilities for concentration rather than to diminish them. With the concentration there are associated certain subsidiary studies, such as languages for science. Such a scheme of professional training should be directed to a clear end congenial to the student. It is not necessary to elaborate the qualifications of these statements. Such a training must, of course, have the width requisite for its end. But its design should not be complicated by the consideration of other ends. This professional training can only touch one side of education. Its centre of gravity lies in the intellect, and its chief tool is the printed book. The centre of gravity of the other side of training should lie in intuition without an analytical divorce from the total environment. Its object is immediate apprehension with the minimum of eviscerating analysis. The type of generality, which above all is wanted, is the appreciation of variety of value. I mean an aesthetic growth. There is something between the gross specialised values of the mere practical man, and the thin specialised values of the mere scholar. Both types have missed something; and if you add together the two sets of values, you do not obtain the missing elements. What is wanted is an appreciation of the infinite variety of vivid values achieved by an organism in its proper environment. When you understand all about the sun and all about the atmosphere and all about the rotation of the earth, you may still miss the radiance of the sunset. There is no substitute for the direct perception of the concrete achievement of a thing in its actuality. We want concrete fact with a high light thrown on what is relevant to its preciousness.

What I mean is art and aesthetic education. It is, however, art in such a general sense of the term that I hardly like to call it by that name. Art is a special example. What we want is to draw out habits of aesthetic apprehension. According to the metaphysical doctrine which I have been developing, to do so is to increase the depth of individuality. The analysis of reality indicates the two factors, activity emerging into individualised aesthetic value. Also the emergent value is the measure of the individualisation of the activity. We must foster the creative initiative towards the maintenance of objective values. You will not obtain the apprehension without the initiative, or the initiative without the apprehension. As soon as you get towards the concrete, you cannot exclude action. Sensitiveness without impulse spells decadence, and impulse without sensitiveness spells brutality. I am using the word "sensitiveness" in its most general signification, so as to include apprehension of what lies beyond oneself; that is to say, sensitiveness to all the facts of the case. Thus "art" in the general sense which I require is any selection by which the concrete facts are so arranged as to elicit attention to particular values which are realisable by them. For example, the mere disposing of the human body and the eyesight so as to get a good view of a sunset is a simple form of artistic selection. The habit of art is the habit of enjoying vivid values.

But, in this sense, art concerns more than sunsets. A factory, with its machinery, its community of operatives, its social service to the general population, its dependence upon organising and designing genius, its potentialities as a source of wealth to the holders of its stock is an organism exhibiting a variety of vivid values. What we want to train is the habit of apprehending such an organism in its completeness. It is very arguable that the science of political economy, as studied in its first period after the death of Adam Smith (1790), did more harm than good. It destroyed many economic fallacies, and taught how to think about the economic revolution then in progress. But it riveted on men a certain set of abstractions which were disastrous in their influence on modern mentality. It dehumanised industry. This is only one example of a general danger inherent in modern science. Its methodological procedure is exclusive and intolerant, and rightly so. It fixes attention on a definite group of abstractions, neglects everything else, and elicits every scrap of information and theory which is relevant to what it has retained. This method is triumphant, provided that the abstractions are judicious. But, however triumphant, the triumph is within limits. The neglect of these limits leads to disastrous oversights. The anti-rationalism of science is partly justified, as a preservation of its useful methodology; it is partly mere irrational prejudice. Modern professionalism is the training of minds to conform to the methodology. The historical revolt of the seventeenth century, and the earlier reaction towards naturalism, were examples of transcending the abstractions which fascinated educated society in the Middle Ages. These early ages had an ideal of rationalism, but they failed in its pursuit. For they neglected to note that the methodology of reasoning requires the limitations involved in the abstract. Accordingly, the true rationalism must always transcend itself by recurrence to the concrete in search of inspiration. A self-satisfied rationalism is in effect a form of anti-rationalism. It means an arbitrary halt at a particular set of abstractions. This was the case with science.

There are two principles inherent in the very nature of things, recurring in some particular embodiments whatever field we explore—the spirit of change, and the spirit of conservation. There can be nothing real without both. Mere change without conservation is a passage from nothing to nothing. Its final integration yields mere transient nonentity. Mere conservation without change cannot conserve. For after all, there is a flux of circumstance, and the freshness of being evaporates under mere repetition. The character of existent reality is composed of organisms enduring through the flux of things. The low type of organisms have achieved a self-identity dominating their whole physical life. Electrons, molecules, crystals, belong to this type. They exhibit a massive and complete sameness. In the higher types, where life appears, there is greater complexity. Thus, though there is a complex, enduring pattern, it has retreated into deeper recesses of the total fact. In a sense, the self-identity of a human being is more abstract than that of a crystal. It is the life of the spirit. It relates rather to the individualisation of the creative activity; so that the changing circumstances received from the environment, are differentiated from the living personality, and are thought of as forming its perceived field. In truth, the field of perception and the perceiving mind are abstractions which, in the concrete, combine into the successive bodily events. The psychological field, as restricted to sense-objects and passing emotions, is the minor permanence, barely rescued from the non-entity of mere change; and the mind is the major permanence, permeating that complete field, whose endurance is the living soul. But the soul would wither without fertilisation from its transient experiences. The secret of the higher organisms lies in their two grades of permanences. By this means the freshness of the environment is absorbed into the permanence of the soul. The changing environment is no longer, by reason of its variety, an enemy to the endurance of the organism. The pattern of the higher organism has retreated into the recesses of the individualised activity. It has become a uniform way of dealing with circumstances; and this way is only strengthened by having a proper variety of circumstances to deal with.

This fertilisation of the soul is the reason for the necessity of art. A static value, however serious and important, becomes unendurable by its appalling monotony of endurance. The soul cries aloud for release into change. It suffers the agonies of claustrophobia. The transitions of humour, wit, irreverence, play, sleep, and—above all—of art are necessary for it. Great art is the arrangement of the environment so as to provide for the soul vivid, but transient, values. Human beings require something which absorbs them for a time, something out of the routine which they can stare at. But you cannot subdivide life, except in the abstract analysis of thought. Accordingly, the great art is more than a transient refreshment. It is something which adds to the permanent richness of the soul's self-attainment. It justifies itself both by its immediate enjoyment, and also by its discipline of the inmost being. Its discipline is not distinct from enjoyment, but by reason of it. It transforms the soul into the permanent realisation of values extending beyond its former self. This element of transition in art is shown by the restlessness exhibited in its history. An epoch gets saturated by the masterpieces of any one style. Something new must be discovered. The human being wanders on. Yet there is a balance in things. Mere change before the attainment of adequacy of achievement, either in quality or output, is destructive of greatness. But the importance of a living art, which moves on and yet leaves its permanent mark, can hardly be exaggerated.

In regard to the aesthetic needs of civilised society the reactions of science have so far been unfortunate. Its materialistic basis has directed attention to *things* as opposed to *values*. The antithesis is a false one, if taken in a concrete sense. But it is valid at the abstract level of ordinary thought. This misplaced emphasis coalesced with the abstractions of political economy, which are in fact the abstractions in terms of which commercial affairs are carried on. Thus all thought concerned with social organisation expressed itself in terms of material things and of capital. Ultimate values were excluded. They were politely bowed to, and then handed over to the clergy to be kept for Sundays. A creed of competitive business morality was evolved, in some respects curiously high; but entirely devoid of consideration for the value of human life. The workmen were conceived as mere hands, drawn from the pool of labour. To God's question, men gave the answer of Cain—"Am I my brother's keeper?"; and they incurred Cain's guilt. This was the atmosphere in which the industrial revolution was accomplished in England, and to a large extent elsewhere. The internal history of England during the last half century has been an endeavour slowly and painfully to undo the evils wrought in the first stage of the new epoch. It may be that civilisation will never recover from the bad climate which enveloped the introduction of machinery. This climate pervaded the whole commercial system of the progressive northern European races. It was partly the result of aesthetic errors of Protestantism and partly the result of scientific materialism, and partly the result of the natural greed of mankind, and partly the result of the abstractions of political economy. An illustration of my point is to be found in Macaulay's Essay criticising Southey's *Colloquies on Society*. It was written in 1830. Now Macaulay was a very favourable example of men living at that date, or at any date. He had genius; he was kind-hearted, honourable, and a reformer. This is the extract:—"We are told, that our age has invented atrocities beyond the imagination of our fathers; that society has been brought into a state compared with which extermination would be a blessing; and all because the dwellings of cotton-spinners are naked and rectangular. Mr. Southey has found out a way he tells us, in which the effects of manufactures and agriculture may be compared. And what is this way? To stand on a hill, to look at a cottage and a factory, and to see which is the prettier."

Southey seems to have said many silly things in his book; but, so far as this extract is concerned, he could make a good case for himself if he returned to earth after the lapse of nearly a century. The evils of the early industrial system are now a commonplace of knowledge. The point which I am insisting on is the stone-blind eye with which even the best men of that time regarded the importance of aesthetics in a nation's life. I do not believe that we have as yet nearly achieved the right estimate. A contributory cause, of substantial efficacy to produce this disastrous error, was the scientific creed that matter in motion is the one concrete reality in nature; so that aesthetic values form an adventitious, irrelevant addition.

There is another side to this picture of the possibilities of decadence. At the present moment a discussion is raging as to the future of civilisation in the novel circumstances of rapid scientific and technological advance. The evils of the future have been diagnosed in various ways, the loss of religious faith, the malignant use of material power, the degradation attending a differential birth rate favouring the lower types of humanity, the suppression of aesthetic creativeness. Without doubt, these are all evils, dangerous and threatening. But they are not new. From the dawn of history, mankind has always been losing its religious faith, has always suffered from the malignant use of material power, has always suffered from the infertility of its best intellectual types, has always witnessed the periodical decadence of art. In the reign of the Egyptian king, Tutankhamen, there was raging a desperate religious struggle between Modernists and Fundamentalists; the cave pictures exhibit a phase of delicate aesthetic achievement as superseded by a period of comparative vulgarity; the religious leaders, the great thinkers, the great poets and authors, the whole clerical caste in the Middle Ages, have been notably infertile; finally, if we attend to what actually has happened in the past, and disregard romantic visions of democracies, aristocracies, kings, generals, armies, and merchants, material power has generally been wielded with blindness, obstinacy and selfishness, often with brutal malignancy. And yet, mankind has progressed. Even if you take a tiny oasis of peculiar excellence, the type of modern man who would have most chance of happiness in ancient Greece at its best period is probably (as now) an average professional heavy-weight boxer, and not an average Greek scholar from Oxford or Germany. Indeed, the main use of the Oxford scholar would have been his capability of writing an ode in glorification of the boxer. Nothing does more harm in unnerving men for their duties in the present, than the attention devoted to the points of excellence in the past as compared with the average failure of the present day.

But, after all, there have been real periods of decadence; and at the present time, as at other epochs, society is decaying, and there is need for preservative action. Professionals are not new in the world. But in the past, professionals have formed unprogressive castes. The point is that professionalism has now been mated with progress. The world is now faced with a self-evolving system, which it cannot stop. There are dangers and advantages in this situation. It is obvious that the gain in material power affords opportunity for social betterment. If mankind can rise to the occasion, there lies in front a golden age of beneficent creativeness. But material power in itself is ethically neutral. It can equally well work in the wrong direction. The problem is not how to produce great men, but how to produce great societies. The great society will put up the men for the occasions. The materialistic philosophy emphasised the given quantity of material, and thence derivatively the given nature of the environment. It thus operated most unfortunately upon the social conscience of mankind. For it directed almost exclusive attention to the aspect of struggle for existence in a fixed environment. To a large extent the environment is fixed, and to this extent there is a struggle for existence. It is folly to look at the universe through rose-tinted spectacles. We must admit the struggle. The question is, who is to be eliminated. In so far as we are educators, we have to have clear ideas upon that point; for it settles the type to be produced and the practical ethics to be inculcated.

But during the last three generations, the exclusive direction of attention to this aspect of things has been a disaster of the first magnitude. The watchwords of the nineteenth century have been, struggle for existence, competition, class warfare, commercial antagonism between nations, military warfare. The struggle for existence has been construed into the gospel of hate. The full conclusion to be drawn from a philosophy of evolution is fortunately of a more balanced character. Successful organisms modify their environment. Those organisms are successful which modify their environments so as to assist each other. This law is exemplified in nature on a vast scale. For example, the North American Indians accepted their environment, with the result that a scanty population barely succeeded in maintaining themselves over the whole continent. The European races when they arrived in the same continent pursued an opposite policy. They at once cooperated in modifying their environment. The result is that a population more than twenty times that of the Indian population now occupies the same territory, and the continent is not yet full. Again, there are associations of different species which mutually cooperate. This differentiation of species is exhibited in the simplest physical entities, such as the association between electrons and positive nuclei, and in the whole realm of animate nature. The trees in a Brazilian forest depend upon the association of various species of organisms, each of which is mutually dependent on the other species. A single tree by itself is dependent upon all the adverse chances of shifting circumstances. The wind stunts it: the variations in temperature check its foliage: the rains denude its soil: its leaves are blown away and are lost for the purpose of fertilisation. You may obtain individual specimens of fine trees either in exceptional circumstances, or where human cultivation has intervened. But in nature the normal way in which trees flourish is by their association in a forest. Each tree may lose something of its individual perfection of growth, but they mutually assist each other in preserving the conditions for survival. The soil is preserved and shaded; and the microbes necessary for its fertility are neither scorched, nor frozen, nor washed away. A forest is the triumph of the organisation of mutually dependent species. Further a species of microbes which kills the forest, also exterminates itself. Again the two sexes exhibit the same advantage of differentiation. In the history of the world, the prize has not gone to those species which specialised in methods of violence, or even in defensive armour. In fact, nature began with producing animals encased in hard shells for defence against the ills of life. It also experimented in size. But smaller animals, without external armour, warm-blooded, sensitive, and alert, have cleared these monsters off the face of the earth. Also, the lions and tigers are not the successful species. There is something in the ready use of force which defeats its own object. Its main defect is that it bars cooperation. Every organism requires an environment of friends, partly to shield it from violent changes, and partly to supply it with its wants. The Gospel of Force is incompatible with a social life. By *force,* I mean *antagonism* in its most general sense.

Almost equally dangerous is the Gospel of Uniformity. The differences between the nations and races of mankind are required to preserve the conditions under which higher development is possible. One main factor in the upward trend of animal life has been the power of wandering. Perhaps this is why the armour-plated monsters fared badly. They could not wander. Animals wander into new conditions. They have to adapt themselves or die. Mankind has wandered from the trees to the plains, from the plains to the seacoast, from climate to climate, from continent to continent, and from habit of life to habit of life. When man ceases to wander, he will cease to ascend in the scale of being. Physical wandering is still important, but greater still is the power of man's spiritual adventures—adventures of thought, adventures of passionate feeling, adventures of aesthetic experience. A diversification among human communities is essential for the provision of the incentive and material for the Odyssey of the human spirit. Other nations of different habits are not enemies: they are godsends. Men require of their neighbours something sufficiently akin to be understood, something sufficiently different to provoke attention, and something great enough to command admiration. We must not expect, however, all the virtues. We should even be satisfied if there is something odd enough to be interesting.

Modern science has imposed on humanity the necessity for wandering. Its progressive thought and its progressive technology make the transition through time, from generation to generation, a true migration into uncharted seas of adventure. The very benefit of wandering is that it is dangerous and needs skill to avert evils. We must expect, therefore, that the future will disclose dangers. It is the business of the future to be dangerous; and it is among the merits of science that it equips the future for its duties. The prosperous middle classes, who ruled the nineteenth century, placed an excessive value upon placidity of existence. They refused to face the necessities for social reform imposed by the new industrial system, and they are now refusing to face the necessities for intellectual reform imposed by the new knowledge. The middle class pessimism over the future of the world comes from a confusion between civilisation and security. In the immediate future there will be less security than in the immediate past, less stability. It must be admitted that there is a degree of instability which is inconsistent with civilisation. But, on the whole, the great ages have been unstable ages.

I have endeavoured in these lectures to give a record of a great adventure in the region of thought. It was shared in by all the races of western Europe. It developed with the slowness of a mass movement. Half a century is its unit of time. The tale is the epic of an episode in the manifestation of reason. It tells how a particular direction of reason emerges in a race by the long preparation of antecedent epochs, how after its birth its subject-matter gradually unfolds itself, how it attains its triumphs, how its influence moulds the very springs of action of mankind, and finally how at its moment of supreme success its limitations disclose themselves and call for a renewed exercise of the creative imagination. The moral of the tale is the power of reason, its decisive influence on the life of humanity. The great conquerors, from Alexander to Caesar, and from Caesar to Napoleon, influenced profoundly the lives of subsequent generations. But the total effect of this influence shrinks to insignificance, if compared to the entire transformation of human habits and human mentality produced by the long line of men of thought from Thales to the present day, men individually powerless, but ultimately the rulers of the world.